CIVILIZATION IN THE WEST

CONTEMPORARY EUROPE

Land Elevation

Feet		Meters
13,123		4,000
6,562		2,000
3,281		1,000
1,640		500
656		200
0		0
Below sea level		Below sea level

0   250   500 mi.

0   250   500 km

ICELAND

Norwegian Sea

Arctic Circle

FAROE IS.

SHETLAND IS.

HEBRIDES IS.

ORKNEY IS.

KJØLEN MOUNTAINS

SCANDINAVIAN PENIN

NORWAY

SWEDEN

L. Vänern

L. Vättern

Scotland

Northern Ireland

UNITED KINGDOM

North Sea

JUTLAND PENINSULA

DENMARK

Balti

BRITISH ISLES

IRELAND

Elbe R.

NORTH EU

Celtic Sea

Wales

England

NETHERLANDS

RUHR VALLEY

GERMANY

POL

Oder R.

50°N

Thames R.

English Channel

BELGIUM

Rhine R.

CZECH REPUBLIC

SLOVA

ATLANTIC OCEAN

BRITTANY PENINSULA

Loire R.

Seine R.

LUXEMBOURG

LIECHTENSTEIN

Danube R.

HUN

HUM

Bay of Biscay

FRANCE

SWITZERLAND

L. Geneva

A L P S

AUSTRIA

SLOVENIA

Drava R.

CENTRAL MASSIF

Rhône R.

Po R.

CROATIA

Sava R.

Garonne R.

ITALY

SAN MARINO

BOSNIA & HERZEGOVINA

40°N

Duero R.

Ebro R.

PYRENEES

APENNINES

Adriatic Sea

DINARIC ALP

ANDORRA

MONACO

IBERIAN PENINSULA

CORSICA

PORTUGAL

Tagus R.

SPAIN

Guadiana R.

Guadalquivir R.

SARDINIA

BALEARIC ISLANDS

Tyrrhenian Sea

ALB

Ionia Sea

SIERRA NEVADA

Strait of Gibraltar

Mediterranean Sea

SICILY

AFRICA

MALTA

20°E 40°E 60°E 80°E 100°E 120°E 140°E 160°E

ARCTIC OCEAN

Barents Sea

Laptev Sea

SCANDINAVIA

NORTH EUROPEAN PLAIN *Volga R.* URAL MTS. *Ob R.* S I B E R I A *Yenisey R.* *Lena R.*

EUROPE *Danube* *Aral Sea*

ALPS CAUCASUS MTS. *Caspian Sea* A S I A GOBI (DESERT) L. *Baikal* *Amur R.*

Black Sea ZAGROS MTS. *Sea of Okhotsk*

Mediterranean Sea *Tigris R.* TIBETAN PLATEAU *Huang He R.* JAPAN

Euphrates R. HIMALAYA MTS. *Chiang Jiang R.* *Sea of Japan*

HARA SERT) *Nile R.* *Red Sea* ARABIAN DESERT *Indus R.* THAR DESERT *Ganges R.* East China Sea Tropic of Cancer

SUDAN *Persian Gulf* DECCAN PLATEAU *Mekong R.* South China Sea PHILIPPINES PACIFIC OCEAN

AFRICA ETHIOPIAN HIGHLANDS *Arabian Sea* Bay of Bengal

Zaire R. CONGO BASIN *Victoria* BORNEO I N D O N E S I A NEW GUINEA

Congo SUMATRA

INDIAN OCEAN JAVA

Zambezi R. MADAGASCAR

KALAHARI DESERT GREAT SANDY DESERT

Tropic of Capricorn **AUSTRALIA** GREAT VICTORIA DESERT *Darling R.*

Cape of Good Hope NEW ZEALAND

CONTEMPORARY WORLD

Land Elevation

Feet		Meters
10,123		4,000
6,562		2,000
3,281		1,000
1,640		500
0		0
Below sea level		Below sea level

Ice-covered

0 ___ 1,000 ___ 2,000 mi.
0 ___ 1,000 ___ 2,000 km

Robinson Projection

ANTARCTICA

CIVILIZATION IN THE WEST

Seventh Edition

Volume B: From 1350 To 1850

Mark Kishlansky
Harvard University

Patrick Geary
University of California, Los Angeles

Patricia O'Brien
University of California, Los Angeles

PEARSON
Longman

New York   San Francisco   Boston
London   Toronto   Sydney   Tokyo   Singapore   Madrid
Mexico City   Munich   Paris   Cape Town   Hong Kong   Montreal

Senior Acquisitions Editor: Janet Lanphier
Assistant Development Manager: David Kear
Development Editor: Barbara Conover
Executive Marketing Manager: Sue Westmoreland
Supplements Editor: Brian Belardi
Media Editor: Melissa Edwards
Production Manager: Donna DeBenedictis
Project Coordination, Text Design, and Electronic Page Makeup: Elm Street Publishing Services, Inc.
Cover Designer/Manager: John Callahan
Cover Image: Scala/Art Resource, NY/Galleria Nazionale, Parma, Italy
Photo Researcher: Vivette Porges
Manufacturing Buyer: Lucy Hebard
Printer and Binder: Quebecor World/Dubuque
Cover Printer: Phoenix Color Corporation

For permission to use copyrighted material, grateful acknowledgment is made to the copyright holders on pp. C-1–C-3, which are hereby made part of this copyright page.

Library of Congress Cataloging-in-Publication Data
Kishlansky, Mark A.
    Civilization in the West/Mark Kishlansky, Patrick Geary, Patricia O'Brien.—7ed.
        p. cm.
    Includes bibliographical references and index.
    ISBN 978–0–205–55684–7 (single v. ed.)—ISBN 978–0–205–55685–4 (v. I)—ISBN 978–0–205–55686–1 (v. II)—ISBN 978–0–205–55687–8 (v. A)—ISBN 978–0–205–55688–5 (v. B)—ISBN 978–0–205–55689–2 (v. C)
    1. Civilization, Western—History—Textbooks. I. Geary, Patrick J., 1948-II. O'Brien, Patricia, 1945-III.Title.

CB245.K546 2008
909'.09821—dc22

Please visit us at http://www.ablongman.com/kishlansky

ISBN-13: 978–0–205–55684–7   ISBN-10: 0–205–55684–1 (Combined Volume)
ISBN-13: 978–0–205–55685–4   ISBN-10: 0–205–55685–X (Volume I)
ISBN-13: 978–0–205–55686–1   ISBN-10: 0–205–55686–8 (Volume II)
ISBN-13: 978–0–205–55687–8   ISBN-10: 0–205–55687–6 (Volume A)
ISBN-13: 978–0–205–55688–5   ISBN-10: 0–205–55688–4 (Volume B)
ISBN-13: 978–0–205–55689–2   ISBN-10: 0–205–55689–2 (Volume C)
ISBN-13: 978–0–13–600706–7   ISBN-10: 0–13–600706–6 (Advanced Placement* Edition, Since 1300)

*Advanced Placement Program and AP are registered trademarks of The College Board, which was not involved in the production of, and does not endorse, this book.

3 4 5 6 7 8 9 10—QWD—10 09

BRIEF CONTENTS

DETAILED CONTENTS

Note: Each chapter ends with Questions for Review, Key Terms, Discovering Western Civilization Online, and Suggestions for Further Reading.

DOCUMENTS

MAPS

CHRONOLOGIES, GENEALOGIES, AND FIGURES

PREFACE

In planning *Civilization in the West,* our aim was to write a book that students would *want* to read. Throughout our years of planning, writing, revising, rewriting, and meeting together, this was our constant overriding concern. Would students read our book? Would it be effective in conveying information while stimulating the imagination? Would it work for a variety of Western civilization courses with different levels and formats? It was not easy to keep this concern in the forefront throughout the long months of composition, but it was easy to receive the reactions of scores of reviewers to this simple question: "Would students *want* to read these chapters?" Whenever we received a resounding "No!" we began again—not just rewriting but rethinking how to present material that might be too complex in argument or detail or that might simply seem too remote to engage the contemporary student. Although all three of us were putting in long hours in front of computers, we quickly learned that we were engaged in a teaching rather than a writing exercise. And though the work was demanding, it was not unrewarding. We hope that you will recognize and come to share with us the excitement and enthusiasm we felt in creating this text. We have enjoyed writing it, and we want students to enjoy reading it.

From the reactions to our first six editions, they have. We have received literally hundreds of cards and letters from adopters and users of *Civilization in the West.* The response has been both overwhelming and gratifying. It has also been constructive. Along with praise, we have received significant suggestions for making each subsequent edition stronger. Topics such as the Crusades, the Enlightenment, and imperialism have been reorganized to present them more clearly. Subjects such as the ancient Hebrews, Napoleon, and German unification have been given more space and emphasis. New features have been added to freshen the book and keep abreast of current scholarship, and more than 100 excerpts from primary sources are presented to give students a feel for the concreteness of the past. We believe that the seventh edition of *Civilization in the West* not only preserves the much-praised quality of its predecessors but also enhances it.

APPROACH

We made a number of decisions early in the project that we believed contributed to our goal. First, we were *not* writing an encyclopedia on Western civilization. Information was not to be included in a chapter unless it related to the themes of that chapter. There was to be no information for information's sake, and each of us was called upon to defend the inclusion of names, dates, and events whenever we met to critique one another's chapters. We found, to our surprise, that by adhering to the principle that information included must contribute to or illustrate a particular point or dominating theme, we provided as much, if not more, material than books that habitually list names, places, and dates without any other context.

Second, we were committed to integrating the history of ordinary men and women into our narrative. We believe that isolated sections, placed at the end of chapters, that deal with the experiences of women or minority groups in a particular era profoundly distort historical experience. We called this technique *caboosing,* and whenever we found ourselves segregating women or families or the masses, we stepped back and asked how we might recast our treatment of historical events to account for a diversity of actors. How did ordinary men, women, and children affect the course of historical events? How did historical events affect the fabric of daily life for men, women, and children from all walks of life? We tried to rethink critical historical problems of civilization as gendered phenomena. To assist us in the endeavor, we engaged two reviewers whose sole responsibility was to evaluate our chapters for the integration of those social groups into our discussion.

We took the same approach to the coverage of central and eastern Europe that we did to women and minorities. Even before the epochal events of 1989 that returned this region to the forefront of international attention, we realized that in too many textbooks the Slavic world was treated as marginal to the history of Western civilization. Thus, with the help of a specialist reviewer, we worked to integrate more of the history of eastern Europe into our text than is found in most others, and to do so in a way that presented the regions, their cultures, and their institutions as integral rather than peripheral to Western civilization.

To construct a book that students would *want* to read, we needed to develop fresh ideas about how to involve them with the material, how to transform them from passive recipients to active participants. We borrowed from computer science the concept of being "user-friendly." We wanted to find ways to stimulate the imagination of the student, and the more we experimented with different techniques, the more we realized that the most effective way to do this was visually. It is not true that contemporary students cannot be taught effectively by the written word; it is only true that they cannot be taught as effectively as they can by the combination of words and images. From the beginning, we realized that a text produced in full color was essential to the features we most wanted to use: the pictorial chapter openers; the large number of maps; the geographical tours of Europe at certain times in history; and the two-page special feature essays, each with its own illustration.

FEATURES

It is hard to have a new idea when writing a textbook. So many authors have come before, each attempting to do something more effective, more innovative than his or her predecessor. However, we feel that the following features enhance students' understanding of Western civilization.

CHAPTER 21

INDUSTRIAL EUROPE

PORTRAIT OF AN AGE
THE RAILROAD

The Normandy train has reached Paris. The coast and the capital are once again connected. Passengers in their city finery disembark and are greeted by others who have awaited their scheduled arrival. Workmen stand ready to unload freight, porters to carry luggage. Steam billows forth from the resting engine, which is ...
engine stares as enj...
Renaissance portrait. Ye...
Saint-
is as n...
trait o...

THE VISUAL RECORD
ual in...
The...
aroun...
are in...
massive frame of the st...
all formed from iron—...
miracle product of indu...
glass panels became as ...
cities as stone cathedral...
tions changed the shap...
travel changed the lives ...
There had never b...
Romans had hitched fo...
century Europeans hitc...
The technology of o...
changed in 2000 years. C...
able, and expensive, an...
and muddy, rutted road...
horses with alarming ...
inside, where they we...
breathed the dust that t...
Second-class passenger...
and risking life and lim...
Railway travel was a...
cheaper, and safer. O...
time, space, and, abov...
what once were distan...

came trips, and the travel holiday was born. Commerce was transformed, as was the way in which it was conducted. Large quantities of goods could be shipped quickly from place to place; orders could instantly be filled. The whole notion of locality changed, as salesmen could board a morn-

al of the Normandy Train, Gare Saint-Lazare, 1877

...) in his obituary for the passing of horse ... r speed, we saw it, we felt it. This speed ... of blind, insensate agencies, that had no ... ut was incarnated in the fiery eyeballs of ... rutes."

... railways, like the fruits of industrializa- ...eet. As the nineteenth century progressed, ...ubt that, year by year, one way of life was ...other. More and more laborers were leav-

618

groups, and even whole societies. It was an engine racing down a track that only occasionally ended as placidly as did the Normandy train at the Gare Saint-Lazarre.

LOOKING AHEAD

As this chapter will discuss, industrialization began in Great Britain, spurred by its mineral wealth and entrepreneurial skill. It

The Visual Record: Pictorial Chapter Openers

It is probably the case that somewhere there has been a text that has used a chapter-opening feature similar to the one we use here. What we can say with certainty is that nothing else we experimented with, no other technique we attempted, has had such an immediate and positive impact on our readers or has so fulfilled our goal of involving the students in learning as *The Visual Record* pictorial chapter openers.

An illustration—a painting, a photograph, a picture, an artifact, an edifice—appears at the beginning of each chapter, accompanied by text through which we explore the picture, guiding students across a canvas or helping them see in an artifact or a piece of architecture details that are not immediately apparent. It is the direct combination of text and image that allows us to achieve this effect, to "unfold" both an illustration and a theme. In some chapters we highlight details, pulling out a section of the original picture to take a closer look. In others we attempt to shock the viewer into the recognition of horror or of beauty. Some chapter-opening images are designed to transport students back in time, to make them ask the question, "What was it like to be there?" All of the opening images have been chosen to illustrate a dominant theme within the chapter, and the dramatic and lingering impression they make helps reinforce that theme. A *Looking Ahead* section provides a brief overview of chapter coverage and further strengthens the connection between the subject of the opener and the major topics and themes of the chapter.

NEW! Image Discovery

Our commitment to using visual materials to enhance learning is seen throughout the book and is reinforced in the seventh edition with a new feature, *Image Discovery.* In *Image Discovery,* students are asked to approach an image as if it were a text. Appearing in each chapter, *Image Discoveries* guide students through suggestive questions to interrogate the image, understand its context, and unpack its multiple meanings.

Map Program

We have taken a similar image-based approach to our *presentation of geography.* When teachers of Western civilization courses are surveyed, no single area of need is cited more often than that of geographical knowledge. Students simply have no mental image of Europe, no familiarity with those geophysical features that are a fundamental part of the geopolitical realities of Western history. We realized that maps, carefully planned and skillfully executed, would be an important component of our text.

Map Discovery

To complement the standard map program of the text, we have two additional map-based features. The first is *Map Discovery.* This feature, which appears two to three times per chapter, offers specially designed maps with supporting caption information and questions designed to engage students in analyzing the map data and making larger connections to chapter discussions. We have found that focusing students' attention on the details of what a map shows and asking them to consider why that information is important is an effective way to strengthen critical thinking skills as well as to expand geographical knowledge.

Geographical Tours of Europe

The second map feature is the *Geographical Tours of Europe.* Six times in the book, we pause in the narrative to take a tour of Europe. Sometimes we follow an emperor as he tours his realm; sometimes we examine the impact of a peace treaty; sometimes we follow the travels of a merchant. Whatever the thematic occasion, our intention is to guide the student around the changing contours of the geography of Western history. In order to do this effectively, we worked with our cartographer to develop small, detailed maps to complement the overview map that appears at the beginning of each tour section. We know that only the most motivated students will turn back several pages to locate on a map a place mentioned in the text. Using small maps allows us to integrate maps directly into the relevant text, thus relieving students of the sometimes frustrating experience of attempting to locate not only a specific place on a map but perhaps even the relevant map itself. We have also added labels to all the tour maps and have included in-text references to direct students to relevant maps at specific points in the narrative of the tour. The great number of maps throughout the text, the specially designed geographical tour of Europe feature, and the ancillary programs of map transparencies and workbook exercises combine to provide the strongest possible program for teaching historical geography.

IMAGE DISCOVERY

Living with the Bomb.
This photo from the early 1950s shows an American family installed in their fallout shelter, intended to protect them from a nuclear blast. These shelters were built below ground or in basements. Note the supplies on hand. From your knowledge of the effects of atomic bombs on Japan, how realistic were people's hopes that radioactive fallout could be avoided? Why were photos like this one common in the 1950s in the United States? Why is this family smiling?

MAP DISCOVERY

Population Loss in Germany During the Thirty Years' War
Notice the pattern of population loss during the war. Where was it heaviest? Where was it lightest? Based on the chapter discussion, how might the intervention of Sweden into the war help explain this pattern?

THE STAINLESS STAR OF WISDOM'S DISCIPLINE

Public philosophers were prized citizens of every ancient city. The austere teachers, distinguished by their black robes, were courted by the wealthy as tutors of their sons and by the powerful for the benefit of their wisdom. But in the early fifth century, Alexandria, long famed for its great museum and rival schools, boasted a philosopher with a difference: Hypatia (ca. 370–415), a woman famed for her wisdom and described by one sup[...] "mother, sister, teacher, benefi[...] all things." Her controversial ca[...] terrible death summarize the c[...] ity and factionalism of late a[...]

As was the case with many o[...] fessional philosophers, Hypati[...] had [...] reno[...] philo[...] befor[...] speci[...] astro[...] math[...] divin[...] and Neoplatonic philosophy, [...] wrote commentaries on math[...] and astronomical treatises, [...]

est praise—and her greatest criticism—for her practice of philosophy. Popular teachers are often controversial, and as a pagan, as a woman, and as a philosopher in the turbulent world of late antiquity, Hypatia was the center of more than her share. But philosophers were more than teachers in antiquity. Because of their deep learning, their

A CLOSER LOOK

THE WEST AND THE WIDER WORLD

WORLD TRADE CENTERS

Trade is older than civilization, and almost as old are specialized buildings where trade is carried on. When the World Trade Centers in New York City were destroyed on September 11, 2001, the terrorist attack was aimed at a symbol of American economic power. But like other trade centers throughout the centuries, these buildings contained a truly international community: citizens of eighty countries were among the victims. The tragedy struck at the United States but wounded a global community of business, finance, trade, and civilization.

Specialized buildings for international trade were well established in Asia, Europe, and Africa by the thirteenth century. Merchants needed protection from bandits, judicial organizations

■ The Twin Towers of the World Trade Center.

to s[...] niz[...] par[...] loca[...] me[...] cili[...] of [...] cor[...] the [...] was[...] gro[...] and[...] for [...] at [...] Ber[...] cha[...] row[...] old[...]

sim[...] spe[...] thr[...] the [...] off[...] cha[...] the [...] nes[...] Pol[...] firs[...]

■ The Tithe Grange at Provins, France.   ■ Merchant houses on the old wharf o[...]

THE TREATY OF VERSAILLES

*Of the various treaties negotiating the peace at the end of World War I, the Treaty of Versailles, signed in 1919, was the most important. This treaty dealt with Germany as a defeated nation and was signed in the great Versailles palace outside of Paris in the same location where in 1871 Germany as victor signed a treaty with its defeated enemy, France, at the close of the short Franco-Prussian War (see pp. 694). In the 1919 treaty, the Allies, represented by President Woodrow Wilson of the United States, Prime Minister David Lloyd George of Great Britain, Prime Minister Georges Clemenceau of France, and Prime Minister Vittorio Orlando of Italy, imposed sole blame for the war on Germany and its expansionist aims. According to the treaty, the war was Germany's fault, and Germany must pay reparations for all the destruction of Allied property by its military. Germany lost territories and suffered a greatly reduced military capability. Especially burdensome was article 231 of the treaty, which came to be known as the **War Guilt Clause**, which spelled out Germany's responsibility and the basis for the need to make restitution.*

Focus Questions

In article 42, for whose benefit were the left and right banks of the Rhine demilitarized? How many different forms of reparation can you identify in the articles cited here? For whose benefit was the German navy scaled back? Examine carefully article 231—the War Guilt Clause. What is your judgment of its validity in light of what you know about the causes of the war?

Part III. Political Clauses for Europe

Article 42. Germany is forbidden to maintain or construct any fortifications either on the left bank of the Rhine or on the right bank to the west of a line drawn 50 kilometers to the east of the Rhine. . . .

Article 45. As compensation for the destruction of the coal-mines in the north of France and as part payment towards the total reparation due from Germany for the damage resulting from the war, Germany cedes to France in full and absolute possession, with exclusive rights of exploita-

Article 89. Poland undertakes to accord freedom of transit to persons, goods, vessels, carriages, wagons, and mails in transit between East Prussia and the rest of Germany over Polish territory, including territorial waters, and to treat them at least as favorably as the persons, goods, vessels, carriages, wagons, and mails respectively of Polish or of any other more favored nationality, origin, importation, starting-point, or ownership as regards facilities, restrictions and all other matters. . . .

Part IV. German Rights and Interests Outside Germany

Article 119. Germany renounces in favor of the Principal Allied and Associated Powers all her rights and titles over her overseas possessions. (This renunciation includes Germany's concessions in China.) . . .

Part V. Military, Naval, and Air Claims

Article 159. The German military forces shall be demobilized and reduced as prescribed hereinafter.

Article 160. (1) By a date which must not be later than

A Closer Look

Another technique we have employed to engage students with historical subjects is the two-page *A Closer Look* special feature that appears in many chapters. *A Closer Look* focuses on an event, phenomenon, or personality chosen to enhance the student's sense that history is something that is real and alive. The features are written more dramatically and sympathetically, with a greater sense of wonder than would be appropriate in the body of the text. The prose style and the accompanying illustration are designed to captivate the reader. To help the student relate personally and directly to a historical event, we have highlighted figures such as Hypatia of Alexandria, Isabella of Castile, and Sigmund Freud.

The West and the Wider World

To engage students with historical subjects, two-page *The West and the Wider World* essays that appear 11 times in the book. These essays focus on instances of dynamic cultural encounters and exchanges between the West and the non-West at different points in history. The topics for this feature were chosen to enhance the student's sense of connections among the events, phenomena, politics, and products of the West and the wider world. At the end of each feature, we have included questions to spark class discussion and to reinforce such connections.

Documents

Civilization in the West contains selections from primary sources designed to stimulate students' interest in history by allowing them to hear the past speak in its own voice. We have tried to provide a mixture of "canonical" texts along with those illustrating the lives of ordinary people in order to demonstrate the variety of materials that form the building blocks of historical narrative. Each selection is accompanied by an explanatory headnote that identifies the author and work and provides the necessary historical context. Following the headnote are two to three *Focus Questions* to guide students' reading and to spark critical thinking. Most of the extracts relate directly to the discussion within the chapter, thus providing the student with a fuller understanding of a significant thinker or event.

Discovering Western Civilization Online

Discovering Western Civilization Online encourages students to further explore Western civilization. These end-of-chapter Website resources link students to documents, images, and cultural sites currently not included in the text.

Questions for Review

Although a standard feature in many texts, the *Questions for Review* in *Civilization in the West* nonetheless are worth noting. They do not provide just a factual review of the chapter. Instead, they prompt students to think critically about the major topics in the chapter and to pull together for themselves some conclusions about the events and peoples of the time.

CHANGES IN THE NEW EDITION

In the seventh edition, we have made significant changes in content and coverage.

NEW! Image Discovery

Appearing in every chapter, new *Image Discovery* features ask students to approach an image as if it were a text. The feature challenges readers to move from a passive mode of information absorption to an active analysis of the visual and material evidence of the past. Through suggestive questions, Image Discoveries guide students to interrogate the image, understand its context, and unpack its multiple meanings. Examples include "A Revolution in Warfare" in Chapter 2, which uses a Corinthian vase depicting hoplites to explore questions of training and warfare; the painting *The Milch Cow* in Chapter 14, which allows for an examination of the politics surrounding the Netherlands in the late sixteenth century; and a photograph in Chapter 28 of Nazi soldiers seizing Jews in Warsaw, which speaks to the experience and expectations of the captured.

Content Updates

The past may not change, but both our understanding of the past and the questions we need to ask about it change constantly. We have taken the opportunity of a new edition to project our history back in time as well as to explore more closely the entangled nature of human history. In the first chapter, a new *The West and the Wider World* feature, confronts the growing consensus that history begins not with Sumer but with the Paleolithic. Here we explore the exciting frontiers of history, genetics, and archaeology that attempt to understand the complex waves of migrations out of Africa that ultimately populated the planet. Elsewhere we explore those extraordinary crossroads of cultural and economic exchange that were trade centers where merchants from Europe, Asia, and Africa have sought the safety and peace necessary to tie together the great civilizations of the world.

Throughout the early chapters we have pruned, eliminating unnecessary and potentially distracting detail while fine tuning content in response to the input from readers and users of previous editions. The addition of the *Image Discovery* feature has provided the opportunity for a broad range of analysis. In some, as in Chapter 3, we ask readers to compare a Hellenistic statue with a classical one; in Chapter 7 we ask them to reflect on how the profession of faith inscribed on Jerusalem's Haram al-Sharif or The Dome of the Rock might be understood as challenging Christian belief. In others, we encourage readers to make use of what they have learned in the text to interpret the images with which they are confronted.

In the middle chapters of the book the authors have continued their efforts to expand the boundaries of Europe and to relate its experiences to those of the wider world. A new feature on the Columbian Exchange highlights the interactive nature of the European encounter with Atlantic populations. It emphasizes the biological and economic impact of discoveries, the disastrous consequences of interchanged diseases, and the enhancements of new products and tools. Pigs and cattle were brought to the new world, potatoes and tomatoes to the old.

Europe's encounters with non-Europeans in the early modern period were not limited to discoveries. The centuries-old struggle between the Ottoman and Holy Roman empires continued deep into the seventeenth century. It reached its apex with the siege of Vienna in 1676—an event that might have transformed European history had it turned out differently. Throughout this section the text has been updated to reflect new historical discoveries and to account for reinterpretations of familiar events. A special effort has been made to enhance sections on the biological sciences.

In the modern chapters, beginning with Chapter 20, attention has been given to updating coverage and information and incorporating the latest bibliographic information. The new *Image Discovery* feature for these chapters (Chapters 20 through 30) includes political cartoons and caricature in understanding how visual images and symbols are a central feature of modern political life beginning in the late eighteenth century. *Image Discovery* has also allowed the authors to interrogate the role of photography in shaping modern consciousness.

One of the great challenges has been the proper inclusion of the United States in the story of *Civilization in the West* from the French Revolution to the war on terrorism. Greater attention to the United States in the story of *Civilization in the West* recognizes the expanding concept of the West as an idea rather than a place. There is expanded treatment of the U.S. role especially in the post–World War II period with the Cold War and the subsequent decline of the Soviet Union. The global context of political, religious, intellectual, and social changes has resulted in increased coverage of Afghanistan, China, South Africa, and India to understand the phenomenon of change in the West. For example, the return of the Taliban changes earlier interpretations about the gains of democratic government in Afghanistan. And the work of Mahatma Gandhi is included in a new way here (in *The West and the Wider World*) to show the influences of ideas in Asia on political discourse in other nations.

The changing nature of ethnicity and nationalism in the contemporary world has required not only updating information but also reconsidering interpretations of the rapid historic changes of the post–Cold War world. Contemporary events such as the trial and death of Saddam Hussein and the civil war in Iraq require new perspectives on the war on terrorism in the final chapter. The chapters that cover the modern period in general are influenced by the weight of contemporary events that continually require reframing and revisiting conclusions.

New West and the Wider World

Two-page *The West and the Wider World* essays explore instances of dynamic cultural encounters and exchanges between the West and the non-West at different points in history. Understanding the importance of viewing the West within this larger context, we have added in this edition six new essays throughout the text: Chapter 1, "The First European Immigrants"; Chapter 10, "World Trade Centers"; Chapter 12, "The Columbian Exchange"; Chapter 16, "The Siege of Vienna"; Chapter 25, "Babylon Discovered"; and Chapter 29, "Mahatma Gandhi's Legacy."

Key Terms and Glossary

In each chapter, key terms are highlighted in boldface type to alert students to principal concepts and events discussed in the chapter. A page-referenced list of the key terms is included at the end of the chapter to help students review the main ideas and events covered in the chapter. A glossary at the end of the book provides definitions for the key terms. In this edition, we have added over 60 new terms.

New Documents

Nine new documents have been added in this edition as well. Chapter 3 now includes an excerpt from Plato's "The Apology" that presents Socrates in his summation to the Athenian jury; Chapter 7 includes Usamah ibn Munqidh's observations in "An Arab in Crusader Jerusalem"; in Chapter 8, Gregory of Tours describes a conflict between two families from Tournai that ultimately destroyed them both; in Chapter 14, in "The Heart and Stomach of a King," Queen Elizabeth rallies her subjects to oppose the invasion of England by the Spanish Armada; Chapter 19 now contains excerpts from Voltaire's great comic novel, *Candide*; the *Treaty of Versailles* is excerpted in Chapter 26; and Chapter 30 now includes both Václav Havel's address to Czechoslovakia from 1 January 1990 and a press release from London Mayor Ken Livingstone regarding his commitment, and that of 21 other mayors from major cities around the world, to reducing greenhouse gases.

New Visual Record Essays

Six new *The Visual Record* pictorial essays were developed for the seventh edition as well. Chapter 3: Classical and Hellenistic Greece, 500–100 B.C.E. opens with a pictorial essay on the Parthenon and Pericles, the man responsible for its construction; Chapter 9: The High Middle Ages, 900–1300 begins with an essay on a portion of the Bayeux tapestry that may well subvert the story of the Battle of Hastings as told by the victors; Chapter 11: The Italian Renaissance opens with an exploration of Leonardo da Vinci's *Last Supper*; Chapter 20: The French Revolution and the Napoleonic Era, 1789–1815 begins with an essay on Jacques-Louis David's *The Oath of the Tennis Court*, which captures the spirit of a key moment in the history of democracy; Chapter 21: Industrial Europe begins with an examination of the transformative power of the railroad as alluded to in Claude Monet's *La Gare Saint-Lazarre*; and Chapter 23: State Building and Social Change in Europe, 1850–1871 opens with an examination of the construction and meaning of London's extraordinary Crystal Palace of 1851.

ACKNOWLEDGMENTS

We want to thank the many conscientious historians who gave generously of their time and knowledge to review our manuscript. We would like to thank the reviewers of the first six editions as well as those of the current edition. Their valuable critiques and suggestions have contributed greatly to the final product. We are grateful to the following:

Achilles Aavraamides, *Iowa State University;* Meredith L. Adams, *Southwest Missouri State University;* Joseph Aieta, III, *Lasell College;* Ken Albala, *University of the Pacific;* Patricia Ali, *Morris College;* Gerald D. Anderson, *North Dakota State University;* Arthur H. Auten, *University of Hartford;* Suzanne Balch-Lindsay, *Eastern New Mexico University;* Sharon Bannister, *University of Findlay;* John W. Barker, *University of Wisconsin;* Patrick Bass, *Mount Union College;* William H. Beik, *Northern Illinois University;* Jean K. Berger, *University of Wisconsin, Fox Valley;* Patrice Berger, *University of Nebraska;* Lenard R. Berlanstein, *University of Virginia;* Raymond Birn, *University of Oregon;* Donna Bohanan, *Auburn University;* Werner Braatz, *University of Wisconsin, Oshkosh;* Thomas A. Brady, Jr., *University of Oregon;* Anthony M. Brescia, *Nassau Community College;* Elaine G. Breslaw, *Morgan State University;* Ronald S. Brockway, *Regis University;* April Brooks, *South Dakota State University;* Daniel Patrick Brown, *Moorpark College;* Ronald A. Brown, *Charles County Community College;* Blaine T. Browne, *Broward Community College;* Susan Carrafiello, *Wright State University;* Kathleen S. Carter, *High Point University;* Robert Carver, *University of Missouri, Rolla;* Edward J. Champlin, *Princeton University;* Stephanie Evans Christelow, *Western Washington University;* Sister Dorita Clifford, BVM, *University of San Francisco;* Gary B. Cohen, *University of Oklahoma;* Robert Cole, *Utah State University;* Jan M. Copes, *Cleveland State University;* John J. Contreni, *Purdue University;* Tim Crain, *University of Wisconsin, Stout;* Norman Delaney, *Del Mar College;* Samuel E. Dicks, *Emporia State University;* Andrew Donson, *University of Massachusetts, Amherst;* Frederick Dotolo, *St. John Fisher College;* Frederick Dumin, *Washington State University;* Janusz Duzinkiewicz, *Purdue University;* Laird Easton, *California State University, Chico;* Brian Elsesser, *Saint Louis University;* Dianne E. Farrell, *Moorhead State University;* Margot C. Finn, *Emory University;* Allan W. Fletcher, *Boise State University;* Luci Fortunato De Lisle, *Bridgewater State College;* Elizabeth L. Furdell, *University of North Florida;* Thomas W. Gallant, *University of Florida;* Bryan Ganaway, *University of Illinois;* Frank Garosi, *California State University, Sacramento;* Lorne E. Glaim, *Pacific Union College;* Joseph J. Godson, *Hudson Valley Community College;* Sue Helder Goliber, *Mount St. Mary's College;* Manuel G. Gonzales, *Diablo Valley College;* David Graf, *University of Miami;* Louis Haas, *Duquesne University;* Eric Haines, *Bellevue Community College;* David Halahmy, *Cypress College;* Paul Halliday, *University of Virginia;* Margaretta S. Handke, *Mankato State University;* David A. Harnett, *University of San Francisco;* Paul B. Harvey, Jr., *Pennsylvania State University;* Benjamin Hett, *Hunter College;* Neil Heyman, *San Diego State University;* Daniel W. Hollis, *Jacksonville State University;* Kenneth G. Holum, *University of Maryland;* Patricia Howe, *University of St. Thomas;* David Hudson, *California State University, Fresno;* Mark M. Hull, *Saint Louis University;* John Hymes, *Horry-Georgetown Technical College;* Charles Ingrao, *Purdue University;* George F. Jewsbury, *Oklahoma State University;* Cynthia Jones, *University of Missouri—Kansas City;* Donald G. Jones, *University of Central Arkansas;* William R. Jones, *University of New Hampshire;* Richard W. Kaeuper, *University of Rochester;* David Kaiser, *Carnegie-Mellon University;* Jeff Kaufmann, *Muscatine Community College;* Carolyn Kay, *Trent University;* John S. Kemp, *Truckee Meadows Community College;* William R. Keylor, *Boston University;* Joseph Kicklighter, *Auburn University;* Charles L. Killinger, III, *Valencia Community College;* Alan M. Kirshner, *Ohlone College;* Charlene Kiser, *Milligan College;* Barbara Klemm, *Broward Community College;* Janilyn M. Kocher, *Richland Community College;* Alexandra Korros, *Xavier University;* Cynthia Kosso, *Northern Arizona University;* Lara Kriegel, *Florida International University;* Lisa M. Lane, *Mira Costa College;* Lawrence Langer, *University of Connecticut;* David C. Large, *Montana State University;* Catherine Lawrence, *Messiah College;* Bryan LeBeau, *Creighton University;* Erik

Lindseth, *Indiana University–Purdue University Indianapolis;* Robert B. Luehrs, *Fort Hays State University;* Donna J. Maier, *University of Northern Iowa;* Margaret Malamud, *New Mexico State University;* Roberta T. Manning, *Boston College;* Lyle McAlister, *University of Florida;* Therese M. McBride, *College of the Holy Cross;* David K. McQuilkin, *Bridgewater College;* Victor V. Minasian, *College of Marin;* David B. Mock, *Tallahassee Community College;* Don Mohr, *University of Alaska–Anchorage,* Robert Moeller, *University of California, Irvine;* Elise Moentmann, *University of Portland;* R. Scott Moore, *University of Dayton;* Ann E. Moyer, *University of Pennsylvania;* Pierce C. Mullen, *Montana State University;* John A. Nichols, *Slippery Rock University;* Thomas F. X. Noble, *University of Virginia;* J. Ronald Oakley, *Davidson County Community College;* Bruce K. O'Brien, *Mary Washington College;* Dennis H. O'Brien, *West Virginia University;* Maura O'Connor, *University of Cincinnati;* Richard A. Oehling, *Assumption College;* James H. Overfield, *University of Vermont;* Catherine Patterson, *University of Houston;* Sue Patrick, *University of Wisconsin, Barron County;* Peter C. Piccillo, *Rhode Island College;* Peter O'M. Pierson, *Santa Clara University;* Alisa Plant, *Tulane University;* Theophilus Prousis, *University of North Florida;* Marlette Rebhorn, *Austin Community College;* Kimberly D. S. Reiter, *Stetson University;* Jack B. Ridley, *University of Missouri, Rolla;* Salvador Rivera, *State University of New York Cobleskill;* Thomas Robisheaux, *Duke University;* Constance M. Rousseau, *Providence College;* Thomas J. Runyan, *Cleveland State University;* John P. Ryan, *Kansas City Community College;* Geraldine Ryder, *Ocean County College;* Joanne Schneider, *Rhode Island College;* Steven Schroeder, *Indiana University of Pennsylvania;* Steven C. Seyer, *Lehigh County Community College;* Lixin Shao, *University of Minnesota, Duluth;* George H. Shriver, *Georgia Southern University;* Ellen J. Skinner, *Pace University;* Bonnie Smith, *University of Rochester;* Patrick Smith, *Broward Community College;* James Smither, *Grand Valley State University;* Sherill Spaar, *East Central University;* Ilicia Sprey, *Saint Joseph's College;* Charles R. Sullivan, *University of Dallas;* Peter N. Stearns, *Carnegie-Mellon University;* Saulius Suziedelis, *Millersville University;* Darryl B. Sycher, *Columbus State Community College;* Roger Tate, *Somerset Community College;* Janet A. Thompson, *Tallahassee Community College;* Anne-Marie Thornton, *Bilkent University;* Donna L. Van Raaphorst, *Cuyahoga Community College;* James Vanstone, *John Abbot College;* George S. Vascik, *Miami University, Hamilton;* Steven Vincent, *North Carolina State University;* Richard A. Voeltz, *Cameron University;* Faith Wallis, *McGill University;* Sydney Watts, *University of Richmond;* Eric Weissman, *Golden West College;* Christine White, *Pennsylvania State University;* Vance Youmans, *Spokane Falls Community College;* William Harry Zee, *Gloucester County College.*

Each author also received invaluable assistance and encouragement from many colleagues, friends, and family members over the years of research, reflection, writing, and revising that went into the making of this text.

Mark Kishlansky thanks Ann Adams, Robert Bartlett, Ray Birn, David Buisseret, Ted Cook, Frank Conaway, Constantine Fasolt, James Hankins, Katherine Haskins, Richard Hellie, Matthew Kishlansky, Donna Marder, Mary Beth Rose, Victor Stater, Jeanne Thiel, and the staffs of the Joseph Regenstein Library, the Newberry Library, and the Widener and Lamont Libraries at Harvard.

Patrick Geary thanks Mary, Catherine, and Anne Geary for their patience, support, and encouragement; he also thanks Anne Picard, Dale Schofield, Hans Hummer, Jared Poley, and Richard Mowrer for their able assistance throughout the project.

Patricia O'Brien thanks Elizabeth Sagias for her encouragement and enthusiasm throughout the project and Robert Moeller for his keen eye for organization and his suggestions for writing a gendered history. She is especially grateful to her assistants Susan Beals and Carolyn Drago for keeping her on track throughout the project.

All the authors thank Janet Lanphier, senior acquisitions editor, Barbara Conover, development editor, and Heather Johnson, project editor at Elm Street Publishing Services, Inc., for producing a beautiful book. Thanks are also due to Melissa Edwards, for her work in producing the media supplements that accompany this volume, and Brian Belardi who worked on the print supplements.

Mark Kishlansky
Patrick Geary
Patricia O'Brien

SUPPLEMENTS

For Qualified College Adopters

- **Instructor's Manual** This thorough instructor's manual includes an introductory essay on teaching Western civilization and a bibliographic essay on the use of primary sources for class discussion and analytical thinking. Each chapter contains a chapter summary, key terms and important geographic locations, discussion questions, and an annotated list of films (not supplied by Longman).
- **Test Bank** This supplement contains more than 1,200 multiple-choice, true/false, and essay questions. Multiple-choice and true/false questions are referenced by topic and text page number.
- **Computerized Test Bank** This flexible, easy-to-master assessment program includes all of the items in the printed test bank and allows instructors to select specific questions, edit them, and add their own items to create exams.
- **Instructor Resource Center (IRC)** (www.ablongman.com/irc) Through the Instructor Resource Center, instructors can log into premium online products, browse and download book-specific instructor resources, and receive immediate access and instructions to installing course management content.
- **Research Navigator and Research Navigator Guide** Research Navigator is a comprehensive website offering EBSCO's ContentSelect Academic Journal & Abstract Database, the *New York Times* Search-by-Subject Archive, *Financial Times* Article Archive and Company Financials, and "Best of the Web" Link Library. The Research Navigator Guide provides your students with access to the Website and includes reference material and hints about conducting online research.
- **Study Card for Western Civilization** Colorful, affordable, and packed with useful information, Longman's Study Cards make studying easier, more efficient, and more enjoyable.
- **Digital Transparency Masters** A set of full-color transparency masters drawn from *Civilization in the West*, Seventh Edition. Available exclusively on the IRC.

- **History Video Program** A list of more than 100 videos from which qualified college adopters can choose. Restrictions apply.
- **History Digital Media Archive CD-ROM** This CD-ROM contains electronic images and interactive and static maps, along with media elements such as video. It is fully customizable and ready for classroom presentation. All images and maps are available in PowerPoint™ as well.
- **Interpretations of the Western World** General Editor Mark Kishlansky has prepared a customizable database of secondary source readings. Selections are grouped topically so that instructors can assign readings that illustrate different points of view about a given historical debate.

For Students

- **Study Guide** Available in two volumes, each chapter in the study guide includes a summary; a timeline activity; map and geography questions; key terms, people, and events; and identification, multiple-choice, and critical-thinking questions.
- **Western Civilization Map Workbook** These two volumes test and reinforce basic geography literacy while building critical-thinking skills.
- **Longman Atlas of Western Civilization** This 52-page atlas features carefully selected historical maps that provide comprehensive coverage for the major historical periods.
- **A Short Guide to Writing About History,** Sixth Edition Written by Richard Marius, late of Harvard University, and Melvin E. Page, Eastern Tennessee State University, and Melvin E. Page, Eastern Tennessee State University, this engaging and practical text helps students get beyond merely compiling dates and facts. Covering both brief essays and the documented resource paper, the text explores the writing and researching processes, identifies different modes of historical writing, including argument, and concludes with guidelines for improving style.

MyHistoryLab (www.myhistorylab.com)

MyHistoryLab provides students with an online package complete with the electronic textbook and numerous study aids. With several hundred primary sources, many of which are assignable and link to a gradebook, pre- and post-tests that link to a gradebook and result in individualized study plans, videos and images, as well as map activities with gradable quizzes, the site offers students a unique, interactive experience that brings history to life. The comprehensive site also includes a History Bookshelf with fifty of the most commonly assigned books in history classes and a History Toolkit with tutorials and helpful links. Other features include gradable assignments and chapter review materials; a Test Bank; and Research Navigator.

MyHistoryKit (www.myhistorykit.com)

MyHistoryKit for Western Civilization is an access-code-protected course-based website that contains a sampling of Longman's premium history content. This website includes practice tests to challenge students' knowledge of the material, flashcards that aid in studying, and media and primary source activities (documents, maps, video and audio clips, and more) that report to an online gradebook. Also included in MyHistoryKit are Research Navigator and Writing About History, both of which provide assistance with and access to powerful and reliable research material.

The Western Civilization Study Site (www.longmanwesterncivilization.com)

Students can take advantage of this open-access online course companion that includes practice tests, Web links, and flash cards that cover the scope of topics covered in a typical Western civilization class.

Longman Library of World Biography Series

Pocket-sized and brief, each biography in the Library of World Biography series relates the life of its subject to the broader themes and developments of the time. Series titles include: ***Ahmad al-Mansur: Islamic Visionary*** by Richard Smith (Ferrum College); ***Alexander the Great: Legacy of a Conqueror*** by Winthrop Lindsay Adams (University of Utah); ***Benito Mussolini: The First Fascist*** by Anthony L. Cardoza (Loyola University); ***Fukuzawa Yūkichi: From Samurai to Capitalist*** by Helen M. Hopper (University of Pittsburgh); ***Ignatius of Loyola: Founder of the Jesuits*** by John Patrick Donnelly (Marquette University); ***Jacques Coeur: Entrepreneur and King's Bursar*** by Kathryn L. Reyerson (University of Minnesota); ***Katô Shidzue: A Japanese Feminist*** by Helen M. Hopper (University of Pittsburgh); ***Simón Bolívar: Liberation and Disappointment*** by David Bushnell (University of Florida); ***Vasco da Gama: Renaissance Crusader*** by Glenn J. Ames (University of Toledo); and ***Zheng He: China and the Oceans in the Early Ming, 1405–1433*** by Edward Dreyer (University of Miami).

Penguin-Longman Partnership

The partnership between Penguin Books and Longman Publishers offers a discount on a wide range of titles when bundled with any Longman history survey textbook. Visit www.ablongman.com/penguin for more information.

ABOUT THE AUTHORS

MARK KISHLANSKY   Mark Kishlansky is Frank B. Baird, Jr., Professor of English and European History at Harvard University, where he has taught Western Civilization and courses in the CORE program for general education. He has also been awarded Harvard's Hoopes Prize for undergraduate teaching. Professor Kishlansky served as Associate Dean of the Faculty from 1999–2001. Before joining the Harvard faculty he taught for sixteen years at the University of Chicago where he was a member of the Committee on Social Thought. Professor Kishlansky is a specialist on seventeenth-century English political history and has written, among other works, *A Monarchy Transformed, The Rise of the New Model Army,* and *Parliamentary Selection: Social and Political Choice in Early Modern England.* From 1984–1991 he was editor of the *Journal of British Studies.* He is currently writing a history of the reign of Charles I entitled *The Death of Kings.* He is the General Editor of Pearson Custom Publishing's primary source databases for Western and World Civilization.

PATRICK GEARY   Holding a Ph.D. in Medieval Studies from Yale University, Patrick Geary has broad experience in interdisciplinary approaches to European history and civilization. He has served as the director of the Medieval Institute at the University of Notre Dame as well as director for the Center for Medieval and Renaissance Studies at UCLA where he is currently professor of history. He has also held positions at the University of Florida and Princeton University and has taught at the École des Hautes Études en Sciences Sociales in Paris, at the University of Vienna, and at the Central European University in Budapest. He has coordinated and participated in programs for history teachers in Pennsylvania, Florida, and California, and has co-authored a television series on medieval knights. His many publications include *Readings in Medieval History; Before France and Germany: The Creation and Transformation of the Merovingian World; Furta Sacra: Thefts of Relics in the Central Middle Ages;* and *The Myth of Nations: The Medieval Origins of Europe.*

PATRICIA O'BRIEN   Between 1995 and 1999, Patricia O'Brien worked to foster collaborative interdisciplinary research in the humanities as director of the University of California Humanities Research Institute. Between 1999 and 2004, she held the position of Dean of the College of Humanities, Arts, and Social Sciences at the University of California, Riverside. She has also held appointments at the University of California, Irvine, Yale University, and at the École des Hautes Études en Sciences Sociales in Paris. Currently Professor O'Brien is the Executive Dean of the UCLA College of Letters and Sciences. Professor O'Brien is a specialist in modern French cultural and social history and has published widely on the history of crime, punishment, cultural theory, urban history, and gender issues. Representative publications include *The Promise of Punishment: Prisons in Nineteenth-Century France;* "The Kleptomania Diagnosis: Bourgeois Women and Theft in Late Nineteenth-Century France" in *Expanding the Past: A Reader in Social History;* and "Michel Foucault's History of Culture" in *The New Cultural History,* edited by Lynn Hunt. Professor O'Brien's commitment to this textbook grew out of her own teaching experiences in large, introductory Western Civilization courses. She has benefited from the contributions of her students and fellow instructors in her approach to the study of Western Civilization in the modern period.

CIVILIZATION IN THE WEST

INTRODUCTION
THE IDEA OF WESTERN CIVILIZATION

The West is an idea. It is not visible from space. An astronaut viewing the blue-and-white terrestrial sphere can make out the form of Africa, bounded by the Atlantic, the Indian Ocean, the Red Sea, and the Mediterranean. Australia, the Americas, and even Antarctica are distinct patches of blue-green in the darker waters that surround them. But nothing comparable separates Europe from Asia, East from West. Viewed from 100 miles up, the West itself is invisible. Although astronauts can see the great Eurasian landmass curving around the Northern Hemisphere, the Ural Mountains—the theoretical boundary between East and West—appear but faintly from space. Certainly they are less impressive than the towering Himalayas, the Alps, or even the Caucasus. People, not geology, determined that the Urals should be the arbitrary boundary between Europe and Asia.

Even this determination took centuries. Originally, Europe was a name that referred only to central Greece. Gradually, Greeks extended it to include the whole Greek mainland and then the landmass to the north. Later, Roman explorers and soldiers carried Europe north and west to its modern boundaries. Asia too grew with time. Initially, Asia was only that small portion of what is today Turkey inland from the Aegean Sea. Gradually, as Greek explorers came to know of lands farther east, north, and south, they expanded their understanding of Asia to include everything east of the Don River to the north and the Red Sea to the south.

Western civilization is as much an idea as the West itself. Under the right conditions, astronauts can see the Great Wall of China snaking its way from the edge of the Himalayas to the Yellow Sea. No comparable physical legacy of the West is so massive that its details can be discerned from space. Nor are Western achievements rooted forever in one corner of the world. What we call Western civilization belongs to no particular place. Its location has changed since the origins of civilization, that is, the cultural and social traditions characteristic of the *civitas*, or city. "Western" cities appeared first outside what Europeans and Americans arbitrarily term *the West*, in the Tigris and Euphrates river basins in present-day Iraq and Iran, a region we today call the Middle East. These areas have never lost their urban traditions, but in time other cities in North Africa, Greece, and Italy adapted and expanded this heritage in different ways. If we focus on this peculiar adaptation and expansion in this book, it is not because of some intrinsic superiority but only because the developments in Europe after the birth of Jesus become more significant than those of Egypt and Mesopotamia for understanding our contemporary culture.

Until the sixteenth century c.e., the western end of the Eurasian landmass—what we think of as western Europe—was the crucible in which disparate cultural and intellectual traditions of the Near East, the Mediterranean, and the north were smelted into a new and powerful alloy. Then "the West" expanded beyond the confines of Europe, carried by the ships of merchants and adventurers to India, Africa, China, and the Americas.

Western technology for harnessing nature, Western forms of economic and political organization, Western styles of art and music are—for good or ill—dominant influences in world civilization. Japan is a leading power in the Western traditions of capitalist commerce and technology. China, the most populous country in the world, adheres to Marxist so-

North America seeking a better life but often find poverty, hostility, and racism instead. Finally, the advances of Western civilization endanger our very existence. Technology pollutes the world's air, water, and soil, and nuclear arms threaten the destruction of all civilization. And yet these are the same advances that allow us to lengthen life expectancy, harness the forces of nature, and conquer disease. It is the same technology that allows us to view our world from outer space.

cialist principles —a European political tradition. Millions of people in Africa, Asia, and the Americas follow the religions of Islam and Christianity. Both are monotheistic faiths that developed from Judaism in the cradle of Western civilization.

Many of today's most pressing problems are also part of the legacy of the Western tradition. The remnants of European colonialism have left deep hostilities throughout the world. The integration of developing nations into the world economy keeps much of humanity in a seemingly hopeless cycle of poverty as the wealth of poor countries goes to pay interest on loans from Europe and America. Western material goods lure millions of people from their traditional worlds into the sprawl of third-world cities. Hatred of Western civilization is a central, ideological tenet that inspired the attacks on symbols of American economic and military strength on September 11, 2001, and that fuels anti-Western terrorism around the world. The West itself faces a crisis. Impoverished citizens of former colonies flock to Europe and

How did we get here? In this book we attempt to answer that question. The history of Western civilization is not simply the triumphal story of progress, the creation of a better world. Even in areas in which we can see development—such as technology, communications, and social complexity—change is not always for the better. It would be equally inaccurate, however, to view the course of Western civilization as a progressive decline from a mythical golden age of the human race. The roughly 300 generations since the origins of civilization have bequeathed a rich and contradictory heritage to the present. Inherited political and social institutions, cultural forms, and religious and philosophical traditions form the framework within which the future must be created. The past does not determine the future, but it is the raw material from which the future will be made. To use this legacy properly, we must first understand it, not because the past is the key to the future, but because understanding yesterday frees us to create tomorrow.

11 THE ITALIAN RENAISSANCE

DINING AL FRESCO

LEONARDO DA VINCI'S *LAST SUPPER*

No period of Western history is better known for its artwork than that of the Italian Renaissance. It was an age with a taste for opulence and a purse to satisfy its hunger. Masters competed against each other for the most lucrative commissions. Leonardo da Vinci learned his trade in Florence, but at the age of 30 he offered his services as a military engineer to the warrior Duke of Milan. Four years later he was established as a court artist.

THE VISUAL RECORD His most important commission came in 1495 when he was instructed to decorate the wall of the new Dominican dining hall in the church of Santa Maria delle Grazie. The church was to house the tomb of the duke and his family, and Leonardo was commissioned to decorate it with a painting appropriate for the grandeur of the Sforza family and the practical purpose for which the room was to be used. He chose as his theme the Passover meal of Jesus and his Apostles.

Although *The Last Supper* was a conventional scene for a dining hall, Leonardo did not paint it conventionally. Rather than represent a group dining at leisure, he captured a moment of agitation, just after Jesus proclaimed that one of the Apostles would betray him. As you look at the picture, on the far right, you see that Matthew points back to Jesus as if to say, "Did you hear that?" At the center right, Thomas raises his finger and James sweeps his hand as if to proclaim their innocence. The three Apostles at the far left are obviously dumbstruck; Andrew holds both of his hands out as if trying to repel the thought. At the center left, Peter whispers something

to John, who appears lost in concentration. Only Judas does not seem shocked by the revelation. Seated in the forefront on the left, he clutches a purse in one hand while his left hand and Jesus' right hand reach for the same bowl of wine. Every face and gesture have a story to tell, and Leonardo shows the Apostles as naturally human rather than as the idealized biblical figures of previous portrayals.

The Last Supper tells a story, but it is also designed for the contemplation of the Dominicans as they dined. Thus the painting contains much Christian symbolism, some of it deliberately ambiguous to stimulate thought. The position of the hands of Jesus, palm up and palm down, has led to centuries of speculation, while the feminine features of John have recently been the subject of a pulp-fiction sensation. The Apostles are arranged in four groups of three, the key number in the Christian doctrine of the Trinity. The groups themselves are organized in variously shaped triangles, as is the figure of Jesus in the center. The scene takes place in front of three painted windows and three decorated arches containing the arms of the dukes of Milan.

Jesus is the centerpiece of the painting in every possible way. During restoration a nail was found in the wall at the center of his right eye. It is supposed that Leonardo ran strings from that nail to determine the place of the other figures, for the lines of perspective all emanate from there. Jesus expresses serenity in contrast to the Apostles' agitation. The window directly behind his head gives the impression of surrounding him in a halo. Most interestingly, the figure of Jesus is larger than that of any of the others, though the

■ Leonardo da Vinci's *The Last Supper* (1495). A conventional scene of dining, yet one full of symbolism, in which da Vinci masterfully captures a crucial moment for Christianity.

arrangement of the group does not make this emphasis immediately obvious.

Perhaps because of all of these qualities, *The Last Supper* was an immediate sensation. But Leonardo had made a tragic mistake. In an attempt to create bolder colors, he shunned the traditional technique of fresco painting in which the paint was applied while the plaster was wet and hardened into it. Instead, using a mixture of egg whites and oil, Leonardo applied the paint to a dry surface. At first the experiment was a success and the reds, golds, and aquamarines stood out as in no other wall painting. But in less than 25 years, the paint began to crack and flake. Down through the centuries retouching and restoring were constantly necessary and very little of what remains on the wall of the church of Santa Maria delle Grazie today is what Leonardo put there more than five hundred years ago.

LOOKING AHEAD

The Last Supper *is but one of many masterpieces produced on the Italian peninsula during the centuries dubbed the Renaissance. In this chapter we shall see how philosophy, art, architecture, and literature enjoyed a remarkable development in the Italian city-states and how Renaissance ideals were exported throughout the Continent and came to define the age.*

RENAISSANCE SOCIETY

Perhaps the most surprising result of the Black Death was the way in which European society revived itself in the succeeding centuries. Even at the height of the plague, a spirit of revitalization was evident in the works of artists and writers. Petrarch (1304–1374), the great humanist poet and scholar, was among the first to differentiate the new age in which he was living from two earlier ones: the **classical** world of Greece and Rome, which he admired, and the subsequent Dark Ages, which he detested. That spirit of self-awareness is one of the defining characteristics of the **Renaissance.** "It is but in our own day that men dare boast that they see the dawn of better things," wrote Matteo Palmieri (1406–1475). Like many others, Marsilio Ficino (1433–1499), a Florentine physician and philosopher who translated Plato and dabbled in astrology, dubbed his times a golden age: "This century, like a golden age, has restored to light the liberal arts, which were almost extinct: grammar, poetry, rhetoric, painting, sculpture, architecture, and music." The Renaissance was a new age by self-assertion. In that self-assertion, wave after wave of artistic celebration of the human spirit found its wellspring and created a legacy that is still vibrant 500 years later.

What was the Renaissance? A French word for an Italian phenomenon, *renaissance* literally means "rebirth." The word captures both the emphasis on humanity that characterized Renaissance thinking and the renewed fascination with the classical world. The Renaissance revered things classical, which to them meant ancient Latin and Greek history and literature. But the Renaissance was an age rather than an event. There is no moment at which the Middle Ages ended, and late medieval society was artistically creative, socially well developed, and economically diverse. Yet eventually the pace of change accelerated, and it is best to think of the Renaissance

as an era of rapid transitions. Encompassing the two centuries between 1350 and 1550, it passed through three distinct phases. The first, from 1350 to 1400, was characterized by a declining population, the uncovering of classical texts, and experimentation in a variety of art forms. The second phase, from 1400 to 1500, was distinguished by the creation of a set of cultural values and artistic and literary achievements that defined Renaissance style. The large Italian city-states developed stable and coherent forms of government, and the warfare between them gradually ended. In the final period, from 1500 to 1550, invasions from France and Spain transformed Italian political life, and the ideas and techniques of Italian writers and artists radiated to all points of the Continent. Renaissance ideas and achievements spread throughout western Europe and were particularly important in Holland, but they are best studied where they first developed, on the Italian peninsula.

The Urban Environment

The Italian peninsula differed sharply from other areas of Europe in the extent to which it was urban. By the late Middle Ages nearly one in four Italians lived in a town, in contrast to one in ten elsewhere. Not even the plague did much to change that ratio. There were more Italian cities and more people in them. By 1500, seven of the ten largest cities in the West were in Italy. Naples, Venice, and Milan, each with a population of more than 100,000, led the rest. But not every city was a great metropolis, and it was the numerous smaller towns, with populations nearer to 1000, that gave the Italian peninsula its urban character. Cities also served as convenient centers of judicial and ecclesiastical power.

Cities acted as central places around which a cluster of large and small villages was organized. Urban areas, especially the small towns, provided markets for the agricultural produce of the countryside and for the manufactured goods of the urban artisans. This structure allowed for the specialization in agricultural and industrial life that increased both productivity and wages. Cities also caught the runoff of rural population, especially the surplus of younger sons and daughters who could not be accommodated on the farms. Cities grew by migration rather than by natural increase. Thus the areas surrounding a city were critical to its prosperity and survival. The urban system was a network of cities encompassed by towns and encircled by rural villages. Florence, the dominant city in the region of Tuscany, exemplifies that relationship. Although it possessed two-thirds of its region's wealth, Florence contained only 14 percent of the regional population. The surrounding countryside was agriculturally rich because marketing costs were low and demand for foodstuffs was high. Smaller cities channeled their local produce and trade to Florence.

Urban populations were organized far differently from rural ones. On the farms, the central distinctions involved ownership of land. Some farmers owned their estates outright and left them intact to their heirs. Others were involved in a

MAP DISCOVERY

Largest Cities

- ■ 125,000 and over
- ▲ 100,000 to 125,000
- ● 50,000 to 100,000
- ○ 25,000 to 50,000
- Boundary of the Holy Roman Empire

Largest Cities in Western Europe, ca. 1500

Examine the locations of western Europe's largest cities at the beginning of the sixteenth century. Where were these cities concentrated? What was the least urbanized part of Europe? Based on this information, why do you suppose the Mediterranean Sea was considered the center of Europe? What was distinctive about the Holy Roman Empire?

sharecropping system by which absentee owners of land supplied working capital in return for half of the farm's produce. A great gulf in wealth separated owners from sharecroppers, but within the groups the gaps were not as great. There were gradations, but those ordinarily were temporary conditions that bad harvests, generous dowries, or divided inheritances balanced out over time.

In the city, however, distinctions were based first on occupation, which largely corresponded to social position and wealth. Cities began as markets, and the privilege to participate in the market defined citizens. City governments provided protection for consumers and producers by creating monopolies through which standards for craftsmanship were maintained and profits for craftsmen were guaranteed. The monopolies were called guilds or companies. Each large city had its own hierarchy of guilds. At the top were the important manufacturing groups—clothiers, metalworkers, and the like. Just below them were bankers, merchants, and the administrators of civic and Church holdings. At the bottom were grocers, masons, and other skilled workers. Roughly speaking, all of those within the guild structure, from bottom to top, lived comfortably. Yet the majority of urban inhabitants were not members of guilds. Many managed to eke out a living as wage laborers; many more were simply destitute. As a group, the poor constituted as much as half of the entire population. Most were dependent upon civic and private charity for their survival.

The disparities between rich and poor were overwhelming. The concentration of wealth in the hands of an ever-narrowing group of families and favored guilds characterized every large city. One reason for that was the extreme instability of economic life. Prices and wages fluctuated wildly in response to local circumstance. After an epidemic of plague, wages climbed and the prices of consumer goods tumbled. A bad harvest sent food prices skyrocketing. Only those able to even out the extreme swings by stockpiling goods in times of plenty and consuming them in times of want were safe. Capital, however initially accumulated, was the key to continued wealth. Monopolies ensured the profitability of trade and manufacturing, but only those with sufficient capital could engage in either. In Florence, for example, 10 percent of the families controlled 90 percent of the wealth, with an even more extreme concentration at the top. The combined wealth of the richest 100 Florentine families was greater than the combined wealth of 87 percent of the city's population.

Production and Consumption

The concentration of wealth and the way in which it was used defined the Renaissance economy. Economic life is bound up in the relationship between resources and desires, or, as economists would have it, supply and demand. The late medieval economy, despite the development of international banking and long-distance trade, was still an economy of primary producers: between 70 and 90 percent of Europe's population was involved in subsistence agriculture. Even in Italy, which contained the greatest concentration of urban areas in the world, agriculture predominated. The manufacture of clothing was the only other significant economic activity. Moreover, most of what was produced was for local consumption rather than for the marketplace. The relationship between supply and demand was precisely measured by the full or empty stomach. Even in good times, more than 80 percent of the population lived at subsistence level with food, clothing, and shelter their only expenses. Thus, when the market economy of the Renaissance is discussed, it actually is the circumstances of the few rather than the many that are under discussion.

The defining characteristic of the early Renaissance economy was population change. Recurring waves of plague kept population levels low for more than a century. Between 1350 and 1450, one in every six years was characterized by an unusually high mortality rate. At the end of that period, for example, Florence's population was only a quarter of what it had been at the beginning. The dramatic reduction in population depressed economic growth. Until 1460 the major sectors of the economy were stagnant. Only after the sustained population increase toward the end of the fifteenth century did the

general economy revive. Until then, in both agriculture and manufacturing, supply outstripped demand.

On the farms, overabundance resulted from two related developments, the concentration of surviving farmers on the best land and the enlargement of their holdings. In the shops, finished products outnumbered the consumers who survived the epidemics. Overproduction meant lower prices for basic commodities, and the decline in population meant higher wages for labor. The result was that, at the lowest levels of society, survivors found it easier to earn their living and even to create a surplus than had their parents. For a time, the lot of the masses improved.

But for investors, such economic conditions meant that neither agriculture nor cloth making were particularly attractive. Expensive investments in land or equipment for sharecropping were paid back in inexpensive grain. High wages for the few surviving skilled workers brought a return only in cheap cloth. In such circumstances, consumption was more attractive than investment. It was not merely the perceived shortage in profitable investments that brought on the increase in conspicuous consumption during the fifteenth century. In the psychological atmosphere created by unpredictable, swift, and deadly epidemics, luxurious living seemed an appropriate response. Moreover, although tax rates increased, houses and personal property remained exempt, making luxury goods attractive investments. Even those at the lowest levels of society eagerly purchased whatever their meager means permitted.

For those reasons, the production and consumption of luxuries soared. By the middle of the fourteenth century, Florence was known for its silks and jewelry as much as for its cloth. Venice became a European center for the glass industry, especially for the finely ground glass that was used in eye-

■ Skilled workers in cities contributed greatly to European economic growth in the late medieval period. This scene shows the manufacture of cannons in a Florentine foundry.

glasses. Production of specialty crops such as sugar, saffron, fruits, and high-quality wine expanded. International trade increasingly centered on acquiring Eastern specialities, resulting in the serious outflow of gold and silver that enriched first the Byzantine and then the Ottoman emperors.

The Experience of Life

Luxury helped improve a life that for rich and poor alike was short and uncertain. Nature was still people's most potent enemy. Renaissance children who survived infancy found their lives governed by parentage and by gender. In parentage, the great divide was between those who lived with surplus and those who lived at subsistence. The first category encompassed the wealthiest bankers and merchants down to those who owned their own farms or engaged in small urban crafts. The vast majority of urban and rural dwellers comprised the second category. About the children of the poor we know very little other than that their survival was unlikely. If they did not die at birth or shortly afterward, they might be abandoned—especially if female—to the growing number of orphanages in the cities, waste away from lack of nutrition, or fall prey to ordinary childhood diseases for which there were no treatments. Eldest sons were favored; younger daughters were disadvantaged. In poor families, however, this favoritism meant little more than early apprenticeship to day labor in the city or farm labor in the countryside. Girls were frequently sent out as domestic servants far from the family home.

Childhood. Children of the wealthy had better chances for survival than did children of the poor. For children of the wealthy, childhood might begin with "milk parents," life in the home of the family of a wet nurse who would breast-feed the baby through infancy. Only the very wealthy could afford a live-in wet nurse, which would increase the child's chances of survival. Again, daughters were more likely to be sent far from home and least likely to have their nursing supervised. The use of wet nurses not only emancipated parents from the daily care of infants, it also allowed them to resume sexual relations. Nursing women refrained from sex in the belief that it affected their milk.

During the period between weaning and apprenticeship, Renaissance children lived with their families. There was no typical Renaissance family. Nuclear families—parents and their children under one roof—were probably more common than extended families, which might include grandparents and other relatives. But the composition of the family changed over the course of the life cycle and included times in which married children or grandparents were present and other times when a single parent and small children were the only members. Moreover, even nuclear families commonly contained stepparents and stepchildren as well as domestic servants or apprentices. Thus a child returning to the parental household was as likely to form emotional bonds with older siblings as with parents.

Sons inherited the family business and its most important possessions—tools of the trade or beasts of labor for the farm. Inheritance customs varied. In some places only the eldest son received the equipment of the family occupation; in others, such as Tuscany, all the sons shared it. Still, in the first 15 years of life, the most-favored children would have spent between one-third and one-half of their time outside the household in which they had been born.

Marriage and the Family. Expectations for daughters centered on their chances of marriage. For a girl, dowry was everything. If a girl's father could provide a handsome one, her future was secure; if not, the alternatives were a convent, which would take a small bequest, or a match lower down the social scale, where the quality of life deteriorated rapidly. Daughters of poor families entered domestic service in order to have a dowry provided by their masters. The dowry was taken to the household of the husband. There the couple resided until they established their own separate family. If the husband died, it was to his parental household that the widow returned.

DOCUMENT

The Office and Dutie of an Husband

Women married in late adolescence, usually around the age of 20. Among the wealthy, marriages were perceived as familial alliances and business transactions rather than love matches. The dowry was an investment on which fathers expected a return, and while the bride might have some choice, it was severely limited. Compatibility was not a central feature in matchmaking. Husbands were, on average, ten years older than their wives and likely to leave them widows. In the early fifteenth century, about one-fourth of all adult women in Florence were widows, many without prospects of remarriage.

Life experiences differed for males. Men married later—near the age of 25 on the farms, nearer the age of 30 in the cities—because of the cost of setting up in trade or on the land. Late marriage meant long supervision under the watchful eye of father or master, an extended period between adolescence and adulthood. The reputation that Renaissance cities gained for homosexuality and licentiousness must be viewed in light of the advanced age at which males married. The level of sexual frustration was high, and its outlet in ritual violence and rape was also high.

The establishment of one's own household through marriage was a late rite of passage, considering the expectations of early death. Men came of age at 30 but were thought to be old by 50. Thus for men marriage and parenthood took place in middle age rather than in youth. Valued all their lives more highly than their sisters, male heads of households were the source of all power in their domiciles, in their shops, and in the state. They were responsible for overseeing every aspect of the upbringing of their children, even choosing wet nurses for their infants and spouses for their daughters. But their wives were essential partners who governed domestic life. Women labored not only at the hearth, but in the fields and shops as well. Their economic contribution to the well-being of the family was critical, both in the dowry they brought at marriage

ON THE FAMILY

Leon Battista Alberti wrote a number of important tracts that set out the general principles of a subject, including On Architecture, *which was considered the basic text for 300 years. His writings on the family bring insight into the nature of a patriarchal, male-dominated institution.*

Focus Questions

According to Alberti, why is it important for men to look for an "honorable manner" when choosing a wife? What role would Alberti see the wife playing in a marriage?

They say that in choosing a wife one looks for beauty, parentage, and riches. . . . Among the most essential criteria of beauty in a woman is an honorable manner. Even a wild, prodigal, greasy, drunken woman may be beautiful of feature, but no one would call her a beautiful wife. A woman worthy of praise must show first of all in her conduct, modesty, and purity. Marius, the illustrious Roman, said in that first speech of his to the Roman people: "Of women we require purity, of men labor." And I certainly agree. There is nothing more disgusting than a coarse and dirty woman. Who is stupid enough not to see clearly that a woman who does not care for neatness and cleanliness in her appearance, not only in her dress and body but in all her behavior and language, is by no means well mannered? How can it be anything but obvious that a bad-mannered woman is also rarely virtuous? We shall consider elsewhere the harm that comes to a family from women who lack virtue, for I myself do not know which is the worse fate for a family, total celibacy or a single dishonored woman. In a bride, therefore, a man must first seek beauty of mind, that is, good conduct and virtue.

In her body he must seek not only loveliness, grace, and charm but must also choose a woman who is well made for bearing children, with the kind of constitution that promises to make them strong and big. There's an old proverb, "When you pick your wife, you choose your children." All her virtues will in fact shine brighter still in beautiful children. It is a well-known saying among poets: "Beautiful character dwells in a beautiful body." The natural philosophers require that a woman be neither thin nor very fat. Those laden with fat are subject to coldness and constipation and slow to conceive. They say that a woman should have a joyful nature, fresh and lively in her blood and her whole being. They have no objections to a dark girl. They do reject girls with a frowning black visage, however. They have no liking for either the undersized or the overlarge and lean. They find that a woman is most suited to bear children if she is fairly big and has limbs of ample length. They always have a preference for youth, based on a number of arguments which I need not expound here, but particularly on the point that a young girl has a more adaptable mind. Young girls are pure by virtue of their age and have not developed any spitefulness. They are by nature modest and free of vice. They quickly learn to accept affectionately and unresistingly the habits and wishes of their husbands.

From Leon Battista Alberti, *On the Family.*

and in the labor they contributed to the household. If their wives died, men with young children remarried quickly. While there were many bachelors, there were few widowers.

In most cases death came suddenly. Epidemic diseases, of which plague was the most virulent, struck with fearful regularity. Even in the absence of a serious outbreak, there were always deaths in town and country attributable to the plague. Epidemics struck harder at the young—children and adolescents, who were the majority of the population—and hardest in the summer months, when other viruses and bacteria weakened the population. Influenza must have been the second largest cause of death, although that can only be speculated in the absence of proper records. Medical treatment was more likely to hasten death than to prolong life. Lorenzo de' Medici's physician prescribed powdered pearls for the Florentine ruler's gout. After that Lorenzo complained more of stomach pains than of gout. Such remedies revealed a belief in the harmony of nature and the healing power of rare substances. The remedies were not silly or superstitious, but they were not effective either. Starvation was rare, less because of food shortage than because the seriously undernourished were more likely to succumb to disease than to famine. In urban areas, the government would intervene to provide grain from public storehouses at times of extreme shortage; in the countryside, large landholders commonly exercised the same function.

The Quality of Life

Although life may have been difficult during the Renaissance, it was not unfulfilling. Despite constant toil and frequent hardship, people of the Renaissance had reason to believe that their lives were better than those of their ancestors and that their children's lives would be better still. On the most basic

■ Double portraits of husbands and wives showed the union of individuals and of families. In this ca. 1465 diptych of Frederico da Montefeltro, the Duke of Urbino, and his wife Battista Sforza, artist Piero della Francesca shows the couple facing each other against the distant backdrop of the territory they ruled. Their union joined the Montefeltro family ruling the small duchy of Urbino in central Italy with the powerful Sforza family that ruled Milan. The wealthy couple was also a generous patron of the artist.

level, health improved and, for those who survived plague, life expectancy increased. Better health was related to better diet. Improvement came from two sources: the relative surplus of grain throughout the fifteenth century and the wider variety of foods consumed. Bread remained the most widely consumed foodstuff, but even subsistence consumers were beginning to supplement their diet with meat and dairy products. There was more pork and lamb in the diet of ordinary people in the fifteenth century than there would be for the next 400 years. At the upper levels of society, sweet wine and citrus fruits helped offset the lack of vegetables. The diversification of diet resulted from improvements in transportation and communication, which brought more goods and services to a growing number of towns in the chain that linked the regional centers to the rural countryside.

As in the Middle Ages, the Church remained the spatial, spiritual, and social center of people's lives. Though Renaissance society became more worldly in outlook, this worldliness took place within the context of an absorbing de-

votional life. There was not yet any separation between faith and reason. The Church provided explanations for both the mysterious and the mundane. The clergy performed the rituals of baptism, marriage, and burial that measured the passage of life. Religious symbols also adorned the flags of militia troops, the emblems of guilds, and the regalia of the city itself. The Church preserved holy relics that were venerated for their power to protect the city or to endow it with particular skills and resources. Through its holy days as much as through its rituals, the Church helped to channel leisure activities into community celebrations.

A growing sense of civic pride and individual accomplishment were underlying characteristics of the Italian Renaissance, enhanced by the development of social cohesion and community solidarity that both Church and city-state fostered. It is commonly held that the Renaissance was both elitist and male dominated, that it was an experience separate from that of the society at large. There can be no question that it was the rich who commissioned works of art and that it was the highly skilled male craftsmen who executed them. But neither lived in a social vacuum. The Renaissance was not the result of the efforts of a privileged few. Family values that permitted early apprenticeships in surrogate households and that emphasized the continuity of crafts from one generation to the next made possible the skilled artists of the Renaissance cities. The stress on the production of luxury goods placed higher value upon individual skills and therefore upon excellence in workmanship. Church and state sought to express social values through representational art. One of the chief purposes of wall murals was to instruct the unlettered in religion, to help them visualize the central episodes in Christian history and thus increase the pleasure they derived from their faith. The grandiose architecture and statuary that adorned central places were designed to enhance civic pride, nurture loyalty, and communicate the protective power of public institutions.

For ordinary people, the world of the Renaissance was not much different from the world of the Middle Ages. Although urban areas grew, providing a wider variety of occupations and a varied material life, most people continued to scratch a meager living from the soil. The crucial difference from generation to generation was the degree of infectious diseases and the rate of rising or falling population. For the lucky ones there was surplus, for the unfortunate there was dearth. Within those confines, men were privileged over women, having greater security, status, and monopolizing power. But the tightly knit organization of family life protected the weak and the poor, while the Church provided faith, hope, and charity.

RENAISSANCE ART

In every age, artistic achievement represents a combination of individual talent and predominant social ideals. Artists may be at the leading edge of the society in which they live, but it is the spirit of that society that they capture in word, song, or image. Artistic disciplines also have their own technical development. Individually, Renaissance artists were attempting to solve problems of perspective and three-dimensionality that had defeated their predecessors. But the particular techniques or experiments that interested them owed as much to the social context as they did to the artistic one. For example, the urban character of Italian government led to the need for civic architecture—public buildings on a grand scale. The celebration of individual achievement led to the explosive growth of portraiture. Not surprisingly, major technological breakthroughs were achieved in both areas. Nor should the brilliance of the artists themselves be underestimated. To deny genius is to deprecate humanity. What needs to be explained is not the existence of a Leonardo or a Michelangelo but their coexistence.

The relationship between artist and social context was all the more important in the Renaissance, when artists were closely tied to the crafts and trades of urban society and to the demands of clients who commissioned their work. Although it was the elite who patronized art, it was skilled tradesmen who

produced it. Artists normally followed the pattern of any craftsman—an apprenticeship begun as a teenager and a long period of training and work in a master's shop. That form of education gave the aspiring artist a practical rather than a theoretical bent and a keen appreciation for the business side of art. Studios were identified with particular styles and competed for commissions from clients, especially the Church. Wealthy individuals commissioned art as investments, as marks of personal distinction, and as displays of public piety. They got what they paid for, usually entering into detailed contracts that stipulated the quality of materials and the amount of work done by the master. Isabella d'Este (1474–1539), one of the great patrons of Renaissance artists, wrote hundreds of letters specifying the details of the works she commissioned. She once sent an artist threads of the exact dimensions of the pictures she had ordered. Demand for art was high. The vast public works projects needed buildings, the new piazzas (public squares) and palazzos (private houses) needed statuary, and the long walls of churches needed murals.

The survival of so many Renaissance masterpieces allows us to reconstruct the stages by which the remarkable artistic achievements of the era took place. Although advances were made in a variety of fields during the Renaissance, the three outstanding areas were architecture, sculpture, and painting. Whereas modern artists would consider each a separate discipline, Renaissance artists crossed their boundaries without hesitation. Not only could the artists work with a variety of materials, their intensive and varied apprenticeships taught them to apply the technical solutions of one field to the problems of another. Few Renaissance artists confined themselves to one area of artistic expression, and many created works of enduring beauty in more than one medium. Was the greatest achievement of Michelangelo his sculpture of David, his paintings on the ceiling of the Sistine Chapel, or his design for the dome of Saint Peter's? Only a century of interdisciplinary cross-fertilization could have prepared the artistic world for such a feat.

An Architect, a Sculptor, and a Painter

The century that culminated in Michelangelo's extraordinary achievements began with the work of three Florentine masters who deeply influenced one another's development: Brunelleschi (1377–1446), Donatello (1386–1466), and Masaccio (1401–1428). In the Renaissance, the dominant artistic discipline was architecture. Buildings were the most expensive investment patrons could make, and the technical knowledge necessary for their successful construction was immense. Not only did the architect design a building, he also served as its general contractor, its construction supervisor, and its inspector. Moreover, the architect's design determined the amount and the scale of the statuary and decorative paintings to be incorporated. By 1400 the Gothic style of building had dominated western Europe for more than two centuries. Its pointed arches, vaulted ceilings, and slender spires had simplified building by removing the heavy walls formerly

IMAGE DISCOVERY

Philosophers and Painters

Raphael's fresco *The School of Athens* depicts the meeting of great minds of antiquity and of the Renaissance. The scene takes place in a dome, one of the architectural achievements of the ancient Mediterranean that was revived in the Renaissance. What might Raphael have sought to communicate by using ancient-turned-modern architecture to frame his gathering? Raphael depicts several distinct groups of learned men in active discussion. Do you think their topics differ? What can you determine about their discussions from the picture? For instance, why is the bearded man in the lower-right corner holding a globe? Which group is most important? The man with a long, white beard at the center of the painting, leading the largest group, is thought to be both Plato and Leonardo da Vinci. How would placing an ancient philosopher and a Renaissance man in the same body relate to Raphael's use of a dome as the setting for the school?

thought necessary to support great structures. Gothic construction permitted greater height, a characteristic especially desirable in cathedrals, which stretched toward the heavens. Although the buildings themselves were simplified, the techniques for erecting them became more complex. By the fifteenth century, architects had turned their techniques into an intricate style. They became obsessed by angular arches, elaborate vaultings and buttresses, and long, pointed spires.

It was Brunelleschi who decisively challenged the principles of Gothic architecture by recombining its basic elements with those of classical structures. His achievement was less an innovation than a radical synthesis of old and new. Basing his designs on geometric principles, Brunelleschi reintroduced planes and spheres as dominant motifs. His greatest work was the dome on the cathedral in Florence, begun in 1420. His design was simple but bold. The windows at the base of the dome of the cathedral illustrate Brunelleschi's geometric technique. Circular windows are set inside a square of panels, which in turn are set inside a rectangle. The facades are dominated by columns and rounded arches, proportionally spaced from a central perspective. Brunelleschi is generally credited with having been the first Renaissance artist to have understood and made use of perspective, though it was immediately put to more dramatic effect in sculpture and painting.

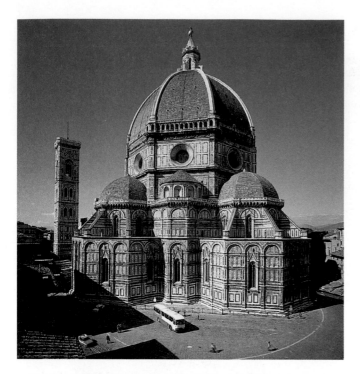

■ Florence Cathedral was begun by Arnolfo di Cambio in 1296. The nave was finished about 1350 and the dome, designed by Brunelleschi, was added in the 1420s. This view shows the dome and the apse end of the cathedral.

The sculptor's study was the human form in all of its three-dimensional complexity. The survival of Roman and Hellenistic pieces, mostly bold and muscular torsos, meant that the influence of classical art was most direct in sculpture. Donatello translated the classical styles into more naturalistic forms. His technique is evident in the long flowing robes that distinguish most of his works. Donatello sculpted the cloth, not in the stylized angularity of the past in which the creases were as sharp as sword blades, but in the natural fashion in which cloth hung. Donatello also revived the freestanding statue, which demanded greater attention to human anatomy because it was viewed from many angles. *Judith Slaying Holofernes* (1455) is an outstanding example of Donatello's use of geometric proportion and perspective. Each side of the piece captures a different vision of Judith in action. In addition, Donatello led the revival of the equestrian statue, sculpting the Venetian captain-general Gattamelata for a public square in Padua. The enormous bronze horse and rider (1445–1450) borrowed from surviving first- and second-century Roman models but relied upon the standpoint of the viewer to achieve its overpowering effect. The use of **linear perspective,** a technique applying principles of geometry to create the illusion of depth and dimension on a flat surface, was also a characteristic of Donatello's dramatic works. His breathtaking bas-relief altar scenes of the miracles of Saint Anthony in Padua, which resemble nothing so much as a canvas cast in bronze, utilize linear perspective and architectural elements to make the flattened relief panels spring to life.

The altar scenes clearly evince the unmistakable influence of the paintings of Masaccio. Although he lived fewer than 30 years, Masaccio created an enduring legacy. His frescoes in the Brancacci Chapel in Florence were studied and sketched by all the great artists of the next generation, who unreservedly praised his naturalism. What most claims the attention of the modern viewer is Masaccio's shading of light and shadow and his brilliant use of linear perspective to create the illusion that a flat surface has three dimensions. Masaccio worked with standard Christian themes, but he brought an entirely novel approach to them all. In an adoration scene he portrayed a middle-aged Madonna and a dwarfish baby Jesus; in a painting of Saint Peter paying tribute money he used his own likeness as the face of one of the Apostles. His two best-known works are *The Expulsion of Adam and Eve* (ca. 1425) and *The Holy Trinity* (1425). In *The Expulsion of Adam and Eve,* Masaccio has left an unforgettable image of the fall from grace in Eve's primeval anguish. Her deep eyes and hollow mouth are accentuated by casting the source of light downward and shading what otherwise would be lighted. In *The Holy Trinity,* Masaccio provides the classic example of the use of linear perspective. In the painting, the ceiling of a Brunelleschi-designed temple recedes to a vanishing point beyond the head of God, creating the simultaneous illusion of height and depth.

■ Donatello's bronze statue *Judith Slaying Holofernes* symbolized the Florentines' love of liberty and hatred of tyranny.

■ In this fresco, *The Expulsion of Adam and Eve* (ca. 1425), Masaccio's mastery of perspective helps create the illusion of movement, as an angel drives the grieving Adam and Eve out of paradise into the world.

Renaissance Style

By the middle of the fifteenth century, a recognizable Renaissance style had triumphed. Florence continued to lead the way, although ideas, techniques, and influences had spread throughout the Italian peninsula and even to the north and west. The outstanding architect of the period was Leon Battista Alberti (1404–1472), whose treatise *On Architecture* (1452) remained the most influential work on the subject until the eighteenth century. Alberti consecrated the geometric principles laid down by Brunelleschi and infused them with a humanist spirit. He revived the classical dictum that a building, like a body, should have an even number of supports and, like a head, an odd number of openings, which furthered precise geometric calculations in scale and design. But it was in civic architecture that Alberti made his most significant contributions. There he demonstrated how classical forms could be applied to traditional living space by being made purely decorative. His facade of the Palazzo Rucellai uses columns and arches not as building supports, but as embellishments that give geometric harmony to the building's appearance.

No sculptor challenged the preeminence of Donatello for another 50 years, but in painting there were many contenders for the garlands worn by Masaccio. The first was Piero della Francesca (ca. 1420–1492) who, though trained in the tradition of Masaccio, broke new ground in his concern for the visual unity of his paintings. From portraits to processions to his stunning fresco *The Resurrection* (ca. 1463), Piero concentrated upon the most technical aspects of composition. He was influenced by Alberti's ideas about the geometry of form, and it is said that his measurements and calculations for various parts of *The Resurrection* took more time than the painting itself. Another challenger was Sandro Botticelli (1445–1510), whose classical themes, sensitive portraits, and bright colors set him apart from the line of Florentine painters with whom he studied. His mythologies, *The Birth of Venus* and *Primavera* (both ca. 1478), depart markedly from the naturalism inspired by Masaccio. Botticelli's paintings have a dreamlike quality, an unreality highlighted by the beautiful faces and lithe figures of his characters.

Botticelli's concern with beauty and personality is also seen in the paintings of Leonardo da Vinci (1452–1519), whose creative genius embodied the Renaissance ideal of the "universal man." Leonardo's achievements in scientific, technical, and artistic endeavors read like a list of all of the subjects known during the Renaissance. His detailed anatomical drawings and the method he devised for rendering them, his botanical observations, and his engineering inventions (including models for the tank and the airplane) testify to his unrestrained curiosity. His paintings reveal the scientific application of mathematics to matters of proportion and perspective. The dramatic fresco *The Last Supper* (ca. 1495–1498), for example, takes the traditional scene of Jesus and his disciples at a long table and divides it into four groups of three, each with its

DOCUMENT

Vasari on Leonardo da Vinci

■ Botticelli's *Primavera* (Spring), also called *Garden of Venus*. Venus, in the center, is attended by the three Graces and by Cupid, Flora, Chloris, and Zephyr. Botticelli's figures have a dreamlike quality, an unreality highlighted by their beautiful faces and lithe figures.

own separate action, leaving Jesus to dominate the center of the picture by balancing its two sides. Leonardo's psychological portrait *La Gioconda* (1503–1506), popularly called the *Mona Lisa*, is quite possibly the best-known picture in the Western world.

From Brunelleschi to Alberti, from Masaccio to Leonardo da Vinci, Renaissance artists placed a unique stamp upon visual culture. By reviving classical themes, geometric principles, and a spirit of human vitality, they broke decisively from the dominant medieval traditions. Art became a source of individual and collective pride, produced by masters but consumed by all. Cities and wealthy patrons commissioned great works of art for public display. New buildings rose everywhere, adorned with the statues and murals that still stand as a testimony to generations of artists.

Michelangelo

The artistic achievements of the Renaissance culminated in the creative outpourings of Michelangelo Buonarroti (1475–1564). It is almost as if the age itself had produced a summation of how it wished to be remembered. Uncharacteristically, Michelangelo came from a family of standing in Florentine society and gained his apprenticeship over the opposition of his father. He claimed to have imbibed his love of sculpture from the milk of his wet nurse, who was the wife of a stonecutter. In 1490, Michelangelo gained a place in the household of Lorenzo de' Medici, thus avoiding the long years of apprenticeship during which someone else's style was implanted upon a young artist.

In 1496, Michelangelo moved to Rome. There his abilities as a sculptor brought him a commission from a French cardinal for a religious work in the classical style, which Michelangelo named the **Pietà**. Although it was his first attempt at sculpting a work of religious art, Michelangelo would never surpass it in beauty or composition. The *Pietà* created a sensation in Rome, and by the time that Michelangelo returned to Florence in 1501, at the age of 26, he was already acknowledged as one of the great sculptors of his day. He was immediately commissioned to work on an enormous block of marble that had been quarried nearly a half-century before and had defeated the talents of a series of carvers. He worked continuously for three years on his *David* (1501–1504), a piece that completed the union between classical and Renaissance styles. Michelangelo's giant nude gives eloquent expression to his belief that the human body was the "mortal veil" of the soul.

Although Michelangelo always believed himself to be primarily a sculptor, his next outstanding work was in the field of painting. In 1508, Pope Julius II commissioned Michelangelo to decorate the small ceremonial chapel that had been built next to the new papal residence. The initial plan called for figures of the 12 apostles to adorn the ceiling, but Michelangelo soon launched a more ambitious scheme: to portray, in an extended narrative, human creation and those Old Testament events that foreshadowed the birth of Jesus. Everything about the execution of the Sistine Chapel paintings was extraordinary. First, Michelangelo framed his scenes within the architecture of a massive classical temple. In this way he was able to give the impression of having flattened the rounded surface ment for the grave of Saint Peter. The basework had already been laid, and drawings for the building's completion had been made 30 years earlier by Donato Bramante. Michelangelo altered the plans in an effort to bring more light inside the church and provide a more majestic facade outside. His main contribution, however, was the design of the great dome, which centered the interior of the church on Saint Peter's grave. More than the height, it is the harmony of Michelangelo's design that creates the sense of the building thrusting upward like a Gothic cathedral of old. The dome on Saint Peter's was the largest then known and provided the model, in succeeding generations, for Saint Paul's Cathedral in London and the U.S. Capitol building in Washington, DC.

Renaissance art served Renaissance society. It reflected both its concrete achievements and its visionary ideals. It was a synthesis of old and new, building upon classical models, particularly in sculpture and architecture, but adding newly discovered techniques and skills. Demanding patrons such as Pope Julius II, who commonly interrupted Michelangelo's work on the Sistine Chapel with criticisms and suggestions, fueled the remarkable growth in both the quantity and quality

■ Michelangelo, *Pietà* (1498–1499). The sculptor's contract for the piece called for it to be "the most beautiful work in marble which exists today in Rome." Michelangelo made several trips to Carrara to find the highest quality marble for the *Pietà*.

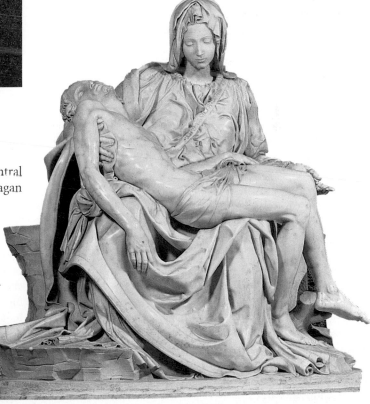

on which he worked. Then, on the two sides of the central panels, he represented figures of Hebrew prophets and pagan Sybils as sculptured marble statues. Finally, within the center panels came his fresco scenes of the events of the creation and of human history from the Fall to the Flood. His representations were simple and compelling: the fingers of God and Adam nearly touching; Eve with one leg still emerging from Adam's side; the half-human snake in the temptation. All are majestically evocative.

The *Pietà*, the *David*, and the paintings of the Sistine Chapel were the work of youth. Michelangelo's crowning achievement—the building of Saint Peter's—was undertaken at the age of 71. The purpose of the church was to provide a suitable monu-

■ The creation of Adam and Eve, a detail from Michelangelo's frescoes on the ceiling of the Sistine Chapel. The Sistine frescoes had become obscured by dirt and layers of varnish and glue applied at various times over the years. In the 1980s they were cleaned to reveal their original colors.

of Renaissance art. When Giorgio Vasari (1511–1574) came to write his *Lives of the Most Eminent Painters, Sculptors, and Architects* (1550), he found more than 200 artists worthy of distinction. But Renaissance artists did more than construct and adorn buildings and celebrate and beautify spiritual life. Inevitably their work expressed the ideals and aspirations of the society in which they lived, the new emphasis upon learning and knowledge; upon the here and now rather than the hereafter; and, most importantly, upon humanity and its capacity for growth and perfection.

RENAISSANCE IDEALS

Renaissance thought went hand in glove with Renaissance art. Scholars and philosophers searched the works of the ancients to find the principles on which to build a better life. They scoured monastic libraries for forgotten manuscripts, discovering among other things Greek poetry and history, the works of Homer and Plato, and Aristotle's *Poetics.* Their rigorous appli-

cation of scholarly procedures for the collection and collation of those texts was one of the most important contributions of the Renaissance intellectuals who came to be known as **humanists.** Humanism developed in reaction to an intellectual world that was centered on the Church and dominated by otherworldly concerns. Humanism was secular in outlook, though by no means was it antireligious.

Humanists celebrated worldly achievements. Pico della Mirandola's *Oration on the Dignity of Man* (1486) is the best known of a multitude of Renaissance writings influenced by the discovery of the works of Plato. Pico believed that people could perfect their existence on earth because humans were divinely endowed with the capacity to determine their own fate: "O highest and most marvelous felicity of man! To him it is granted to have whatever he chooses, to be whatever he wills."

Thus humanists studied and taught the humanities—the skills of disciplines such as **philology,** the art of language, and **rhetoric,** the art of expression. Although they were mostly laypeople, humanists applied their learning to both religious and secular studies. Humanists were not antireligious.

THE RENAISSANCE MAN

Giorgio Vasari celebrated the creativity of the artists who made Italy the center of cultural activity in the Later Middle Ages. His commemoration of their achievements through the medium of biographies helped to create the aura that still surrounds Renaissance art.

Focus Questions

What makes Leonardo such an exemplary "Renaissance man"? Does Vasari see Leonardo as someone who excels in many separate fields, or does he see the different arts and sciences as unified?

The most heavenly gifts seem to be showered on certain human beings. Sometimes supernaturally, marvelously, they all congregate in one individual. Beauty, grace, and talent are combined in such bounty that in whatever that man undertakes, he outdistances all other men and proves himself to be specially endowed by the hand of God. He owes his pre-eminence not to human teaching or human power. This was seen and acknowledged by all men in the case of Leonardo da Vinci, who had, besides the beauty of his person (which was such that it has never been sufficiently extolled), an indescribable grace in every effortless act and deed. His talent was so rare that he mastered any subject to which he turned his attention. Extraordinary strength and remarkable facility were here combined. He had a mind of regal boldness and magnanimous daring. His gifts were such that his celebrity was worldwide, not only in his own day, but even more after his death, and so will continue until the end of time.

Leonardo was frequently occupied in the preparation of plans to remove mountains or to pierce them with tunnels from plain to plain. By means of levers, cranes, and screws, he showed how to lift or move great weights. Designing dredging machines and inventing the means of drawing water from the greatest depths were among the speculations from which he never rested. Many drawings of these projects exist which are cherished by those who practice our arts. . . .

Leonardo, with his profound comprehension of art, began many things that he never completed, because it seemed to him that perfection must elude him. He frequently formed in his imagination enterprises so difficult and so subtle that they could not be entirely realized and worthily executed by human hands. His conceptions were varied to infinity. In natural philosophy, among other things, he examined plants and observed the stars—the movements of the planets, the variations of the moon, and the course of the sun. . . .

From Giorgio Vasari, *Lives of the Most Eminent Painters, Sculptors, and Architects.*

Although they reacted strongly against Scholasticism (see Chapter 14), they were heavily indebted to the work of medieval churchmen, and most were devoutly religious. Nor were they hostile to the Church. Petrarch, Leonardo Bruni, and Leon Battista Alberti were all employed by the papal court at some time in their careers, as was Lorenzo Valla, the most influential of the humanists. Their interest in human achievement and human potential must be set beside their religious beliefs. As Petrarch stated quite succinctly: "Christ is my God; Cicero is the prince of the language I use."

Humanists and the Liberal Arts

The most important achievements of humanist scholars centered on ancient texts. It was the humanists' goal to discover as much as had survived from the ancient world and to provide texts of classical authors that were as full and accurate as possible.

Studying the Classical World.   Although much was already known of the Latin classics, few of the central works of ancient Greece had been uncovered. Humanists preserved that heritage by reviving the study of the Greek language and by translating Greek authors into Latin. After the fall of Constantinople in 1453, Italy became the center for Greek studies as Byzantine scholars fled the Ottoman conquerors. Humanists also introduced historical methods in studying and evaluating texts, establishing principles for determining which of many manuscript copies of an ancient text was the oldest, the most accurate, and the least corrupted by copyists. That was of immense importance in studying the writings of the ancient Fathers of the Church, many of whose manuscripts had not been examined for centuries. They believed that the study of the "liberal arts" should be undertaken for its own sake. That belief gave a powerful boost to the ideal of the perfectability of the individual that appeared in so many other aspects of Renaissance culture.

Humanists furthered the secularization of Renaissance society through their emphasis on the study of the classical world. The rediscovery of Latin texts during the Later Middle Ages spurred interest in all things ancient. Petrarch, who is rightly called the father of humanism, revered the great Roman

Petrarch, *Letters to Cicero*

rhetorician Cicero above all others. For Petrarch, Cicero's legacy was eloquence. He stressed that in his correspondence with the leading scholars of his day and taught it to those who would succeed him. From 1350 to 1450, Cicero was the dominant model for Renaissance poets and orators. The leading humanist in the generation after Petrarch was Leonardo Bruni (1370–1444), who was reputed to be the greatest Greek scholar of his day. He translated both Plato and Aristotle and did much to advance mastery of classical Greek and foster the ideas of Plato in the late fifteenth century.

Philology and Lorenzo Valla.   The study of the origins of words, their meaning, and their proper grammatical usage may seem an unusual foundation for one of the most vital of all European intellectual movements. But philology was the humanists' chief concern and can be best illustrated by the work of Lorenzo Valla (1407–1457). Valla was brought up in Rome, where he was largely self-educated, although according to the prescriptions of the Florentine humanists. Valla entered the service of Alfonso I, king of Naples, and applied his humanistic training to affairs of state. The kingdom of Naples bordered on the Papal States, and its kings were in continual conflict with the papacy. The pope asserted the right to withhold recognition of the king, a right that was based upon the jurisdictional authority supposedly ceded to the papacy by the Emperor Constantine in the fourth century. The so-called Donation of Constantine had long been a matter of dispute, and its authenticity had been challenged frequently in the Middle Ages. But those challenges were made on political grounds, and the arguments of papal supporters were as strenuous as those of papal opponents. Valla settled the matter definitively. Applying historical and philological critiques to the text of the Donation, Valla proved that it could not have been written earlier than the eighth century, 400 years after Constantine's death. He exposed words and terms that had not existed in Roman times, such as *fief* and *satrap,* and thus proved beyond doubt that the Donation was a forgery and papal claims based upon it were without merit.

Civic Humanism.   Valla's career demonstrates the impact of humanist values on practical affairs. Although humanists were scholars, they made no distinction between an active and a contemplative life. A life of scholarship was a life of public service. They saw their studies as means of improving themselves and their society: "Man is born in order to be useful to man." That **civic humanism** is best expressed in the writings of Leon Battista Alberti (1404–1472), whose treatise *On the Family* (1443) is a classic study of the new urban values, especially prudence and thrift. Alberti extolled the virtues of "the fatherland, the public good, and the benefit of all citizens." An architect, a mathematician, a poet, a playwright, a musician, and an inventor, Alberti was one of the great virtuosi of the Renaissance.

Alberti's own life might have served as a model for the most influential of all Renaissance tracts, Baldesar Castiglione's *The Courtier* (1528). While Alberti directed his lessons to the private lives of successful urban families, Castiglione (1478–1529) directed his to the public life of the aspiring elite. In Castiglione's view, the perfect courtier was as much born as made: "Besides his noble birth I would have the Courtier endowed by nature not only with talent and beauty of person and feature, but with a certain grace and air that shall make him at first sight pleasing." Everything that the courtier did was to maintain his pleasing grace and his public reputation. *The Courtier* was an etiquette book, and in it Castiglione prescribed every detail of the education necessary for the ideal state servant, from table manners to artistic attainments. Although each talent was to be acquired through careful study and application, it was to be manifested with *sprezzatura,* a natural ease and superiority that was the essence of the gentleman.

Renaissance Science

As the spirit of the Renaissance looked back to the classical world and ahead to the achievements that would come from the adaptation of ancient wisdom, so Renaissance scientific inquiry was focused in two directions. The first was text-based knowledge derived from recovered works mainly from classical Greece; the second was experiment-based knowledge achieved through observation. Texts dominated the life sciences, especially medicine and biology; experimentation enriched the physical sciences such as engineering and cartography. But it is important to realize that both ways of knowing blended together. Doctors were instructed by the classics but increasingly learned their anatomy by dissection. Navigators carried the works of Ptolemy on voyages of discovery but amended his maps and charts with what they found in practice.

The biological sciences were given new life by the recovery of the writings of Hippocrates and Galen. Medicine became a subject for learned inquiry and the medical school at Padua was considered the greatest in Europe. The work of Hippocrates concerned diagnosing common diseases and attempting to find treatments. Galen's studies of the human body, rediscovered, formed the basis for a new interest in anatomy and led to experiments in human dissection in the most advanced universities. Such experimentation improved knowledge of the skeleton and the placement of the organs, which led to medical advances in setting broken bones and treating injuries. Galen taught that the body was composed of **humors**—yellow bile, black bile, phlegm, and blood—that corresponded to the four elements of life—earth, air, water, and fire. In the healthy body the humors were well mixed together, but in the diseased body there was an imbalance. This understanding explains why doctors attempted to cure disease by the use of leeches or the practice of "bleeding," cutting open a vein and allowing blood to run out. The extraction of blood was believed to aid in restoring the balance of the humors and thus the health of the body.

Whereas the life sciences were advanced through attention to ancient texts, engineering developed through the experiences of Renaissance craftsmen and artists who were attempting to solve practical problems of proportion, stability, and height in the buildings, bridges, and ultimately domes that they built. Most of the important advances in engineering were actually made in the service of military ventures. The science of ballistics advanced through greater mathematical precision in studying the relationship between speed and trajectory in the shooting of artillery. It was Leonardo da Vinci who attempted to apply a theory of mechanics to Renaissance warfare, and he made drawings for the creation of war machines such as tanks and flying machines such as airplanes, though, of course, neither were produced during his lifetime. But he was expert in building working models of machines, in advising princes on their fortifications, and in suggesting improvements in the art of gunnery. All of his contributions were made by experimentation rather than through text-based learning. Wherever he went, Leonardo built workshops to construct models and kept careful notebooks of the results of his trials. This spirit of experimentation would ultimately lead to the birth of a recognizably scientific method in the next century.

■ Portrait of Niccolò Machiavelli, who expounded his theory of statecraft in *The Prince*.

■ Baldassare Castiglione sat for this portrait, painted by his friend Raphael, in 1515.

Machiavelli and Politics

At the same time that Castiglione was drafting a blueprint for the idealized courtier, Niccolò Machiavelli (1469–1527) was laying the foundation for the realistic sixteenth-century ruler. No Renaissance work has been more important or more controversial than Machiavelli's *The Prince* (1513). Its vivid prose, its epigrammatic advice—"Men must either be pampered or crushed"—and its clinical dissection of power politics have attracted generation after generation of readers. With Machiavelli began the science of politics.

DOCUMENT

Machiavelli, *The Prince*

Machiavelli came from an established Florentine family and entered state service as an assistant to one of his teachers, who then recommended him for the important office of secretary to the Council of Ten, the organ of Florentine government that had responsibility for war and diplomacy. Machiavelli devoted all his energies and his entire intellect to his career. He was a tireless correspondent, and he began to collect materials for various tracts on military matters. He also planned out a prospective history in which to celebrate the greatness of the Florentine Republic that he served.

THE LION AND THE FOX

Niccolò Machiavelli wrote The Prince *in 1513 while he was under house arrest. It is one of the classics of Western political theory in which the author separates the political from the moral.*

Focus Questions
According to Machiavelli, why is honesty not always the best policy? For a ruler, how valuable a tactic is a show of strength?

Everyone understands how praiseworthy it is in a prince to keep faith, and to live uprightly and not craftily. Nevertheless we see, from what has taken place in our own days, that princes who have set little store by their word, but have known how to overreach men by their cunning, have accomplished great things, and in the end got the better of those who trusted to honest dealing.

Be it known, then, that there are two ways of contending—one in accordance with the laws, the other by force; the first of which is proper to men, the second to beasts.

But since the first method is often ineffectual, it becomes necessary to resort to the second. A prince should, therefore, understand how to use well both the man and the beast. . . . But inasmuch as a prince should know how to use the beast's nature wisely, he ought of beasts to choose both the lion and the fox; for the lion cannot guard himself from the toils, nor the fox from wolves. He must therefore be a fox to discern toils, and a lion to drive off wolves.

To rely wholly on the lion is unwise; and for this reason a prudent prince neither can nor ought to keep his word when to keep it is hurtful to him and the causes which led him to pledge it are removed. If all men were good, this would not be good advice, but since they are dishonest and do not keep faith with you, you in return need not keep faith with them.

From Niccolò Machiavelli, *The Prince.*

But as suddenly as Machiavelli rose to his position of power and influence, he fell from it. The militia that he had advocated and in part organized was soundly defeated by the Spaniards, and the Florentine Republic fell. Machiavelli was summarily dismissed from office in 1512 and was imprisoned and tortured the following year. Released and banished from the city, he retired to a small country estate and turned his restless energies to writing. Immediately he began work on what became his two greatest works, *The Prince* and the *Discourses on Livy* (1519).

Machiavelli has left a haunting portrait of his life in exile, and it is important to understand how intertwined his studies of ancient and modern politics were.

On the coming of evening, I return to my house and enter my study; and at the door I take off the day's clothing, covered with mud and dust, and put on garments regal and courtly; and reclothed appropriately, I enter the ancient courts of ancient men, where, received by them with affection, I feed on that food which only is mine and which I was born for. For four hours of time I do not feel boredom, I forget every trouble, I do not dread poverty, I am not frightened by death; entirely I give myself over to them.

In this state of mind *The Prince* was composed.

The Prince is a handbook for a ruler who would establish a lasting government. It attempts to set down principles culled from historical examples and contemporary events to aid the prince in attaining and maintaining power. By study of those precepts and by their swift and forceful application, Machiavelli believed that the prince might even control fortune itself. *The Prince* is purely secular in content and philosophy. Where the medieval writer of a manual for princes would have stressed the divine foundations of the state, Machiavelli asserted the human bases: "The chief foundations on which all states rest are good laws and good arms." What made *The Prince* so remarkable in its day, and what continues to enliven debate over it, is that Machiavelli was able to separate all ethical considerations from his analysis. Whether that resulted from cynicism or from his own expressed desire for realism, Machiavelli uncompromisingly instructed the would-be ruler to be half man and half beast—to conquer neighbors, to murder enemies, and to deceive friends. Steeped in the humanist ideals of fame and *virtù*—a combination of virtue and virtuosity, of valor, character, and ability—he sought to reestablish Italian rule and place government upon a stable, scientific basis that would end the perpetual conflict among the Italian city-states.

The careers of both Lorenzo Valla and Niccolò Machiavelli illustrate how humanists were able to bring the study of the liberal arts into the service of the state. Valla's philological studies had a vital impact on diplomacy; Machiavelli's historical studies were directly applicable to warfare. Humanists created a demand for learning that helps account for the growth of universities, the spread of literacy, and the rise of printing. They also created a hunger for knowledge that characterized intellectual life for nearly two centuries.

MAP DISCOVERY

Italy, 1494

Notice how Italy was organized into city-states at the end of the fifteenth century. Which were the largest city-states? Which city-states seem most susceptible to foreign invasion? Which states had the best positioning for trade? When the wars of Italy began in 1494 (discussed later in this chapter), France sided with Milan against Naples, Florence, and the Papal States. Based on the positions of the combatants, what do you think would have been the likeliest route for the French invasion? Which city-states could the French avoid fighting?

THE POLITICS OF THE ITALIAN CITY-STATES

Like studs on a leather boot, **city-states** dotted the Italian peninsula. They differed in size, shape, and form. Some were large seaports, others small inland villages; some cut wide swaths across the plains, others were tiny islands. The absence of a unifying central authority in Italy, resulting from the collapse of the Holy Roman Empire and the papal schism, allowed ancient guilds and confraternities to transform themselves into self-governing societies. By the beginning of the fifteenth century the Italian city-states were the center of power, wealth, and culture in the Christian world.

That dominion rested on several conditions. First, Italy's geographical position favored the exchange of resources and goods between the East and the West. Until the fifteenth century, and despite the crusading efforts of medieval popes, the East and the West fortified each other. A great circular trade had developed, encompassing the Byzantine Empire, the North African coastal states, and the Mediterranean nations of western Europe. The Italian peninsula dominated the circumference of that circle. Its port cities, Genoa and Venice especially, became great maritime powers through their trade in spices and minerals. Second, just beyond the peninsula to the north lay the vast and populous territories of the Holy Roman Empire. There the continuous need for manufactured goods, especially cloths and metals, was filled by long caravans that traveled from Italy through the Alps. Milan specialized in metal crafts. Florence was a financial capital as well as a center for the manufacture of fine luxury goods. Finally, the city-states and their surrounding areas were agriculturally self-sufficient.

Because of their accomplishments, there has been a tendency to think of the Italian city-states as small nations. Even the term *city-state* implies national identity. Each city-state governed itself according to its own rules and customs, and each defined itself in isolation from the larger regional or tribal associations that once prevailed. Indeed, the struggles of the city-states against one another speak eloquently of their local self-identification. Italy was neither a nation nor a people.

The Five Powers

Although there were dozens of Italian city-states, by the early fifteenth century five had emerged to dominate the politics of the peninsula. In the south was the kingdom of Naples, the only city-state governed by a hereditary monarchy. Its politics were mired by conflicts over its succession, and it was not until the Spaniard Alfonso I of Aragon (1442–1458) secured the throne in 1443 that peace was restored. Bordering Naples were the Papal States, whose capital was Rome but whose territories stretched far to the north and lay on both sides of the spiny Apennine mountain chain that extends down the center of the peninsula. Throughout the fourteenth and early fifteenth centuries, the territories under the nominal control of the Church were largely independent and included such thriving city-states as Bologna, Ferrara, and Urbino. Even in Rome the weakened papacy had to contend with noble families for control of the city.

The three remaining dominant city-states were clustered together in the north. Florence, center of Renaissance culture, was one of the wealthiest cities of Europe before the devastations of the plague and the sustained economic downturn of the late fourteenth century. The city itself was inland and its main waterway, the Arno, ran to the sea through Pisa, whose subjugation in 1406 was a turning point in Florentine history. Nominally Florence was a republic, but during the fifteenth century it was ruled in effect by its principal banking family, the Medici.

To the north of Florence was the duchy of Milan, the major city in Lombardy. It too was landlocked, cut off from the sea by Genoa. But Milan's economic life was oriented northward to the Swiss and German towns beyond the Alps, and its major concern was preventing foreign invasions. The most warlike of the Italian cities, Milan was a despotism, ruled for nearly two centuries by the Visconti family.

The last of the five powers was the republic of Venice. Ideally situated at the head of the Adriatic Sea, Venice became the leading maritime power of the age. Until the fifteenth century, Venice had been less interested in securing a landed empire than in dominating a seaborne one. Its outposts along the Greek and Dalmatian coasts, and its favored position in Constantinople, were the source of vast mercantile wealth. The republic was ruled by a hereditary elite—headed by an elected **doge,** who was the chief magistrate of Venice—and a variety of small elected councils.

The political history of the Italian peninsula during the late fourteenth and early fifteenth centuries is one of unrelieved turmoil. Everywhere, the governments of the city-states were threatened by foreign invaders, internal conspiracies, or popular revolts. By the middle of the fifteenth century, however, two trends were apparent amid the political chaos. The first was the consolidation of strong centralized governments within the large city-states. The governments took different forms but yielded a similar result—internal political stability. The return of the popes to Rome after the Great Schism restored the pope to the head of his temporal estates and began a long period of papal dominance over Rome and its satellite territories. In Milan, one of the great military leaders of the day, Francesco Sforza (1401–1466), seized the reins of power. The succession of King Alfonso I in Naples ended a half century of civil war. In both Florence and Venice, the grip that the political elite held over high offices was tightened by placing greater power in small advisory councils and, in Florence, by the ascent to power of the Medici family. That process, known as the rise of signorial rule, made possible the establishment of a balance of power within the Italian peninsula.

It was the leaders of the Italian city-states who first perfected the art of diplomacy. Constant warfare necessitated continual alliances, and by the end of the fourteenth century the large city-states had begun the practice of keeping resident ambassadors at the major seats of power. That enhanced communication, a principal challenge in Renaissance diplomacy, and also provided leaders with accurate information about the conditions of potential allies and enemies. Diplomacy was both an offensive and a defensive weapon, especially because the city-states hired their soldiers as contract labor. The mercenary armies, whose leaders were known as *condottieri* from the name of their contract, were both expensive and dangerous to maintain. If they did not bankrupt their employers, they might desert them or, even worse, turn on them.

Venice: A Seaborne Empire

Water was the source of the prosperity of Venice. Located at the head of the Adriatic Sea, the city was formed by a web of lagoons. Through its center snaked the Grand Canal, whose banks were lined with large and small buildings that celebrated its civic and mercantile power. At the Piazza San Marco stood the vast palace of the doge, elected leader of the republic, and the Basilica of Saint Mark, a domed church built in the Byzantine style. At the Rialto were the stalls of the bankers and moneylenders, less grand perhaps but no less important. There, too, were the auction blocks for the profitable trade in European slaves, eastern European serfs, and battlefield captives who were sold into service in Egypt or Byzantium. On the eastern edge of the island city was the Arsenal, erected in the twelfth century to house the shipbuilding and arms manufacturing industries. Three centuries later it was the industrial marvel of the world, where the Venetian great galleys were constructed with assembly-line precision.

Its prosperity based on trade rather than conquest, Venice enjoyed many natural advantages. Its position at the head of the Adriatic permitted access to the raw materials of both the East and the West. The rich Alpine timberland beyond the city provided the hardwoods necessary for shipbuilding. The hinterland population were steady consumers of grain, cloth, and the new manufactured goods—glass, silk, jewelry, and cottons—that came pouring onto the market in the Later Middle Ages.

But the success of Venice owed more to its own achievements than to its rich inheritances. "It is the most triumphant city I have ever seen," wrote the Frenchman Philippe de Commynes at the end of the fifteenth century. The triumph of the Venetian state was the triumph of dedicated efficiency. The heart of its success lay in the way in which it organized its trade and its government. The key to Venetian trade was its privileged position with the Byzantine Empire. Through a treaty with the Byzantines, Venetian traders gained a competitive edge in the spice trade with the East. Venetians were the largest group of resident Europeans in Constantinople, and their personal contacts with Eastern traders were an important part of their success. The spice trade was so lucrative that special ships were built to accommodate it. The galleys were constructed at public expense and doubled as the Venetian navy in times of war. By controlling the ships, the government strictly regulated the spice trade.

Like its trade, Venetian government was also designed to disperse power. Although it was known as the Most Serene Republic, Venice was not a republic in the sense that the term is used today; rather, it was an oligarchy—a government administered by a restricted group. Political power was vested in a Great Council whose membership had been fixed at the end of the thirteenth century. All males whose fathers enjoyed the privilege of membership in the Great Council were registered at birth in the "Book of Gold" and became members of the Great Council when adults. There were no further distinctions of rank within the nobility, whose members varied widely in wealth and intermarried freely with other groups in the society. From the body of the Great Council, which numbered about 2,500 at the end of the fifteenth century, was chosen the Senate—a council about one-tenth the size, whose members served a one-year term. It was from the Senate that the true officers of government were selected: the doge, who was chosen for life; and members of a number of small councils, who administered affairs and advised the doge. Members of the councils were chosen by secret ballot in an elaborate process by which nominators were selected at random. Terms of office on the councils were extremely short in order to limit factionalism and to prevent any individual from gaining too much power. Venetian-style republicanism was admired throughout Europe.

With its mercantile families firmly in control of government and trade, Venice created an overseas empire in the East during the thirteenth and fourteenth centuries. Naval supremacy, based largely on technological advances that made long-distance and winter voyages possible, allowed the Venetians to offer protection to strategic outposts in return for either privileges or tribute. But in the fifteenth century, Venice turned to the West. In a dramatic reversal of its centuries-old policy, it began a process of conquest in Italy, an empire on terra firma, as Venetian islanders called it. There were several reasons for this new policy. First, the Venetian

navy was no longer the unsurpassed power that it once had been. More importantly, mainland expansion offered new opportunities for Venice. Not all Venetians were traders, and the new industries that were being developed in the city could readily benefit from control of mainland markets. So could those Venetian nobles employed to administer the conquered lands. They argued persuasively that the supply of raw materials and foodstuffs on which Venetian trade ultimately depended should be secured by the republic itself. Most decisively of all, opportunity was knocking. In Milan, Visconti rule was weakening and the Milanese territories were ripe for picking.

Venice reaped a rich harvest. For the first half of the fifteenth century, the Most Serene Republic engaged in unremitting warfare. Its successes were remarkable. It pushed out to the north to occupy all the lands between the city and the Habsburg territories; it pushed to the east until it straddled the entire head of the Adriatic; and it pushed to the west almost as far as Milan itself. Venetian victories resulted from both the traditional use of hired mercenaries and from the Venetians' own ingenuity at naval warfare. Although Venice was creating a landed empire, the course of expansion, especially in Lombardy, was along river routes. At the Arsenal were built new oared vessels armed with artillery for river sieges. Soon the captured territories were paying for continued expansion. The Western conquests in particular brought large populations under Venetian control, which, along with their potential as a market, provided a ready source of taxation. By the end of the fifteenth century, the mainland dominions of Venice were contributing nearly 40 percent of the city's revenue at a cost far smaller than that of the naval empire a century earlier. Venice had become the most powerful city-state in Italy.

Florence: Spinning Cloth into Gold

"What city, not merely in Italy, but in all the world . . . is more proud in its palazzi, more bedecked with churches, more beautiful in its architecture, more imposing in its gates, richer in piazzas, happier in its wide streets, greater in its people, more glorious in its citizenry, more inexhaustible in wealth, more fertile in its fields?" So boasted the humanist Coluccio Salutati (1331–1406) in 1403 during one of the most calamitous periods in Florentine history. Salutati's boastings were not unusual; the Florentines' mythical view of their homeland as savior of Christianity and as heir to the republican greatness of Rome was everywhere apparent. And it seemed to be most vigorously expressed in the city's darkest moments.

Florentine prosperity was built on two foundations: money and wool. Beginning in the thirteenth century, Florentine bankers were among the wealthiest and most powerful in the world. Initially their position was established through support of the papacy in its long struggle with the Holy Roman Empire. Florentine financiers established banks in all the capitals of Europe and the East, though their seats in

Rome and Naples were probably most important. In the Middle Ages, bankers had served more functions than simply handling and exchanging money. Most were also tied to mercantile adventures and underwrote industrial activity. So it was in Florence, where international bankers purchased high-quality wool to be manufactured into the world's finest woven cloth. At its height before the plague, the cloth industry employed nearly 30,000 workers, providing jobs at all levels of society, from the rural women who spun the wool into yarn at piecework wages to the highly paid weavers and dyers whose skills made Florentine cloth so highly prized.

The activities of both commerce and cloth manufacture depended on external conditions, and thus the wealth of Florence was potentially unstable. In the mid-fourteenth century instability came with the plague that devastated the city. Nearly 40 percent of the entire population was lost in the single year 1348, and recurring outbreaks continued to ravage the already weakened survivors. Loss of workers and loss of markets seriously disrupted manufacturing. By 1380, cloth production had fallen to less than a quarter of pre-plague levels. On the heels of plague came wars. The property of Florentine bankers and merchants abroad was an easy target. Thirty years of warfare with Milan, interrupted by only a single decade of peace (1413–1423), resulted in total bankruptcy for many of the city's leading commercial families. More significantly, the costs of warfare, offensive and defensive, created a massive public debt. Every Florentine of means owned shares of the debt, and the republic was continually devising new methods for borrowing and staving off crises of repayment. Small wonder that the republic turned for aid to the wealthiest banking family in Europe, the Medici.

The ability of the Medici to secure a century-long dynasty in a government that did not have a head of state is just one of the mysteries surrounding the history of the remarkable family. Cosimo de' Medici (1389–1464) was one of the richest men in Christendom when he returned to the city in 1434 after a brief exile. His leading position in government rested upon supporters who were able to gain a controlling influence on the Signoria, the ruling Council in Florence's republican form of government. Cosimo built his party carefully, recruiting followers among the artisans whom he employed and even paying delinquent taxes to maintain the eligibility of his voters. Most importantly, emergency powers were invoked to reduce the number of citizens qualified to vote for the Signoria until the majority were Medici backers.

Cosimo was a practical man. He raised his children along humanist principles and was a great patron of artists and intellectuals. He collected books and paintings, endowed libraries, and spent lavishly on his own palace, the Palazzo Medici, which after his death was transformed into the very center of Florentine cultural life. Cosimo's position as an international banker brought him into contact with the heads of other Italian city-states and enabled him to negotiate peace treaties.

It was Cosimo's grandson Lorenzo (1449–1492) who linked the family's name to that of the age. Lorenzo was trained to

■ The patriarch of the great Florentine banking family, Cosimo de' Medici, portrayed here by Pontormo, was the dominant force in the city's politics from 1434 until his death in 1464.

hold office as if he had been a prince rather than a citizen of a republic. His own father ruled for five years and used his son as a diplomat in order to acquaint him with the leaders of Europe. Diplomacy was Lorenzo's greatest achievement. He held strong humanist values instilled in him by his mother, Lucrezia Tornabuoni, who organized his education. He wrote poetry and drama and even entered competitions for architectural designs. But Lorenzo's chief contribution to artistic life as it reached its height in Florence was to facilitate its production. He brought Michelangelo and other leading artists to his garden; he brought Pico della Mirandola and other leading humanists to his table. He secured commissions for Florentine artists throughout the Italian peninsula, ensuring the spread of their influence and the continued regeneration of artistic creativity in Florence itself.

Lorenzo was generally regarded as the leading citizen of Florence, and that was true in terms of both his wealth and his influence. He did not rule from high office, though he maintained the party that his grandfather had built and even extended it through wartime emergency measures. His power was based on his personality and reputation, a charisma enhanced when he survived an assassination attempt in which

FIORENZA

■ A view of Florence in 1490. The Duomo of the Florence Cathedral dominates the small city, which is already built up on both sides of the Arno River.

his brother was killed. His diplomatic abilities were the key to his survival. Almost immediately after Lorenzo came to power, Naples and the papacy began a war with Florence, a war that was costly to the Florentines in both taxation and lost territory. In 1479, Lorenzo traveled to Naples and personally convinced the Neapolitan king to sign a separate treaty, which restored the Italian balance of power and ensured continued Medici rule in Florence. Soon Lorenzo even had a treaty with the pope that allowed for the recovery of lost territories and the expansion of Florentine influence. But two years after his death, the Italian peninsula was plunged into wars that turned it from the center of European civilization into one of its lesser satellites.

The End of Italian Hegemony, 1450–1527

In the course of the Renaissance, western Europe was Italianized. For a century, the city-states dominated the trade routes that connected the East and the West. Venetian and Genoese merchants exchanged spices and minerals from the Black Sea to the North Sea, enriching the material life of three continents. They brought wool from England and Spain to the skilled artisans in the Low Countries and Florence. Italian manufactures such as Milanese artillery, Florentine silk, and Venetian glass were prized above all others. The ducat and the florin, two Italian coins, were universally accepted in an age when every petty prince minted his own money. The Italian peninsula exported culture in the same way that it exported goods. Humanism quickly spread across the Alps, aided by the recent invention of printing (which the Venetians soon domi-

nated), while Renaissance standards of artistic achievement were known worldwide and everywhere imitated. The city-states shared their technology as well. The compass and the navigational chart, projection maps, double entry bookkeeping, eyeglasses, the telescope—all profoundly influenced what could be achieved and what could be hoped for. In this spirit, Christopher Columbus—a Genoese seaman—successfully crossed the Atlantic under the Spanish flag, and Amerigo Vespucci—a Florentine merchant—gave his name to the newly discovered continents.

Political and Military Unrest. But it was not in Italy that the rewards of innovation or the satisfactions of achievement were enjoyed. There the seeds of political turmoil and military imperialism, combined with the rise of the Ottoman Turks, were to reap a not-unexpected harvest. In 1454, the five powers agreed to the Peace of Lodi, which established two balanced alliances, one between Florence and Milan, the other between Venice and Naples. The states, along with the papacy, pledged mutual nonaggression, a policy that lasted for nearly 40 years. But the Peace of Lodi did not bring peace. It only halted the long period in which the major city-states struggled against one another. Under cover of the peace, the large states continued the process of swallowing up their smaller neighbors and creating quasi-empires. It was a policy of imperialism as aggressive as that of any in the modern era. Civilian populations were overrun, local leaders exiled or exterminated, tribute monies taken, and taxes levied. Each of the five states either increased its mainland territories or strengthened its hold upon them.

■ Paolo Uccello, *Niccolò da Tolentino at the Battle of San Romano* (ca. 1435–1450). The painting represents the early stages of a 1432 battle between the Florentines and the Sienese at San Romano. The Florentine condottiere, Niccolò da Tolentino, on a white horse, dominates the center of the scene.

By the end of the fifteenth century the city-states eyed one another greedily and warily. Each expected the others to begin a peninsula-wide war for hegemony and took the steps that ultimately ensured the contest. Perhaps the most unusual aspect of the imperialism of the city-states was that it had been restricted to the Italian peninsula. Each of the major powers shared the dream of recapturing the glory that was Rome. Although the Venetians had expanded abroad, their acquisitions had not come through conquest or occupation. In their Greek and Dalmatian territories, local law and custom continued to govern under the benevolent eye of Venetian administrators. But in their mainland territories, the Venetians were as ruthless as the Florentines were in Pisa or as Cesare Borgia was in Romagna when he consolidated the Papal States by fire and sword. Long years of siege and occupation had militarized the Italian city-states. Venice and Florence balanced their budgets on the backs of their captured territories, Milan had been engaged in constant war for decades, and even the papacy was militarily aggressive.

The Italian Decline.   The Italians were no longer alone. The most remarkable military leader of the age was not a Renaissance *condottieri* but an Ottoman prince, Mehmed II (1451–1481), who conquered Constantinople and Athens and

threatened Rome itself. The rise of the Ottomans (whose name is derived from that of Osman, their original tribal leader) is one of the most compelling stories in world history. Little more than a warrior tribe at the beginning of the fourteenth century, 150 years later the Ottomans had replaced stagnant Byzantine rule with a virile and potent empire. First they gobbled up towns and cities in a wide arc around Constantinople. Then they fed upon the Balkans and the eastern kingdoms of Hungary and Poland. By 1400, they were a presence in all the territory that stretched from the Black Sea to the Aegean; by 1450, they were its master.

Venice was most directly affected by the Ottoman advance. Not only was its favored position in Eastern trade threatened, but during a prolonged war at the end of the fifteenth century, the Venetians lost many of their most important commercial outposts. Ottoman might closed off the markets of eastern Europe. Islands in the Aegean Sea and seaports along the Dalmatian coast fell to the Turks in alarming succession. By 1480, Venetian naval supremacy was a thing of the past. (See "A Closer Look: The Fall of Constantinople," pp. 342–343.)

The Italian city-states might have met this challenge from the East had they been able to unite in opposing it. Successive popes pleaded for holy wars to halt the advance of the Turks, which was compared in officially inspired propaganda to an

THE SIEGE OF CONSTANTINOPLE

Mehmed II (1432–1481) was one of the great military geniuses of world history. He consolidated the expansion of the Ottoman Empire in Asia Minor and in 1453 organized the siege of Constantinople. He personally directed the combined land and naval assault and brilliantly improvised the tactics that led to the fall of the city. The fall of Constantinople to the Ottomans was a watershed. Kritovoulos was a Greek who entered the service of Mehmed II, probably after the siege. Though he was not an eyewitness of the fall of Constantinople, he gathered numerous accounts together in composing his history. In this selection he refers to the defenders of the city as Romans because Constantinople was what remained of the Roman Empire.

Focus Questions

How did Mehmed get his ships into the harbor at Constantinople? Why was Mehmed's scheme for moving the ships so important in the siege of Constantinople?

Sultan Mehmed considered it necessary in preparation for his next move to get possession of the harbor and open the Horn for his own ships to sail in. So, since every effort and device of his had failed to force the entrance, he made a wise decision, and one worthy of his intellect and power. It succeeded in accomplishing his purpose and in putting an end to all uncertainties.

He ordered the commanders of the vessels to construct as quickly as possible glideways leading from the outer sea to the inner sea. . . . He brought up the ships and placed large cradles under them, with stays against each of their sides to hold them up. And having under-girded them well with ropes, he fastened long cables to the corners and gave them to the soldiers to drag, some of them by hand, and others by certain machines and capstans.

So the ships were dragged along very swiftly. And their crews, as they followed them, rejoiced at the event and boasted of it. Then they manned the ships on the land as if they were on the sea. Some of them hoisted the sails with a shout, as if they were setting sail, and the breeze caught the sails and bellied them out. Others seated themselves on the benches, holding the oars in their hands and moving them as if rowing. And the commanders, running along by the sockets of the masts with whistlings and shouting, and with their whips beating the oarsmen on the benches, ordered them to row. The ships, borne along over the land as if on the sea, were some of them being pulled up the ascent to the top of the hill while others were being hauled down the slope into the harbor, lowering the sails with shouting and great noise.

It was a strange spectacle, and unbelievable in the telling except to those who actually did see it—the sight of ships borne along on the mainland as if sailing on the sea, with their crews and their sails and all their equipment. I believe this was a much greater feat than the cutting of a canal across at Athos by Xerxes, and much stranger to see and to hear about.

The Romans, when they saw such an unheard-of thing actually happen, and warships lying at anchor in the Horn—which they never would have suspected—were astounded at the impossibility of the spectacle, and were overcome by the greatest consternation and perplexity. They did not know what to do now, but were in despair. In fact they had left unguarded the walls along the Horn for a distance of about thirty stadia, and even so they did not have enough men for the rest of the walls, either for defense or for attack, whether citizens or men from elsewhere. Instead, two or even three battlements had but a single defender.

And now, when this sea-wall also became open to attack and had to be guarded, they were compelled to strip the other battlements and bring men there. This constituted a manifest danger, since the defenders were taken away from the rest of the wall while those remaining were not enough to guard it, being so few.

From Kritovoulos, *The History of Mehmed the Conqueror.*

CASE STUDY

Two Views on the Fall of Constantinople

outbreak of plague. The fall of Constantinople in 1453 was an event of epochal proportions for Europeans, many believing that it foreshadowed the end of the world. "A thing terrible to relate and to be deplored by all who have in them any spark of humanity. The splendor and glory of the East has been captured, despoiled, ravaged and completely sacked by the most inhuman barbarians," the Venetian doge was informed. Yet it was Italians rather than Ottomans who plunged the Italian peninsula into the wars from which it never recovered.

The Wars of Italy (1494–1529) began when Naples, Florence, and the Papal States united against Milan. At first the alliance seemed little more than another shift in the balance of power. But rather than call upon Venice to redress the situation, the Milanese leader, Ludovico il Moro, sought help from the French. An army of French cavalry and Swiss mercenaries, led by Charles VIII of France (1483–1498), invaded the Italian peninsula in 1494. With Milanese support, the French swept all before them. Florence was forced to surrender Pisa, a humiliation that led to the overthrow of the

THE FALL OF CONSTANTINOPLE

The prayers of the devout were fervent on Easter Sunday in 1453. The Christians of Constantinople knew that it was only a matter of time before the last remaining stronghold of the Byzantine Empire came under siege. For decades the ring of Ottoman conquests had narrowed around the holy city until it alone stood out against the Turkish sultan. Constantinople, the bridge between Europe and Asia, was tottering. The once teeming center of Eastern Christianity had never recovered from the epidemics of the fourteenth century, and now dwindling revenues matched the dwindling population.

Perhaps it was that impoverishment that had kept the Turks at bay. Constantinople was still the best fortified city in the world. Shaped like the head of a horse, it was surrounded by water on all but one side, and that side was protected by two stout rings of walls separated by a trench lined with stones. No cannon forged in the West could dent the battlements, and no navy could hope to force its way through the narrow mouth of the Golden Horn. Thus an uneasy peace existed between sultan and emperor. It was shattered in 1451 with the accession of a new sultan, the 19-year-old Mehmed II. Mehmed's imagination was fired by the ancient prophecies that a Muslim would rule the East. Only Constantinople was a fitting capital for such an empire, and Mehmed immediately began preparations for its conquest.

A CLOSER LOOK

In 1452 Mehmed had constructed a fortress at the narrow mouth of the Bosporus and demanded tribute from all ships that entered the Golden Horn. The Byzantine emperor sent ambassadors to Mehmed to protest that aggression; Mehmed returned their severed heads. When the first Venetian convoy refused to lower its sails, Mehmed's artillery efficiently sank one of the galleys with a single shot. The Turks now controlled access to the city for trade and supplies. An attack the following spring seemed certain.

The emperor appealed far and wide for aid: to the Venetians and Genoese to protect their trade and to the pope to defend Christianity. The Europeans were willing, but as yet they were unable. They did not think that the Ottomans could assemble an army before summer. By then an Italian armada could dislodge the Ottoman fortress and reinforce the city with trained fighting men.

But they hadn't reckoned with Mehmed. While the Italians bickered over the cost of the expedition and Christians everywhere made ready to celebrate Holy Week, the Ottomans assembled a vast army of fighters and laborers and a huge train of weapons and supplies. Among them was the largest cannon ever cast, with a 26-foot barrel that shot a 1200-pound ball. Fifty teams of oxen and 200 men took two months to pull it in place.

Mehmed's forces—which eventually numbered more than 150,000, of which 60,000 were soldiers—assembled around the walls of Constantinople on 5 April. During the next week a great flotilla sailed up the Bosporus and anchored just out of reach of the

Byzantine warships in the Golden Horn. A census taken inside the city revealed that there were only 7000 able-bodied defenders—about 5000 Greek residents and 2000 foreigners, mostly Genoese and Venetians. The Italians were the only true soldiers among them.

Although the defenders were vastly outnumbered, they still held the military advantage. As long as their ships controlled the entrance to the Golden Horn, they could limit the Ottoman attack to only one side of the city, where all of the best defenders could be massed. The Byzantines cast a boom—an iron chain supported by wooden floats—across the mouth of the Horn to forestall a naval attack. By the middle of April, the Turks had begun their land assault. Each day great guns pounded the walls of the city, and each night residents worked frantically to repair the damage. Everyone contributed. Old women wove baskets in which children carried stones. Monks and nuns packed mud and cut branches to shore up the breaches in the wall. The Turks suffered heavily each time they attempted to follow a cannon shot with a massed charge, but the attack took its toll among the defenders as well. No one was safe from the flaming arrows and catapulted stones flung over the city's walls. Choking black smoke filled the air as the huge cannon shook the foundations of the city and treated its stout stone walls as if they were plaster. Nevertheless, for the first month of siege the defenders held their own.

The stubborn defense of the city infuriated Mehmed. As long as there was only one point of attack, the defenders could resist indefinitely. The line of assault had to be extended, and this could only be done by sea. With the boom effectively impregnable and with Italian seamen superior to the Turks, the prospects seemed dim. But what could not be achieved by force might be achieved by intelligence. Mehmed devised a plan to carry a number of smaller ships across land and then to float them behind the Christian fleet. Protected by land forces, the ships could be used as a staging point for another line of attack. Thousands of workers built huge wooden rollers, which were greased with animal fat. Under cover of darkness and the smoke of cannon fire, 72 ships were pulled up the steep hills and pushed down into the sea. Once they were safely anchored, a pontoon bridge was built and cannons were trained on the seaward walls of the city.

By then the city had withstood siege for nearly six weeks without any significant reinforcement. At the end of May there was a sudden lull. A messenger from the sultan arrived to demand surrender. The choice was clear. If the city were taken by force, the customary three days of unrestricted pillage would be allowed; if it yielded, the sultan pledged to protect the property of all who desired to remain under his rule. The emperor replied feebly that no one who had ever laid siege to Constantinople had enjoyed a long life. He was ready to die in defense of his capital.

On 30 May the final assault began. Mehmed knew that his advantage lay in numbers. First, he sent in waves of irregular troops, mostly captured slaves and Christians, who suffered great losses and were finally driven back by the weakened defenders. Next, better-trained warriors

■ This fifteenth-century illustration shows the siege of Constantinople by the Turks.

attacked and widened the breaches made by the irregulars. Finally came the crack Janissaries, the sultan's elite warriors, disciplined from birth to fight. It was the Janissaries who found a small door left open at the base of the wall. In they rushed, quickly overwhelming the first line of defenders and battering their way through the weaker second walls. By dawn the Ottoman flag was raised over the battlements and the sack of Constantinople had begun.

There was no need for the customary three days of pillage. By the end of the first day there was nothing left worth taking. The churches and monasteries had been looted and defaced, the priests and nuns murdered or defiled, and thousands of civilians had been captured to be sold into slavery. Large areas of the city smoldered from countless fires. The bastion of Eastern Christendom was no more.

Medici and the establishment of French sovereignty. The Papal States were next to be occupied, and within a year Charles had conquered Naples without engaging the Italians in a single significant battle. Unfortunately, the Milanese were not the only ones who could play at the game of foreign alliances. Next, it was the turn of the Venetians and the pope to unite and call upon the services of King Ferdinand of Aragon and the Holy Roman Emperor. Italy was now a battleground in what became a total European war for dynastic supremacy. The city-states used their foreign allies to settle old scores and to extend their own mainland empires. At the turn of the century Naples was dismembered. In 1509, the pope conspired to organize the most powerful combination of forces yet known against Venice. All the "terra firma" possessions of the Most Serene Republic were lost, but by a combination of good fortune and skilled diplomacy Venice itself survived. Florence was less fortunate, becoming a pawn first of the French and then of the Spanish. The final blow to Italian hegemony was the sack of Rome in 1527, when German mercenaries fulfilled the fears of what the "infidels" would do to the Holy City.

Surveying the wreckage of the Italian wars, Machiavelli ended *The Prince* with a plea for a leader to emerge to restore Italian freedom and recreate the unity of the ancient Roman Republic. He concluded with these lines from Petrarch:

> *Then virtue boldly shall engage*
> *And swiftly vanquish barbarous rage,*
> *Proving that ancient and heroic pride*
> *In true Italian hearts had never died.*

CONCLUSION

The revival of "ancient and heroic pride" fueled the Italian Renaissance. The sense of living in a new age, the spirit of human achievement, and the curiosity and wonderment of writers and artists all characterized the Renaissance. The desire to recreate the glories of Rome was not Machiavelli's alone. It could be seen in the palaces of the Italian aristocracy; in the papal rebuilding of the Holy City; and in the military ambitions of princes. But the legacy of empire, of "ancient and heroic pride," had passed out of Italian hands.

QUESTIONS FOR REVIEW

1. What social and cultural conditions were peculiar to the Italian peninsula, and how might those conditions have contributed to the Renaissance?
2. What were the principal characteristics of the Renaissance style in the visual arts?
3. What is humanism, and why was the study of languages so important to the humanists?
4. In what ways did the ideas of Niccolò Machiavelli reflect the reality of politics in the city-states of Renaissance Italy?

KEY TERMS

city-states, *p. 335*	humors, *p. 332*
civic humanism, *p. 332*	linear perspective, *p. 326*
classical, *p. 318*	philology, *p. 330*
condottieri, *p. 336*	*Pietà*, *p. 328*
doge, *p. 336*	Renaissance, *p. 318*
humanists, *p. 330*	rhetoric, *p. 330*

DISCOVERING WESTERN CIVILIZATION ONLINE

You can obtain more information about the Italian Renaissance at the Websites listed below. See also the Companion Website that accompanies this text, www.ablongman.com/kishlansky, which contains an online study guide and additional resources.

Renaissance Society

NM's Creative Impulse: Renaissance
www.history.evansville.net/renaissa.html#Resources
A site of links to a wide array of subjects relating to the era of the Renaissance. A good starting point.

The Florentine Republic
www.mega.it/eng/egui/epo/secrepu.htm
The history of the Florentine Republic with links to major tourist attractions and buildings. Brief biographies of important Florentine citizens can also be found.

The History of Costume—Index
www.siue.edu/COSTUMES/COSTUME5_INDEX.HTML
Part of a site devoted to the history of dress. This page shows examples of the clothing worn by different classes as well as in different countries during the fifteenth and sixteenth centuries.

Renaissance Art

Renaissance Art
www.anu.edu.au/ArtHistory/renart/pics.art/index_1.html
A pictorial guide to the major artists of the Italian Renaissance and their works. Thumbnail representations lead to links on specific pieces.

Leon Battista Alberti—Great Buildings Online
www.greatbuildings.com/architects/Leon_Battista_Alberti.html
A page devoted to Alberti's architecture with a brief biography and links to pictures.

Michelangelo Buonarroti
www.mega.it/eng/egui/pers/micbuon.htm
A Website devoted to Michelangelo with a variety of links to text and images of Renaissance Florence.

WebMuseum: The Italian Renaissance (1420–1600)
www.ibiblio.org/wm/paint/tl/it-ren/
Reproductions of Renaissance art, with accompanying text.

SUGGESTIONS FOR FURTHER READING

General Reading

P. Burke, *Culture and Society in Renaissance Italy* (Princeton, NJ: Princeton University Press, 1999). A good introduction to social and intellectual developments.

Paul Grendler, ed., *Encyclopedia of the Renaissance* (New York: Scribners, 1999). Reference for all aspects of the Renaissance.

Denys Hay, *The Italian Renaissance* (Cambridge, England: Cambridge University Press, 1977). The best first book to read, an elegant interpretive essay.

John M. Najemy, ed. *Italy in the Age of the Renaissance: 1300–1550* (Oxford: 2005). A collection of essays written by experts on the Italian Renaissance that provide an engaging and thorough introduction to many aspects of Renaissance Italy.

Renaissance Society

Carlo Cipolla, *Before the Industrial Revolution: European Society and Economy, 1000–1700,* 3rd ed. (New York: W. W. Norton, 1994). A sweeping survey of social and economic developments across the centuries.

J. R. Hale, *Renaissance Europe: The Individual and Society* (Berkeley: University of California Press, 1978). A lively study placing great Renaissance figures in their social context.

D. Herlihy and C. Klapisch-Zuber, *Tuscans and Their Families* (New Haven, CT: Yale University Press, 1985). A difficult but rewarding study of the social and demographic history of Florence and its environs.

Margaret L. King, *Women of the Renaissance* (Chicago: University of Chicago Press, 1991). A study by a leading women's historian.

Richard MacKenney, *Renaissances: The Cultures of Italy, c. 1300–c. 1600* (Palgrave Macmillan, 2004). A specialist argues for the diversity and plurality of cultures and experiences in Italy between the fourteenth and seventeenth centuries.

Renaissance Art

Michael Baxandall, *Painting and Experience in Fifteenth-Century Italy* (Oxford: Oxford University Press, 1972). A study of the relationship between painters and their patrons and of how and why art was produced.

Anthony Grafton, *Leon Battista Alberti: Master Builder of the Italian Renaissance* (New York: Hill and Wang, 2000). A lucid biographical study of a truly renaissance man.

Frederick Hartt, *History of Italian Renaissance Art* (Englewood Cliffs, NJ: Prentice-Hall, 1974). The most comprehensive survey, with hundreds of plates.

Howard Hibbard, *Michelangelo* (New York: Harper & Row, 1974). A compelling biography of an obsessed genius.

Lisa Jardine and Jerry Brotton, *Global Interests: Renaissance Art Between East and West* (Ithaca, NY: Cornell University Press, 2000). A bold argument about Renaissance art and its relation to Ottoman culture.

Michael Levey, *Early Renaissance* (London: Penguin, 1967). A concise survey of art, clearly written and authoritative.

Linda Murray, *High Renaissance and Mannerism* (London: Thames & Hudson, 1985). The best introduction to late Renaissance art.

Renaissance Ideals

Hans Baron, *The Crisis of the Early Italian Renaissance* (Princeton, NJ: Princeton University Press, 1966). One of the most influential intellectual histories of the period.

George Holmes, *The Florentine Enlightenment,* 2nd ed. (Oxford: Clarendon Press, 1992). A new edition of the best study of intellectual developments in Florence.

Quentin Skinner, *Machiavelli* (Oxford: Oxford University Press, 1981). A brief but brilliant biography.

The Politics of the Italian City-States

Gene Brucker, *Florence, The Golden Age 1138–1737* (Berkeley: University of California Press, 1998). The best single-volume introduction to Florentine history with excellent illustrations.

J. R. Hale, *Florence and the Medici* (London: Thames & Hudson, 1977). A compelling account of the relationship between a city and its most powerful citizens.

Frederic C. Lane, *Venice: A Maritime Republic* (Baltimore, MD: Johns Hopkins University Press, 1973). A complete history of Venice that stresses its naval and mercantile developments.

Lauro Martines, *Power and Imagination: City-States in Renaissance Italy* (New York: Alfred A. Knopf, 1979). An important interpretation of the politics of the Italian powers.

Lauro Martines, *Scourge and Fire: Savonarola in Renaissance Italy* (Jonathan Cape, 2006). An exciting new biography of the charismatic preacher Savonarola who called for religious and political reform in the 1490s.

Eugene F. Rice, Jr., *The Foundations of Early Modern Europe, 1460–1559,* 2nd ed. (New York: W. W. Norton, 1994). The best short synthetic work.

Charles Stinger, *The Renaissance in Rome* (Bloomington, IN: University of Indiana Press, 1998). A thorough account of one of the great ages in the history of Rome.

For a list of additional titles related to this chapter's topics, please see http://www.ablongman.com/kishlansky.

THE EUROPEAN EMPIRES

ASTRIDE THE WORLD
THE AGE OF MONARCHIES

Henry VIII lived large. He was a bear of a man, famed for his ability to hunt all day while wearing out a pack of trained horses, for his prowess in wrestling bouts, including one with King Francis I of France, and, of course, for having six wives. His accomplishments as a leader were equally impressive. Bequeathed a surplus by his father, Henry spent lavishly in an attempt to restore England to European prominence. He allied with Spain to fight France and with France to fight Spain and ran an expensive but futile campaign to be elected Holy Roman Emperor. He sponsored humanist thinkers and brought them to his court from all over Europe. He also encouraged the new learning at the Universities of Oxford and Cambridge, and during his reign Sir Thomas More wrote *Utopia*, one of the classic works of English literature. Henry's generals decisively defeated the Scots, England's troublesome northern neighbor, and his ministers successfully completed the integration of Wales into the English crown.

THE VISUAL RECORD

In 1532, when his attempt to secure an annulment of his first marriage failed, Henry dissolved England's ties to the Church of Rome declaring that "this realm of England is an Empire"—the first statement of British imperial ambition. He had Parliament declare him Supreme Head of the Church in England and then helped himself to the vast holdings of the Catholic religious orders. Perhaps as much as a third of all of the land in England was forfeited to the crown when the monasteries and chantries were dissolved. Though Henry VIII shared his plunder with his loyal nobility and gentry, the lion's share was his. Henry's own religious beliefs remained shrouded in mystery, but he guided his nation toward the Protestantism that would bloom under his son Edward VI and his daughter Elizabeth I.

Henry VIII has passed through the ages as the very symbol of a monarch, an image captured by the German portrait painter Hans Holbein. Holbein was born into a family of painters and settled among the Swiss in Basel to practice his craft before being invited to the English court in the mid-1530s. His great skill was in rendering subjects true to life and his paintings of the Henrician court and its leading members such as Thomas More and Thomas Cromwell rival the works of Italian Renaissance portraiturists. But none were more memorable than the artist's numerous studies of Henry himself. Holbein was able to capture both the ferocity and the grandeur of the king.

Ironically, one of Holbein's most powerful, and most famous, portraits of Henry did not survive the seventeenth century. Part of a mural that Holbein painted in Henry's Whitehall Palace in 1537, the original work was lost when the palace burned in 1698. However, as Holbein's followers had copied the grand painting, and earlier sketches of it by Holbein himself also survived, we still have a strong visual record of Holbein's vision of the king. The image shown here is a vibrant copy of the Whitehall Palace original, painted on oak panels, likely in the mid-sixteenth century. In this portrait, Henry stands with straight legs astride suggesting the solidity of tree trunks, one arm bent at the elbow as if in defiance of all comers. There is not even a suggestion of doubt as the king thrusts out his chest and fixes the viewer with a penetrating stare. The artist represents the sumptuousness of Henry's court in the monarch's clothing. Fabric literally encases him, flowing in folds and gathers of intricate design and the costliest material. Furs drape over his doublet and

■ Henry VIII portrait, after Hans Holbein.

elaborately embroidered red cloak. Enormous rubies bedeck not only his great gold chain but his hat and vest, running down both sleeves, all to create an overwhelming sense of opulence. Even the protruding codpiece is meant to convey the potency of a king who had finally sired a male heir. Every detail conveys the impression of a monarch at the height of his power.

LOOKING AHEAD

This image of Henry VIII is among the most recognizable from an age of monarchy that began in the sixteenth century and coincided with the consolidations of nations in western Europe and their expansion into all corners of the globe. Everywhere small principalities and kingdoms were absorbed by their larger and more powerful neighbors, and Europe's military might was on display as far east as India and as far west as Peru. Though England played but a small part in a century dominated by Spain and France, even its monarch could believe that he bestrode the world like a colossus.

EUROPEAN ENCOUNTERS

The sixteenth century was an age of exploration. Knowledge bequeathed from the past created curiosity about the present. Technological change made long sea voyages possible, and the demands of commerce provided incentives. Ottoman expansion on the southern and eastern frontiers of the Continent, however, threatened access to the goods of the East on which Europeans had come to rely. Spices were rare and expensive, but they were not merely luxuries. While nobles and rich merchants consumed them lavishly to enhance their reputations of wealth and generosity, spices had many practical uses. Some acted as preservatives, some as flavorings, and others were used as perfumes to battle the noxious gases that rose from urban streets and invaded homes and workplaces. The drugs of the East, the nature of which we can only guess at, helped soothe chronic ill health. The demand for all of the "spices" continued to rise at a greater rate than their supply. There was more than a fortune to be made by anyone who could participate in the trade.

Eastern spices were expensive. Most European manufactured goods had little utility in the East. Woven wool, which was the staple of Western industry, was too heavy to be worn in Eastern climes. Both silk and cotton came from the East and were more expertly spun there. Even Western jewelry relied upon imported stones. Metalwork was an attractive commodity for export, but providing Ottomans or other Muslims with weapons to wage holy wars against Christian Europe posed problems of policy and morality. And once the Ottomans began to cast great bronze cannons of their own, European arms were less eagerly sought. Western gold and silver flowed steadily east. As supplies of precious metals dwindled, economic growth in Europe slowed. Throughout the fifteenth century, ever larger amounts of Western specie were necessary to purchase ever smaller amounts of Eastern commodities. Europe faced a severe shortage of gold and silver, a shortage that threatened its standard of living and its prospects for economic growth. The search was on to discover new sources of gold.

Africa and a Passage to India

It was the Portuguese who made the first dramatic breakthroughs in exploration and colonization. Perched on the southwestern tip of Europe, Portugal was an agriculturally poor and sparsely populated nation. Among its few marketable commodities were fish and wine. The Portuguese had long been sea explorers, especially in the Atlantic Ocean, where they had established bases in the Azores and Madeira islands. Their small ships, known as **caravels**, were ideal for ocean travel, and their navigators were among the most skillful in the world. Yet they were unable to participate in the lucrative Mediterranean trade in bullion and spices until the expanding power of the Ottomans threatened the traditional eastern sea routes.

Prince Henry the Navigator. In the early fifteenth century, the Portuguese gained a foothold in northern Africa and used it to stage voyages along the continent's unexplored western coast. Like most explorers, the Portuguese were motivated by an unself-conscious mixture of faith and greed. Establishing southern bases would enable them to surround their Muslim enemies and give them access to the African bullion trade. The Portuguese navigator Bartolomeu Dias (ca. 1450–1500) summarized those goals succinctly: "To give light to those who are in darkness and to grow rich." Under the energetic leadership of Prince Henry the Navigator (1394–1460), the Portuguese pushed steadily southward. Prince Henry studied navigational techniques, accumulated detailed accounts of voyages, and encouraged the creation of accurate maps of the African coastline.

Prince Henry's systematic program paid off in the next generation. By the 1480s, Portuguese outposts had reached almost to the equator, and in 1487 Bartolomeu Dias rounded the tip of Africa and opened the eastern African shores to Portuguese traders. The aim of the enterprises was access to Asia rather than Africa. Dias might have reached India if his crew had not mutinied and forced him to return home. A decade later, Vasco da Gama (ca. 1460–1524) rounded the Cape of Good Hope and crossed into the Indian Ocean. His journey took two years, but when he returned to Lisbon in 1499 laden with the most valuable spices of the East, Portuguese ambitions were achieved.

Spanish and Portuguese Explorations, 1400–1600

Larger expeditions followed, one of which, blown off course, touched the South American coast of Brazil. Brazil was soon subsumed within the Portuguese dominions.

The Beginnings of the Slave Trade. The exploration of the African coast also brought the Portuguese into contact with Muslim traders who had developed connections between North Africa and the middle of the continent. They bartered for gold, ivory, and exotic spices, exchanging colorful cloth, metalwork, and other manufactured goods. They also bartered for slaves. Slavery was a common feature of the cultures that interacted in

Africa. Europeans had used slaves in ancient times and had developed a theory that justified slavery by capture. Muslims were dependent upon them for their armies and bought many slaves from European sources. Africans enslaved those who were captured in tribal wars and sold them out of Africa, first to Muslim traders and then to the Portuguese. There was nothing new about slavery in the West, especially if the slaves were not Christians. The popes who granted Portugal a monopoly on European trade in Africa also sanctioned the trade in African slaves upon the condition that those enslaved had not converted to Christianity.

The slave trade began almost immediately. At first African slaves were imported to Europe as a curiosity and were purchased by wealthy families. But the discovery of the Azores and the Canary Islands provided a much more valuable use for the enslaved Africans. Their ability to labor in intense heat fitted them for agricultural work in the new sugar fields that were being developed in these Atlantic islands. By the 1470s it was estimated that over a thousand African slaves a year were being imported into Portugal and that a significant percentage of those were sold to Spanish masters who also saw their value in farming. Originally, the slaves were purchased either from Muslim traders or directly from African

MAP DISCOVERY

Portuguese Explorations

Examine the routes of the Portuguese explorers. What was their strategy of exploration? How long did it take for explorers to round the tip of Africa? What was the ultimate goal of Portuguese seafarers?

tribal leaders. As the trade became more sophisticated and more competitive, slaves could no longer be bartered for trinkets. Horses became the preferred medium of exchange, and Prince Henry the Navigator financed the trade until his death. Thereafter, the right to trade in slaves was sold to private entrepreneurs, and they were less scrupulous in their methods. Soon the Portuguese were simply conducting raids on coastal villages to capture as many Africans as they could cram on to their boats.

In these early decades, slaves were viewed as just another trading commodity and valued only in regard to their profit. Ships were still small, voyages still risky, and capital still scarce. Traders carried whatever items were most in demand,

and the agricultural use of African slaves was limited by the small amount of commercial agriculture undertaken by Europeans. The Portuguese held a monopoly on transporting slaves from Africa, but the trade soon centered in Seville where Italians dominated it. This was a significant, if unplanned development. Seville would soon become the center of the Spanish overseas empire, and the Spanish colonies in America would soon become the destination for most of the African slaves bought by Europeans.

The Asian Trade. The Portuguese came to the East as traders rather than as conquerors. Building on their experi-

MOLVQVES

PETITE IAVE

GRANDE IAVE

K DE LINDE ORIENTALE

■ This sixteenth-century map of Java and the Moluccas shows European traders bartering for spices. At the upper left, a ship laden with the rich cargo sails for markets in Europe.

ence in West Africa, they developed a policy of establishing military outposts to protect their investments and subduing native populations only when necessary. Throughout the East the Portuguese took advantage of local feuds to gain allies, and they established trading compounds that were easily defensible. The Portuguese general Alfonso de Albuquerque (1453–1515) understood the need for strategically placed garrisons and conquered the vital ports of the Middle East and India. By the first decade of the sixteenth century, the Portuguese were masters of a vast empire, which spanned both the eastern and western coasts of Africa and the western shores of India. Most importantly, the Portuguese controlled Ceylon and Indonesia, the precious Spice Islands from which came cloves, cinnamon, and pepper. Almost overnight, Lisbon became one of the trading capitals of the world, tripling in population between 1500 and 1550.

It was northern Europe that was to harvest what Portugal had sown. The long voyages around Africa were costly and dangerous. Moreover, the expense of maintaining a far-flung empire ate into the profits of trade at the same time that the increased volume necessary to make the voyages worthwhile drove down spice prices. Between 1501 and 1505, more than 80 ships and 7000 men sailed from Portugal to the East. The vast commitment was underwritten by Flemish, German, and Italian bankers. Soon Antwerp replaced Lisbon as the marketplace for Asian spices. Ironically, it was in the accidental discovery of Brazil rather than in Asia that the Portuguese were rewarded for the enterprise of their explorers.

Mundus Novus

Whereas most of Portugal's resources were devoted to the Asian trade, those of the Spanish kingdom came to be concentrated in the New World. Although larger and richer than its eastern neighbor, Spain had been segmented into a number of small kingdoms and principalities and divided between Christians and Muslims. Not until the end of the fifteenth century, when the crowns of Aragon and Castile were united and the Muslims expelled from Granada, could the Spanish concentrate their resources. By then they were far behind in establishing commercial enterprises. With Portugal dominating the African route to India, Queen Isabella of Castile was persuaded to take an interest in a western route by a Genoese adventurer, Christopher Columbus ca. (1446–1506).

Christopher Columbus. Like all well-informed people of his day, Columbus believed that the world was round. By carefully calculating routes and distances, he concluded that a western track would be shorter and less expensive than the path that the Portuguese were breaking around Africa. Columbus's conclusions were based partly on conventional knowledge and partly on his own self-assurance. All were wholly erroneous. He misjudged the size of the globe by 25 percent and the distance of the journey by 400 percent. But he persevered against all odds. Columbus sailed westward into the unknown in 1492, and on 12 October he landed in the Bahamas, on an island that he named San Salvador. He had encountered a *Mundus Novus*, a New World.

DOCUMENT

Christopher Columbus, Letter from the New World

Initially, Columbus's discovery was a disappointment. He had gone in search of a western passage to the Indies, but he had failed to return to Spain laden with Eastern spices. Despite his own belief that the islands he had discovered lay just off the coast of Japan, it was soon apparent that he had found an altogether unknown landmass. Columbus's own explorations and those of his successors continued to focus on discovering a route to the Indies. That was all the more imperative once the Portuguese succeeded in finding the passage around Africa. In 1494, the **Treaty of Tordesillas** had confirmed Portugal's right to the eastern route to the Indies as well as to any undiscovered lands east of an imaginary line fixed west of the Cape Verde Islands. That entitled Portugal to Brazil; the Spanish received whatever lay west of the line. At the time few doubted that Portugal had the better end of the bargain.

But Spanish-backed explorations soon proved the value of the new lands. Using the Caribbean Islands as a staging ground, successive explorers uncovered the vast coastline of Central and South America. In 1513, Vasco Núñez de Balboa (1475–1517) crossed the land passage in Panama and became the first European to view the Pacific Ocean. The discovery of this ocean refueled Spanish ambitions to find a western passage to the Indies.

Ferdinand Magellan. In 1519, Ferdinand Magellan (ca. 1480–1521), a Portuguese mariner in the service of Spain, set sail in pursuit of Columbus's goal of reaching the Spice Islands by sailing westward. His voyage, which he did not live to complete, remains the most astounding of the age. After making the Atlantic crossing, Magellan resupplied his fleet in Brazil. Then his ships began the long southerly run toward the tip of South America, though he had no idea of the length of the continent. Suppressing mutinies and overcoming ship-

wrecks and desertions, Magellan finally found the straits that still bear his name. That crossing was the most difficult of all; the 300 miles took 38 terrifying days to navigate.

The Pacific voyage was equally remarkable. The sailors went nearly four months without taking on fresh food or water. Survival was miraculous. "We drank yellow water and often ate sawdust. Rats were sold for half a ducat a piece."

When Magellan finally reached land, in the Philippines, his foolhardy decision to become involved in a local war cost him his life. It was left to his navigator, Sebastian Elcano (ca. 1476–1526), to complete the journey. In 1522, three years and one month after setting out, Elcano returned to Spain with a single ship and 18 survivors of the crew of 280. But in his hold were spices of greater value than the cost of the expedition, and in his return was practical proof that the world was round.

The circumnavigation of Magellan and Elcano brought to an end the first stage of the Spanish exploration of the New World. Columbus's dreams were realized, but the vastness of

A MOMENTOUS DISCOVERY

Christopher Columbus seemingly needs no introduction. His name has forever been associated with the European discovery of the New World, although the meaning of that discovery has continually been contested. In the summer of 1492, Columbus sailed west from the Canary Islands believing that he would reach the coast of China. Instead he landed on an island in the Caribbean. This passage, from a letter addressed to the royal treasurer of Spain, contains his first impressions of the people he encountered.

Focus Questions

How do the indigenous people respond to Columbus and his men? Why is Columbus so interested in the tools and clothing of the natives?

A letter addressed to the noble Lord Raphael Sanchez, *Treasurer to their most invincible Majesties, Ferdinand and Isabella, King and Queen of Spain, by Christopher Columbus, to whom our age is greatly indebted, treating of the islands of India recently discovered beyond the Ganges, to explore which he had been sent eight months before under the auspices and at the expense of their said Majesties.*

The inhabitants of both sexes in this island, and in all the others which I have seen, or of which I have received information, go always naked as they were born, with the exception of some of the women, who use the covering of a leaf, or small bough, or an apron of cotton which they prepare for that purpose. None of them are possessed of any iron, neither have they weapons, being unacquainted with, and indeed incompetent to use them, not from any deformity of body (for they are well-formed), but because they are timid and full of fear.

They carry however in lieu of arms, canes dried in the sun, on the ends of which they fix heads of dried wood

sharpened to a point, and even these they dare not use habitually; for it has often occurred when I have sent two or three of my men to any of the villages to speak with the natives, that they have come out in a disorderly troop, and have fled in such haste at the approach of our men, that the fathers forsook their children and the children their fathers. This timidity did not arise from any loss or injury that they had received from us; for, on the contrary, I gave to all I approached whatever articles I had about me, such as cloth and many other things, taking nothing of theirs in return: but they are naturally timid and fearful. As soon however as they see that they are safe, and have laid aside all fear, they are very simple and honest, and exceedingly liberal with all they have; none of them refusing any thing he may possess when he is asked for it, but on the contrary inviting us to ask them. They exhibit great love towards all others in preference to themselves: they also give objects of great value for trifles, and content themselves with very little or nothing in return.

Such are the events which I have briefly described. Farewell.

Lisbon, the 14th of March.
CHRISTOPHER COLUMBUS,
Admiral of the Fleet of the Ocean.

Christopher Columbus, *Letter from the First Voyage* (1493).

THE COLUMBIAN EXCHANGE

The encounters between Europeans and native Americans were a cultural and intellectual event of the first magnitude, likely stirring the imaginations of native tribesmen as much as those of European writers. These people had been separated for millennia, ever since the ice bridge in the Bering Sea ceased to be a conduit between North America and Asia. Their civilizations had developed along entirely different paths, and their first encounters must have mixed curiosity and fear in equal parts. The Europeans left extensive records of the differences they observed in sexual mores, attitudes toward property, and social organization. Native Americans must have made similar observations even if they were lost to posterity. Each civilization had much to teach the other though their ability to communicate with one another was limited at best.

THE WEST AND THE WIDER WORLD

The encounters were also a biological and ecological event and both had far reaching and long-lasting consequences. Each culture introduced the other to new diseases and to unknown plants and animals. Historians have labeled this aspect of the European discoveries the **Columbian Exchange**.

The mixing of populations that had been historically separate had effects that no one could have foreseen. First and foremost were issues of public health. Although it is believed that the Americas were originally settled by migration across a land bridge that connected Russia to Alaska, those who made the trek were few and over many generations they had lost their immunity to diseases they may have encountered in Europe. When the Spanish explorers arrived in the Caribbean islands, they carried agents of their common diseases such as measles, influenza, and especially smallpox. These diseases raged in European population centers and killed thousands each year, but those who survived them carried lifetime immunity. The native populations of the Americas endured their first exposure to these diseases all at once, and millions succumbed in the first half-century of contact. From the Caribbean to Peru, the microbes that Europeans unknowingly carried in their bodies decimated native populations.

Similarly, it was believed that Europeans first contracted the venereal disease syphilis through sexual encounters with American women. Though experts still debate whether syphilis originated in the New World it is agreed there was an epidemic of the disease in western Europe after the explorers returned home. It began in Naples in 1494 shortly after the return of Columbus's crew and spread with devastating rapidity throughout western Europe. In the first generations of infection, syphilis erupted quickly, spread rapidly, and was often fatal. In its final states it resulted in a form of mental illness that attracted the attention of numerous Renaissance physicians.

Disease was not the only unanticipated exchange that resulted from the encounters. On their ships the Spanish explorers brought horses, pigs, cows, and other domesticated animals unknown in the Americas. Native populations had no work beast sturdier than the llama, an animal barely able to carry two hundred pounds of weight and comparatively slow of foot. The lack of beasts of burden had a profound effect on the organization of Native American agriculture. Whereas European plow teams could clear trees and turn over earth with great efficiency, Americans had to accomplish these tasks by their own hands. Moreover, their range of travel was limited to what they could traverse by foot. European horses could cover many more miles at a faster speed than even the best conditioned American runners. The arrival of horses and oxen changed patterns of work among native populations almost instantly, and it eventually transformed entire cultures. Nowhere was horse culture more evident than in North America where once sedentary tribes became skilled hunters. The horses bred by North American Indians could easily outrun the herds of buffalo that roamed the Great Plains. The newly introduced animals provided hides for clothing and shelter, fat for candles and soaps, and meat that supplemented a protein-poor diet and improved the lives of generations of North Americans. Beef and pork consumption also rose dramatically in Mexico and Peru where earlier a diet of meat consisted entirely of wild turkey.

Nor was the exchange of food one-sided. Indeed, the foodstuffs of the New World proved of lasting significance to Europeans. Beginning in the 1550s, men who in later centuries would be called botanists and zoologists began to make the voyage to the Americas, hoping to discover new plants and animals that could be exported back to Europe. They catalogued thousands of unknown species, a small number of which were suited to the different climates and soils of Europe. The Jesuit missionary Jose de Acosta (1539–1600) traveled through what are now Mexico, Chile, and Peru observing the nature of the land, of the peoples who lived at altitude in the Andes, and of the many plants that were put to use as medicines and food. His book, *The Natural and Moral History of the Indies* (1590), was an immediate best seller, read for its scientific value as much as for its description of his exotic discoveries. Among these was the Aztec use of the cocoa bean to make a rich, bitter drink. Cocoa was so prized that the beans were used for exchange and to pay taxes and the Aztecs reserved the drink for their nobility. It was commonly flavored with seeds from an orchid

■ The meeting between Montezuma and Cortés in 1519. The initial encounters between Europeans and native Americans had far-reaching social, biological, and ecological consequences.

known to the natives as vanilla. Both cocoa and vanilla were exported by the Spanish back to Europe though it took several generations before they were able to master their uses. The combination of the ground bitter cocoa beans with sugar and milk made a drink called chocolate which became a European-wide fad in the eighteenth century.

If one part of the Columbian food exchanges yielded treats, another part yielded staples. One of these was a small yellow fruit that had been cultivated by the Mayans and was used in cooking in Central America. When it was exported to Europe it thrived in the hot Mediterranean climates of Spain and Italy. The Italians called it *pomodoro*- the yellow apple—but Native Americans called it tomato. Though some commentators thought it was poisonous, Italian peasants were soon using it in soups and developing sauces from its rich fruit. By the eighteenth century it was a staple of southern Italian cooking, was grown in

France, and was used as a condiment in Spain. A close relative to the tomato was an even more important South American foodstuff, the potato. This was a food so nutritious that laborers could nearly survive on it alone. It could be cooked in accordance with any local custom, boiled, fried, or simply thrown into a fire. Potatoes needed little land for cultivation and little care once they were planted. Both characteristics made them perfect staples for peasant diets. They took hold quickly in central Europe where population pressure had reduced the size of farms and became a standard in German cooking. They were the most important crop in Ireland as well, where the poor survived on almost nothing else.

The Columbian Exchange was a global event that altered the nature of American and European societies. It was, of course, a much greater shock to the Native Americans who endured epidemic disease, military conquest, and occupation. Their great civilizations were ultimately obliterated, in

South and Central America by the Spanish, in North America by the British and the French. The wealth they dug from the mines of the Andes financed two centuries of continental warfare as Spain vied for European supremacy. But Europeans too were changed by the encounters. Millions of them emigrated to begin new lives in the Americas and to build societies that were profoundly influenced by the natives who had preceded them.

QUESTIONS FOR DISCUSSION

Why were the diseases brought by Europeans to America so devastating? What diseases did the native peoples spread to their visitors? What was the consequence of native peoples' lack of work animals? What effect did the introduction of horses have on their societies? How did the Columbian Exchange ultimately change native and European populations?

the Pacific Ocean made a western passage to the Indies uneconomical. In 1529, the Spanish crown relinquished to the Portuguese its claims to the Spice Islands for a cash settlement. By then, trading spices was less alluring than mining gold and silver.

The Spanish Conquests

At the same moment that Magellan's voyage closed one stage of Spanish exploration, the exploits of Hernando Cortés (1485–1547) opened another. The Spanish colonized the New World along the model of their reconquest of Spain. Individuals were given control over land and the people on it in return for military service. The interests of the crown were threefold: to convert the natives to Christianity; to extend sovereignty over new dominions; and to gain some measure of profit from the venture. The colonial entrepreneurs had a singular interest—to grow rich. By and large, the colonizers came from the lower orders of Spanish society. Even the original captains and governors were drawn from groups, like younger sons of the nobility, that would have had little opportunity for rule in Castile. They undertook great risks in expectation of great rewards.

Thus many of the protective measures taken by the crown to ensure orderly colonization and fair treatment of the natives were ineffective in practice. During the first decades of the sixteenth century, Spanish captains and their followers subdued the Indian populations of the Caribbean Islands and put them to work on the agricultural haciendas that they had carved out for themselves. As early as 1498, Castilian women began arriving in the New World. Their presence helped change the character of the settlement towns from wild frontier garrisons to civilized settlements. Younger daughters of the lesser nobility, guided and guarded by chaperones, came to find husbands among the successful **conquistadores**. Some

of the women ultimately inherited huge estates and participated fully in the forging of Spanish America.

Life on the hacienda, even in relative ease with a Castilian wife and family, did not always satisfy the ambitions of the Spanish colonizers. Hernando Cortés was one such conquistador. Having participated in the conquest of Cuba, Cortés sought an independent command to lead an expedition into the hinterland of Central America, where a fabulous empire was rumored to exist. Gathering a force of 600 men, Cortés sailed across the Gulf of Mexico in 1519; established a fort at Vera Cruz, where he garrisoned 200 men; and then sank his boats so that none of his company could turn back. With 400 soldiers, he began his quest. The company marched 250 miles through steamy jungles and over rugged mountains before glimpsing the first signs of the great Aztec civilization.

The Aztec Empire was a loose confederation of native tribes that the Aztecs had conquered during the previous century. They were ruled by the emperor Montezuma II (1502–1520) from his capital at Tenochtitlán, a marvelous city built of stone and baked clay in the middle of a lake. Invited to an audience with the Aztec emperor, Cortés and his men saw vast stores of gold and silver.

The conquest of the Aztecs took almost a year. Nearly 100,000 natives from the tribes that the Aztecs had conquered supported the Spanish assault. Cortés's cavalry terrified the Aztecs. They had never seen horses or iron armaments. Cortés also benefited from the Aztec practice of taking battlefield captives to be used in religious sacrifices. That allowed many Spanish soldiers, who would otherwise have been killed, to be rescued and to fight again.

By 1522, Cortés was master of an area larger than all of Spain. But the cost in native lives was staggering. In 30 years a population of approximately 25 million had been reduced to

DOCUMENT

Cortés's Letter to Charles V

■ A sixteenth-century Tenochtitlán drawing of Cortés marching on the Aztec capital at Tenochtitlán. Cortés, the bearded figure third from right, is accompanied by the Indian princess Malinche, who served as his interpreter, and the Moorish servant Estevanico. Barefoot soldiers and Indian porters bring up the rear.

THE HALLS OF MONTEZUMA

Bernal Díaz del Castillo (ca. 1492–1581) was one of the soldiers who accompanied Hernando Cortés on the conquest of the Aztecs. Díaz wrote The True History of the Conquest of New Mexico *to refute what he regarded as inaccurate accounts of the conquest. In this passage he describes the Aztec gods from a Christian point of view and shows how difficult it was for the Europeans to understand the different cultures they were encountering.*

Focus Questions

Díaz describes the Aztec gods as devils and idols. What does this view reveal about the Europeans' way of thinking? Why would Cortés want to see Montezuma's gods, and why does Montezuma show them to him?

Then Cortés said to Montezuma . . ."Your Highness is indeed a great prince, and it has delighted us to see your cities. Now that we are here in your temple, will you show us your gods?"

Montezuma replied that he would first have to consult with his priests. After he had spoken with them, he bade us enter a small tower room, a kind of hall where there were two altars with very richly painted planks on the ceiling. On each altar there were two giant figures, their bodies very tall and stout. The first one, to the right, they said was Uichilobos, their god of war. It had a very broad face with monstrous, horrible eyes, and the whole body was covered with precious stones, gold, and pearls that were stuck on with a paste they make in this country out of roots. The body was circled with great snakes made of gold and precious stones, and in one hand he held a bow and in the other some arrows. A small idol standing by him they said was his page; he held a short lance and a shield rich with gold and precious stones. Around the neck of Uichilobos were silver Indian faces and things that we took to be the hearts of these Indians, made of gold and decorated with many precious blue stones. There were braziers with copal incense, and they were burning in them the hearts of three Indians they had sacrificed that day. All the walls and floor were black with crusted blood, and the whole place stank.

To the left stood another great figure, the height of Uichilobos, with the face of a bear and glittering eyes made of their mirrors, which they call *tezcal*. It was decorated with precious stones the same as Uichilobos, for they said that the two were brothers. This Tezcatepuca was the god of hell and had charge of the souls of the Mexicans. His body was girded with figures like little devils, with snakelike tails. The walls were so crusted with blood and the floor was so bathed in it that in the slaughterhouses of Castile there was no such stink. They had offered to this idol five hearts from the day's sacrifices. . . .

Our captain said to Montezuma, half laughingly, "Lord Montezuma, I do not understand how such a great prince and wise man as yourself can have failed to come to the conclusion that these idols of yours are not gods, but evil things—devils is the term for them. . . ."

The two priests with Montezuma looked hostile, and Montezuma replied with annoyance, "Señor Malinche, if I had thought that you would so insult my gods, I would not have shown them to you. We think they are very good, for they give us health, water, good seedtimes and weather, and all the victories we desire. We must worship and make sacrifices to them. Please do not say another word to their dishonor."

From Bernal Díaz, The True History of the Conquest of New Mexico *(1552–1568).*

---

less than 2 million. Most of the loss was due to exposure to European diseases such as smallpox, typhoid, and measles, against which the natives were helpless. Their labor-intensive system of agriculture could not survive the rapid decrease in population, and famine followed pestilence.

This tragic sequence was repeated everywhere the Europeans appeared. In 1531, Francisco Pizarro (ca. 1475–1541) matched Cortés's feat when he conquered the Peruvian Empire of the Incas. That conquest vastly extended the territory under Spanish control and became the true source of profit for the crown when a huge silver mine was discovered in 1545 at Potosí in what is now southern Bolivia. The gold and silver that poured into Spain in the next quarter century helped support Spanish dynastic ambitions in Europe. During the course of the sixteenth century, more than 200,000 Spaniards migrated across the ocean. Perhaps one in ten was a woman who married and set up a family. In succeeding generations, the settlers created huge haciendas built on the forced labor of black African slaves, who proved better able to endure the rigors of mining and farming than did the natives.

The Legacy of the Encounters

By the seventeenth century, long-distance trade had begun to integrate the regions of the world into a single marketplace. Slaves bought in Africa mined silver in South America. The bullion was shipped to Spain, where it was distributed across Europe. Most went to Amsterdam to settle Spanish debts, Dutch bankers having replaced the Italians as the paymasters of Europe. From Holland the silver traveled east to the Baltic Sea—the Dutch lifeline where vital stores of grain and timber

MAP DISCOVERY

Claims of Spain and Portugal to Overseas Empires

Examine the voyages of discovery and the claims to overseas empires. How did Portuguese and Spanish explorations differ? What was the effect of the Treaty of Tordesillas on their travel and claims? Why was it believed at the time that Portugal was the more powerful empire?

were purchased for home consumption. Even more of this African-mined Spanish silver, traded by the Dutch, was carried to Asia to buy spices in the Spice Islands, cottons in India, and silk in China. Millions of ounces of silver flowed from South America to Asia via the European trading routes. On the return voyage, Indian cottons were traded in Africa to purchase slaves for the South American silver mines. (See "The West and the Wider World: The Columbian Exchange," pp. 352–353.)

Gold, God, and Glory.   Gold, God, and glory neatly summarized the motives of the European explorers. Perhaps it is not necessary to delve any further. The gold of Africa and the silver of South America enriched the Western nations. Christian missions arose wherever the European empires touched down: among Africans, Asians, and Native Americans. And glory there was in plenty. The feats of the European explorers were recounted in story and song. The *Lusiads* (1572) by Luiz de Camões (ca. 1524–1580), one of the greatest works of Portuguese literature, celebrated the new age. "They were men of no ordinary stature, equally at home in war and in dangers of every kind: they founded a new king-

■ These engravings by Theodore de Bry accompanied a 1599 English edition of *The Destruction of the Indies* by Bartolomé de las Casas. They illustrated acts of Spanish cruelty and so bolstered Las Casas's argument by engendering sympathy for the Native American population.

dom among distant peoples, and made it great." In the achievement of exploration and conquest, the modern world had finally surpassed the ancients. "Let us hear no more then of Ulysses and Aeneas and their long journeyings, no more of Alexander and Trajan and their famous victories. My theme is the daring and renown of the Portuguese, to whom Neptune and Mars alike give homage."

The feats of exploration were worthy of celebration. In less than 50 years, tenacious European seafarers found passages to the east and continents to the west. In doing so they overcame terrors both real and imagined. Hazardous journeys in uncharted waters took their toll in men and ships. The odds of surviving a voyage of exploration were no better than those of surviving an epidemic of plague. Nearly two-thirds of da Gama's crew perished on the passage to India. The 40 men that Columbus left on Hispaniola, almost half his company, disappeared without a trace. Only one of the five ships that set out with Magellan in 1519 returned to Spain. "If you want to learn how to pray, go to sea" was a Portuguese proverb that needed no explanation.

IMAGE DISCOVERY

Smallpox: Death and Disease

This sixteenth-century drawing from the Aztec *Codex Florentino* depicts Native Americans suffering smallpox. Europeans often survived smallpox, but Americans had never encountered it before European contact and so had no immunity. As a result, smallpox devastated the native population. How might deaths from smallpox have affected the European conquest of America? After the conquest, Aztec survivors of the fall of Tenochtitlán developed these illustrations for a history of the conquest by Spanish church authorities. Does it seem that this image was created by Aztecs who may have lost family members to smallpox? Why, or why not? Why would the Spanish church have wanted to understand smallpox in America?

Yet all of these dangers were overcome. The expansion of Europe was a feat of technology. Advances in navigational skills, especially in dead reckoning and later in calculating latitude from the position of the sun, were essential preconditions for covering the distances that were to be traveled. So were the more sophisticated ship designs. The magnetic compass and the astrolabe were indispensable tools. New methods for the making of maps and charts, and the popular interest in them, fueled both ambitions and abilities. It was a mapmaker who named the newly found continents after Amerigo Vespucci (1451–1512), the Italian explorer who voyaged to Brazil for the Portuguese. It may have been an accident that Columbus found the New World, but it was no coincidence that he was able to land in the same place three more times.

European Reflections. Riches and converts, power and glory, all came in the wake of exploration. But in the process of exploring new lands and new cultures, Europe also discovered itself. It learned something of its own aspirations. Early Portuguese voyagers went in quest of the mythical Prester John, a saintly figure who was said to rule a heaven on earth in the middle of Africa. The first children born on Madeira were named Adam and Eve, though that slave plantation of sugar and wine was an unlikely Garden of Eden. The optimism of those who searched for the fountain of youth in the Florida swamps was not only that they would find it there, but that a long life was worth living. Contact with the cultures of the New World also forced a different kind of thinking about life in the old one. The supposed customs of strange lands also provided the setting for one of the great works of English social criticism, Sir Thomas More's *Utopia* (1516).

Europe also discovered and revealed a darker side of itself in the age of exploration. Accompanying the boundless optimism and assertive self-confidence that made so much possible was a tragic arrogance toward and callous disregard of native races. Portuguese travelers described Africans as "dog-faced, dog-toothed people, satyrs, wild men, and cannibals." Such attitudes helped justify enslavement. The European conquests were both brutal and wasteful. The Dominican priest Bartolomé de Las Casas (1474–1566) championed the cause of the native inhabitants at the court of the Spanish kings. His *Apologetic History of the Indies* (1550) highlighted the complexity of native society even as he witnessed its destruction. The German artist Albrecht Dürer (1471–1528) marveled at the "subtle ingenuity of the men in those distant lands" after viewing a display of Aztec art.

DOCUMENT

Laws on Good Treatment of the Indians

But few Europeans were so enlightened about native society. Although Europeans encountered heritages that were in some ways richer than their own, only the most farsighted Westerners could see that there was more value in the preservation of the heritages than in their demolition. The Portuguese spice trade did not depend upon the indiscriminate destruction of eastern ports. The obliteration of millions of Aztecs and Incas was not a necessary result of the fever for gold and silver. The destruction was wanton. It revealed the

■ Contact with cultures of the New World forced Europeans into a different way of thinking about the old world. In this detail from *The Cognoscenti*, a seventeenth-century Flemish painting, English scholars and navigators examine European encounters with new lands and new cultures.

rapaciousness, greed, and cruelty of the Portuguese and Spanish conquerors. Those were the impulses of the Crusades rather than of the Renaissance.

GEOGRAPHICAL TOUR
Europe in 1500: The Age of the New Monarchies

Just as the map of the world was changing as a result of the voyages of exploration, so the map of Europe was changing as a result of the activities of princes. The early sixteenth century was the age of the prince, the first great stage of nation building that would last for the next 300 years. The **New Monarchies,** as they are sometimes called, consolidated territories that were divided culturally, linguistically, and histori-

cally. The states of Europe were political units, and they were forged by political means: by diplomacy, by marriage, and, most commonly, by war. The national system that we take for granted when thinking about Europe is a relatively recent development. Before we can observe its beginnings, we must first have a picture of Europe as it existed in 1500 (see **Map A**). At that time it was composed of nearly 500 distinct political units.

Europe is a concept. Like all concepts, it is difficult to define. The vast plain that stretches from the Netherlands to the steppes of Russia presents few natural barriers to migration. Only in the south did geographical forces stem the flow of humanity. The Carpathian Mountains created a basin for the settlement of Slavic peoples that extended down to the Black Sea. The Alps provided a boundary for French, Germanic, and Italian settlements. The Pyrenees defined the Iberian Peninsula, with a mixture of African and European peoples.

Boundaries of Eastern Europe

In the East, three great empires had created the political geography that could be said to define a European boundary: the Mongol, the Ottoman, and the Russian. During the early Middle Ages, Mongol warriors had swept across the Asian steppes and conquered most of central and southern Russia. By the sixteenth century, the Mongol Empire was disintegrating, its lands divided into a number of separate states called *khanates*. The khanate of the Crimea, with lands around the northern shores of the Black Sea, created the southeastern border of Europe (see **Map B**).

The Ottoman territories defined the southern boundary. By 1450, the Ottomans controlled all of Byzantium and Greece, dominating an area from the Black Sea to the Aegean. Fifty years later, they had conquered nearly all the lands between the Aegean and the Adriatic seas. A perilous frontier was established on the Balkan Peninsula. There the principali-

ties of Moldavia, Wallachia, Transylvania, and Hungary (see **Map B**) held out against the Ottomans for another quarter century before being overrun.

The Russian state defined the eastern boundary of Europe. Russia too had been a great territorial unit in the Middle Ages, centered at Kiev in the west and stretching eastward into Asia. The advance of the Mongols in the thirteenth century had contracted the eastern part of Russia, and its western domains had disintegrated under the practice of dividing the ruling prince's inheritance among his sons. In 1500, Europe reached as far east as the principality of Muscovy. There the heritage of East and West mingled. In some periods of history, Russia's ties with the West were more important; at other times, Russia retreated into isolation from Europe.

The northern borders of eastern Europe centered on the Baltic Sea, one of the most important trading routes of the early modern era (see **Map B**). On the northern coasts lay the Scandinavian nations of Sweden, Norway, and Denmark.

■ **Map A. Europe in 1500.** While the western part of Europe had taken on its modern features, central and eastern Europe continued to change their boundaries.

■ **Map B. Eastern Europe.** This map shows eastern Europe before the consolidation of Russia. The Duchy of Lithuania had reached the height of its power and stretched from the Baltic to the Black Sea.

These loosely confederated nations had a single king throughout the fifteenth century. Denmark, the southernmost of the three, was also the richest and most powerful. It enjoyed a favorable trading position on both the North and Baltic seas and social and economic integration with the Germanic states on its border. On the southern side of the Baltic Sea lay the dominions of the Teutonic Knights, physically divided by the large state of Poland-Lithuania. The Teutonic territories, in the valuable Baltic region of Prussia, had been colonized by German crusaders in the thirteenth century.

Poland-Lithuania comprised an enormous territory that covered the length of Europe from the Baltic to the Black Sea (see **Map B**). The crowns of the two nations had been joined at the end of the fourteenth century, and their dynastic history was tied up with the nations of Bohemia and Hungary to their west and south. Whereas Bohemia was increasingly drawn into the affairs of central Europe, Hungary remained more Eastern in orientation, partly because the Bohemians gave nominal allegiance to the Holy Roman Emperor and partly because the Ottoman conquests had engulfed a large part of the Hungarian territories. At the end of the fifteenth century, Poland, Lithuania, Bohemia, and Hungary were all ruled by the same family, the Jagiellons.

Mongols and Ottomans to the south, Russians in the east, Scandinavia in the north, Poland-Lithuania in the center, and Hungary in the west: such were the contours of the eastern portion of Europe. Its lands were, on the whole, less fertile than those farther west, and its climate was more severe. It was a sparsely populated region. Its wealth lay in the Baltic fish-

eries, in the Hungarian and Bohemian silver mines, and in the enormous Russian forests, where wood and its by-products were plentiful. Except in the southern portions of Poland and central Bohemia, the region was agriculturally poor.

Central Europe

The middle of the continent was defined by the Holy Roman Empire and occupied almost entirely by Germanic peoples (see **Map C**). In length, the empire covered the territory from the North and Baltic seas to the Adriatic and the Mediterranean, where the Italian city-states were located. In width, it stretched from Bohemia to Burgundy. Politically, central Europe comprised a bewildering array of principalities, Church lands, and free towns. By the end of the fifteenth century, the Holy Roman Empire was an empire in name only. The large states of Brandenburg, Bohemia, and Bavaria resembled the political units of the East. In the south, the Alps provided an effective physical boundary, which allowed the Archduchy of Austria and the Swiss Confederation to follow their own separate paths. Stretching across the center of the empire, from the Elbe River to the North Sea, was a jumble of petty states. Great cities such as Nüremberg and Ulm in the

■ **Map C. Central Europe.** This map of Central Europe shows the boundaries of the Holy Roman Empire.

south, Bremen and Hamburg in the north, and Frankfurt and Cologne in the west were free municipalities. Large sections of the northwestern part of the empire were governed by the Church through resident bishops. Farther to the west were the prosperous Low Countries: Holland and its port of Amsterdam, Brabant and its port of Antwerp. In the southwest, the empire extended in some places as far as the Rhone River and included the rich estates of Luxembourg, Lorraine, and Burgundy (see **Map C**).

The riches of the empire made it the focal point of Europe. Nearly 15 million people lived within its borders. Its agriculture varied from the olive- and wine-producing areas in the southwest to the great granaries in its center. Rich mineral deposits and large reserves of timber made the German lands industrially advanced. The European iron industry was centered there, and the empire was the arms manufacturer for the Western world. The empire was also a great commercial center, heir to the Hanseatic League of the Middle Ages. Its northern and western ports teemed with trade, and its merchants were replacing the Italians as the leading international bankers.

Like the Empire, the Italian peninsula was divided into a diverse collection of small city-states (see **Map C**). During the course of the fifteenth century, five city-states had emerged as most powerful (see Chapter 11). In the north were Florence, Venice, and the Duchy of Milan. In the south was Rome, spiritual center of Catholicism and residence of the pope. Although Roman and papal governments were separate jurisdictions, in fact their fates were bound together. Papal lands stretched far to the north of Rome, and wars to defend or expand them were Roman as well as papal ventures. The kingdom of Naples—the breadbasket of the Mediterranean—occupied the southernmost part of Italy and included the agriculturally rich island of Sicily.

Western Europe

The Iberian Peninsula, the French territories, and the British Isles formed the westernmost borders of Europe (see **Map D**). Separated from France in the north by the Pyrenees, the Iberian Peninsula is surrounded by the Atlantic Ocean and the Mediterranean Sea on the west and east. But neither its protective mountain barrier nor its ample coastline was its most significant geographical feature during its formative period. Rather, it was the fact that Iberia is separated from North Africa only by the easily navigable Strait of Gibraltar. During the Middle Ages, the peninsula was overrun by North African Muslims, whom the Spanish called Moors. From the eighth to the fifteenth centuries, Iberian history was dominated by the **reconquista**—the recapture and re-Christianization of the conquered territories. The reconquest was finally completed in 1492, when the Moors were pushed out of Granada and the Jews were expelled from Spain. At the end of the fifteenth century, the Iberian Peninsula contained several separate kingdoms. The most important were Portugal—the only Continental nation to have the same borders in 1500 as it does

■ **Map D. Western Europe.** Western Europe was already consolidated into nation-states.

today—on the western coast; Aragon, with its Mediterranean ports of Barcelona and Valencia; and Castile, the largest of the Iberian states (see **Map D**). The marriage of King Ferdinand of Aragon and Queen Isabella of Castile in 1469 had joined the crowns of Aragon and Castile, but the two kingdoms remained separate.

The remnants of ancient Gaul were also favored by a maritime location. Like those of Iberia, French coasts are located along the Mediterranean Sea and the Atlantic Ocean. France's eastern boundaries touched the empire; its southern mountain border touched Spain. To the northwest, Britain was less than 30 miles from France across the English Channel. Toward the end of the fifteenth century, France was still divided into many small fiefs. The royal domain centered on Paris and extended to Champagne in the east and Normandy in the west (see **Map D**). South of this area, however, from Orléans to Brittany, were principalities that had long been contested between England and France. Nor was the rich central plain yet integrated into the royal domain. Agriculturally, French lands were the richest in Europe. France enjoyed both Mediterranean and Atlantic climates, which suited the growing of the widest variety of foodstuffs. Its population of approximately 13 million was second only to that of the empire.

Across the Channel lay Britain (composed of England, Scotland, and Wales) and Ireland (see **Map D**). Britain had been settled by an array of European colonizers—Romans, Danes, Angles, and Saxons—before being conquered in the eleventh century by the French Normans. From that time, it was protected by the rough waters of the English Channel and the North Sea and allowed to develop a distinct cultural and political heritage. Wales to the west and Scotland to the north were still separate nations at the beginning of the sixteenth century. Both were mountainous lands with harsh climates and few natural advantages. They were sparsely populated. Although Ireland, too, was sparsely populated, it contained several rich agricultural areas especially suited for dairying and grazing.

In 1500, Europe exhibited a remarkable diversity of political and geographical forms. Huge states in the east, tiny principalities in the center, emerging nations in the west, all seemingly had little in common. There was as yet no state system and no clear group of dominant powers. The western migration of the Germanic peoples appeared to be over, but their consolidation was as yet unimagined. The Iberians struggled to expel the Moors, the Hungarians to hold back the Ottomans. Everywhere one looked there was fragmentation and disarray. Yet in less than a half century the largest empire yet known in the West would be formed. States would come to be consolidated and dynasties established all over the Continent. And with the rise of the state would come the dream of dominion, an empire over all of Europe.

THE FORMATION OF STATES

It was Machiavelli who identified the prince as the agent of change in the process of state formation. He believed that the successful prince could bring unity to his lands, security to his borders, and prosperity to his subjects. The unsuccessful prince brought nothing but ruin.

A process as long and as complex as the formation of nations, however, depends on more than the will of individuals. Factors such as geography, population, and natural resources are all important. So too are the structures through which human activity is channeled. The ways in which families are organized and wealth is transmitted from generation to generation can result in large estates with similar customs or small estates with varying ones. The manner in which social groups are formed and controlled can mean that power is centralized or dispersed. The beliefs of ordinary people and the way they practice them can define who is a part of a community and who is not. All these elements and many others affected the way in which European states began to take shape at the end of the fifteenth century. Despite these complexities, we should not lose sight of the simple truth of Machiavelli's observations. In the first stages of the consolidation of European nations, the role of the prince was crucial.

Indeed, in the middle of the fifteenth century there were many factors working against the formation of large states in Europe. The most obvious involved simple things such as transportation and communication. The distance that could be covered quickly was very small. In wet and cold seasons, travel was nearly impossible. The emperor Charles V sat in Burgundy for two months awaiting a favorable wind to take him to his newly inherited kingdom of Spain. Similarly, directives from the center of the states to the localities were slow to arrive and slower still to be adopted. Large areas were difficult to control and to defend. Distinct languages or dialects also made for difficulties in communication. Only the most educated could use Latin as a common written language, and separate languages contributed to separate cultures. Customary practices, common ancestry, and shared experiences helped define a sense of community through which small states defined themselves.

To the natural forces that acted to maintain the existence of small units of government were added invented ones. To succeed, a prince had to establish supremacy over a number of rivals. For the most part, states were inherited. In some places it was customary to follow the rule of primogeniture—inheritance by the eldest son. In others, estates were split among sons, or among children of both sexes. Some traditions, like those of the French, excluded inheritance through women; others, like the Castilian, treated women's claims as equal to men's. Short lives meant prolonged disputes about inheritance. Rulers had to defend their thrones from any number of rivals with strong claims to legitimacy.

Rulers also had to defend themselves from the ambitions of their mightiest subjects. Dukes could dream only one dream. The constant warfare of the European nobility was one of the central features of the Later Middle Ages. To avoid resort to arms, princes and peers entered into all manner of alliances, using their children as pawns and the marriage bed as the chessboard. Rulers also faced independent institutions within their states, powerful organizations that had to be won over or crushed. The long process of taming the Church was well advanced by the end of the fifteenth century and about to enter a new stage. Fortified towns presented a different problem. They possessed both the manpower and wealth necessary to raise and maintain armies. They also jealously guarded their privileges. Rulers who could not tax their towns could not rule their state. Finally, most kingdoms had assemblies that represented the propertied classes, especially in matters of taxation. Some, such as the English Parliament and the Spanish Cortes, were strong; others, such as the Imperial Diet and the French Estates-General, were weak. But everywhere they posed an obstacle to the extension of the power of princes.

In combination, these factors slowed and shaped the process of state formation. But neither separately nor together were they powerful enough to overcome it. The fragmentation of Europe into so many small units of government made some consolidation inevitable; and as the first large states took shape, the position of smaller neighbors grew ever more precarious.

This consolidation was especially true by the end of the fifteenth century because of the increase in the destructive power of warfare. Technological advances in cannonry and in the skills of gunners and engineers made medieval fortifications untenable. The fall of Constantinople was as much a military watershed as it was a political one. Gunpowder decisively changed battlefield tactics. It made heavy armor obsolete and allowed for the development of a different type of warfare. Not only could lightly armored horses and riders inflict more damage upon one another, but now they were mobile enough to be used against infantry. Infantry armed with long pikes or small muskets became the crucial components of armies that were growing ever larger. Systems of supply were better, sources of small arms were more available, and the rewards of conquest were more tangible. What could not be inherited or married could be conquered.

Eastern Configurations

The interplay of factors that encouraged and inhibited the formation of states is most easily observed in the eastern parts of Europe. There the different paths taken by Muscovy and Poland-Lithuania stand in contrast. At the beginning of the sixteenth century, the principality of Muscovy was the largest European political unit. Muscovy had established itself as the heir to the ancient state of Russia through conquest, shrewd political alliances, and the good fortune of its princes to be blessed with long reigns. Muscovy's growth was phenomenal. Under Ivan III, "the Great" (1462–1505), Muscovy expanded to the north and west. During a long series of wars it annexed Novgorod and large parts of Livonia and Lithuania. Its military successes were almost unbroken, but so too were its diplomatic triumphs. Ivan the Great preferred pacification to conquest, though when necessary he could conquer with great brutality. Between 1460 and 1530, Muscovy increased its landed territory by 1.5 million square miles.

A number of factors led to the rise of Muscovy. External threats had diminished. First, the deterioration of the Mongol Empire that had dominated south-central Russia allowed Ivan to escape the yoke of Mongol rule that the Russian princes had worn for centuries. Second, the fall of Constantinople made Muscovy the heir to Eastern Christendom, successor to the Roman and Byzantine empires. Ivan's marriage to Sophia, niece of the last emperor of Byzantium, cemented the connection. Sophia brought both Italian artisans and Byzantine customs to the Russian court, helping Ivan open his contacts with the wider world.

Ivan the Terrible.   What made the expansion of Muscovy so impressive was that land once gained was never lost. The military and political achievements of Ivan the Great were furthered by his son Vasili and his more famous grandson Ivan IV, "the Terrible" (1533–1584). Ivan IV defeated the Mongols on his southeastern border and incorporated the entire Volga river basin into Muscovy. But his greatest ambition was to gain a port on the Baltic Sea and establish a northern outlet for commerce. His objective was to conquer Livonia. Nearly three decades of warfare between Muscovy and Poland-Lithuania—with which Livonia had allied itself—resulted in large territorial gains, but Muscovy always fell short of the real prize. And Ivan's northern campaigns seriously weakened the defense of the south. In 1571, the Crimean Tatars advanced from their territories on Muscovy's southwestern border and inflicted a powerful psychological blow when they burned the city of Moscow. Although the Tatars were eventually driven off Muscovite soil, expansion in both north and south was at an end for the next 75 years.

By the reign of Ivan IV, Muscovite society was divided roughly into three groups: the hereditary nobility known as the *boyars*, the military service class, and the peasantry who were bound to the land. There was no large mercantile presence in Muscovy and its urban component remained small. The boyars, who were powerful landlords of great estates, owed little to the tsar. They inherited their lands and did not necessarily benefit from expansion and conquest. Members of the military service class, on the other hand, were bound to the success of the crown. Their military service was a requirement for the possession of their estates, which were granted out of lands gained through territorial expansion. Ivan IV used members of the military service class as legislative advisers and elevated them in his parliamentary council (the Zemsky Sobor), which also included representatives of the nobility, clergy, and towns.

Unlike his grandfather, Ivan IV had an abiding mistrust of the boyars. They had held power when he was a child, and it was rumored that his mother had been poisoned by them. It was in his treatment of the boyars that he earned the nickname "the Terrible." During his brutal suppression of supposed conspiracies, several thousand families were massacred by Ivan's own orders and thousands more by the violent excesses of his agents. Ivan constantly imagined plots against himself, and many of the men who served him met horrible deaths. He also forcibly relocated boyar families, stripping them of their lands in one place but granting them new lands elsewhere.

All those measures contributed to the breakdown of local networks of influence and power and to a disruption of local governance. But they also made possible a system of central administration, one of Ivan IV's most important achievements. He created departments of state to deal with the various tasks of administration, which resulted in more efficient management of revenues and of the military. Ivan IV promoted the interests of the military service class over those of the boyars, but he did not destroy the nobility. New boyars were created, especially in conquered territories, and those new families owed their positions and loyalty to the prince. Both the boyars and the military benefited from Ivan's policy of binding the great mass of people to the land. Russian peasants had few political or economic rights in comparison to those of Western peasants, but during the early sixteenth century even the meager rights Russian peasants had were curtailed. The right of peasants to move from the estate of one lord to that of another was suspended, all but binding the peasantry to the land. The serfdom made possible the prolonged absence of military leaders from their estates and contributed to the creation of the military service class. But it also made imperative the costly system of coercing agricultural and industrial labor. In the long term, serfdom retarded the development of the Muscovite economy by removing incentive from large landholders to make investments in commerce or to improve agricultural production.

Poland-Lithuania. The growth of an enlarged and centralized Muscovy stands in contrast to the experiences of Poland-Lithuania during the same period. At the end of the fifteenth century, Casimir IV (1447–1492) ruled the kingdom of Poland and the grand duchy of Lithuania. His son Vladislav II ruled Bohemia (1471–1516) and Hungary (1490–1516). Had the four states been permanently consolidated they could have become an effective barrier to Ottoman expansion in the south and Russian expansion in the east. But the union of crowns had never been the union of states. The union of crowns had taken place during the previous century by political alliances, diplomatic marriages, and the consent of the nobility. Such arrange-

■ A miniature painted by a Krakow artist about 1510 depicts the final act of the coronation rite: The king in majesty is surrounded by his court while a *Te Deum* is sung. The knights in the foreground bear the standards of Poland and Lithuania.

ments kept peace among the four neighbors, but they kept any one of them from becoming a dominant partner.

While the Polish-Lithuanian monarchs enjoyed longevity similar to that of the Muscovites, those who ruled Hungary and Bohemia were not so fortunate: by the sixteenth century a number of claimants to both crowns existed. The competition was handled by diplomacy rather than war. The accession of Vladislav II, for example, was accompanied by large concessions, first to the Bohemian towns and later to the Hungarian nobility. The formal union of the Polish and Lithuanian crowns in 1569 also involved the decentralization of power and the strengthening of the rights of the nobility in both countries. In the end, the states split apart. The Russians took much of Lithuania, the Ottomans much of Hungary. Bohemia, which in the fifteenth century had been ruled more by its nobles than its king, was absorbed into the Habsburg territories after 1526.

There were many reasons why a unified state did not appear in east-central Europe. In the first place, external forces disrupted territorial and political arrangements, and wars with the Ottomans and the Russians absorbed resources. Second, the princes faced rivals to their crowns. Although Casimir IV was able to place his son on the thrones of both Bohemia and Hungary, he managed to do so against the powerful claims of the Habsburg princes, who continued to intrigue against the Jagiellons. The contests for power necessitated concessions to leading citizens, which decreased the ability of the princes to centralize their kingdoms or to effect real unification among them. The nobility of Hungary, Bohemia, and Poland-Lithuania all developed strong local interests that increased over time. In Bohemia, Vladislav II was king in name only, and even in Poland the nobility won confirmation of its rights and privileges from the monarchy. War, rivalries for power, and a strong nobility prevented any one prince from dominating the area as the princes of Muscovy dominated theirs.

The Western Powers

Just as in the east, there was no single pattern to the consolidation of the large western European states. They, too, were internally fragmented and externally imperiled. While England had to overcome the ruin of decades of civil war, France and Spain faced the challenges of invasion and occupation. Western European princes struggled against powerful institutions and individuals within their states. Some they conquered, others they absorbed. Each nation formed its state differently: England by administrative centralization, France by good fortune, and Spain by dynastic marriage. Yet in 1450 few imagined that any one of these states would succeed.

The Taming of England. Alone among European states, England suffered no threat of foreign invasion during the fifteenth century. The island fortress might easily have become the first consolidated European state were it not for the ambitions of the nobility and the weakness of the crown. For thirty years, the English aristocracy fought over the spoils of a helpless monarch. The Wars of the Roses (1455–1485), as they came to be called, were as much a free-for-all among the English peerage as they were a contest for the throne between the houses of Lancaster and York. At their center was an attempt by the dukes of York to wrest the crown from the mad and ineffective Lancastrian king Henry VI (1422–1461). All around the edges was the continuation of local and family feuds that had little connection to the dynastic struggle.

Three decades of intermittent warfare had predictable results. The houses of Lancaster and York were both destroyed. Edward IV (1461–1483) succeeded in gaining the crown for the House of York, but he was never able to wear it securely. When he died, his children, including his heir, Edward V (1483), were placed in the protection of their uncle Richard III (1483–1485). It was protection that they did not survive. The two boys disappeared, reputedly murdered in the Tower of London, and Richard declared himself king. Richard's usurpation led to civil war, and he was killed by the forces of Henry Tudor at the battle of Bosworth Field in 1485. By the end of the Wars of the Roses, the monarchy had lost both revenue and prestige, and the aristocracy had stored up bitter memories for the future.

It was left to Henry Tudor to pick up the pieces of the kingdom. As legend has it, he picked up the crown off a bramble bush. The two chief obstacles to his determination to consolidate the English state were the power of the nobility and the poverty of the monarchy. No English monarch had held secure title to the throne for more than a century. Henry Tudor, as Henry VII (1485–1509), put an end to the dynastic instability at once. He married Elizabeth of York, in whose heirs would rest the legitimate claim to the throne. Their children were indisputable successors to the crown. He also began the long process of taming his over-mighty subjects. Traitors were hung and turncoats rewarded. He and his son Henry VIII (1509–1547) adroitly created a new peerage, which soon was as numerous as the old feudal aristocracy. The new nobles owed their titles and loyalty to the Tudors. They were favored with offices and spoils and were relied upon to suppress both popular and aristocratic rebellions.

The financial problems of the English monarchy were not so easily overcome. In theory and practice an English king was supposed to live "of his own," that is, off the revenues from his own estates. In normal circumstances, royal revenue did not come from the king's subjects. The English landed classes had established the principle that only on extraordinary occasions were they to be required to contribute to the maintenance of government. The principle was defended through their representative institution—the Parliament. When the kings of England wanted to tax their subjects, they had first to gain the assent of Parliament. Although Parliaments did grant requests for extraordinary revenue, especially for national defense, they did so grudgingly. The English landed elites were not exempt from taxation, but they were able to control the amount of taxes they paid.

The inability of the crown to extract its living from its subjects made it more dependent on the efficient management of its own estates. Thus English state building depended upon the growth of centralized institutions that could oversee royal lands and collect royal customs. Gradually, medieval institutions such as the Exchequer were supplanted by newer organs that were better able to adjust to modern methods of accounting, record keeping, and enforcement. Henry VII sent ministers to view and value royal lands. He ordered the cataloging and collection of feudal obligations. Ship cargoes were inspected thoroughly and every last penny of customs charged. Whether Henry's reputation for greed and rapacity was warranted, it was undeniable that he squeezed as much as could be taken from a not very juicy inheritance. His financial problems limited both domestic and foreign policy.

It was not until the middle of the next reign that the English monarchy was again solvent. As a result of his dispute with the papacy over his divorce from Catherine of Aragon and marriage to Anne Boleyn, Henry VIII confiscated the enormous wealth of the Catholic Church, and with one stroke solved the crown's monetary problems (see Chapter 13). But the real contribution that Henry and his chief minister, Thomas Cromwell (ca.

■ Portrait of Anne Boleyn, the second wife of Henry VIII, by an unknown artist. Anne lost favor with Henry when she delivered a daughter instead of the son he expected. Anne made other enemies at court and in 1536 was convicted of adultery and beheaded.

LAST WORDS

Anne Boleyn was the second wife of Henry VIII and the mother of Elizabeth I. Henry's desire to have a son and his passion for Anne resulted in his divorce from Catherine of Aragon and England's formal break with the Roman Catholic Church. When Anne bore only a daughter, she too became dispensable. She was convicted of adultery and incest and executed in 1536. Here are her last words.

Focus Questions

How does Anne respond in her scaffold speech to the charges against her? What does Anne mean when she condemns "the cruel law of the land" at the same time as she praises "the King my sovereign lord"?

Good friends, I am not come here to excuse or to justify myself, for as much as I know full well that aught that I could say in my defense doth not appertain unto you, and that I could draw no hope of life from the same. But I come here only to die, and thus to yield myself humbly to the will of the King my lord. And if in my life I did ever offend the King's grace, surely with my death I do now atone for the same. And I blame not my judges, nor any other manner of person, nor anything save the cruel law of the land by which I die. But be this, and be my faults as they may, I beseech you all, good friends, to pray for the life of the King my sovereign lord and yours, who is one of the best princes on the face of the earth, and who hath always treated me so well that better could not be; wherefore I submit to death with a good will, humbly asking pardon of the world.

Anne Boleyn, scaffold speech.

1485–1540), made to forming an English state was the way in which the windfall was administered. Cromwell accelerated the process of centralizing government that had begun under Edward IV. He divided administration according to its functions by creating separate departments of state, modeled upon courts. The new departments were responsible for record keeping, revenue collection, and law enforcement. Each had a distinct jurisdiction and a permanent, trained staff. Cromwell coordinated the work of the distinct departments by expanding the power of the Privy Council, which included the heads of the administrative bodies. Through a long evolution, the Privy Council came to serve as the king's executive body. Cromwell also saw the importance of Parliament as a legislative body. Through Parliament, royal policy could be turned into statutes that had the assent of the political nation. If Parliament was well managed, issues that were potentially controversial could be defused. Laws passed by Parliament were more easily enforced locally than were proclamations issued by the king. By the end of Henry VIII's reign, the English monarchy was strong enough to withstand the succession of a child king, precisely the circumstance that had plunged the nation into civil war a century earlier.

The Unification of France. Perhaps the most remarkable thing about the unification of France is that it took place at all. The forces working against the consolidation of a French state were formidable. France was surrounded by aggressive and powerful neighbors with whom it was frequently at war. Its greatest nobles were semi-independent princes who were constant rivals for the throne and consistent opponents of the extension of royal power. The French people were deeply suspicious of the pretensions of the monarchy. **Provincialism** was not simply negative; it was a fierce pride of and loyalty to-

■ This painting by an anonymous Flemish artist of the wedding of Philip the Good, duke of Burgundy, and Isabella of Portugal evokes the courtly style and aspirations of fifteenth-century Burgundy.

ward local customs and institutions that had deep roots within communities. Furthermore, France was splintered by profound regional differences. The north and south were divided by culture and by language (*the langue d'oc* in the south and the *langue d'oïl* in the north). As late as the fifteenth century, a French king needed a translator to communicate with officials from his southern lands.

The first obstacles that were overcome were the external threats to French security. For more than a century, the throne of France had been contested by the kings of England. The so-called Hundred Years' War, which was fought intermittently between 1337 and 1453, originated in a dispute over the inheritance of the French crown and English possessions in Gascony in southern France (see Chapter 10). The war was fought on

THE KINGDOM OF FRANCE

Claude de Seyssel (ca. 1450–1519) was a legal scholar and professor at the University of Turin. He came from the duchy of Savoy, a small state that mixed French and Italian peoples and culture. Seyssel thus learned about the French monarchy as an outsider and wrote The Monarchy of France *as a book of counsel for French kings. In this passage he explains and defends the Salic law, which prohibited legitimate title to the French throne from passing through a woman. The legal documents that supposedly established Salic law were fakes.*

Focus Questions

Why is it "excellent" that the French throne cannot pass to a woman? What conditions are desirable in order for a state to be stable and prosper?

Without going too deeply into the disputes of the philosophers, we may presuppose three kinds of political rule: monarchy under a single person, aristocracy under a certain number of the better sort, and democracy the popular state. Of these, according to the true and most widespread opinion, monarchy is the best if the prince is good and has the sense, the experience, and the good will to govern justly. That rarely comes to pass, however, because with such authority and license it is hard to follow the right course and hold fairly the balance of justice. The second state seems the more reasonable and praiseworthy since it is more lasting, better founded, and easier to bear, being comprised of the persons selected by the assembly or a part of them. Such persons are, moreover, subject to corruption and change, at least to the extent that, when there are several bad and inadequate men among them, the better sort, being their superiors, can repress their boldness and thwart their unreasonable enterprises. As to the popular state, it has always been turbulent, dangerous, and hostile to the better sort. Nevertheless, the aristocratic state is often transformed into oligarchy, a monopoly by covetous and ambitious folk, who, though chosen as the wisest and most prudent of the people to rule and to govern the people well, care only for their particular profit. So when all is said, none of these states can possibly be perpetual, for ordinary in the course of time they get worse, especially when they go on growing, so that often one [by disorder] rises from the other.

The first special trait that I find good is that this realm passes by masculine succession and, by virtue of the law which the French call Salic, cannot fall into the hands of a woman. This is excellent, for by falling into the feminine line it can come into the power of a foreigner, a pernicious and dangerous thing, since a ruler from a foreign nation is of a different rearing and condition, of different customs, different language, and a different way of life from the men of the lands he comes to rule. He ordinarily, therefore, wishes to advance those of his nation, to grant them the most important authority in the handling of affairs, and to prefer them to honors and profits. Moreover, he always has more love for and faith in them and so conforms more to their customs and ways than to the customs of the land to which he has newly come, whence there always follows envy and dissension between the natives and the foreigners and indignation against the princes, as has often been seen by experience, and is seen all the time. When the succession goes from male to male, the heir is always certain and is of the same blood as those who formerly ruled, so the subjects have the very same love and reverence for him as for his predecessors. Even though he be related only distantly and the dead king have daughters, yet without deviation or scruple the people turn to him as soon as the other has ceased to be, and there is no disturbance or difficulty. So it went at the death of King Charles VIII and of King Louis XII recently deceased. Although in former times there were great quarrels and differences on such occasions, which brought great wars, persecutions, and desolations to the realm, nevertheless, these differences were not the reason for the troubles but the pretext, although well known to be frivolous and ill founded. In the end matters must have been redressed and so established that there can never again be dissensions and difficulties on this score. [In order to demonstrate what I said about the perfection of the monarchy of France I have included in this account] the state of France as it is now, joining the old laws, customs, and observances with the new and more recent.

From Claude de Seyssel, *The Monarchy of France* (1515).

French soil, and by the early fifteenth century English conquests in north-central France extended from Normandy to the borders of the Holy Roman Empire. Two of the largest French cities, Paris and Bordeaux, were in English hands.

Nor was England the only threat to the security of the French monarchy. On France's eastern border, in a long arching semicircle, were the estates of the dukes of Burgundy. The dukes of Burgundy and the kings of France shared a common ancestry—both were of the House of Valois. Still, the sons of brothers in one generation were only cousins in the next, and the two branches of the family grew apart. The original Burgundian inheritance was in the southeast, centered at Dijon. A good marriage and good fortune brought to the first duke the rich northern province of Flanders. For the next hundred years, the aim of the dukes of Burgundy was to unite their divided estates. While England and France were locked in deadly embrace, Burgundy systematically grew. It absorbed territory from both the Holy Roman Empire and France. To little pieces gained through marriages were added little pieces taken through force. As the second half of the fifteenth century began, the court of the duke of Burgundy was the glittering jewel of Europe, the heir of the Italian Renaissance. Wealthy and powerful, it stood poised to achieve what had once only been dreamed: the unification of the Burgundian lands. The conquest of Lorraine finally connected the ducal estates in one long, unbroken string.

But it was a string stretched taut. The power of Burgundy threatened its neighbors in all directions. Both France and the empire were too weak to resist its expansion, but the confederation of Swiss towns to the southwest of Burgundy was not. Fearing a Burgundian advance against them, a number of independent Swiss towns pooled their resources to raise a large army. In a series of stunning military victories, Swiss forces repelled the Burgundians from their lands and demolished their armies. Charles the Bold, the last Valois duke of Burgundy, fell at the Battle of Nancy in 1477. His estates were quickly dismembered. France recovered its ancestral ter-

ritories, including Burgundy, and through no effort of its own was now secure on its eastern border.

The king most associated with the consolidation of France was Louis XI (1461–1483). He inherited an estate exhausted by warfare and civil strife. More by chance than by plan, he vastly extended the territories under the dominion of the French crown and, more importantly, subdued the nobility. Louis XI was as cunning as he was peculiar. In an age in which royalty was expressed through magnificence, Louis sported an old felt hat and a well-worn coat. His enemies constantly underestimated his abilities, which earned him the nickname "the Spider." But during the course of his reign, Louis XI gradually won back what he had been forced to give away. Years of fighting both the English and each other left the ranks of the French aris-

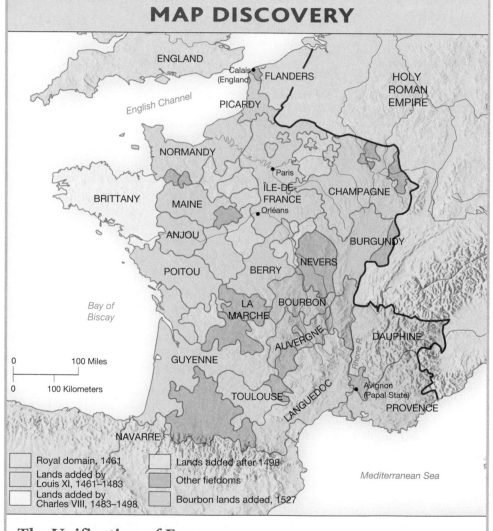

MAP DISCOVERY

The Unification of France

Notice how France grew piecemeal rather than by acquiring large additions of adjacent estates. Which monarch added the most land to the state? Contrast the acquisitions made by Louis XI and those made by the Bourbons. Notice how France was not a unified geographical unit even after its so-called unification.

tocracy depleted. As blood spilled on the battlefields, the stocks of fathers and sons ran low. Estates, to which no male heirs existed, fell forfeit to the king. In that manner, the crown absorbed Anjou and Maine in the northwest and Provence in the south. More importantly, Louis XI ultimately obtained control of the two greatest independent fiefs, Brittany and Orléans. He managed the feat by arranging the marriage of his son Charles to the heiress of Brittany and of his daughter Jeanne to the heir of Orléans. When in 1527 the lands of the duke of Bourbon fell to the crown, the French monarch ruled a unified state.

The consolidation of France was not simply the result of the incorporation of diverse pieces of territory into the domain of the king. More than in any other state, the experience in France demonstrated how a state could be formed without the designs of a great leader. Neither Louis XI nor his son Charles VIII (1483–1498) was a nation builder. Louis's main objective was always to preserve his estate. His good fortune saved him from the consequences of many ill-conceived policies. But no amount of luck could make up for Louis's failure to obtain the Burgundian Low Countries for France after the death of Charles the Bold in 1477. The marriage of Mary of Burgundy to Maximilian of Habsburg was one of the great turning points in European history. It initiated the struggle for control of the Low Countries that endured for more than two centuries.

The long years of war established the principle of royal taxation that was so essential to the process of state building in France. It enabled the monarchy to raise money for defense and for consolidation. Because of the strength of the nobles, most taxation fell only on the commoners, the so-called third estate. The *taille* was a direct tax on property from which the nobility and clergy were exempt. The *gabelle* was a consumption tax on the purchase of salt in most parts of the kingdom, and the *aide* was a tax on a variety of commodities, including meat and wine. The consumption taxes were paid by all members of the third estate no matter how poor they might be. Although there was much complaint about taxes, the French monarchy established a broad base for taxation and a high degree of compliance long before any other European nation.

Along with money went soldiers, fighting men necessary to repel the English and to defend the crown against rebels and traitors. Again the French monarchy was the first to establish the principle of a national army, raised and directed from the center but quartered and equipped regionally. From the nobility were recruited the cavalry, from the towns and countryside the massive infantry. Fortified towns received privileges in return for military service to the king. Originally, towns were required to provide artillery, but constant troubles with the nobility had led the kings of France to establish their own store of heavy guns. The towns supplied small arms, pikes, and swords, and later pistols and muskets. By the beginning of the sixteenth century, the French monarch could raise and equip an army of his own.

The Marriages of Spain. Before the sixteenth century there was little prospect of a single nation emerging on the Iberian Peninsula. North African Muslims, called Moors, oc-

cupied the province of Gra[nada]
kingdom of Portugal do[minated]
Spanish peoples were div[ided]
states. The two most imp[ortant]
wealthiest kingdom, and[]
number of quasi-indep[endent]
tained its own laws an[d]
languages (not includ[ing]
sions. Furthermore, th[e]
Castile was, above all, determin[ed]
Islamic Spain and to convert its large Jewish p[opulation to]
Christianity. Aragon played in the high-stakes game for pow[er]
in the Mediterranean, claiming sovereignty over Sicily and Naples and exercising that sovereignty whenever it could.

A happy teenage marriage brought together the unhappy kingdoms of Castile and Aragon. When Ferdinand of Aragon and Isabella of Castile secretly exchanged wedding vows in 1469, both their homelands were rent by civil war. In Castile, Isabella's brother, Henry IV (1454–1474), struggled unsuccessfully against the powerful Castilian nobility. In Aragon, Ferdinand's father, John II (1458–1479), faced a revolt by the rich province of Catalonia on one side and the territorial ambitions of Louis XI of France on the other. Joining the heirs increased the resources of both kingdoms. Ferdinand took an active role in the pacification of Castile, while Castilian riches allowed him to defend Aragon from invasion. In 1479, the two crowns were united and the Catholic monarchs, as they were called, ruled the two kingdoms jointly. But the unification of the crowns of Castile and Aragon was not the same as the formation of a single state between them. Local privileges were zealously guarded, especially in Aragon, where the representative institutions of the towns—the Cortes—were aggressively independent. Their attitude is best expressed in the oath of the townspeople of Saragossa: "We accept you as our king provided you observe all our liberties and laws; and if not, not." The powerful Castilian nobility never accepted Ferdinand as their king and refused him the crown after Isabella's death.

But Ferdinand and Isabella (1479–1516) took the first steps toward forging a Spanish state. Their most notable achievement was the final recovery of the lands that had been conquered by the Moors. For centuries, the Spanish kingdoms had fought against the North African Muslims, who had conquered large areas of the southern peninsula. The reconquista was characterized by short bursts of warfare followed by long periods of wary coexistence. By the middle of the fifteenth century, the Moorish territory had been reduced to the province of Granada, but civil strife in Castile heightened the possibility of a new Moorish offensive. "We no longer mint gold, only steel," was how a Moorish ruler replied to Isabella's demand for the traditional payment of tribute money. The final stages of the reconquista began in 1482 and lasted for a decade. The struggle was waged as a holy war and was financed in part by grants from the pope and the Christian princes of Europe. It was a bloody undertaking. The Moorish population of nearly 500,000 was reduced to 100,000 before

...ada finally fell and the province was ab-
...le.

...quista played an important part in creating a na-
...ty for the Christian peoples of Spain. In order to
...n and money for the war effort, Ferdinand and
... mobilized their nobility and town governments and
...ed a central organization to oversee the invasion.
...rdinand was actively involved in the warfare, gaining the respect of the hostile Castilian nobles in the process. The conquered territories were used to reward those who had aided
the effort, though the crown maintained control and jurisdiction over most of the province. But the idea of the holy war
also had a darker side and an unanticipated consequence. The
Jewish population that had lived peacefully in both Castile
and Aragon became another object of hostility. Many Jews
had risen to prominence in government and in skilled professions. Others, who had accepted conversion to Christianity
and were known as *conversos*, had become among the most
powerful figures in Church and state.

Both groups were now attacked. The conversos fell prey to
a special Church tribunal created to examine their sincere devotion to Catholicism. This was the **Spanish Inquisition**,
which, though it used traditional judicial practices—torture
to gain confessions, public humiliation to show contrition,
and burnings at the stake to maintain purity—used them on a
scale never before seen. Thousands of conversos were killed,
and many more families had their wealth confiscated to be
used for the reconquista. In 1492, the Jews themselves were
expelled from Spain. Although the reconquista and the expulsion of the Jews and the Moors inflicted great suffering upon
victims and incalculable loss to the Castilian economy, both
events enhanced the prestige of the Catholic monarchs.

In many ways, Ferdinand and Isabella had trodden the
paths of the medieval monarchy. They relied upon personal
contact with their people more than upon the use of a centralized administration. They frequently dispensed justice
personally, sitting in court and accepting petitions from their
subjects. Quite remarkably, they had no permanent residence
and traveled the length and breadth of their kingdoms.
Isabella is said to have visited every town in Castile, and it is
entirely possible that a majority of the population of both
kingdoms actually saw their monarchs at one time or another.
Queen Isabella was venerated in Castile, where women's right
to inheritance remained strong. Ferdinand's absences from
Aragon were always a source of contention between him and
the Cortes of the towns, yet he was careful to provide regents
to preside in his absence and regularly returned to visit his native kingdom. He was not an absentee monarch.

The joint presence of Ferdinand and Isabella in the provinces
of Spain was symbolic of the unity that they wanted to achieve.
Despite the great obstacles, they were intent on bringing about a
more permanent blending. Ferdinand made Castilian the official language of government in Aragon and even appointed
Castilians to Aragonese posts. He and Isabella actively encouraged the intermarriage of the two aristocracies and the expansion of the number of wealthy nobles who held land in both
kingdoms. A single coinage, stamped with the heads of both
monarchs, was established for both kingdoms. Nevertheless, the
measures did not unify Spain or erase the centuries' long tradition of hostility among the diverse Iberian peoples.

It was left to the heirs of Ferdinand and Isabella to forge together the Spanish kingdoms, and the process was a painful one.
The hostility to a foreign monarch that both the Castilian nobility and the Aragonese towns had shown to Ferdinand and

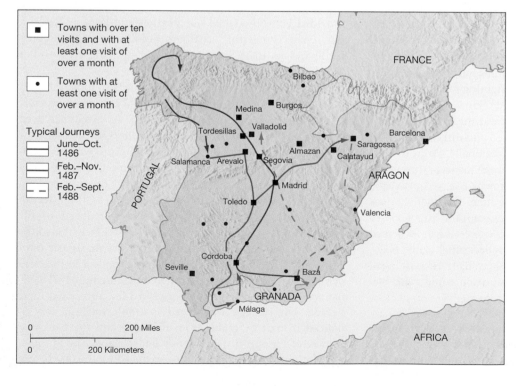

The Travels of Ferdinand and Isabella. Early modern monarchs did not reside solely in a capital city but moved around their territories to consolidate their power and ensure the loyalty of their subjects.

Isabella increased dramatically at the accession of their grandson, who became the Emperor Charles V (1516–1556). Charles had been born and raised in the Low Countries, where he ruled over Burgundy and the Netherlands. Through a series of dynastic accidents, he became heir to the Spanish crown with its possessions in the New World and to the vast Habsburg estates that included Austria. Charles established his rule in Spain gradually. For a time he was forced to share power in Castile and to suppress a disorganized aristocratic rebellion.

Because of his foreign obligations, Charles was frequently absent from Spain. During those periods he governed through regents and royal councils that did much to centralize administration. Although Castile and Aragon had separate councils, they were organized similarly and had greater contact than before. Charles V realized the importance of Spain, especially of Castile, in his empire. He learned Castilian and spent more time there than in any other part of his empire, calling it "the head of all the rest." Like Ferdinand and Isabella, he traveled throughout Castile and Aragon; unlike them, he established a more permanent bureaucratic court, modeled on that of Burgundy, and placed able Spaniards at the head of its departments. That smoothed over the long periods when Charles was abroad, especially the thirteen years between 1543 and 1556.

Yet neither his personal efforts to rule as a Spanish monarch nor those of his able administrators were the most important factor in uniting the Spanish kingdoms of Iberia. Rather it was the fact that Charles V brought Spain to the forefront of European affairs in the sixteenth century. Spanish prowess, whether in arms or in culture, became a source of national pride that helped erode regional identity. Gold and silver from the New World helped finance Charles's great empire. Whether or not he dreamed of uniting all of Europe under his rule, Charles V fulfilled nearly all of the ancient territorial ambitions of the Spanish kingdoms. In Italy, he prosecuted Aragonese claims to Sicily and Naples; in the north he held on firmly to the kingdom of Navarre, which had been annexed by Ferdinand and which secured Spain's border with France. In the south, he blocked off Ottoman and Muslim expansion. The reign of Charles V ushered in the dawn of Spain's golden age.

THE DYNASTIC STRUGGLES

The formation of large states throughout Europe led inevitably to conflicts among them. Long chains of marriages among the families of the European princes meant that sooner or later the larger powers would lay claim to the same inheritances and test the matter by force. Thus the sixteenth century was a period of almost unrelieved general warfare that took the whole of the Continent as its theater. Advances in technology made war more efficient and more expensive. They also made it more horrible. The use of artillery against infantry increased the number of deaths and maiming injuries, as did the replacement of the arrow with the bullet. As the size of armies increased, so did casualties. Nearly 60,000 men met at Marignano in 1515, where it took 30 French cavalry charges and 28 consecutive hours of bat-

tle before the Swiss infantry was driven from the field. The slaughter of French nobility at Pavia in 1525 was the largest in a century, while the Turkish sultan Suleiman the Magnificent recorded the burial of 24,000 Hungarian soldiers after the battle of Mohacs in 1526.

Power and Glory

The frequency with which offensive war was waged in the sixteenth century raises a number of questions about the militaristic values of the age. Valor remained greatly prized—a Renaissance virtue inherited from the crusading zeal and chivalric ideals of the Middle Ages. Princes saw valor as a personal attribute and sought to do great deeds. Ferdinand of Aragon and Francis I of France (1515–1547) won fame for their exploits in war. Charles the Bold and Louis II of Hungary were less fortunate: their battlefield deaths led to the breakup of their states. Wars were fought to further the interests of princes rather than the interests of national sovereignty or international

■ Titian, *Charles V on Horseback* (1548). The portrait commemorates the Emperor's victory in the Battle of Mülberg in 1547. The portrait is less that of a victorious hero, but rather that of a forceful individual girded to contend against his enemies.

Christianity. Wars certainly were not fought in the interests of their subjects. States were an extension of a prince's heritage: what rulers sought in battle was a part of the historical and familial rights that defined themselves and their subjects. The wars of the sixteenth century were dynastic wars.

The New Monarchs waged war and defended their territories in new ways. Internal security depended on locally raised forces or hired mercenaries. Both required money, which was becoming available in unprecedented quantities as a result of the increasing prosperity of the early sixteenth century and the windfall of gold and silver from the New World. Professional soldiers, of whom the Swiss and Germans were the most noteworthy, sold their services to the highest bidders. Developments in transport and supply enabled campaigns to take place far from the center of a state. Finally, communications were improving. The need for knowledge about potential rivals or allies had the effect of expanding the European system of diplomacy. Resident agents were established in all the European capitals, and they had a decisive impact upon war and peace. Their dispatches formed the most reliable source of information about the strengths of armies or the weaknesses of governments, about the birth of heirs or the death of princes.

Personality also played a part in the international warfare of the early sixteenth century. The three most consistent protagonists—Charles V, Francis I, and Henry VIII—were of similar age and outlook. Each came unexpectedly to his throne in the full flush of youth, eager for combat and glory. The three were self-consciously rivals, each jealous of the other's successes, each triumphant in the other's failures. Henry VIII and Francis I held wrestling bouts when they met in 1520. Francis I challenged Charles V to single combat after the French king's humiliating imprisonment in Madrid in 1526. As the three monarchs aged together, their youthful wars of conquest matured into strategic warfare designed to maintain a continental balance of power.

The Italian Wars

The struggle for supremacy in Europe in the sixteenth century pitted the French House of Valois against the far-flung estates of the Habsburg Empire. Yet the wars took place in Italy. The

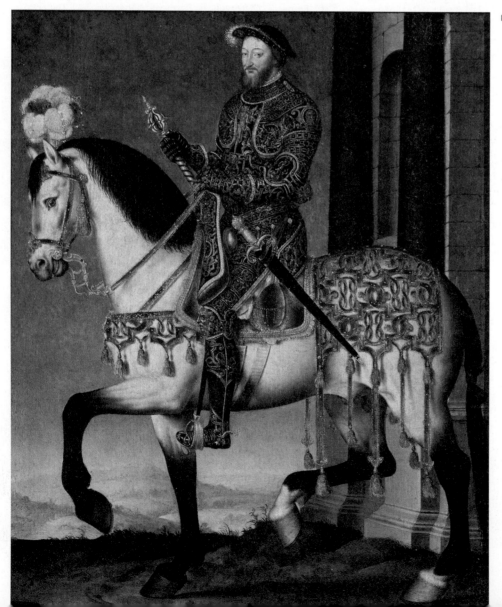

■ Jean Clouet, *Francis I on Horseback* (sixteenth century). Rivalry between Francis and Charles V plunged Europe into decades of war.

rivalries among the larger Italian city-states proved fertile ground for the newly consolidated European monarchies. Both French and Spanish monarchs had remote but legitimate claims to the kingdom of Naples in southern Italy. In 1494, the French king, Charles VIII, took up an invitation from the ruler of Milan to intervene in Italian affairs. His campaign was an unqualified, if fleeting, success. He marched the length of the Italian peninsula, overthrew the Medici in Florence, forced the pope to open the gates of Rome, and finally seized the crown of Naples. The occupation was accomplished without a single great battle and lasted until the warring Italian city-states realized that they had more to fear from the French than from one another. Once that happened, Charles VIII beat a hasty retreat. But the French appetite for Italian territory was not sated. Soon a deal was struck with Ferdinand of Aragon to divide the kingdom of Naples in two. In the end, Spain wound up with all of Naples and France was left with nothing but debts and grievances.

Thus, when Francis I came to the French throne and Charles V to the Spanish, Naples was just one of several potential sources of friction. Not only had Ferdinand betrayed the French in Naples, he had also broken a long-standing peace on the Franco-Spanish border by conquering the independent but French-speaking kingdom of Navarre. Francis could be expected to avenge both slights. Charles, on the other hand, was the direct heir of the dukes of Burgundy. From his childhood he had longed for the restoration of his ancestral lands, including Burgundy itself, which had been gobbled up by Louis XI after the death of Charles the Bold. Competition between Francis and Charles became all the more ferocious when Charles's grandfather, the Holy Roman Emperor Maximilian I (1486–1519), died in 1519. Both monarchs launched a vigorous campaign for the honor of succeeding him.

For nearly a century the Holy Roman Emperor had come from the Austrian ruling family, and there was little reason to believe that Charles V, who now inherited the Habsburg lands in Austria and Germany, would not also succeed to the eminent but empty dignity. Almost as soon as he took up the imperial mantle, Charles V was determined to challenge Francis I in Italy.

The key to such a challenge was the construction of alliances among the various Italian city-states and most especially with England, whose aid both Charles and Francis sought to enlist in the early 1520s. Henry VII had found foreign alliances a ready source of cash, and he was always eager to enter into them so long as they did not involve raising armies and fighting wars. Henry VIII was made of sterner stuff. He longed to reconquer France and to cut a figure on the European scene. Despite the fact that his initial Continental adventures had emptied his treasury without fulfilling his dreams, Henry remained eager for war. He was also flattered to find himself the object of attention by both Valois and Habsburg emissaries. Charles V made two separate trips to London, while Henry crossed the Channel in 1520 to meet Francis I in one of the gaudiest displays of conspicuous consumption that the century would witness, appropriately known as the Field of the Cloth of Gold.

■ The Italian Wars with Key Battle Sites. Italy was overrun in the sixteenth century and became a battleground for the dynastic struggles of the French, the Spanish, and the Imperial forces.

The result of the diplomatic intrigues was an alliance between England and the Holy Roman Empire. English and Burgundian forces would stage an invasion of northern France while Spanish and German troops would again attempt to dislodge the French forces from Italy. The strategy worked better than anyone could have imagined. In 1523, Charles's forces gained a foothold in Milan by taking the heavily fortified town of Pavia. Two years later Francis was ready to strike back. At the head of his own royal guards, he massed Swiss mercenaries and French infantry outside Pavia and made ready for a swift assault. Instead, a large imperial army arrived to relieve the town, and in the subsequent battle the French suffered a shattering defeat. Francis I was captured.

The victory at Pavia, which occurred on Charles V's twenty-fifth birthday, seemingly made him master of all of Europe. His ally Henry VIII urged an immediate invasion and dismemberment of France and began raising an army to spearhead the attack. But Charles's position was much less secure than it appeared. The Ottomans threatened his Hungarian territories, and the Protestants threatened his German lands. He could not afford a war of conquest in France. His hope now was to reach an agreement with Francis I for a lasting European peace, and for that purpose the French king was brought in captivity to Madrid.

It is doubtful that there was ever any real chance for peace between Habsburg and Valois after the battle of Pavia.

■ The Battle of Pavia in 1525, shown in this tapestry, gave Spain a decisive victory over its French rivals. Francis I was captured and imprisoned in Madrid where he was forced to accept a humiliating peace treaty.

Francis's personal humiliation and Charles's military position were both too strong to allow for a permanent settlement in which Habsburgs ruled in Milan and Naples. But it was neither political nor personal considerations that were the source of another 30 years of continuous European warfare. Rather it was Charles's demand that Burgundy be returned to him. Although Francis was hardly in a position to bargain, he held out on this issue for as long as possible and secretly prepared a disavowal of the final agreement before it was made. By the Treaty of Madrid in 1526, Francis I yielded Burgundy and recognized the Spanish conquest of Navarre and Spanish rule in Naples. The agreement was sealed by the marriage of Francis to Charles's sister, Eleanor of Portugal. But marriage was not sufficient security for such a complete capitulation. To secure his release from Spain, Francis was required to leave behind as hostages his seven- and eight-year-old sons until the treaty was fulfilled. For three years, the children languished in Spanish captivity.

No sooner had he set foot upon French soil than Francis I renounced the Treaty of Madrid. Despite the threat that it posed to his children, Francis argued that the terms had been extracted against his will, and he even gained the approval of the pope for violating his oath. Setting France on a war footing, he began seeking new allies. Henry VIII, disappointed with the meager spoils of his last venture, switched sides. So too did a number of Italian city-states, including Rome. Most importantly, Francis I entered into an alliance with the Ottoman sultan, Suleiman the Magnificent (1520–1566), whose armies were pressing against the southeastern borders of the Holy Roman Empire. In the year following Pavia, the Ottomans secured an equally decisive triumph at Mohacs, captured Budapest, and threatened Vienna, the eastern capital of the Habsburg lands. Almost overnight Charles V had been turned from hunter into hunted. The Ottoman threat demanded immediate attention in Germany, the French and English were preparing to strike in the Low Countries, and the Italian wars continued. In 1527, Charles's unpaid German mercenaries stormed through Rome, sacked the papal capital, and captured the pope. Christian Europe was mortified.

The struggle for European mastery ground on for decades. The Treaty of Cateau-Cambrésis in 1559 brought to a close 60 years of conflict. In the end the French were no more capable of dislodging the Habsburgs from Italy than were the Habsburgs of forcing the Ottomans out of Hungary. The great stores of silver that poured into Castile from the New World were consumed in the fires of Continental warfare. In 1557, both France and Spain declared bankruptcy to avoid foreclosures by their creditors. For the French, the Italian wars were disastrous. They seriously undermined the state's financial base, eroded confidence in the monarchy, and thinned the ranks of the ruling nobility. The adventure begun by Charles VIII in search of glory brought France nearly to ruin. It ended with fitting irony. After the death of Francis I, his son Henry II (1547–1559) continued the struggle. Henry never forgave his

■ This Ottoman painting depicts the defeat of the Hungarians at the hands of the sultan's army at Mohacs in 1526. The prominence of artillery and muskets in the painting reflects the impact of technological advances on warfare.

father for abandoning him in Spain, and he sought revenge on Charles V, who had been his jailer. He regarded the Treaty of Cateau-Cambrésis as a victory and celebrated it with great pomp and pageantry. Among the feasts and festivities were athletic competitions for the king's courtiers and attendants. Henry II entered the jousting tournament and was killed there.

CONCLUSION

Charles V died in his bed. The long years of war made clear that the dream to dominate Europe could only be a dream. He split apart his empire and granted to his brother, Ferdinand I (1558–1564), the Austrian and German lands and the mantle of the Holy Roman Emperor. To his son Philip II (1556–1598) he ceded the Low Countries, Spain and the New World, Naples, and his Italian conquests. In 1555, Charles abdicated all of his titles and retired to a monastery to live out his final

days. The cares of an empire that once stretched from Peru to Vienna were lifted from his shoulders. Beginning with his voyage to Castile in 1517, he had made ten trips to the Netherlands, nine to Germany, seven to Italy, six to Spain, four to France, two to England, and two to Africa. "My life has been one long journey," he told those who witnessed him relinquish his crowns. On 21 September 1558, he finally rested forever.

QUESTIONS FOR REVIEW

1. What impulses in European society were revealed by the global exploration and conquests of the Portuguese and the Spanish?
2. What qualities characterized the "New Monarchies" and what are some of the best examples of such princely states?
3. How and why did the experience of political and territorial unification differ in England, France, and Spain?
4. How did war between the great European monarchies contribute to unity within each?

KEY TERMS

caravels, *p. 348*

Columbian Exchange, *p. 352*

conquistadores, *p. 355*

Lusiads, p. 357

New Monarchies, *p. 359*

provincialism, *p. 367*

reconquista, *p. 362*

Spanish Inquisition, *p. 371*

Treaty of Tordesillas, *p. 350*

DISCOVERING WESTERN CIVILIZATION ONLINE

You can obtain more information about the European empires at the Websites listed below. See also the Companion Website that accompanies this text, www.ablongman.com/kishlansky, which contains an online study guide and additional resources.

European Encounters

Discoverers Web
www.win.tue.nl/cs/fm/engels/discovery/
A site devoted to all ages of discovery with maps, short biographies, and time lines. There are links to the writings of Columbus, Cortés, and other early voyagers.

The Columbus Navigation Homepage
www1.minn.net/~keithp/
Everything you ever wanted to know about Christopher Columbus.

1492: An Ongoing Voyage
www.loc.gov/exhibits/1492
A Library of Congress online exhibit on the causes and consequences of European exploration and expansion.

Christopher Columbus—A Culinary History
www.castellobanfi.com/features/story_3.html
A site devoted to the food and drink associated with a long ocean voyage in the fifteenth century.

Medieval Sourcebook: Exploration and Expansion
www.fordham.edu/halsall/sbook1z.html
Dozens of primary sources relating to the voyages of discovery.

The Formation of States

Henry VIII: Intrigue in the Tudor Court
www.archsoc.com/games/Henry.html
A board game that teaches both history and strategy.

SUGGESTIONS FOR FURTHER READING

General Reading

David Nicholas, *The Transformation of Europe 1300–1600* (New York: Oxford University Press, 1999). A comprehensive survey that emphasizes continuities between the sixteenth century and the preceding period.

Eugene Rice, *The Foundations of Early Modern Europe, 1460–1559*, 2nd ed. (New York: Norton, 1994). An outstanding synthesis.

European Encounters

C. R. Boxer, *The Portuguese Seaborne Empire, 1415–1825* (London: Hutchinson, 1968). The best history of the first of the explorer nations.

Natalie Zemon Davis. *Trickster Travels: A Sixteenth-Century Muslim Between Worlds* (New York: Hill and Wang, 2006). A gripping life of the travel writer and biographer known as Leo Africanus.

J. H. Elliott. *Empires of the Atlantic World: Britain and Spain in America 1492–1830* (New Haven: Yale, 2006). A comparative account of Spanish and British imperialism and colonization in the New World.

J. H. Elliott, *The Old World and the New, 1492–1650* (Cambridge: Cambridge University Press, 1970). A brilliant look at the reception of knowledge about the New World by Europeans.

Felipe Fernandez-Armesto, *Columbus* (Oxford: Oxford University Press, 1991). The best of the recent studies. Reliable, stimulating, and up-to-date.

Anthony Pagden, *Lords of All the World: Ideologies of Empire in Spain, Britain and France, c. 1500–c. 1800* (New Haven, CT: Yale University Press, 1995). A fresh look at the ideas behind the European encounter with the New World.

Hugh Thomas, *Rivers of Gold: The Rise of the Spanish Empire* (London: Widenfeld & Nicholson, 2004). A breathtaking retelling of Spain's New World Empire.

Geographical Tour—Europe in 1500: The Age of the New Monarchies

N. J. G. Pounds, *An Historical Geography of Europe, 1500–1800* (Cambridge: Cambridge University Press, 1990). A remarkable survey of the relationship between geography and history.

Daniel Waley, *Later Medieval Europe* (London: Longman, 1985). A good brief account.

The Formation of States

Robert Bucholz and Newton Key. *Early Modern England 1485–1714: A Narrative History* (Blackwell Publishers, 2003). The latest survey of the reigns of the Tudors and Stuarts in England.

S. B. Chrimes, *Henry VII* (Berkeley: University of California Press, 1972). A traditional biography of the first Tudor.

Robert O. Crummey, *The Formation of Muscovy, 1304–1613* (London: Longman, 1987). The best one-volume history.

Norman Davies, *God's Playground: A History of Poland, Vol. 1, The Origins to 1795* (New York: Columbia University Press, 1982). The best treatment in English of a complex history.

Bernard Guenée, *States and Rulers in Later Medieval Europe* (London: Basil Blackwell, 1985). An engaging argument about the forces that helped shape the state system in Europe.

Henry Kamen, *The Spanish Inquisition: A Historical Revision* (New Haven, CT: Yale University Press, 1998). The most recent assessment of the power and activities of the Inquisition.

Paul M. Kendall, *Louis XI: The Universal Spider* (New York: Norton, 1971). A highly entertaining account of an unusual monarch.

John Lynch, *Spain, 1516–1598: From Nation State to World Empire* (Cambridge, MA: Blackwell Publishers, 1994). The best survey.

J. H. Shennan, *The Origins of the Modern European State, 1450–1725* (London: Hutchinson, 1974). An analytic account of the rise of the state.

The Dynastic Struggles

J. R. Hale, *War and Society in Renaissance Europe* (Stroud, England: Sutton, 1998). Assesses the impact of war on the political and social history of early modern Europe.

Robert Knecht. *The Valois: Kings of France 1328–1589* (Hambledon and London, 2005). A history of the dynasty under which France was established as a major European power.

William Maltby, *The Reign of Charles V* (New York: Palgrave, 2002). The most recent study of one of Europe's great emperors.

David Potter, *A History of France, 1460–1560* (London: Macmillan, 1995). A reliable survey that connects medieval and early modern developments.

J. J. Scarisbrick, *Henry VIII* (New Haven: Yale University Press, 1997). The definitive biography.

For a list of additional titles related to this chapter's topics, please see http://www.ablongman.com/kishlansky.

THE REFORM OF RELIGION

SOLA SCRIPTURA

THE BIBLE AND THE REFORMATION

THE VISUAL RECORD

"In the beginning was the word, and the word was with God, and the word was God." In no other period of European history was this text of the apostle John so appropriate. Men and women shared a consuming desire to hear and to read the Word of God as set down in the Bible. In the early sixteenth century, Europeans developed an insatiable appetite for the Bible. Scriptures rolled off printing presses in every shape and form, from the great vellum tomes of Gutenberg pictured here to pocket Bibles that soldiers carried into battle. They came in every imaginable language. Before 1500 there were 14 complete Bibles printed in German, 4 each in Italian, French, and Spanish, 1 in Czech, and even 1 in Flemish.

There were hundreds more editions in Latin, the official Vulgate Bible first translated by Saint Jerome in the fourth century. Whole translations and editions of the Bible were only part of the story. Separate sections, especially the Psalms and the first books of the Old Testament, were printed by the thousands. There were 24 French editions of the Old Testament before an entirely new translation appeared in 1530. When Martin Luther began his own German translation of the Bible in 1522, it immediately became an international best seller. In 25 years it went into 430 editions. It is estimated that 1 million German Bibles were printed in the first half of the sixteenth century—a time when Europe had a German-speaking population of about 15 million people, 90 percent of whom were illiterate.

■ Pages from a Gutenberg Bible printed in the 1450s.

Bible owning was no fad. It was but one element in a new devotional outlook that was sweeping the Continent and that would have far-reaching consequences for European society during the next 150 years. A renewed spirituality was everywhere to be seen. It was expressed in a desire to change the traditional practices and structures of the Roman Church. It was expressed in a desire to have learned and responsible ministers to tend to the needs of their parishioners. It was expressed in a desire to establish godly families, godly cities, and godly kingdoms. Sometimes it took the form of sarcasm and bitter denunciations; sometimes it took the form of quiet devotion and pious living. The need for reform was everywhere felt; the demand for reform was everywhere heard. It came from within the Roman Church as much as from without. The inspiration for reform was based on the Word of God. Scholars, following humanist principles, worked on biblical translations in an attempt to bring a purer text to light. Biblical commentary dominated the writings of churchmen as never before. Woodcut pictures depicting scenes from the life of Jesus or from the Old Testament were printed in untold quantities for the edification of the unlettered. For the first time, common people could, in their own dwellings, contemplate representations of the lives of the saints. Many of the Bibles that were printed in vernacular— that is, in the languages spoken in the various European states rather than in Latin—were interleaved with illustrations of the central events of Christian history. Preachers spoke to newly aware audiences and relied on biblical texts to draw out their message. Study groups, especially in urban areas, proliferated so that the literate could read and learn together. Bible reading became a part of family life, one that mothers and fathers could share with their children and their servants.

■ Detail of pages from a Gutenberg Bible.

LOOKING AHEAD

Sola scriptura—by the word alone—became the battle cry of religious reform. As we will see in this chapter, in the early decades of the sixteenth century Europeans experienced one of the greatest of all religious rebirths: the Protestant Reformation. The **Reformation** was a movement to purify the Catholic Church that resulted in the creation of new religious denominations in Europe collectively known as Protestants from their protest against Roman Catholic practices. But the Catholic Church experienced its own renewal as well. Figures such as Luther, Calvin, and Ignatius of Loyola were part of the most remarkable generation of religious leaders since the foundation of Christianity.

THE INTELLECTUAL REFORMATION

There is nothing as powerful as an idea whose time has come. But the coming of ideas has a history as complex as the ideas themselves. In the early sixteenth century, reformers throughout western Europe preached new ideas about religious doctrine and religious practice. At first the ideas took the form of a sustained critique of the Roman Catholic Church, but soon they developed a momentum of their own. Some reformers remained within traditional Catholicism; others moved outside and founded new Protestant churches. Whether Catholic or Protestant, wherever the movement for religious reform appeared it was fed by new ideas. But if new ideas were to supplant old ones, they had to be communicated—not only heard and repeated but accurately recorded and understood. That was made possible by the development of the technology of printing, which appeared in Germany in the late fifteenth century and rapidly spread across Europe in the succeeding decades. Yet printing was as much a result as it was a cause of the spread of ideas. The humanist call for a return to the study of the classics and for the creation of accurate texts, first heard in Italy, aroused scholars and leaders in all of the European states. Their appetite for manuscripts exhausted the abilities of the scribes and booksellers who reproduced texts. Printing responded to that demand.

The Print Revolution

The development of printing did not cause religious reform, but it is difficult to see how reform would have progressed in its absence. The campaign to change the doctrine and practice of Catholicism was waged through the press, with millions of flyers and pamphlets distributed across Europe to spread the new ideas. One-third of all books sold in Germany between 1518 and 1525 were written by Luther. But the ways in which printing came to be used by religious reformers could hardly

■ An early German print shop. The man at the left operates the screw press while an apprentice (right) stacks the printed sheets. The man in the back is setting type for the next impression.

have been foreseen by the artisans, bankers, and booksellers who together created one of the true technological revolutions in Western history.

Printing was not invented. It developed as a result of progress made in a number of allied industries, of which papermaking and goldsmithing were the most important. Scholars and university students needed copies of manuscripts. Their need led to the development of a trade in bookselling that flourished in almost every university town. The process of reproduction was slowed by difficulties in obtaining the sheepskins and calfskins on which the manuscripts were written. It took the skins of 300 sheep to produce a single Bible. In the early fifteenth century, copyists began to substitute paper made from linen rags for the expensive vellum skins. A number of German artisans experimented with using movable metal type to make exact reproductions of manuscripts on paper. Paper took a better impression and provided an absolutely smooth surface, which was essential for pressing the image. In the 1450s, in Mainz, Johannes Gutenberg (ca. 1400–1468) and his partners published their famous Bibles.

The association of early printing with goldsmithing resulted from the high level of technical skill that was necessary to create the hard metal stamps from which the softer metal type was produced. Printing was an expensive business. The investment in type and in paper was considerable. Only the press itself was cheap. Any corn or wine press could be used to bring the long flat sheets of paper down upon a wooden frame filled with ink-coated metal type. Booksellers initially put up the capital needed to cast the stamps, mold the type, and buy the paper. They bound the printed pages and found the markets to distribute them. At first sales were slow. Printed books were considered inferior to handwritten manuscripts. Nor at first were printed books less expensive. Bibles like those printed by Gutenberg were major investments, equivalent to purchasing a house today. Many printing shops

quickly went bankrupt as they misjudged their markets and were unable to pay back their loans.

Still, once it was begun, printing spread like wildfire. By 1480, more than 110 towns had established presses, most in Italy and Germany. After that the pace quickened. By the beginning of the sixteenth century, Venice and Paris were the centers of the industry, with the Paris presses producing more than three hundred new titles annually. Most of the early printed works were either religious or classical. Bibles, church service books, and the commentaries of the Church fathers were most common. Cicero topped the list of classical authors.

What is most amazing about the printing revolution is how rapidly printing came to be a basic part of life. In the first

MAP DISCOVERY

The Spread of Printing

Examine the locations and dates of early printing. Where were the earliest printing presses concentrated? How did printing spread? Why do you think Rome had a press established before Florence?

40 years after the presses began, perhaps as many as 20 million books were produced and distributed. Printing changed the habits of teachers and students, and therefore the possibilities of education. It altered the methods by which the state conducted its business. It affected both legal training and legal proceedings. Compilations of laws could now be widely distributed and more uniformly enforced. Printing had a similar effect on the development of scientific study. The printing press popularized the discoveries of the New World and contributed to the reproduction of more accurate charts and maps, which in turn facilitated further discovery. Printing also helped standardize language—both Latin and vernacular—by frequent repetition of preferred usage and spelling. Perhaps most importantly, printing created an international intellectual community whose ideas could be dispersed the length and breadth of the Continent. The printing press enhanced the value of ideas and of thinking. Nothing could be more central to the reform of religion.

Christian Humanism

Many of the ideas that spread across Europe as the result of the printing revolution originated in Italian humanism (see Chapter 11). The revival of classical literature, with its concern for purity in language and eloquence in style, was one of the most admired achievements of the Renaissance. Students from all over Europe who descended upon Italian universities to study medicine and law came away with a strong dose of philology, rhetoric, moral philosophy, and the other liberal arts. Their heads were filled with the new learning. By the beginning of the sixteenth century, the force of humanism was felt strongly in northern and western Europe, where it was grafted on to the dominant strains of traditional theological teaching. The combination was a new and powerful intellectual movement known as **Christian humanism**.

Christian humanism was a program of reform rather than a philosophy. It aimed to make better Christians through better education. Humanists were especially interested in the education of women. "For what is more fruitful than the good education and order of women, the one half of all mankind," wrote Thomas More (1478–1535). Humanists helped found schools for girls and advocated that they be trained in the same subjects as boys. Thomas More raised his daughters to be among the educated elite of England, and they enjoyed international renown. The Spanish humanist Juan Luis Vives (1492–1540) wrote *The Instruction of a Christian Woman* (1523), a handbook for women of the elite orders commissioned by Catherine of Aragon. Renowned women scholars even held places at Italian universities. Humanist educational principles posed an implicit challenge to Roman Catholicism. Schools had once been the monopoly of the Church, which used them to train clergymen. The Church had founded them and kept them afloat in good times and in bad. Literacy itself had been preserved over the centuries so that the gospel could be propagated.

By the sixteenth century those purposes had been transformed. Schools now trained many who were not destined for careers in the Church, and literacy served the needs of the state, the aristocracy, and the merchant classes. More importantly, as the humanists perfected their techniques of scholarship, the Church continued to rely upon traditional methods of training and traditional texts. The dominant manner of teaching at the schools and universities was known as Scholasticism. Passages of biblical texts were studied through the commentaries of generations of Church fathers. Rote memorization of the opinions of others was more highly valued than critical thinking. Argument took place by formal disputation of questions on which the Church fathers disagreed. Disputed questions became more and more obscure. Even if Scholastics did not debate the question, "How many angels can dance on the head of a pin?" it seemed to many humanists that they might as well have. The Vulgate Bible was used throughout Western Christendom. It was now a thousand years old.

The Humanist Movement

Many humanist criticisms of Church teaching focused on its failure to inspire individuals to live a Christian life. Humanist writers were especially scathing about popular practices that bordered on superstition, such as pilgrimages to holy places or the worship of relics from the early history of the Church. Such beliefs became the butt of popular humor: "If the fragments [of the Lord's Cross] were joined together they would seem a full load for a freighter. And yet the Lord carried his whole cross." Christian humanists wanted to inspire Christians. As the great Dutch humanist Desiderius Erasmus observed, "To be learned is the lot of only a few; but no one is unable to be a Christian, no one is unable to be pious." The ironic strain in humanist writing is most closely associated with Erasmus, but it is also visible in the humanist social criticism of Sir Thomas More's *Utopia*. (See "A Closer Look: Utopia," pp. 384–385.)

DOCUMENT

Sir Thomas More, *Utopia*

Christian humanism was an international movement. The humanists formed the elite of the intellectual world of the sixteenth century, and their services were sought by princes and peers as well as by the most distinguished universities. In fact, the New Monarchs supported the humanists and protected them from their critics. Marguerite of Navarre, sister of Francis I, was an accomplished writer who frequently interceded on behalf of the leading French humanists. Ferdinand of Aragon, Henry VIII, and the Holy Roman Emperors Maximilian I and Charles V all brought humanists to their courts and aided their projects. Maria of Hungary and Mary and Elizabeth Tudor were trained in humanist principles and participated in humanist literary achievements.

The centerpiece of humanist reforms was the translation of Christian texts. Armed with skills in Greek and Latin, informed by scholars of Hebrew and Aramaic, humanist writers prepared new editions of the books of the Bible and of the writings of the early Church fathers. Their favorite method was side-by-side translation. The Polyglot—literally "many languages"—Bible that was produced in 1522 at the University of Alcala took a team of scholars 15 years to complete. They gathered together copies of all known biblical manuscripts and rigorously compared their texts. They established the principle that inconsistencies among Latin manuscripts were to be resolved by reference to Greek texts, and difficulties in Greek texts by reference to Hebrew texts. The result was six elegantly printed volumes that allowed scholars to compare the texts. The Old Testament was printed in three parallel columns of Hebrew, Latin Vulgate, and Greek. The New Testament was printed in double columns, with the Greek text on one side and the Vulgate on the other. The Greek edition of the Bible and its establishment as a text superior to the Vulgate caused an immediate sensation throughout humanist and Church circles.

The Wit of Erasmus

Although the Polyglot Bible contained the first completed Greek edition of the New Testament, it was not the first published one. That distinction belongs to the man whose name is most closely associated with the idea of Christian humanism: Desiderius Erasmus of Rotterdam (ca. 1466–1536). Orphaned at an early age, Erasmus was educated by the Brothers of the Common Life, a lay brotherhood that specialized in schooling children and preparing them for a monastic life. Marked out early by his quick wit, pleasant though strong personality, and extraordinary intellectual gifts, Erasmus en-

tered a monastery and was then allowed to travel to pursue his studies, first in France and then in England.

In England, Erasmus learned of new techniques for instructing children both in classical knowledge and in Christian morals, and he became particularly interested in the education of women. He dedicated a number of his later writings to women patrons who were accomplished humanist scholars. While in England, Erasmus decided to compose a short satire on the lines of his conversations with Thomas More, extolling what was silly and condemning what was wise. The result was *In Praise of Folly* (1509), a work that became one of the first best sellers in publishing history.

Before his visit to England, Erasmus had worked solely on Latin translations, but he came to realize the importance of recovering the Greek texts of the early Church fathers. At the age of 30, he began the arduous task of learning ancient Greek and devoted his energies to a study of the writings of Saint Jerome, the principal compiler of the Vulgate, and to preparing an edition of the Greek text of the Bible. Erasmus's New Testament and his edition of the writings of Saint Jerome both appeared in 1516. Coming from the pen of the most renowned intellectual in Europe, they were an immediate success.

Erasmus devoted his life to restoring the direct connection between the individual Christian and the textual basis of Christian doctrine. Although he is called the father of biblical criticism, Erasmus was not a theologian. He was more interested in the practical impact of ideas than in the ideas themselves. His scathing attacks upon the Scholastics, popular superstition, and the pretensions of the traditionalists in the Church and the universities all aimed at the same goal: to restore the experiences of

A DUTCH WIT

In Praise of Folly (1500) was a witty satire on the abuses to be found in the Catholic Church. Desiderius Erasmus wrote it on a lark to be presented to his friend, Sir Thomas More, on whose name its Greek title puns. It was probably the first best seller of the age of printing.

Focus Questions

How do the follies of priests and theologians differ, and how are they similar? Is this piece a satire of religion?

These various forms of foolishness so pervade the whole life of Christians that even the priests themselves find no objection to admitting, not to say fostering, them, since they do not fail to perceive how many tidy little sums accrue to them from such sources. But what if some odious philosopher should chime in and say, as is quite true: "You will not die badly if you live well. You are redeeming your sins when you add to the sum that you contribute a hearty detestation of evil doers: then you may spare yourself tears, vigils, invocations, fasts, and all that kind of life. You may rely upon any saint to aid you when once you begin to imitate his life."

As for the theologians, perhaps the less said the better on this gloomy and dangerous theme, since they are a style of man who show themselves exceeding supercilious and irritable unless they can heap up six hundred conclusions about you and force you to recant; and if you refuse, they promptly brand you as a heretic—for it is their custom to terrify by their thunderings those whom they dislike. It must be confessed that no other group of fools are so reluctant to acknowledge Folly's benefits toward them, although I have many titles to their gratitude, for I make them so in love with themselves that they seem to be happily exalted to the third heaven, whence they look down with something like pity upon all other mortals, wandering about on the earth like mere cattle.

From Erasmus, *In Praise of Folly.*

UTOPIA

"It is a general rule that the more different anything is from what people are used to, the harder it is to accept." So warned the imaginary traveler, Raphael Hythloday as he described Utopia, a fabulous society he had visited in the New World. Utopian society was different indeed. In Utopia, all property was held in common; there were no social classes; families were extended to include grandparents, in-laws, and flocks of children; and all work and most social activities were regulated by the state. Utopians were rarely tempted to sin. Everyone wore the same practical clothes to abolish vanity. "No matter how delicate the thread, they say a sheep wore it once and still was nothing but a sheep." Everyone ate the same food in large common halls to abolish jealousy. "A man would be stupid to take the trouble to prepare a worse meal at home when he had a sumptuous one near at hand in the hall." To abolish greed, Utopians scorned gold and silver. "Criminals who are to bear through life the mark of some disgraceful act are forced to wear golden rings on their ears, golden bands on their fingers, golden chains around their necks, and even golden crowns on their heads." Utopians lived harmoniously in planned cities, honored their elders, cared for their sick, and brought up their children to love learning and respect hard work. They "lead a life as free of anxiety and as full of joy as possible."

There were many ways in which Christian humanists attempted to in-struct their contemporaries to lead a joyful life. None has proved more enduring than the imaginary community Sir Thomas More created in *Utopia,* a social satire so convincing that a Catholic priest sought to become its bishop and sea travelers tried to learn its location. More's creation has proven so compelling that it has given its name to the entire genre of dreamworlds that followed in its wake. His vision of a carefully planned and permanently contented society has passed into our language, but in a way that would not have pleased the author. Now, utopian has a wistful ring. It is a label for impractical ideals that will never come to pass, a name for well-meaning but misguided daydreams. For More, as for his generation of humanists, the goal of teaching Christians to lead a Christian life was neither wistful nor impractical.

Sir Thomas More was a London lawyer by vocation but a humanist scholar by avocation. His father practiced law and planned a similar career for his son. But More's stay at Oxford University coincided with the first flush of humanist enthusiasm there, especially in the study of Greek. More proved so able that his father removed him to London in fear that reading Greek would turn him away from Catholicism. More was as good at law school as he had been at the university, and he was soon singled out as one of the best lawyers of his day. But in his spare time he continued to study the classics and became part of the growing humanist circle in London. There he met Erasmus, who was to become his lifelong friend.

Erasmus left a vivid portrait of More. "His complexion is fair, his face being rather blond than pale; his hair is auburn inclining to black, his eyes a bluish gray. It is a face more expressive of pleasantry than of gravity or dignity. He seems to be born and made for friendship, his extraordinary kindness and sweetness of temper are such as to cheer the dullest spirit."

More wrote *Utopia* in 1516, before he embarked upon the public career that would result in his becoming Chancellor of England, Speaker of the House of Commons, Privy Councilor and companion to Henry VIII, and finally a victim of the king's divorce and assumption of the title Supreme Head of the Church of England. More's life was ended on the chopping block, and his death was mourned by humanists throughout Europe.

The community that More described in *Utopia* combined Plato's republic with a Christian monastery and was informed by travelers' tales of the New World. But More's Utopia resembled nothing so much as England. The real and the imaginary, the serious and the absurd intermingle to disguise the author's point of view. *Utopia* is written in the form of a dialogue in which the author pretends to be one of the characters. On a visit to Antwerp, the character More is introduced to an imaginary traveler named Raphael Hythloday. During a long evening, Hythloday related a tale of a remarkable society that he encountered on his voyages. Utopia was a self-sufficient island, protected from invasion by the sea and thus able to develop its social customs without interference.

Hythloday contrasted the practices of the Utopians with those of contemporary Europeans. For example, where European peasants or craftsmen worked for fourteen hours a day, Utopians worked for only six. But all Utopians worked. There were no idle aristocrats with their marauding retainers, no priests and monks and nuns, no beggars unable to find jobs. Moreover, there was no surplus of workers in one field and shortage in another. For two years, each Utopian worked on a farm. After that, Utopians practiced a craft according to the needs of the city. Both males and females were educated to serve the community. Women were trained in less strenuous but no less essential trades such as weaving or spinning. The population of cities was strictly controlled so that there was neither poverty nor homelessness. In their spare time Utopians engaged in uplifting activities such as music, gardening, or artistic pursuits. Severe punishment awaited transgressors, but in contrast to the European practice of executing thieves, Utopian criminals were enslaved so that they could work for the restitution of the wrongs that they committed. Even as slaves they lived well, with good food and much leisure. Though they had not the benefit of Christian religion, the Utopians believed in a single divinity as well as an afterlife and their worship was simple and natural.

More's *Utopia* was written in Latin, but the name of the island and its central places were all Greek words. For More's humanist friends the joke was plain. Utopia meant "nowhere" in Greek and Hythloday meant "peddler of nonsense." Humanist interest in the New World and in the strange native customs of the Amerindians made it a logical setting for an idealized commu-

A woodcut of the island of Utopia by Ambrosius Holbein, from the 1518 edition of Sir Thomas More's *Utopia*.

nity. But *Utopia* was a model for a Christian community, one in which the seven deadly sins had all been abolished and replaced by a life led according to the Golden Rule, where people did attempt to do to others what they wished done to themselves. By ironic contrast with the unfulfilling life led by Europeans, grasping for riches, the simple life of the Utopians held great attraction. By comparing the success of heathen Utopians with the failure of Christian Europeans, More called upon his contemporaries to reform their own lives. The purpose of *Utopia* was not to advocate the abolition of wealth and property but to demonstrate that a society founded upon Christian principles would become truly Christian.

■ Hans Holbein's 1523 portrait depicts Erasmus in profile, absorbed in his work rather than looking in the direction of the viewer.

Christ to the center of Christianity. Many of Erasmus's popular writings were how-to books—how to improve one's manners, how to speak Latin properly, how to write letters—he even propounded 22 rules on how to lead a Christian life. Although his patrons were the rich and his language was Latin, Erasmus also hoped to reach men and women lower down the social order, those whom he believed the Church had failed to educate. "The doctrine of Christ casts aside no age, no sex, no fortune or position in life. It keeps no one at a distance."

THE LUTHERAN REFORMATION

On the surface, the Roman Catholic Church appeared as strong as ever at the end of the fifteenth century. The growth of universities and the spread of the new learning had helped create a better-educated clergy. The printing press proved an even greater boon to the Church than it had to the humanists by making widely available both instructional manuals for priests and up-to-date service books for congregations. The prosperity of European societies enhanced the prosperity of the Church. In Rome, successive late medieval popes had

managed to protect Church interests in the wake of the disintegration of the autonomous power of the Italian city-states. That was a remarkable feat. Popes had become first diplomats and then warriors in order to repel French and Spanish invaders. Although Rome had been invaded, it had never been conquered. And it was more beautiful than ever, as the greatest artists and artisans of the Renaissance had built and adorned its churches. Pilgrims came in the hundreds of thousands to bask in its glory. On the surface all was calm.

Yet everywhere in Europe the cry was for reform. Reform the venal papacy and its money-sucking bishops. Reform the ignorant clergy and the sacrilegious priests. Raise up the fallen nuns and the wayward friars. Wherever people turned, they saw abuses. Parish livings were sold to the highest bidder to raise money. That was simony. Rich appointments were given to the kinsmen of powerful Church leaders rather than to those most qualified. That was nepotism. Individual clergymen accumulated numerous positions whose responsibilities they could not fulfill. That was pluralism. Some priests who took the vow of chastity lived openly with their concubines. Some mendicants who took the vow of poverty dressed in silk and ate from golden plates.

Yet the cry for reform that pierced the states of Europe at the beginning of the sixteenth century was a cry not so much of anguish as of hope. It came at a moment when people from all walks of life demanded greater spiritual fulfillment and held those whose vocation it was to provide such fulfillment to higher standards of achievement. It was expectation rather than experience that powered the demands for reform.

The Spark of Reform

Europe was becoming more religious. The signs of religious fervor were everywhere. Cities hired preachers to expound the gospel. Pilgrims to the shrines of saints clogged the roadways every spring and summer. It is estimated that 140,000 people visited the relics at Aachen on one day in 1496. Rome remained the greatest attraction, but pilgrims covered the Continent. The shrine of the apostle Saint James at Compostela in Spain was believed to cure the ill. Endowments of masses for the dead increased. Henry VII of England provided money for 10,000 masses to be said for his soul. Even moderately well-to-do city merchants might bequeath funds for several hundred. The chantries, where such services were performed, became overburdened by the "arithmetical piety," as there were neither enough priests nor enough altars to supply the demand.

People wanted more from the Church than the Church could possibly give them. Humanists condemned visits to the shrines as superstitious; pilgrims demanded that the relics be made more accessible. Reformers complained of pluralism; the clergy complained that they could not live on the salary of a single office. In one English diocese, 60 percent of all parish incomes were inadequate to live on. Civic authorities demanded that the established Church take greater responsibility for good works; the pope demanded that civic authorities help pay for them.

Contradiction and paradox dominated the movements for reform. Although the most vocal critics of the Church complained that its discipline was too lax, for many ordinary people its demands were too rigorous. The obligations of penance and confession weighed heavily upon them. Church doctrine held that sins had to be washed away before the souls of the dead could enter heaven. Until then they suffered in purgatory. Sins were cleansed through penance—the performance of acts of contrition assigned after confession. Despite the rule that confession must be made at least annually, it is doubtful if many Catholics entered the confessional for years on end. This is not to say that they were unconcerned about their sins or did not desire to do penance for them. Rather, it was the ordeal of the confession itself that kept many people away. "Have you skipped mass? Have you dressed proudly? Have you thought of committing adultery? Have you insulted or cursed your parents? Have you failed to offer prayers, give alms, and endow masses for departed parents?" These were just a few of the uncomfortable questions that priests were instructed to pose in confession. In towns, merchants were asked about their trading practices, shopkeepers about the quality of their goods. Magistrates were questioned about their attitudes to the clergy, intellectuals about their attitudes to the pope.

Thus it is hardly surprising that the sale of **indulgences** became a popular substitute for **penance and confession**. An indulgence was a portion of the treasury of good works performed by righteous Christians throughout the ages. They could be granted to those who desired to atone for their sins. Strictly speaking, an indulgence supplemented penance rather than substituted for it. It was effective only for the contrite—for sinners who repented of their sins. But as the practice of granting indulgences spread, the subtle distinction largely disappeared. Indulgences came to be viewed as pardons and the gift given to the Church in return as payment. "So soon as coin in coffer rings, the soul from purgatory springs." Indulgences were bought by the living to cleanse the sins of the dead, and some people even bought indulgences in anticipation of sins they had not yet committed.

By the sixteenth century, to limit abuses by local Church authorities, only the pope, through his agents, could grant indulgences. And their sale had become big business. Indulgences were one of the first items printed on Gutenberg's press. Popes used special occasions to offer an indulgence for pilgrimages to Rome or for contributions to special papal projects. Other indulgences were licensed locally, usually at the shrines of saints or at churches that contained relics—one reason why pilgrimages became increasingly popular. Frederick III, "the Wise" (1463–1525), ruler of Saxony, was one of the largest collectors of relics in Europe. At its height, his collection contained 17,000 different items, including a branch of Moses' burning bush, straw from Christ's manger, and 35 fragments of the true cross. Together, his relics

■ An anonymous caricature of Johann Tetzel, whose sale of an indulgence inspired Martin Luther's Ninety-five Theses. Tetzel answered with 122 theses of his own but was rebuked and disowned by the Catholics.

carried remission for sins that would otherwise have taken more than a quarter of a million years in purgatory to be cleansed.

The indulgence controversy was a symptom rather than a cause of the explosion of feelings that erupted in the small German town of Wittenberg in the year 1517. In that year, the pope was offering an indulgence to help finance the rebuilding of Saint Peter's Basilica in Rome. The pope chose Prince Albert of Brandenburg (1490–1545) to distribute the indulgence in Germany, and Albert hired the Dominican friar Johann Tetzel (ca. 1465–1519) to preach its benefits. Tetzel offered little warning about the theological niceties of indulgences to those who paid to mitigate their own sins or alleviate the suffering of their ancestors whose souls resided in purgatory.

Enthusiasm for the indulgence spread to the neighboring state of Saxony, where Frederick banned its sale. His great collection of relics carried their own indulgences, and Tetzel offered unwelcome competition. But Saxons flocked into Brandenburg to make their purchases. By the end of October, Tetzel was not very far from Wittenberg Castle, where Frederick's relics were housed. On All Saints' Day the relics would be opened to view and, with the harvest done, one of the largest crowds of the year would gather to see them. On the night before, Martin Luther (1483–1546), a professor of theology at Wittenberg University, posted on the door of the castle church Ninety-five Theses attacking indulgences and their sale.

Aside from the timing of Luther's action, there was nothing unusual about the posting of theses. In the Scholastic tradition of disputation, scholars presented propositions, or theses, for debate and challenged all comers to argue with them in a public forum. Luther's theses were controversial, but—as that was the whole point of offering them for discussion—they were meant to be. Only circumstance moved Luther's theses from the academic to the public sphere. Already there was growing concern among clergy and theologians about Tetzel's blatant sale of indulgences. Hordes of purchasers believed that they were buying unconditional remission of sin. In the late summer and early fall of 1517, the frenzy to buy indulgences had reached gold-rush proportions, and individual priests and monks began to sound the alarm: an indulgence without contrition was worthless.

Luther's theses focused that concern and finally communicated it beyond the walls of the Church and university. The theses were immediately translated into German and spread throughout the Holy Roman Empire by humanists who had long criticized practices such as the sale of indulgences as superstitious. Prospective buyers became wary; past purchasers became angry. They had been duped again by the Church, by the priests who took their money, and by the Italian pope who cared nothing for honest, hardworking Germans. But Prince Albert and the pope needed the income. They could not stand by while sales collapsed and anticlerical and antipapal sentiment grew. Luther and his theses would have to be challenged.

Martin Luther's Faith

Martin Luther was not a man to challenge lightly. Although he was only an obscure German professor, he had already marked himself out to all who knew him. In his youth, Luther was an exceptionally able student whose father sent him to the best schools in preparation for a career in law. But Martin had his own ideas about his future, which were made more vivid when he was nearly struck by lightning. Against the wishes of his father, he entered an Augustinian monastery, wholeheartedly followed the strict program of his order, and was ordained a priest in 1507. Intellectually gifted, he went on to study at the university, first at Erfurt and then at Wittenberg, where he received his doctorate and was appointed to the theology faculty in 1512.

A professor at the age of 29, he also served as priest at the castle church, where he preached each week. He attracted powerful patrons in the university and gained a reputation as an outstanding teacher. He began to be picked for administrative posts and became overseer of 11 Augustinian monasteries. His skills in disputation were so widely recognized that he was sent to Rome to argue a case on behalf of his order. Each task he was given he fulfilled beyond expectation; at every step he proved himself ready to go higher.

In all outward appearances, Luther was successful and contented. But beneath this tranquil exterior lay a soul in torment. As he rose in others' estimation, he sank in his own. Through beating and fasting he mortified his flesh. Through vigil and prayer he nourished his soul. Through study and contemplation he honed his intellect. Still he could find no peace. Despite his devotion, he could not erase his sense of sin; he could not convince himself that the righteousness God demanded of him was a righteousness he could achieve. "I

■ Catholics and Protestants alike used religious images to slander their opponents. Here Catholic propaganda portrays Martin Luther as the devil in academic disguise come to tempt Jesus.

was one who terribly feared the last judgment and who nevertheless with all my heart wished to be saved."

Knowledge of his salvation came to Luther through study. His internal agonies led him to ponder over and over again the biblical passages that described the righteousness of God. In the intellectual tradition in which he had been trained, that righteousness was equated with law. The righteous person either followed God's law or was punished by God's wrath. It was that understanding that tormented him. "I thought that I had to perform good works till at last through them Jesus would become a friend and gracious to me." But no amount of good works could overcome Luther's feelings of guilt for his sins. Like a man caught in a net, the more he struggled the more entangled he became. For years he wrestled with his problem. Almost from the moment he began lecturing in 1512 he searched for the key to the freedom of his own soul.

Even before he wrote his Ninety-five Theses, Luther had made the first breakthrough by a unique reading of the writings of Saint Paul. "I pondered night and day until I understood the connection between the righteousness of God and the sentence 'The just shall live by faith.' Then I grasped that the justice of God is the righteousness by which through grace and pure mercy, God justifies us through faith. Immediately I felt that I had been reborn and that I had passed through wide open doors into paradise!" Finally he realized that the righteousness of God was not a burden that humans carried, but a gift that God bestowed. It could not be earned by good works but was freely given. It was this belief that fortified Luther during his years of struggle with both civil and Church powers.

Over the next several years, Luther refined his spiritual philosophy and drew out the implications of his newfound beliefs. His religion was shaped by three interconnected tenets. First came justification by faith alone—*sola fide*. An individual's everlasting salvation came from faith in God's goodness rather than from the performance of good works. Sin was ever present and inescapable. It could not be washed away by penance, and it could not be forgiven by indulgence. Second, faith in God's mercy came only through the knowledge and contemplation of the Word of God—*sola scriptura*. All that was needed to understand the justice and mercy of God was contained in the Bible, the sole authority in all things spiritual. Reading the Word, hearing the Word, expounding upon and studying the Word—that was the path to faith, and through faith to salvation. Third, all who believed in God's righteousness and had achieved their faith through the study of the Bible were equal in God's eyes. No longer was it necessary for men and women to renounce their worldly existence and take up a life consumed by spiritual works. Neither pope nor priest, neither monk nor nun, could achieve a higher level of spirituality than the most ordinary citizen. The priesthood was of all believers. Each followed his or her own calling in life and found his or her own faith through Scripture. Ministers and preachers were valuable because they could help others learn God's Word. But they could not confer faith.

Luther's spiritual rebirth and the theology that developed from it posed a fundamental challenge to the Roman Catholic Church. The doctrine of justification by faith alone called into question the Church's emphasis upon the primacy of works—that is, receiving the sacraments administered by the priests and performing acts of charity and devotion. The doctrine that faith was achieved through Scripture weakened the mediating power of the Church by making salvation an individual rather than a collective event. The doctrine of the equality of all believers struck at the vast establishment of religious houses as well as the spiritual hierarchy of the Church from the lowest priest to the pope. Although for centuries the Roman Catholic Church had met doctrinal challenges and had absorbed many seemingly unorthodox ideas, Luther's theology could not be among them. It struck too deeply at the roots of belief, practice, and structure. If Luther was right, then the Roman Catholic Church must be wrong.

Yet for all of the transforming power of the apparently simple ideas, it was not Luther alone who initiated the reform of religion. Before Luther, countless thousands strove for salvation. Justification by faith alone provided an alternative to the combination of works and faith that many Roman Catholics found too difficult to fulfill. Luther's insistence that faith comes only through the study of the Word of God was facilitated by the new learning and the invention of printing. The printing press prepared the ground for the dissemination of his thought as much as it disseminated it. That was a result of the Renaissance. Luther's hope for the creation of a spiritual elite, confirmed in their faith and confident of their salvation, readily appealed to the citizens of hundreds of German towns who had already made of themselves a social and economic elite. That was a result of the growth of towns. The idea of the equality of all believers meant that all were equally responsible for fulfilling God's commandments. That set secular rulers on an equal footing with the pope at a moment in Western history when they were already challenging papal power in matters of both Church and state. That was a result of the formation of states. For all of the painful soul-searching by which he came to his shattering insight, there was embodied in Luther the culmination of changes of which he was only dimly aware.

Lutheranism

The first to feel the seriousness of Luther's challenge to the established order was the reformer himself. The head of his order, a papal legate, and finally the Emperor Charles V all called for Luther to recant his views on indulgences. Excommunicated by Pope Leo X in 1521, Luther was ordered by Charles V to appear before the diet, or assembly, in Worms. The emperor demanded that Luther retract his teachings. Infuriatingly, Luther replied that, if he could be shown the places in the Bible that contradicted his views, he would gladly change them. "I cannot and I will not retract anything, since it is neither safe nor right to go against conscience. I cannot do otherwise." In fact, during the three years between the posting of his theses and his appearance before the emperor, Luther came to conclusions much more radical than his initial attack on indulgences. Preparing to contend with papal representatives about the pope's right to issue indulgences, Luther came to believe that the papacy was a human rather than a divine invention. Therefore he denounced both the papacy and the general councils of the Church. In his *Address to the Christian Nobility of the German Nation* (1520), he called upon the princes to take the reform of religion into their own hands. No longer was there hope of compromise. Charles V declared Luther an enemy of the empire. In both Church and state he was now an outlaw.

But Luther had attracted powerful supporters as well as powerful enemies. Prince Frederick III of Saxony consistently intervened on his behalf, and the delicate international situation forced Luther's chief antagonists to move more slowly than they might have wanted. The pope hoped first to keep Charles V off the imperial throne and then to maintain a united front with the German princes against him. Charles V, already locked in his lifelong struggle with the French, needed German military support and peace in his German territories. Those factors consistently played into Luther's hands.

While pope and emperor were otherwise occupied, Luther refined his ideas and thus was able to hold his own in the theological debates in which he won important converts. More importantly, as time passed Luther's reputation grew, not only in Germany, but all over Europe. Between 1517 and 1520 he published 30 works, all of which achieved massive sales. Yet Luther alone could not sustain what came to be called Lutheranism. The Roman Catholic Church had met heresy before and knew how to deal with it. What turned Luther's theology into a movement—which after 1529 came to be known as Protestantism—was the support he received among German princes and within German cities.

Martin Luther, The German Mass

Princes and Cities.

There were many reasons that individual princes turned to Luther's theology. First and foremost was sincere religious conviction. Matters of the hereafter were a pressing concern in a world in which the average life span was 30 years and nearly all natural phenomena were inexplicable. And they were more pressing still among the educated elites inspired by the new learning and confident of their power to reason critically. Yet there were secular reasons as well. The formation of large states had provided a model for civil government. On a smaller scale, German princes worked to centralize their administration, protect themselves from predatory neighbors, and increase their revenues. They had long suffered under the burden of papal exactions. Taxes and gifts flowed south to a papacy dominated by Italians. Luther's call for civil rulers to lead their own churches meant that civil rulers could keep their own revenues.

The Reformation spread particularly well in the German cities, especially those the emperor had granted the status of freedom from the rule of any prince. Once Protestant ideas were established, entire towns adopted them. The cities had long struggled with the tension of the separate jurisdictions of state and Church. Much urban property was owned by the Church and thus exempt from taxation and law enforcement, and the clergy constituted a significant proportion of urban populations. Reformed religion stressed the equality of clergy and laity, and thus the indisputable power of civil authorities. Paradoxically, it was because the cities contained large numbers of priests that Luther's ideas reached them quickly. Many of his earliest students served urban congregations and began to develop doctrines and practices that, though based on Luther's ideas, were adapted to the circumstances of city life. The reform clergy became integrated into the life of the city in a way that the Catholic clergy had not. They married the daughters of citizens, became citizens themselves, and trained their children in the guilds. Moreover, the imperial free cities were also the center of the printing trade and home to many of the most noted humanists who were initially important in spreading Luther's ideas.

LUTHER ON MARRIAGE

Martin Luther wrote thousands of pages of theological and devotional literature in establishing a new religious movement. His simple style and everyday examples made his message accessible to hundreds of thousands of ordinary people. In this selection from his tract On Good Works *(1520), he compares the relationship of the husband and wife to that of the Christian and Christ.*

Focus Questions

Why are "good works" not of primary importance in a Christian's relationship with God? Does Luther leave a role for the Church in his ideal of the relationship between a Christian and God?

We can understand this whole matter [of good works] by an obvious human example. When husband and wife are fond of one another and live together in love and in confidence in one another, and each believes truly in the other, who shall teach them how they should act, what they should do or leave undone, say or not say, think or not think? Their own insight tells them all that need be, and more too. There is no distinction in their "works" for one another. They do the long, hard, and heavy tasks as willingly as the slight and easy things, and moreover they act with glad, peaceful, and secure hearts and are altogether free and unconstrained. But when doubt comes they begin to ask what is best, and begin to distinguish between their acts in order to gain the other's favor, and go about with troubled and heavy hearts, perhaps well-nigh in despair or driven to downright desperation.

So the Christian who lives in confidence toward God knows what things he should do, and does all gladly and freely, not with a view to accumulating merit and good works, but because it is his great joy to please God and to serve him without thought of reward, contented if he but do God's will. On the contrary, he who is not at one with God, or is in doubt, will begin to be anxious how he may satisfy God and justify himself by his works. He runs off on a pilgrimage to St. James of Compostella, to Rome, to Jerusalem—here, there, anywhere; prays to St. Bridget, or some other saint, fasts this day and that, confesses here and confesses there, asks this man and that, but finds no peace.

From Martin Luther, On Good Works.

Luther's message held great appeal for the middle orders in the towns. While it was necessary for the leader of a state to support reform if it was to survive, in the cities it was the petty burghers, lesser merchants, tradesmen, and artisans who led the movements that ultimately gained the approval of city governments. The groups resented the privileges given to priests and members of religious orders who paid no taxes and were exempt from the obligations of citizenship. The level of anticlericalism, always high in Germany, was especially acute in cities that were suffering economic difficulties. Pressure from ordinary people and petty traders forced town leaders into action. The evangelism of reforming ministers created converts and an atmosphere of reform. Support from members of the ruling oligarchy both mobilized the pressures and capitalized upon them. Town governments secured their own autonomy over the Church, tightening their grip upon the institutions of social control and enhancing the social and economic authority of their members. Once Protestant, city governments took over many of the religious houses, often converting them into schools or hostels for the poor. Former monks were allowed to enter trades and to become citizens. Former nuns were encouraged to marry. Luther himself married an ex-nun after the dissolution of her convent.

The Appeal for Women.   Religious reform appealed to women as well as men, but it affected them differently. Noblewomen were among the most important defenders of Protestant reformers, especially in states in which the prince opposed it. Marguerite of Navarre (1492–1549), sister of Francis I, frequently intervened with her brother on behalf of individual Lutherans who fell afoul of Church authorities. She created her own court in the south of France and stocked it with both humanists and Protestants. Her devotional poem *Mirror of the Sinful Soul* (1533) inspired women reformers and was translated into English by Elizabeth I. Mary of Hungary (1505–1558) served a similar role in the Holy Roman Empire. Sister of both Charles V and Ferdinand I, queen of Hungary, and later regent of the Netherlands, she acted as patron to Hungarian reformers. Although Mary was more humanist than Protestant, Luther dedicated an edition of the Psalms to her, and she read a number of his works. Her independent religious views infuriated both of her brothers. Bona (1493–1558), wife of Sigismund I of Poland, was especially important in eastern reform. An Italian by birth, Bona was a central figure in spreading both Renaissance art and humanist learning in Poland. She became one of the largest independent landowners in the state and initiated widespread agricultural and economic reforms. Her private confessor was one of Poland's leading Protestants.

Luther's reforms also offered much to women who were not so highly placed in society. The doctrine of the equality of all believers put men and women on an equal spiritual footing, even if it did nothing to break the male monopoly of the ministry. But the most important difference that Protestantism made to ordinary women was in the private rather than the public sphere. Family life became the center of faith when sal-

■ A portrait of Marguerite de Valois, queen of Navarre, the cultured and talented sister of King Francis I.

vation was removed from the control of the Church. Luther's marriage led him to a deeper appreciation of the importance of the wife and mother in the family's spirituality. "Next to God's word there is no more precious treasure than holy matrimony."

By following humanist teaching on the importance of educating women of the upper orders and by encouraging literacy, the reformers did much that was uplifting. Girls' schools were founded in a number of German cities, and townswomen could use their newly acquired skills in their roles as shopkeepers, family accountants, and teachers of their children. But there were losses as well as gains. The attack on the worship of saints, and especially of the Virgin Mary, removed female images from religion. Protestantism was male dominated in a way that Catholicism was not. Moreover, the emphasis upon reading the Bible tended to reinforce the image of women as weak and inherently sinful. The dissolution of the convents took away from women the one institution that valued their gender and allowed them to pursue a spiritual life outside marriage.

The Spread of Lutheranism

By the end of the 1520s, the Holy Roman Empire was divided between cities and states that accepted reformed religion and those that adhered to Roman Catholicism. Printing presses, traveling merchants, and hordes of students who claimed—not always accurately—to have attended Luther's lectures or sermons spread the message. Large German communities across northern Europe, mostly founded as trading outposts, became focal points for the penetration of reformist ideas. In Livonia, the Teutonic Knights established a Lutheran form of worship that soon took hold all along the shores of the Baltic. Lutheran-inspired reformers seized control of the Polish port city of Gdansk, which they held for a short time, while neighboring Prussia officially established a Lutheran church. Polish translations of Luther's writings were disseminated into Poland-Lithuania, and Protestant communities were established as far south as Krakow.

Merchants and students carried Luther's ideas into Scandinavia, but there the importance of political leaders was crucial. Christian III (1534–1559) of Denmark had been present at the Diet of Worms when Luther made his famous reply to Charles V. Christian was deeply impressed by the reformer, and after a ruinous civil war, he confiscated the property of the Catholic Church in Denmark and created a reformed religion under Luther's direct supervision.

Paradoxically, Lutheranism came to Sweden as part of an effort to throw off the yoke of

MAP DISCOVERY

Intensity of green represents the approximate strength of Lutheranism

The Spread of Lutheranism

Observe the extent of Lutheranism across Europe in the sixteenth century. Where was Lutheranism concentrated? Notice how Lutheranism swept through entire states. How was Europe divided between Protestants and Catholics?

Danish dominance. There, too, direct connection with Luther provided the first impulses. Olaus Petri (1493–1552) had studied at Wittenberg and returned to preach Lutheran doctrine among the large German merchant community in Stockholm. He was a trained humanist who used both Erasmus's Greek New Testament and Luther's German one to prepare his Swedish translation (1526). When Gustav I Vasa (1523–1560) led a successful uprising against the Danes and became king of Sweden, he encouraged the spread of Protestant ideas and allowed Petri to continue his Swedish translations of the mass and the Lutheran service. Under the protection of the monarchy, Lutheranism flourished in Scandinavia, where it remains the dominant religion to this day.

As important as Protestant ideas were in northern and central Europe, it was in the Swiss towns of the Holy Roman Empire that they proved most fertile. Here was planted the second generation of reformers, theologians who drew radical new conclusions from Luther's insights. In the east, Huldrych Zwingli (1484–1531) brought reformed religion to the town of Zürich. Educated at the University of Basel and deeply influenced by humanist thought early in his career, Zwingli was a preacher among the Swiss mercenary troops that fought for the empire. In 1516, he met Erasmus in Basel and under his influence began a study of the Greek writings of the Church fathers and of the New Testament. Zwingli was also influenced by reports of Luther's defiance of the pope, for his own

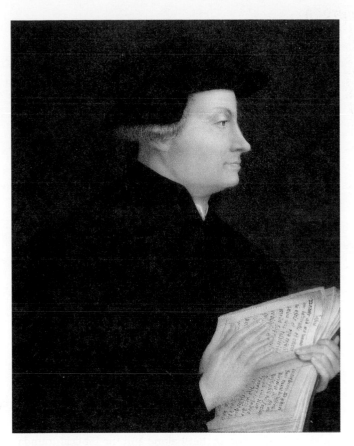

■ Huldrych Zwingli was a scholarly humanist deeply influenced by Erasmus. He led the Reformation in Zürich, the most important Swiss town.

antipapal views were already developing. Perhaps most decisively for his early development, in 1519 Zwingli was stricken by plague. In his life-and-death struggle he came to a profoundly personal realization of the power of God's mercy.

Those experiences became the basis for the reform theology Zwingli preached in Zürich. He believed that the Church had to recover its earlier purity and to reject the innovations in practices brought in by successive popes and general councils. He stressed the equality of believers, justification by faith alone, and the sufficiency of the gospel as authority for church practice. He attacked indulgences, penance, clerical celibacy, prayers to the Virgin, statues and images in churches, and a long list of other abuses. He also stressed that the mass was to be viewed as a commemorative event rather than one that involved the real presence of Christ. He preferred to call the service the Lord's Supper. His arguments were so effective that the town council adopted them as the basis for a reform of religion.

The principles Zwingli preached quickly spread to neighboring Swiss states. He participated in formal religious disputations in both Bern and Basel. In both places, his plea for a simple, unadorned religious practice met widespread approval. Practical as well as theological, Zwingli's reforms were carried out by the civil government with which he allied himself. That

was not the same as the protection that princes had given to Lutherans. Rather, in the places that came under Zwingli's influence there was an important integration of church and state. Zwingli organized a formal military alliance of the Protestant Swiss towns. For him, the Bible carried a social message, and it is fitting that he died on the battlefield defending the state. He stressed the divine origins of civil government and the importance of the magistrate as an agent of Christian reform: "A church without the magistrate is mutilated and incomplete." That theocratic idea—that the leaders of the state and the leaders of the church were linked together—became the basis for further social and political reform.

THE PROTESTANT REFORMATION

By the middle of the 1530s, Protestant reform had entered a new stage. Luther did not intend to form a new religion; his struggle had been with Rome. Before he could build, he had to tear down—his religion was one of protest. Most of his energy was expended in attack and counterattack. The second generation of reformers faced a different task. The new reformers were the church builders who had to systematize doctrine for a generation that had already accepted religious reform. Their challenge was to draw out the logic of reformed ideas and to create enduring structures for reformed churches. The problems they faced were as much institutional as doctrinal. How was the new church to be governed in the absence of the traditional hierarchy? How could discipline be enforced when members of the reformed community went astray? What was the proper relationship between the community of believers and civil authority? Whatever the failings of the Roman Catholic Church, it had ready answers to those critical questions. The first generation of reformers had thrown out the stagnant bathwater of ecclesiastical abuses; it was left to the second generation to discover if they had thrown out the baby and the bathtub as well.

Geneva and Calvin

The Reformation came late to Geneva. In the sixteenth century, Geneva was under the dual government of the Duchy of Savoy, which owned most of the surrounding rural areas, and the Catholic bishop of the town, who was frequently a Savoy client. The Genevans also had their own town council, which traditionally struggled for power against the bishop. By the 1530s the council had gained the upper hand. The council confiscated Church lands and institutions, secularized the Church's legal powers, and forced the bishop and most of his administrators to flee the city. War with Savoy inevitably followed, and Geneva would certainly have been crushed into submission had it not been for its alliance with neighboring Bern, a potent military power among the Swiss towns.

Geneva was saved and was free to follow its own course in religious matters. Under Zwingli's influence, Bern had become Protestant, and it might have been expected that Geneva

■ John Calvin, who published a major theological and political polemic and developed an alternative to Lutheranism before he turned thirty, is shown here as a young man.

would adopt that model even though French rather than German was the predominant language of the city. Some Protestant preachers arrived in Geneva to propagate reformed religion, and after a public disputation the town council abolished the mass. In 1536, the adult male citizens of the city voted to become Protestant. But as yet there was no reformer in Geneva to establish a Protestant program and no clear definition of what that program might be.

Martin Luther had started out to become a lawyer and ended up a priest. John Calvin started out to become a priest and ended up a lawyer. The difference tells much about each man. Calvin (1509–1564) was born in France, the son of a bishop's secretary. His education was based on humanist principles, and he learned Greek and Hebrew, studied theology, and received a legal degree from the University of Orléans. Around the age of 20 he converted to Lutheranism. He described the experience as "unexpected," but it had predictable results. Francis I had determined to root Protestants out of France, and Calvin fled Paris. Persecution of Protestants continued in France, and one of Calvin's close friends was burned for heresy. The events left an indelible impression upon him. In 1535, he left France for Basel, where he wrote and published the first edition of his *Institutes of the Christian Religion* (1536), a defense of French Protestants against persecution. Directed toward Francis I, it set out "the whole sum of godliness and whatever it is necessary to know of

the doctrine of salvation." Calvin returned briefly to France to wind up his personal affairs and then decided to settle in Strasbourg, where he could retire from public affairs and live out his days as a scholar.

To Calvin, providence guided all human action. He could have no better evidence for that belief than what happened next. War between France and the Holy Roman Empire clogged the major highways to Strasbourg. Soldiers constantly menaced travelers, and Protestants could expect the worst from both sides. Thus Calvin and his companions detoured around the armies and passed through Geneva. How Calvin's presence there came to be known remains a mystery, but when Guillaume Farel (1489–1565), one of Geneva's leading Protestant reformers, heard of it, he quickly made his way to the inn where Calvin was staying. Farel implored Calvin to remain in Geneva and lead its reformation. Calvin was not interested. Farel tried every means of persuasion he knew until, in exasperation, Farel declared that God would curse Calvin's retirement if, Calvin wrote, "I should withdraw and refuse to help when the necessity was so urgent. By this imprecation I was so terror-struck that I gave up the journey that I had undertaken." For a quarter of a century, Calvin labored to bring order to the Genevan church.

Calvin's greatest contributions to religious reform came in church structure and discipline. He had studied the writings of the first generation of reformers and accepted without question justification by faith alone and the biblical foundation of religious authority. Like Luther and Zwingli, he believed that salvation came from God's grace. But more strongly than his predecessors he believed that the gift of faith was granted only to some and that each individual's salvation or damnation was predestined before birth. "We call predestination God's eternal decree. For all are not created in equal condition; rather, eternal life is fore-ordained for some, eternal damnation for others." The doctrine of **predestination** was a traditional one, but Calvin emphasized it differently and brought it to the center of the problem of faith. "Many are called but few are chosen," Calvin quoted from the Bible. Those who were predestined to salvation, "the elect," were obliged to govern; those who were predestined to damnation were obliged to be governed. Thus, for the church that Calvin erected, discipline was the central concern.

DOCUMENT

Calvin on Predestination

Calvin structured the institution of the Genevan church in four parts. First were the pastors who preached the Word to their congregations. There were fewer than 10 pastors in Geneva in the early 1540s and fewer than 20 by the time of Calvin's death—a far cry from the 500 priests who had administered the sacraments there under Catholicism. While the pastors preached, the doctors, the second element in Calvin's church, studied and wrote. The doctors were scholars who mastered the difficult portions of the Bible and who increased the stock of learned pastors by their teaching. In the beginning, Calvin was the only Genevan doctor, but after he helped to establish the University of Geneva in 1559, there was a ready supply of learned theologians.

THE ETERNAL DECREE

John Calvin was born in France but led the Reformation in the Swiss town of Geneva. He was one of the leaders of the second generation of reformers, whose task was to refine the structure of church doctrine. Calvinism was propounded in his Institutes of the Christian Religion *(1534), from which this section on the doctrine of predestination is taken.*

Focus Questions

According to Calvin, why is everyone contaminated by sin? What power do humans have over their spiritual destiny?

We must be content with this—that such gifts as it pleased the Lord to have bestowed upon the nature of man he vested in Adam; and therefore when Adam lost them after he had received them, he lost them not only from himself but also from us all. . . . Therefore from a rotten root rose up rotten branches, which sent their rottenness into the twigs that sprang out of them; for so were the children corrupted in their father that they in turn infected their children. . . .

And the apostle Paul himself expressly witnesseth that therefore death came upon all men, because all men have sinned and are wrapped in original sin and defiled with the spots thereof. And therefore the very infants themselves, since they bring with them their own damnation from their mothers' womb, are bound not by another's but by their own fault. For although they have not as yet brought forth the fruits of their own iniquity, yet they have the seeds thereof enclosed within them; yea, their whole nature is a certain seed of sin, therefore it cannot but be hateful and abominable to God. . . .

Predestination we call the eternal decree of God, whereby he has determined with himself what he wills to become of every man. For all are not created to like estate; but to some eternal life and to some eternal damnation is foreordained. Therefore as every man is created to the one or the other end, so we say that he is predestinate either to life or to death.

From John Calvin, *Institutes of the Christian Religion.*

Pastors and doctors made up the top tier of the official church; deacons and elders the lower. Deacons, the third element in Calvin's four-part structure, were laymen chosen by the congregation to oversee the institutions of social welfare run by the church. Those institutions included the hospitals and schools that cared for the sick and the poor and instructed the young. The last element was the elders of the church, who were its governors in all moral matters. They were the most controversial part of Calvin's establishment and the most fundamental. They had the power to discipline. Chosen from among the elite of the city, the 12 elders enforced the strict Calvinist moral code that extended into all aspects of private life. The elders and the pastors met each week in a body known as the consistory to examine violations of God's laws; for them was reserved the ultimate sanction of excommunication. Offenses ranged from trivial superstitions—a woman wrapping a walnut containing a spider around the neck of her sick husband—to cases of blasphemy. Sexual offenses were the most common. Adultery and fornication were vigorously suppressed, and prostitutes, who had nearly become a recognized guild in the early sixteenth century, were expelled from Geneva.

The structure that Calvin gave to the Genevan church soon became the basis for reforms throughout the Continent. The Calvinist church was self-governing, independent of the state, and therefore capable of surviving and even flourishing in a hostile environment. Expanded in several subsequent editions, *Institutes of the Christian Religion* became the most influential work of Protestant theology. It had begun as an effort to extend Protestantism to France, and Calvin never abandoned hope that his homeland would be converted. Waves of Calvinist-educated pastors returned to France in the mid-sixteenth century and established churches along Calvinist lines. Calvinism spread north to Scotland and the Low Countries, where it became the basis for Dutch Protestantism, and east to Poland, where it flourished in Lithuania and Hungary. It reached places untouched by Luther and revitalized reform where Lutheranism had been suppressed. Perhaps its greatest impact was in Britain, where the Reformation took place not once but twice.

The English Reformation

The king of England wanted a divorce. Henry VIII had been married to Catherine of Aragon (1485–1536) as long as he had been king, and she had borne him no male heir to carry on his line. Catherine of Aragon had done her duty: in ten years she had given birth to six children and endured several miscarriages. Yet only one daughter, Mary, survived. Nothing so important as the lack of a male heir could happen by accident, and Henry came to believe that it was God's punishment for his marriage. Catherine had been married first to Henry's older brother, who had died as a teenager, and there was at least one scriptural prohibition against marrying a brother's wife. A papal dispensation had been provided for the marriage, and now Henry wanted a papal dispensation for an annulment. For three years his case ground its way through the papal courts. Catherine of Aragon was the aunt of the

An allegorical painting of Edward VI triumphing over the Pope, shown lying at the king's feet. To Edward's left is his Privy Council. His father, Henry VIII, gestures to the young king from his deathbed.

Emperor Charles V, and the emperor had taken her side in the controversy. With imperial power in Italy at its height, the pope was content to hear all of the complex legal and biblical precedents argued at leisure.

By 1533, Henry could wait no longer. He had already impregnated Anne Boleyn (ca. 1507–1536), one of the ladies-in-waiting at his court. If the child—which Henry was certain would be a boy—was to be legitimate, a marriage would have to take place at once. Legislation was prepared in Parliament to prevent papal interference in the decisions of England's courts, and Thomas Cranmer (1489–1556), archbishop of Canterbury, England's highest ecclesiastical officer, agreed to annul Henry's first marriage and celebrate his second. That was the first step in a complete break with Rome. Under the guidance of Thomas Cromwell (ca. 1485–1540), the English Parliament passed statute after statute that made Henry supreme head of the church in England and owner of its vast wealth. Monasteries were dissolved and a Lutheran service was introduced. England's first reformation came as a result of the "King's Great Matter." On 7 September 1533, Anne Boleyn gave birth not to the expected son, but to a daughter, the future Queen Elizabeth I.

The Church of England.   Henry's reformation was an act of state, but the English Reformation was not. There was an English tradition of dissent from the Roman Church that stretched back to the fourteenth century and that had survived even the most determined efforts to suppress it. Anticlericalism was especially virulent in the towns, where citizens refused to pay fees to priests for performing services such as burial. And humanist ideas flourished in England, where Thomas More, John Colet, and a host of others sup-

ported both the new learning and its efforts to reform spiritual life. The English were as susceptible as other Europeans to Luther's ideas, which crossed the Channel with German merchants and English travelers. Luther's attack on ritual and the mass and his emphasis on Scripture and faith found many recruits in London and the northern port towns.

Protestantism had grown slowly in England because it had been vigorously repressed. Like Francis I and Charles V, Henry VIII had viewed actual attacks on the established church as potential attacks on the established state. The consolidation of the Tudor monarchy was too recent for him not to be concerned with its stability. Henry had earned the title "Defender of the Faith" from the pope in 1521 for authoring an attack on Luther. Bonfires of Lutheran books had lighted the English skies. Small groups of Protestants at Cambridge and Oxford universities had been sniffed out and hunted down by Henry's agents. Some had made public recantations; some had fled to the Continent; one—Thomas Bilney—went to the stake. The first published English translation of the New Testament, made by William Tyndale in 1525, had to be smuggled into England. As sensitivity to the abuses of the Church grew and Lutheran ideas spread, official censorship and persecution sharpened.

Henry's divorce unleashed a groundswell of support for religious change. The king's own religious beliefs remained a secret, but Anne Boleyn and Thomas Cromwell sponsored Lutheran reforms and Thomas Cranmer put them into practice. Religion was legislated through Parliament, and the valuable estates of the Church were sold to the gentry. The practices found favor with both the legal profession and the landed elites and made Protestantism more palatable among those conservative groups. It was in the reign of Edward VI

TEMPLE DE LYON, NOMME PARADIS.

■ This painting depicts a Calvinist service in Lyon, France, in 1564. The men and women are segregated, and the worshipers are seated according to rank. An hourglass times the preacher's sermon.

Pilgrimage of Grace, posed the most serious threat to the English Crown since the Wars of the Roses. Gentry and common people opposed the dissolution of the monasteries and feared for provision for their spiritual needs. Henry's ability to suppress the Pilgrimage of Grace owed more to his political power than to the conversion of his governing classes to Protestantism. Edward VI's government faced a similar uprising in 1549 when it attempted to introduce a new and more Protestant prayer book. Catholicism continued to flourish in England, surviving underground during the reigns of Henry and Edward and reemerging under Mary I (1553–1558).

The Successors of Henry VIII.   Mary Tudor was her mother's child. The first woman to rule England, she held to the Catholic beliefs in which Catherine of Aragon had raised her, and she vowed to bring the nation back to her mother's church. When Edward VI died, the English ruling elite opted for political legitimacy rather than religious ideology in supporting Mary against a Protestant pretender to the throne. The new queen was as good as her word. She reestablished papal sovereignty, abolished Protestant worship, and introduced a crash program of education in the universities to train a new generation of priests. The one thing that Mary could not achieve was restoration of monastic properties and Church lands: they had been scattered irretrievably and any attempt at confiscation from the landed elite would surely have been met with insurrection. Mary had to be content with reestablishing orthodoxy. She fought fire with fire. Catholic retribution for the blood of their martyrs was not long in coming. Cranmer and three other bishops were burned for heresy, and more than 270 others, mostly commoners, were consigned to the flames.

Nearly 800 Protestants fled the country rather than suffer a similar fate. The Marian exiles, as they came to be called, settled in a number of reformed communities, Zürich, Frankfurt, and Geneva among them. There they imbibed the second generation of Protestant ideas, especially Calvinism, and from there they began a propaganda campaign to keep reformed religion alive in England. It was the Marian exiles who were chiefly responsible for the second English reformation, which began in 1558 when Mary died and her half-sister, Elizabeth I (1558–1603), came to the throne.

Under Elizabeth, England returned to Protestantism. The rapid reversals of established religion were more than disconcerting to laity and clergy alike. Imagine the experience of ordinary churchgoers. For all their lives they had prayed to the Virgin Mary for aid and comfort. One day all images of the Virgin disappeared from the church. The Latin mass was re-

(1547–1553), Henry's son by his third wife, that the central doctrinal and devotional changes were made. Although they were Protestant in tenor, there remained compromises and deliberate ambiguities. The chantries were abolished, and with them masses for the dead. Church service was now conducted in English, and the first two English prayer books were created. The mass was reinterpreted along Zwinglian lines and became the Lord's Supper, the altar became the communion table, and the priest became the minister. Preaching became the center of the church service, and concern over the education of learned ministers resulted in commissions to examine and reform the clergy.

Beginning in the 1530s, state repression turned against Catholics. Those who would not swear the new oaths of allegiance or recognize the legality of Henry VIII's marriage suffered for their beliefs as the early Protestants had suffered for theirs. Thomas More and more than 40 others paid with their lives for their opposition. Others took up arms against the government, marrying economic and political grievances to religious ones. An uprising in the north in 1536, known as the placed by a whole new English service. Then the Latin mass returned and back came the images of the Virgin. Five years later the Virgin was gone again and the English service was restored. Imagine the plight of a clergyman who questioned the vow of chastity in the 1540s. Prohibited from marrying under Henry VIII, he was encouraged to marry under Edward VI. When Mary came to the throne, he had to put his wife aside and deny the legitimacy of his children. At Elizabeth's accession he was married again—if he could find his wife and if she had not taken another husband. The Elizabethan reforms put an end to those uncertainties.

But what was reestablished was not what had come before. Even the most advanced reforms during Edward's reign now seemed too moderate for the returning exiles. Against Elizabeth's wishes, the English church adopted the Calvinist doctrine of predestination and the simplification (but not wholesale reorganization) of the structure of the church. But it did not become a model of thoroughgoing reformation. The Thirty-nine Articles (1563) continued the English tradition of compromising points of disputed doctrine and of maintaining traditional practices wherever possible. The Calvinism that the exiles learned abroad was more demanding than the Calvinism that the queen practiced at home.

The Reformation of the Radicals

Schism breeds schism. That was the stick with which Catholic Church and civil authorities beat Luther from the beginning. By attacking the authority of the established church and flouting the authority of the established state, he was fomenting social upheaval. It was a charge to which he was particularly sensitive. He insisted that his own ideas buttressed rather than subverted authority, especially civil authority, under whose protection he had placed the Church. As early as 1525, peasants in Swabia appealed to Luther for support in their social rebellion. They based some of their most controversial demands, such as the abolition of tithes and labor service, on biblical authority. Luther offered them no comfort. "Let every person be subject to the governing authorities with fear and reverence," he quoted from the Bible while instructing rebels to lay down their arms and await their just rewards in heaven.

■ This engraving from the *Chronicle of the Peasants' War* by Abbot Murer presents a Catholic interpretation of the peasants' actions as they pillaged the Monastery of Weissenau.

■ Anabaptist leaders persecuted at Münster endured the torture of being confined in cages hung from the church belfry.

But Luther's ideas had a life of their own. He clashed with Erasmus over free will and with Zwingli over the mass. Toward the end of his life he felt he was holding back the floodgates against the second generation of Protestant thinkers. Time and again serious reformers wanted to take one or another of his doctrines further than he was willing to go himself. The water was seeping in everywhere.

The most dangerous threat to the establishment of an orthodox Protestantism came from groups who were described, not very precisely, as **Anabaptists.** *Anabaptist* was a term of abuse. Although it identified people who practiced adult baptism—literally, "baptism again"—the label was mainly used to tar religious opponents with the brush of extremism. For more than a hundred years it defined the outcast from the Protestant fold. New ideas were branded Anabaptist to discredit them; religious enthusiasts were labeled Anabaptists to expel them. Catholics and Protestants both used the term to describe what they were not, and thereby defined what they were.

Anabaptists appeared in a number of German and Swiss towns in the 1520s. Taking seriously the doctrine of justification by faith, Anabaptists argued that only believers could be members of the true church of God. Those who were not of God could not be members of his church. While Catholics, Lutherans, and Calvinists incorporated all members of society into the church, Anabaptists excluded all but true believers. Anabaptists reasoned that baptism was a sacrament for adults rather than infants. Although the practice was as much symbolic as substantive, it was a practice that horrified others. Infant baptism was a core doctrine for both Catholics and Protestants. It was one of only two sacraments that remained in reformed reli-

gion. It symbolized the acceptance of Christ, and without it eternal salvation was impossible. Luther, Zwingli, and Calvin agreed that infant baptism was biblical in origin and all wrote vigorously in its defense. It was a doctrine with practical import. Unbaptized infants who died could not be accepted in heaven, and infant mortality was appallingly common.

Thus the doctrine of Anabaptism posed a psychological as well as a doctrinal threat to the reformers. But the practice of adult baptism paled in significance to many of the other conclusions that religious radicals derived from the principle of *sola scriptura*—by the Word alone. Some groups argued the case that since true Christians were only those who had faith, all others must be cast out of the church. Those true Christians formed small separate sects. Many believed that their lives were guided by the Holy Spirit, who directed them from within. Both men and women could give testimony of revelations that appeared to them or of mystical experiences. Some went further and denied the power of civil authority over true believers. They would have nothing to do with the state, refusing to pay taxes, perform military obligations, or give oaths: "The Sword must not be used by Christians even in self-defense. Neither should Christians go to law or undertake magisterial duties." Some argued for the community of goods among believers and rejected private property. Others literally followed passages in the Old Testament that suggested polygamy and promiscuity.

Wherever they settled, the small bands of believers were persecuted to the brutal extent of the laws of heresy. Catholics burned them, Protestants drowned them, and they were stoned and clubbed out of their communities. Although Anabaptists were never a large group within the context of the

Protestant churches, they represented an alternative to mainstream views—whether Lutheran or Calvinist—that was both attractive and persistent. There was enough substance in their ideas and enough sincerity in their patient sufferings that they continued to recruit followers as they were driven from town to town, from Germany into the Swiss cities, from Switzerland into Bohemia and Hungary.

There, on the eastern edges of the Holy Roman Empire, the largest groups of Anabaptists finally settled. Although all practiced adult baptism, only some held goods in common or remained pacifist. Charismatic leaders such as Balthasar Hubmaier (1485–1528) and Jacob Hutter (d. 1536) spread Anabaptism to Moravia in southern Bohemia, where they converted a number of the nobility to their views. They procured land for their communities, which came to be known as the Moravian Brethren. The Moravian Anabaptists ultimately split on the question of pacifism when the advancing Turkish armies posed the problem starkly. Anabaptists remained a target of offi-

cial persecution, and Hubmaier, Hutter, and a number of other leaders met violent deaths. But the Moravian communities were able to survive and to spread their movement throughout Hungary and Poland. Independent groups existed in England and throughout northwest Europe, where Menno Simons (1496–1561), a Dutch Anabaptist, spent his life organizing bands of followers who came to be known as Mennonites.

THE CATHOLIC REFORMATION

Like a rolling wave, Protestant reform slapped up across the face of Europe, but the rock of the Roman Catholic Church endured. Although pieces of the universal church crumbled away in northern Germany, Switzerland, Bohemia, Scandinavia, England, and Scotland, the dense mass remained in southern Germany, Italy, Poland-Lithuania, Spain, France, and Ireland. Catholics felt the same impulses toward a more

IMAGE DISCOVERY

Fishing for Souls

This allegorical painting by Adriaen van de Velde shows Protestants (on the left) and Catholics (on the right) vying for the souls of Christians. What does the painting indicate about the painter's view of the Reformation? In the water, parties from both banks try to drag men and women into their boats. What might entering a boat signify? The painter's use of fishing boats and water alludes to Jesus' promise to make his fisherman disciples "fishers of men." Would it have been unusual for an early modern painter to use biblical imagery in his work? Do you suppose Adriaen van de Velde would have used biblical imagery if he were not depicting a religious controversy?

fulfilling religious life as did Protestants and complained of the same abuses of clerical, state, and papal powers. But the Catholic response was to reform the Church from within. A new personal piety was stressed, which led to the founding of additional spiritual orders. The ecclesiastical hierarchy became more concerned with pastoral care and initiated reforms of the clergy at the parish level. The challenge of converting other races, Asians and Native Americans especially, led to the formation of missionary orders and to a new emphasis on preaching and education. Protestantism itself revitalized Catholicism. Pope and emperor met the challenge of religious reform with all of the resources at their disposal. If anything, Roman Catholicism was stronger at the end of the era of religious reformation than it had been at the beginning.

The Spiritual Revival

The quest for individual spiritual fulfillment dominated later medieval Roman Catholicism. Erasmus, Luther, and Zwingli were all influenced by a Catholic spiritual movement known as the **New Piety**. It was propagated in Germany by the Brethren of the Common Life, a lay organization that stressed the importance of personal meditation upon the life of Jesus. *The Imitation of Christ* (1427), the central text of the New Piety, commonly attributed to Thomas à Kempis

(1379–1471), was among the most influential works of the later Middle Ages, with 70 editions printed before 1500. The Brethren taught that a Christian life should be lived according to Jesus' dictates as expressed in the Sermon on the Mount. They instructed their pupils to lead a simple ascetic life with personal devotion at its core. Those were the lessons that the young Erasmus found so liberating and the young Luther so stifling.

The New Piety, with its emphasis on a simple personal form of religious practice, was a central influence upon Christian humanism. It is important to realize that humanism developed within the context of Catholic education and that many churchmen embraced the new learning and supported educational reform or patronized works of humanist scholarship. The Polyglot Bible, the first new translation project of the sixteenth century, was organized by Cardinal Jiménez de Cisneros (1436–1517), Archbishop of Toledo and Primate of Spain. The greatest educational reformer in England, John Colet (1467–1519), was dean of Saint Paul's, London's cathedral church. Without any of his famed irony, Erasmus dedicated his Greek Bible to the pope. Although they set out to reform education and to provide better texts through which Christian learning could be accomplished, the leading Christian humanists remained within the Catholic Church even after many of their criticisms formed the basis of Protestant reforms.

HEAVENLY VISION

Teresa of Ávila was a Carmelite nun whose life became a model of spirituality for Spanish Catholics in the seventeenth century. She founded a number of monasteries and convents and wrote popular devotional literature. Her autobiography was published after her death.

Focus Questions

How does Teresa explain God's sympathy for humans? How does she see God's manner as different from that of earthly rulers?

My love of, and trust in, our Lord, after I had seen Him in a vision, began to grow, for my converse with Him was so continual. I saw that, though He was God, He was man also; that He is not surprised at the frailties of men; that He understands our miserable nature, liable to fall continually, because of the first sin, for the reparation of which He had come. I could speak to Him as a friend, though He is my Lord, because I do not consider Him as one of our earthly lords, who affect a power they do not possess, who give audience at fixed hours, and to whom only certain persons may speak. If a poor man have any business with these, it will cost him many goings and comings, and currying favour with others, together with much pain and labour before he can speak to them. Ah, if such a one has business with a king! Poor people, not of gentle blood, cannot ap-

proach him, for they must apply to those who are his friends; and certainly these are not persons who tread the world under their feet; for they who do this speak the truth, fear nothing, and ought to fear nothing; they are not courtiers, because it is not the custom of a court, where they must be silent about those things they dislike, must not even dare to think about them, lest they should fall into disgrace.

O my Lord! O my King! who can describe Thy Majesty? It is impossible not to see that Thou art Thyself the great Ruler of all, that the beholding of Thy Majesty fills men with awe. But I am filled with greater awe, O my Lord, when I consider Thy humility and the love Thou hast for such as I am. We can converse and speak with Thee about everything whenever we will; and when we lose our first fear and awe at the vision of Thy Majesty, we have a greater dread of offending Thee—not arising out of the fear of punishment, O my Lord, for that is as nothing in comparison with the loss of Thee!

From *The Life of St. Teresa of Ávila* (1611).

The combination of piety and humanism imbued the ecclesiastical reforms initiated by Church leaders. Archbishop Jiménez de Cisneros, who also served as Inquisitor-General of the Spanish Inquisition, undertook a wide-ranging reorganization of Spanish religious life in the late fifteenth century. Although not every project was successful, Jiménez de Cisneros's program took much of the sting out of Protestant attacks on clerical abuse, and there was never a serious Protestant movement in Spain.

The most influential reforming bishop was Gian Matteo Giberti (1495–1543) of Verona. Like Jiménez de Cisneros, Giberti believed that a bishop must be a pastor rather than an administrator. After a period of service in Rome, Giberti returned to live in his diocese and made regular visits to all of its parishes. Using his own frugal life as an example, Giberti rigorously enforced vows, residency, and the pastoral duties of the clergy. "The priests in this diocese are marked men; the unworthy are removed from their offices; the jails are full of their concubines; sermons for the people are preached incessantly and study is encouraged," came the report after one of his tours. He founded almshouses to aid the poor and orphanages to house the homeless. In Verona, Giberti established a printing press, which turned out editions of the central works of Roman Catholicism, especially the writings of Augustine.

The most important indication of the reforming spirit within the Roman Church was the foundation of new religious orders in the early sixteenth century. Devotion to a spiritual life of sacrifice was the chief characteristic of the lay and clerical orders that had flourished throughout the Middle Ages. In one French diocese, the number of clergy quadrupled in the last half of the fifteenth century, and while entrants to the traditional orders of Franciscans and Dominicans did not rise as quickly, the growth of lay communities such as the Brethren of the Common Life attested to the continuing appeal of Catholic devotionalism.

Devotionalism was particularly strong in Italy, where new orders received papal charters. The Capuchins were founded by the Italian peasant Matteo de Bascio (ca. 1495–1552). He sought to follow the strictest rule of the life of Saint Francis of Assisi, a path that even the so-called Observant Franciscans had found too arduous. Bascio won admiration for his charitable works among the poor and the victims of the plague in the late 1520s and ultimately secured approval for the establishment of a small community devoted to penance and good works.

The spiritual revival spread all over Catholic Europe and was not limited to male orders. In Spain, Saint Teresa of Ávila (1515–1582) led the reform of the Carmelites. From an early age she had had mystical visions and had entered a convent near her home. But her real spiritual awakening came when she was 40. She believed that women had to withdraw totally from the world around them in order to achieve true devotion. Against the wishes of the male superiors of her order, she founded a convent to put her beliefs into practice and began writing devotional tracts such as *The Way of Perfection* (1583). Teresa was ultimately granted the right to establish convents throughout Castile, and she supervised the organi-

■ Gian Lorenzo Bernini, *The Ecstasy of St. Teresa.* In this work, depicting the ecstatic vision of St. Teresa of Ávila, the sixteenth-century Spanish Carmelite reformer, the saint floats toward heaven on seemingly weightless marble as an angel is about to pierce her breast with a burning arrow. The artist's creation depicts a mystic vision St. Teresa experienced and described in her writings.

zation of 16 religious houses for women. In 1535, Angela Merici (ca. 1474–1540) established another female order. The Ursulines were one of the most original of the new foundations, composed of young unmarried girls who remained with their families but lived chaste lives devoted to the instruction of other women. The group met monthly and submitted to the discipline of a superior, but otherwise they rejected both the cloistered monastic life and vows. The Ursuline movement, begun in northern Italy, spread into France and helped provide women with education and with moral role models.

Loyola's Pilgrimage

At first sight, Saint Ignatius Loyola (1491–1556) appears an unlikely candidate to lead one of the most vital movements for religious reform in the sixteenth century. The thirteenth child of a Spanish noble family, Loyola trained for a military life in the service of Castile. He began his career as an administrative official and then became a soldier. In 1521, he was one of the garrison defenders when the French besieged Pamplona. A cannonball shattered his leg, and he was carried home for a long enforced convalescence. There he slowly and carefully read the only books in the castle, a life of Jesus and a history of the saints. His reading inspired him. Before he had sought glory and renown in battle. But when he compared the truly heroic deeds of the saints to his own vainglorious exploits, he decided to give his life over to spirituality.

Loyola was not a man to do things by halves. He resolved to model his life on the sufferings of the saints about whom he had read. He renounced his worldly goods and endured a year-long regimen of physical abstinence and spiritual nourishment in the town of Manresa. He deprived himself of food and sleep for long periods and underwent a regimen of seven hours of daily prayer, supplemented by nearly continuous religious contemplation. "But when he went to bed, great enlightenment, great spiritual consolations often came to him, so that he lost much of the time he had intended for sleeping." During that period of intense concentration he first began to have visions, which later culminated in a mystical experience in which Jesus called him directly to his service.

Like Luther, Loyola was tormented by his inability to achieve grace through penance, but unlike Luther he redoubled his efforts. At Manresa, Loyola encountered *The Imitation of Christ*, which profoundly influenced his conversion. He recorded the techniques he used during this vigil in *The Spiritual Exercises*, which became a handbook for Catholic devotion. In 1523, crippled and barefoot, he made a pilgrimage to Jerusalem, where he intended to stay and battle the infidel. But he was dissuaded from that course and returned to Spain intent upon becoming a priest.

By this time, Loyola had adopted a distinctive garb that attracted both followers and suspicion. Twice the Spanish ecclesiastical authorities summoned him to be examined for heresy. In 1528, he decided to complete his studies in France. Education in France brought with it a broadening of horizons that was so important in the movement that Loyola was to found. He entered the same college that Calvin had just left, and it is more than likely that he came into contact with the Protestant and humanist ideas that were then in vogue. Given his own devotional experiences, Protestantism held little attraction. While in France, Loyola and a small group of his friends decided to form a brotherhood after they became priests. They devoted themselves to the cure of souls and took personal vows of poverty, chastity, and obedience to the pope. On a pilgrimage to Rome, Loyola and his followers again attracted the attention of ecclesiastical authorities. Loyola explained his mission to them and in 1540 won the approval of Pope Paul III to establish a new holy order, the Society of Jesus.

Ignatius Loyola, Rules for Thinking with the Church

Loyola's Society was founded at a time when the spiritual needs of the Church were being extended beyond the confines of Europe. Loyola volunteered his followers, who came to be known as Jesuits, to serve in the remotest parts of the world, and that offer was soon accepted. One disciple, Francis Xavier (1506–1552), was sent to Portugal, where he embarked on an expedition to the East. For ten years, Xavier made converts to Catholicism in the Portuguese port cities in the East, and then in India and Japan. Other Jesuits became missionaries to the New World, where they offered Christian consolation to the Native American communities. By 1556, the Society of Jesus had grown from 10 to 1000, and Loyola had become a full-time administrator in Rome.

Loyola never abandoned the military images that had dominated his youth. He thought of the world as an all-consuming struggle between the forces of God and Satan: "It is my will to conquer the whole world and all of my enemies." He enlisted his followers in military terms. The Jesuits were "soldiers of God" who served "beneath the banner of the Cross." Loyola's most fundamental innovation in those years

■ Rubens's (1577–1640) *The Miracles of Saint Ignatius Loyola*. Founder of the Society of Jesus, Loyola prepared his Jesuit recruits for an active, rather than a contemplative, life.

was the founding of schools to train recruits for his order. Jesuit training was rigorous. The period of the novitiate was extended and a second period of secular education was added. Since they were being prepared for an active rather than a contemplative life, Jesuits were not cloistered during their training. At first Loyola wanted to train only those who wanted to be missionaries. When that proved impractical, Jesuit schools were opened to the laity and lay education became one of the Jesuits' most important functions. Loyola lived to see the establishment of nearly a hundred colleges and seminaries and the spread of his order throughout the world. He died while at prayer.

The Counter-Reformation

The Jesuits were both the culmination of one wave of Catholic reform and the advance guard of another. They combined the piety and devotion that stretched from medieval mysticism through humanism, diocesan reforms, and the foundations of new spiritual orders. But they also represented an aggressive Catholic response that was determined to meet Protestantism head on and repel it—the **Counter-Reformation**. This was the Church Militant. Old instruments like the Inquisition were revived, and new weapons such as the Index of Prohibited Books were forged. But the problems of fighting Protestantism were not only those of combating Protestant ideas. Like oil and water, politics and religion failed to combine. The emperor and the hierarchy of the German church, where Protestantism was strong, demanded thoroughgoing reform of the Catholic Church; the pope and the hierarchy of the Italian church, where Protestantism was weak, resisted the call. As head of the Catholic Church, the pope was distressed by the spread of heresy in the lands of the empire. As head of a large Italian city-state, the pope was consoled by the weakening of the power of his Spanish rival. Brothers in Christ, pope and emperor were mortal enemies in everything else. Throughout the Catholic states of Germany

came the urgent cry for a reforming council of the Church. But the voices were muffled as they crossed the Alps and made their way down the Italian peninsula.

At the instigation of the emperor, the first serious preparations for a general council of the Church were made in the 1530s. The papacy warded it off. The complexities of interna-

■ The Council of Trent met from 1545–1563 and corrected a number of abuses of the Church, including the sale of indulgences, and stressed the obligations of priests and bishops to preach to their congregations. No concessions, however, were made to Protestants. This painting is attributed to Titian.

tional diplomacy were one factor—the French king was even less anxious to bring peace to the empire than was the pope—and the complexities of papal politics were another. The powers of a general council in relation to the powers of the papacy had never been clarified. Councils were usually the product of crises, and crises were never the best times to settle constitutional matters. Hard cases make bad law. After the advent and spread of Protestantism, successive popes had little reason to believe that in that gravest crisis of all a council would be mindful of papal prerogatives. In fact, Catholic reformers were as bitter in their denunciations of papal abuses as were Protestants. The second attempt to arrange a general council of the Church occurred in the early 1540s. Again the papacy warded it off.

Those factors ensured that when a general council of the Church did finally meet, its task would not be an easy one. The emperor wanted the council in Germany; the pope wanted it in Italy. The northern churches, French and German alike, wanted reforms of the papacy; the papacy wanted a restatement of orthodox doctrine. The Spanish church wanted reform along the principles set down by Jiménez de Cisneros—for example, that bishops must be made resident in their dioceses. The papacy needed bishops to serve as administrators in Rome. Many princes whose states were divided among Catholics and Protestants wanted compromises that might accommodate both. Ferdinand I, King of Bohemia, saw the council as an opportunity to bring the Hussites back into the fold. He wanted to allow the laity

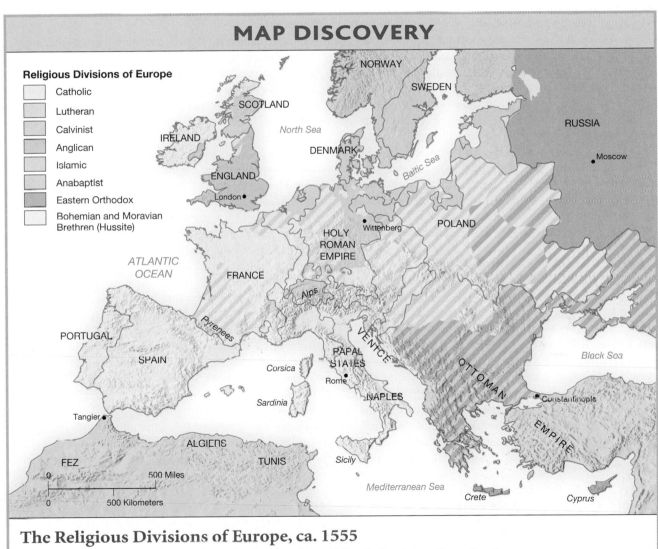

MAP DISCOVERY

Religious Divisions of Europe

- Catholic
- Lutheran
- Calvinist
- Anglican
- Islamic
- Anabaptist
- Eastern Orthodox
- Bohemian and Moravian Brethren (Hussite)

The Religious Divisions of Europe, ca. 1555

Which was the largest religious denomination by the middle of the sixteenth century? Which states were most at risk of internal religious warfare? Notice the difference in the ways in which Lutheranism and Calvinism spread. Where did Catholicism remain untouched by the new religions?

to take both the bread and the wine at communion and the clergy to marry. Charles V and the German bishops wanted the leading Protestant church authorities to offer their own compromises on doctrine that might form a basis for reuniting the empire. The papacy wanted traditional Church doctrine reasserted.

The general council of the Church that finally met in Trent from 1545 to 1563 thus had nearly unlimited potential for disaster. It began in compromise—Trent was an Italian town under the government of the emperor—but ended in total victory for the views of the papacy. For all of the papacy's seeming weaknesses—the defections of England and the rich north German territories cut into papal revenues and Italy was under Spanish occupation—an Italian pope always held the upper hand at the council. Fewer than a third of the delegates came from outside Italy. The French looked upon the council suspiciously and played only a minor role, and the emperor forbade his bishops to attend after the council moved to Bologna. While 270 bishops attended one or another of the council's sessions, 187 of them were Italians.

DOCUMENT

Council of Trent

Yet for all of the difficulties, the councillors at Trent made some real progress. They corrected a number of abuses, of which the sale of indulgences was the most substantive. They formulated rules for the better regulation of parish priests and stressed the obligation of priests and bishops to preach to their congregations. Following the work of Jiménez de Cisneros and Giberti, they emphasized the pastoral function of the clergy. On the heels of the success of the Jesuits, they ordered seminaries to be founded in all dioceses where there was not already a university so that priests could receive sufficient education to perform their duties. They prepared a new modern and uniform Catholic service and centralized and updated the Index of Prohibited Books to include Protestant writings from all over the Continent.

The Council of Trent made no concessions whatever to Protestants, moderate or radical. The councillors attempted to turn back every doctrinal innovation of the previous 40 years. Although Protestant theologians attended one of the council's sessions, their views were totally repudiated and efforts at compromise, which were supported by a number of Catholics on the council, were rejected. The councillors upheld justification by faith and works over justification by faith alone. They confirmed the truth of Scripture and the traditions of the Church against Scripture alone. They declared the Vulgate the only acceptable text of the Bible and encouraged vast bonfires of Greek and Hebrew Scriptures in an effort to undo the great scholarly achievements of the humanists. They reaffirmed the seven sacraments and the doctrine of the miracle of the Eucharist. They upheld clerical celibacy. The redefinition of traditional Roman Catholicism drew the doctrinal lines clearly and ended decades of confusion. But it also meant that the differences between Catholics and Protestants could now be settled only by the sword.

The Empire Strikes Back

Warfare dominated the reform of religion almost from its beginning. The burnings, drownings, and executions by which both Catholics and Protestants attempted to maintain religious purity were but raindrops compared to the sea of blood that was shed in sieges and on battlefields beginning in the 1530s. Neither side was capable of waging an all-out war against the other, but they fought intermittently for 25 years. The Catholic divisions were clear. The Holy Roman Empire continued to be engaged in the west with its archenemy France, and in the south with the ever-expanding Ottoman Empire. Charles V needed not only peace within his own German realms, but also positive support for his offensive and defensive campaigns. He could never devote his full resources to suppressing Protestant dissent.

Yet there was never a united Protestant front to suppress. The north German towns and principalities that accepted Lutheranism in the 1520s had had a long history of warfare among themselves. Princes stored up grievances from past wars and contested inheritances; cities stored up jealousies from commercial rivalries and special privileges. Added to that was the division between Luther and Zwingli over doctrinal issues that effectively separated the German and Swiss components of the Reformation from each other. Each faction formed its own political league, and the division almost certainly cost Zwingli his life in 1531, when Zürich was left to stand by itself against imperial allies.

Although both the Protestant and the Catholic sides were internally weak, it was the greater responsibilities of Charles V that allowed for the uneasy periods of peace. Each pause gave the Protestant reformers new life. Lutheranism continued to spread in the northern part of the Holy Roman Empire, and Zwinglian reform in the south. Charles V asked the papacy to convoke a general council and the Protestants to stop evangelizing in new territories. But Protestant leaders were no more capable of halting the spread of the Reformation than were Catholics. Thus each violation of each uneasy truce seemed to prove treachery. In 1546, just after Luther's death, both sides raised armies in preparation for renewed fighting. In the first stage of war, Charles V scored a decisive victory, capturing the two leading Protestant princes and conquering Saxony and Thuringia, the homeland of Lutheran reform.

MAP

Religious Diversity in Western Europe

Charles V's greatest victories were always preludes to his gravest defeats. The remaining Protestant princes were driven into the arms of the French, who placed dynastic interests above religious concerns. Again Europe was plunged into general conflict, with the French invading the German states from the west, the Turks from the south, and the Protestant princes from the north. Charles V, now an old and broken man, was forced to flee through the Alps in the dead of winter and was brought to the bargaining table soon after. Through the Peace of Augsburg in 1555, the emperor agreed to allow the princes of Germany to establish the religion of their people. Protestant princes would govern Protestant states, Catholic princes Catholic states. The Peace of Augsburg ended 40 years of religious struggle in Germany.

CONCLUSION

In 1547, the then-victorious Charles V stood at the grave of Martin Luther. Luther had been buried in the shadow of the church in which he had been baptized, and now other shadows darkened his plot. Imperial troops were masters of all Saxony and were preparing to turn back the religious clock in Luther's homeland. The emperor was advised to have Luther's body exhumed and burned to carry out 25 years too late the Edict of Worms that had made Luther an outlaw from church and state. But Charles V was no longer the self-confident young emperor who had been faced down by the Saxon monk on that long-ago day. Popes had come and gone, and his warrior rivals Francis I and Henry VIII were both dead. He alone survived. He had little stomach for the petty revenge that he might now exact upon the man who more than any other had ruined whatever hope there might have been for a united empire dominant over all of Europe. "I do not make war on dead men," Charles declared as he turned away from the reformer's grave. But the ghosts of Luther and Zwingli, of Calvin and Ignatius of Loyola were not so easily laid to rest. For another century, they would haunt a Europe that could do nothing else but make war on dead men.

QUESTIONS FOR REVIEW

1. How did humanism prepare the way for the Protestant Reformation?
2. What motivated Martin Luther?
3. What were the differences among the reforming ideas of Luther, Zwingli, and Calvin?
4. How did the Catholic Church respond to the challenges posed by the Protestant Reformation?

KEY TERMS

Anabaptists, *p. 399*

Christian humanism, *p. 382*

Counter-Reformation, *p. 404*

indulgences, *p. 387*

New Piety, *p. 401*

penance and confession, *p. 387*

predestination, *p. 394*

Reformation, *p. 379*

sola fide, *p. 389*

sola scriptura, *p. 379*

DISCOVERING WESTERN CIVILIZATION ONLINE

You can obtain more information about the reform of religion at the Websites listed below. See also the Companion Website that accompanies this text, www.ablongman.com/kishlansky, which contains an online study guide and additional resources.

The Lutheran Reformation

Lutherstadt Wittenberg, Martin Luther
www.wittenberg.de/e/seiten/personen/luther.html
A site devoted to Martin Luther and the city of Wittenberg. Texts of the famous Ninety-five Theses and other of Luther's writings as well as pictures of locations associated with the Lutheran reformation.

The Protestant Reformation

The Reformation Guide
www.educ.msu.edu/homepages/laurence/reformation/index.htm
The Reformation guide is the best starting place for information about all aspects of the Protestant Reformation. Dozens of links to follow.

Discovery and Reformation
www.wsu.edu/~dee/REFORM/REFORM.HTM
A primarily text-based site created by Washington State University, with profiles of key individuals and explanations of the issues at stake.

Project Wittenberg
www.iclnet.org/pub/resources/text/wittenberg/wittenberg-home.html
The home page of Project Wittenberg, containing a large number of texts (including hymns) by Luther and other Reformers.

Tudor History
tudorhistory.org/
A site with links to a variety of subjects relating to England under the Tudors. Biographies of the kings and queens, bibliographies, maps, and documents.

Reformation Picture Gallery
www.mun.ca/rels/hrollmann/reform/pics/pics.html
Contemporary pictures of leading reformers and the places associated with the Protestant Reformation. Excellent reproductions, especially from woodcuts.

Internet Modern History Sourcebook: Reformation Europe
www.fordham.edu/halsall/mod/modsbook02.html
Sources for both the Reformation and Counter-Reformation with links to other valuable sites.

SUGGESTIONS FOR FURTHER READING

General Reading
Owen Chadwick, *The Reformation* (London: Penguin Books, 1972). An elegant and disarmingly simple history of religious change.

Patrick Collinson, *The Reformation: A History* (New York: Modern Library, 2004). A recent, accessible account of early modern religious upheaval.

Diarmaid MacCulloch, *The Reformation* (London: Viking, 2003). A vastly impressive survey of the Reformation from a leading scholar.

Steven Ozment, *The Age of Reform, 1250–1550* (New Haven, CT: Yale University Press, 1980). An important interpretation of an epoch of religious change.

James D. Tracy, *Europe's Reformations, 1450–1650* (Rowman and Littlefield, 2005). A leading scholar examines intellectual, religious, political, and social processes that provoked religious reform and change.

The Intellectual Reformation

E. Eisenstein, *The Printing Revolution in Early Modern Europe* (Cambridge: Cambridge University Press, 1983). An abridged edition of a larger work that examines the impact of printing upon European society.

Adrian Johns, *The Nature of the Book: Print and Knowledge in the Making* (Chicago: University of Chicago Press, 1998). A major new synthesis with an unusual interpretation.

Anthony Levi, *Renaissance and Reformation: The Intellectual Genesis* (New Haven, CT: Yale, 2004) A new interpretation of European intellectual culture in the early modern period.

R. W. Scribner, *For the Sake of Simple Folk* (Cambridge: Cambridge University Press, 1994). A study of the impact of the Reformation on common people. Especially good on the iconography of reform.

James Tracy, *Erasmus of the Low Countries* (Berkeley: University of California, 1996). A brief biography of the great Dutch humanist.

The Lutheran Reformation

Roland Bainton, *Here I Stand* (New York: New American Library, 1968). The single most compelling biography of Luther.

Bernd Moeller, *Imperial Cities and the Reformation* (Durham, NC: Labyrinth Press, 1982). A central work that defines the connection between Protestantism and urban reform.

Heiko Oberman, *Luther: Man Between God and the Devil* (New York: Doubleday, 1992). English translation of one of the best German biographies of Luther. Sets Luther within the context of late medieval spirituality.

G. R. Potter, *Huldrych Zwingli* (New York: St. Martin's Press, 1984). A difficult but important study of the great Swiss reformer.

Lyndal Roper, *The Holy Household: Women and Morals in Reformation Augsburg* (Oxford: Oxford University Press, 1991). The best work to show the impact of the Reformation on family life and women.

R. W. Scribner, *The German Reformation* (Atlantic Highlands, NJ: Humanities Press, 1986). An excellent introduction, especially to the social history of the Reformation.

The Protestant Reformation

G.W. Bernard, *The King's Reformation: Henry VIII and the Remaking of the English Church* (New Haven, CT: Yale, 2005). An account of the decisive event in early modern English history, emphasizing King Henry's personal desire for reformed religion.

William Bouwsma, *John Calvin* (Oxford: Oxford University Press, 1988). A study that places Calvin within the context of the social and intellectual movements of the sixteenth century.

Claus-Peter Clasen, *Anabaptism, A Social History, 1525–1618* (Ithaca, NY: Cornell University Press, 1972). An important study of the Anabaptist movement.

A. G. Dickens, *The English Reformation*, 2d ed. (London: Batsford, 1989). The classic study of reform in England.

Peter Marshall, *Reformation England, 1480–1642* (Hodder Arnold, 2003). A lucid and thoughtful narrative of religious change in early modern England.

J. J. Scarisbrick, *Henry VIII* (Berkeley: University of California Press, 1968). The classic biography of the larger-than-life monarch.

The Catholic Reformation

Jean Delumeau, *Catholicism Between Luther and Voltaire* (Philadelphia: Westminster Press, 1977). An important reinterpretation of the Counter-Reformation.

Carlos Eire, *From Madrid to Purgatory* (Cambridge: Cambridge University Press, 1995). A brilliant study of the Spanish culture of death during the Counter-Reformation.

W. W. Meissner, *Ignatius of Loyola: The Psychology of a Saint* (New Haven, CT: Yale University Press, 1994). A searching study of the founding spirit of the Counter-Reformation.

John W. O'Malley, *Trent and All That: Renaming Catholicism in the Early Modern Era* (Cambridge, MA: Harvard University Press, 2000). A re-examination of Catholicism in the century surrounding the Council of Trent.

A. D. Wright, *The Counter-Reformation* (New York: St. Martin's Press, 1984). A comprehensive survey.

For a list of additional titles related to this chapter's topics, please see http://www.ablongman.com/kishlansky.

14

EUROPE AT WAR, 1555–1648

THE MASSACRE OF THE INNOCENTS
WAR AND EUROPEAN SOCIETY

THE VISUAL RECORD

"War is one of the scourges with which it has pleased God to afflict men," wrote Cardinal Richelieu (1585–1642), the French minister who played no small part in spreading the scourge. War was a constant of European society and penetrated to its very core. It dominated all aspects of life. It enhanced the power of the state; it defined gender roles; it consumed lives, treasure, and commodities ravenously. War affected every member of society from combatants to civilians. There were no innocent bystanders. Grain in the fields was destroyed because it was food for soldiers; houses were burned because they provided shelter for soldiers. Civilians were killed for aiding the enemy or holding out against demands for their treasure and supplies. Able-bodied men were taken forcibly to serve as conscripts, leaving women to plant and harvest as best they could.

There was nothing new about war in the middle of the sixteenth century. The early part of the century had witnessed the dynastic struggle between the Habsburgs and the House of Valois as well as the beginnings of the religious struggle between Catholics and Protestants. But the wars that dominated Europe from 1555 to 1648 brought together the worst of both of the conflicts. War was fought on a larger scale, it was more brutal and more expensive, and it claimed more victims, civilians and combatants alike. During this century, war extended throughout the Continent. Dynastic strife, rebellion, and international rivalries joined together with the ongoing struggle over religion. Ambition and faith were an explosive mixture. The French endured 40 years of civil war; the Spanish 80 years of fighting with the Dutch. The battle for hegemony in the east led to dynastic strife for decades on end as Poles, Russians, and Swedes pressed their rival claims to each other's crowns. Finally, in 1618, the separate theaters of war came together in one of the most brutal and terrifying episodes of destruction in European history: the Thirty Years' War.

Neither the ancient temple nor the Roman costume can conceal the immediacy of the picture shown here. It is as painful to look at now as it was when it was created more than 375 years

ago. Painted by Nicolas Poussin (1594–1665) at the height of the Thirty Years' War, *The Massacre of the Innocents* remains a horrifying composition of power, terror, and despair. The cruel and senseless slaughter of the innocent baby that is about to take place is echoed throughout the canvas. In the background between the executioner's legs can be seen a mother clasping her own child tightly and anticipating the fall of the sword. In the background on the right, another mother turns away from the scene and carries her infant to safety. In the foreground strides a mother holding her dead child. She tears at her hair and cries in anguish. To a culture in which the image of mother and child—of Mary and Jesus—was one of sublime peacefulness and inexpressible joy, the contrast could hardly be more shocking.

The picture graphically displays the cruelty of the soldier, the helplessness of the child, and the horror of the mother. By his grip on the mother's hair and his foot on the baby's throat, the warrior shows his brute power. The mother's futile effort to stop the sword illustrates her powerlessness. She scratches uselessly at the soldier's back. Naked, the baby boy raises his hands as if to surrender to the inevitable, as if to reinforce his innocence.

To study Europe at war, we must enter into a world of politics and diplomacy, of issues and principles, of judgment and error. We must talk about armies in terms of their cost and numbers, of generals in terms of their strategy and tactics, and of battles in terms of winners and losers. There can be no doubt that the future of Europe was decisively shaped by the century of wholesale slaughter during which dynastic and religious fervor finally ran its course.

LOOKING AHEAD

As we will see in this chapter, warfare in the seventeenth century decisively reshaped power relations of families and states. Protestantism survived after nearly a century of military challenge, and the power of the great Habsburg dynasty was finally crushed. In its place rose France, England, and Holland, and a new chapter of European conflict began.

■ Nicolas Poussin, *The Massacre of the Innocents* (1632–1634).

THE CRISES OF THE WESTERN STATES

"Un roi, une foi, une loi"—one king, one faith, one law. That was a prescription that members of all European states accepted without question in the sixteenth century. Society was an integrated whole, equally dependent upon monarchical, ecclesiastical, and civil authority for its effective survival. A European state could no more tolerate the presence of two churches than it could the presence of two kings. But the Reformation had created two churches.

In Germany, where the problem first arose, the Peace of Augsburg (1555) enacted the most logical solution. The religion of the ruler was to be the religion of the subjects. Princes, town governments, and bishops would determine faith. Not surprisingly, the policy was more convenient for rulers than for the ruled. Sudden conversions of princes, a hallmark of Protestantism, threw the state into disarray. Those closely identified with Catholicism and those who firmly believed in its doctrines had no choice but to move to a neighboring Catholic community and begin again. Given the dependence of ordinary people upon networks of kin and neighbors, enforced migration was devastating. Protestant minorities in Catholic states suffered the same fate. The enmity between the two groups came as much from bitter experience as from differences of belief.

Thus compromises that might have brought Protestants back into a reformed Catholic Church were doomed from the start. Doomed too was the practical solution of toleration. To the modern mind, toleration seems so logical that it is difficult to understand why it took over a century of bloodshed before it came to be grudgingly accepted by those countries most bitterly divided. But toleration was not a practical solution in a society that admitted no principle of organization other than one king, one faith. In such a world, toleration was even more threatening than warfare. Pope Clement VIII (1592–1605) described liberty of conscience as "the worst thing in the world." Those who advocated limited forms of toleration were universally despised. Those occasions during which toleration was a reluctant basis for a cease-fire were moments for catching breath before resuming the struggle for total victory. Only Poland-Lithuania, Hungary, and a few German states experimented with religious toleration during the sixteenth century.

■ This scene depicts the mistreatment of French Catholics by the Protestants in the town of Angoulême. They were deprived of all nourishment, dragged over a taut rope, and then slowly roasted at the stake.

The crises of the western European states that stretched from the middle of the sixteenth century to the middle of the seventeenth were as much internal and domestic as they were external and international. In France, a half century of religious warfare sapped the strength of both the monarchy and the nation. In Spain, the protracted revolt of the Netherlands drained men, money, and spirit from the most powerful nation in Europe. Decades of intermittent warfare turned the golden age of Spain to lead and hastened the decline of the Spanish Empire. Each crisis had its own causes and its own history. Yet it was no coincidence that they occurred together or that they starkly posed the conflict between the authority of the state and the conscience of the individual. The century between the Peace of Augsburg (1555) and the Peace of Westphalia (1648) was the century of total war.

The French Wars of Religion

No wars are more terrible than civil wars. They tear at the very fabric of society, rending its institutions and destroying the delicate web of relationships that underlie all communal life. The nation is divided; communities break into factions; families are destroyed. Civil wars are wars of passion. Issues become elevated into causes and principles that form the rallying cry of heroic self-sacrifice or wanton destruction. Civil wars feed on themselves. Each act of war becomes an outrage to be revenged, each act of revenge a new outrage. Passions run deep and, however primitive, the rules for the civilized conduct of war are quickly broken. The loss of lives and property is stag-

gering, but the loss of communal identity is greater still. Generations pass before societies recover from their civil wars. Such was the case with the **French wars of religion.**

The Spread of Calvinism and Religious Division. Protestantism came late to France. It was not until after Calvin reformed the church in Geneva and began to export his brand of Protestantism that French society began to divide along religious lines. By 1560 there were more than 2000 Protestant congregations in France, whose membership totaled nearly 10 percent of the French population. Calvin and his successors concentrated their efforts on large provincial towns and had their greatest success among the middle ranks of urban society—merchants, traders, and artisans. They also found a receptive audience among aristocratic women, who eventually converted their husbands and their sons.

The wars of religion, however, were brought on by more than the rapid spread of Calvinism. Equally important was the vacuum of power that had been created when Henry II

Religious Divisions in France During the Wars of Religion

What was the dominant religion of France? Notice the relationship between the location of Paris and the Huguenot strongholds. Based on region of influence, which religion controlled trade with England and in the Mediterranean?

Catherine de Médicis (1519–1598), the wife of Henry II of France, was the real power behind the throne during the reigns of her sons Charles IX (1560–1574) and Henry III (1574–1589). Her overriding concern was to ensure her sons' succession and to preserve the power of the monarchy.

(1547–1559) died in a jousting tournament. Surviving Henry were his extraordinary widow, Catherine de Médicis, three daughters, and four sons, the oldest of whom, Francis II (1559–1560), was only 15. Under the influence of his beautiful young wife, Mary, Queen of Scots, Francis II allowed the Guise family to dominate the great offices of state and to exclude their rivals from power. The Guises controlled the two most powerful institutions of the state, the army and the Church.

The Guises were staunchly Catholic, and among their enemies were the Bourbons, princes of the blood with a direct claim to the French throne but also a family with powerful Protestant members. The revelation of a Protestant plot to remove the king from Paris provided the Guises with an opportunity to eliminate their most potent rivals. The Bourbon duc de Condé, the leading Protestant peer of the realm, was sentenced to death. But five days before Condé's execution, Francis II died and Guise power evaporated. The new king, Charles IX (1560–1574), was only ten years old and firmly under the grip of his mother, Catherine de Médicis, who now declared herself regent of France. (See "A Closer Look: The Monstrous Regiment of Women," pp. 416–417.)

Civil War. Condé's death sentence convinced him that the Guises would stop at nothing to gain their ambitions. Force would have to be met with force. Protestants and Catholics alike raised armies, and in 1562 civil war erupted. Once the wars began, the leading Protestant peers fled the court, but the position of the Guises was not altogether secure. Henry Bourbon, king of Navarre, was the next in line to succeed to the throne should Charles IX and his two brothers die without male heirs. Henry had been raised in the Protestant faith by his mother, Jeanne d'Albret, whose own mother, Marguerite of Navarre, was among the earliest protectors of the French Protestants. The objectives of the **Huguenots,** as the French Calvinists came to be called, were less clear-cut. The townspeople wanted the right to practice their faith, the clergy wanted the right to preach and make converts, and the nobility wanted their rightful place in local government. Almost from the beginning, the Huguenots were on the defensive, fighting to preserve what they already had and to avoid annihilation.

The inconclusive nature of the early battles might have allowed for the pragmatic solution sought by Catherine de

Painting of the Saint Bartholomew's Day Massacre. The massacre began in Paris on 24 August 1572, and the violence soon spread throughout France.

Médicis had it not been for the assassination of the duc de Guise in 1563 by a Protestant fanatic. That act added a personal vendetta to the religious passions of the Catholic leaders. They encouraged the slaughter of Huguenot congregations and openly planned the murder of Huguenot leaders. Protestants gave as good as they got. In open defiance of Valois dynastic interests, the Guises courted support from Spain, while the Huguenots imported Swiss and German mercenaries to fight in France. Noble factions and irreconcilable religious differences were pulling the government apart.

The Saint Bartholomew's Day Massacre. By 1570 Catherine was ready to attempt another reconciliation. She announced her plans for a marriage between her daughter Margaret and Henry of Navarre, a marriage that would symbolize the spirit of conciliation between the crown and the Huguenots. The marriage was to take place in Paris during August 1572. The arrival of Huguenot leaders from all over France to attend the marriage ceremony presented an opportunity of a different kind to the Guises and their supporters. If leading Huguenots could be assassinated in Paris, the Protestant cause might collapse and the truce that the wedding signified might be turned instead into a Catholic triumph.

DOCUMENT

Massacre of St. Bartholomew

Saint Bartholomew was the apostle that Jesus described as a man without guile. Ironically, it was on his feast day that the Huguenots who had innocently come to celebrate Henry's marriage were led like lambs to the slaughter. On 24 August 1572, the streets of Paris ran red with Huguenot blood. Although frenzied, the slaughter was inefficient. Henry of Navarre and a number of other important Huguenots escaped the carnage and returned to their urban strongholds. In the following weeks, the violence spread from Paris to the countryside and thousands of Protestants paid for their beliefs with their lives. Until the French Revolution, no event in French history would evoke as much passion as the memory of the Saint Bartholomew's Day Massacre.

One King, Two Faiths

The Saint Bartholomew's Day Massacre was a transforming event in many ways. In the first place, it prolonged the wars. A whole new generation of Huguenots now had an emotional attachment to the continuation of warfare: their fathers and brothers had been mercilessly slaughtered. By itself, the event was shocking enough; in the atmosphere of anticipated reconciliation created by the wedding, it screamed out for revenge. And the target for retaliation was no longer limited to the Guises and their followers. By accepting the results of the massacre, the monarchy sanctioned it and spilled Huguenot blood on itself. For more than a decade, Catherine de Médicis had maintained a distance between the crown and the leaders of the Catholic movement. That distance no longer existed.

GENEALOGY

The Houses of Valois and Bourbon of France

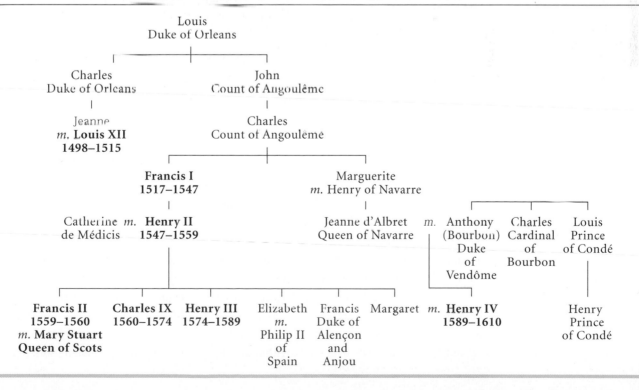

THE MONSTROUS REGIMENT OF WOMEN

"To promote a woman to bear rule, superiority, dominion or empire above any realm, nation, or city is repugnant to nature, contumely to God, and the subversion of good order, of all equity and justice." So wrote the Scottish theologian John Knox (1513–1572) in *The First Blast of the Trumpet Against the Monstrous Regiment of Women* (1558). Although he made his points more emphatically than many others, Knox was only repeating the commonplace notions of his day. He could quote Aristotle and Aquinas as well as a host of secular authorities to demonstrate female inadequacies: "Nature, I say, doth paint them forth to be weak, frail, impatient, feeble, and foolish." He could quote Saint Paul along with the ancient Fathers of the Church to demonstrate the "proper" place of women—

A CLOSER LOOK

"Man is not of the woman, but the woman of the man."

But no stacking up of authorities, no matter how numerous or revered, could erase the fact that all over Europe in the sixteenth century women could and did rule. In the Netherlands, Mary, Queen of Hungary (1531–1552), and Margaret of Parma (1559–1567) were successful regents. Jeanne d'Albret (1562–1572) was queen of the tiny state of Navarre, territory claimed by both France and Spain but kept independent by that remarkable woman. Catherine de Médicis (1560–1589), wife of one king of France and mother of three others, was the effective ruler of that nation for nearly 30 years. Mary, Queen of Scots (1542–1587), was the nominal ruler of Scotland almost from her birth. England was ruled by two very different women, the Catholic Mary I (1553–1558) and her Protestant half-sister Elizabeth I (1558–1603).

The problems faced by this long list of queens and regents were more than just the ordinary cares of government. The belief that women were inherently inferior in intelligence, strength, and character was so pervasive that, for men like Knox, a woman ruler was almost a contradiction in terms. Yet this was not the view taken by everyone, and female rule had its defenders as well as its detractors. One set of objections was overcome by the traditional medieval theory of the two bodies of the monarch. That argument was developed to reconcile the divine origins and functions of monarchs with their very real human frailties. In the theory of the two bodies, there was the body natural and the body politic. Both were joined together in the person of the ruler, but the attributes of each could be separated. Rule of a woman did nothing to disrupt this notion. In fact, it made it easier to argue that the frailties of the body natural of a woman were in no way related to the strengths of the body politic of a monarch.

While such ideas might help a female ruler win the acceptance of her subjects, they did little to invigorate her own sense of her role. Female rulers often strained against the straitjacket that definitions of gender placed them in. When angered, Elizabeth I would proclaim that she had more courage than her father, Henry VIII, "though I am only a woman." Mary, Queen of Scots, once revealed that her only regret was that she "was not a man to know what life it was to lie all night in the fields or to walk with a buckler and a broadsword." Some queens assumed masculine traits, riding in armor or leading forces to battle. Elizabeth's presence in armor at the threat of the landing of the Spanish Armada was viewed as one of the heroic moments of her reign. Other women rulers combined characteristics that were usually separated by gender definitions. Margaret of Parma was considered one of the most accomplished horse riders of her day. After leading her courtiers through woods and fields at breakneck speed, she would then attend council meetings and work on her needlepoint. Mary, Queen of Scots, loved hawking, a traditional kingly sport, in the Scottish wilds. After relishing the hawk's destruction of its prey, she liked to negotiate matters of state by beginning with tears and entreaties and ending with accusations and threats. The effect was more than disconcerting.

Women were no more or less successful as rulers than were men. Women's achievements, like men's, depended upon strength of character and the circumstances of the times. All the women rulers of the sixteenth century had received outstanding educations. Whether raised Catholic or Protestant, each was trained in Latin as well as modern languages, in the liberal arts, and in fine arts. Mary and Elizabeth Tudor of England wrote poetry and played musical instruments with considerable accomplishment. Mary, Queen of Scots, who was raised at the court of France, was considered particularly apt at learning, praise not often accorded a foreigner by the French. Catherine de Médicis, orphaned as an infant, was raised in convents and instructed in the new learning by Italian nuns. It was said that her political instincts were in her blood: Machiavelli had dedicated *The Prince* to her father. Marguerite of Navarre chose one of the leading French humanists to supervise the training of her daughter, Jeanne d'Albret.

Mary, Queen of Scots, was the only one of the female rulers born to rule. She was the sole survivor of her father, who died shortly after her birth. Mary and Elizabeth Tudor came to their thrones after the death of their younger brother Edward VI; Mary of Hungary and Margaret of Parma came to theirs as princesses of the House of Habsburg. The rule of Catherine de Médicis was the most unexpected of all. Her vigorous husband, Henry II, died during a jousting tournament, and her eldest son, Francis II, husband of Mary, Queen of Scots, died the following year. Instead of retirement as a respected queen dowager (the widow of a previous king), Catherine de Médicis was forced into the vortex of French politics to protect the rights of her ten-year-old son, Charles IX.

For most of the queens and regents, marriage was of central importance to their position. Both Mary, Queen of Hungary, and Mary, Queen of Scots, married kings whose reigns were exceedingly brief. Lewis of Hungary died at the battle of Mohács in 1526, just four years after Mary had become his queen. Mary, Queen of Scots, was widowed even sooner, and throughout the rest of her remarkable career schemed to remarry. To strengthen her claim to the throne of England, she married the Scottish Lord Darnley. When he proved unsatisfactory to her plans, she plotted his murder and then married one of his assassins. When that husband died, she sought a match with a powerful English lord who might help her capture Elizabeth's throne. The intrigues finally

■ The Latin inscription in this portrait of Mary, Queen of Scots, indicates that it was painted when she had been a prisoner in England for ten years.

led to her execution in England in 1587. Mary Tudor married Philip II of Spain in hope of reestablishing Catholicism in England through a permanent alliance with the most powerful Catholic state in Europe. Her dreams went unfulfilled when she failed to produce an heir, and the throne passed to her sister, Elizabeth, who, alone among the women rulers of the period, did not marry.

Unfortunately, the accomplishments of women rulers did little to dispel prejudices against women as a whole or to alter the definition of gender roles. Except for Mary, Queen of Scots, whose principal achievement was to provide an heir to the English throne, all the queens and regents of the sixteenth century were successful rulers. Margaret of Parma steered the careful middle course in the conflict between Spain and the Netherlands. She opposed the intervention of the Duke of Alba, and, had her advice been followed, the 80 years of war between Spain and the Netherlands might have been avoided. Catherine de Médicis held the crown of France on the heads of her sons, navigated the treacherous waters of civil war, and provided the model for religious toleration that finally was adopted in the Edict of Nantes. Elizabeth I of England became one of the most beloved rulers in that nation's history. A crafty politician who learned to balance the factions at her court and who turned the aristocracy into a service class for the crown, she brought nearly a half century of stability to England at a time when the rest of Europe was in flames.

The Theory of Resistance. The Huguenots could not continue to maintain the fiction that they were fighting against the king's evil advisers rather than against the king. After Saint Bartholomew's Day, Huguenot theorists began to develop the idea that resistance to a monarch whose actions violated divine commandments or civil rights was lawful. For the first time, Huguenot writers provided a justification for rebellion. Perhaps most importantly, a genuine revulsion against the massacres swept the nation. A number of Catholic peers now joined with the Huguenots to protest the excesses of the crown and the Guises. Those Catholics came to be called **politiques** from their desire for a practical settlement of the wars. They were led by the duc d'Anjou, next in line to the throne after Henry III (1574–1589) became king.

Against them, in Paris and a number of other towns, the **Catholic League** was formed, a society that pledged its first allegiance to religion. The League took up where the Saint Bartholomew's Day Massacre left off, and the slaughter of ordinary people who unluckily professed the wrong religion continued. Matters grew worse in 1584, when Anjou died. With each passing year it was becoming apparent that Henry III would produce no male heir. After Anjou's death, the Huguenot Henry of Navarre was the next in line for the throne. Catholic Leaguers talked openly of altering the royal succession and began to develop theories of lawful resistance to monarchical power. By 1585, when the final civil war began—the war of the three Henrys, named for Henry III, Henry Guise, and Henry of Navarre—the crown was in the weakest possible position. Paris and the Catholic towns were controlled by the League, the Protestant strongholds by Henry of Navarre. King Henry III could not abandon his capital or his religion, but neither could he gain control of the Catholic party. The extremism of the Leaguers kept the politiques away from court, and without the politiques, there could be no settlement.

In December 1588, Henry III summoned Henry Guise and Guise's brother to a meeting in the royal bedchamber. There they were murdered by the king's order. The politiques were blamed for the murders—revenge was taken on a number of them—and Henry III was forced to flee his capital. Paris was still firmly in the hands of the League, and Henry was in danger of becoming a king without a country. He made a pact with Henry of Navarre, and together royalist and Huguenot forces besieged Paris. All supplies were cut off from the city and only the arrival of a Spanish army prevented its fall. In 1589, Catherine de Médicis died, her ambition to reestablish the authority of the monarchy in shambles, and in the same year a fanatic priest gained revenge for the murder of the Guises by assassinating Henry III.

Henry IV. Now Henry of Navarre came into his inheritance. After nearly 30 years of continuous civil war, it was certain that a Huguenot could never rule France. The League had already proclaimed a Catholic rival as king, and the pope excommunicated Henry of Navarre and absolved France from loyalty to him. If Henry was to become king of all France, he would have

■ Although Henry IV probably never said, "Paris is worth a mass," his conversion to Roman Catholicism, depicted here, was instrumental in securing his kingship and ending the French wars of religion.

to become a Catholic king. It is not clear when Henry made the decision to accept the Catholic faith—"Paris is worth a mass," he reportedly declared—but he did not announce his decision at once. Rather he strengthened his forces, tightened his bonds with the politiques, and urged his countrymen to expel the Spanish invaders. He finally made his conversion public and in 1594 was crowned Henry IV (1589–1610). A war-weary nation was willing to accept the sincerity of its new king rather than endure a seemingly endless struggle. Most of the leading peers on both sides were nearly bankrupt, and Henry IV was willing to pay large cash settlements to all those who would return to their estates and pledge allegiance to him.

In 1598, Henry proclaimed the **Edict of Nantes,** which granted limited toleration to the Huguenots. It was the culmination of decades of attempts to find a solution to the existence of two religions in one state. It was a compromise that satisfied no one, but it was a compromise that everyone could accept. One king, two faiths was as apt a description of Henry IV as it was of the settlement. Yet neither Henry's conversion nor the Edict of Nantes stilled the passions that had spawned and sustained the French wars of religion. Sporadic fighting between Catholics and Huguenots continued, and fanatics on both sides fanned the flames of religious hatred. Henry IV survived 18 attempts on his life before he was finally felled by an assassin's knife in 1610, but by then he had reestablished the monarchy and brought a semblance of peace to France.

The World of Philip II

By the middle of the sixteenth century, Spain was the greatest power in Europe. The dominions of Philip II (1556–1598) of Spain stretched from the Atlantic to the Pacific; his continental territories included the Netherlands in the north and Milan and Naples in Italy. In 1580, Philip became king of Portugal, uniting all the states of the Iberian peninsula. With the addition of Portugal's Atlantic ports and its sizable fleet, Spanish maritime power was now unsurpassed. Spain was also a great cultural and intellectual center. The fashions and tastes of its golden age dominated all the courts of Europe.

Great power meant great responsibilities, and few monarchs took their tasks more seriously than did Philip II. Trained from

childhood for the cares of office, he exceeded all expectations. Philip II earned his reputation as "King of Paper" by maintaining a grueling work schedule. Up at eight and at mass soon afterward, he met with his advisers and visitors on official business until noon. After a brief lunch, he began the real business of the day, the study of the mountains of papers that his empire generated. Although summaries were prepared of the hundreds of documents he handled each day, Philip II frequently read and annotated the longer originals. No detail was too small to escape his attention. His workday often lasted ten hours or longer. Even when he was traveling, his secretaries carried huge chests of state papers that Philip studied in his carriage and annotated on a portable desk that always accompanied him.

There was good reason why the slightly stooped king appeared as if he had the weight of the world on his shoulders. In the Mediterranean, Spain alone stood out against the expansion of Ottoman power. The sultan's navy continually threatened to turn the Mediterranean into a Turkish lake, while his armies at-

GENEALOGY
The Family of Charles V

■ This image depicts the clash of the once-feared Spanish Armada and the English navy in 1588. The defeat of the Spanish Armada dealt a serious blow to Spain's standing in Europe.

tempted to capture and hold Italian soil. All Europe shuddered at the news of each Ottoman advance. Popes called for holy wars against the Turks, but only Philip heeded the cry. From nearly the moment that he inherited the Spanish crown, he took up the challenge of defending European Christianity. For more than a decade, Philip maintained costly coastal garrisons in North Africa and Italy and assembled large fleets and larger armies to discourage or repel Turkish invasions. The sparring could not go on indefinitely, and in 1571 both sides prepared for a decisive battle. A combined Spanish and Italian force of more than 300

THE HEART AND STOMACH OF A KING

In 1588 Queen Elizabeth rallied her subjects to oppose the invasion of England by the mighty Spanish Armada. This is part of the speech she made before the troops that were gathered in Kent.

Focus Questions

What are the images that Elizabeth uses to appeal to her people? Why does she compare herself to a king?

My loving people, we have been persuaded by some, that are careful of our safety, to take heed how we commit ourselves to armed multitudes, for fear of treachery; but I assure you, I do not desire to live to distrust my faithful and loving people. Let tyrants fear; I have always so behaved myself that, under God, I have placed my chiefest strength and safeguard in the loyal hearts and good will of my subjects. And therefore I am come amongst you at this time, not as for my recreation or sport, but being resolved, in the midst and heat of the battle, to live or die amongst you all; to lay down, for my God, and for my kingdom, and for my people, my honor and my

blood, even the dust. I know I have but the body of a weak and feeble woman; but I have the heart and stomach of a king, and of a king of England, too; and think foul scorn that Parma or Spain, or any prince of Europe, should dare to invade the borders of my realms: to which, rather than any dishonor should grow by me, I myself will take up arms; I myself will be your general, judge, and rewarder of every one of your virtues in the field. I know already, by your forwardness, that you have deserved rewards and crowns; and we do assure you, on the word of a prince, they shall be duly paid you. In the mean my lieutenant general, General Leicester, shall be in my stead, than whom never prince commanded a more noble and worthy subject; not doubting by your obedience to my general, by your concord in the camp, and by your valor in the field, we shall shortly have a famous victory over the enemies of my God, of my kingdom, and of my people.

ships and 80,000 men met an even larger Ottoman flotilla off the coast of Greece. The Spanish naval victory at Lepanto was considered one of the great events of the sixteenth century, celebrated in story and song for the next 300 years. Although the Turks continued to menace the Mediterranean islands, Lepanto marked the end of Ottoman advances.

Philip was equally aggressive against the English Protestants. For a brief time he had been king in England through his marriage to Mary I (1553–1558). He encouraged Mary's efforts to restore the Catholic Church in England and supported her policies of repression. When Mary died and Elizabeth I (1558–1603) rejected his marriage proposal, his limited rule in England came to an end. From then on, England and Spain entered a long period of hostility. English pirates raided Spanish treasure ships returning to Europe, and Elizabeth covertly aided both French and Dutch Protestants. Finally, in 1588, Philip decided upon invasion. A great fleet set sail from the Portuguese coast to the Netherlands, where a large Spanish army stood waiting to be conveyed to England.

The **Spanish Armada** was composed of more than 130 ships, many of them the pride of the Spanish and Portuguese navies. They were bigger and stronger than anything possessed by the English, whose forces were largely merchant vessels hastily converted for battle. But the English ships were faster and more easily maneuverable in the unpredictable winds of the English Channel. They also contained guns that could easily be reloaded for multiple firings, while the Spanish guns were designed to discharge only one broadside before hand-to-hand combat ensued. With those advantages the English were able to prevent the Armada from reaching port in the Netherlands and to destroy many individual ships as they were blown off course. The defeat of the Spanish Armada was less a military than a psychological blow to Philip II: he could more easily replace ships than restore confidence in Spanish power.

DOCUMENT
Reports on the Spanish Armada

The Burgundian Inheritance

Confidence was all the more necessary when Philip II faced the gravest crisis of his reign: the revolt of the Netherlands. Although Philip's father, Charles V, had amassed a great empire, he had begun only as the duke of

Burgundy. Charles's Burgundian inheritance encompassed a diverse territory in the northwestern corner of Europe. The 17 separate provinces of the territory were called the Netherlands, or the Low Countries, because of the flooding that kept large portions of them under water. The Netherlands was one of the richest and most populous regions of Europe, an international leader in manufacturing, banking, and commerce. Antwerp and Amsterdam were bustling port cities with access to the North Sea; inland were the prosperous industrial towns of Ghent and Brussels. The preeminence of the Netherlands was all the more remarkable because the provinces themselves were divided geographically, culturally, and linguistically. Rivers, lakes, and flooded plains separated the southern provinces, where French was the background and language of the inhabitants, from the northern ones, where Germans had settled and Dutch was spoken. Charles V attempted to unify the provinces by removing them from the jurisdiction of the Holy Roman Empire and establishing a separate regency under his eldest son, Philip II. Thus the future of the Netherlands was tied to Spain and the New World when Philip II set sail for Castile in 1559 to claim the crown of Spain.

Although Philip II had every intention of returning to the Low Countries, in fact the Netherlands had seen the last of

MAP DISCOVERY

Habsburg Lands at the Abdication of Charles V
Notice how dispersed were the states controlled by Charles V when he abdicated the throne in 1556. Why do you think he divided his empire between his son Philip II and his brother Ferdinand I? What made it possible for the Netherlands to revolt against Spanish control?

their king. Philip left his half-sister, Margaret of Parma, as regent, providing her with a talented group of Spanish administrators to carry out policies that were to be formulated in Madrid. As Philip's own grasp on the affairs of the Netherlands loosened, so did the loyalty of the native nobility to the absent monarch. The resentments that built up were traditional ones—hostility to foreigners, distrust of royal advisers, and contempt for policies that lacked understanding of local conditions. All of the discontents came together over Philip's religious policies.

The Low Countries had accepted the Peace of Augsburg in a spirit of conciliation in which it was never intended. There Catholics, Lutherans, Anabaptists, and Calvinists peaceably coexisted. As in France, the situation changed dramatically with the spread of Calvinism. The heavy concentration of urban populations in the Low Countries provided the natural habitat for Calvinist preachers, who made converts across the entire social spectrum. As Charles V, Holy Roman Emperor, he may have made his peace with Protestants, but as Charles I, king of Spain, he had not. Charles V had maintained the purity of the Spanish Catholic Church through a sensible combination of reform and repression.

Philip II intended to pursue a similar policy in the Low Countries. With papal approval he initiated a scheme to reform the hierarchy of the Church by expanding the number of bishops, and he invited the Jesuits to establish schools for orthodox learning. Simultaneously, he strengthened the power of the Inquisition and ordered the enforcement of the decrees of the Council of Trent. The Protestants sought the protection of their local nobility who—Catholic or Protestant—had their own reasons for opposing provincial nobility, and magistrates resented both the policies that were being pursued and the fact that they disregarded local autonomy. Town governors and noblemen refused to cooperate in implementing the new laws. Leading Protestants such as Prince William of Orange, one of the largest landholders in the Netherlands, and Count Egmont, an outstanding military leader, urged Margaret to adopt a policy of toleration along the lines of the Peace of Augsburg and made clear that they would resign from office rather than support anything else.

The Revolt of the Netherlands

The passive resistance of nobles and magistrates was soon matched by the active resistance of the Calvinists. Unable to enforce Philip's policy, Margaret and her advisers agreed to a limited toleration. But in the summer of 1566, before it could be put into effect, bands of Calvinists unleashed a storm of iconoclasm in the provinces, breaking stained glass windows and statues of the Virgin and the saints, which they claimed were idolatrous. Catholic churches were stormed and turned into Calvinist meeting houses. Local authorities were helpless in the face of determined Calvinists and apathetic Catholics; they could not protect Church property. Iconoclasm gave way to open revolt. Fearing social rebellion, even the leading Protestant noblemen took part in suppressing the riots.

Rebellion and War. In Spain, the events in the Netherlands were treated for what they were: open rebellion. Despite the fact that Margaret had already restored order, Philip II was determined to punish the rebels and enforce the heresy laws. A large military force under the command of the Duke of Alba (1507–1582)—whose record of success was matched only by his record of brutality—was sent from Spain as an army of occupation. As befit a warrior who had made his reputation leading imperial troops against the Lutherans, Alba gave no quarter to the Protestants of the Netherlands.

■ Portrait of Philip II by Titian (ca. 1554). Philip tried for 12 years to suppress rebellion in the Protestant Netherlands, and he sent troops to aid Catholic forces in battle with the Huguenots in France. He fared badly in his attempts to deal with England, his Spanish Armada suffering a humiliating defeat in 1588 that marked the beginning of the decline of Spanish power.

CANNIBALS

Michel de Montaigne (1533–1592) came from a wealthy family in the Bordeaux region of France and ultimately inherited the chateau from which his name derives. Before his early retirement he worked in the legal profession. His Essays *(1572–1588) combined humanist learning with the new philosophy of skepticism. The following excerpt, from "Of Cannibals," shows both his penetrating intelligence and his detached observation of the world around him. His description of the practices of cannibals was an explicit critique of his own European countrymen.*

Focus Questions

In what ways does Montaigne profess sympathy with the inhabitants of the New World? What constitutes barbarism for him?

These nations, then, seem to me barbarous in this sense, that they have been fashioned very little by the human mind, and are still very close to their original naturalness. The laws of nature still rule them, very little corrupted by ours; and they are in such a state of purity that I am sometimes vexed that they were unknown earlier, in the days when there were men able to judge them better than we. I am sorry that Lycurgus and Plato did not know of them; for it seems to me that what we actually see in these nations surpasses not only all the pictures in which poets have idealized the golden age and all their inventions in imagining a happy state of man, but also the conceptions and the very desire of philosophy. . . .

For the rest, they live in a country with a very pleasant and temperate climate, so that according to my witnesses it is rare to see a sick man there; and they have assured me that they never saw one palsied, bleary-eyed, toothless, or bent with age. They are settled along the sea and shut in on the land side by great high mountains, with a stretch about a hundred leagues wide in between. They have a great abundance of fish and flesh which bear no resemblance to ours, and they eat them with no other artifice than cooking.

They have their wars with the nations beyond the mountains, further inland, to which they go quite naked, with no other arms than bows or wooden swords ending in a sharp point, in the manner of the tongues of our boar spears. It is astonishing what firmness they show in their combats, which never end but in slaughter and bloodshed; for as to routs and terror, they know nothing of either.

Each man brings back as his trophy the head of the enemy he has killed, and sets it up at the entrance to his dwelling. After they have treated their prisoners well for a long time with all the hospitality they can think of, each man who has a prisoner calls a great assembly of his acquaintances. He ties a rope to one of the prisoner's arms by the end of which he holds him, a few steps away, for fear of being hurt, and gives his dearest friend the other arm to hold in the same way; and these two, in the presence of the whole assembly, kill him with their swords. This done, they roast him and eat him in common and send some pieces to their absent friends. This is not, as people think, for nourishment, as of old the Scythians used to do; it is to betoken an extreme revenge. And the proof of this came when they saw the Portuguese, who had joined forces with their adversaries, inflict a different kind of death on them when they took them prisoner, which was to bury them up to the waist, shoot the rest of their body full of arrows, and afterward hang them. They thought that these people from the other world, being men who had sown the knowledge of many vices among their neighbors and were much greater masters than themselves in every sort of wickedness, did not adopt this sort of vengeance without some reason, and that it must be more painful than their own; so they began to give up their old method and to follow this one.

I am not sorry that we notice the barbarous horror of such acts, but I am heartily sorry that, judging their faults rightly, we should be so blind to our own. I think there is more barbarity in eating a man alive than in eating him dead; and in tearing by tortures and the rack a body still full of feeling, in roasting a man bit by bit, in having him bitten and mangled by dogs and swine (as we have not only read but seen within fresh memory, not among ancient enemies, but among neighbors and fellow citizens, and what is worse, on the pretext of piety and religion), than in roasting and eating him after he is dead. . . .

So we may well call these people barbarians, in respect to the rules of reason, but not in respect to ourselves, who surpass them in every kind of barbarity.

Their warfare is wholly noble and generous, and as excusable and beautiful as this human disease can be; its only basis among them is their rivalry in valor. They are not fighting for the conquest of new lands, for they still enjoy that natural abundance that provides them without toil and trouble with all necessary things in such profusion that they have no wish to enlarge their boundaries. They are still in that happy state of desiring only as much as their natural needs demand; anything beyond that is superfluous to them. . . . Truly here are real savages by our standards, for either they must be thoroughly so, or we must be; there is an amazing distance between their character and ours.

From Montaigne, "Of Cannibals."

START

OUT

"Everyone must be made to live in constant fear of the roof breaking down over his head," he wrote.

Alba lured Count Egmont and other Protestant noblemen to Brussels, where he publicly executed them in 1568. He also established a military court to punish participants in the rebellion, a court that came to be called the Council of Blood. The Council handed down more than 9000 convictions, a thousand of which carried the death penalty. As many as 60,000 Protestants fled beyond Alba's jurisdiction. Alba next made an example of several small towns that had been implicated in the iconoclasm. He allowed his soldiers to pillage the towns at will before slaughtering their entire populations and razing them to the ground. By the end of 1568, royal policy had gained a sullen acceptance in the Netherlands, but the hostilities did not end. For the next 80 years, with only occasional truces, Spain and the Netherlands were at war.

The Protestants Rebel. Alba's policies drove the Protestants into rebellion. That forced the Spanish government to maintain its army by raising taxes from those provinces that had remained loyal. Soon the loyal provinces too were in revolt, not over religion, but over taxation and local autonomy. Tax resistance and fear of an invasion from France left Alba unprepared for the series of successful assaults Protestants launched in the northern provinces during 1572. Protestant generals established a perma-

Michel de Montaigne, *Essays*

nent base in the northwestern provinces of Holland and Zeeland. By 1575 the Protestants had gained a stronghold that they would never relinquish. Prince William of Orange assumed

CHRONOLOGY

Revolt of the Netherlands

1559	Margaret of Parma named regent of the Netherlands
1566	Calvinist iconoclasm begins revolt
1567	Duke of Alba arrives in Netherlands and establishes Council of Blood
1568	Protestant Count Egmont executed
1572	Protestants capture Holland and Zeeland
1573	Alba relieved of his command
1576	Sack of Antwerp; pacification of Ghent
1581	Catholic and Protestant provinces split
1585	Spanish forces take Brussels and Antwerp
1609	Twelve Years' Truce

■ The Revolt of the Netherlands, 1555. The consolidation of the Low Countries under Charles V brought together lands with different languages, cultures, and forms of government.

■ The Revolt of the Netherlands, 1609. By the beginning of the seventeenth century, the union had broken apart and the northern provinces had won independence from Spain.

the leadership of the two provinces that were now united against the tyranny of Philip's rule.

Spanish government was collapsing all over the Netherlands. William ruled in the north and the States-General, a parliamentary body composed of representatives from the separate provinces, ruled in the south. Margaret of Parma had resigned in disgust at Alba's tactics, and Alba had been relieved of his command when his tactics had failed. No one was in control of the Spanish army. The soldiers, who had gone years with only partial pay, now roamed the southern provinces looking for plunder. Brussels and Ghent both had been targets, and in 1576 the worst atrocities of all occurred when mutinous Spanish troops sacked Antwerp. One of the wealthiest cities in Europe, home to the most important mercantile and banking establishments in the world, Antwerp was torn apart like a roasted pig. The rampage lasted for days. When it ended, more than 7000 people had been slaughtered and nearly a third of the city burned to the ground.

The "Spanish fury" in Antwerp effectively ended Philip's rule over his Burgundian inheritance. The Protestants had established a permanent home in the north. The States-General had established its ability to rule in the south, and Spanish policy had been totally discredited. To achieve a settlement, the Pacification of Ghent of 1576, the Spanish government conceded local autonomy in taxation, the central role of the States-General in legislation, and the immediate withdrawal of all Spanish troops from the Low Countries. Five southern provinces pledged to remain Catholic and to accept the authority of the king's regent. The rift between the provinces was soon followed by a permanent split. In 1581, one group of provinces voted to depose Philip II, while a second group decided to remain loyal to him.

Philip II refused to accept the dismemberment of his inheritance and refused to recognize the independent Dutch state that now existed in Holland. Throughout the 1580s and 1590s, military expeditions attempted to re-unite the southern provinces and to conquer the northern ones. But Spanish military successes in the south were outweighed by the long-term failure of Spanish objectives in the north. In 1609, Spain and the Netherlands concluded the Twelve Years' Truce, which tacitly recognized the existence of the state of Holland. By the beginning of the seventeenth century, Holland was not only an independent state, it was one of the greatest rivals of Spain and Portugal for the fruits of empire.

THE STRUGGLES IN EASTERN EUROPE

In eastern Europe, dynastic struggles outweighed the problems created by religious reform. Muscovy remained the bulwark of Eastern Orthodox Christianity, immune from the struggles over the Roman faith. Protestantism did spread into Poland-

IMAGE DISCOVERY

The Cow, as Political Symbol

This painting, *The Milch Cow,* illustrates the politics surrounding the Netherlands in the later sixteenth century. Philip II of Spain is riding on the cow. What do you think that says about Spain's relationship to the Netherlands? Why would the painter have depicted William of Orange, ruler of the Netherlands, under the cow and milking it? Elizabeth I is feeding the cow, and the King of France stands behind it, gripping its tail and collecting its droppings. Note the sizes of the figures; Philip II is smaller than Elizabeth I. Since this is not a reflection of their actual dimensions, what might this mean? What does the picture indicate about the painter's political leanings?

Lithuania, but unlike its reception in the west, its presence was tolerated by the Polish state. The spread of dissent was checked not by repression, but by a vigorous Catholic reformation led by the Jesuits. The domestic crises in the east were crises of state rather than of church. In Muscovy, the disputed succession that followed the death of Ivan the Terrible plunged the state into anarchy and civil war. Centuries of conflict between Poland-Lithuania and Muscovy came to a head with the Poles' desperate gamble to seize control of their massive eastern neighbor. War between Poland-Lithuania and Muscovy inevitably dominated the politics of the entire region. The Baltic states, of which Sweden was to become the most important, had their own ambitions for territory and economic gain. They soon joined the fray, making alliances in return for concessions and conquering small pieces of the mainland.

Kings and Diets in Poland

Until the end of the sixteenth century, Poland-Lithuania was the dominant power in the eastern part of Europe. It was economically healthy and militarily strong. Through its Baltic ports, especially Gdansk, Poland played a central role in international commerce and a dominant role in the northern grain trade. The vast size of the Polish state made defense difficult, and during the course of the sixteenth century it had lost lands to Muscovy in the east and to the Crimean Tatars in the south. But the permanent union with Lithuania in 1569 and the gradual absorption of the Baltic region of Livonia more than compensated for the losses. Matters of war and peace, of taxation and reform, were placed under the strict supervision of the **Polish Diet**, a parliamentary body that represented the

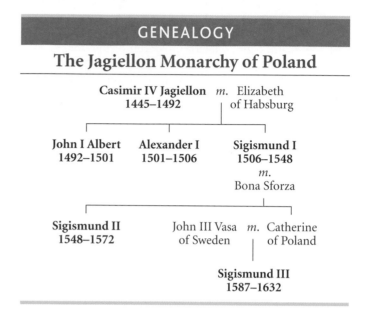

GENEALOGY

The Jagiellon Monarchy of Poland

Casimir IV Jagiellon *m.* Elizabeth
1445–1492   of Habsburg

John I Albert   **Alexander I**   **Sigismund I**
1492–1501   **1501–1506**   **1506–1548**
                                        m.
                                    Bona Sforza

Sigismund II   John III Vasa *m.* Catherine
1548–1572   of Sweden   of Poland

                        Sigismund III
                        1587–1632

■ Eastern Europe (ca. 1550) after the Consolidation of Russia and the Growth of Poland. The eastern part of Europe was still sparsely populated and economically underdeveloped.

■ Portrait of Sigismund III, who was elected to the Polish throne in 1587. Also the hereditary heir to the Crown of Sweden, Sigismund brought Poland into war with Sweden in an effort to reclaim his crown.

Polish landed elite. The Diet also carefully controlled religious policy. Roman Catholicism was the principal religion in Poland, but the state tolerated numerous Protestant and Eastern creeds. In the Warsaw Confederation of 1573, the Polish gentry vowed, "We who differ in matters of religion will keep the peace among ourselves."

The biological failure of the Jagiellon monarchy in Poland ended that nation's most successful line of kings. Without a natural heir, the Polish nobility and gentry, who officially elected the monarch, had to peddle their throne among the princes of Europe. When Sigismund III (1587–1632) was elected to the Polish throne in 1587, he was also heir to the crown of Sweden. Sigismund accepted the prohibitions against religious repression that were outlined in the Warsaw Confederation, but he actively encouraged the establishment of Jesuit schools, the expansion of monastic orders, and the strengthening of the Roman Catholic Church.

All those policies enjoyed the approval of the Polish ruling classes. But the Diet would not support Sigismund's efforts to gain control of the Swedish crown, which he inherited in 1592 but from which he was deposed three years later. If Sigismund triumphed in Sweden, all Poland would get was a part-time monarch. The Polish Diet consistently refused to give the king

the funds he would need to invade Sweden successfully. Nevertheless, Sigismund mounted several unsuccessful campaigns against the Swedes that sapped Polish money and manpower.

Muscovy's Time of Troubles

The wars of Ivan the Great and Ivan the Terrible in the fifteenth and sixteenth centuries were waged to secure agricultural territory in the west and a Baltic port in the north; both objectives came at the expense of Poland-Lithuania. But following the death of Ivan the Terrible in 1584, the Muscovite state began to disintegrate. For years it had been held together only by conquest and fear. Ivan's conflicts with the boyars, the hereditary nobility, had created an aristocracy unwilling and unable to come to the aid of his successors. By 1601, the crown was plunged into a crisis of legitimacy known as the **Time of Troubles.** Ivan had murdered his heir in a fit of anger and left his half-witted son to inherit the throne, which led to a vacuum of power at the center as well as a struggle for the spoils of government. Private armies ruled great swaths of the state and pretenders to the crown—all claiming to be Dimitri, the lost brother of the last legitimate tsar—appeared everywhere. Ambitious groups of boyars backed their own claimants to the throne. So, too, did ambitious foreigners who eagerly sought to carve up Muscovite possessions.

Muscovy's Time of Troubles was Poland's moment of opportunity. While anarchy and civil war raged, Poland looked to regain the territory that it had lost to Muscovy during the previous century. Sigismund abandoned war with Sweden in order to intervene in the struggle for the Russian crown. Polish forces crossed into Muscovy and Sigismund's generals backed one of the strongest of the false Dimitris, but their plan to put him on the throne failed when he was assassinated. Sigismund used the death of the last false Dimitri as a pretext to assert his own claim to the Muscovite crown. More Polish forces poured across the frontier. In 1610, they took Moscow and Sigismund proclaimed himself tsar, intending to unite the two massive states.

The Russian boyars, so long divided, now rose against the Polish enemy. The Polish garrison in Moscow was starved into submission, and a native Russian, Michael Romanov (1613–1645), was chosen tsar by an assembly of landholders, the Zemsky Sobor. He made a humiliating peace with the Swedes—who had also taken advantage of the Time of Troubles to invade Muscovy's Baltic provinces—in return for Swedish assistance against the Poles. Intermittent fighting continued for another 20 years. In the end, Poland agreed to peace and a separate Muscovite state, but only in exchange for large territorial concessions.

The Rise of Sweden

Sweden's rise to power during the seventeenth century was as startling as it was swift. Until the Reformation, Sweden had been part of the Scandinavian confederation ruled by the

Danes. Although the Swedes had a measure of autonomy, they were very much a junior partner in Baltic affairs. Denmark controlled the narrow sound that linked the Baltic with the North Sea, and its prosperity derived from the tolls it collected on imports and exports. When, in 1523, Gustav I Vasa led the uprising of the Swedish aristocracy that ended Danish domination, he won the right to rule over a poor, sparsely populated state with few towns or developed seaports. The Vasas ruled Sweden in conjunction with the aristocracy. Although the throne was hereditary, the part played by the nobility in elevating Gustav I Vasa (1523–1560) gave the nobles a powerful voice in Swedish affairs. Through the council of state, known as the Rad, the Swedish nobility exerted a strong check on the monarch. Sweden's aggressive foreign policy began accidentally. When in the 1550s the Teutonic Knights found themselves no longer capable of ruling in Livonia, the Baltic seaports that had been under their dominion scrambled for new alliances. Muscovy and Poland-Lithuania were the logical choices, but the town of Reval, an important outlet for Russian trade near the mouth of the Gulf of Finland, asked Sweden for protection. After some hesitation, since the occupation of territory on the southern shores of the Baltic would involve great expense, Sweden fortified Reval in 1560. A decade later, Swedish forces captured Narva, farther to the east, and consolidated their hold on the Livonian coast. By occupying the most important ports on the Gulf of Finland, Sweden could control a sizable portion of the

■ Michael Romanov was chosen to be tsar in 1613. His father, the Patriarch Philaret of Moscow, acted as joint ruler with Michael until the patriarch's death in 1633.

■ The Rise of Russia. Russia grew through the addition of large units of territory comprising millions of square acres.

Muscovite trade. As the Swedes secured the northern Livonian ports, more of the Muscovy trade moved to the south and passed through Riga, which would have to be captured or blockaded if the Swedes were to control commerce in the eastern Baltic.

Sigismund's aggressive alliance with the Polish Jesuits persuaded the Swedish nobility that he would undermine their Lutheran church. Sigismund was deposed in favor of his uncle Charles IX (1604–1611). War with Poland resulted from Sigismund's efforts to regain the Swedish crown. The Swedes used the opportunity to blockade Riga and to occupy more Livonian territory. The Swedish navy was far superior to any force that the Poles could assemble, but on land Polish forces were masters. The Swedish invasion force suffered a crushing defeat and had to retreat to its coastal enclaves. The Poles now had an opportunity to retake all of Livonia but, as always, the Polish Diet was reluctant to finance Sigismund's wars. Furthermore, Sigismund had his eyes on a bigger prize. Rather than follow up its Swedish victory, Poland invaded Muscovy.

Meanwhile, the blockade of Riga and the assembly of a large Swedish fleet in the Baltic threatened Denmark. The Danes continued to claim sovereignty over Sweden and took the opportunity of the Polish-Swedish conflict to reassert it.

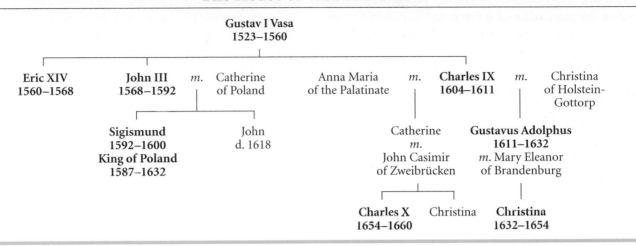

GENEALOGY

The House of Vasa of Sweden

Gustav I Vasa
1523–1560

Eric XIV
1560–1568

John III
1568–1592 *m.* Catherine of Poland

Anna Maria of the Palatinate *m.* **Charles IX 1604–1611** *m.* Christina of Holstein-Gottorp

Sigismund
1592–1600
King of Poland
1587–1632

John
d. 1618

Catherine
m.
John Casimir of Zweibrücken

Gustavus Adolphus 1611–1632
m. Mary Eleanor of Brandenburg

Charles X
1654–1660

Christina

Christina
1632–1654

In 1611, under the energetic leadership of the Danish king Christian IV (1588–1648), Denmark invaded Sweden from both the east and the west. The Danes captured the towns of Kalmar and Alvsborg and threatened to take Stockholm. To end the Danish war, Sweden accepted humiliating terms in 1613, renouncing all claims to the northern coasts and recognizing Danish control of the Arctic trading route.

In 1611, during the middle of the Danish war, Charles IX died and was succeeded by his son Gustavus Adolphus (1611–1632). Unlike his father and cousin before him, who had come by chance to the Swedish throne, Gustavus Adolphus was raised to be king. Gruff and affable by turns, he was one of the leading Protestant princes of his day, in every way a match for Christian IV of Denmark. Gustavus's greatest skills were military, and he inherited an ample navy and an effective army. Unlike nearly every other European state, Sweden raised its forces from its own citizens. Gustavus introduced new weapons such as the light mobile gun and reshaped his army into standard-size squadrons and regiments, which were easier to administer and deploy.

The calamitous wars inherited from his father occupied Gustavus during the early years of his reign. He was forced to conclude the humiliating peace with the Danes in 1613 and to go to war with the Russians in 1614 in order to secure the Baltic coastal estates that had been promised in 1609. Gustavus's first military initiative was to resume war with Poland in order to force Sigismund to renounce his claim to the Swedish throne. In 1621, Gustavus landed in Livonia and within two weeks had captured Riga, the capstone of Sweden's Baltic ambitions. Occupation of Riga increased Swedish control of the Muscovy trade and deprived Denmark of a significant portion of its customs duties. Gustavus now claimed Riga as a Swedish port and successfully demanded that ships sailing from there pay tolls to Sweden rather than Denmark. The capture of Riga firmly established Sweden as a coequal Baltic power.

■ The Rise of Sweden. For the only time in its history, Sweden acquired territories on the European mainland.

By the mid-seventeenth century, the Sweden of Gustavus Adolphus was well on its way to international prominence. The capture of Riga gave Sweden complete control of the eastern Baltic and ended Polish pretensions to the Swedish throne. A negotiated settlement with the Danes over the collection of tolls enhanced Swedish prestige and increased Sweden's commercial prosperity. Moreover, Gustavus's marriage into the family of the Protestant rulers of Prussia gave Sweden a presence in Germany as well. For the time being, Sweden faced east. But the storm clouds of religious warfare were already bursting over the Holy Roman Empire. Gustavus Adolphus now took his place among the Protestant princes of Europe, and Sweden ranked among the leading Protestant powers.

THE THIRTY YEARS' WAR, 1618–1648

Perhaps it was just a matter of time before the isolated conflicts that dotted the corners of Europe were joined together. In 1609, Spain and the Dutch Republic had signed a truce that was to last until 1621. In more than 40 years of nearly continuous fighting, the Dutch had carved out a state in the northern Netherlands. They used the truce to consolidate their position and increase their prosperity, largely at the expense of Spain and Portugal. Thus, to the insult of rebellion was added the injury of commercial competition. Spain had reluctantly accepted Dutch independence, but Philip III (1598–1621) never abandoned the objective of recovering his Burgundian inheritance. By the start of the seventeenth century, Philip had good reasons for hope. Beginning in the 1580s, Spanish forces had reconquered the southern provinces of the Netherlands. The prosperous towns of Brussels, Antwerp, and Ghent were again under Spanish control, and they provided a springboard for another invasion.

The Twelve Years' Truce gave Spain time to prepare for the final assault. During this time, Philip III attempted to resolve all of Spain's other European conflicts so that he could then give full attention to a resumption of the Dutch war. Circumstance smiled upon his efforts. In 1603, the pacific James I (1603–1625) came to the English throne. Secure in his island state, James I desired peace among all Christian princes. He quickly concluded the war with Spain that had begun with the invasion of the Spanish Armada and entered into negotiations to marry his heir to a Spanish princess. In 1610, the bellicose Henry IV of France was felled by an assassin's knife. French plans to renew war with Spain were abandoned with the accession of the eight-year-old Louis XIII (1610–1643). As the sands of the Twelve Years' Truce ran out, Spain and the Netherlands readied for war. But not even the greatest empire in Europe could control its own destiny. War was in the air all over the Continent, and not everyone could wait until 1621. The **Thirty Years' War** was about to begin.

Bohemia Revolts

The Peace of Augsburg had served the German states well. The principle that the religion of the ruler was the religion of the state complicated the political life of the Holy Roman Empire, but it also pacified it. Although rulers had the right to enforce uniformity on their subjects, in practice many of the larger states toler-

ated more than one religion. By the beginning of the seventeenth century, Catholicism and Protestantism had achieved a rough equality within the German states, symbolized by the fact that of the seven electors who chose the Holy Roman Emperor, three were Catholic, three Protestant, and the seventh was the emperor himself, acting as king of Bohemia. The situation was not unwelcome to the leaders of the Austrian Habsburg family who succeeded Emperor Charles V. By necessity, the eastern Habsburgs were more tolerant than their Spanish kinfolk. Protestants fought the Ottomans with as much zeal as did Catholics, and the Ottomans were the empire's more potent enemy. The unofficial policy of toleration not only helped the Austrian Habsburgs defend their state, it allowed them to expand it. The head of their house was elected king of Bohemia and king of Hungary, both states with large Protestant populations.

A Fatal Election.   In 1617, Mathias, the childless Holy Roman Emperor, began making plans for his cousin, Ferdinand Habsburg, to succeed him. In order to ensure a Catholic majority among the electors, the emperor relin-

CHRONOLOGY
The Thirty Years' War

1618	Defenestration of Prague
1619	Ferdinand Habsburg elected Holy Roman Emperor; Frederick of the Palatinate accepts the crown of Bohemia
1620	Catholic victory at Battle of the White Mountain
1621	End of Twelve Years' Truce; war between Spain and Netherlands
1626	Danes form Protestant alliance under Christian IV
1627	Spain declares bankruptcy
1630	Gustavus Adolphus leads Swedish forces into Germany
1631	Sack of Magdeburg; Protestant victory at Breitenfeld
1632	Protestant victory at Lützen; death of Gustavus Adolphus
1635	France declares war on Spain
1640	Portugal secedes from Spain
1643	Battle of Rocroi; French forces repel Spaniards
1648	Peace of Westphalia

WAR IS HELL

No source has better captured the brutality of the Thirty Years' War than the novel Simplicissimus *(1669). In a series of loosely connected episodes, the hero (whose name means "the simplest of the simple") is snatched from his village to serve in marauding armies whose confrontations with local villagers are usually more horrifying than the episode narrated here.*

Focus Questions

How do the peasants respond to the troopers' actions? What does this passage suggest about the breadth of the average villager's experience?

These troopers were even now ready to march, and had the pastor fastened by a rope to lead him away. Some cried, "Shoot him down, the rogue!" Others would have mercy from him. But he, lifting up his hands to heaven, begged, for the sake of the Last Judgment, for forbearance and Christian compassion, but in vain; for one of them rode down and dealt him such a blow on the head that he fell flat, and commended his soul to God. Nor did the remainder of the captured peasants fare any better. But even when it seemed these troopers, in their cruel tyranny, had clean lost their wits, came such a swarm of armed peasants out of the wood, that it seemed a wasps'-nest had been stirred. And these began to yell so frightfully and so furiously to attack with sword and musket that all my hair stood on end; and never had I been at such a merrymaking before: for the peasants of the Spessart and the Vogelsberg are as little wont as are the Hessians and men of the Sauerland and the Black Forest to let themselves be crowed over on their own dunghill. So away went the troopers, and not only left behind the cattle they had captured, but threw away bag and baggage also, and so cast all their booty to the winds lest themselves should become booty for the peasants: yet some of them fell into their hands. This sport took from me well-nigh all desire to see the world, for I thought, if 'tis all like this, then is the wilderness far more pleasant.

From Hans Von Grimmelshausen, *The Adventurous Simplicissimus.*

quished his Bohemian title and pressed for Ferdinand's election as the new king of Bohemia. Ferdinand was Catholic, very devout, and very committed. He had been educated by Jesuits and practiced what had been preached to him. On his own estates, Ferdinand abandoned the policy of toleration. Jesuit schools were founded and the precepts of the Council of Trent were enforced. Protestant preachers were barred from their offices, Protestant books were publicly burned, and thousands of common people were forced to flee, many into nearby Bohemia, where Protestants constituted the majority of the population.

Thus Ferdinand's election as king of Bohemia was no foregone conclusion. Although in the end the Protestant nobles of Bohemia could not prevent his election, they forced the new king to accept the strictest limitations upon his political and religious powers. But once elected, Ferdinand had not the slightest intention of honoring the provisions that had been thrust upon him. His opponents were equally strong willed. When Ferdinand violated Protestant religious liberties, a group of noblemen marched to the royal palace in Prague in May 1618, found two of the king's chief advisers, and hurled them out an upper-story window. The officials' lives—if not their dignity—were preserved by the pile of manure in which they landed.

The Defenestration of Prague, as the incident came to be known, initiated a Protestant counteroffensive throughout the Habsburg lands. Fear of Ferdinand's policies led to Protestant uprisings in Hungary as well as Bohemia. Those who seized control of the government declared Ferdinand deposed and the throne vacant, but they had no candidate to accept their crown. When Emperor Mathias died in 1619, the stalemate was broken. Ferdinand succeeded to the imperial title as Ferdinand II (1619–1637) and Frederick V, one of the Protestant electors, accepted the Bohemian crown.

Frederick V, the "Winter King."   Frederick was a sincere but weak Calvinist whose credentials were much stronger than his abilities. His mother was a daughter of Prince William of Orange and his wife, Elizabeth, a daughter of James I of England. It was widely believed that it was Elizabeth's resolution that she would "rather eat sauerkraut with a King than roast meat with an Elector" that decided the issue. No decision could have been more disastrous for the fate of Europe. Frederick ruled a geographically divided German state known as the Palatinate. One hundred miles separated the two segments of his lands, but both were strategically important. The Lower Palatinate bordered on the Catholic Spanish Netherlands and the Upper Palatinate on Catholic Bavaria.

Once Frederick accepted the Bohemian crown, he was faced with a war on three fronts. It was over almost before it began. At the Battle of the White Mountain in 1620, Ferdinand's Catholic forces annihilated Frederick's army. Frederick and Elizabeth fled north, first to Denmark and then to Holland. Bohemia was left to face the wrath of Ferdinand, the victorious king and emperor. The retribution was horrible. Mercenaries who had fought for Ferdinand II were allowed to sack Prague for a week. Elective monarchy was abolished, and Bohemia became part of the hereditary Habsburg lands. Free peasants were enserfed and subjected to imperial law. Those nobles who had supported Frederick lost their lands and their privileges. Calvinism was repressed and thoroughly rooted out, consolidating forever the Catholic character of Bohemia. Frederick's estates were carved up and his rights as elector transferred to the Catholic duke of Bavaria. The Battle of the White Mountain was a turning point in the history of central Europe.

The War Widens

For the Habsburgs, religious and dynastic interests were inseparable. Ferdinand II and Philip III of Spain fought for their beliefs and for their patrimony. Their victory gave them more than they could have expected: Ferdinand swallowed up Bohemia and strengthened his position in the empire, and Philip gained possession of a vital link in his supply route between Italy and the Netherlands. The Habsburgs were now more dangerous than ever. Ferdinand's aggressive Catholicism threatened the Protestant princes of Germany, who prudently began to seek allies outside the empire. Spanish expansion threatened France. The occupation of the Lower Palatinate placed a ring of Spanish armies around the French borders from the Pyrenees to the Low Countries. The French too searched for allies. But French opinion remained divided over which was the greater evil: Spain or Protestantism.

The Danes Respond.   Frederick, now in Holland, refused to accept the judgment of battle. He lobbied for a grand alliance to repel the Spaniards from the Lower Palatinate and to restore the religious balance in the empire. Although his personal cause met with little sympathy, his political logic was impeccable, especially after Spain again declared war upon the Dutch in 1621. A grand Protestant alliance—secretly supported by the French—brought together England, Holland, a number of German states, and Denmark. It was the Danes who led this potentially powerful coalition. In 1626, a large Danish army under the command of King Christian IV engaged imperial forces on German soil. But Danish forces could not match the superior numbers and the superior leadership of the Catholic mercenary forces under the command of the ruthless and brilliant Count Albrecht von Wallenstein (1583–1634). In 1629, the Danes withdrew from the empire and sued for peace.

If the Catholic victory at the White Mountain in 1620 threatened the well-being of German Protestantism, the Catholic triumph over the Danes threatened its survival. More powerful than ever, Ferdinand II determined to turn the religious clock back to the state of affairs that had existed when the Peace of Augsburg was concluded in 1555. He demanded that all lands that had then been Catholic but had since become Protestant be returned to the fold. He also proclaimed that as the Peace of Augsburg made no provision for the toleration of Calvinists, they would no longer be tolerated in the empire. Those policies together constituted a virtual revolution in the religious affairs of the German states, and they proved impossible to impose. Ferdinand succeeded in only one thing—he united Lutherans and Calvinists against him.

Protestant Gains.   In 1630, King Gustavus Adolphus of Sweden decided to enter the German conflict. To protect Swedish interests, he reasoned, he must defend the Protestant states of northern Germany. Moreover, France was willing to pay much of the cost of a war against Ferdinand. The French

■ Gustavus Adolphus of Sweden, shown at the battle of Breitenfeld in 1631. The battle was the first important Protestant victory of the Thirty Years' War. Gustavus died on the battlefield at Lützen in the following year.

FIRE AND SWORD

No event of the Thirty Years' War had a greater effect on public opinion than the annihilation of the Protestant city of Magdeburg in 1631. Dozens of pamphlets and woodcuts, including this anonymous account, detailed the slaughter of civilians and the devastation of property. It was commonly believed that neither a human nor an animal escaped the destruction.

Focus Questions

What motivated those who destroyed Magdeburg? What is the writer trying to achieve with this account?

Thus it came about that the city and all its inhabitants fell into the hands of the enemy, whose violence and cruelty were due in part to their common hatred of the adherents of the Augsburg Confession, and in part to their being imbittered by the chain shot which had been fired at them and by the derision and insults that the Magdeburgers had heaped upon them from the ramparts.

Then was there naught but beating and burning, plundering, torture, and murder. Most especially was every one of the enemy bent on securing much booty. When a marauding party entered a house, if its master had anything to give he might thereby purchase respite and protection for himself and his family till the next man, who also wanted something, should come along. . . .

Thus in a single day this noble and famous city, the pride of the whole country, went up in fire and smoke; and the remnant of its citizens, with their wives and children, were taken prisoners and driven away by the enemy with a noise of weeping and wailing that could be heard from afar, while the cinders and ashes from the town were carried by the wind to Wanzleben, Egeln, and still more distant places. . . .

too felt the pressure of increasing imperial and Spanish power. Gustavus Adolphus had more success gaining the support of Catholic France than he did gaining the support of the Protestant German princes. Saxony and Brandenburg, the two largest states, feared the consequences of renewed war. Gustavus believed that he could defend the north German states from Ferdinand's aggression and by doing so protect Sweden's Baltic empire. "I seek not my own advantage in this war, nor any gain save the security of my Kingdom," he lectured the reluctant Germans. It was a farsighted strategy. In fact, the only thing he could not foresee when he landed in Germany early in 1630 was how successful his intervention would be.

While Gustavus Adolphus struggled to construct his alliance, imperial forces continued their triumphant progress. In 1631 they besieged, captured, and put to the torch the town of Magdeburg. In a war noted for cruelty between combatants and atrocities against civilians, the destruction of Magdeburg set new standards. Perhaps three-fourths of the 40,000 inhabitants of the town were slaughtered—"in the midst of a horrible din of heart-rending shrieks and cries they were tortured and put to death in so cruel a manner that no words would suffice to describe nor no tears to bewail it," was the report in one pamphlet. The sack of Magdeburg marked a turning point in Protestant fortunes. It gave the international Protestant community a unifying symbol that enhanced Gustavus's military efforts. Hundreds of pamphlets, woodcuts, and newspaper accounts brought the horror of Magdeburg home to Protestants throughout the Continent. Brandenburg and Saxony joined Gustavus Adolphus, not only enlarging his forces, but allowing him to open a second front in Bohemia. He would soon have 140,000 men under his command, only 13,000 of whom were Swedish. In the autumn of 1631, the combination overwhelmed the imperial armies. Gustavus won a decisive triumph at Breitenfeld, while the Saxons occupied Prague. For the first time since 1618, Protestant forces were ascendant, and they brought the war into the Catholic heartland of the empire.

Gustavus Adolphus lost no time in pressing his advantage. The Swedes marched west to the Rhine, easily conquering the richest of the Catholic cities and retaking the Lower Palatinate. In early 1632, Protestant forces plundered Bavaria. It was the Bavarian ruler Maximilian who had gained most from the years of war. His troops had occupied the Upper Palatinate, and he had received Frederick's rights as imperial elector in return for support of Ferdinand. Moreover, Maximilian had played a double game of negotiating with the French for neutrality and with the emperor for the spoils of victory. So there was poetic justice when Maximilian's state was invaded, his castles looted, and his lands plundered. But there was no justice at all for the wretched inhabitants of that stronghold of German Catholicism. Town and countryside were laid waste. Not until the winter of 1632 did the armies of Gustavus and Wallenstein finally meet. At the battle of Lützen the Swedes won the field but lost their beloved king. Wounded in the leg, the back, and the head, Gustavus Adolphus died. In less

MAP DISCOVERY

Percentage Loss:

| No Change | Up to 10 | 11–20 | 21–30 | 31–40 | 41–50 | Over 50 |

Population Loss in Germany During the Thirty Years' War

Notice the pattern of population loss during the war. Where was it heaviest? Where was it lightest? Based on the chapter discussion, how might the intervention of Sweden into the war help explain this pattern?

The Long Quest for Peace

The Thirty Years' War was barely half over when Gustavus Adolphus fell at Lützen. But from that time forward, its central European phase receded in importance. The final stages of the war involved the resumption of the century-old struggle between France and Spain. When the Twelve Years' Truce expired in 1621, Spain again declared war upon the Dutch. Philip III's hopes of concentrating all his resources against Holland had been disappointed by the outbreak of war in central Europe. Not until after the Bohemian revolt had been repressed did the Spanish army begin the long, laborious process of besieging the well-fortified and well-defended towns of the Netherlands. The resumption of war in the Netherlands, combined with the continued successes of Habsburg forces in central Europe, convinced Louis XIII and his chief minister, Cardinal Richelieu, that the time for active French involvement in European affairs was at hand. Throughout the early stages of the war, France had secretly aided anti-Habsburg forces. The time had come to take an open stand. In 1635, France declared war on Spain.

Neither country was prepared for large-scale military action, and neither could afford it. The war resembled nothing so much as two punch-drunk fighters pounding each other, both receiving as much punishment as they inflicted. France took the offensive first, invading the Spanish Netherlands. In 1636, a Spanish army struck back, pushing to within 25 miles of Paris before it was repelled. Both sides soon began to search for a settlement, but pride prevented them from laying down their gloves. Spain toppled first. Its economy in shambles and its citizens in revolt over high prices and higher taxes, it could no longer maintain its many-fronted war. The Swedes again defeated imperial forces in Germany, the Dutch destroyed much of Spain's Atlantic fleet in 1639, and the

than two years he had decisively transformed the course of the war and the course of Europe's future. Protestant forces now occupied most of central and northern Germany. Ferdinand's ability to redraw the religious map of the empire was at an end.

■ This painting by Jan Brueghel (1568–1625) and Sebastien Vranx (1573–1647) evokes the ravaging of the countryside by the belligerent armies between battles in the Thirty Years' War.

Portuguese rose up against the union of crowns that had brought them nothing but expense and the loss of crucial portions of their empire. In 1640, the Portuguese regained their independence. In 1643, Spain gambled once more on a knockout blow against the French. But at the battle of Rocroi, exhausted French troops held out and the Spanish invasion failed.

By then the desire for peace was universal. Most of the main combatants had long since perished: Philip III, ever optimistic, in 1621; Frederick V, an exile to the end, in 1632; Gustavus Adolphus, killed at Lützen in the same year; Wallenstein, murdered by order of Ferdinand II in 1634; Ferdinand himself in 1637; and Louis XIII in 1643, five days before the French triumph at Rocroi. Those who succeeded them had not the same passions, and after so many decades the longing for peace was the strongest emotion on the Continent. At the beginning of 1648, Spain and the Netherlands concluded their 80 years of fighting. The bilateral agreement broke the logjam. One by one, the combatants agreed to end their hostilities with one another, and soon the stage was set for a Continentwide settlement.

A series of agreements, collectively known as the Peace of Westphalia, established the outlines of the political geography of Europe for the next century. Its focus was on the Holy Roman Empire, and it reflected Protestant successes in the final two decades of war. Sweden gained further territories on the Baltic, making it master of the north German ports. France, too, gained in territory and prestige. It kept the vital towns in the Lower Palatinate through which Spanish men and material had moved, and though it did not agree to come to terms with Spain immediately, France's fear of encir-

clement was at an end. The Dutch gained statehood through official recognition by Spain and through the power they had displayed in building and maintaining an overseas empire.

Territorial boundaries were reestablished as they had existed in 1624, giving the Habsburgs control of both Bohemia and Hungary. The independence of the Swiss cantons was now officially recognized, as were the rights of Calvinists to the protection of the Peace of Augsburg, which again was to govern the religious affairs of the empire. Two of the larger German states were strengthened to balance the emperor's power. Bavaria was allowed to retain the Upper Palatinate, and Brandenburg, which ceded some of its coastal territory to Sweden, gained extensive territories in the east.

The emperor's political control over the German states was also weakened. German rulers were given independent authority over their states, and the imperial Diet, rather than the emperor, was empowered to settle disputes. Thus weakened, future emperors ruled in the Habsburg territorial lands with little ability to control, influence, or even arbitrate German affairs. The judgment that the Holy Roman Empire was neither holy, nor Roman, nor an empire was now irrevocably true.

CONCLUSION

The Peace of Westphalia put the pieces of the map of European states back together. Protestantism and Catholicism now coexisted and there was to be little further change in the geography of religion. The northwest of Europe—England, Holland,

☐	Spanish dominions
☐	Austrian dominions
■	Swedish dominions
■	Brandenburg–Prussia
▬	Boundary of the Holy Roman Empire

■ The Peace of Westphalia, 1648. The agreement recognized the new boundaries of European states that included an independent Portugal and the United Netherlands. It also recognized the growth of the Ottoman Empire into the Balkans.

Scandinavia, and the north German states—was Protestant, while the south was Catholic. The empire of the German peoples was at an end, the Austro-Hungarian Empire at a beginning. Holland and Sweden had become international powers; Spain and Denmark faded from prominence. Muscovy began a long period of isolation from the west, attempting to restore a semblance of government to its people. But if the negotiators at Westphalia could resolve the political and religious ambitions that gave rise to a century of nearly continuous warfare, they could do nothing to eradicate the effects of war itself. The devastation of humanity in the name of God with which the reform of religion had begun was exhausted. The costs were horrific. The population of Germany fell from 15 million in 1600 to 11 million in 1650. The armies brought destruction of all kinds in their wake. Plague again raged in Europe—the town of Augsburg lost 18,000 inhabitants in the early 1630s. Famine, too,

returned to a continent that 50 years earlier had been self-sufficient in grain. The war played havoc with all of the economies that it touched. Inflation, devaluation of coinage, and huge public and private debts were all directly attributable to the years of fighting. And the toll taken on the spirit of those generations that never knew peace is incalculable.

QUESTIONS FOR REVIEW

1. How was Henry IV able to bring peace to France after decades of civil war?
2. What were the political and religious connections between the Armada launched against England by Philip II and the revolt of the Netherlands?
3. How did Sweden rise to become one of Europe's great powers in the first half of the seventeenth century?

4. How did religion help spark and spread the Thirty Years' War?

5. What were the effects of the Peace of Westphalia on political arrangements in the heart of Europe?

KEY TERMS

Catholic League, *p. 418*

Edict of Nantes, *p. 418*

French wars of religion, *p. 413*

Huguenots, *p. 414*

Polish Diet, *p. 426*

politiques, *p. 418*

Spanish Armada, *p. 421*

Thirty Years' War, *p. 430*

Time of Troubles, *p. 427*

DISCOVERING WESTERN CIVILIZATION ONLINE

You can obtain more information about Europe at war at the Websites listed below. See also the Companion Website that accompanies this text, www.ablongman.com/kishlansky, which contains an online study guide and additional resources.

The Crises of the Western States

Internet Modern History Sourcebook: Early Modern West

www.fordham.edu/halsall/mod/modsbook1.html#Conflict

Links to documents on the French wars of religion, the invasion of the Spanish Armada, and the Thirty Years' War.

WebMuseum: The Northern Renaissance (1500–1615)

www.ibiblio.org/wm/paint/tl/north-ren/

Links to pictures and portraits from the late sixteenth and early seventeenth centuries.

Pieter Bruegel the Elder: *The Triumph of Death*

www.ibiblio.org/wm/paint/auth/bruegel/death.jpg

A Web page depicting Peter Brueghel's *Triumph of Death*, one of the most evocative paintings of the destruction wrought by warfare in early modern Europe.

The Thirty Years' War, 1618–1648

The Avalon Project: Treaty of Westphalia

www.yale.edu/lawweb/avalon/westphal.htm

The full text of the Treaty of Westphalia that ended the Thirty Years' War.

SUGGESTIONS FOR FURTHER READING

General Reading

M. S. Anderson, *The Origins of the Modern European State System, 1494–1618* (London: Longman, 1998). A survey of developments stressing war and diplomacy across all of Europe.

Jan de Vries, *The European Economy in an Age of Crisis* (Cambridge: Cambridge University Press, 1976). A comprehensive study of economic development, including long-distance trade and commercial change.

J. H. Elliott, *Europe Divided, 1559–1598* (New York: Harper & Row, 1968). An outstanding synthesis of European politics in the second half of the sixteenth century.

Mark Konnert, *Early Modern Europe: The Age of Religious War, 1559–1715* (Peterborough: Ontario Broadview Press, 2006). Konnert examines political wars and their religious motivations within their social, economic, and intellectual contexts.

Geoffrey Parker, *Europe in Crisis, 1598–1648* (London: William Collins and Sons, 1979). Compelling study of European states in the early seventeenth century.

The Crises of the Western States

Susan Brigden, *New Worlds, Lost Worlds: The Rule of the Tudors, 1485–1603* (New York: Viking, 2001). The latest volume in the new Penguin History of Britain series.

J. A. Guy, *Tudor England* (Oxford: Oxford University Press, 1988). A magisterial survey by the leading scholar of Tudor England.

Mack P. Holt, *The French Wars of Religion, 1562–1629* (New York: Cambridge, 2005). An important work integrating popular and court experience during the French wars of religion.

Henry Kamen, *Spain, 1469–1714* (London: Longman, 1983). A thorough survey with valuable interpretations.

Robert Kingdon, *Myths about the St. Bartholomew's Day Massacres, 1572–1576* (Cambridge, MA: Harvard University Press, 1988). A study of the impact of a central event in the history of France.

R. J. Knecht, *The French Civil Wars, 1562–1598* (New York: Pearson Education, 2000). A compact survey of the religious, social, and political dimensions of the conflicts that raged in France through the second half of the sixteenth century.

John Lynch, *Spain, 1516–1598: From Nation State to World Empire* (Cambridge, MA: Blackwell Publishers, 1994). An up-to-date survey.

Garrett Mattingly, *The Armada* (Boston: Houghton Mifflin, 1959). Still the classic account, despite recent reinterpretations.

Geoffrey Parker, *The Dutch Revolt* (London: Penguin Books, 1977). An outstanding account of the tangle of events that comprised the revolts of the Netherlands.

Geoffrey Parker, *Philip II* (Boston: Little, Brown, 1978). The best introduction.

Michael Roberts, *Gustavus Adolphus and the Rise of Sweden* (London: English Universities Press, 1973). A highly readable account of Sweden's rise to power.

C. V. Wedgwood, *William the Silent, William of Nassau, Prince of Orange, 1533–1584* (New York: Norton, 1968). A stylish biography.

Alison Weir, *Elizabeth the Queen* (London: J. Cape, 1998). A lively biography of the great queen.

The Struggles in Eastern Europe

Robert Frost, *The Northern Wars: War, State and Society in Northeastern Europe, 1558–1721* (New York: Longman, 2000) Examining an oft-neglected sector of European political history, a noted historian explains how Sweden and Poland lost their hegemony to Russia and Prussia during the course of the seventeenth century.

David Kirby, *Northern Europe in the Early Modern Period: The Baltic World, 1492–1772* (London: Longman, 1990). The best single volume on Baltic politics.

S. F. Platonov, *The Time of Troubles* (Lawrence: University Press of Kansas, 1970). A good narrative of the disintegration of the Muscovite state.

Michael Roberts, *The Swedish Imperial Experience* (Cambridge: Cambridge University Press, 1979). Reflections on Swedish history by the preeminent historian of early modern Sweden.

The Thirty Years' War

J. H. Elliott, *Richelieu and Olivares* (Cambridge: Cambridge University Press, 1984). A comparison of statesmen and statesmanship in the early seventeenth century.

Peter Limm, *The Thirty Years' War* (London: Longman, 1984). An excellent brief survey with documents.

Geoffrey Parker, ed., *The Thirty Years' War*, 2d ed. (London: Routledge, 1997). A revised edition of the standard survey of the conflict.

Geoffrey Parker, *The World Crisis: Thirty Years of War, Famine, Plague, Regicide, and Radicalism, 1635–1665* (London: Perseus, 2007). A dynamic, broad history of a tumultuous three decades by a prize-winning military historian.

For a list of additional titles related to this chapter's topics, please see http://www.ablongman.com/kishlansky.

15 THE EXPERIENCES OF LIFE IN EARLY MODERN EUROPE, 1500–1650

HAYMAKING

AGRICULTURE IN A EUROPEAN COMMUNITY

THE VISUAL RECORD

It is summer in the Low Countries. The trees are full, the meadows green; flowers rise in clumps and bushes hang heavy with fruit. The day has dawned brightly for haymaking. Yesterday the long meadow was mowed, and today the hay will be gathered and the first fruits and vegetables of the season harvested. From throughout the village families come together to labor. Twice each summer the grass is cut, dried, and stacked. Some of it will be left in the fields for the animals until autumn; some will be carried into large lofts and stored for the winter.

The scene of communal farming shown here was repeated with little variation throughout Europe in the early modern era. The village pictured is fairly prosperous with at least three horses and a large wheeled cart in view. Horses were still a luxury for farmers; they could be used for transportation as well as labor, but they were weaker than oxen and had to be fed grain rather than grass. The houses of the village also suggest comfort. The one at the far right is typical. It contains one floor for living and a loft for storage. The chimney separates a kitchen in the back from the long hall where the family works, sleeps, and entertains itself. The bed—it was not uncommon for there to be only one for the whole family—would be near the fireplace, and would be restuffed with straw after the harvest. The long end of the hall, farthest from heat and light, would be home to the family's animals once winter set in. But in summer it was a luxurious space where children could play or parents could claim a little privacy.

The church is easily distinguished by its steeple and is made of brick. The steeple has 16 windows, probably all set with expensive glass and even some stained glass. The church would have been built over several generations at considerable cost to the villagers. Even the most prosperous houses in the far meadow are made of timber and thatch. The layout of the buildings shows how the village must have grown. The original settlement was all on the rise above the church. The houses nearer the center of the picture were added later, perhaps to allow the sons of the more prosperous village farmers to begin their own families before their parents' deaths.

In the center of the scene are a large number of laborers. Four men with pitchforks load the cart while two women sweep the hay that falls back into new piles. Throughout the field, men and women, distinguished only by their clothing,

■ Detail of women laborers.

■ *Haymaking* (ca. 1565) by Pieter Brueghel.

rake hay into large stacks for successive loadings of the cart. At least 25 individuals work at these tasks. Men perform the heaviest work of loading the haycart and hammering the scythes while men and women share all the other work. Although no children appear in the scene, some are undoubtedly at work picking berries and beans.

The scenes of physical labor remind us that the life of ordinary people in the early modern period was neither romantic nor despondent, neither quaint nor primitive. It had its own joys and sorrows, its own triumphs and failures, its own measures of progress and decay. By today's standards, a sixteenth-century prince endured greater material hardships than a twentieth-century welfare recipient. There was no running water, no central heating, no lavatories, no electricity. There was no relief for toothache, headache, or numbing pain. Travel was dangerous and exhausting. There was no protection from the open air, and many nights were spent on the bare ground. Waiting for winds to sail was more tedious than waiting to board a plane. Entertainment was sparse, and the court jester would have been little match for stereo and video. Though we cannot help but be struck by the differences, we will not understand very much about the experience of life in sixteenth-century Europe if we judge it by our own standard of living.

LOOKING AHEAD

In this chapter, we will examine the social and economic conditions of early modern European society, dominated as it was by extreme change, and often, hardship. We will see how population growth put pressure on the European economy and how the rich became richer as food prices rose. We will also see how European governments were overwhelmed by changes they could only dimly perceive.

ECONOMIC LIFE

There was no typical sixteenth-century European. Travelers' accounts and ambassadors' reports indicate that contemporaries were constantly surprised by the habits and possessions of other Europeans. Language, custom, geography, and material conditions separated peoples in one place from those in another. Contrasts between social groups were more striking still. A Muscovite boyar had more in common with an English nobleman than either had with his country's peasants. A Spanish goldsmith and a German brass maker lived remarkably similar lives when compared to the life of a shepherd anywhere in Europe. No matter how carefully historians attempt to distinguish between country and town life, between social or occupational groups, or between men and women, they are still smoothing out edges that are very rough, still turning individuals into aggregates, still sacrificing the particular for the general. No French peasant family ever had 3.5 children even if, on average, they all did. There was no typical sixteenth-century European.

But there were experiences that most Europeans shared and common structures through which their activities were channeled that separated them from their predecessors and their successors. There was a distinctive sixteenth-century experience that we can easily discern and that they could dimly perceive. Much of it was a natural progression in which one generation improved upon the situation of another. Agriculture increased: more land was cleared, more crops were grown, and better tools were crafted. Some of the experience was natural regression. Irreplaceable resources were lost: more trees were felled, more soil was eroded, and more fresh water was polluted. But some of what was distinctive about sixteenth-century life resulted from dynamic changes in economic and social conditions. The century-long population explosion and increase in commodity prices fundamentally altered people's lives. Not since the Black Death had Europe experienced so thorough a transformation in its economic development and its social organization. Change and reactions to change became dominant themes of everyday life.

Rural Life

In the early modern era, as much as 90 percent of the European population lived on farms or in small towns in which farming was the principal occupation. Villages were small and relatively isolated, even in densely populated regions such as Italy and the Low Countries. They might range in size from 100 families, as was common in France and Spain, to fewer than 20 families, which was the average size of Hungarian villages. The villages, large or small, prosperous or poor, were the bedrock of the sixteenth-century state. A sur-

IMAGE DISCOVERY

A Rural Scene: Social or Religious?

This picture depicts the slaughtering of a hog, which required winter weather, and baking in a communal oven, which happened year-round. Why do you suppose impoverished peasants caught the blood from the slit throat of the hog? The illustration comes from a sixteenth-century calendar of religious observances and devotions. Would the readers of this calendar have participated in scenes like those pictured? Why or why not?

plus peasant population fed the insatiable appetite of towns for laborers and of crowns for soldiers. The manor, the parish, and the rural administrative district were the institutional infrastructures of Europe. Each organized the peasantry for its own purposes. Manorial rents supported the lifestyle of the nobility; parish tithes supported the works of the Church; local taxes supported the power of the state. Rents, tithes, and taxes easily absorbed more than half of the wealth produced by the land. From the remaining half, the peasants had to make provisions for their present and their future.

To survive, the village community had to be self-sufficient. In good times there was enough to eat and some to save for the future. Hard times meant hunger and starvation. Both conditions were accepted as part of the natural order, and both occurred regularly. One in every three harvests was bad; one in every five was disastrous. Bad harvests came in succession. Depending upon the soil and crop, between one-fifth and one-half of the grain harvested had to be saved as seed for the next planting season. When hunger was worst, people faced the agonizing choice of eating or saving their seed corn.

The Sixteenth-Century Household.   Hunger and cold were the constant companions of the average European. In Scandinavia and Muscovy, winter posed as great a threat to survival as did starvation. There the stove and garments made from animal fur were essential requirements, as were the hearth and the woolen tunic in the south. Everywhere in Europe, homes were inadequate shelter against the cold and damp. Most were built of wood and roofed in thatch. Inside walls were patched with dried mud and sometimes covered with bark or animal skins. Windows were few and narrow.

Piled leaves or straw, which could easily be replaced, covered the ground and acted as insulation. The typical house was one long room with a stone hearth at the end. The hearth provided both heat and light and belched forth soot and smoke through a brick chimney.

People had relatively few household possessions. The essential piece of furniture was the wooden chest, which was used for storage. A typical family could keep all of its belongings in the chest, which could then be buried or carried away in times of danger. The chest could also serve as a table or bench or as a sideboard on which food could be placed. Tables and stools were becoming more common during the sixteenth century, though chairs were still a great luxury. Most domestic activities, of which cooking, eating, and sleeping were dominant, took place close to the ground, and squatting, kneeling, and sitting were the usual postures of family members. All other family possessions related to food production. Iron spits and pots, or at least metal rings and clamps for wooden ones, were treasured goods that were passed from generation to generation. Most other implements were wooden. Long-handled spoons; boards known as trenchers, which were used for cutting and eating; and one large cup and bowl were the basic stock of the kitchen. The family ate from the long trencher and passed the bowl and cup. Knives were essential farm tools that doubled for kitchen and mealtime duty, but forks were still a curiosity.

Reliance on Agriculture.   Peasant life centered on agriculture. Technology and technique varied little across the continent, but there were significant differences depending upon climate and soil. The lives of those who grew crops contrasted

■ This picture, painted in 1530, shows farmworkers threshing grain. The figure at the door seems to be an overseer. He has just sold a sack of grain, indicating the transition from a system of self-sufficient manors to a market economy.

with the experiences of those who raised animals. Across the great plain, the breadbasket that stretched from the Low Countries to Poland-Lithuania, the most common form of crop growing was still the **three-field rotation** system. In that method, winter crops such as wheat or rye were planted in one field; spring crops such as barley, peas, or beans were planted in another; and the third field was left fallow. More than 80 percent of what was grown on the farm was consumed on the farm. Most of the grain was baked into the coarse black bread that was the monotonous fare of the peasant diet. Two to three pounds a day for an adult male was an average allotment when grain was readily available. Beer and gruels of grain and skimmed milk or water flavored with fruit juice supplemented peasant fare. In one form or another, grain provided more than 75 percent of the calories in a typical diet.

The warm climate and dry weather of Mediterranean Europe favored a two-crop rotation system. With less water and stronger sunlight, half the land had to be left fallow each year to restore its nutrients. There fruit, especially grapes and olives, was an essential supplement to diet. With smaller cereal crops, wine replaced beer as a nutritious beverage. The fermentation of grapes and grain into wine and beer also provided convenient ways of storing foodstuffs, a constant problem during the winter and early spring. Wine and olive oil were also luxury products and were most commonly exchanged for meat, which was less plentiful on southern European farms.

Animal husbandry was the main occupation in the third agricultural area of Europe, the mountainous and hilly regions. Sheep were the most common animal that Europeans raised. Sheep provided the raw material for almost all clothing, their skins were used for parchment and as window coverings, and they were a ready source of inexpensive meat. They were bred in hundreds of thousands, migrating across large areas of grazing land, especially in western Europe,

where their wool was the main export of both England and Spain. Pigs were domestic animals prevalent in woodland settlements. They foraged for food and were kept, like poultry, for slaughter. Cattle, on the other hand, were essential farm animals. "The fundamentals of the home," wrote the Spanish poet Luis de Leon (1527–1591), "are the woman and the ox, the ox to plow and the woman to manage things." In the dairying areas of Europe, cattle produced milk, cheese, and butter; in Hungary and Bohemia, the great breeding center of the Continent, they were raised for export; and almost everywhere else they were used as beasts of burden.

Because agriculture was the principal occupation of Europeans, land was the principal resource. Most land was owned, not by those who worked it, but by lords who let it out in various ways. The land was still divided into manors, and the manor lord, or **seigneur,** was still responsible for maintaining order, administering justice, and arbitrating disputes. Although the personal bonds between lords and tenants were gradually loosening, political and economic ties were as strong as ever. In western Europe, peasants generally owned between a third and a half of the land they worked, while eastern European peasants owned little if any land. But by the sixteenth century, almost all peasants enjoyed security of tenure on the land they worked. In return for various forms of rents, they used the land as they saw fit and could hand it down to their children. Rents were only occasionally paid in coin, although money rents became more common as the century progressed. More frequently, the lord received a fixed proportion of the yield of the land or received labor from the peasant. Labor service was being replaced by monetary payments in northern and western Europe, but it continued in the east, where it was known as the **robot.** German and Hungarian peasants normally owed two or three days' labor on the lord's estate each week, while Polish peasants might owe as many as

■ Painting of a town market by Italian painter Leandro da Ponte Bassano (1557–1622). In sixteenth-century Europe, towns were centers of commercial activity, and such scenes of bartering and buying goods were common.

LIVING BY ONE'S WITS

The Life of Lazarillo des Tormes (1554) is among the first modern novels, one of a variety of sixteenth-century Spanish stories that are called picaresque *after the wandering beggars that are their heroes. Although the picaresque novel was a fictional account, much of the descriptive detail accurately portrays the social conditions for the vast majority of the Spanish population in the so-called Golden Age.*

Focus Questions

Why is it so important for Lazarillo to use his cunning? Why is the reader encouraged to sympathize with the narrator?

We began our journey, and in a few days he taught me thieves' jargon, and when he saw me to be of a good wit, was well pleased, and used to say: "Gold or silver I cannot give thee, but I will show thee many pointers about life." And it was so; for after God this man gave me my life, and although blind lighted and guided me in the career of living.

He used to carry bread and everything else in a linen sack which closed at the mouth with an iron ring and a padlock and key, and when he put things in and took them out, it was with so much attention, so well counted, that the whole world wouldn't have been equal to making it a crumb less. But I would take what stingy bit he gave me, and finish it in less than two mouthfuls. After he had fastened the lock and stopped worrying about it, thinking me to be engaged in other things, by a little seam, which I unsewed and sewed up again many times in the side of the sack, I used to bleed the miserly sack, taking out bread—not measured quantities but good pieces—and slices of bacon and sausage; and thus would seek a convenient time to make good the devilish state of want which the wicked blind man left me in.

When we ate he used to put a little jug of wine near him. I would quickly seize it and give it a couple of silent kisses and return it to its place; but this plan didn't work long, for he noticed the deficiency in his draughts, and in order to keep his wine safe, he never after let go the jug, but kept hold of the handle. But there is no lode-stone that draws things to it so strongly as I with a long rye straw, which I had prepared for that purpose, and placing which in the mouth of the jug, I would suck up the wine to a fare-ye-well. But the villain was so clever that I think he heard me; and from then on he changed procedure and set his jug between his legs and covered it with his hand, and thus drank secure.

We were at Escalona, town of the Duke of that ilk, in an inn, and he gave me a piece of sausage to roast. When he had basted the sausage and eaten the basting, he took a maravedi from his purse and bade me fetch wine from the tavern. The devil put the occasion before my eyes, which, as the saying is, makes the thief; and it was this: there lay by the fire a small turnip, rather long and bad, and which must have been thrown there because it was not fit for the stew. And as nobody was there at the time but him and me alone, as I had an appetite whetted by having got the toothsome odour of the sausage inside me (the only part, as I knew, that I had to enjoy myself with), not considering what might follow, all fear set aside in order to comply with desire—while the blind man was taking the money out of his purse, I took the sausage, and quickly put the above-mentioned turnip on the spit, which my master grasped, when he had given me the money for the wine, and began to turn before the fire, trying to roast what through its demerit had escaped being boiled. I went for the wine, and on the way did not delay in despatching the sausage, and when I came back I found the sinner of a blind man holding the turnip ready between two slices of bread, for he had not yet recognized it, because he had not tried it with his hand. When he took the slices of bread and bit into them, thinking to get part of the sausage too, he found himself chilled by the chilly turnip.

From *Lazarillo des Tormes.*

---

four days. Labor service tied the peasants to the land they worked. Eastern European peasants were less mobile than peasants in the west, and as a result towns were fewer and smaller in the east.

Town Life

In the country, men and women worked to the natural rhythm of the day: up at the cock's crow, at work in the cooler hours, at rest in the hotter ones. Rain and cold kept them idle; sunlight kept them busy. Each season brought its own activity.

In the town the bell tolled every hour. In the summer the laborers gathered at the town gates at four in the morning, in the winter at seven. The bell signaled the time for morning and afternoon meals as well as the hour to lay down tools and return home. Wages were paid for hours worked: 7 in winter, as many as 16 in June and July.

The Heart of Commerce.   In all towns there was an official guild structure that organized and regulated labor. Rules laid down the requirements for training, the standards for quality, and the conditions for exchange. Only those officially sanctioned could work in trades, and each trade could perform only specified tasks. In the German town of Nüremberg, a sword maker could not make knives nor could a pin maker make thimbles. Specialization went even further in London, Paris, and other large cities.

While the life of the peasant community turned on self-sufficiency, that of the town turned on interdependence. Exchange was the medium that transformed labor and skill into food and shelter. The town was one large marketplace in which the circulation of goods dictated the survival of the residents. Men and women in towns worked as hard as did those on farms, but town dwellers received a more varied and more comfortable life in return. However, that did not mean that hunger and hardship were unknown in towns. Urban poverty was endemic and grew worse as the century wore on. In most towns, as much as a quarter of the entire population might be destitute, living from casual day labor, charity, or crime. But even for those people, food was more readily available in greater varieties than in the countryside, and the institutional network of support for the poor and homeless was stronger. In Lyon, the overseers of the poor distributed a daily ration of a pound and a half of bread, more than half of what a farm laborer would consume. The urban poor more often fell victim to disease than to starvation.

Towns were distinguished by the variety of occupations that existed within them. The preparation and exchange of food dominated small market towns. Peasants would bring in their finest produce for sale and exchange it for vital manufactured goods such as iron spits and pots for cooking or metal and leather tools for farm work. In smaller towns, there was as much barter as sale; in larger places, money was exchanged for commodities. Women dominated the food trades in most market towns, trading, buying, and selling in the shop fronts that occupied the bottom story of their houses. Because of their skills in food preparation, they were better able to obtain the best prices and advantageously display the best goods.

The Work Force. In larger towns, the specialization of labor was more intense and wage earning more essential. Large traders dominated the major occupations such as baking, brewing, and cloth manufacture, leaving distribution in the hands of the family economy, where there might still be a significant element of bartering. Piecework handicrafts became the staple for less prosperous town families, who prepared raw materials for the large manufacturers or finished products before their sale. Occupations were usually organized geographically, with metal or glassworking taking place in one quarter of the town, brewing or baking in another. There was a strong family and kin network to the occupations, as each craft required long years of technical training, which was handed down from parents to children.

Most town dwellers, however, lived by unskilled labor. The most lucrative occupations were strictly controlled, so those who flocked to towns in search of employment usually hired themselves out as day laborers, hauling and lifting goods onto carts or boats, stacking materials at building sites, or delivering water and food. After the first decades of the sixteenth century, the supply of laborers exceeded the amount of work to occupy them, and town authorities were constantly attempting to expel them. The most fortunate might succeed in becoming servants.

Domestic service was a critical source of household labor. Even families on the margins of subsistence employed ser-

■ Van Schwanerburg (1537–1614), *The Spinners*. Workers spinning and weaving wool. Labor in large towns was often specialized into occupations such as baking, brewing, and cloth manufacture.

MAP DISCOVERY

Grain Supply and Trade in Sixteenth-Century Europe

Where were the breadbaskets of Europe located? What was the relationship between urban areas and grain supply? How did grain move from suppliers to consumers?

Grain surplus areas

Grain deficit areas

Grain trade routes

0   500 Miles
0   500 Kilometers

Economic Change

Over the course of the sixteenth century, the European population increased by about a third, with much of the growth taking place in the first 50 years. Rough estimates suggest the rise to have been from about 80 to 105 million. Patterns of growth varied by region. The population of the eastern part of Europe seems to have increased more steadily across the century, while western Europe experienced a population explosion in the early decades. The population of France may have doubled between 1450 and 1550, from 10 to 20 million. The population of England nearly doubled between 1500 and 1600, from more than 2 million to more than 4 million. Castile, the largest region in Spain, grew 50 percent in 50 years. Europe had finally recovered from the devastation of the Black Death, and by 1600 its population was greater than it had ever been. Demographic growth was even more dramatic in the cities. In 1500, only four cities had populations greater than 100,000; in 1600, there were eight. Naples grew from 150,000 to 280,000, and both Paris and London to more than 200,000 inhabitants. Fifteen large cities more than doubled their populations, with London experiencing a phenomenal 400 percent increase.

The rise in population dramatically affected the lives of ordinary Europeans. In the early part of the century, the first phase of growth brought prosperity. The land was still not farmed to capacity, and extra hands meant increased productivity. As there was uncultivated land that could be plowed, convenient room for new housing, and enough commons and woodlands to be shared, the population increase was a welcome development. Even when rural communities began to reach their natural limits as people's needs pressed against nature's resources, opportunity still existed in the burgeoning towns and cities. At first the cycle was beneficial. Surplus on the farms led to economic growth in the towns. Growth in the towns meant more opportunities for those on the farms. More food supported more workers, and more

vants to undertake the innumerable household tasks, which allowed parents to pursue their primary occupations. Everything was done by hand and on foot, and extra pairs of each were essential. In Münster at mid-century, there were 400 servants for 1000 households. Domestics were not apprentices, though they might aspire to become apprentices to the trade followed in the family with whom they lived. If they had kinship bonds in the town, apprenticeship was a likely outcome. But more commonly, domestics remained household servants, frequently changing employers in hope of more comfortable housing and better food.

MAP DISCOVERY

People per square mile

- Over 60
- 30 to 60
- 10 to 30
- Under 10

Population Density in Europe, ca. 1600

Which were the most populated parts of Europe at the beginning of the seventeenth century? Which were the least populated? What was the relationship between population and access to water routes?

European Population Density, c. 1600

workers produced more goods and services, which were exchanged for more food.

The first waves of migrants to the towns found opportunity everywhere. Even the most lucrative textile and provisioning trades were recruiting new members, and apprenticeships were easy to find. A shortage of casual labor kept wages at a decent rate. Successful migrants encouraged kin from their villages to move to the towns and sponsored their start in trade or service. For a while, rural families did not have to make elaborate preparations to provide for their younger sons and daughters: they could be sent to the towns. Instead of saving every extra penny to give their children a start in life, farmers could purchase some luxury goods or expand their landholdings.

Such an opportunity could not last. With more mouths to feed, more crops had to be planted. Since the most productive land was already under the plow, new fields were carved from less fertile areas. In some villages, land was taken from the common waste, the woodlands or scrublands that were used for animal forage and domestic fuel. The land was less suitable for crops, and it became unavailable for other important uses.

As workers continued to flood into the towns, real wages began to fall, not only among the unskilled but throughout the work force. A black market in labor developed to take advantage of the surplus population. In terms of purchasing power, the wages of a craftsman in the building trade in

■ The new money economy inspired this satirical portrait by Quentin Massys. It shows a moneylender counting his receipts while his wife is distracted from her Bible by the pile of coins. Many such merchants won fame and power and even titles.

England fell by one-half during the sixteenth century. A French stonemason, a highly paid skilled laborer, could buy 33 pounds of bread with his daily wage in 1480; by 1550 he could buy fewer than 10. Peasants in the French region of Languedoc who hired out for farm labor lost 56 percent of their purchasing power during the century. Only reapers, who were the physically strongest agricultural laborers, appear to have kept pace with inflation; grape pickers, among the least skilled, endured declines of up to 300 or 400 percent.

The fall in real wages took place against a backdrop of inflation that has come to be called the **Price Revolution**. Between 1500 and 1650, cereal prices increased between five- and sixfold, manufactured goods between two- and threefold. Most of the rapid increase came in the second half of the sixteenth century, a result of both population growth and the import of precious metals from the New World. Sixteenth-century governments understood little about the relationship between money supply and prices. Gold and silver from America flooded the international economy, raising commodity prices. As prices rose so did the deficits of the state, which was the largest purchaser of both agricultural and manufactured goods. With huge deficits, states began to devalue their coins in the mistaken belief that this would lower their debt. But debased coinage resulted in still higher prices, and higher prices resulted in greater debt. The Price

Revolution was felt throughout the Continent and played havoc with government finances, international trade, and the lives of ordinary people.

A 500 percent inflation in agricultural products over a century is not much by modern standards. Compounded, the rate averages less than 2 percent a year. But the Price Revolution did not take place in a modern society or within a modern market economy. In the sixteenth century, that level of rising prices disrupted everything. In the Spanish town of Seville, almost all buildings were rented on 99-year leases to the families who lived and worked in them. That was a fairly common practice throughout Europe. It meant that a landlord who rented a butcher shop and living quarters in 1501 could not raise the rent until 1600! Similarly, lords frequently held the right to purchase agricultural produce at specified prices. That system, similar to today's commodity market, helped both lords and peasants plan ahead. It ensured the lord a steady supply and the peasant a steady market. But it assumed steady prices. Until the middle of the seventeenth century, the king of England had the right to purchase wheat at prices set 300 years earlier.

Thus an enduring increase in prices created profound social dislocation. Some people became destitute; others became rich beyond their dreams. The towns were particularly hard hit, for they exchanged manufactured goods for food and thus suffered when grain prices rose faster than those of other commodities. Landholders who derived their income from rents were squeezed; those who received payment in kind reaped a windfall of more valuable agricultural goods. Peasants were largely protected from the rise in food prices, but they were not insulated from its consequences. As long as they consumed what they raised, the nominal value of commodities was of no great matter. But if some part of their subsistence had to be obtained by labor, they were in grave peril.

There was now an enormous incentive to produce a surplus for market and to begin to specialize in particular grains that were in high demand. Every small scrap of land that individual peasant families could bring under cultivation would now yield foodstuffs that could be exchanged for manufactured luxury goods. The tendency for all peasants to hold roughly equivalent amounts of land abruptly ceased. The fortunate could become prosperous by selling their surplus. The unfortunate found ready purchasers for their strips and common rights. Villagers began to be divided into those who held large amounts of land and sold their surplus at a profit and those who held small amounts of land and hired themselves out as laborers to their more fortunate neighbors.

The beneficial cycle now turned vicious. Those who had sold out and left the land looking for prosperity in the towns were forced to return to the land as agrarian laborers. In western Europe, they became the landless poor, seasonal migrants without the safety net of rooted communal life. In eastern Europe, labor service enriched the landed nobility, who were able to sell stores of grain in the export market. They used the law to tie the peasants to the land in order to ensure that grain would be cultivated for the market. Poland-Lithuania became a major supplier of cereals to northern Europe, and Gdansk became the most important agricultural seaport in the world. But agricultural surplus from the east could not make up for the great shortfall in the west. By the beginning of the seventeenth century, the western European states faced a crisis of subsistence. Everyone was hungry; many were starving.

SOCIAL LIFE

Social organization combines elements of tradition, belief, and function, but the elements are so fused together that it is impossible to determine where one ends and the other begins. Society is a human construct, subject to the strengths and frailties of its creators. The basic assumption of sixteenth-century European society was inequality, and its basic form of social organization was stratification. The group, rather than the individual, was the predominant unit in society. The first level of the social order was the family and the household; then came the village or town community; and finally the gradations of ranks and orders of society at large. Elaborate rituals helped define membership in each of the groups, from the marriage ceremony to the initiation rites of citizens and to the processions and ceremonial displays of the nobility. All stressed the significance of the rights and obligations of different levels of society. Each group had its own place in the social order and each performed its own essential function. Society was the sum of its parts.

The traditional social organization was severely tested over the course of the early modern period. Economic change reshaped ideas of mobility and drew sharper distinctions between rural and urban life. The growth of towns and their domination of the countryside around them challenged beliefs about the primacy of agricultural production and the subordinate nature of trade and commerce. The rise to new

wealth and prominence of some social groups challenged traditional elites' hold on power and prestige. The transformation of landholding patterns in the villages challenged the stability of rural communities. The rising numbers of both urban and rural poor challenged the institutions of charitable relief and posed the threat of crime and disorder. Eventually those developments led to bloody confrontations between social groups.

Social Constructs

Hierarchy was the dominant principle of social organization in the early modern era. Hierarchy existed at every level, from the basic distinction between lords and commoners to the fastidious complexity of the ranks of the nobility. The hierarchy of masters, journeymen, and apprentices dominated trades; trades themselves existed in a hierarchy. In the hierarchy of civic government, each official held a place in an ascending order, up to the elite of councillors and mayors. On the land was the hierarchy of freeholder, laborer, and leaseholder among the peasants. The family itself was hierarchically organized, with the wife subordinate to her husband, the children to their parents, and the apprentices and servants to their master and mistress. "All things observe degree, priority and place," Shakespeare wrote of both natural and human order in *Troilus and Cressida* (1601–1602). "Take but degree away, untune that string, and hark what discord follows."

Status, rather than wealth, determined the social hierarchy. It conferred privileges and exacted responsibilities according to rank. Status was everywhere apparent. It was confirmed in social conventions such as bowing and hat doffing. In towns and cities the clothing that people were allowed to wear—even the foods that they were allowed to eat—reflected status. Status was signified in titles: not just in the ranks of the nobility or between nobles and commoners, but even in ordinary communities masters and mistresses, goodmen and good-

■ Festivals disrupted the dreary routine of village life with games and feasting. The Christian or popular reason for the festival was often less important than the festival's value as a source of merriment and affirmation of solidarity.

wives, squires and ladies, adopted the English equivalents of European titles. The acceptance of status was an everyday, uncomplicated, unreflective act, similar to stopping at a red light. Inequality was a fact of European social life that was as unquestioned as it was unquestionable.

Images that people used to describe both the natural world and their social world reinforced the functional nature of hierarchy. The first, and most elaborate image, was that of the **Great Chain of Being**. The Great Chain was a description of the universe in which everything had a place, from God at the top of the chain to inanimate objects like rocks at the bottom. Complex accounts of the chain listed the seven orders of angels, the multiple ranks of humans, even the degrees of animals and plants, from which lions emerged as kings of the jungle. Spanish botanists were dispatched to the New World to help identify the unknown flora and fauna in terms of their places in the chain. Native Americans were first thought to be the lost tribes of Israel, as they were the only humans missing from traditional accounts of the chain. For ordinary people, the Great Chain of Being expressed the belief that all life was interconnected, that every link was a part of a divinely ordered universe and was as necessary as every other.

The second metaphor used to describe society stressed the notion of interdependency even more strongly. This was the image of the Body Politic, in which the head ruled, the arms protected, the stomach nourished, and the feet labored. The image described a small community as well as a large state. In the state, the king was the head, the Church the soul, the nobles the arms, the artisans the hands, and the peasants the feet. Each performed its own function, and each function was essential to the health of the body. Like the Great Chain of Being, the Body Politic was a profoundly conservative concept of social organization. Taken literally, it precluded the idea of social mobility, of people rising or falling from one group to another.

Social Structure

The Great Chain of Being and the Body Politic were static concepts of social organization. But in the early modern era, European society was in a state of dynamic change. Fundamentally, all European societies were divided into nobles and commoners. That basic distinction existed throughout the Continent, although relationships between the two orders differed from place to place.

The Nobles.   Nobility was a legal status that conferred certain privileges upon its holders. The first was rank and title, a well-defined place at the top of the social order that was passed from one generation to the next. Each rank had its own privileges and each was clearly demarcated from the next by behavior, dress, and title. The escutcheon—the coat of arms—was a universally recognized symbol of rank and family connection. The coat of arms was woven in garments; emblazoned on windows, carriages, and household goods; and displayed on banners during formal processions. Although

there were various systems of title in use across the Continent and the nobility of one state could not claim noble privileges in another state, the hierarchy of prince, duke, earl, count, and baron was roughly standard.

Because rulers conferred the titles on individuals, elevating some to higher ranks and others from commoner to noble, the nobility was a political order as well as a social one. Political privileges were among the nobility's most important attributes. In many countries, the highest offices of the state and the military were reserved for members of the nobility. In Poland, for example, all offices were held by noblemen. It was a privilege that could work both ways, either restricting officeholders to those already ennobled or, as in town councils in France and Spain, ennobling those who achieved certain offices. The nobility was also granted rights of political participation in the deliberative bodies of the state. In England, the peerage was defined as all those who were summoned to the House of Lords. In most parts of central Europe, the nobility alone composed the diets that advised the monarch. In the Holy Roman Empire, the rank of imperial free knights allowed the nobility to separate itself entirely from the jurisdiction of towns or individual principalities.

Finally, members of the nobility held economic privileges, a result both of their rank and of their role as lords on the lands they owned. In almost every state, the nobility was exempt from most taxation. That was an area in which the interests of the nobles conflicted directly with those of the ruler. The larger the number of tax exemptions for the nobility, the stronger was its power in relation to the monarch. Tax exemptions of the nobility were most extensive in eastern and central Europe. There the crowns were elective rather than hereditary, allowing the nobles to bargain their support. The Polish nobility was exempt from the salt tax, the alcohol tax, and all internal tolls and customs. As Polish agriculture developed into an export industry, exemption from tolls gave the nobility a competitive advantage over merchants in the marketing of goods. The Hungarian nobility was exempt from all direct taxes, including the land tax. The nobility in western Europe enjoyed fewer immunities but not necessarily less valuable ones. French nobles were exempt from the taille, Spanish nobles from the hearth tax.

Privileges implied obligations. Initially the nobility was the warrior caste of the state and its primary obligations were to raise, equip, and lead troops into battle. Much of the great wealth that nobles possessed was at the service of the ruler during times of war, and war was a perpetual activity. By the sixteenth century, the military needs of the state had far surpassed the military power of its nobility. Warfare had become a national enterprise that required central coordination. Nobles became administrators as much as warriors, though it is fair to say that many did both. The French nobility came to be divided into the nobility of the sword and the nobility of the robe—that is, warriors and officeholders. The old military nobility could hardly understand the new service nobility. "I have continually been astounded," one of them remarked, "that so many young men could thus amuse themselves in a law court, since ordinarily youthful blood is boiling." A glorious battlefield death was still an ideal for most of Europe's noblemen.

Town Elite and Gentry.   The principal distinction in sixteenth-century society was between lord and commoners, but it was not the only one. In both town and countryside a new social group was emerging. It had neither the legal nor the social privileges of nobility, but it performed many of the same functions. Over the course of the century the group carved out a place that was clearly distinct from that of the commoners, even if it was not clearly identical to the lords. It was most evident in the towns, for the towns remained a separate unit of social organization in most states. Towns enjoyed many of the same political and economic privileges as the nobility. In many states, the towns sent representatives to meet with the nobles and the king and were the most important part of national deliberative assemblies such as the English Parliament, the French Estates, or the Spanish Cortes. Towns were granted legal rights to govern their own citizens, to engage in trade, and to defend themselves by raising and storing arms. Although they paid a large share of most taxes, towns also received large tax concessions.

Yet, as individuals, members of the town elite held no special status in society at large. Some were among the richest people in the state—great bankers and merchants who were wealthier than dukes—but they had to devise their own systems of honor and prestige. In Venice, the *Book of Gold* distinguished the local elite from the ranks of ordinary citizens. Members of the "Old Families," who monopolized the highest civic offices, ruled Nüremberg. In France and Spain, some of the highest officers of leading towns were granted noble status, such as the "honored citizens" of Barcelona who were ennobled by King Ferdinand of Aragon. German burghers, as prosperous townsmen were called, remained caught in a state between noble and common, despised from above because they worked with their hands, envied from below for their wealth and comfort. In Münster, many withdrew from urban affairs and sought the privileges of the lower nobility.

In rural society, the transformation of agricultural holdings in many places also created a group that fit uncomfortably between lords and commoners. The accumulation of larger and larger estates through purchase from the nobility, the state, or the Church made lords—in the sense of landowners with tenants—out of many who were not lords in rank. They received rents and dues from their tenants, admin-

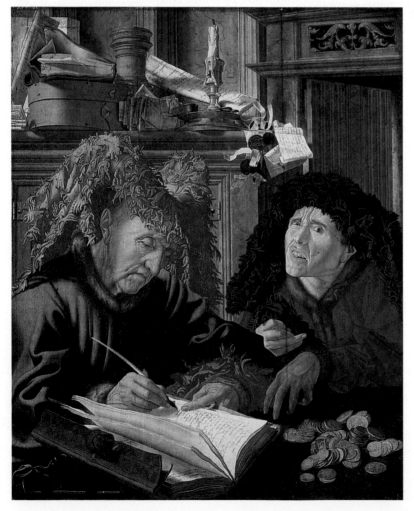

■ Marinus van Reymerswaele, *The Two Tax Gatherers.* The figure on the left is a city treasurer who is posting in the book an account of the city's revenues from taxes on wine, beer, fish, and other commodities. The painting is probably a satirical composition intended to expose the iniquity of covetousness, usury, or extortion.

istered their estates, and preserved the so-called moral economy that sustained the peasants during hard times. In England, the group came to be known as the gentry, and there were parallel groups in Spain, France, and the empire. The gentry aspired to the privileges of the nobility. In England, members of the gentry had the right to have a coat of arms and could be knighted. But knighthoods were not hereditary and did not confer membership in the House of Lords. In Spain, the caballeros and hidalgos gained noble privileges but were still of lower status than the grandees. The gentry aped the habits of the nobility, often outdoing nobles in lavish displays of wealth and spending.

In towns, the order of rank below the elite pertained as much to the kind of work that one performed as it did to the level at which it was undertaken. The critical division in town life was between those who had the freedom of the city—citizens—and those who did not. Citizenship was restricted to membership in certain occupations and was closely regulated. It could be purchased, especially by members of learned professions whose services were becoming vital in the early modern era, but most citizenship was earned by becoming a master in one of the guilds after a long period of apprenticeship and training. Only males could be citizens. In Germany, the feminine equivalent for the word used to denote a male citizen in good standing meant "prostitute"! But women who were married to citizens enjoyed their husbands' privileges, and widows of citizens could pass the privileges to their new husbands when they remarried. In both town and countryside, the privileges and obligations of each social group were the glue that held communities together.

Social Change

In the sixteenth century, social commentators believed that change was transforming the world in which they lived. In 1600, a Spanish observer blamed the rise of the rich commoners for the ills of the world: "They have obtained a particular status, that of a self-made group; and since they belong neither to the rich nor to the poor nor to the middle, they have thrown the state into the confusion we now see it in." An Englishman commenting on the rise of the gentry could give no better definition of its status than to say that a gentleman was one who lived like a gentleman. The challenge that the new nobility of the robe posed to the old nobility of the sword poisoned relations between the two segments of the French ruling elite. The military service class in Muscovy, who were of more use to the Muscovite princes than were the traditional landed nobility, posed an even greater threat to the privileges of the boyars.

The New Rich.   Pressures on the ruling elites of European society came from above as well as below. The expansion of the state and the power of the prince frequently came as a result of direct conflict with the nobility. Only in east-central Europe—in Hungary, Bohemia, and Poland-Lithuania, where towns were small and urban elites weak—did the consolidation of the state actually enhance the privileges of the traditional noble orders.

There were many reasons why the traditional European social hierarchy was transformed during the course of the early modern era. In the first place, population increase necessitated an expansion of the ruling orders. With more people to govern, there had to be more governors who could perform the military, political, and social functions of the state. The traditional nobility grew slowly, as titles could be passed to only one son and intermarriage within the group was very high. Second, opportunities to accumulate wealth expanded dramatically with the Price Revolution. Traditionally, wealth was calculated in land and tenants rather than in the possession of liquid assets such as gold and silver. But with the increase in commodity prices, surplus producers could rapidly improve their economic position. What previously might have taken a generation or two of good fortune to amass could now be gathered seemingly overnight. Moreover, state service became a source of unlimited riches. The profits to be made from tax collecting, officeholding, or administering the law could easily surpass those to be made from landholding, especially after the economic downturn at the end of the century. The newly rich clamored for privileges, and many were in a position to lobby rulers effectively for them. Across European society the nobility grew, fed from fortunes made on the land, in trade, and in office.

The New Poor.   Social change was equally apparent at the bottom of the social scale, but there it could not be so easily absorbed. The continuous population growth created a group of landless poor who squatted in villages and clogged the streets of towns and cities. Although poverty was not a new development of the early modern era, its growth created new problems. Rough estimates suggest that as many as a quarter of all Europeans were destitute. That was a staggering figure in great cities. There were tens of thousands of destitute people in London or Paris, where, it was observed, "the crowds of poor were so great that one could not pass through the streets."

Traditionally, local communities cared for their poor. Widows, orphans, and the handicapped, who would normally constitute more than half the poor in a village or town, were viewed as the "deserving poor," worthy of the care of the community through the Church or through private almsgiving. Catholic communities such as Venice created a system of private charity that paralleled the institutions of the Church. Although Protestant communities took charity out of the control of the church, they were no less concerned about the plight of the deserving poor. In England, a special tax, the poor rate, supported the poor and provided them with subsistence until they remarried or found employment. Perhaps the most elaborate system of all existed in the French town of Lyon where all the poor were registered and given identity cards. Each Sunday they would receive a week's worth of food and money. Young girls were provided with dowries, and young boys were taught crafts. Vagrants

■ A scene of peasant life in France during the prosperous reign of Louis XIV, by the genre painter Louis le Nain.

from the surrounding countryside were given one week's allotment to enable them to travel on. But Lyon's enlightened system was only for the deserving poor, and as the century progressed it was overwhelmed.

Charity was an obligation of the community, but as the sixteenth century progressed, the number of people who lived on the margins of subsistence grew beyond the ability of the local community to care for them. Perhaps more importantly, many of those who now begged for alms fell outside the traditional categories of the deserving poor. In England, they were called the sturdy beggars, men and women capable of working but incapable of finding more than occasional labor. To support themselves and their families, they left their native communities in search of employment and thus forfeited their claims on local charity. Most wound up in the towns and cities, where they slept and begged in the streets. Some disfigured themselves to enhance their abilities as beggars. As strangers they had no claim on local charity; as able-bodied workers they had no claim on local sympathy. Poor mothers abandoned their newborn infants on the steps of foundling hospitals or the houses of the rich. It is estimated that 10 percent of all newborn babies in the Spanish city of Valladolid were abandoned.

The problem of crime complicated the problems of poverty and vagrancy. Increasing population and increasing wealth equaled increasing crime; the addition of the poor to the equation aggravated the situation. The poor, destitute outsiders to the community, without visible means of support, were the easiest targets of official retribution. Throughout the century, numerous European states passed vagrancy laws in an effort to alleviate the problem of the wandering poor. In England, the poor were whipped from village to village until they were returned home. The sturdy beggars were branded with the letter *V* on their chests to identify them as vagrants,

and therefore as potential criminals. Both Venetian and Dutch vagrants were regularly rounded up for galley service, while vagrants in Hungary were sold into slavery. Physical mutilation was used as an ineffective method of deterrence; thieves had fingers chopped off—which made it impossible for them to perform manual labor, and thus likely to steal again. Sexual offenses were criminalized—especially bastardy, since the birth of illegitimate children placed an immediate burden on the community. Prostitutes, who had long been tolerated and regulated in towns, were now persecuted. Rape increased. Capital punishment was reserved for the worst crimes—murder, incest, and grand larceny being most common—but, not surprisingly, executions were carried out mostly on outsiders to the community, with single women, the poor, and the vagrant being the most frequent victims.

Peasant Revolts

The economic and social changes of the sixteenth century bore serious consequences. Most telling was the upswing of violent confrontations between peasants and their lords. There was more than one difference between rich and poor in sixteenth-century society, but when conflict arose between them the important difference was that the wealthy controlled the means of coercion: the military and the law. Across Europe, and with alarming regularity, peasants took up arms to defend themselves from what they saw as violations of traditional rights and obligations. Peasant revolts were not hunger riots. Although they frequently occurred in periods of want, after bad harvests or marauding armies had impoverished villages, peasant revolts were not desperate attacks against warehouses or grain silos. Nor did those who took part in them form undisciplined mobs. Most revolts chose leaders, drew up peti-

■ Rebellious peasants gathered under a standard called the Banner of the Shoe. Here they surround a knight.

tions of grievances, and organized the rank and file into a semblance of military order. Leaders were literate—usually drawn from the lower clergy or minor gentry rather than from the peasantry—political demands were moderate, and tactics were sophisticated. But peasant revolts so profoundly threatened the social order that they were met with the severest repression. Confronted with the execution of their estate agents, rent strikes, and confiscation of their property, lords responded as if they were at war. Veteran soldiers and trained mercenaries were called out to fight peasant armies composed mostly of raw recruits. The results were horrifying.

Agrarian Changes. It is essential to realize that while peasants revolted against their lords, fundamentally their anger and frustration were products of agrarian changes that could be neither controlled nor understood. As population increased and market production expanded, many of the traditional rights and obligations of lords and peasants became oppressive. One example is that of forest rights. On most estates, the forests surrounding a village belonged to the lord. Commonly the village had its own woodlands in which animals foraged and fuel and building material were available. As the population increased, more farms came into existence. New land was put under the plow, and grain fields pressed up against the forest. There were more animals in the village, and some of them were let loose to consume the young sprouts and saplings. Soon there was not enough food for the wild game that was among the lord's most valuable property. So the game began to feed on the peasants' crops, which were now placed so appetizingly close to the forests. It was a capital crime for a peasant to kill wild game, but peasants couldn't allow the game to consume their crops.

A similar conflict arose over enclosing crop fields. An **enclosure** was a device—normally a fence or hedge that surrounded an area—to keep a parcel of land separate from the planted strips of land owned by the villagers. The parcel could be used for grazing animals or raising a specialty crop for the market. But an enclosure destroyed the traditional form of village agriculture, whereby decisions on which crops to plant were made communally. It became one of the chief grievances of the English peasants. But while enclosures broke up the old field system in many villages, they were a logical response to the transformation of land ownership that had already taken place. As more land was accumulated by fewer families, it made less sense for them to work widely scattered strips all over the village. If a family could consolidate its holdings by swaps and sales, it could gain an estate large enough to be used for both crops and grazing. An enclosed estate allowed wealthy farmers to grow more luxury crops for market or to raise only sheep on a field that had once been used for grain.

Enclosure was a process that both lord and rich peasant undertook, but it drove the smallholders from the land and was thus a source of bitter resentment for the poorer peasants. It was easy to protest the greed of the lords who, owning the most land, were the most successful enclosers. But enclosures were more a result of the process in which villages came to be characterized by a very small elite of large landholders and a very large mass of smallholders and landless poor. They were an effect rather than a cause.

From Hungary to England, peasant revolts brought social and economic change into sharp relief. A call for a crusade against Ottoman advances in 1514 provided the opportunity for Hungarian peasants to revolt against their noble landlords. Thousands dropped their plowshares and grasped the sword of a holy war. However, in fact, war against the Ottomans did not materialize. Instead, the mobilized peasants, under the leadership of disaffected army officers and clergymen, issued grievances against the labor service that they owed to their lords as well as numerous violations of customary agricultural practices. Their revolt turned into a civil war that was crushed with great brutality. In England, severe economic conditions led to a series

THE PEASANTS' REVOLT

In 1524 and 1525, a series of local protests over economic conditions coalesced into one of the largest concerted peasant uprisings in German history. The Peasants' Revolt was not a disorganized uprising of the hungry and dispossessed, but rather a carefully coordinated movement that attempted to win widespread social reforms. The Twelve Articles of the Peasants of Swabia show both the nature of the peasants' grievances and their ability to articulate them.

Focus Questions

On what grounds do the peasants base their pleas? Why are religious and economic issues so intertwined for these peasants?

The First Article. First, it is our humble petition and desire, as also our will and resolution, that in the future we should have power and authority so that each community should choose and appoint a pastor, and that we should have the right to depose him should he conduct himself improperly. The pastor thus chosen should teach us the gospel pure and simple, without any addition, doctrine, or ordinance of man.

The Second Article. According as the just tithe is established by the Old Testament and fulfilled in the New, we are ready and willing to pay the fair tithe of grain. . . . We will that for the future our church provost, whomsoever the community may appoint, shall gather and receive this tithe. . . .

The Tenth Article. In the tenth place, we are aggrieved by the appropriation by individuals of meadows and fields which at one time belonged to a community. These we will take again into our own hands. . . .

Conclusion. In the twelfth place, it is our conclusion and final resolution that if any one or more of the articles here set forth should not be in agreement with the word of God, as we think they are, such article we will willingly retract if it is proved really to be against the word of God by a clear explanation of the Scripture.

From the Twelve Articles of the Peasants of Swabia.

---

of revolts in 1549. Participants in the Western Rising, who succeeded in storming the town of Exeter, also combined religious and economic grievances. Cornish rebels added a social dimension with their slogan "Kill the gentlemen." In eastern England, Ket's Rebellion arose from peasant opposition to enclosure. The rebels occupied Norwich, the second largest city in the realm, but their aspirations were for reform rather than revolution. They, like the Hungarian peasants, were crushed by well-trained forces.

Uprising in Germany. The complexity of the peasants' problems is perhaps best revealed in the series of uprisings that are known collectively as the German Peasants' War. It was by far the most widespread peasant revolt of the sixteenth century, involving tens of thousands of peasants, and it combined a whole series of agrarian grievances with an awareness of the new religious spirit preached by Martin Luther. Luther condemned both lords and peasants: the lords for their rapaciousness, the peasants for their rebelliousness. Although he had a large following among the peasants, his advice that earthly oppression be passively accepted was not followed. The Peasants' War was directed against secular and ecclesiastical lords, and the rebels attacked both economic and religious abuses. Their combination of demands, such as the community's right to select its own minister and the community's right to cut wood freely, attracted a wide following in the villages and small towns of southern and central Germany. The printed demands of the peasantry, the most famous of which was the Twelve Articles of the Peasants of Swabia (1525), helped spread the movement far beyond its original

bounds. The peasants organized themselves into large armies led by experienced soldiers. Initially they were able to besiege castles and abbeys and plunder lords' estates. Ultimately, those movements that refused compromise were ruthlessly crushed. By conservative estimates, more than 100,000 peasants were slaughtered during and after the war, many to serve as warning against future uprisings.

At base, the demands of the peasantry addressed the agrarian changes that were transforming German villages. Population growth was creating more poor villagers who could only hire out as laborers but who demanded a share of common grazing and woodlands. Because the presence of the poor increased the taxable wealth of the village, they were advantageous to the lord. But the strain they placed on resources was felt by both the subsistence and the surplus farmers. Tensions within the village were all the greater because the landless members were the kin of the landed—sons and daughters, brothers and sisters. If they were to be settled properly on the land, then the lord would have to let the village expand. If they were to be kept on the margins of subsistence, then the more prosperous villagers would have to be able to control their numbers and their conduct. In either case, the peasants needed more direct responsibility for governing the village than existed in their traditional relationship with their lord. Thus the grievances of the peasants of Swabia demanded release of the village peasantry from the status of serfs. They wanted to be allowed to move off the land, to marry out of the village without penalty, and to be free of the death taxes that further impoverished their children. The concessions would make it easier for the excess population to adjust to new conditions. They also wanted stable rents fixed at fair rates, a limit placed on labor service, and a return to the ancient customs that governed relations between lords and peasants. All the proposals were backed by an appeal to Christian principles of love and charity. They were profoundly conservative.

PRIVATE AND COMMUNITY LIFE

The great events of the sixteenth century—the discovery of the New World, the consolidation of states, the increasing incidence and ferocity of war, the reform of religion—all had profound impact on the lives of ordinary people. However slowly and intermittently these developments penetrated to isolated village communities, they were inextricably bound up with the experiences and the worldview of all Europeans. The states offered more protection and demanded more resources. Taxes increased, and tax collecting became more efficient. Wars took village boys and made them soldiers. Armies brought devastation to thousands of communities. The New World offered new opportunities, brought new products, and increased the wealth of the Continent. Religious reform, both Protestant and Catholic, penetrated into popular beliefs and personal piety. All the sweeping changes blurred the distinction between public and private life.

Still, the transformations wrought by political and intellectual developments were not necessarily the most important ones in people's lives. The lives of most Europeans centered on births and deaths, on the harvest, and on the social relations in their communities. For them, great events were the successful crop, the marriage of an heir, or the festivals that marked the progress of the year. Their beliefs were based as much on the customs they learned as children as on the religion they learned at church. Their strongest loyalties were to family and community rather than to church or state.

The Family

Sixteenth-century life centered on the family. The family was a crucial organizing principle for Europeans of all social ranks, and it served a variety of functions. In the most obvious sense, the family was the primary kin group. European families were predominantly nuclear, composed of a married couple and their children. In western Europe, a small number of families contained the adult siblings of the family head, uncles and aunts who had not yet established their own families. That pattern was more common in the east, especially in Hungary and Muscovy, where taxation was based on households and thus encouraged extended families. There, several nuclear families might live under the same roof. Yet however

■ Jan Vermeer's *The Milkmaid* (1658–1660) shows a domestic servant absorbed in her household tasks. Homes were sparsely furnished, though this family was rich enough to possess a table, an earthenware bowl and jug, and a footstove that held hot coals (seen on the floor behind the maid).

families were composed, kinship had a wider orbit than just parents and children. In-laws, step-relations, and cousins were considered part of the kin group and could be called upon for support in a variety of contexts, from charity to employment and business partnerships. In towns, such family connections created large and powerful clans.

A FEMININE PERSPECTIVE

Arcangela Tarabotti was born in Venice in the early seventeenth century. Her family did not have the means to provide her with a sufficient dowry, so she was sent to live in a Catholic convent, where she unhappily remained for the rest of her life. She wrote two major works. The first, Monastic Hell, *gives the flavor of her attitude toward her fate. The second was* Innocence Undone, *from which the following excerpt is taken.*

Focus Questions

What does Tarabotti point to as evidence of female superiority? Why do you think Tarabotti concentrates on the biblical account of the Creation?

Since woman is the epitome of all perfections, she is the last of the works of God, as far as material creation is concerned, but otherwise she dates from the beginning, and is the first-generated of all creatures, generated by the breath of God himself, as the Holy Spirit inferred, through the mouth of Solomon in the Ecclesiastes where he introduces the Most Holy Virgin to sing of herself: *The Lord possessed me in the beginning of his ways, before he made any thing from the beginning.*

This creature, although a woman, did not need to be made with a rib taken from man, because, so to speak, she was born before the beginning of time as well as before men, who, blinded by their ambition to dominate the world alone, astutely fail to mention this infallible truth, that the woman has existed in the Divine mind from the beginning. *I was set up from eternity, and of old before the earth was made. The depths were not as yet, and I was already conceived.*

They cannot deny the fact, although their malice prevents them from speaking it openly; but let us try to make them admit, in accordance with the Holy Scriptures rather than with some ill-informed preachers, that the woman made the man perfect and not vice versa.

After the Supreme Being created the world and all the animals (as I have said before), the text says *And God saw all the things that he had made; and they were very good.* Foreseeing that the man without woman would be the compendium of all imperfections, God said: *It is not good for man to be alone: let us make him a help like unto himself.* And therefore he created a companion for him that would be the universal glory of humanity and make him rich with merits.

Almighty God, having kept the creation of the woman as the last act of his wonderful work, desired to bestow privileges upon her, reinforce her graces and gladden the whole world with her splendour. If the supreme Architect's greatness, wisdom and love towards us shone brightly in his other works, he planned to make the woman, this excellent last addition to his splendid construction, capable of filling with wonder whoever looked at her. He therefore gave her the strength to subdue and dominate the proudest and wildest hearts and hold them in sweet captivity by a mere glance or else by the power of her pure modesty. God formed Man, who is so proud, in the field of Damascus; and from one of his ribs he formed woman in the garden of Eden.

If I were not a female, I would deduce from this that the woman, both because of her composition and because of the place in which she was created, is nobler, gentler, stronger and worthier than the man.

What is true strength anyway, if not domination over one's feelings and mastery over one's passions? And who is better at this than the female sex, always virtuous and capable of resisting every temptation to commit or even think evil things? Is there anything more fragile than your head? Compare it to the strength of a rib, the hard bone that is the material from which we were created, and you will be disappointed. Anyone knows that women show more strength than men when they conceive and give birth, by tirelessly carrying all that weight around for nine months.

But you cruel men, who always go around preaching evil for good and good for evil, you pride yourselves in your strength because, like the inhuman creatures you are, you fight and kill each other like wild beasts. . . .Thus, if strength is the ability to bear misfortunes and insults, how can you call yourselves strong when you shed other people's blood sometimes for no reason at all and take the life of innocent creatures at the slightest provocation of a word or a suspicion?

Strength is not mere violence; it requires an indomitable soul, steadfast and constant in Christian fortitude. How can you, o most inconstant ones, ever boast of such virtù? Improperly and deceitfully you have called yourselves virtuous, because only those who fill the world with people and virtù can be called strong.

And those are women. Listen to Solomon, whose words about women reinforce my argument: *Strength and dignity are her clothing.*

From Tarabotti, *Innocence Undone.*

In a different sense, family was lineage, the connections between preceding and succeeding generations. That was an important concept among the upper ranks of society, where ancient lineage, genuine or fabricated, was a valued component of nobility. That concept of family imparted a sense of stability and longevity in a world in which individual life was short. Even in peasant communities, however, lineage existed in the form of the family farm, that is, the strips in the field that were passed from generation to generation and named for the family that owned them. The village's fields and landmarks also bore the names of individual families, and membership in one of the ancient families of the village was a mark of social distinction.

The family was also an economic unit. In this sense, family overlapped with the household—all those who lived under the same roof, including servants and apprentices. In its economic functions, the family was the basic unit for the production, accumulation, and transmission of wealth. Occupation determined the organization of the economic family. Every member of the household had his or her own functions that were essential to the survival of the unit. Tasks were divided by gender and by age, but there was far more intermixture than is traditionally assumed. On farms, women worked at nearly every occupation with the exception of mowing and plowing. In towns, they were vital to the success of shops and trades, though they were denied training in the skilled crafts. As laborers, they worked in the town fields—for little more than half the wages of men performing the same tasks—and in carrying and delivering goods and materials. Children contributed to the economic vitality of the household from an early age.

Finally, the family was the primary unit of social organization. In the family, children were educated and the social values of hierarchy and discipline were taught. Authority in the family was strictly organized in a set of three overlapping categories. At the top was the husband, head of the household, who ruled over his wife, children, and servants. All members of the family owed obedience to the head. The family was like "a little commonwealth," as English writers put it, in which the adult male was the governor and all others the governed. But two other categories of relationships in the family dispersed the authority. Children owed obedience to their parents, male or female. In this role, the wife and mother was governor as well as governed. Similarly, servants owed obedience to both master and mistress. Male apprentices were under the authority of the wife, mother, and mistress of the household. The importance of the family as a social unit was underscored by the fact that people unattached to families attracted suspicion in sixteenth-century society. Single men were often viewed as potential criminals; single women as potential prostitutes. Both lived outside the discipline and social control of families.

Although the population of Europe was increasing in the early modern era, families were not large. Throughout northern and western Europe, the size of the typical family was two adults and three or four children. Late marriages and breast-feeding helped control family size: the former restricted the number of childbearing years while the latter increased the space between pregnancies. Women married around age 25, men slightly later. A woman could expect about 15 fertile years and seven or eight pregnancies if neither she nor her husband died in the interim.

■ In an age of high infant mortality and short life expectancy, women were expected to bear many children to ensure family continuity. This embroidery depicts a mother with her thirteen daughters.

Only three or four children were likely to survive beyond the age of ten. In her fertile years, a woman was constantly occupied with infants. She was either about to give birth or about to become pregnant. If she used a wet nurse rather than feed her own babies, as many women in the upper ranks of society did, then she was likely to have 10 or 12 pregnancies during her fertile years and correspondingly more surviving children.

Constant pregnancy and child care may help explain some of the gender roles that men and women assumed in the early modern era. Biblical injunctions and traditional stereotypes help explain others. Pregnant or not, women's labor was a vital part of the domestic economy, especially until the first surviving children were strong enough to assume their share. The woman's sphere was the household. On the farm, she was in charge of the preparation of food, the care of domestic animals, the care and education of children, and the manufacture and cleaning of the family's clothing. In towns, women supervised the shop that was part of the household. They sold goods, kept accounts, and directed the work of domestics or apprentices. Mothers trained their daughters to perform the tasks in the same way that fathers trained their sons to work the fields or ply their craft.

CASE STUDY

The Ideal Wife

The man's sphere was public—the fields in rural areas, the streets in towns. Men plowed, planted, and did the heavy reaping work of farming. They made and maintained essential farm equipment and had charge of the large farm animals. They marketed surplus produce and made the few purchases of equipment or luxury goods. Men performed the labor service that was normally due the lord of the estate, attended the local courts in various capacities, and organized the affairs of the village. In towns, men engaged in heavy labor, procured materials for craft work, and marketed their product if it was not sold in the household shop. Only men could be citizens of the towns or full members of most craft guilds, and only men were involved in civic government.

The separation of men and women into the public and the domestic spheres meant that marriage was a blending of complementary skills. Each partner brought to the marriage essential knowledge and abilities that were fundamental to the economic success of the union. Except in the largest towns, nearly everyone was married for at least a part of his or her life. Remarriage was more common for men than women, however, because a man continued to control the family's property after the death of his wife, whereas a widow might have only a share of it after bequests to children and provisions for apprentices. In the French town of Nantes, a quarter of the annual weddings were remarriages.

■ A woodcut from *De Conceptu et generatione hominis* (1554), a famous sixteenth-century handbook for midwives. During the birth, astrologers cast the infant's horoscope in the background.

Communities

Despite its central place in all aspects of sixteenth-century life, the family was a fragile and impermanent institution. Even without divorce—permitted in Protestant communities, though never very common—marriages were short. The early death of one of the partners abbreviated the life of the natural family. New marriage partners or social welfare to aid the indigent was sought from within the wider community. On the farm, that community was the rural village; in the town, it was the ward, quarter, or parish in which the family lived. Community life must not be romanticized. Interpersonal violence, lawsuits, and feuds were extraordinarily common in both rural and urban communities. The community was not an idyllic haven of charity and love, where everyone knew and respected neighbors and worked toward a common goal. Like every other aspect of society, the community was socially and economically stratified, gender roles were segregated, and resources were inequitably divided. But the community was the place where people found their social identity. It provided marriage partners for its families, charity for its poor, and a local culture for all of its inhabitants.

Communities were bound together by the authorities who ruled them and by their common activities. But they were also bound together by their own social customs. Early modern communities used a number of ceremonial occasions as opportunities for expressing solidarity and confirming, in one way or another, the values to which they adhered. In rural parishes there was the annual perambulation, a walk around the village fields that usually occurred before planting began. It was led by the priest, who carried with him any particularly sacred objects that the parish possessed. Behind him followed the village farmers, in some places all members of the village who were capable of walking the distance. The perambulation had many purposes. The priest blessed the fields and prayed for a bountiful crop; the farmers surveyed their own strips and any damage that had been done to the fields during the winter; the community defined its geographical space in distinction to the space of others; and all the individuals who took part reaffirmed their shared identity with others in the village.

In towns, ceremonial processions were far more elaborate. Processions might take place on saints' days in Catholic communities or on anniversaries of town liberties. The order of the march, the clothing worn by the participants, and the objects displayed reflected the strict hierarchies of the town's local organizations. In Catholic towns, the religious orders led the town governors in their robes of office. Following the governors were the members of guilds, each guild placed according to its rank of importance and each organized by masters, journeymen, and apprentices. In some towns, the wives of citizens marched in procession; in others, they were accorded special places from which to view the ceremony. Village and civic ceremonies normally ended with communal feasting and dancing, which were the most popular forms of recreation.

Weddings and Festivals.

Not all ceremonial occasions were so formal. The most common ceremony was the wedding, a rite of passage that was simultaneously significant to the individual, the family, and the community. The wedding was a public event that combined a religious ceremony and a community procession with feasting and festivity. It took different forms in different parts of Europe and in different social groups. But whether eastern or western, noble or common, the wedding was celebrated as the moment when the couple entered fully into the community. Marriage involved more than just the union of bride and groom. Parents were a central feature in the event, both in arranging the economic aspects of the union—dowry and inheritance—and in approving the occasion. Many couples were engaged long before they were married, and in many places it was the engagement that was most important to the individuals and the wedding that was most important to the community. One German townsman described how he "had taken a wife but they have not held the wedding yet."

Traditional weddings involved the formal transfer of property, an important event in rural communities, where the ownership of strips of land or common rights concerned everyone. The bridal dowry and the groom's inheritance were formally exchanged during the wedding, even if both were small. The public procession—"the marriage in the streets" as it was

■ Jan van Eyck, *The Marriage of Giovanni Arnolfini and Giovanna Cenami*. This outstanding fifteenth-century painting of a nuptial scene teems with symbols, including the religious symbols of the rosary, the roundels on the mirror frame, and the post of the chair. The little dog in the foreground may represent fidelity, and the candles in the chandelier may be a symbol of marriage. The mirror reflects the image of two witnesses, who would have been standing where spectators viewing the picture would stand. The inscription on the wall, "Jan van Eyck was here, 1434," suggests that one of the figures is a self-portrait of the artist.

sometimes called in towns—proclaimed the union throughout the community and was considered to be as important as the religious ceremony. It was followed by a feast as abundant as the families of bride and groom could afford. In peasant communities, gifts of food for the feast were as common as were gifts to the couple. There were always provisions made that excess food should be sent to the poor or unfortunate after the wedding.

Weddings also legitimated sexual relations. Many of the dances and ceremonies that followed the feast symbolized the sexual congress. Among German burghers it was traditional for the bride to bring the bed to her new home, and bridal beds were passed from mothers to daughters. Among the nobility, the consummation of the marriage was a vital part of the wedding, for without it the union could be annulled. Finally, the marriage inaugurated both bride and groom into new roles in the community. Their place at the wedding table next to their parents elevated them to the status of adults.

Other ceremonies were equally important in creating a shared sense of identity within the community. In both town and countryside, the year was divided by a number of festivals that defined the rhythm of toil and rest. They coincided with both the seasonal divisions of agricultural life and the central events of the Christian calendar. There was no essential difference between the popular and Christian elements in festivals, however strongly the official church insisted upon one. Christmas and Easter were probably the most widely observed Christian holidays, but **Carnival,** which preceded Lent, was a frenzied round of feasts and parties that resulted in a disproportionate number of births nine months later. The Twelve Days of Christmas, which inaugurated the slow, short days of winter, were only loosely attached to the birth of Jesus and were even abolished by some Protestant churches. The rites of May, which celebrated the rebirth of spring, were filled with sexual play among the young adults of the community. Youth groups went "a-Maying" by placing flowers at the homes of marriageable girls, electing a Queen of the May, and dancing and reveling before the hard work of planting. All Hallows' Eve was a celebration for the community's dead, whose spirits were believed to have wandered the village on that night, visiting kin and neighbors.

Festivals helped maintain the sense of community that might be weakened during the long months of increased work or enforced indoor activity. They were first and foremost celebrations in which feasting, dancing, and play were central. But they also served as safety valves for the pressures and conflicts that built up over the year. Group and individual sports, such as soccer or wrestling, frequently served to channel aggressions. Village elders would arbitrate disputes, and marriage alliances or property transactions would be arranged.

Festivals further cemented the political cohesion of the community. Seating arrangements reflected the hierarchy of the community, and public punishment of offenders reinforced deference and social and sexual mores. Youth groups, or even the village women, might band together to shame a promiscuous woman or to place horns on the head of a cuckolded husband. Sometimes a man who had been beaten or abused by his wife, or who had simply failed to enforce obedience from her, was forced to ride backward on a horse or donkey to symbolize the misrule in his family. At such processions, which the French called *charivaris* and the English *skimmingtons*, rough music was played and the offense of the individual or couple was elaborately recreated. (See "A Closer Look: Sex and the Married Man," pp. 464–465.) Such forms of community ritual worked not only to punish offenders but also to reinforce the social and sexual values of the village as a whole.

■ Carnivals were occasions for games and feasting. In this painting, *Struggle Between Carnival and Lent,* Pieter Brueghel the Elder depicts a contest between the fasting and other forms of self-denial during Lent (the period of fasting and penitence before Easter) and the tempting attractions of Carnival.

Popular Beliefs and the Persecution of Witches

Ceremony and festival are reminders that sixteenth-century Europe was still a preliterate society. Despite the introduction of printing and the millions of books that were produced during the period, the vast majority of Europeans conducted their affairs without the benefit of literacy. Their culture was oral and visual. They had need of an exact memory, and they developed a shorthand of adages, charms, and spells that helped them organize their activities and pass down their knowledge. It is difficult for us to recreate that mental world, in which almost all natural events were unpredictable and in which there was little certainty. Outside a small circle of intellectuals, there was little effective knowledge about either human or celestial bodies. The mysteries of the sun, moon, and stars were as deep as those of health and sickness. But ordinary people did not live in a constant state of terror and anxiety. They used the knowledge they did have to form a view of the universe that conformed to their experiences and that responded to their hopes. Although many of their beliefs seem mere superstitions, they allowed people to form a coherent explanation of the natural world and of their relationship to it.

Magical Practices.   The people's beliefs blended Christian teaching and folk wisdom with a strong strain of magic. Popular belief in magic could be found everywhere in Europe, and it operated in much the same way as science does today. Only skilled

THE DEVIL'S DUE

Evidence of the supernatural world abounded for the people of premodern Europe. Natural disasters such as plague and human disasters such as war promoted fear of witchcraft. When the world seemed out of balance and the forces of good retreated before the forces of evil, people sought someone to blame for their troubles. Witches were an obvious choice. Accused witches were most commonly women on the margins of society. Once brought before the authorities, many admitted their traffic with Satan, especially under torture. The Witch Hammer is a set of detailed instructions for the rooting out of witches, including procedures to induce their confessions.

Focus Questions

What is the point of torture, punishment, or investigation? Is the suspected witch seen as being in control of his or her magic?

The method of beginning an examination by torture is as follows: First, the jailers prepare the implements of torture, then they strip the prisoner (if it be a woman, she has already been stripped by other women, upright and of good report). This stripping is lest some means of witchcraft may have been sewed into the clothing—such as often, taught by the Devil, they prepare from the bodies of unbaptized infants, [murdered] that they may forfeit salvation. And when the implements of torture have been prepared, the judge, both in person and through other good men zealous in the faith, tries to persuade the prisoner to confess the truth freely; but, if he will not confess, he bids attendants make the prisoner fast to the strappado or some other implement of torture. The attendants obey forthwith, yet with feigned agitation. Then, at the prayer of some of those present, the prisoner is loosed again and is taken aside and once more persuaded to confess, being led to believe that he will in that case not be put to death.

But if, neither by threats nor by promises such as these, the witch cannot be induced to speak the truth, then the jailers must carry out the sentence, and torture the prisoner according to the accepted methods, with more or less of severity as the delinquent's crime may demand. And, while he is being tortured, he must be questioned on the articles of accusation, and this frequently and persistently, beginning with the lighter charges—for he will more readily confess the lighter than the heavier. And, while this is being done, the notary must write down everything in his record of the trial—how the prisoner is tortured, on what points he is questioned, and how he answers.

And note that, if he confesses under the torture, he must afterward be conducted to another place, that he may confirm it and certify that it was not due alone to the force of the torture.

But, if the prisoner will not confess the truth satisfactorily, other sorts of tortures must be placed before him, with the statement that, unless he will confess the truth, he must endure these also. But, if not even thus he can be brought into terror and to the truth, then the next day or the next but one is to be set for a *continuation* of the tortures—not a *repetition*, for they must not be repeated unless new evidence be produced. . . .

And during the interval, before the day assigned, the judge, in person or through approved men, must in the manner above described try to persuade the prisoner to confess, promising her (if there is aught to be gained by this promise) that her life shall be spared.

The judge shall see to it, moreover, that throughout this interval guards are constantly with the prisoner, so that she may not be left alone; because she will be visited by the Devil and tempted into suicide.

From The Witch Hammer.

SEX AND THE MARRIED MAN

On 27 May 1618 the peace of the small hamlet of Quemerford, in the west of England, was shattered by the appearance of a large crowd from the neighboring market town of Calne. Men marched with fowling pieces and muskets to a cacophony of drums, clanging pots, whistles, and shouts. Among them, on a red horse, rode an outlandishly costumed man—a smock covering his body; on his head a nightcap with two long shoehorns tied to his ears; and on his face a false beard made from a deer's tail. The crowd escorted the rider to the home of Thomas Mills, who worked in Calne as a cutler. There they stopped. Guns were discharged into the air; an even greater clamor of rough music arose from drums, pipes, and metal objects; and when Mills opened his door, members of the crowd waved aloft the horns of goats or rams mounted on sticks. Then a few strong men entered the house; seized hold of his wife, Agnes; and dragged her to a village mud hole where she was ducked and covered in filth. She was rescued from being set on the horse and ridden to Calne.

A CLOSER LOOK

That event, known as a **skimmington** in the west of England and a charivari in France, was a shaming ritual. It was an element of popular culture that took place against the wishes of local authorities and without their connivance. Its purpose was twofold: to identify and punish sexual misconduct and to maintain the male-dominated gender system. The shaming rituals resulted from conduct that the male members of the community believed threatened local order (few women are known to have taken part in the events). In France, most charivaris were conducted against husbands who were beaten by their wives; in England, many skimmingtons were directed against husbands whose wives had been unfaithful. In both they were designed to shame men into disciplining women and to warn women to remain obedient.

Although skimmingtons and charivaris differed from place to place, all contained similar elements which were designed to invert normal behavior in one way or another. The rough music symbolized the disharmony of a household in which the woman dominated, either by her physical conduct—adultery or husband beating—or her verbal conduct—cursing or abusing her husband or other men. The music was made with everyday objects rather than instruments, and pots and pans were universally present. The "riding" of the husband was another common feature. In many rituals, the "husband," played by a neighbor, was placed facing the tail of the horse or donkey to symbolize the backwardness of his behavior. In some, a "wife," also acted by a neighbor, rode behind the man and beat him with a stick or, in England, with the long-handled ladle used to skim cream that was known as a skimmington. In the end, the real husband or wife was captured, the man to ride in shame throughout the town, the woman to be sat on a cucking stool and dunked in water.

The presence of horns on the male riding the horse and on sticks carried by members of the crowd or worn atop their heads was the universal symbol of adultery. The cuckold—a word derived from the name of a promiscuous female bird—was an object of derision throughout European society. Codes of conduct from noble to peasant stressed the importance of female sexual fidelity in maintaining the purity of bloodlines and the order of the household. The cuckold was shorn of his masculinity; he had lost his "horns," in common parlance. His personal indignity was a cause for jest and insult, but the disorderliness implicit in the conduct of his wife was a cause for community concern. In local society, reputation was equated with personal worth, and no one had less reputation than the cuckold. Among the nobility, duels were fought over the slightest suggestion of a wife's unfaithfulness, while among ordinary folks the raising of the forefinger and pinkie—the sign of horns—initiated brawls.

The skimmington or charivari combined festive play with the enforcement of social norms. It was rough justice, as the objects of shame were allowed neither explanation nor defense. They were guilty by common fame, that is, by the report of their neighbors and the gossip of the local alehouse rather than by any examination of evidence. Women who yelled at their husbands were sometimes assumed to have beaten them; women who had beaten their husbands were assumed to have cuckolded them. The crimes were all interrelated, and protestations of innocence were useless. The crowds that gathered to perform the ceremony usually had bolstered their courage at the local tavern, and among them were village toughs and those who held grudges against the targeted family. Assault, property damage, and theft occasionally accompanied a skim-

■ Scene of a shaming ritual, with the object of derision wearing horns and riding a donkey.

mington. But most of the crowd was there to have a bit of sport and revel in the discomfort of the victims. Their conduct was the inverse of a legal procedure, as disorderly as the conduct of those to be punished. However, their purpose was not to turn the world upside down, but to set it right side up again by restoring the dominance of husbands over wives.

While shaming rituals like the charivari and the skimmington had a long history in Europe, they seem to have exploded into prominence in the late sixteenth and early seventeenth centuries. Population pressures and economic hardship are two conventional explanations for why there were greater local tensions during that period. Skimmingtons and charivaris frequently had rough edges, with some participants motivated by hatred or revenge. But it is also likely that there were more inversion rituals because there was more inversion. Women were taking a larger role in economic affairs and were becoming increasingly literate and active in religion, especially in Protestant countries. Assertive, independent women threatened the male-dominated social order as much as demographic and social change. That the threats were most identified with sexual misconduct and with the stripping of a husband's masculinity was hardly surprising. The image of the obedient female was conventionally the image of chastity. Thus the image of the independent female had to become one of promiscuity. Through the use of skimmingtons and charivaris, men attempted to restore norms of sexual conduct and gender relations that were increasingly under attack. As one English poet put it:

Ill fares the hapless family that shows
A cock that's silent, and a Hen that crows.
I know not which live more unnatural lives,
Obedient husbands, or commanding wives.

practitioners could perform magic. It was a technical subject that combined expertise in the properties of plants and animals with theories about the composition of human and heavenly bodies. It had its own language, a mixture of ancient words and sounds with significant numbers and catchphrases. Magicians specialized: some concentrated on herbs and plants, others on the diseases of the body. Alchemists worked with rocks and minerals, astrologers with the movement of the stars. Witches were thought to understand the properties of animals especially well. The witches of Shakespeare's *Macbeth* chanted their exotic recipe for witch's gruel:

> *Eye of newt and toe of frog,*
> *Wool of bat and tongue of dog,*
> *Adder's fork and blindworm's sting,*
> *Lizard's leg and owlet's wing,*
> *For a charm of powerful trouble,*
> *Like a hell-broth boil and bubble.*

Magical practices appealed to people at all levels of society. The wealthy favored astrology and paid handsomely to discover which days and months were the most auspicious for marriages and investments. So-called cunning men predicted the future for those of the lower orders who would not be able to give an astrologer such vital information as the date of their birth or to pay exorbitant fees. The poorest villagers sought the aid of herbalists to help control the constant aches and pains of daily life. Sorcerers and wizards were called upon in more extreme circumstances, such as a threatened harvest or matters of life and death. The magicians competed with the remedies offered by the Church. Special prayers and visits to the shrines of particular saints were believed to have similar curative value. Magical and Christian beliefs did not oppose each other; they existed on a continuum and were practiced simultaneously. In some French villages, for example, four-leaf clovers were considered especially powerful if they were found on a particular saint's day. It was not until the end of the century, when Protestant and Catholic leaders condemned magical practices and began a campaign to root them out, that magic and religion came into conflict.

Magical practices served a variety of purposes. Healing was the most common, and many "magical" brews were effective remedies of the minor ailments for which they were prescribed. Most village magicians were women because it was believed that women had unique knowledge and understanding of the body. Women were also familiar with the properties of the herbs from which most remedies were derived. Magic was also used for predictive purposes. Certain charms and rituals were believed to have the power to affect the weather, the crops, and even human events. As always, affairs of the heart were as important as those of the stomach. Magicians advised the lovesick on potions and spells that would gain them the object of their desires. Cats were particularly associated with love spells, as were the petals of certain flowers. "He loves me, he loves me not" was more than a child's game. Magic was believed to have the power to alter the course of nature, and it could be used for both good and evil purposes.

The Witch Craze.   Magic for evil was black magic, or witchcraft, which utilized beliefs in the presence of spiritual forces in nature. Witches were believed to possess special powers that put them into contact with the devil and the forces of evil, which they could then use for their own purposes. Belief in the prevalence of good and evil spirits was Christian as well as magical. But the Church had gradually consigned the operation of the devil to the afterlife and removed his direct agency from earthly affairs. Beginning in the late fifteenth century, Church authorities began to prosecute large numbers of suspected witches. By

■ This woodcut from the sixteenth-century *History of the Northern People* by Olaus Magnus shows a devil carrying off a witch, whose protests and gestures beseeching help go unheeded by her fellow villagers in the background.

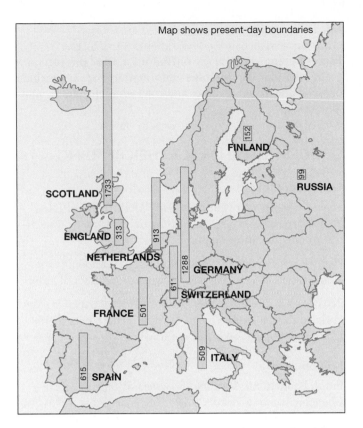

Map shows present-day boundaries

FINLAND 152

RUSSIA 99

SCOTLAND 1733

ENGLAND 313

NETHERLANDS 913

GERMANY 1288

SWITZERLAND 61

FRANCE 501

SPAIN 615

ITALY 509

■ Witchcraft Persecutions. There were more trials for witchcraft in Calvinist Scotland than in all of Spain and France combined.

blemish. Another strand of explanation lies in the fact that single women existed on the fringes of society, isolated and exploited by the community at large. Their occult abilities thus became a protective mechanism that gave them a function within the community while they remained outside it.

It is difficult to know how important black magical beliefs were in ordinary communities. Most of the daily magic that was practiced was the mixture of charms, potions, and prayers that mingled magical, medical, and Christian beliefs. But as the century progressed, more and more notice was taken of black magic. Misfortunes that befell particular families or social groups were blamed upon the activities of witches. The campaign of the established churches to root out magic was largely directed against witches. The churches transposed witches' supposed abilities to communicate with the devil into the charge that they worshipped the devil. Because there was such widespread belief in the presence of diabolical spirits and in the capabilities of witches to control them, Protestant and Catholic church courts could easily find witnesses to testify in support of the charges against individual witches. Yet wherever sufficient evidence exists to understand the circumstances of witchcraft prosecutions, it is clear that the community itself was under some form of social or economic stress. Sacrificing a marginal member of the community might have been the means to restore village solidarity.

the end of the sixteenth century, there was a continentwide witchcraze. Unexplained misfortune or simple malice could set off accusations that might include dozens or even hundreds of suspected witches. Confessions were obtained under torture, as were further accusations. In the period from 1550 to 1650, there were more than 30,000 prosecutions in Germany alone.

Witches were usually women, most often those unmarried or widowed. Although male sorcerers and wizards were thought to have powers over evil spirits, by the sixteenth century it was females who served as the mediators between humans and the diabolical. In a sample of more than 7000 cases of witchcraft prosecuted in early modern Europe, more than 80 percent of the defendants were women. There is no clear explanation why women fulfilled this important and powerful role. Belief in women's special powers over the body through their singular ability to give birth is certainly one part of the explanation, for many stories about the origins of witches suggest that they were children fathered by the devil and left to be raised by women. The sexual element of union with the devil and the common belief that older women were sexually aggressive combined to threaten male sexual dominance. Witches were also believed to have peculiar physical characteristics. A group of Italian witches, male and female, was distinguished by having been born with a caul (a membrane around their heads that was removed after birth). Accused witches were strip-searched to find the devil's mark, which might be any bodily

CONCLUSION

Population growth, economic diversification, and social change characterized life in early modern Europe. It was a century of extremes. The poor were getting poorer and the rich were getting richer. The early part of the century has been called the golden age of the peasantry; the later part has been called the crisis of subsistence. At all levels of the social scale, the lives of grandparents and grandchildren were dramatically different. For surplus producers, the quality of life improved throughout the century. The market economy expanded. Agricultural surplus was exchanged for more land and a wider variety of consumer goods. Children could be provided with an education, and domestic and agricultural labor was cheap and plentiful. For subsistence producers, the quality of life eroded. In the first half of the century, their diet contained more meat than it would for the next 300 years. Their children could be absorbed on new farms or sent to towns where there was a shortage of both skilled and unskilled labor. But gradually the outlook turned bleak. The land could support no more new families, and the towns needed no more labor. As wages fell and prices rose, peasants in western Europe were caught between the crushing burdens of taxation from lord, state, and church and the all-too-frequent catastrophes of poor harvests, epidemic disease, and warfare. In eastern Europe, the peasantry was tied to the land in a new serfdom that provided minimum subsistence in return for the loss of freedom and opportunity. When peasants anywhere rose up against those conditions, they were cut down and swept away like new-mown hay.

QUESTIONS FOR REVIEW

1. What physical forces and social customs shaped the everyday life of Europe's rural population?
2. What was the nature of demographic change in the sixteenth century, and what was its impact on the European economy?
3. How are the terms "stratification," "hierarchy," and "status" useful for understanding social relations in early modern Europe?
4. How were the different roles of men and women within the family reflected in the different lives of men and women in the wider community?

KEY TERMS

Carnival, *p. 462*

enclosure, *p. 455*

Great Chain of Being, *p. 451*

Price Revolution, *p. 449*

robot, p. 444

seigneur, p. 444

skimmington, *p. 464*

three-field rotation, *p. 444*

DISCOVERING WESTERN CIVILIZATION ONLINE

You can obtain more information about life in early modern Europe at the Websites listed below. See also the Companion Website that accompanies this text, www.ablongman.com/kishlansky, which contains an online study guide and additional resources.

Social Life

Internet Modern History Sourcebook: Everyday Life in Premodern Europe

www.fordham.edu/halsall/mod/modsbook04.html

A site with links to sources, pictures, and accounts of everyday life in early modern Europe. A good place to start.

Modern History Sourcebook: Social Conditions in 17th Century France

www.fordham.edu/halsall/mod/17france-soc.html

Documents illustrating social conditions in early modern France.

Private Life

Witchcraft

www2.kenyon.edu/projects/margin/witch.htm

A site with links to sources concerning European witchcraft. Also includes suggestions for further reading and a brief overview of the subject.

Witches and Witchcraft

Womenshistory.about.com/cs/witches

This site offers historical information about witches and witchcraft in Europe and America and includes links to related sites.

Life in Tudor England

englishhistory.net/tudor/tudorlife.html

Part of a comprehensive site on Tudor England, this section on life in Tudor England offers information on topics including food and drink, pastimes and entertainment, and mental illness.

SUGGESTIONS FOR FURTHER READING

General Reading

Peter Burke, *Popular Culture in Early Modern Europe* (New York: Harper & Row, 1978). A lively survey of cultural activities among the European populace.

Henry Kamen, *European Society, 1500–1700* (London: Hutchinson, 2000). A general survey of European social history.

Peter Laslett, *The World We Have Lost: Further Explored* (New York: Scribners, 1984). One of the pioneering works on the family and population history of England.

Economic Life

Judith Bennett, *Ale, Beer, and Brewsters: Women's Work in a Changing World* (Oxford: Oxford University Press, 1996). An important study of the role of women in one of the most traditional trades.

Fernand Braudel, *Civilization and Capitalism: The Structures of Everyday Life* (New York: Harper & Row, 1981). Part of a larger work filled with fascinating detail about the social behavior of humankind during the early modern period.

Emmanuel Le Roy Ladurie, *The French Peasantry, 1450–1660* (London: Scholar Press, 1987). A complex study of the lives of the French peasantry.

Peter Musgrave, *The Early Modern European Economy* (New York: St. Martin's Press, 1999). A multidimensional survey of economic life.

Merry E. Wiesner-Hanks, *Early Modern Europe, 1450–1789* (Cambridge: Cambridge University Press, 2006). A new thematic synthesis of the early modern period, emphasizing gender and social relations. This history treats the "margins" of Europe, discussing oft-neglected Scandinavia as well as the Ottoman Empire.

Social Life

Yves-Marie Bercé, *Revolt and Revolution in Early Modern Europe* (New York: St. Martin's Press, 1987). A study of the structure of uprisings throughout Europe by a leading French historian.

Natalie Zemon Davis, *Women on the Margins: Three Seventeenth-Century Lives* (Cambridge, MA: Harvard University Press, 1995). Three short and stimulating biographies of early modern European women by a leading historian of popular culture.

Jonathan Dewald, *The European Nobility 1400–1800* (Cambridge: Cambridge University Press, 1996). An outstanding survey based on a wide range of sources.

Edward Muir, *Ritual in Early Modern Europe* (Cambridge: Cambridge University Press, 2005). A new and expanded edition of a classic study examining the importance of rites and habits in early modern Europe. Muir has added material on rituals among women and argued forcefully for the persistence of traditional ritual well into the eighteenth century.

Barry Reay, *Popular Cultures in England, 1550–1750* (New York: Addison Wesley Longman, 1998). A sound and insightful thematic survey.

E. M. W. Tillyard, *The Elizabethan World Picture* (New York: Harper & Row, 1960). The classic account of the social constructs of English society.

Private Life

Roger Chartier, ed., *A History of Private Life, Vol. 3, Passions of the Renaissance* (Cambridge, MA: Harvard University Press, 1989). A lavishly illustrated study of the habits, mores, and structures of private life from the fifteenth to the eighteenth centuries.

Stuart Clark, *Thinking with Demons: The Idea of Witchcraft in Early Modern Europe* (Oxford: Oxford University Press, 1997). A sensitive reading of the sources for the study of witchcraft.

Beatrice Gottlieb, *The Family in the Western World from the Black Death to the Industrial Age* (Oxford: Oxford University Press, 1994). An outstanding introduction to the transformations in the lives of families.

R. A. Houston, *Literacy in Early Modern Europe* (London: Longman, 1988). How literacy and education became part of popular culture from 1500 to 1800.

Gary Jensen, *The Path of the Devil: A Study of Early Modern Witch Hunts* (Oxford: Rowman and Littlefield, 2006). The author compares witch hunts throughout Europe in the early modern era and analyzes them in relation to their cultural context.

Brian Levack, *The Witch-Hunt in Early Modern Europe* (New York: Longman, 2006). A study of the causes and meaning of the persecution of European witches in the sixteenth and seventeenth centuries.

R. Muchembled, *Popular Culture and Elite Culture in France, 1400–1750* (Baton Rouge: Louisiana State University Press, 1985). A detailed treatment of the practices of two conflicting cultures.

Steven Ozment, *Ancestors: The Loving Family in Old Europe* (Cambridge, MA: Harvard University Press, 2001). A brief and accessible survey by a leading historian, making a spirited defense of early modern family life against historians who have portrayed the premodern family in grim terms.

D. Underdown, *Revel, Riot, and Rebellion* (Oxford: Oxford University Press, 1985). An engaging study of popular culture and its relationship to social and economic structures in England.

Merry E. Wiesner, *Women and Gender in Early Modern Europe* (Cambridge: Cambridge University Press, 1993). The best introduction to European women's history.

For a list of additional titles related to this chapter's topics, please see http://www.ablongman.com/kishlansky.

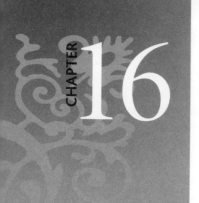

16 THE ROYAL STATE IN THE SEVENTEENTH CENTURY

FIT FOR A KING

THE GRANDEUR OF THE EUROPEAN MONARCHY

Behold Versailles: the greatest palace of the greatest king of the greatest state in seventeenth-century Europe. Everything about it was stupendous, a reflection of the grandeur of Louis XIV and of France. Sculptured gardens in dazzling geometric forms stretched for acres, scenting the air with exotic perfumes. Nearly as beautiful as the grounds were the 1400 fountains, especially the circular basins of Apollo and Latona, the sun god and his mother. The hundreds of water jets that sprayed at Versailles defied nature

THE VISUAL RECORD

as well as the senses, for the locale was not well irrigated and water had to be pumped through elaborate mechanical works all the way from the Seine. Gardens and fountains provided the setting for the enormous palace with its hundreds of rooms for both use and show. Five thousand people, a tenth of whom served the king alone, inhabited the palace. Thousands of others flocked there daily. Most lived in the adjacent town, which had grown from a few hundred people to more than 40,000 in a single generation. The royal stables quartered 12,000 horses and hundreds of carriages. The cost of all that magnificence was equally astounding. Fragmentary accounts indicate that construction costs were more than 100 million French pounds. Louis XIV ordered the official receipts burned.

Like the marble of the palace, nature itself was chiseled to the requirements of the king. Forests were pared to make leafy avenues or trimmed to conform to the geometric patterns of the gardens. In spring and summer, groves of orange trees grown in tubs were everywhere; in winter and fall they were housed indoors at great expense. Life-size statues and giant carved urns lined the carefully planned walkways that led to breathtaking views or sheltered grottoes. A cross-shaped artificial canal, more than a mile long, dominated the western end of the park. Italian gondolas skimmed along its surface, carrying visitors to the zoo and aviary on one side or to the king's private chateau on the other.

But that great pile of bricks and stone, of marble and precious metals, expressed the contradictions of its age as well as its grandeur. The seventeenth century was an era in which the rich got richer and the poor got poorer. It was a time when the monarchical state expanded its power and prestige even as it faced grave challenges to its very existence. It was an epoch of unrelenting war amid a nearly universal desire for lasting peace. Thus it was fitting that the prodigious monument was uncomfortable to live in, so unpleasant that Louis had a separate chateau built on the grounds as a quiet retreat. His wife and his mistresses complained constantly of accommodations in which all interior comforts had been subordinated to the external facade of the building. Versailles was a seat of state as well as the home of the monarch, and it is revealing that the private was sacrificed to the public.

The duc de Saint-Simon, who passed much of his time at Versailles, was well aware of the contradictions: "The beautiful and the ugly were sown together, the vast and the constricted." Soldiers, artisans, and the merely curious clogged the three great avenues that led from Paris to the palace. When the king dined in public, hordes of Parisians drove out for the spectacle, filing past the monarch as if he were an exhibit at a museum. The site itself was poorly drained. "Its mud is black and stinking with a stench so penetrating that you can smell it for several leagues around." The orange groves and the stone urns filled with flower petals were more practical than beautiful: they masked the stench of sewage that was particularly noxious in the heat and the rain. Even the gardens were too vast to be enjoyed. In the planted areas, the smell of flowers was overpowering while the acres of mown lawn proved unattractive to an aristocracy little given to physical exercise. "The gardens were admired and avoided," Saint-Simon observed acidly. In those contrasts of failure amid achievement, Versailles stands as an apt symbol of its age: a gaudy mask to hide the wrinkles of the royal state.

■ Pierre Patel the Elder, *View of Versailles*, 1668.

LOOKING AHEAD

The great palaces of European absolute monarchs were designed to intimidate those who visited them. They were the representation of royal power at its apex. As we will learn in this chapter, not since Rome's emperors were at the height of their glory had power been more concentrated in the hands of rulers, and what they had consolidated over centuries they now had to protect against competing dynasties or rebellious subjects.

Portraits of rulers in action and repose conveyed the central message. Elizabeth I was depicted bestriding a map of England or clutching a rainbow and wearing a gown woven of eyes and ears to signify her power to see and hear her subjects. The Flemish painter Sir Anthony Van Dyck (1599–1641) created powerful images of three generations of Stuart kings of England. He was court painter to Charles I, whose qualities he portrayed with great sympathy and not a little exaggeration. Diego Velázquez (1599–1660) was court painter to Philip IV of Spain. His series of equestrian portraits of the Habsburgs—

- Queen Elizabeth I of England. This portrait was commissioned by Sir Henry Lee to commemorate the queen's visit to his estate at Ditchley. Here the queen, shown standing on a map of England, is the very image of Gloriana—ageless and indomitable.

THE RISE OF THE ROYAL STATE

The religious and dynastic wars that dominated the early part of the seventeenth century had a profound impact upon the western European states. Not only did they cause terrible suffering and deprivation, but they also demanded efficient and better centralized states to conduct them. War was both a product of the European state system and a cause of its continued development. As armies grew in size, the resources necessary to maintain them grew in volume. As the battlefield spread from state to state, defense became government's most important function. More and more power was absorbed by the monarch and his chief advisers; more and more of the traditional privileges of aristocracy and towns were eroded. At the center of the rising states, particularly in western Europe, were the king and his court. In the provinces were tax collectors and military recruiters.

Divine Kings

"There is a divinity that doth hedge a king," wrote Shakespeare. Never was that hedge more luxuriant than in the seventeenth century. In the early sixteenth century, monarchs treated their states and their subjects as personal property. Correspondingly, rulers were praised in personal terms: for their virtue, wisdom, or strength. By the early seventeenth century, the monarchy had been transformed into an office of state. Now rulers embodied their nation and, no matter what their personal characteristics, they were held in awe because they were monarchs.

Thus, as rulers lost direct personal control over their patrimony, they gained indirect symbolic control over their nation. The symbolic power was to be seen everywhere. By the beginning of the seventeenth century, monarchs had set permanent seats of government attended by vast courts of officials, place seekers, and servants. The idea of the capital city emerged, with Madrid, London, Paris, and Vienna as the models. There the grandiose style of the ruler stood proxy for the wealth and glory of the nation. Great display bespoke great pride, and great pride was translated into great strength.

kings, queens, princes, and princesses—exude the spirit of the seventeenth-century monarchy, the grandeur and pomp, the power and self-assurance. Peter Paul Rubens (1577–1640) represented 21 separate episodes in the life of Marie de Médicis, queen regent of France.

The themes of writers were no different than those of artists. Monarchy was glorified in a variety of forms of literary representation. National history, particularly of recent events, enjoyed wide popularity. Its avowed purpose was to draw the connection between the past and the present glories of the state. One of the most popular French histories of the period was entitled *On the Excellence of the Kings and the Kingdom of France*. Francis Bacon (1561–1626), who is remembered more as a philosopher and scientist, wrote a laudatory history of Henry VII, founder of the Tudor dynasty.

In England it was a period of renaissance. Poets, playwrights, historians, and philosophers by the dozens gravitated to the English court. One of the most remarkable of them was Ben Jonson (1572–1637). He began life as a bricklayer, fought against the Spanish in Flanders, and then turned to acting and writing. His wit and talent brought him to court, where he made his mark by writing and staging masques, light entertainment that included music, dance, pantomime, and acting. Jonson's masques were distinguished by their lavish productions and exotic costumes and the inventive set designs of the great architect Inigo Jones (1573–1652). They were frequently staged at Christmastime and starred members of the court as players. The masques took the grandeur of England and its rulers for their themes.

Shakespeare and Kingship. The role of William Shakespeare (1564–1616) in the celebration of monarchy was more ambiguous. Like Jonson, Shakespeare came from an ordinary family, had little formal education, and began his astonishing career as an actor and producer of theater. He soon began to write as well as direct his plays, and his company, the King's Players, received royal patronage. He set many of his plays at the courts of princes, and even comedies such as *The Tempest* (1611) and *Measure for Measure* (1604) centered on the power of the ruler to dispense justice and to bring peace to his subjects. Both plays were staged at court. Shakespeare's history plays focused entirely on the character of kings. In *Richard II* (1597) and *Henry VI* (three parts, 1591–1594) Shakespeare exposed the harm that weak rulers inflicted on their states, while in *Henry IV* (two parts, 1598–1600) and *Henry V* (1599) he highlighted the benefits to be derived from strong rulers.

Shakespeare's tragedies made the point in a different way. The tragic flaw in the personality of rulers exposed the world around them to ruin. In *Macbeth* (1606), the flaw was ambition. Macbeth killed to become a king and had to keep on killing to remain one. In *Hamlet* (1602), the tragic flaw was irresolution. The inability of the Prince of Denmark to act decisively and reclaim the crown that was his by right brought his state to the brink of collapse. Shakespeare's plays were viewed in London theaters by members of all social classes, and his concentration on the affairs of rulers helped reinforce their dominating importance in the lives of all of their subjects.

Monarchy and Law.   The political theory of the **divine right of kings** further enhanced the importance of monarchs. The theory held that the institution of monarchy had been created by God and that the monarch functioned as God's representative on earth. One clear statement of divine right theory was actually written by a king, James VI of Scotland, who later became James I of England (1603–1625). In *The True Law of Free Monarchies* (1598), James reasoned that God had placed kings on earth to rule and that he would judge them in heaven for their transgressions.

James I on Divine Right of Kings

The idea of the divine origin of monarchy was uncontroversial, and it was espoused not only by kings. One of the few things that the French Estates-General actually agreed upon during its meeting in 1614—the last for more than 175 years—was the statement: "The king is sovereign in France and holds his crown from God only." That sentiment echoed the commonplace view of French political theorists. The greatest writer on the subject, Jean Bodin (1530–1596), called the king "God's image on earth." In *The Six Books of the Commonwealth* (1576), Bodin defined the essence of the monarch's power: "The principal mark of sovereign majesty is essentially the right to impose laws on subjects generally without their consent."

Although at first glance the theory of the divine right of kings appears to be a blueprint for arbitrary rule, in fact it was yoked together with a number of principles that restrained the conduct of the monarch. As James I pointed out, God had charged kings with obligations: "to minister justice; to establish good laws; and to procure peace."

The Court and the Courtiers

For all of the bravura of divine right theory, far more was expected of kings than they could possibly deliver. The day-to-day affairs of government had grown beyond the capacity of any monarch to handle them. The expansion in the powers of the western states absorbed more officials than ever. At the beginning of the sixteenth century, the French court of Francis I employed 622 officers; at the beginning of the seventeenth century, the court of Henry IV employed more than 1500. Yet the difference was not only in size. Members of the seventeenth-century court were becoming servants of the state as well as of the monarch.

Like everything else in seventeenth-century government, the court revolved around the monarch. The monarch appointed, promoted, and dismissed officeholders at will. As befit that type of personal government, most monarchs chose a single individual to act as a funnel for private and public business. That person was the "favorite," whose role combined varying proportions of best friend, right-hand man, and hired gun. Some favorites, such as Cardinal Richelieu of France and Spain's Count-Duke Olivares, were able to transform themselves into chief ministers with a political philosophy and a

THE DIVINITY THAT DOTH HEDGE A KING

William Shakespeare's history play of the reign of Richard II tells the story of a rebellion against a lawful monarch. It was banned from production during Elizabeth's reign.

Focus Questions

What does Carlisle mean when he refers to the "power that made you king?" Where does Richard claim his army will come from to defeat Bolingbroke?

KING RICHARD II

Needs must I like it well: I weep for joy
To stand upon my kingdom once again.
Dear earth, I do salute thee with my hand,
Though rebels wound thee with their horses' hoofs:
As a long-parted mother with her child
Plays fondly with her tears and smiles in meeting,
So, weeping, smiling, greet I thee, my earth,
And do thee favours with my royal hands.
Feed not thy sovereign's foe, my gentle earth,
Nor with thy sweets comfort his ravenous sense;
But let thy spiders, that suck up thy venom,
And heavy-gaited toads lie in their way,
Doing annoyance to the treacherous feet
Which with usurping steps do trample thee:
Yield stinging nettles to mine enemies;
And when they from thy bosom pluck a flower,
Guard it, I pray thee, with a lurking adder
Whose double tongue may with a mortal touch
Throw death upon thy sovereign's enemies.
Mock not my senseless conjuration, lords:
This earth shall have a feeling and these stones
Prove armed soldiers, ere her native king
Shall falter under foul rebellion's arms.

BISHOP OF CARLISLE

Fear not, my lord: that Power that made you king
Hath power to keep you king in spite of all.
The means that heaven yields must be embraced,
And not neglected; else, if heaven would,

And we will not, heaven's offer we refuse,
The proffer'd means of succor and redress.

DUKE OF AUMERLE

He means, my lord, that we are too remiss;
Whilst Bolingbroke, through our security,
Grows strong and great in substance and in power.

KING RICHARD II

Discomfortable cousin! know'st thou not
That when the searching eye of heaven is hid,
Behind the globe, that lights the lower world,
Then thieves and robbers range abroad unseen
In murders and in outrage, boldly here;
But when from under this terrestrial ball
He fires the proud tops of the eastern pines
And darts his light through every guilty hole,
Then murders, treasons and detested sins,
The cloak of night being pluck'd from off their backs,
Stand bare and naked, trembling at themselves?
So when this thief, this traitor Bolingbroke,
Who all this while hath revell'd in the night
Whilst we were wandering with the antipodes,
Shall see us rising in our throne, the east,
His treasons will sit blushing in his face,
Not able to endure the sight of day,
But self-affrighted tremble at his sin.
Not all the water in the rough rude sea
Can wash the balm off from an anointed king;
The breath of worldly men cannot depose
The deputy elected by the Lord:
For every man that Bolingbroke hath press'd
To lift shrewd steel against our golden crown,
God for his Richard hath in heavenly pay
A glorious angel: then, if angels fight,
Weak men must fall, for heaven still guards the right.

From William Shakespeare, Richard II, Act III, scene II.

---

vision of government. Others, like the English duke of Buckingham, simply remained royal companions. Favorites walked a not very tight rope. They could retain their balance only as long as they retained their influence with the monarch. Richelieu claimed that it was "more difficult to dominate the four square feet of the king's study than the affairs of Europe." The parallel careers of Richelieu, Olivares, and Buckingham neatly illustrate the dangers and opportunities of the office.

Cardinal Richelieu (1585–1642) was born into a French noble family of minor importance. A younger son, he trained

for the law and then for a position that his family owned in the Church; he was made a cardinal in 1622. After skillful participation in the meeting of the Estates-General of 1614, Richelieu was given a court post through the patronage of Queen Marie de Médicis, mother of Louis XIII. The two men made a good match. Louis XIII hated the work of ruling and Richelieu loved little else.

Although Richelieu received great favor from the king—he became a duke and amassed the largest private fortune in France—his position rested on his managerial abilities. Richelieu never enjoyed a close personal relationship with his building a court faction. His objective was to maintain the greatness of Spain, whose fortunes, like his moods, waxed and waned. Like Richelieu, Olivares attempted to further the process of centralizing royal power, which was not very advanced in Spain. Olivares's plans for a nationally recruited and financed army ended in disaster. His efforts at tax reform went unrewarded. He advocated the aggressive foreign policy that mired Spain in the Thirty Years' War and 80 years of war in the Netherlands. As domestic and foreign crises mounted, Philip IV could not resist the pressure to dismiss his chief minister. In 1643, Olivares was removed from office and two years later, physically exhausted and mentally deranged, he died.

The duke of Buckingham (1592–1628) was also a younger son, but not of the English nobility. He received the aimless education of a country gentleman, spending several years in France learning the graces of fashion and dancing. Reputedly one of the most handsome men in Europe, Buckingham hung

■ The Spanish master Diego Velázquez painted this portrait of the Count-Duke Olivares.

■ This portrait of Richelieu by Philippe de Champaigne shows the cardinal's intellectual power and controlled determination.

monarch, and he never felt that his position was secure. In 1630, Marie de Médicis turned against him, and he very nearly was ousted from office. His last years were filled with suppressing plots to undermine his power or to take his life.

Count-Duke Olivares (1587–1645) was a younger son of a lesser branch of a great Spanish noble family. By the time he was 20 he had become a courtier with a title, a large fortune, and, most unusually, a university education. Olivares became the favorite of King Philip IV (1621–1665). He was elevated to the highest rank of the nobility and lost no time consolidating his position.

Olivares used his closeness to the monarch to gain court appointments for his relatives and political supporters, but he was more interested in establishing political policy than in

■ George Villiers, duke of Buckingham. The royal favorite virtually ruled England between 1618 and 1628. The general rejoicing at his death embittered the king and helped bring about the 11 years' rule without Parliament.

enemies at every turn. Those increased dramatically when James I died in 1625. But Buckingham succeeded where so many others had failed by becoming the favorite and chief minister of the new king, Charles I (1625–1649). His accumulation of power and patronage proceeded unabated, as did the enmity he aroused. But Charles I stood firmly behind him. In 1628, a discontented naval officer finally accomplished what the most powerful men in England could not: Buckingham was assassinated. While Charles I wept inconsolably at the news, ordinary Londoners drank to the health of his killer.

The Taxing Demands of War

More than anything else, war propelled the consolidation of the state. Whether offensive or defensive, continuous or intermittent, successful or calamitous, war was the irresistible force of the seventeenth-century monarchy. War taxation was its immovable object. Perhaps half of all revenue of the western states went to finance war. To maintain its armies and navies, its fortresses and outposts, the state had to squeeze every penny from its subjects. Old taxes had to be collected more efficiently; new taxes had to be introduced and enforced. As one Spanish jurist observed, in a familiar refrain, "There can be no peace without arms, no arms without money, and no money without taxation." However, the unprecedented demands for money by the state were always resisted. The privileged challenged the legality of levying taxes; the unprivileged did whatever they could to avoid paying them.

The claims and counterclaims of subjects and sovereigns were very strong. Armies had grown bigger and more expensive. In 1625, Philip IV had nearly 300,000 men in arms throughout his empire. The expense of maintaining Spanish fortresses alone had quintupled since the time of Philip II. Not only were there more men to pay, equip, and supply, but the cost of war materials continued to rise with inflation. Similarly, the cost of food and fodder rose. Marauding armies might be able to plunder sufficient grain during the spring and autumn, but they still consumed massive amounts of meat and drink that could not be supplied locally.

In fact, the inability of the lower orders of European society to finance a century of warfare was clear from the beginning. In Spain and France, the principal problem was that so much of the wealth of the nation was beyond the reach of traditional royal taxation. The nobility and many of the most important towns had long achieved exemption from basic taxes on consumption and wealth. European taxation was regressive, falling most heavily on those least able to pay. Rulers and subjects alike recognized the inequities of the system. Regime after regime began with plans to overhaul the national system of taxation before settling for propping up new emergency levies against the rotting foundations of the old structure. Nevertheless, the fiscal crisis that the European wars provoked did result in an expansion of state taxation.

Fiscal Expedients.   In France, for example, royal expenditures rose 60 percent during the first two decades of the seven-

about the fringes of the English court until his looks and charm brought him to the attention of Queen Anne, James I's wife. She recommended him for a minor office that gave him frequent access to the king. Buckingham quickly caught the eye of James I, and his rise was meteoric. In less than seven years he went from commoner to duke, the highest rank of the English nobility.

Along with his titles, Buckingham acquired political power. He assumed a large number of royal offices, among them Admiral of the Navy, and placed his relatives and dependents in many others. Buckingham took his obligations seriously. He began a reform of naval administration, for example, but his rise to power had been so sudden that he found teenth century, while the yield from the *taille,* the crown's basic commodity tax, remained constant. Thus the crown was forced to search for new revenues, the most important of which was the ***paulette,*** a tax on officeholding. To raise money, especially in emergencies, the crown had been forced to sell government offices, until by the seventeenth century a majority of offices had been obtained by direct purchase. The sale of an office provided a one-time windfall for the crown, but after that the cost of salaries and benefits was a perpetual drain. Draining, too, were the administrative costs of potentially inefficient officeholders. Many purchased their posts as an investment and treated them as personal property. For an annual payment of one-sixtieth of the value of the office, the paulette allowed the current holder to sell or bequeath it as desired. Henry IV instituted the *paulette* in 1604, and it became a vital source of royal revenue as well as an acute source of aristocratic and legal complaint. In the early 1620s, revenue from the sale of offices amounted to one-third of the crown's income.

The purchase of office was inherently corrupt, but it was not necessarily inefficient. Sons who were to inherit offices could be trained for their posts, if for no other reason than to operate them profitably. The crown received money from classes in society that were generally beyond the reach of taxation, while members of those classes received power, prestige, and experience in public service. As long as profit and efficiency went hand in hand, both officeholder and monarch might be well served. Unfortunately, it was the king rather than his officers who had the greatest incentive to manipulate the system. The more offices that could be created, the larger the income from the paulette. During fiscal emergencies it was a temptation to which all French monarchs succumbed.

"Fiscal emergency" was just another name for the routine problems of the Spanish monarchy. As the greatest military power in Europe, Spain necessarily had the greatest military budget, and thus the most extensive system of taxation. The crown taxed both domestic and imperial trade and took a healthy share of the gold and silver that continued to be mined in America. But all the revenues fell short of the state's needs. In the 1590s, Philip II established an important new source of internal taxation. In an agreement with the Cortes of Castile, he introduced the *milliones,* a tax on consumption that was to yield millions of ducats a year for war costs. An extremely regressive measure, the milliones taxed the sale of meat, wine, and oil—the basic elements of diet. The tax, which hit urban areas particularly hard, was originally designed to last only six years. But the crises that the crown pleaded in the 1590s were even deeper at the turn of the century. The milliones became a permanent tax and a permanent grievance throughout Castile.

Taxation in England.   By contrast, the English crown was never able to persuade Parliament to grant permanent additional revenues. Although uninvolved in European conflicts, England was not immune from military spending. War with Ireland in the 1590s and with Spain between 1588 and 1604 depleted the reserves that the crown had obtained when Henry VIII dissolved the monasteries. Disastrous wars against France

and Spain in the 1620s provoked fiscal crisis for a monarchy that had few direct sources of revenue. While the great wealth of the kingdom was in land, the chief sources of revenue for the crown were in trade. In the early seventeenth century, customs duties, or *impositions,* became a lucrative source of income when the judges ruled that the king could determine which commodities could be taxed and at what rate. Impositions fell heavily upon the merchant classes and urban consumers, but unlike the milliones, impositions were placed on luxury import goods rather than on basic commodities.

Because so much of the crown's revenues derived from commerce and because foreign invasion could only come from the sea, the most pressing military need of the English monarchy was for naval defense. Even during the Armada crisis, the largest part of the English fleet had been made up of private merchant ships pressed into service through the emergency tax of Ship Money, which was a tax on each port town to hire a merchant ship and fit it out for war. In the 1630s, Charles I revived Ship Money and extended it to all English localities. His innovation aroused much opposition from the gentry, especially after his refusal to call Parliament into session to have the tax confirmed.

Still, no matter how much new revenue was provided for war finance, more was needed. New taxes and increased rates of traditional taxation created suffering and a sense of grievance throughout the western European states. Opposition to taxation was not based on greed: the state's right to tax was not yet an established principle. Monarchs received certain forms of revenue in return for grants of immunities and privileges to powerful groups in their state. The state's efforts to go beyond the restricted grants were viewed as theft of private property. In the case of Ship Money, challengers argued that the king had no right to what belonged to his subjects except in a case of national emergency. That was a claim that the king accepted, arguing that such an emergency existed in the presence of pirates who were attacking English shipping. But if Charles I did not make a convincing claim for national emergency, the monarchs of France and Spain, the princes of Germany, and the rulers of the states of eastern Europe all did.

Throughout the seventeenth century, monarchy solidified itself as a form of government. The king's authority came from God, but his power came from his people. By administering justice, assembling armies, and extracting resources through taxation, the monarch ruled as well as governed. The richer the king and the more powerful his might, the more potent was his state. Europeans began to identify themselves as citizens of a nation and to see themselves in distinction to other nations.

THE CRISES OF THE ROYAL STATE

The expansion of the functions, duties, and powers of the state in the early seventeenth century was not universally welcomed in European societies. The growth of central government came at the expense of local rights and privileges held by corporate bodies such as the Church and the towns or by

EUROPEAN POPULATION DATA (IN MILLIONS)

Year	1550	1575	1600	1625	1650	1675	1700
England	3.0	—	4.0	4.5	—	5.8	5.8
France	—	20.0	—	—	—	—	19.3
Italy	11.0	13.0	13.0	13.0	12.0	11.5	12.5
Russia	9.0	—	11.0	8.0	9.5	13.0	16.0
Spain	6.3	—	7.6	—	5.2	—	7.0
All Europe	85.0	95.0	100.0	100.0	80.0	90.0	100.0

individuals such as provincial officials and aristocrats. The state proved a powerful competitor, especially in the contest for the meager surplus produced on the land. As rents and prices stabilized in the early seventeenth century after a long period of inflation, taxation increased, slowly at first and then at a pace with the gathering momentum of the Thirty Years' War. State exactions burdened all segments of society. Peasants lost the small benefit that rising prices had conferred on producers. The surplus that parents had once passed on to children was now taken by the state. Local officials, never altogether popular, came to be seen as parasites and were easy targets for peasant rebellions. Larger landholders, whose prosperity depended on rents and services from an increasingly impoverished peasantry, suffered along with their tenants. Even the great magnates were appalled by the state's insatiable appetite.

Taxation was not the only thing that aroused opposition. Social and economic regulation meant more laws. More laws meant more lawyers and agents of enforcement. State regulation may have been more efficient (though many believed it was more efficient only for the state) but it was certainly disruptive. It was also expensive at a time when the fragile European economy was in a phase of decline. The early seventeenth century was a time of hunger in most of western Europe. Subtle changes in climate reduced the length of growing seasons and the size of crops. Bad harvests in the 1620s and 1640s left disease and starvation in their wake. And the wars ground on.

By the middle of the seventeenth century, a European crisis was taking shape, though its timing and forms differed from place to place. Rural protests, such as grain riots and mob assaults on local institutions, had a long history in all of the European states. Popular revolt was not the product of mindless despair, but rather the natural form of political action for those who fell outside the institutionalized political process. Bread riots and tax revolts became increasingly common in the early seventeenth century. More significantly, as the focus of discontent moved from local institutions to the state, the forms of revolt changed. So, too, did the participants. Members of the political elite began to formulate their own grievances against the expansion of state power. A theory of resistance, first developed in the French wars of religion, came to be applied to political tyranny and posed a direct challenge to the idea of the divine right of kings. By the 1640s, all those forces had converged, and rebellion exploded across the Continent. In Spain, the ancient kingdoms of Catalonia and Portugal asserted their independence from Castilian rule; in France, members of the aristocracy rose against a child monarch and his regent. In Italy, revolts rocked Naples and Sicily. In England, a constitutional crisis gave way to civil war, and then to the first political revolution in European history.

The Need to Resist

Europeans lived more precariously in the seventeenth century than in any period since the Black Death. One benchmark of crisis was population decline. In the Mediterranean, Spain's population fell from 8.5 to 7 million and Italy's population from 13 to 11 million. The ravages of the Thirty Years' War were most clearly felt in central Europe: Germany lost nearly a third of its people, Bohemia nearly half. Northwestern Europe—England, the Netherlands, and France—was hardest hit in the first half of the century and only gradually recovered by 1700. Population decline had many causes and, rather remarkably, direct casualties from warfare were a very small component. The indirect effects of war—the disruption of agriculture and the spread of disease—were far more devastating. Spain alone lost a half million people at the turn of the century and another half million between 1647 and 1652. Severe outbreaks of plague in 1625 and in 1665 hit England, while France endured three consecutive years of epidemics, from 1629 to 1631.

All sectors of the European economy, from agriculture to trade, stagnated or declined in the early seventeenth century. Not surprisingly, peasants were hardest hit. The surplus from good harvests did not remain in rural communities to act as a buffer for bad ones. Tens of thousands died during the two great subsistence crises in the late 1620s and the late 1640s. Predictably, acute economic crisis led to rural revolt. As the

French peasants reeled from visitations of plague, frost, and floods, the French state was raising the taille, the tax that fell most heavily on the lower orders. A series of French rural revolts in the late 1630s focused on opposition to tax increases. The Nu-Pieds—"the barefooted"—rose against changes in the salt tax; others rose against new levies on wine. The revolts began in the same way: with the murder of a local tax official, the organization of a peasant militia, and the recruitment of local clergy and notables. The rebels forced temporary concessions from local authorities, but they never achieved lasting reforms. Each revolt ended with the reimposition of order by the state. In England, the largest rural protests, like the Midland Revolt of 1607, centered on opposition to the enclosure of grain fields and their conversion to pasture.

The most spectacular popular uprisings occurred in Spanish-occupied Italy. In the spring of 1647, the Sicilian city of Palermo exploded under the pressure of a disastrous harvest, rising food prices, and relentless taxation. A city of 130,000 inhabitants, Palermo imported nearly all of its foodstuffs. As grain prices rose, the city government subsidized the price of bread, running up huge debts in the process. When the town governors could no longer afford the subsidies, they decided to reduce the size of the loaf rather than increase its price. This did not fool the women of the city, who rioted when the first undersized loaves were placed on sale. Soon the entire city was in revolt. "Long live the king and down with taxes!" became the rebel slogan. Commoners who were not part of the urban power structure led the revolt in Palermo. For a time they achieved the abolition of Spanish taxes on basic foodstuffs. Their success provided the model for a similar uprising in Naples, the largest city in Europe. The Neapolitan revolt began in 1647 after the Spanish placed a tax on fruit. A crowd gathered to protest the new imposition, burned the customs house, and murdered several local officials. The protesters were led first by a fisherman and then by a blacksmith, and again the rebels achieved the temporary suspension of Spanish taxation. But neither of the Italian urban revolts could attract support from the local governors or the nobility. Both uprisings were eventually crushed.

The Right to Resist

Rural and urban revolts by members of the lower orders of European society were doomed to failure. Not only did the state control vast military resources, but it could count on the loyalty of the governing classes to suppress local disorder. It was only when local elites rebelled and joined their social and political discontent to the economic grievances of the peasants that the state faced a genuine crisis. Traditionally, aristocratic rebellion focused on the legitimacy rather than the power of the state. Claimants to the throne initiated civil wars for the prize of the crown. By the early seventeenth century, however, hereditary monarchy was too firmly entrenched to be threatened by aristocratic rebellions. When Elizabeth I of England died without an heir, the throne passed to her cousin, James I, without even a murmur of discontent. The assassination of Henry IV in 1610 left a child on the French throne, yet it provoked little more than intrigue over which aristocratic faction would advise him. The principles of hereditary monarchy and the divine right of kings laid an unshakable foundation for royal legitimacy. But if the monarch's right to rule could no longer be challenged, was the method of rule equally unassailable? Were subjects bound to their sovereign in all cases whatsoever?

Resistance Theory.   Luther and Calvin had preached a doctrine of passive obedience. **Magistrates** ruled by divine

■ War, famine, and disease all contributed to population decline in the seventeenth century. This broadsheet shows the weekly burial of plague victims in London during a severe outbreak in 1665.

will and had to be obeyed in all things, they argued. Both left a tiny crack in the door of absolute submission, however, by recognizing the right of lesser magistrates to resist their superiors if divine law was violated. It was during the French civil wars that a broader theory of resistance began to develop. In attempting to defend themselves from accusations that they were rebels, a number of Huguenot writers responded with an argument that accepted the divine right of kings but limited royal power. They claimed that kings were placed on earth by God to uphold piety and justice. When they failed to do so, lesser magistrates were obliged to resist them. As God would not institute tyranny, oppressive monarchs could not be acting by divine right. Therefore, the king who violated divine law could be punished. In the most influential of such writings, *A Defense of Liberty Against Tyrants* (1579), Philippe Duplessis-Mornay (1549–1623) took the critical next step and argued that the king who violated the law of the land could also be resisted.

In the writings of both Huguenot and Dutch Protestants there remained strict limits to the right to resist. Those authors accepted all the premises of divine right theory and restricted resistance to other divinely ordained magistrates. Obedience tied society together at all levels, and loosening any of the knots might unravel everything. In fact, one crucial binding had already come loose when the arguments used to justify resistance in matters of religion came to be applied to matters of state. Logic soon drove the argument further. If it was the duty of lesser magistrates to resist monarchical tyranny, why was it not the duty of all citizens to do so? That was a question posed not by a Protestant rebel, but by a Jesuit professor, Juan de Mariana (1536–1624). In *The King and the Education of the King* (1598), Mariana described how human government developed from the need of individuals to have leaders to act for their convenience and well-being. The magistrates were established by the people and then legitimated by God. Magistrates were nothing other than the people's representatives, and if it was the duty of magistrates to resist the tyranny of monarchs, then it must also be the duty of every individual citizen. "If the sacred fatherland is falling into ruins, he who tries to kill the tyrant will be acting in no ways unjustly."

There remained one more vital link in the chain, which was supplied by the great English poet John Milton (1608–1674) in his defense of the English Revolution. Milton built upon traditional resistance theory as it had developed over the previous 50 years. Kings were instituted by the people to uphold piety and justice. Lesser magistrates had the right to resist monarchs. An unjust king forfeited his divine right and was to be punished as any ordinary citizen. In *The Tenure of Kings and Magistrates* (1649), Milton expanded upon the conventional idea that society was formed by a covenant, or contract, between ruler and ruled. The king in his coronation oath promised to uphold the laws of the land and rule for the benefit of his subjects. The subjects promised to obey. Failure by either side to meet obligations broke the contract.

Resistance and Rebellion. By the middle of the seventeenth century, resistance theory provided the intellectual justification for a number of different attacks on monarchical authority. In 1640, simultaneous rebellions in the ancient kingdoms of Portugal and Catalonia threatened the Spanish monarchy. The Portuguese successfully dissolved the rather artificial bonds that had been created by Philip II and resumed their separate national identity. Catalonia, the easternmost province of Spain, which Ferdinand of Aragon had brought to the union of crowns in the fifteenth century, presented a more serious challenge. Throughout the 1620s, Catalonia, with its rich Mediterranean city of Barcelona, had consistently rebuffed Olivares's attempts to consolidate the Spanish provinces. The Catalonian Cortes—the representative institution of the towns—refused to make even small contributions to the Union of Arms or to successive appeals for emergency tax increases. Catalonian leaders feared that the demands were only the thin edge of the wedge. They did not want their province to go the way of Castile, where taxation was as much an epidemic as plague.

Catalonia relied on its ancient laws to fend off demands for contributions to the Spanish military effort. But soon the province was embroiled in the French war, and Olivares was forced to bring troops into Catalonia. The presence of the soldiers and their conduct inflamed the local population. In the spring of 1640 an unconnected series of peasant uprisings took place. Soldiers and royal officials were slain, and the Spanish viceroy of the province was murdered. But the violence was not directed only against outsiders. Attacks on wealthy citizens raised the specter of social revolt.

At that point a peasant uprising broadened into a provincial rebellion. The political leaders of Barcelona not only decided to approve the rebellion but decided to lead it. They declared that Philip IV had violated the fundamental laws of Catalonia and that as a consequence their allegiance to the crown of Spain was dissolved. They turned to Louis XIII of France, offering him sovereignty if he would preserve their liberties. In fact, the Catalonians simply exchanged a devil they knew for one they did not. The French happily sent troops into Barcelona to repel a Spanish attempt to crush the rebellion, and then two armies occupied Catalonia. The Catalonian rebellion lasted for 12 years. When the Spanish finally took Barcelona in 1652, both rebels and ruler were exhausted from the struggle.

The revolt of the Catalonians posed a greater external threat to the Spanish monarchy than it did an internal one. In contrast, the French **Fronde,** an aristocratic rebellion that began in 1648, was more directly a challenge to the underlying authority of the state. It too began in response to fiscal crises brought on by war. Throughout the 1640s the French state had tottered on the edge of bankruptcy. It had used every means of creative financing that its ministers could devise, mortgaging as much of the future as anyone would buy. Still, it was necessary to raise traditional taxes and institute new ones. The first tactic revived peasant revolts, especially in the early years of the decade; the second led to the Fronde.

■ Anne of Austria acted as a regent during her son's minority, though in practice she delegated most power to her adviser Cardinal Mazarin. This painting emphasizes the piety of the royal family, as Anne, Louis, and his younger brother Philippe kneel in prayer against a backdrop of God, Jesus, and their heavenly and worldly servants.

The Fronde was a rebellion against the regency government of Louis XIV (1643–1715), who was only four years old when he inherited the French throne. His mother, Anne of Austria (1601–1666), ruled as regent with the help of her Italian adviser, Cardinal Mazarin (1602–1661). In the circumstances of war, agricultural crisis, and financial stringency, no regency government was popular, but Anne and Mazarin made the worst of a bad situation. They initiated new taxes on officeholders, Parisian landowners, and the nobility. Soon all three united against them, led by the Parlement of Paris, the highest court in the land, in which new decrees of taxation had to be registered. When the **Parlement** refused to register a number of the new taxes proposed by the government and soon insisted on the right to control the crown's financial policy, Anne and Mazarin struck back by arresting a number of leading members of the Parlement. But in 1648 barricades went up in Paris, and the court, along with the nine-year-old king, fled the capital. Quickly the Fronde—which took its name from the slingshots that children used to hurl stones at carriages—became an aristocratic revolt aimed not at the king, but at his advisers. Demands for Mazarin's resignation, removal of the new taxes, and greater participation in government by nobles and Parlement were coupled with profuse statements of loyalty to the king.

The duc de Condé, leader of the Parisian insurgents, courted Spanish aid against Mazarin's forces, and the cardinal was forced to make concessions in order to prevent a Spanish invasion of France. The leaders of the Fronde agreed that the crown must overhaul its finances and recognize the rights of the administrative nobility to participate in formulating royal policy, but they had no concrete proposals to accomplish either aim. Nor could they control the deteriorating political situation in Paris and a number of provincial capitals where urban and rural riots followed the upper-class attack upon the state. The catastrophic winter of 1652, with its combination of harvest failure, intense cold, and epidemic disease, brought the crisis to a head. Louis XIV was declared old enough to rule and his forces recaptured Paris, where he was welcomed as a savior. Born of frustration, fear, and greed, the Fronde accomplished little. It demonstrated only that the French aristocracy remained an independent force in politics. Like the Catalonian revolt, it revealed the fragility of the absolute state on the one hand, yet its underlying stability on the other.

The English Civil War

On the surface, it is difficult to understand why the most profound challenge to monarchical authority took place in England. Among the nations of Europe, England alone enjoyed peace in the early seventeenth century. Except for a brief period around 1620, the English economy sputtered along. The monarchy itself was stable. James I had succeeded his cousin Elizabeth I without challenge and already had as many children as the Tudors had produced in nearly a century.

James I. James I was not a lovable monarch, but he was capable, astute, and generous. In the eyes of his critics he had two great faults: he succeeded a legend and he was Scottish. There was little he could do about either. Elizabeth I had ruled England successfully for more than 40 years. As the economy soured and the state tilted toward bankruptcy in the 1590s, the queen remained above criticism. She sold off royal lands worth thousands of pounds and ran up huge debts at the turn of the century, yet the gleaming myth of the glorious virgin queen tarnished not the least bit. When she died, the general population wept openly and the governing elite breathed a collective sigh of relief. There was so much to be done to set things right.

At first, James I endeared himself to the English gentry and aristocracy by showering them with the gift of social elevation. On his way to London from Scotland, the first of the Stuart kings knighted thousands of gentlemen who had waited in vain for favor from the queen. He promoted peers and created new titles to meet the pent-up demands of decades of stinginess. But he showered favor equally on his own countrymen, members of his royal Scottish court who accompanied him to England. A strong strain of ethnic prejudice combined with the disappointed hopes of English courtiers to generate immediate hostility to the new regime. If Elizabeth could do no wrong, James could do little right. Although he relied upon Elizabeth's most trusted ministers to guide state business, James was soon plunged into financial and political difficulties. He never escaped from either.

Charles I. James's financial problems resulted directly from the fact that the tax base of the English monarchy was undervalued. For decades the monarchy had staved off a crisis by selling lands that had been confiscated from the Church in the mid-sixteenth century. But that solution reduced the crown's long-term revenues and made it dependent on extraordinary grants of taxation from Parliament. Royal demands for money were met by parliamentary demands for political reform, and the differing objectives provoked unintentional political controversies in the 1620s. The most significant, in 1628, during the reign of Charles I, led to the formulation of the Petition of Right, which restated the traditional English freedoms from arbitrary arrest and imprisonment (habeas corpus), nonparliamentary taxation, and the confiscation of property by martial law.

IMAGE DISCOVERY

Commoner or King? Charles I at the Hunt
The artist Anthony Van Dyck painted this picture of Charles I in 1635, only a few years before his kingdoms revolted. Here, Charles is depicted in a rustic location, without crown, scepter, or other trappings of monarchy. Does he still look like a king? Charles was not, in fact, unusually fond of hunting. Why, then, would he have chosen to be painted this way? What might the drooping head of his horse have signified to seventeenth-century viewers? Remember, this was painted before anyone could have known that England, Scotland, or Ireland would revolt.

Religious problems mounted on top of economic and political difficulties. Demands were made for thoroughgoing church reforms by groups and individuals who had little in common apart from the name given to them by their detractors: **Puritans.** One of the most contentious issues raised by

A SHORT, SHARP SHOCK

Charles I was executed at Westminster on a bitter January afternoon in 1649. This excerpt comes from an eyewitness account of his last moments. Charles, who was accompanied on the scaffold by the bishop of London, discovered that the chopping block was very short so that he could be held down if he resisted.

Focus Questions

Is Charles resigned to his execution? In what ways is the divine right of kings commented upon in this passage?

And to the executioner he said, "I shall say but very short prayers, and when I thrust out my hands—"

Then he called to the bishop for his cap, and having put it on, asked the executioner, "Does my hair trouble you?" who desired him to put it all under his cap; which, as he was doing by the help of the bishop and the executioner, he turned to the bishop, and said, "I have a good cause, and a gracious God on my side."

The bishop said, "There is but one stage more, which, though turbulent and troublesome, yet is a very short one. You may consider it will soon carry you a very great way; it will carry you from earth to heaven; and there you shall find to your great joy the prize you hasten to, a crown of glory."

The king adjoins, "I go from a corruptible to an incorruptible crown; where no disturbance can be, no disturbance in the world."

The bishop. "You are exchanged from a temporal to an eternal crown—a good exchange."

Then the king asked the executioner, "Is my hair well?" . . . and looking upon the block, said . . . "You must set it fast."

The executioner. "It is fast, sir."

King. "It might have been a little higher."

Executioner. "It can be no higher, sir."

King. "When I put out my hands this way, then—"

Then having said a few words to himself, as he stood, with hands and eyes lifted up, immediately stooping down he laid his neck upon the block; and the executioner, again putting his hair under his cap, his Majesty, thinking he had been going to strike, bade him, "Stay for the sign."

Executioner. "Yes, I will, and it please your Majesty."

After a very short pause, his Majesty stretching forth his hands, the executioner at one blow severed his head from his body; which, being held up and showed to the people, was with his body put into a coffin covered with black velvet and carried into his lodging.

His blood was taken up by divers persons for different ends: by some as trophies of their villainy; by others as relics of a martyr; and in some hath had the same effect, by the blessing of God, which was often found in his sacred touch when living.

Puritans was the survival in the Anglican church of the Catholic hierarchy of archbishops and bishops. They demanded the abolition of this episcopal form of government and its replacement with a presbyterial system similar to that in Scotland, in which congregations nominated their own representatives to a national assembly. As the king was the supreme head of the English church, an attack upon church structure was an attack upon the monarchy. "No bishop, no king," James I declared as he rejected the first formal attempts at reform. But neither James I nor his son, Charles I, opposed religious reform. They, too, wanted a better educated clergy, a plain and decorous worship service, and godly citizens. But to achieve their reforms they strengthened episcopal power. In the 1620s, Archbishop William Laud (1573–1645) rose to power in the English church by espousing a Calvinism so moderate that many denied it was Calvinism at all. Laud preached the beauty of holiness and strove to reintroduce decoration in the church and a formal decorum in the service. One of Laud's first projects after he was appointed archbishop of Canterbury was to establish a consistent divine service in England and Scotland by creating new prayer books.

It fell to the unfortunate dean of St. Giles Cathedral in Edinburgh to introduce the new Scottish prayer book in 1637. The reaction was immediate: someone threw a stool at his head and dozens of women screamed that "popery" was being brought to Scotland. There were riots by citizens and resistance to the use of the new prayer book by clergy and the nobility. To Charles I the opposition was rebellion, and he began to raise forces to suppress it. But Scottish soldiers were far more determined to preserve their religious practice than were English soldiers to impose the king's. By the end of 1640, a Scottish army had successfully invaded England.

Now the fiscal and political problems of the Stuart monarchs came into play. For 11 years, Charles I had managed to do what he was in theory supposed to do: live from his own revenues. He had accomplished that by a combination of economy and the revival of ancient feudal rights that struck hard at the governing classes. He levied fines for unheard-of offenses, expanded traditional taxes, and added a brutal efficiency to the collection of revenue. While these expedients sufficed during peacetime, they could not support an army and war. Charles I was again dependent on grants from Parliament, which he reluctantly summoned in 1640.

MAP DISCOVERY

| | Areas controlled by Royalists | | Areas controlled by Parliamentarians | ★ | Major battles |

English Civil War

How would you describe the geographical divisions at the beginning of the war in 1642? Who appears to have been winning the war by December 1643? How did the war progress between 1644 and 1645?

The Long Parliament.   The **Long Parliament,** which met in November 1640 and sat for 13 years, saw little urgency in levying taxes to repel the Scots. After all, the Scots were resisting Laud's religious innovations, and there were many Englishmen who believed that they should be resisted. More to the point, members of Parliament had a host of political grievances to be redressed before they granted the king his money. Parliament proposed a number of constitutional reforms that Charles I reluctantly accepted. The Long Parliament would not be dismissed without its own consent. In the future, Parliaments would be summoned once every three years. Due process in common law would be observed, and the ancient taxes that the crown had revived would be abolished. To show its seriousness of purpose, Parliament, as the highest court in the land, tried and executed Charles's leading political adviser, the Earl of Strafford, and imprisoned Archbishop Laud.

At first Charles I could do nothing but bide his time and accept the assaults on his power and authority, believing that once he had crushed the Scots he would be able to bargain from a position of strength. But as the months passed, it became clear that Parliament had no intention of providing him with money or forces. Rather, the members sought to negotiate with the Scots themselves and to continue to demand concessions from the king as long as the Scottish threat remained. By the end of 1641, Charles's patience had worn thin. He bungled an attempt to arrest the leaders of the House of Commons, but he successfully spirited his wife and children out of London. Then he too left the capital and headed north where, in the summer of 1642, he raised the royal standard

and declared the leaders of Parliament rebels and traitors. England was plunged into civil war.

Parliament had finally pushed too hard, and its members now found themselves in the unprecedented situation of having to fight a war against their sovereign, a war that few of them wanted and that hardly anyone believed they could win. One of the Parliament's generals summed up the futility of the situation: "If we defeat the king ninety-nine times, yet still he is king. But if he defeat us once we will all be hanged as traitors." Nevertheless, there were strong passions on both sides. Parliamentarians believed that they were fighting to defend their religion, their liberties, and the rule of law. Royalists believed they were fighting to defend their monarch, their church, and social stability. After nearly three years of inconclusive fighting, in June 1645 Parliament won a decisive victory at Naseby and brought the war to an end the following summer. The king was in captivity, bishops had been abolished, a Presbyterian church had been established, and limitations were placed on royal power. All that remained necessary to end three years of civil war was the king's agreement to abide by the judgment of battle.

But Charles I had no intention of surrendering either his religion or his authority. Despite the rebels' successes, they could not rule without him, and he would concede nothing as long as opportunities to maneuver remained. In 1647 there were opportunities galore. The war had proved ruinously expensive to Parliament. It owed enormous sums to the Scots, to its own soldiers, and to the governors of London. Each of those elements had its own objectives in a final settlement of the war, and they were not altogether compatible. London

■ Print of the 1649 execution of Charles I, who was tried and found guilty of treason. As the ax fell, one witness recorded, "such a groan as I never heard before and hope never to hear again" broke forth from the crowd. With the king's execution, England was declared to be a commonwealth, and the monarchy was abolished.

feared the parliamentary army, unpaid and camped dangerously close to the capital. The Scots and the English Presbyterians in Parliament feared that the religious settlement already made would be sacrificed by those known as Independents, who desired a more decentralized church. The Independents feared that they would be persecuted just as harshly by the Presbyterians as they had been by the king. In fact, the war had settled nothing.

The English Revolutions

Charles I happily played both ends against the middle until the army decisively ended the game. In June 1647, soldiers kidnapped the king and demanded that Parliament pay their arrears, protect them from legal retribution, and recognize their service to the nation. Those in Parliament who opposed the army's intervention were impeached, and when London Presbyterians rose up against the army's show of force, troops moved in to occupy the city. The civil war, which had come so close to resolution in 1647, had now become a military revolution. Religious and political radicals flocked to the army and encouraged the soldiers to support their programs and resist disbandment. New fighting broke out in 1648 as Charles encouraged his supporters to resume the war. But forces under

the command of Sir Thomas Fairfax (1612–1671) and Oliver Cromwell (1599–1658) easily crushed the royalist uprisings in England and Scotland. The army then demanded that Charles I be brought to justice for his treacherous conduct both before and during the war. When the majority in Parliament refused, still hoping against hope to reach an accommodation with the king, the soldiers again acted decisively. In December 1648, army regiments were sent to London to purge the two houses of Parliament of those who opposed the army's demands. The remaining members, contemptuously called the Rump Parliament, voted to bring the king to trial for his crimes against the liberties of his subjects. On 30 January 1649, Charles I was executed and England was declared to be a commonwealth. The monarchy and the House of Lords were abolished, and the nation was to be governed by what was left of the membership of the House of Commons.

DOCUMENT

Cromwell Abolishes Monarchy

Oliver Cromwell. For four years, the members of the Rump Parliament struggled with proposals for a new constitution while balancing the demands of moderate and radical reformers and an increasingly hostile army. It achieved little other than to raise the level of frustration. In 1653, Oliver Cromwell, with the support of the army's senior officers, forcibly dissolved the Rump and became the leader of the revolutionary government. At first he ruled along with a Parliament hand-picked from among the supporters of the commonwealth. When Cromwell's Parliament proved no more capable of governing than had the Rump, a written constitution, The Instrument of Government (1653), established a new polity. Cromwell was given the title Lord Protector, and he was to rule along with a freely elected Parliament and an administrative body known as the Council of State.

Cromwell was able to hold the revolutionary cause together through the force of his own personality. A member of the lesser landed elite who had opposed the arbitrary policies of Charles I, he was a devout Puritan who believed in a large measure of religious toleration for Christians. As both a member of Parliament and a senior officer in the army, he had been able to temper the claims of each when they conflicted.

■ The charismatic Oliver Cromwell, Lord Protector of England, wore many hats but was most comfortable under the helmet of a cavalry commander. He is pictured here in his element, armed and on horseback.

Cromwell saw God's hand directing England toward a more glorious future, and he believed that his own actions were divinely ordained: "No man climbs higher than he that knows not whither he goes." Although many urged him to accept the crown of England and begin a new monarchy, Cromwell steadfastly held out for a government in which fundamental authority resided in Parliament. Until his death he defended the achievements of the revolution and held its conflicting constituents together.

But a sense that only a single person could effectively rule a state remained too strong for the reforms of the revolutionary regimes to have much chance of success. When Cromwell died in 1658 it was only natural that his eldest son, Richard, should be proposed as the new Lord Protector despite the fact that Richard had very little experience in either military or civil affairs. Nor did he have the sense of purpose that was his father's greatest source of strength. Without an individual to hold the movement together, the revolution fell apart. In 1659, the army again intervened in civil affairs, dismissing the recently elected Parliament and calling for the restoration of the monarchy to provide stability to the state. After a period of negotiation in which the king agreed to a general amnesty with only a few exceptions, the Stuarts were restored when Charles II (1649–1685) took the throne in 1660.

Twenty years of civil war and revolution had had their effect. Parliament became a permanent part of civil government and now had to be managed rather than ignored. Royal power over taxation and religion was curtailed, although in fact Parliament proved more vigorous in suppressing religious dissent than the monarchy ever had. England was to be a reformed Protestant state, although there remained much dispute about what constituted reform. Absolute monarchy had become constitutional monarchy, with the threat of revolution behind the power of Parliament and the threat of anarchy behind the power of the crown.

The Glorious Revolution. The threats of revolution and of anarchy proved potent in 1685 when James II (1685–1688) came to the throne. A declared Catholic, James attempted to use his power of appointment to foil the constraints that Parliament imposed on him. He elevated Catholics to leading posts in the military and in the central government and began a campaign to pack a new Parliament with his supporters. That proved too much for the governing classes, who entered into negotiations with William, Prince of Orange, husband of Mary Stuart, James's eldest daughter. In 1688, William landed in England with a small force. Without support, James II fled to France, the English throne was declared vacant, and William and Mary were proclaimed king and queen of England. There was little bloodshed in England and little threat of social disorder, and the event soon came to be called the **Glorious Revolution.** Its achievements were set down in the Declaration of Rights (1689), which was presented to William and Mary before they took the throne. The

DOCUMENT

English Bill of Rights

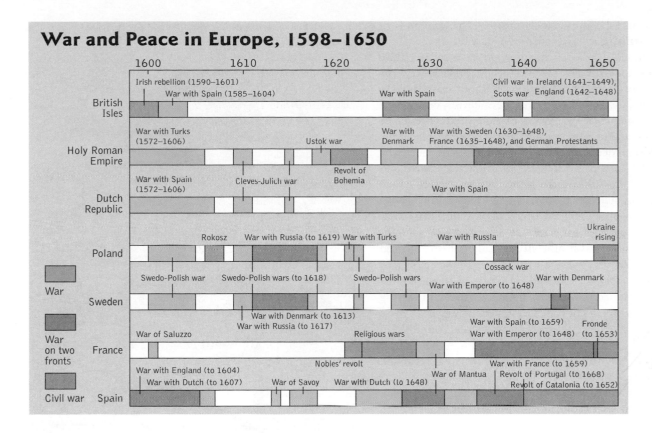

Declaration reasserted the fundamental principles of constitutional monarchy as they had developed over the previous half century. Security of property and the regularity of Parliaments were guaranteed. The Toleration Act (1689) granted religious freedom to nearly all groups of Protestants. The liberties of the subject and the rights of the sovereign were to be in balance.

The events of 1688 in England reversed a trend toward increasing power on the part of the Stuarts and resulted in the development of a unique form of government that a century later would spawn dozens of imitators. John Locke (1632–1704) was the theorist of the Revolution of 1689. He was heir to the century-old debate on resistance, and he carried the doctrine to a new plateau. In *Two Treatises on Civil Government* (1690), Locke developed the contract theory of government. Political society was a compact that individuals entered into freely for their own well-being. It was designed to maintain each person's natural rights—life, liberty, and property. Natural rights were inherent in individuals; they could not be given away. The contract between rulers and subjects was an agreement for the protection of natural rights. "Arbitrary power cannot consist with the ends of society and government. Men would not quit the freedom of the state of nature were it not to preserve their lives, liberties, and fortunes and by stated rules to secure their peace and happiness." When rulers acted arbitrarily, they were to be deposed by their subjects, preferably in the relatively peaceful manner in which James II had been replaced by William III.

The efforts of European monarchies to centralize their power came at the expense of the Church, the aristocracy, and the localities. It was a struggle that took place over decades and was not accomplished easily. In France, the Fronde was an aristocratic backlash; in Spain, the revolt of the Catalonians pitted the Castilian crown against a proud ethnic province. In England, a civil war fought to prevent the encroachments of the crown against the rights of the community gave way to a bloody revolution that combined religious and constitutional grievances—the excesses of monarchy were succeeded by the excesses of parliamentary rule. But the lesson learned by the English ruling elites was that for a nation to enjoy the benefits of a powerful central authority, it was necessary to restrain that authority. The Glorious Revolution of 1689 helped create a constitutional balance between ruler and ruled.

THE ZENITH OF THE ROYAL STATE

The crises of midcentury tested the mettle of the royal states. Over the long term, the crises had two different consequences. First, they provided a check to the exercise of royal power. Fear of recurring rebellions had a chilling effect upon policy, especially taxation. Reforms of financial administration, long overdue, were one of the themes of the later seventeenth century. Even as royal government strengthened itself, it remained concerned about the impact of its policies. Second, the memory of rebellion served to control the ambitions of factious noblemen and town oligarchs.

If nothing else, the episodes of opposition to the rising royal states made clear the universal desire for stable government, which was seen as the responsibility of both subjects and rulers. By the second half of the seventeenth century, effective government was the byword of the royal state. As Louis XIV proclaimed, rule was a trade that had to be constantly studied and practiced. The natural advantages of monarchy had to be merged with the interests of the state's citizens and their desires for wealth, safety, and honor. After so much chaos and instability, the monarchy had to be elevated above the fray of day-to-day politics; it had to become a symbol of the power and glory of the nation. Control no longer meant the greedy grasp of royal officials but rather their practiced guidance of affairs.

In England, Holland, and Sweden, a form of constitutional monarchy developed in which rulers shared power, in varying degrees, with other institutions of state. In England it was Parliament, in Holland the town oligarchies, and in Sweden the nobility. But in most other states in Europe there developed a pure form of royal government known as **absolutism.** Absolute monarchy revived the divine right theories of kingship and added to them a cult of the personality of the ruler. Absolutism was practiced in states as dissimilar as Denmark, Brandenburg-Prussia, and Russia. It reached its zenith in France under Louis XIV, the most powerful of the seventeenth-century monarchs.

The Nature of Absolute Monarchy

Locke's theory of contract provided one solution to the central problem of seventeenth-century government: how to balance the monarch's right to command and the subjects' duty to obey. By establishing a constitutional monarchy in which power was shared between the ruler and a representative assembly of subjects, England found one path out of this thicket. But it was not a path that many others could follow. The English solution was most suited to a state that was largely immune from invasion and land war. Constitutional government required a higher level of political participation of citizens than did an absolute monarchical one. Greater participation in turn meant greater freedom of expression, greater toleration of religious minorities, and greater openness in the institutions of government. All were dangerous. The price that England paid was a half century of governmental instability.

The alternative to constitutional monarchy was absolute monarchy. It too found its greatest theorist in England. Thomas Hobbes (1588–1679) was one of many Englishmen who went into exile in France during the course of the English civil wars. In his greatest work, *Leviathan* (1651), Hobbes argued that before civil society had been formed, humans lived in a savage state of nature, "in a war of every man against every man." That was a ghastly condition without morality or law—"the notions of right and wrong, of justice and injustice have there no place." People came together to form a govern-

■ The title page of the first edition of Thomas Hobbes's *Leviathan*, published in 1651. The huge figure, composed of many tiny human beings, symbolizes the surrender of individual human rights to those of the state.

ment for the most basic of all purposes: self-preservation. Without government they were condemned to a life that was "solitary, poor, nasty, brutish, and short." To escape the state of nature, individuals pooled their power and granted it to a ruler. The terms of the Hobbesian contract were simple. Rulers agreed to rule; subjects agreed to obey. When the contract was intact, people ceased to live in a state of nature. When it was broken, they returned to it. With revolts, rebellions, and revolutions erupting in all parts of Europe, Hobbes's state of nature never seemed very far away.

For most states of Europe in the later seventeenth century, absolute monarchy became not only a necessity but an ideal. The consolidation of power in the hands of the divinely ordained monarch who nevertheless ruled according to principles of law and justice was seen as the perfect form of government. Absolutism was an expression of control rather than of power. If the state was sometimes pictured as a horse, the ab-

THE NATURE OF MAN

Thomas Hobbes's Leviathan *(1651) is one of the classic works of political theory in Western history. Hobbes describes the state of nature as a state of perpetual insecurity from which mankind emerged by surrendering power to a sovereign and thereby creating a political society. Writing in the context of both the English and French civil wars, Hobbes's sovereign held absolute power over life and property which he used to protect and defend his subjects.*

Focus Questions

What is the importance of security to a civilized state? What is Hobbes's view of the nature of man without government?

Whatsoever therefore is consequent to a time of war, where every man is enemy to every man, the same consequent to the time wherein men live without other security than what their own strength and their own invention shall furnish them withal. In such condition there is no place for industry, because the fruit thereof is uncertain: and consequently no culture of the earth; no navigation, nor use of the commodities that may be imported by sea; no commodious building; no instruments of moving and removing such things as require much force; no knowledge of the face of the earth; no account of time; no arts; no letters; no society; and which is worst of all, continual fear, and danger of violent death; and the life of man, solitary, poor, nasty, brutish, and short.

To this war of every man against every man, this also is consequent; that nothing can be unjust. The notions of right and wrong, justice and injustice, have there no place. Where there is no common power, there is no law; where no law, no injustice. Force and fraud are in war the two cardinal virtues. Justice and injustice are none of the faculties neither of the body nor mind. If they were, they might be in a man that were alone in the world, as well as his senses and passions. They are qualities that relate to men in society, not in solitude. It is consequent also to the same condition that there be no propriety, no dominion, no mine and thine distinct; but only that to be every man's that he can get, and for so long as he can keep it. And thus much for the ill condition which man by mere nature is actually placed in; though with a possibility to come out of it, consisting partly in the passions, partly in his reason.

From Thomas Hobbes, *Leviathan.*

---

solute monarch gripped the reins more tightly than the whip. "Many writers have tried to confound absolute government with arbitrary government. But no two things could be more unlike," wrote Bishop Jacques Bossuet (1627–1704), who extolled absolutism in France. The absolute ruler ruled in the interests of his people: "The prince is the public person, the whole state is included in him, the will of all the people is enclosed within his own."

The main features of absolute monarchy were designed to extend royal control. As in the early seventeenth century, the person of the monarch was revered. Courts grew larger and more lavish in an effort to enhance the glory of the monarchy, and thereby of the state. "L'état, c'est moi"—"I am the state"—Louis XIV was supposed to have said. No idea better expresses absolutism's connection between governor and governed. As the king grew in stature, his competitors for power all shrank. Large numbers of nobles were herded together at court under the watchful eye of monarchs who now ruled rather than reigned. The king shed the cloak of his favorites and rolled up his own sleeves to manage state affairs. Representative institutions, especially those that laid claim to control over taxation, were weakened or cast aside for obstructing efficient government and endangering the welfare of the state. Monarchs needed standing armies, permanent forces that could be drilled and trained in the increasingly sophisticated arts of war. Thus the military was expanded and made an integral part of the machinery of government. The

military profession developed within nations, gradually replacing mercenary adventurers who had fought for booty rather than for duty.

Yet the absolute state was never as powerful in practice as it was in theory, nor did it ever exist in its ideal shape. Absolutism was always in the making, never quite made. Its success depended upon a strong monarch who knew his own will and could enforce it. It depended upon unity within the state and the absence or ruthless suppression of religious or political minorities. The absolute ruler needed to control information and ideas, to limit criticism of state policy. Ultimately, the absolute state rested upon the will of its citizens to support it.

Absolutism in the East

Frederick William, the Great Elector of Brandenburg-Prussia (1640–1688), was one of the European princes who made the most effective use of the techniques of absolutism. In 1640, he inherited a scattered and ungovernable collection of territories that had been devastated by the Thirty Years' War. Brandenburg, the richest of his possessions, had lost nearly half of its population. The war had a lasting impact on Frederick William's character. As a child, he had hidden in the woods to escape bands of marauding soldiers; as a teenager, he had followed to its burial the corpse of Gustavus Adolphus, the man he most admired and wished to emulate. A long stay in Holland during the final stages of the Dutch Revolt im-

GENEALOGY

Tsars of Russia

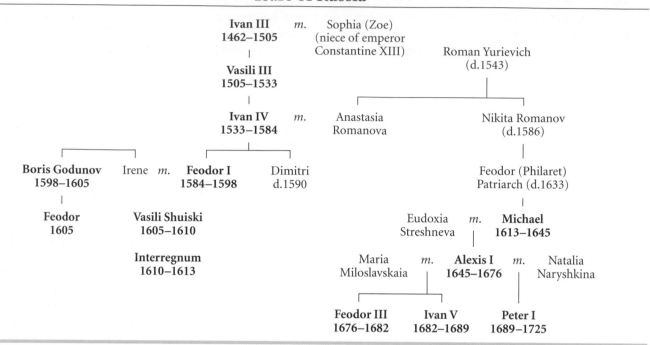

- Ivan III 1462–1505 *m.* Sophia (Zoe) (niece of emperor Constantine XIII)
- Vasili III 1505–1533
- Ivan IV 1533–1584 *m.* Anastasia Romanova
- Boris Godunov 1598–1605
- Irene *m.* Feodor I 1584–1598
- Dimitri d.1590
- Feodor 1605
- Vasili Shuiski 1605–1610
- Interregnum 1610–1613
- Roman Yurievich (d.1543)
- Nikita Romanov (d.1586)
- Feodor (Philaret) Patriarch (d.1633)
- Eudoxia Streshneva *m.* Michael 1613–1645
- Maria Miloslavskaia *m.* Alexis I 1645–1676 *m.* Natalia Naryshkina
- Feodor III 1676–1682
- Ivan V 1682–1689
- Peter I 1689–1725

pressed on him the importance of a strong army and a strong base of revenue to support it.

Frederick William had neither. In 1640, his forces totaled no more than 2500 men, most of them, including the officers, the dregs of German society. Despite the fact that he was surrounded by powerful neighbors—Sweden and Poland both claimed sovereignty over parts of his inheritance—the territories under his control had no tradition of military taxation. The nobility, known as the Junker, enjoyed immunity from almost all forms of direct taxation, and the towns had no obligation to furnish either men or supplies for military operations beyond their walls. When Frederick William attempted to introduce an excise—the kind of commodity tax on consumption that had so successfully financed the Dutch Revolt and the English Revolution—he was initially rebuffed. But military emergency overcame legal precedents. By the 1650s Frederick William had established the excise in the towns, though not on the land.

With the excise as a steady source of revenue, the Great Elector could now create one of the most capable standing armies of the age. The strictest discipline was maintained in the new army, and the Prussian army developed into a feared and efficient fighting machine. Frederick William organized one of the first departments of war to oversee all of the details of the creation of his army, from housing and supplies to the training of young officer candidates. The department was also responsible for the collection of taxes. By integrating military and civilian government, Frederick William was able to create an efficient state bureaucracy that was particularly responsive

■ Peter I wrestled Russia into the West. Sometimes, the unusually big tsar used physical force to do so, such as when he determined that Russian nobles ought to cut off their beards and be clean-shaven in the European fashion of the period.

A CLOSE SHAVE

Peter the Great made many efforts to westernize Russia after his travels in Holland and England. He reformed the navy, built a great seaport at St. Petersburg, and instituted an array of governmental reforms. But nothing was so prominent as or affected ordinary people more than his edicts on beards and clothing. This excerpt was written by Jean Rousset de Missy, a French historian who wrote a popular account of Peter and Russia in the early eighteenth century.

Focus Questions

Why would Peter want Russians to look more like western Europeans? In dealing with his subjects, is Peter acting like Louis XIV?

The tsar labored at the reform of fashions, or, more properly speaking, of dress. Until that time the Russians had always worn long beards, which they cherished and preserved with much care, allowing them to hang down on their bosoms, without even cutting the moustache. With these long beards they wore the hair very short, except the ecclesiastics, who, to distinguish themselves, wore it very long. The tsar, in order to reform that custom, ordered that gentlemen, merchants, and other subjects, except priests and peasants, should each pay a tax of one hundred rubles a year if they wished to keep their beard; the commoners had to pay one kopeck each. Officials were stationed at the gates of the towns to collect that tax, which the Russians regarded as an enormous sin on the part of the tsar and as a thing which tended to the abolition of their religion.

These insinuations, which came from the priests, occasioned the publication of many pamphlets in Moscow, where for that reason alone the tsar was regarded as a tyrant and a pagan; and there were many old Russians who, after having their beards shaved off, saved them preciously, in order to have them placed in their coffins, fearing that they would not be allowed to enter heaven without their beards. As for the young men, they followed the new customs with the more readiness as it made them appear more agreeable to the fair sex.

From the reform in beards we may pass to that of clothes. Their garments, like those of the Orientals, were very long, reaching to the heel. The tsar issued an ordinance abolishing that costume, commanding all the boyars (nobles) and all those who had positions at the court to dress after the French fashion, and likewise to adorn their clothes with gold or silver according to their means. . . .

The same ordinance also provided that in the future women, as well as men, should be invited to entertainments, such as weddings, banquets, and the like, where both sexes should mingle in the same hall, as in Holland and England. It was likewise added that these entertainments should conclude with concerts and dances, but that only those should be admitted who were dressed in English costumes. His Majesty set the example in all these changes.

From "De Missy's Life of Peter."

---

in times of crisis. The creation of the Prussian army was the force that led to the creation of the Prussian state.

The same materials that forged the Prussian state led to the transformation of Russia. Soon after the young tsar Peter I (1682–1725) came to the throne, he realized that he could compete with the western states only by learning to play their game. In 1697, Peter visited the West, ostensibly to build an alliance against the Turks but actually to learn as much as he could about Western military technology. He loved novelty and introduced new agricultural products such as wine and potatoes to his subjects. When he determined that Russians should no longer wear beards, he took a hand in cutting them off. When he was persuaded of the benefits of dentistry, he practiced it himself on his terrified subjects. His campaign to westernize Russia frequently confused the momentous with the inconsequential, but it had an extraordinary impact at all levels of government and society.

Like those of Frederick William, Peter's greatest reforms were military. Peter realized that if Russia were to flourish in a world dominated by war and commerce, it would have to reestablish its hold on the Baltic ports. That meant dislodging the Swedes from the Russian mainland and creating a fleet to protect Russian trade. Neither goal seemed likely. The Swedes were one of the great powers of the age, constant innovators in battlefield tactics and military organization. Peter studied their every campaign. His first wars against the Swedes ended in humiliating defeats, but with each failure came a sharper sense of what was needed to succeed.

First Peter introduced a system of conscription that resulted in the creation of a standing army. Conscripts were branded to inhibit desertion, and a strict discipline was introduced to prepare the soldiers for battle. Peter unified the military command at the top and stratified it in the field. He established promotion based on merit. For the first time, Russian officers were given particular responsibilities to fulfill during both training and battle. Peter created military schools to train cadets for the next generation of officers.

Finally, in 1709, Peter realized his ambitions. At the battle of Poltava, the Russian army routed the Swedes, wounding King Charles XII, annihilating his infantry, and capturing dozens of his leading officers. That night Peter toasted the captured Swedish generals. He claimed that everything he

MAP DISCOVERY

Expansion of Russia Under Peter the Great

Notice the extent of the Russian Empire in 1689 and the territory added by Peter the Great. What was important about the new territory? What was the role of the battle of Poltava in expanding the empire? The route of Peter's trip to western Europe is marked here. Why did he travel where he did? Based on the chapter discussion, what impact did his trip have on the way he ruled his empire?

knew about warfare he had learned from them, and he congratulated them on their success as teachers. After the battle of Poltava, Russia gradually replaced Sweden as the dominant power in the Baltic.

Like everything else about him, Peter the Great's absolutism was uniquely his own. But though Peter's power was unlimited, it was not uncontested. He secularized the Russian Orthodox Church, subjecting it to the control of state power and confiscating much of its wealth in the process. He broke the old military service class, which attempted a coup d'état when Peter was abroad in the 1690s. By the end of his reign, the Russian monarchy was among the strongest in Europe.

The Origins of French Absolutism

Nowhere was absolutism as successfully implanted as in France. Louis XIII (1610–1643) was only eight years old when he came to the throne, and he grew slowly into his role under the tutelage of Cardinal Richelieu. It was Richelieu's vision that stabilized French government. As chief minister,

Richelieu saw clearly that the prosperity and even the survival of France depended upon strengthening royal power. He preached a doctrine of **raison d'état**—reason of state—in which he placed the needs of the nation above the privileges of its most important groups. Richelieu saw three threats to stable royal government: "The Huguenots shared the state, the nobles conducted themselves as if they were not subjects, and the most powerful governors in the provinces acted as if they were sovereign in their office."

Richelieu took measures to control all three. The power of the nobles was the most difficult to attack. The nobles' long tradition of independence from the crown had been enhanced by the wars of religion. Perhaps more importantly, the ancient aristocracy, the nobility of the sword, believed themselves to be in a particularly vulnerable position. Their world was changing and their traditional roles were becoming obsolete. Professional soldiers replaced them at war, professional administrators at government. Mercantile wealth threatened their economic superiority; the growth of the nobility of the robe—lawyers and state officials—threatened their social

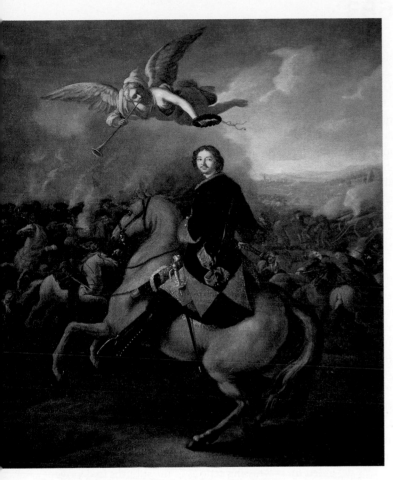

■ The Battle of Poltava (1709) led to the decline of Swedish influence in Europe. Peter the Great is depicted receiving the laurel of victory.

Louis XIII hated the business of government and even neglected his principal responsibility of providing the state with an heir. For years he and his wife slept in separate palaces, and only a freak rainstorm in Paris forced him to spend a night with the queen, Anne of Austria, in 1637. It was the night Louis XIV was conceived. Louis XIII and Richelieu died within six months of each other in 1642 and 1643, and the nation again endured the turmoil of a child king. Richelieu's aggressive policy to curb the nobility and his stringent financial program in the 1630s helped precipitate the Fronde. Louis XIV (1643–1715) was never to forget the terror of the aristocratic rebellion in Paris: how he was forced to flee the capital in the dead of night, how he endured the penury of exile, how he suffered the humiliation of being bossed about by the rebels. He would never forget, and he would have a long time to remember.

Louis le Grand

Not quite five years old when he came to the throne, Louis XIV was tutored by Cardinal Jules Mazarin (1602–1661), Richelieu's successor as chief minister. If anything, Mazarin was more ruthless and less popular than his predecessor. An Italian from a modest background, Mazarin won the money to launch his career at the gaming table. Good fortune seemed to follow him everywhere. He gambled with his life and his career, and each time he raked in the stakes. He died with the largest private fortune that had ever been accumulated by a French citizen, easily surpassing the fortune of Richelieu. Like Richelieu, whom he emulated, Mazarin was an excellent administrator who had learned well the lessons of raison d'état. At the conclusion of the Thirty Years' War, for example, Mazarin refused to make peace with Spain, believing that the time was ripe to deliver a knockout blow to the Spanish Habsburgs.

The King and His Ministers.   In order to pacify the rebellious nobility of the Fronde, who opposed Mazarin's power, Louis XIV was declared to have reached his majority at the age of 13. But it was not until Mazarin died ten years later in 1661 that the king began to rule. Louis was blessed with able and energetic ministers. The two central props of his state—money and might—were in the hands of dynamic men, Jean-Baptiste Colbert (1619–1683) and the Marquis de Louvois (1639–1691). Colbert—to whom credit belongs for the building of the French navy, the reform of French legal codes, and the establishment of national academies of culture—was Louis's chief minister for finance. Colbert's fiscal reforms were so successful that in less than six years a debt of 22 million French pounds had become a surplus of 29 million. Colbert achieved that astonishing feat not by raising taxes but by increasing the efficiency of their collection. Until Louis embarked on his wars, the French state was solvent.

To Louvois, Louis's minister of war, fell the task of reforming the French army. During the Fronde, royal troops were barely capable of defeating the makeshift forces of the nobil-

standing. They were hardly likely to take orders from a royal minister such as Richelieu, especially when he attacked one of the great symbols of their power, the duel.

To limit the power of local officials, Richelieu used central officials, or **intendants**, to examine their conduct and to reform their administration. He made careful appointments of local governors and brought more regions under direct royal control. Against the Huguenots, Richelieu's policy was more subtle. He was less interested in challenging their religion than their autonomy. In 1627, when the English sent a force to aid the Huguenots against the government, Richelieu and Louis XIII abolished the Huguenots' privileges altogether. They were allowed to maintain their religion, but not their special status. They would have no privileges other than to be subjects of the king of France.

Richelieu's program was a vital prelude to the development of absolute monarchy in France. But the cardinal was not a king. Although it is clear that Richelieu did not act without the full support of Louis XIII and clear that the king initiated many reforms for which the cardinal received credit, there can be no doubt that Richelieu was the power behind the throne.

THE SIEGE OF VIENNA—1683

Across the Balkans, for twelve hundred miles, Muslims and Christians stared at each other. The West had seen many decisive encounters in its history, but none had larger stakes than the one at the end of the seventeenth century. Brutal wars punctuated by long periods of uneasy peace had defined relations between Ottoman sultans and Holy Roman emperors. In the eighth century it was the French who had halted the Muslim advance into Europe. In the fifteenth century fortunes had reversed, and the Ottomans had taken Constantinople. Slowly they pressed forward from Asia to the mainland of Europe. For more than a hundred years after the Ottoman victory at Mohacs in 1526, Hungary had been the battlefield, and beyond Hungary stood the imperial capital of Vienna, gateway to Germany and the West.

THE WEST AND THE WIDER WORLD

Vienna, a city of modest wealth by European standards, was thought a glittering prize by the Ottoman diplomats who visited it. Called "the golden apple," it was surely the most desirable of the territories within reach of the Ottoman armies. In 1683 Vienna was still recovering from the devastating effects of the Thirty Years' War. The forty-year-old Emperor Leopold I made it his capital and initiated a building boom and considerable conspicuous consumption. If Sultan Mehmed IV felt the pull of Vienna—his ancestor the great Suleiman had attempted to take it in the sixteenth century—it was now more attractive than ever.

In the camps of the Ottoman army, the Grand Vizier, Kara Mustafa, looked longingly toward the West. When imperial ambassadors arrived in 1682 to renew treaties of peace, Kara Mustafa made demands that were tantamount to war.

Both sides anticipated the oncoming struggle. Emperor Leopold appealed to the princes of Germany for aid only to be rebuffed at every turn. The imperial states feared the French more than they feared the Turks. In desperation Leopold appealed to the young Polish king, Jan III Sobieski. Though Poland was not part of the empire, it had good reason to fear Ottoman expansion. Should Vienna fall, the heart of its state would be open to a deadly thrust. Jan Sobieski set out to raise an army. But Kara Mustafa was raising forces of his own. The Ottoman Empire was a conglomerate of conquered peoples who served the Sultan as circumstances required. Now Africans from Egypt, Tatars from the Steppes of Russia, and Sunnis from Persia all joined the Sultan's feared Janissaries to form a massive army of perhaps as many as 140,000 men. The Viennese garrison consisted of just 11,000 soldiers.

Nevertheless, Vienna was well fortified. After being besieged in 1529, successive emperors strengthened the city's walls and bulwarks. It was defended in the Italian style with a series of outworks that provided a considerable obstacle. The initial wall was built on an in-sloping angle to stop a cavalry incursion and was palisaded with long spears to prevent scaling. This glacis, as it was called, was overhung by a walkway from which defenders could establish a murderous crossfire. Beyond the glacis was a deep moat, and beyond this moat was what was known as a ravelin, an artificial mound with its own twenty-foot-high inward-facing glacis. The ravelin was criss-crossed with trenches from which defenders could emerge or disappear with alarming rapidity. Beyond the ravelin was another treacherous moat, and beyond that the forty-foot-high walls of the city itself. This series of ramparts, moats, and high thick walls gave defenders a decided advantage during the sieges of the seventeenth century. The distance between the farthest outwork and the city walls diminished the effectiveness of artillery while the narrow bottlenecks that pro-

tected each layer of defense diminished the advantage of numbers.

There were only two ways for Kara Mustafa to take Vienna. The first was to starve the city into submission by controlling the suburbs whose farms supplied it. When he brought his great army to the outskirts of Vienna in June 1683, he unleashed independent forces of Magyars and Tatars to ravish the countryside. At the news of their depredations, Emperor Leopold and his court fled the city for fear of being trapped without means of escape. They made it out just in time. By July, Kara Mustafa's tents surrounded the city on every side—his crescent flags flew in all directions. But a passive siege had its disadvantages. The garrison might eventually be starved—and it was not long before even the wealthiest citizens were reduced to eating household pets and rodents—but so, too, might the massive Ottoman army, which could store only what it could carry. Moreover, the emperor's own armies could keep up constant harrassing actions in the suburbs to deprive the Ottomans of supplies.

The second option for taking the city was more aggressive. If the Ottoman troops could not climb over the walls that defended Vienna, perhaps they could tunnel under them. This required a feat of considerable engineering skill. Tunnels had to be designed to begin in many places but to converge under the glacis. There, mines would be exploded to create a breach large enough for warriors to rush through. Additionally, the tunneling yielded mounds of earth that could be piled as high as the outwork walls. When the defenders appeared from their trenches to repel the first wave of assault, Ottoman marksmen could pepper them with shot.

This was the tactic that Kara Mustafa favored. On 26 July, after several days of bombarding the city's walls with artillery, the Grand Vizier summoned the town. He offered the defenders the choice of mercy or death. If they would surrender before the siege began, their lives would be spared. But

■ Jan III Sobieski at Vienna, painted by Jan Matejko.

if they held out, by the established rules of war all of the defenders would be slaughtered, Vienna's wealth would be confiscated, and its defenses would be razed to the ground. Seemingly safe behind their high walls and deep moats, the civic and military leaders of Vienna never hesitated. Kara Mustafa's offer was met with a volley from the city's own guns. The tunnelers were within range and would pay a high price for their efforts.

Meanwhile, Leopold renewed his pleas for assistance. The siege was no longer a theoretical danger and the consequences of the fall of Vienna had to be seriously contemplated. At this eleventh hour the German princes rallied to the aid of their emperor. In the first weeks of August Saxon cavalry headed south and Bavarian forces marched east. They intended to join with the powerful army that Jan Sobieski had raised in Poland. The question was whether they could arrive in time to prevent Vienna's fall. After an enormous tunnel explosion on 12 August allowed Ottoman soldiers to enter the ravelin fifty abreast,

the defenders were forced to abandon the outworks and retreat inside the city's walls. From there they were able temporarily to halt the Muslim advance as every inch of the ravelin and second moat was contested. But by the first week of September mines were exploding under the walls of the city itself and buildings were ablaze in many districts. Disease ravaged soldiers and civilians alike and there were no more than 4000 able defenders left to repulse increasing Ottoman attacks. But repulse them they did. Another week passed and still the city stood.

By now Kara Mustafa was aware that a relief force was within striking distance of his encampment. Rumors exaggerated their numbers wildly, but the reality was sobering enough. The forces commanded by Sobieski numbered 60,000 while Kara Mustafa could rely upon only 28,000 fighting men to oppose them. His auxiliaries were useful for plundering and laboring but not for the life-and-death battle that ensued on 12 September, 1683. More damaging, most of his artillery

was deployed against Vienna and was unavailable at the time of greatest need. The relief of Vienna was almost a foregone conclusion. Imperial forces mowed through the Ottoman battle lines as a scythe in a field of grain, and the Muslims made few stands to slow Sobieski and his allies. Kara Mustafa escaped only because of the desperate sacrifices made by his bodyguard. He carried away the Flag of the Prophet and his store of gold but left behind the myth of Ottoman invincibility. Over the course of the next two decades they would be chased entirely from the Holy Roman Empire and would never again challenge the West for military superiority.

QUESTIONS FOR DISCUSSION

What were the relations between Christians and Muslims prior to the siege of Vienna? What was the nature of the Ottoman army? Why did the Viennese believe they could defend their city? What were the reasons for Jan Sobieski's victory?

■ This Hyacinthe Rigaud portrait of Louis XIV in his coronation robes shows the splendor of *Le Roi Soleil* (the Sun King), who believed himself to be the center of France as the sun is the center of the solar system.

ity. By the end of the reign, the army had grown to 400,000 and its organization had thoroughly been reformed. Louvois introduced new ranks for the field officers who actually led their men into battle, and promotions were distributed by merit rather than purchase. He also solved one of the most serious logistical problems of the age by establishing storehouses of arms and ammunition throughout the realm. The greatest achievements of the reign were built on the backs of fiscal and military reforms, which were themselves a product of the continuing sophistication of French administration.

Louis XIV furthered the practice of relying on professional administrators to supervise the main departments of state and offer advice on matters of policy. He created a separation between courtiers and officeholders and largely excluded the nobility of the sword from the inner circles of government, which were composed of ministers of departments and small councils that handled routine affairs. The councils were connected to the central advisory body of government, the secret council of the king. Within each department, ministers furthered the process of professionalization that led to the advancement of talented clerks, secretaries, and administrators. Although there still remained a large gulf between the promulgation of policy at Versailles and its enforcement in the provinces, it was now a gulf that could be measured and ultimately bridged. Louis XIV built on the institution of the intendant that Richelieu had developed with so much success. Intendants were now a permanent part of government, and their duties expanded from their early responsibilities as coordinators and mediators into areas of policing and tax collection. It was through the intendants that the wishes of central government were made known in the provinces.

The Court of Versailles. Although Louis XIV was well served, it was the king himself who set the tone for French absolutism. "If he was not the greatest king, he was the best actor of majesty that ever filled the throne," wrote an English observer. The acting of majesty was central to Louis's rule. His residence at Versailles was the most glittering court of Europe, renowned for its beauty and splendor. It was built on a scale never before seen, and Louis took a personal interest in making sure it was fit for a king. When the court and king moved there permanently in 1682, Versailles became the envy of the Continent. But behind the imposing facade of Versailles stood a well-thought-out plan for domestic and international rule.

Louis XIV attempted to tame the French nobles by requiring their attendance at his court. Louis established a system of court etiquette so complex that constant study was necessary to prevent humiliation. While the nobility studied decorum they could not plot rebellion. At Versailles one never knocked on a door; one scratched with a fingernail. That insignificant custom had to be learned and remembered—it was useless anywhere else—and practiced if one hoped for the favor of the king. Leading noblemen of France rose at dawn so that they could watch Louis be awakened and hear him speak his first words. Dozens followed him from hall to gallery and from gallery to chamber as he washed, dressed, prayed, and ate.

That aura of court culture was equally successful in the royal art of diplomacy. During Louis's reign, France replaced Spain as the greatest nation in Europe. Massive royal patronage of art, science, and thought brought French culture to new heights.

The French language replaced Latin as the universal European tongue. It was also spoken at the court's of the Holy Roman Emperor in Vienna and the tsar in Moscow. France was the richest and most populous European state, and Louis's absolute rule finally harnessed the resources to a single purpose. France became a commercial power rivaling the Netherlands, a naval power rivaling England, and a military power without peer. It was not only for effect that Louis took the

DOCUMENT

Louis XIV Writes to His Son

LE ROY DE FRANCE.
l'Home immortel Chef de la S.te Ligue.

Mon soleil par sa force eclaira l'heretique.
Il chassa tout d'un coup les brouillards de Calvin:
Non pas par un Zele divin,
Mais a fin de cacher ma fine Politique.

■ A symbolic drawing shows how heretics will be driven from France by the Sun King. Such a policy proved shortsighted, however, as thousands of Huguenot émigrés enriched Louis's potential enemies with their valuable skills.

image of the sun as his own. In court, in the nation, and throughout Europe, everything revolved around him.

France's rise to preeminence in Europe was undoubtedly the greatest accomplishment of the absolute monarchy of Louis XIV. But it did not come without costs. Louis XIV made his share of mistakes, which were magnified by the awe in which his opinions were held. His aggressive foreign policy ultimately bankrupted the crown. But without doubt his greatest error was to persecute the Huguenots. As an absolute ruler, Louis believed that it was necessary to have absolute conformity and obedience. The existence of the Huguenots, with their separate communities and distinct forms of worship, seemed an affront to his authority. Almost from the beginning, Louis allowed the persecution of Protestants, despite the protection provided by the Edict of Nantes. Protestant churches were pulled down, conversions to Catholicism were bought with the lure of immunities from taxation, and children were separated from their families to be brought up in Catholic schools. Finally, in 1685 Louis XIV revoked the Edict of Nantes. All forms of Protestant worship were outlawed, and

the ministers who were not hunted down and killed were forced into exile. Despite a ban on Protestant emigration, more than 200,000 Huguenots fled the country, many of them carrying irreplaceable skills with them to Holland and England in the west and Brandenburg in the east.

Supporters of the monarchy celebrated the revocation of the Edict of Nantes as an act of piety. Religious toleration in seventeenth-century Europe was still a policy of expediency rather than of principle. Even the English, who prided themselves on developing the concept of toleration, and the Dutch, who welcomed Jews to Amsterdam, would not officially tolerate Catholics. But the persecution of the Huguenots was a social and political disaster for France. Those who fled to other Protestant states spread the stories of atrocities that stiffened European resolve against Louis. Those who remained became an embittered minority who pulled at the fabric of the state at every chance. Nor did the official abolition of Protestantism have much effect upon its existence. Against the policies, the Huguenots held firm to their beliefs. There were well more than a million French Protestants, undoubtedly the largest religious minority in any state. Huguenots simply went underground, practicing their religion secretly and gradually replacing their numbers. No absolutism, however powerful, could succeed in eradicating religious beliefs.

CONCLUSION

Louis XIV gave his name to the age that he and his nation dominated, but he was not its only towering figure. The Great Elector, Peter the Great, Louis the Great—so they were judged by posterity, kings who had forged nations for a new age. Their style of rule showed the royal state at its height, still revolving around the king but more and more dependent upon permanent institutions of government that followed their own imperatives. The absolute state harnessed the economic and intellectual resources of the nation to the political will of the monarch. It did so to ensure survival in a dangerous world. But while monarchs ruled as well as reigned, they did so by incorporating vital elements of the state into the process of government. In England, the importance of the landholding classes was recognized in the constitutional powers of Parliament. In Prussia, the military power of the Junker was asserted through command in the army, the most important institution of the state. In France, Louis XIV coopted many nobles at his court while making use of a talented pool of lawyers, clergymen, and administrators in his government. A delicate balance existed between the will of the king and the will of the state, a balance that would soon lead the continental powers into economic competition and military confrontation.

QUESTIONS FOR REVIEW

1. How did war in the seventeenth century contribute to the creation of more powerful monarchical states?

2. What religious and political ideas were developed to justify resistance to monarchical authority?

3. What political and religious problems combined to bring England to civil war, and what results did the conflict produce in English government?

4. How did rulers such as Frederick William of Brandenburg, Peter the Great, and Louis XIV and theorists such as Hobbes and Bossuet justify absolute monarchical power?

KEY TERMS

absolutism, *p. 488*

divine right of kings, *p. 473*

Fronde, *p. 480*

Glorious Revolution, *p. 486*

intendants, *p. 493*

Long Parliament, *p. 484*

magistrates, *p. 479*

Parlement, *p. 481*

paulette, *p. 477*

Puritans, *p. 482*

raison d'état, *p. 492*

DISCOVERING WESTERN CIVILIZATION ONLINE

You can obtain more information about the royal state in the seventeenth century at the Websites listed below. See also the Companion Website that accompanies this text, www.ablongman.com/kishlansky, which contains an online study guide and additional resources.

The Crises of the Royal State

Internet Modern History Sourcebook: Constitutional States

www.fordham.edu/halsall/mod/modsbook06.html

Links to sources relating to the reign of Charles I and the revolution against him.

The Execution of Charles I

www.baylor.edu/BIC/WCIII/Essays/charles.1.html

Excerpts from primary sources describing the execution of Charles I.

The Zenith of the Royal State

Baroque Living History Society: L'Age d'Or & Kirke's Lambs

www.kipar.org/

A site on the Golden Age of France in the seventeenth century but with extensive links to English and Dutch materials on a variety of subjects.

Chateau de Versailles

www.chateauversailles.fr/en

The Website of Versailles, with views of the gardens and rooms inside the palace. (Version of site in English.)

Creating French Culture

www.loc.gov/exhibits/bnf/bnf0005.html

The Library of Congress's exhibition on the Age of Absolutism shows manuscripts, medals, and portraits of leading figures at the French court.

Peter the Great

www.historylearningsite.co.UK/peter_the_great.htm

Follow the links for a complete history of Peter's reign, including his military and domestic reforms.

SUGGESTIONS FOR FURTHER READING

General Reading

Perry Anderson, *Lineages of the Absolutist State* (London: NLB Books, 1974). A sociological study of the role of absolutism in the development of the Western world.

Euan Cameron, ed., *Early Modern Europe: An Oxford History* (New York: Oxford University Press, 1999). Up-to-date essays by leading historians with well-chosen topics and illustrations.

Thomas Munck, *Seventeenth-Century Europe, 1598–1700* (New York: St. Martin's Press, 1990). A thorough survey.

David Sturdy, *Fractured Europe 1600–1721* (Oxford: Blackwell Publishers, 2002). A thorough survey of the complex military and political events of the long seventeenth century.

The Rise of the Royal State

Yves-Marie Bercé, *The Birth of Absolutism* (London: Macmillan, 1996). A history of France from the reign of Louis XIV to the eve of the Revolution by a leading historian of France.

J. H. Elliott, *Richelieu and Olivares* (Cambridge: Cambridge University Press, 1984). A brilliant dual portrait.

J. H. Elliott and Jonathan Brown, *A Palace for a King* (New Haven, CT: Yale University Press, 1980). An outstanding work on the building and decorating of a Spanish palace.

Alan James, *The Origins of French Absolutism, 1598–1661* (New York: Longman, 2006). A concise assessment of the development of the French government in a crucial period, directed toward college students.

Graham Parry, *The Golden Age Restor'd* (New York: St. Martin's Press, 1981). A study of English court culture in the reigns of James I and Charles I.

The Crises of the Royal State

Jonathan Israel, ed., *The Anglo-Dutch Moment* (Cambridge: Cambridge University Press, 1991). Essays by an international team of scholars on the European dimensions of the Revolution of 1688.

M. A. Kishlansky, *A Monarchy Transformed* (London: Penguin Books, 1996). The most accessible survey of a remarkable era.

G. Parker and L. Smith, eds., *The General Crisis of the Seventeenth Century* (London: Routledge & Kegan Paul, 1978). A collection of essays on the problem of the general crisis.

Quentin Skinner, *The Foundations of Modern Political Thought,* 2 vols. (Cambridge: Cambridge University Press, 1978). A seminal work on the history of ideas from Machiavelli to Calvin.

W. A. Speck, *The Revolution of 1688* (Oxford: Oxford University Press, 1988). The best single volume on the event that transformed England into a global power.

Lawrence Stone, *The Causes of the English Revolution* (New York: Harper & Row, 1972). A vigorously argued explanation of why England experienced a revolution in the mid-seventeenth century.

The Zenith of the Royal State

Martyn Bennett, *Oliver Cromwell* (London: Routledge, 2006). The most up-to-date and accessible biography of the man at the center of the English Revolution.

Joseph Bergin, *The Rise of Richelieu* (New Haven, CT: Yale University Press, 1991). A fascinating portrait of a consummate politician.

Peter Burke, *The Fabrication of Louis XIV* (New Haven, CT: Yale University Press, 1992). A compelling account of a man and a myth.

Paul Dukes, *The Making of Russian Absolutism* (London: Longman, 1982). A thorough survey of Russian history in the seventeenth and eighteenth centuries.

Nicholas Henshall, *The Myth of Absolutism: Change and Continuity in Early Modern European Monarchy* (London: Longman, 1992). A searching examination of the problem of absolutism in the western European states.

Vasili Klyuchevsky, *Peter the Great* (London: Random House, 1958). A classic work, still the best study of Peter.

H. W. Koch, *A History of Prussia* (London: Longman, 1978). A comprehensive study of Prussian history, with an excellent chapter on the Great Elector.

Anthony Levi, *Louis XIV* (New York: Carroll and Graf, 2004). An acclaimed new biography of France's most famous ruler.

Geoffrey Parker, *The Military Revolution* (Cambridge: Cambridge University Press, 1988). A lucid discussion of how power was organized and deployed in the early modern state.

John Wolf, *Louis XIV* (New York: Norton, 1968). An outstanding biography of the Sun King.

For a list of additional titles related to this chapter's topics, please see http://www.ablongman.com/kishlansky.

17 SCIENCE AND COMMERCE IN EARLY MODERN EUROPE

REMBRANDT'S LESSONS
ANATOMY AND THE NEW SCIENCE

By the early seventeenth century, interest in scientific investigation had spread out from narrow circles of specialists to embrace educated men and women. One of the more spectacular demonstrations of new knowledge was public dissection, by law performed only on the corpses of criminals. There the secrets of the human body were revealed both for those who were training to be physicians and those who had the requisite fee and strong stomach. Curiosity about the human body was becoming a mark of education. New publications, both scientific and popular, spread ancient wisdom as well as the controversial findings of the moderns. Pictures drawn on the basis of dissections filled the new medical texts, such as the one shown in the photo on the stand at the feet of the corpse in *The Anatomy Lesson of Dr. Nicolaes Tulp* (1632) by Rembrandt van Rijn (1606–1669).

THE VISUAL RECORD

Dr. Tulp's anatomy lesson was not meant for the public. In fact, those gathered around him in various poses of concentration were not students at all. They were members of the Amsterdam company of surgeons, the physicians' guild of the early seventeenth century. The sitters had commissioned the picture, which was a celebration of themselves as well as of the noted Professor Tulp. They hired the young Rembrandt to compose the picture with the assurance that each of the sitters (whose names are written on the paper one of them holds in his hand) would appear as if he alone were the subject of a portrait. Rembrandt succeeded beyond expectation. Each individual was given his due. The expressions on their faces as much as their physical characteristics mark each one out from the group. Yet the portraits were only one part of the painting. The scene that Rembrandt depicted unified them. They became a group by their participation in the anatomy lesson. Rembrandt has chosen a moment of drama to stop the action. Dr. Tulp is demonstrating how the gesture he is making with his left hand would be made by the tendons in the arm of the gruesome cadaver. The central figures of the group are rapt in attention, although only one of them is actually observing the procedure of the dissection. Each listens to Tulp, comparing his own experience and knowledge to that of the professor and the text that stands open.

The Anatomy Lesson established the 25-year-old Rembrandt as one of the most gifted and fashionable painters in Amsterdam. If any people could be said to be consumers of art in seventeenth-century Europe, it was the Dutch. Artists flourished and pictures abounded. Travelers were struck by the presence of artwork in both public and private places and in the homes of even moderately prosperous people. The group portrait, which Rembrandt brought to new levels of expression, was becoming a favorite genre. It was used to celebrate the leaders of Dutch society, who—unlike the leaders of most other European states—were not princes and aristocrats, but rather merchants, guild officials, and professionals. Rembrandt captured a spirit of civic pride in his group portraits. Then it was the surgeons' guild; later it would be the leaders of the cloth merchants' guild, another time a militia company.

Like the leaders of the surgeons' guild, who hung their commissioned portraits in their company's hall, the Dutch Republic swelled with pride in the seventeenth century. Its long war with Spain was finally drawing to a close, and it was time to celebrate the birth of a new state. The Dutch were a trading people, and their trade flourished as much in times of war as in times of peace. Their ships traveled to all parts of the globe, and they dominated the great luxury trades of the age. Bankers and merchants were the backbone of the Dutch Republic. Yet that republic of merchants was also one of the great cultural centers of the Continent. Intellectual creativity was cultivated in the same manner as was a trading partner. In the burgeoning port of Amsterdam, the fastest-growing city in Europe, artists, philosophers, and mathematicians lived cheek by jowl. The free exchange of ideas made Amsterdam home to those exiled for their beliefs. The Dutch practiced religious toleration as did no one else. Catholics, Protestants, and Jews all were welcomed to the Dutch Republic and found that they could pursue their own paths without persecution.

■ Rembrandt van Rijn, *The Anatomy Lesson of Dr. Nicolaes Tulp* (1632).

LOOKING AHEAD

Freedom of thought and freedom of expression helped develop a new spirit of scientific inquiry, like that portrayed in The Anatomy Lesson of Dr. Nicolaes Tulp. *As this chapter will show, maritime* nations such as Holland and England took full advantage of scientific and technological discovery to expand their overseas trade and enrich their citizens. Although much of the new science was seemingly abstract, its practical applications ultimately fueled a new commercial spirit and a new European economy.

THE NEW SCIENCE

And new Philosophy calls all in doubt,
The element of fire is quite put out;
The sun is lost and the earth, and no man's wit
Can well direct him where to look for it.

So wrote the English poet John Donne (1572–1631) about one of the most astonishing yet perplexing moments in the history of Western thought: the emergence of the new science. It was astonishing because it seemed truly new. The discoveries of the stargazers, like those of the sea explorers, challenged people's most basic assumptions and beliefs. Men dropping balls from towers or peering at the skies through a glass claimed that they had disproved thousands of years of certainty about the nature of the universe: "And new Philosophy calls all in doubt." But the new science was perplexing because it seemed to loosen the moorings of everything that educated people thought they knew about their world. Nothing could be more disorienting than to challenge common sense. People needed to do little more than wake up in the morning to know that the sun moved from east to west while the earth stood still. But mathematics, experimentation, and deduction were needed to understand that the earth was in constant motion and that it revolved around the sun—"And no man's wit/ Can well direct him where to look for it."

The **scientific revolution** was the opening of a new era in European history. After two centuries of classical revival, European thinkers had finally come up against the limits of ancient knowledge. Ancient wisdom had served Europeans well, and it was not to be discarded lightly. But one by one, the certainties of the past were being called into question. The explanations of the universe and the natural world that had been advanced by Aristotle and codified by his followers no longer seemed adequate. There were too many contradictions between theory and observation, too many things that did not fit. Yet breaking the hold of Aristotelianism was no easy task. A full century was to pass before even learned people would accept the proofs that the earth revolved around the sun. Even then, the most famous of them—Galileo—had to recant those views or be condemned as a heretic.

The two essential characteristics of the new science were that it was materialistic and mathematical. Its **materialism** was contained in the realization that the universe is composed of matter in motion. That meant that the stars and planets were not made of some perfect ethereal substance but of the same matter that was found on earth. They were thus subject to the same rules of motion as were earthly objects. The mathematics of the new science was contained in the realization that calculation had to replace common sense as the basis for understanding the universe. Mathematics itself was transformed with the invention of logarithms, analytic geometry, and calculus. More importantly, scientific experimentation took the form of measuring repeatable phenomena. When Galileo attempted to develop a theory of acceleration, he rolled a brass ball down an inclined plane and recorded the time and distance of its descent 100 times before he was satisfied with his results.

DOCUMENT

Galileo, Letter to
Grand Duchess
Christina

The new science was also a Europewide movement. The spirit of scientific inquiry flourished everywhere. The main contributors to astronomy were a Pole, a Dane, a German, and an Italian. The founder of medical chemistry was Swiss; the best anatomist was Belgian. England contributed most of all—the founders of modern chemistry, biology, and physics. By and large, the scientists operated outside the traditional seats of learning at the universities. Although most were university trained and not a few taught the traditional Aristotelian subjects, theirs was not an academic movement. Rather, it was a public one made possible by the printing press. Once published, findings became building blocks for scientists throughout the Continent and from one generation to the next. Many discoveries were made in the search for practical solutions to ordinary problems, and what was learned fueled advances in technology and the natural sciences. The new science gave seventeenth-century Europeans a sense that they might finally master the forces of nature.

Heavenly Revolutions

There was much to be said for Aristotle's understanding of the world, for his cosmology. For one thing, it was harmonious. It incorporated a view of the physical world that coincided with a view of the spiritual and moral one. The heavens were unchangeable, and therefore they were better than the earth. The sun, moon, and planets were all faultless spheres, unblemished and immune from decay. Their motion was circular because the circle was the perfect form of motion. The earth was at the center of the universe because it was the heaviest planet and because it was at the center of the Great Chain of Being, between the underworld of spirits and the upper world of gods. The second advantage to the Aristotelian world view was that it was easily incorporated into Christianity.

Aristotle's description of the heavens as being composed of a closed system of crystalline rings that held the sun, moon, and planets in their circular orbits around the earth left room for God and the angels to reside just beyond the last ring.

There were, of course, problems with Aristotle's explanation of the universe as it was preserved in the work of Ptolemy, the greatest of the Greek astronomers. For one thing, if the sun revolved in a perfect circle around the earth, then why were the seasons not perfectly equal? If the planets all revolved around the earth in circles, then why did they look nearer or farther, brighter or darker at different times of year? To solve those problems, a host of ingenious hypotheses were advanced. Perhaps the sun revolved around the earth in an eccentric circle, that is, a circle not centered on the earth. That would account for the differing lengths of seasons. Perhaps the planets revolved in circles that rested on a circle around the earth. Then, when the planet revolved within the larger circle, it would seem nearer and brighter, and when it revolved outside it, it would seem farther away and darker. That was the theory of epicycles. Yet to account for the observable movement of all the known planets, there had to be 55 epicycles. As ingeniously complex as they were, the modifications of Aristotle's views made by the theories of eccentric circles and epicycles had one great virtue: they accurately predicted the movements of the planets. Although they were completely hypothetical, they answered the most troubling questions about the Aristotelian system.

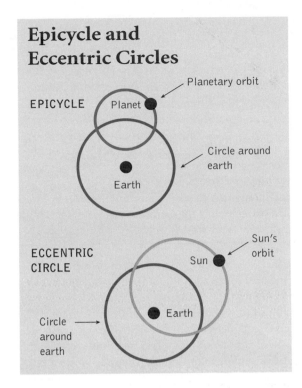

Epicycle and Eccentric Circles

EPICYCLE
- Planetary orbit
- Planet
- Circle around earth
- Earth

ECCENTRIC CIRCLE
- Sun's orbit
- Sun
- Circle around earth
- Earth

■ The theories of epicycles and eccentric circles helped explain the apparent inadequacies of the Aristotelian theory of planetary movement.

■ Andreas Cellarius created this artistic depiction of the solar system in the late seventeenth century. The chart portrays the heliocentric universe described by Copernicus and Galileo and the elliptical orbits of the planets posited by Kepler. An outsized earth is shown in four different positions as it orbits the sun.

STARGAZING

Nicolaus Copernicus was born in Poland and educated at the University of Krakow, which had one of the greatest mathematics faculties of the age. He prepared for a career in the Church, but his abiding interest was the study of astronomy. Through observation and calculation, Copernicus worked out a heliocentric view of the universe in which the earth revolved on an axis and orbited the sun. His pathbreaking work was not published until the year of his death, although he was fully aware of the implications of his discovery.

Focus Questions

What is the problem Copernicus is trying to solve by focusing on the movements of the Earth? In what ways is this passage consistent with the established theories of cosmology?

For, first, the mathematicians are so unsure of the movements of the Sun and Moon that they cannot even explain or observe the constant length of the seasonal year. Secondly, in determining the motions of these and of the other five planets, they use neither the same principles and hypotheses nor the same demonstrations of the apparent motions and revolutions. . . . Nor have they been able thereby to discern or deduce the principal thing—namely the shape of the Universe and the unchangeable symmetry of its parts. . . .

Thus assuming motions, which in my work I ascribe to the Earth, by long and frequent observations I have at last discovered that, if the motions of the rest of the planets be brought into relation with the circulation of the Earth and be reckoned in proportion to the circles of each planet, not only do their phenomena presently ensue, but the orders and magnitudes of all stars and spheres, nay the heavens themselves, become so bound together that nothing in any part thereof could be moved from its place without producing confusion of all the other parts of the Universe as a whole.

From Copernicus, *On the Revolutions of Heavenly Spheres* (1543).

Copernicus.

During the 1490s, Nicolaus Copernicus (1473–1543) came to the Polish University of Krakow, which had one of the leading mathematical faculties in Europe. There they taught the latest astronomical theories and vigorously debated the existence of eccentric circles and epicycles.

Copernicus, On the Revolutions of the Heavenly Spheres

Copernicus came to Krakow for a liberal arts education before pursuing a degree in Church law. He became fascinated by astronomy and puzzled by the debate over planetary motion. Copernicus believed, like Aristotle, that the simplest explanations were the best. If the sun was at the center of the universe and the earth simply another planet in orbit, then many of the most elaborate explanations of planetary motion were unnecessary. "At rest, in the middle of everything is the sun," Copernicus wrote in *On the Revolutions of the Heavenly Spheres* (1543). "For in this most beautiful temple who would place this lamp in another or better position than that from which it can light up the whole thing at the same time?" Because Copernicus accepted most of the rest of the traditional Aristotelian explanation, especially the belief that the planets moved in circles, his sun-centered universe was only slightly better at predicting the position of the planets than the traditional earth-centered one, but Copernicus's idea stimulated other astronomers to make new calculations.

Brahe and Kepler.

Under the patronage of the king of Denmark, Tycho Brahe (1546–1601) built a large observatory to study planetary motion. In 1572, Brahe discovered a nova, a brightly burning star that was previously unknown. The discovery challenged the idea of an immutable universe composed of crystalline rings. In 1577, the appearance of a comet cutting through the supposedly impenetrable rings punched another hole into the old cosmology. Brahe's own views were a hybrid of old and new. He believed that all planets but the earth revolved around the sun and that the sun and the planets revolved around a fixed earth. To demonstrate his theory, Brahe and his students compiled the largest and most accurate mathematical tables of planetary motion yet known. From this research, Brahe's pupil Johannes Kepler (1571–1630), one of the great mathematicians of the age, formulated laws of planetary motion. Kepler discovered that planets orbited the sun in an elliptical rather than a circular path, which accounted for their movements nearer and farther from the earth. More importantly, he demonstrated that there was a precise mathematical relationship between the speed with which a planet revolved and its distance from the sun. Kepler's findings supported the view that the galaxy was heliocentric and that the heavens, like the earth, were made of matter that was subject to physical laws.

Galileo.

What Kepler demonstrated mathematically, the Italian astronomer Galileo Galilei (1564–1642) confirmed by observation. Creating a telescope by using magnifying lenses and a long tube, Galileo saw parts of the heavens that had never been dreamed of before. In 1610, he discovered four moons of Jupiter, proving conclusively that all heavenly bod-

These drawings of Galileo's observations of the phases of the moon accompanied the first draft of his major work, *The Starry Messenger*. In addition to understanding the moon's phases, Galileo also accurately described the topography of the moon; for example, he recognized the bright spots on its face as mountain peaks.

As news of his experiments and discoveries spread, Galileo became famous throughout the Continent, and his support for heliocentrism became a celebrated cause. In 1616, the Roman Catholic Church cautioned him against promoting his views. In 1633, a year after publishing *A Dialogue Between the Two Great Systems of the World*, Galileo was tried by the Inquisition and forced specifically to recant the idea that the earth moves. He spent the rest of his life under house arrest. Galileo insisted that there was nothing in the new science that was anti-Christian. He rejected the view that his discoveries refuted the Bible, arguing that the words of the Bible were often difficult to interpret and that nature was another way in which God revealed himself. In fact, Galileo feared that the

ies did not revolve around the earth. He observed the landscape of the earth's moon and described it as full of mountains, valleys, and rivers. It was of the same imperfect form as the earth itself. He even found spots on the sun, which suggested that it, too, was composed of ordinary matter. Through the telescope, Galileo gazed upon an unimaginable universe: "The Galaxy is nothing else but a mass of innumerable stars," he wrote. Galileo's greatest scientific discoveries had to do with motion—he was the first to posit a law of inertia—but his greatest contribution to the new science was his popularization of the Copernican theory. He took the debate over the structure of the universe to the public, popularizing the discoveries of scientists in his vigorous Italian tracts.

■ Tycho Brahe is pictured here inside his observatory on the Danish island of Hven. He designed and built it for naked-eye monitoring of planetary motion.

Church's opposition to what he deemed as scientific truth could only bring the Church into disrepute.

The Natural World

The new science originated from a number of traditions that were anything but scientific. Inquiry into nature and the environment grew out of the discipline of natural philosophy and was nurtured by spiritual and mystical traditions. Much of the most useful medical knowledge had come from the studies of herbalists; the most reliable calculations of planetary motion had come from astrologers. Although the first laboratories and observatories were developed in aid of the new science, practice in them was as much magical as experimental. For those attempting to unlock the mysteries of the universe, there was no separation between magic and science. Some of the most characteristic features of modern science, such as the stress on ex-

Bacon, *Novum Organum*

perimentation and empirical observation, developed only gradually. What was new about the new science was the determination to develop systems of thought that could help humans understand and control their environment. Thus there was a greater openness and spirit of cooperation about discoveries than in the past, when experiments were conducted secretly and results were kept hidden away.

The most influential of the mystical traditions was that associated with Hermes Trismegistus ("Thrice Greatest"), an Egyptian who was reputed to have lived in the second century C.E. and to have known the secrets of the universe. A body of writings mistakenly attributed to Hermes was discovered during the Renaissance and formed the basis of a Hermetic tradition. The core of Hermetic thinking was belief in a universal spirit that was present in all objects and that spontaneously revealed itself. Kepler was one of many of the new scientists influenced by Hermeticism. His efforts to understand planetary motion derived from his search for a unifying spirit.

THE TELESCOPE

No single individual is as much associated with the scientific revolution as Galileo Galilei. He made formative contributions to mathematics, physics, and astronomy, but he also served as a lightning rod for the dissemination of the newest ideas. He popularized the work of Copernicus and was condemned by the Catholic Church for his views and publications. He ended his life under house arrest. Among his other accomplishments, Galileo was the first to use a telescope to make scientific observations.

Focus Questions

How does Galileo get the idea for building a telescope, and why is that significant? What significance did Galileo's observations about the moon have for contemporary theories of the nature of the universe?

About ten months ago a report reached my ears that a certain Fleming had constructed a spyglass by means of which visible objects, though very distant from the eye of the observer, were distinctly seen as if nearby. Of this truly remarkable effect several experiences were related, to which some persons gave credence while others denied them. A few days later the report was confirmed to me in a letter from a noble Frenchman at Paris, Jacques Badovere, which caused me to apply myself wholeheartedly to inquire into the means by which I might arrive at the invention of a similar instrument. This I did shortly afterwards, my basis being the theory of refraction. First I prepared a tube of lead, at the ends of which I fitted two glass lenses, both plane on one side while on the other side one was spherically convex and the other concave. Then placing my eye near the concave lens I perceived objects satisfactorily large and near, for they appeared three times closer and nine times larger than when seen with the naked eye alone. Next I constructed another one, more accurate, which repre-

sented objects as enlarged more than sixty times. Finally, sparing neither labor nor expense, I succeeded in constructing for myself so excellent an instrument that objects seen by means of it appeared nearly one thousand times larger and over thirty times closer than when regarded with our natural vision.

It would be superfluous to enumerate the number and importance of the advantages of such an instrument at sea as well as on land. But forsaking terrestrial observations, I turned to celestial ones, and first I saw the moon from as near at hand as if it were scarcely two terrestrial radii. . . .

. . . Let us speak first of that surface of the moon which faces us. For greater clarity I distinguish two parts of this surface, a lighter and a darker; the lighter part seems to surround and to pervade the whole hemisphere, while the darker part discolors the moon's surface like a kind of cloud, and makes it appear covered with spots. . . . From observation of these spots repeated many times I have been led to the opinion and conviction that the surface of the moon is not smooth, uniform, and precisely spherical as a great number of philosophers believe it (and the other heavenly bodies) to be, but is uneven, rough, and full of cavities and prominences, being not unlike the face of the earth, relieved by chains of mountains and deep valleys.

From Galileo, *The Starry Messenger* (1610).

■ Paracelsus was a physician and philosopher who rejected Galen's theory that disease was caused by an imbalance of humors in the body. Instead, he argued that diseases each had their own causes and remedies.

Paracelsus.   The Hermetic tradition was central to the work of one of the most curious of the new scientists, the Swiss alchemist Paracelsus (1493–1541). Paracelsus studied with a leading German alchemist before following in his father's footsteps by becoming a physician. Although he worked as a doctor, his true vocation was **alchemy**, the use of fire in the study of metals, and he conducted innumerable experiments designed to extract the essence of particular metals. Paracelsus taught that all matter was composed of combinations of three principles: salt, sulfur, and mercury. That view replaced the traditional belief in the four elements of earth, water, fire, and air.

Although the Paracelsian system was peculiar, it transformed ideas about chemistry and medicine. Paracelsus rejected the theory that disease was caused by an imbalance in the humors of the body—the standard view of Galen, the great Greek physician of the second century C.E. Instead, Paracelsus argued that each disease had its own cause, which could be diagnosed and remedied. Whereas traditional doctors treated disease by bloodletting or sweating to correct the patient's imbalance of humors, Paracelsus prescribed the ingestion of particular chemicals—especially distilled metals such as mercury, arsenic, and antimony—and he favored administering them at propitious astrological moments.

Paracelsus's experimentation with metals and his practice of diagnostic medicine gave a practical turn to the study of alchemy. Efforts to cure new diseases such as syphilis led to the continued study of the chemical properties of substances and to a new confidence about medical science.

Boyle and Chemistry.   Although established physicians and medical faculties rejected Paracelsian cures and methods, his influence spread among ordinary practitioners. It ultimately had a profound impact on the studies of Robert Boyle (1627–1691), an Englishman who helped establish the basis of the science of chemistry. Boyle devoted his energies to raising the study of medical chemistry above that of merely providing recipes for the cure of disease. He worked carefully and recorded each step in his experiments. Boyle's first important work, *The Sceptical Chymist* (1661), attacked both Aristotelian and Paracelsian views of the basic components of the natural world. Boyle rejected both the four humors and the three principles. Instead he favored an atomic explanation in which matter "consisted of little particles of all sizes and shapes." Changes in the particles, which would later be identified as the chemical elements, resulted in changes in matter. Boyle's most important experiments were with gases—a word invented by Paracelsus. He formulated the relationship between the volume and pressure of a gas (Boyle's law) and invented the air pump.

Medical Science.   The new spirit of scientific inquiry also affected medical studies. The study of anatomy through dissection had helped the new scientists reject many of the descriptive errors in Galen's texts. The Belgian doctor Andreas Vesalius (1514–1564), who was physician to the emperor Charles V, published the first modern set of anatomical drawings in 1543, the same year that Copernicus published his work. But accurate knowledge of the composition of the body did not also mean better understanding of its operation. Dead bodies didn't easily yield the secrets of life. Much of what was known about matters as common as reproduction was a combination of ancient wisdom and the practical experiences of midwives and doctors. Both were woefully inadequate.

One of the greatest mysteries was the method by which blood moved through the vital organs. It was generally believed that the blood originated in the liver, traveled to the right side of the heart, and then passed to the left side through invisible pores. Anatomical investigation proved beyond doubt that there was blood in both sides of the heart, but no one could discover the pores through which it passed. William Harvey (1578–1657), an Englishman who had received his medical education in Italy, offered an entirely different explanation. Harvey was employed as royal physician to both James I and Charles I and had one of the most lucrative medical practices in Europe. His real interest, however, was in studying the anatomy of the heart. Harvey examined hearts in more than 40 species before concluding that the heart worked like a pump or, as he put it, a water bellows. Harvey observed that the valves of the heart's chambers allowed the blood to flow in only one direction. He thus concluded that the blood

DE HVMANI CORPORIS FABRICA LIBER II. 197

DECIMA
MVSCV.
LORVM TA-
BVLA.

■ Tenth "Muscle Plate" from Andreas Vesalius's *De Humani Corporis Fabrica (Concerning the Fabric of the Human Body)*, published in 1543. The muscles of the back of the body are laid bare.

important discoveries made possible by use of the microscope was the existence of bacteria. This observation was the work of Antony van Leeuwenhoek, the greatest of all Dutch scientists of the seventeenth century who also first observed blood cells in human tissue. Although Leeuwenhoek, who spent much of his life as a merchant, had no formal training or education, he learned to grind lenses and developed a small single lens microscope that magnified images over two hundred times. He discovered bacteria by examining the plaque between his own teeth. He found, he wrote to the Royal Society in London, "an unbelievably great company of living animalcules, a-swimming more nimbly than any I had ever seen." Though it would be a long time before scientists made the connection between bacteria and disease, the new experimental scientists took the first step.

Sir Isaac Newton. The greatest of all English scientists was the mathematician and physicist Sir Isaac Newton (1642–1727). It was Newton who brought together the various strands of the new science. He merged the materialists and Hermeticists, the astronomers and astrologers, the chemists and alchemists. He made stunning contributions to the sciences of optics, physics, astronomy, and mathematics, and his magnum opus, *Mathematical Principles of Natural Philosophy* (1687), is one of a handful of the most important scientific works ever composed. Most important, Newton solved the single most perplexing problem: If the world was composed of matter in motion, what was motion?

Newton came from a moderately prosperous background and was trained at a local grammar school before entering Cambridge University. There was little in his background or education to suggest his unique talents, and in fact his most important discoveries were not appreciated until years after he had made them. Newton was the first to understand the composition of light, the first to develop a calculus, and the first to build a reflecting telescope. Newton became a professor at Cambridge, but he spent much of his time alone. He made a great study of Hermetic writings and from them revived the mystical notions of attraction and repulsion.

Although Galileo had developed a *theory of inertia*, the idea that a body at rest stays at rest, most materialists believed that motion was inherent in objects. In contrast, Newton believed that motion was the result of the interaction of objects and that it could be calculated mathematically. From his experiments he formulated the concept of force and his famous laws of motion: (1) that objects at rest or of uniform linear motion remain in such a state unless acted upon by an external force; (2) that changes in motion are proportional to force; and (3) that for every action there is an equal and opposite reaction. From the laws of motion, Newton advanced one step further. If the world was no more than matter in motion and if all motion was subject to the same laws, then the movement of the planets could be explained in the same way as the movement of an apple falling from a tree. There was a mathematical relationship between attraction and repulsion—a universal gravitation, as Newton called it—that governed the movement of

was pumped by the heart and circulated throughout the entire body.

But Harvey's theory could not explain how the blood in the heart moved from the arteries to the veins. The explanation was uncovered by Marcello Malpighi using a primitive microscope. Studying the lungs of a frog, Malpighi was able to see a network of tiny blood vessels, the capillaries. The microscope served to advance medical science in a number of areas. While it had probably been invented in Holland, it was Galileo who was able to improve its function so that it could be used for experimentation. Like the telescope, the microscope encouraged precise observation and measurement and thus continued the transformation to experimental science. It was popularized by Robert Hooke whose 1665 book *Micrographia* was internationally acclaimed. Among the most the so-called mechanics colleges, such as Gresham College in London, where the practical applications of mathematics and physics were studied and taught. Navigation was a particular concern of the college, and the faculty established close ties with the Royal Navy and with London merchants.

The establishment of learned scientific societies and practical colleges fulfilled part of the program advocated by Sir Francis Bacon (1561–1626), one of the leading supporters of scientific research in England. In *The Advancement of Learning* (1605), Bacon had proposed a scientific method through inductive empirical experimentation. Bacon believed that experiments should be carefully recorded so that results were both reliable and repeatable. He advocated the open world of the scientist over the secret world of the magician. In his numerous writings, he stressed the practical impact of scientific discovery and even wrote a utopian work in which science appeared as the savior of humanity. Although he was not himself a scientific investigator, Bacon used his considerable influence to support scientific projects in England.

■ The new philosophers attracted the attention of governments as well as scholars. René Descartes traveled to Sweden at the invitation of Queen Christina, with whom he is shown conversing.

■ Sir Isaac Newton provided a clear and comprehensive explanation of the physical universe in mathematical terms. He established the theory of gravity and invented a new kind of mathematics: calculus.

all objects. Newton's theory of gravity joined together Kepler's astronomy and Galileo's physics. The mathematical, materialistic world of the new science was now complete.

Science Enthroned

By the middle of the seventeenth century, the new science was firmly established throughout Europe. Royal and noble patrons supported the enterprise by paying some of the costs of equipment and experimentation. Royal observatories were created for astronomers, colleges of physicians for doctors, and laboratories for chemists. Both England and France established royal societies of learned scientists to meet together and discuss their discoveries. The French Academie des Sciences (1666) was composed of 20 salaried scientists and an equal number of students, representing the different branches of scientific learning. They met twice weekly throughout the year, and each member worked on a project of his own devising. The English Royal Society (1662) boasted some of the greatest minds of the age. It was there that Newton first made public his most important discoveries. Scientific bodies were also formed outside the traditional universities. Those were

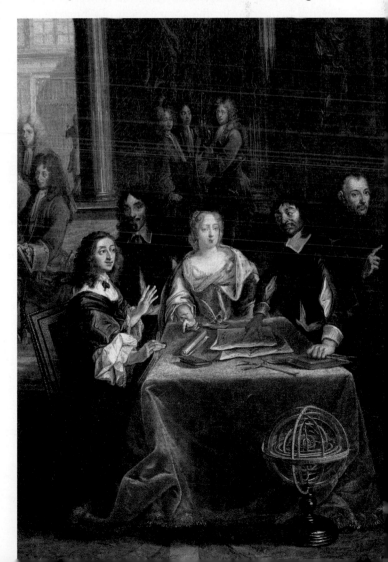

Bacon's support for the new science contrasts markedly with the stance taken by the Roman Catholic Church. Embattled by the Reformation and the wars of religion, the Church had taken the offensive in preserving the core of its heritage. By the early seventeenth century, the missionary work of the Jesuits had won many reconversions and had halted the advance of Protestantism. Now the new science appeared to be another heresy. Not only did it confound ancient wisdom and contradict Church teachings, but it was also a lay movement that was neither directed nor controlled from Rome. The trial of Galileo slowed the momentum of scientific investigation in Catholic countries and starkly posed the conflict between authority and knowledge. But the stand taken by the Church was based on more than narrow self-interest. Ever since Copernicus had published his views, a new skepticism had emerged among European intellectuals. Every year new theories competed with old ones, and dozens of contradictory explanations for the most common phenomena were advanced and debated. The skeptics concluded that nothing was known and nothing was knowable. Their position led inevitably to the most shocking of all possible views: atheism.

There was no necessary link between the new science and an attack upon established religion, as Galileo had argued all along. Few of the leading scientists ever saw a contradiction between their studies and their faith. Sir Robert Boyle endowed a lectureship for the advancement of Christian doctrine and contributed money for the translation of the New Testament into Turkish. Still, by the middle of the century attacks on the Church were increasing, and some blamed the new science for them. Thus it was altogether fitting that one of the leading mathematicians of the day should also provide the method for harmonizing faith and reason.

René Descartes (1596–1650) was the son of a provincial lawyer and judge. He was trained in one of the best Jesuit schools in France before taking a law degree in 1616. Although it was his father's intention that his son practice law, it was René's intention that he become educated in "the school of life." He entered military service in the Dutch Republic, and after the outbreak of the Thirty Years' War served in the Duke of Bavaria's army. Descartes was keenly interested in mathematics, and during his military travels he met and was tutored by a leading Dutch mathematician. For the first time he learned of the new scientific discoveries and of the advances made in mathematics. In 1619, he dreamed that he had discovered the scientific principles of universal knowledge. After the dream, Descartes returned to Holland and began to develop his system. He was on the verge of publishing his views when he learned of the Church's condemnation of Galileo. Reading Galileo's *Dialogue Between the Two Great Systems of the World,* Descartes discovered that he shared many of the same opinions and had worked out mathematical proofs for them. He refrained from publishing until 1637 when he brought out his *Discourse on Method.*

In the *Discourse on Method,* Descartes demonstrated how skepticism could be used to produce certainty. He began by declaring that he would reject everything that could not be clearly proved beyond doubt. Thus he rejected his perception of the material world, the testimony of his senses—all known or imagined opinions. He was left only with doubt. But what was doubt, if not thought, and what was thought, if not the workings of his mind? The only thing of which he could be certain, then, was that he had a mind. Thus his famous formulation: "I think, therefore I am." From this first certainty came another: the knowledge of perfectibility. He knew that he was imperfect and

DESCARTES EXPERIMENTS

René Descartes contributed new observations and theories to the emerging scientific community of the seventeenth century. Published in 1637, his Discourse on Method *presents a system that combines mathematical reasoning with central problems of moral philosophy. The passage here is from the final section of* Discourse, *in which Descartes puts forth his reasons for writing and his ideas for advancing the scientific investigation of nature.*

Focus Questions

According to Descartes, what is the obligation of the scientist to humankind? What kind of philosophy does Descartes oppose?

I have never attributed great significance to what came from my own mind. . . . However, I soon acquired some general notion about physics; and when I began to test them in relation to specific problems and noticed where they can lead and how much they differ from the principles that had been used up to now, I thought I could not keep them hidden without sinning greatly against the law that

obliges us to realize, as much as we can, the general welfare of all people. For they made me see that it was possible to achieve knowledge which would be very useful for life and that, in place of the speculative philosophy by which, knowing the force and actions of fire, water, air, the stars, the heavens and all the other bodies that surround us, as distinctly as we know the various crafts of our artisans, we would be able to use them in the same way for all the applications for which they are appropriate, and thereby make ourselves, as it were, the lords and masters of nature.

René Descartes, *Discourse on Method and Related Writings* (translated by Desmond M. Clarke, Penguin 1999).

that a perfect being had to have placed that knowledge within him. Therefore, a perfect being—God—existed.

Descartes's philosophy, known as **Cartesianism**, rested on the dual existence of matter and mind. Matter was the material world, subject to the incontrovertible laws of mathematics. Mind was the spirit of the creator. Descartes was one of the leading mechanistic philosophers, believing that all objects operated in accord with natural laws. He invented analytic geometry and made important contributions to the sciences of optics and physics on which Newton would later build. Yet it was in his proof that the new science could be harmonized with the old religion that Descartes made his greatest contribution to the advancement of learning. Despite the fact that his later work was condemned by the Catholic Church and that he preferred the safety of Protestant Holland to the uncertainty of his Catholic homeland, Cartesianism became the basis for the unification of science and religion.

"I shall attempt to make myself intelligible to everyone," Descartes wrote. Like many of the new scientists, he preferred the use of vernacular languages to elite Latin, hoping that his work would reach beyond the narrow bounds of high culture. Descartes was one of many new scientists who saw the practical import of what they had learned and who hoped to bring that knowledge to the aid of the material well-being of their contemporaries. John Dee (1527–1608) translated the Greek geometrician Euclid into English so that ordinary people might "find out and devise new works, strange engines and instruments for sundry purposes in the commonwealth." Although many of the breakthrough discoveries of the new scientists would not have practical uses for centuries, the spirit of discovery was to have great impact in an age of commerce and capital. The quest for mathematical certainty led directly to improvements in agriculture, mining, navigation, and industrial activity. It also brought with it a sense of control over the material world that provided a new optimism for generations of Europeans.

EMPIRES OF GOODS

Under the watchful eye of the European states, a worldwide marketplace for the exchange of commodities had been created. First the Dutch and then the English had established monopoly companies to engage in exotic trades in the East. First the Spanish and Portuguese, then the English and French, had established colonial dependencies in the Atlantic that they carefully nurtured in hope of economic gain. Protected trade had flourished beyond the wildest dreams of its promoters. Luxury commodities became staples; new commodities became luxuries. Trade enhanced the material life of all Europeans, although it came at great cost to the Asians, Africans, and Latin Americans whose labor and raw materials were converted into the new crazes of consumption.

While long-distance trade was never as important to the European economy as inland and intracontinental trade, its development in the seventeenth and eighteenth centuries had a profound impact on lifestyles, economic policy, and, ulti-

mately, warfare. The Dutch became the first great commercial power. Their achievements were based on innovative techniques, rational management, and a social and cultural environment that supported mercantile activities. Dutch society was freer than any other; it was open to new capital, new ventures, and new ideas. The Dutch improved the organization of trade by developing the concept of the **entrepôt,** a place where goods were brought for storage before being exchanged. They pioneered in finance by establishing the Bank of Amsterdam. They led in shipbuilding by developing the flyboat, a long, flat-hulled vessel designed specifically to carry bulky cargoes like grain. They traded around the globe with the largest mercantile fleet yet known. It was not until the end of the seventeenth century that England and France surpassed the Dutch. That reversal owed less to new innovations than it did to restrictions on trade. Because the Dutch dominated the European economy, the French and English began to pass laws to eliminate Dutch competition. The English banned imports carried in Dutch ships; the French banned Dutch products. Both policies cut heavily into the Dutch superiority, and both ultimately resulted in commercial warfare.

■ *The Geographer* by Jan Vermeer van Delft, 1669. A Dutch cartographer, holding dividers, is shown surrounded by charts, a globe, and other paraphernalia of his craft. Such cartographers combined the skills of artist and mathematician.

The Marketplace of the World

By the sixteenth century, all the major trading routes had already been opened. The Spanish moved back and forth across the Atlantic; the Dutch and Portuguese sailed around the tip of Africa to the Indian Ocean. The Baltic trade connected the eastern and western parts of Europe as Danes, Swedes, and Dutch exchanged Polish and Russian raw materials for English and French manufactured goods. The Mediterranean, which had dominated world trade for centuries, was still a vital artery of intercontinental trade, but its role was diminishing. In 1600, almost three-quarters of the Asian trade was still land based, much of it carried through the Middle East to the Mediterranean. A century later, nearly all Asian trade was carried directly to western Europe by Dutch and English vessels. Commercial power was shifting to the northern European states just as dramatically as military and political power.

The Evolution of Long-Distance Travel.   The technology associated with commerce achieved no breakthroughs to compare with the great transformations of the fifteenth century, when new techniques of navigation made transatlantic travel possible. It is certainly true that there continued to be improvements. The astronomical findings of the new science were a direct aid to navigation, as were the recorded experiences of so many practiced sea travelers. The materials used to make and maintain ships improved with the importation of pitch and tar from the East and with the greater availability of iron and copper from Scandinavia. It was the Dutch who made the single most important innovation in shipbuilding. To gain maximum profit from their journeys to the Baltic, the Dutch designed the so-called flyboats. Flyboats sacrificed speed and maneuverability, but they were cheap to build and could be manned by small crews. They carried no heavy armaments and were thus well adapted to the serene Baltic trade.

It was unspectacular developments such as the flyboat that had such an impact on seventeenth- and eighteenth-century transcontinental trade. Innovation, organization, and efficient management were the principal elements of what historians

MAP DISCOVERY

Dutch Trade Routes, ca. 1650

The Dutch were the greatest commercial nation of the seventeenth century. According to the trade routes shown here, how would you describe the extent of Dutch trade? Why are there so many trading centers in the East? Based on information provided in the chapter, what were some of the major goods exchanged in the various trade regions? Why did the Dutch not secure major colonial possessions (orange shaded areas) in the East?

have called the commercial revolution. Concerted efforts to maximize opportunities and advantages accounted for the phenomenal growth in the volume and value of commercial exchange. One of the least spectacular and most effective breakthroughs was the replacement of bilateral with **triangular trade.** In bilateral trade, the surplus commodities of one community were exchanged for those of another. The method, of course, restricted the range of trading partners to those with mutually desirable surplus production: England and Italy were unlikely to swap woolens or Sicily and Poland to trade grain. For those with few desirable commodities, bi-

lateral trade meant the exchange of precious metals for goods, and throughout much of the sixteenth and early seventeenth centuries, bullion was by far the most often traded commodity. Triangular trade created a larger pool of desirable goods. British manufactured goods could be traded to Africa for slaves, the slaves could be traded in the West Indies for sugar, and the sugar could be consumed in Britain. Moreover, the merchants involved in shifting the goods from place to place could achieve profits on each exchange. Indeed, their motive in trading could now change from dumping surplus commodities to matching supply and demand.

The Symbols of Trade

This painting of the Custom House Quay, or wharf, in London illustrates how England processed and benefited from trade that passed through its ports. Which of the men in the picture is probably the customs agent responsible for recording goods and collecting tariffs? Why is there a dog on the dock? Note that the sky is mostly clear, but dark clouds are rolling in from the right. What might these signify?

The New Forms of Banking.   Equally important were the changes made in the way trade was financed. As states, cities, and even individuals could stamp their own precious metal, there were hundreds of different European coins with different nominal and metallic values. The influx of American silver further destabilized an already unstable system of exchange. The Bank of Amsterdam was created in 1609 to establish a uniform rate of exchange for the various currencies traded in that city. From that useful function a second developed—transfer, or giro, banking, a system that had been invented in Italy. In **giro banking**, various merchant firms held money on account and issued bills of transfer from one to another. The transfer system meant that merchants in different cities did not have to transport their precious metals or endure long delays in having their accounts settled.

Giro banking also aided the development of bills of exchange, an early form of checking. Bills of exchange were especially important in international trade, as they made large-scale shipments of precious metals to settle trade deficits unnecessary. By the end of the seventeenth century, bills of exchange had become negotiable; that is, they could pass from one merchant to another without being redeemed. There were two disadvantages to the system: ultimately the bill had to return for redemption; when it did, the account on which it was drawn might be empty. The establishment of the Bank of England in 1694 overcame such difficulties. The Bank of England was licensed to issue its own bills of exchange, or bank notes, which were backed by the revenue from specific English taxes. That security of payment was widely sought after, and the Bank of England soon became a clearinghouse for all kinds of bills of exchange. The Bank would buy in bills at a discount, paying less than their face value, and pay out precious metal or its own notes in exchange.

The effects of those and many other small-scale changes in business practice helped fuel prolonged growth in European commerce. It was the European merchant who made that growth possible by accepting the risks of each individual transaction and building up small pools of capital from which successive transactions could take place. Most mercantile ventures were conducted by individuals or families and were based on the specialized trade of a single commodity. Trade offered high returns because it entailed high risks. The long delays in moving goods and their uncertain arrival; the unreliability of agents and the unscrupulousness of other traders; and the inefficiencies in transport and communication all weighed heavily against success. Those who succeeded did so less by luck than by hard work. They used family members to receive shipments. They lowered shipping costs by careful packaging. They lowered protection costs by securing their trade routes. Financial publications lowered the costs of information. Ultimately, lower costs meant lower prices. For centuries luxury goods had dominated intercontinental trade. But by the eighteenth century, European merchants had created a world marketplace in which the luxuries of the past were the common fare of the present.

Consumption Choices

As long-distance trade became more sophisticated, merchants became more sensitive to consumer tastes. Low-volume, high-quality goods such as spices and silks could not support the growing merchant communities in the European states. Those goods were the preserve of the largest trading companies and, more importantly, they had reached saturation levels by the early seventeenth century. The price of pepper, the most used of all spices, fell nearly continuously after 1650. Moreover, triangular trade allowed merchants to provide a better match of supplies and demands. The result was the rise to prominence of a vast array of new commodities, which not only continued the expansion of trade but also reshaped diet, lifestyles, and patterns of consumption. New products came from both East and West. Dutch and English incursions into the Asian trade provoked competition with the Portuguese and expanded the range of commodities that were shipped back to Europe. An aggressive Asian triangle was created in which European bullion bought Indonesian spices that were exchanged for Persian silk and Chinese and Japanese finished goods. In the Atlantic, the English were quick to develop both home and export markets for a variety of new or newly available products.

Commodities from the East.   European trade with Asia had always been designed to satisfy consumer demand rather than to exchange surplus goods. Europeans manufactured little that was desired in Asia, and neither merchants nor governments saw fit to attempt to influence Asian tastes in the way they did those of Europeans. The chief commodity imported to the East was bullion: tons of South American silver, perhaps a third of all that was produced. In return came spices, silk, coffee, jewels, jade, porcelain, dyes, and a wide variety of other exotic goods. By the middle of the seventeenth

century, the Dutch dominated the spice trade, obtaining a virtual monopoly over cinnamon, cloves, nutmeg, and mace and carrying the largest share of pepper. Each year, Europeans consumed perhaps a million pounds of the four great spices and seven million pounds of pepper. Both the Dutch and the English competed for preeminence in the silk trade. The Dutch concentrated on Chinese silk, which they used mostly in trade with Japan. The English established an interest in lower-quality Indian silk spun in Bengal and even hired Italian silk masters to try to teach European techniques to the Indian spinners.

The most important manufactured articles imported from the East to Europe were the lightweight, brightly colored Indian cottons known as calicoes. The Dutch first realized the potential of the cotton market. Until the middle of the seventeenth century, cotton and cotton blended with silk were used in Europe only for wall hangings and table coverings. Colorful Asian chintz contained floral patterns that Europeans still considered exotic. But the material was also soft and smooth to the touch, and it soon replaced linen for use as underwear and close-fitting garments among the well-to-do. The fashion

■ Detail of an Indian textile from the Madras region (ca. 1650). Calicut gave its name to the cotton cloth called calico. This is an example of a "painted Calicut," a wall hanging that shows richly dressed Indian women. (Photograph © 1980 The Metropolitan Museum of Art.)

As popular as coffee became among the European elites, it paled in comparison to the importance of tea as both an import commodity and a basic beverage. While coffee drinking remained the preserve of the wealthy, tea consumption spread throughout European society. It was probably most prevalent in England, where the diet of Chinese tea and West Indian sugar created a virtual revolution in nutrition. The growth in tea consumption was phenomenal. In 1706, England imported 100,000 pounds of tea. By the end of the century, the number had risen to more than 15 million pounds. The English imported most of the tea directly from China, where an open port had been established at Canton. Originally just one of a number of commodities that were carried on an Asian voyage, tea soon became the dominant cargo of the large English merchant ships. Some manufactured goods would be brought to India on the outward voyage in order to fill as much cargo space as possible, but once the ships had loaded the green and black teas, they sailed directly home. Almost all tea was purchased with bullion, as the Chinese had even less use for European goods than did other Asians. It was not until the discovery that the Chinese consumed large quantities of opium, which was grown in India and Southeast Asia, that a triangular trade developed.

Colonial Trade: The Demand for Sugar.

The success of tea was linked to the explosive growth in the development of sugar in Europe's Atlantic colonies. The Portuguese had attempted to cultivate sugar in the Azores at the end of the fifteenth century, but it was not until the settlement of Brazil, whose hot, humid climate was a natural habitat for the cane plants, that widespread cultivation began. The island of Barbados became the first English sugar colony. Barbados turned to sugar production accidentally, when its first attempts to market tobacco failed. The planters modeled their methods on those of Brazil, where African slaves were used to plant, tend, and cut the giant canes from which the sugar was extracted. For reasons that will never be fully understood, the English had an insatiable appetite for sugar's sweetness. It was taken plain, like candy; used in small quantities in almost all types of recipes; and diluted in ever increasing quantities of tea. Hot, sweet tea became a meal for the lower orders of English society, a meal that—unlike beer—provided a quick burst of energy. By 1700, the English were sending home more than 50 million pounds of sugar besides what they were shipping directly to the North American colonies. The quantity doubled by 1730, and still there was no slackening of demand. What might have become a valuable raw material in English trade instead became a staple of consumption.

The African Slave Trade.

The triangular trade of manufactures—largely reexported calicoes—to Africa for slaves, who were exchanged in the West Indies for sugar, became the dominant form of English overseas trade. Colonial production depended upon the enforced labor of hundreds of thousands of Africans. Gold and silver, tobacco, sugar, rice, and indigo

■ *An English Family at Tea* by Joseph Van Aken, ca. 1720. In the eighteenth century, tea imports from China soared as tea-drinking became a domestic ritual in Europe. The enormous popularity of tea also resulted in an increased demand for goods related to its consumption, such as tea tables, porcelain dishes, and silver serving sets.

quickly caught on, and the Dutch began exporting calicoes throughout the Continent. The English and French followed suit, establishing their own trading houses in India and bringing European patterns and designs with them for the Asians to copy. The calico trade was especially lucrative because the piece goods were easy to pack and ship and, unlike consumables, could be stored indefinitely. When the English finally came to dominate the trade in the middle of the eighteenth century, they were shipping more than a million cloths a year into London. The craze for calicoes was so great that both the English and French governments attempted to ban their import to protect their own clothing industries.

Along with the new apparel from the East came new beverages. Coffee, which was first drunk in northern Europe in the early seventeenth century, had become a fashionable drink by the end of the century. Coffeehouses sprang up in the major urban areas of northern Europe. There political and intellectual conversation was as heady as the strong Middle Eastern brew that was served. The Dutch and English both established themselves in the coffee trade, which was centered in the Middle Eastern seaport of Mocha. By the beginning of the eighteenth century, the Dutch had begun to grow their own coffee for export from their island colony of Java, and the two different types of coffee competed for favor.

PLAN OF A SLAVE VESSEL.

THE SLAVE TRADE.

THE motion in the House of Lords made by Lord Denman, on Tuesday night, has naturally revived the interest of the measures for the extinction of this vile traffic of "man-selling and man-stealing." The close of the session is marked by these humane exertions, as was its commencement, in the comprehensive speech of Lord George Bentinck, in the House of Commons, on February 3. His Lordship then held in his hand a communication from Captain Pilkington, of the Royal Navy, on the subject of the slave-trade, accompanied with a plan of one of the slave vessels (which we now Engrave). They were sit-

entertainment enlivened by some most exquisite performances on the national instrument, the harp, much to the delight of all assembled. From the dinner-table the company retired at an early hour to the School-rooms, where the *conversazioni* were held.

WEDNESDAY.

On Wednesday, as the Geological and Natural History Sections were unable to finish the business before them, they each held meetings; but as a great number of members had left Swansea that morning by the *Lord Beresford* steamer, and others were examining the works in the neighbourhood, the Sections were very slightly attended, and the papers communicated were of small general interest.

A dinner, given by Lewis W. Dillwyn, Esq., who is himself one of the oldest members of the Royal Society, may be regarded as the close of the proceedings.

The last General Meeting was held in the afternoon, when it appeared, that, notwithstanding the inferiority of Swansea as respects population, this meeting has added considerably to the funds of the Association.

In concluding our notice of an Association which numbers among its members all the most eminent men in every department of physical and natural science, we cannot but express our satisfaction at the business-like character of this meeting. It is true that it has not startled the world by the announcement of any great discovery; but it will be found, upon examination, to present a fair average rate of progress. The vulnerable points have been less apparent than hitherto; and by the exclusion from the sections of all subjects which were not purely scientific, and by particularly avoiding those communications which have frequently been introduced as mere trading advertisements, of which we witnessed but one, that on gutta percha, which in our opinion should not have

were all commodities based in slave labor. Africans were enslaved by other Africans and then sold to Europeans to be used in the colonies. More than six million black slaves were imported into the Americas during the course of the eighteenth century. While rum and calicoes were the main commodities exchanged for slaves, the African tribes that dominated the slave trade organized a highly competitive market. Every colonial power participated in the lucrative trade. More than three million slaves were imported into the Portuguese colony of Brazil; by the end of the eighteenth century, there were 500,000 slaves and only 35,000 French inhabitants on the sugar island of Saint Domingue. But it was the English, with their sugar colonies of Barbados and Jamaica and their tobacco colonies of Virginia and Maryland, who ultimately came to control the slave trade. The prosperity of Newport, Rhode Island, in North America and the port of Liverpool in Lancashire was built entirely on the slave trade, as were hundreds of plantation fortunes. The sweet tooth of Europe was fed by the sweat of black Africans.

The new commodities flooded into Europe from all parts of the globe. By the middle of the eighteenth century, tea, coffee, cocoa, gin, and rum were among the most popular beverages. All were products that had largely been unknown a century earlier. Among the wealthy, tea was served from porcelain pots imported from China; among all classes it was drunk with sugar imported from America. Beaver hats and Persian silks were fashionable in the upper reaches of society, rabbit caps and calico prints in the lower. New habits were created as new demands were satisfied. Tea and sugar passed from luxury to staple in little more than a generation, and the demand for both products continued to increase. To meet it, the European trading powers needed to create and maintain a powerful and efficient mercantile system.

Dutch Masters

For the nearly 80 years between 1565 and 1648 that the Dutch were at war, they grew ever more prosperous. While the economies of most other European nations were sapped by warfare, the Dutch seemed to draw strength from their interminable conflict with the Spanish Empire. They had the advantage of fighting defensively on land and offensively on sea. Land war was terribly costly to the aggressor, who had to raise large armies, transport them to the site of battles or sieges, and feed them while they were there. The defender simply had to fortify strong places, keep its water routes open to secure supplies, and wait for the weather to change. Sea war—or piracy, depending on one's viewpoint—required much smaller outlays for men and material and promised the rewards of captured prizes. The Dutch became expert at attacking the Spanish silver fleets, hunting like a lion against a herd by singling out the slower and smaller vessels for capture. The Dutch also benefited from the massive immigration into their provinces of Protestants who had lived and worked in the southern provinces. The immigrants brought with them vital skills in manufacturing and large reserves of capital for investment in Dutch commerce.

The Dutch grounded their prosperity on commerce. Excellent craftsmen, they took the lead in the skilled occupations necessary for finishing cloth, refining raw materials, and decorating consumer goods. They were also successful farmers, especially given the small amounts of land with which they had to work and the difficult ecological conditions in which they worked it. But their greatest abilities were in trade.

Although the Dutch Republic comprised seven separate political entities, with a total population of about two million, the province of Holland was preeminent among them. Holland contained more than a quarter of that population, and its trading port of Amsterdam was one of the great cities of Europe. The city had risen dramatically in the seventeenth century, growing from a midsized urban community of 65,000 in 1600 to a metropolis of 170,000 fifty years later. The port was one of the busiest in the world, for it was built to be an entrepôt. Vast warehouses and docks lined its canals. Visitors were impressed by the bustle, the cleanliness, and the businesslike appearance of Amsterdam. There were no great public squares and few recognizable monuments. The central buildings were the Bank and the Exchange, testimony to the dominant activities of the residents.

The Dutch dominated all types of European trade. They carried more English coal than England, more French wine than France, more Swedish iron than Sweden. Dutch ships outnumbered all others in every important port of Europe. Goods were brought to Amsterdam to be redistributed throughout the world. Dutch prosperity rested first upon the Baltic trade. Even after it ceased to expand in the middle of the seventeenth century, the Baltic trade composed more than one-quarter of all of Holland's commercial enterprise. The Dutch also were the leaders in the East Indian trade throughout the seventeenth century. They held a virtual monopoly on the sale of exotic spices and the largest share of the pepper trade. Their imports of cottons, and especially of porcelain, began new consumer fads that soon resulted in the development of European industries. Dutch potteries began to produce china, as lower-quality ceramic goods came to be known. Dutch trade in the Atlantic was of less importance, but the Dutch did have a colonial presence in the New World, controlling a number of small islands and the rapidly growing mainland settlement of New Netherland. Yet the Dutch still dominated the secondary market in tobacco and sugar, becoming the largest processor and refiner of those important commodities.

Trade Routes to Asia

There were many explanations for the unparalleled growth of the small maritime state into one of the greatest of European trading empires. Geography and climate provided one impetus, the lack of sufficient foodstuffs another. Yet there were cultural characteristics as well. One was the openness of Dutch society. Even before the struggle with Spain, the northern provinces had shown a greater inclination toward religious toleration than had most parts of Europe. Amsterdam became a unique center for religious and intellectual exchange. European Jews flocked there, as did Catholic dissidents like Descartes. Those people brought with them a wide range of skills and knowledge, along with capital that could be invested in trade. There was no real nobility among the Dutch, and certainly no set of values that prized investment in land over investment in trade. The French and Spanish nobility looked with scorn upon their mercantile

■ *The Fishmarket at Leiden*, a seventeenth-century painting by Jan Steen, illustrates the importance of the fishing industry and trade to the Dutch economy.

classes and shunned any form of commercial investment; the English, though more open to industry and trade, sank as much of their capital as possible into landed estates and country houses. The Dutch economic elite invested in trade. By the middle of the seventeenth century, the Dutch Republic enjoyed a reputation for cultural creativity that was the envy of the Continent. A truly extraordinary school of Dutch artists led by Rembrandt celebrated the new state born of commerce with vivid portrayals of its people and its prosperity.

Mercantile Organization

Elsewhere in Europe, trade was the king's business. The wealth of the nation was part of the prestige of the monarch, and its rise or fall part of the crown's power. Power and prestige were far more important to absolute rulers than was the profit of merchants. Indeed, in all European states except the Dutch Republic, the activities of merchants were scorned by both the landed elite and the salaried bureaucrats. Leisure was valued by the one and royal service by the other. The pursuit of wealth by buying and selling somehow lacked dignity, yet the activities of the mercantile classes took on increasing importance for the state for two reasons. First, imported goods, especially luxuries, were a noncontroversial target for taxation. Customs duties and excise taxes proliferated all over Europe. Representative assemblies composed of landed elites were usually happy to grant them to the monarch, and merchants could pass them on to consumers in higher prices. Second, the competition for trade was seen as a competition between states rather than individual merchants. Trading privileges involved special arrangements with foreign powers, arrangements that recognized the sovereign power of European monarchs. In this way, trade could bring glory to the state.

Mercantilism.   The competition for power and glory derived from the theory of **mercantilism**, a set of assumptions about economic activity that were commonly held throughout Europe and that guided the policies of almost every government. There were two interrelated ideas. One was that the wealth of a nation resided in its stock of precious metal, and the other was that economic activity was a zero-sum game. There was thought to be a fixed amount of money, a fixed number of commodities, and a fixed amount of consumption. Thus, what one country gained, another lost. If England bought wine from France and paid £100,000 in precious metal for it, then England was £100,000 poorer and France £100,000 richer. If one was to trade profitably, it was absolutely necessary to wind up with a surplus of precious metal. Therefore, it was imperative that governments regulate trade so that the stocks of precious metal were protected from the greed of the merchants. The first and most obvious measure of protection, then, was to prohibit the export of coin except by license, a prohibition that was absolutely unenforceable and was violated more often by government officials than by merchants.

Those ideas about economic activity led to a variety of forms of economic regulation. The most common was the **monopoly**, a grant of special privileges in return for both financial considerations and an agreement to abide by the rules set out by the state. In the context of the seventeenth-century economy, there were a number of advantages to monopolies. First, of course, were those that accrued to the crown. There were direct and indirect revenues: monopolists usually paid considerable fees for their rights, and their activities were easy to monitor for purposes of taxation. The crown could use the grant of monopoly to reward past favors or to purchase future support from powerful individuals. There were also advantages for the monopolists. They could make capital investments with the expectation of long-term gains. That advantage was especially important in attracting investors for risky and expensive ventures such as long-distance trade. Indeed, there were even benefits for the economy as a whole, as monopolies increased productive investment at a time when most capital was being used to purchase land, luxury goods, or offices.

The East India Companies.   Two monopoly companies, the English and the Dutch East India companies, dominated the Asian trade. The English East India Company, founded in 1600 with capital of £30,000, was given the exclusive right to the Asian trade and immediately established itself throughout the Indian Ocean. The Dutch East India Company was formed two years later with ten times the capital of its English counterpart. By the end of the century, the Dutch company employed more than 12,000 people. Both companies were known as **joint-stock companies**, an innovation in the way in which businesses were organized. Subscribers owned a percentage of the total value of the company, based on the number of shares they bought, and were entitled to a distribution of profits on the same basis. Initially, the English company determined profits on single voyages and was supposed to distribute all of its assets to its shareholders after a given period. But changes in legal practice gave the company an identity separate from the individuals that held the shares. Now shares could be exchanged without the breakup of the company as a whole. Both Amsterdam and London soon developed stock markets to trade the shares of monopoly companies.

Both East India companies were remarkably good investments. The Dutch East India Company paid an average dividend of 18 percent for more than 200 years. The value of English East India Company shares rose fivefold in the second half of the seventeenth century alone. Few other monopoly companies achieved a record comparable to that of the East India companies. The English Royal African Company, founded in 1672 to provide slaves for the Spanish colonies, barely recouped costs and was soon superseded by private trade. Even the French East Indian and African companies, which were modeled on the Dutch and English, were forced to abandon their monopolies. The Dutch and English companies were successful not because of their special privileges but because they were able to lower the costs of protecting their ships and cargoes.

Protective Trade Regulations. Monopolies were not the only form of regulation in which seventeenth-century government engaged. For those states with Atlantic colonies, regulation took the form of restricting markets rather than traders. In the 1660s, the English government, alarmed at the growth of Dutch mercantile activity in the New World, passed a series of **Navigation Acts** designed to protect English shipping. Colonial goods—primarily tobacco and sugar—could be shipped to and from England only in English boats. If the French wanted to purchase West Indian sugar, they could not simply send a ship to the English colony of Barbados loaded with French goods and exchange them for sugar. Rather, they had to make their purchases from an English import-export merchant and the goods had to be unloaded in an English port before they could be reloaded to be shipped to France. As a result, the English reexport trade skyrocketed. In the year 1700, reexports amounted to nearly 40 percent of all English commerce. With such a dramatic increase in trading, all moved in English ships, shipbuilding boomed. English coastal towns enjoyed heightened prosperity, as did the great colonial ports of Bristol and Liverpool. For a time, colonial protection proved effective.

French protectionism was as much internal as colonial. The French entered the intercontinental trade later than their North Atlantic rivals, and they were less dependent on trade for their subsistence. Of all the states of Europe, only France could satisfy its needs from its own resources. But to achieve such self-sufficiency required coordination and leadership. In the 1670s, Louis XIV's finance minister, Jean-Baptiste Colbert (1619–1683), developed a plan to bolster the French economy by protecting it against European imports. First Colbert followed the English example of restricting the reexport trade by requiring that imports come to France either in French ships or in the ships of the country from which the goods originated. In addition, he used tariffs to make imported goods unattractive in France. He sponsored a drive to increase French manufacturing, especially of textiles, tapestries, linens, glass, and furniture. To protect the investments in French manufacturing, enormous duties were placed on the import of similar goods manufactured elsewhere. The Venetian glass industry, for example, suffered a serious blow from Colbert's tariffs. English woolen manufacturers were also damaged, and the English sought retaliatory measures. But in fact, the English had already begun to imitate that form of protection. In the early eighteenth century, England attempted to limit the importation of cotton goods from India to prevent the collapse of the domestic clothing industry.

The Navigation Acts and Colbert's program of protective tariffs were directed specifically against Dutch reexporters. The Dutch were the acknowledged leaders in all branches of commerce in the seventeenth century. There were many summers when there were more Dutch vessels in London Harbor than there were English ships. In the 1670s, the Dutch merchant fleet was probably larger than the English, French, Spanish, Portuguese, and German fleets combined! Restrictive navigation practices were one way to combat an advantage that the Dutch had built through heavy capital investment and by breaking away from the prevailing theories about the relationship between wealth and precious metals. The English and French Navigation Acts cut heavily into the Dutch trade,

■ The Dutch East India Company's trading station on the Hooghly River in Bengal, 1665. The station was one of a network of bases the company established throughout its Eastern trading empire.

■ Rembrandt, *The Syndics of the Cloth Guild* (1662). This work was painted for the Drapers' or Cloth Guild and installed at the Guild's headquarters in Amsterdam. The five hatted Syndics look as though they have been caught in a momentary interruption of business. The bareheaded figure in the background is the valet, who unlike the Syndics, was not required to pay for his portrait.

and ultimately both the English and French overtook them. But protectionism had its price. Just as the dynastic wars were succeeded by the wars of religion, so the wars of religion were succeeded by the wars of commerce.

"The discovery of America and that of a passage to the East Indies by the Cape of Good Hope are the two greatest and most important events in the history of mankind." So wrote the great Scottish economist Adam Smith (1723–1790) in *The Wealth of Nations* (1776). For Smith and his generation, the first great age of commerce was coming to an end. The innovations of the Dutch had given way to a settled pattern of international long-distance trade. States now viewed commerce as a part of their national self-interest. They developed overseas empires, which they protected as markets for their goods and sources for their raw materials. The empires were justified by the theory of mercantilism and the demands of a generation of consumers who saw the luxuries of the past as the necessities of the present.

THE WARS OF COMMERCE

The belief that there was a fixed amount of trade in the world was still strong in the late seventeenth century. One country's gains in trade were another's losses. There was not more than enough to go around, and it could not be easily understood how the expansion of one country's trade could benefit all countries. Competition for trade was the same as competition for territory or subjects, part of the struggle by which the

state grew powerful. It was not inevitable that economic competition would lead to warfare, only that restrictive competition would.

Thus the scramble for colonies in the seventeenth century led to commercial warfare in the eighteenth. As the English gradually replaced the Dutch as the leading commercial nation, so the French replaced the English as the leading competitor. Hostility between the English and the French had existed for centuries, and it was not without cause that the commercial wars of the eighteenth century should be likened to the territorial wars of the Middle Ages. The greed of merchants and the glory of princes fueled a struggle for the dominance of world markets that brought European warfare to every corner of the globe.

The Mercantile Wars

Commercial warfare in Europe began between the English and the Dutch in the middle of the seventeenth century. Both had established aggressive overseas trading companies in the Atlantic and in Asia. In the early seventeenth century, the Dutch were the undisputed leaders, their carrying capacity and trade monopolies the greatest in the world. But the English were rising quickly. Their Atlantic colonies began to produce valuable new commodities such as tobacco and sugar, and their Asian trade was expanding decade after decade. Conflict was inevitable, and the result was a series of three naval wars fought between 1652 and 1674. (See "The West and the Wider World: The Nutmeg Wars," pp. 522–523.)

DEFINING COMMERCE

Adam Smith was a Scottish political theorist whose work The Wealth of Nations *(1776) was the first great work of economic analysis in European history. Smith had wide-ranging interests and wrote with equal authority about manufacturing, population, and trade. He was the first to develop the doctrine of free trade, which he called laissez-faire. Smith argued that the government that governed least governed best, and he was an early critic of protective tariffs and monopolies.*

Focus Questions

According to Smith, why are tariffs and monopolies damaging? Why should commerce be a bond rather than a division between nations?

Every individual necessarily labours to render the annual revenue of the society as great as he can. He generally, indeed, neither intends to promote the public interest, nor knows how much he is promoting it. By preferring the support of domestic to that of foreign industry, he intends only his own security; and by directing that industry in such a manner as its produce may be of the greatest value, he intends only his own gain, and he is in this, as in many other cases, led by an invisible hand to promote an end which was no part of his intention. Nor is it always the worse for the society that it was no part of it. By pursuing his own interest he frequently promotes that of the society more effectually than when he really intends to promote it. I have never known much good done by those who affected to trade for the public good. . . .

. . . Each nation has been made to look with an invidious eye upon the prosperity of all the nations with which it trades, and to consider their gain as its own loss. Commerce, which ought naturally to be, among nations as among individuals, a bond of union and friendship, has become the most fertile source of discord and animosity. The capricious ambition of kings and ministers has not, during the present and the preceding century, been more fatal to the repose of Europe, than the impertinent jealousy of merchants and manufacturers. The violence and injustice of the rulers of mankind is an ancient evil, for which, I am afraid, the nature of human affairs can scarce admit of a remedy. But the mean rapacity, the monopolizing spirit of merchants and manufacturers, who neither are, nor ought to be, the rulers of mankind, though it cannot perhaps be corrected, may very easily be prevented from disturbing the tranquility of anybody but themselves. . . .

The natural advantages which one country has over another in producing particular commodities are sometimes so great, that it is acknowledged by all the world to be in vain to struggle with them. . . . Very good grapes can be raised in Scotland, and very good wine too can be made of them at about thirty times the expense for which at least equally good can be brought from foreign countries. Would it be a reasonable law to prohibit the importation of all foreign wines merely to encourage the making of claret and burgundy in Scotland?

From Adam Smith, *The Wealth of Nations* (1776).

The Dutch had little choice but to strike out against English policy, but they also had little chance of overall success. Their spectacular naval victory in 1667, when the Dutch fleet surprised many English warships at port and burned both ships and docks at Chatham, obscured the fact that Dutch commercial superiority was slipping. In 1664, the English conquered New Netherland on the North American mainland and renamed it New York. With that defeat, the Dutch lost their largest colonial possession. The wars were costly to both states, nearly bankrupting the English Crown in 1672. Anglo-Dutch rivalry was finally laid to rest after 1688, when William of Orange, stadtholder of Holland, became William III (1689–1702), king of England.

The Anglo-Dutch commercial wars were just one part of a larger European conflict. Dutch commerce was as threatening to France as it was to England, though in a different way. Under Colbert, France pursued a policy of economic independence. The state supported internal industrial activity through the financing of large workshops and the encouragement of new manufacturing techniques. To protect French products, Colbert levied a series of punitive tariffs on Dutch imports, which severely depressed both trade and manufacture in Holland. Although the Dutch retaliated with restrictive tariffs of their own—in 1672 they banned the import of all French goods for an entire year—the Dutch economy depended on free trade. The Dutch had much more to lose than did France in a battle of protective tariffs.

But the battle that Louis XIV had in mind was to be more deadly than one of tariffs. Greedily he eyed the Spanish Netherlands—to which he had a weak claim through his Habsburg wife—believing that the Dutch stood in the way of his plans. The Dutch had entered into an alliance with the English and Swedes in 1668 to counter French policy, and Louis was determined to crush them in retaliation. He successfully bought off both of Holland's supposed allies, providing cash pensions to the kings of England and Sweden in return for England's active participation and Sweden's passive neutrality in the impending war. In 1672, Louis's army, more

THE NUTMEG WARS

A seed about the size of an acorn connected Portugal, Holland, and England to a small string of islands in the Pacific Ocean and to the eastern seaboard of North America. It created a series of trading wars among the European powers in the seventeenth century and resulted in a number of trade treaties with the leaders of the Banda Islands, in what is now Indonesia. East and West became linked as great European sailing ships made port at the juncture of the Indian and Pacific Oceans in search of the seeds of the tree *Myristica Fragrans*, which grew only on the Banda Islands and which had the singular virtue of producing two rare spices greatly prized by Europeans: mace and, especially, nutmeg.

Flimsy in appearance, the seeds of the *Myristica Fragrans* could be harvested with no greater effort than the shaking of its branches. The husk of the seed pod yielded the delicate spice mace that was used in cookery and as a base for fragrances. The pod itself after husking, drying, and cracking yielded the nutmeg, a versatile spice (some think it is the distinctive ingredient in Coca Cola) that experienced a craze in the first decades of the seventeenth century. Its use as a flavoring was long known in China and South Asia and it had entered the Mediterranean in small quantities through the efforts of Muslim traders. But once the Portuguese started importing it in bulk, around twenty tons a year by the middle of the sixteenth century, merchants and apothecaries began to tout its other virtues. Its fragrance was a desirable mask for the acrid odors of ordinary life when applied either to the skin or to a piece of linen. Its exotic origins suggested mystical power. By the end of the century, when the Dutch entered the trade and annual imports grew toward 100 tons, nutmeg was widely believed to be an aphrodisiac, and since aphrodisiacs work on the mind rather than the body, what was believed was all that mattered. Demand rose and supply fell. By the beginning of the seventeenth century, when the English contested Dutch supremacy in global trade, the two nations were bringing back a staggering 200 to 250 tons from the Bandas. By then nutmeg was a wonder drug indeed, believed capable of curing ailments from headache to the sweating sickness associated with plague. What cost a tenth of a penny a pound on the island docks of the South Seas sold in a London or Amsterdam shop for 7000 times that amount. Small wonder that the greatest trading companies in the world were pooling resources to outfit ships to sail for nutmeg.

Indeed, nutmeg was so valuable to Europeans in the seventeenth century that their quest to obtain it led three nations to dispatch their merchants on eighteen-month journeys from which most never returned. If they did not perish during the long sea voyage around the horn of Africa, along the Coromandel Coast of India, and past the great pepper island of Java, they were imperiled by barely submerged razor-sharp volcanic rocks that guarded the Banda Islands on which the trees flourished. Shifting trade winds also made the islands inaccessible six months a year.

Only those with good guides or good luck laid anchor there. If the merchants survived the dangers of nature, then they faced those of man. Every European captain claimed his nation held exclusive trading rights to these miraculous seeds, and in the open waters of the Pacific Ocean might made right. More than one great sailing ship had its hull punctured by cannon balls, its mast burned by flaming arrows, its crew killed or scuttled by rival merchants.

Even to reach an island port in safety was no guarantee of success. The indigenous peoples were fierce, capable, and resolutely independent. As one Englishman described them, the Bandanese were "men warlike and agile, strong and valiant . . . courteous and affable . . . full of contention amongst themselves, but generally united against the common enemy." Though the islands were small, they were not unified politically. Each village contained its own governing council, which meant that trade was very much a local affair. The Bandanese granted "exclusive" trading rights as often as possible and placidly watched the Europeans squabble over

■ Engraving of the Banda Islands, based on a sixteenth-century map by Theodore de Bry.

THE WEST AND THE WIDER WORLD

522

■ Engraving of a massacre of Dutch soldiers by the Bandanese.

them. In the long months during which the traders waited for the winds to shift so they could depart, misunderstandings and misdeeds were resolved lethally.

The growing popularity of nutmeg in the West and the evolution of trade with European merchants had an enormous impact on the Banda Islands. Though the Bandanese used nutmeg in their cooking, the abundant resource was hardly considered a prized commodity. Until the Portuguese arrived, most nutmeg was carried off the islands in small boats and bartered for ceramics, metalwork, and agricultural products. The Portuguese attempted to control the nutmeg trade as well as to convert local leaders, many of whom were Muslim, to Christianity. While the Portuguese greatly increased the amount of nutmeg that was gathered and shipped, their attempts to prevent the traditional barter trade and to win religious converts led to near constant conflict with the locals. Thus, when the Dutch arrived in 1599 and dispersed the Portuguese fleet, they were welcomed by the Bandanese and were allowed to build a fort where they could store bags of seed and await return voyages.

The Bandanese soon tired of the Dutch as well. By now the islanders had become more sophisticated traders, securing guns, powder, and shot in return for bags of nutmeg, and their conflicts with the Dutch occasionally turned into pitched battles. In 1609, the Bandanese massacred 46 Dutchmen; in 1616 the Dutch invaded Ay Island and slaughtered hundreds of indigenous people. In this environment of conflict, the arrival of the English seemed the answer to a prayer, and local Bandanese leaders entered into contracts to provide these new European visitors with as much nutmeg as they could carry away in exchange for weapons. Just as the leaders

had hoped, the Dutch and the English began to fight each other, the English insisting that the commerce of the seas was open to everyone, the Dutch that they held monopoly rights to nutmeg.

The Dutch were the greater power, and they soon drove the English from all but one of the Banda islands, the small island of Rhun. In 1619 the European nations signed a treaty granting each the territory they held but it had little effect in Banda. The Dutch began a systematic depopulation of the smaller islands, invaded Rhun, and cut down all of its nutmeg trees. In 1621 they assaulted the English fort that was now inhabited by the Bandanese and killed anyone who did not flee into the mountains. Most of the islanders were captured and sold into slavery, replaced in turn by other South Asian slaves.

Not only had the Dutch gained control of the nutmeg trade, they now controlled the nutmegs as well. They offered land on the islands to any Dutch trader who would settle there. Again, in violation of their treaty with the English, they invaded Rhun and destroyed whatever new growth had occurred there. In retaliation, the English attacked a Dutch island outpost half a world away, the set-

tlement of New Amsterdam. In 1667 the two European powers settled their differences with an exchange. The English turned over the Banda island of Rhun, the Dutch the American island of Manhattan. Wily Dutch traders had once purchased it for the derisory sum of $24 worth of trinkets. Now their government traded it away for a volcanic rock where nutmeg would no longer grow, and they were convinced they had gotten the better of the deal. The linking of East and West in seventeenth-century global trade networks had enormous consequences. In the case of nutmeg, the search for seeds had led to half a century of fighting among the Europeans, the decimation of the population of Banda, and Dutch domination of the spice.

QUESTIONS FOR DISCUSSION

Why did Europeans come to the Pacific Islands? How did the organization of Bandanese society create conflict for the Portuguese and Dutch? How did the Bandanese manage to maintain their freedom for half a century after the first Europeans arrived? What was the Dutch solution to threats to their nutmeg monopoly?

■ Some mercantile conflicts existed before European incursions and independent of them. This illustration from an account of Samuel de Champlain's voyages in North America depicts de Champlain assisting his Huron allies in an attack on the Iroquois in part of an ongoing Native American struggle for control of valuable fur-trapping grounds.

than 100,000 strong, invaded the Low Countries and swept all before them. Only the opening of the dikes prevented the French from entering the province of Holland itself.

The French invasion coincided with the third Anglo-Dutch war, and the United Provinces found themselves besieged on land and sea. Their international trade was disrupted, their manufacturing industries were in ruins, and their military budget skyrocketed. Only able diplomacy and skillful military leadership prevented total Dutch demise. A separate peace was made with England, and Spain, whose sovereign territory had been invaded, entered the war on the side of the Dutch, as did a number of German states. Louis's hope for a lightning victory faded, and the war settled into a series of interminable sieges and reliefs of fortified towns. The Dutch finally persuaded France to come to terms in the Treaty of Nijmegen (1678–1679). While Louis XIV retained a number of the territories he had taken from Spain, his armies withdrew from the United Provinces, and he agreed to lift most of the commercial sanctions against Dutch goods. The first phase of mercantile warfare was over.

The Wars of Louis XIV

It was Louis XIV's ambition to restore the ancient Burgundian territories to the French crown and to provide secure northern and eastern borders for his state. Pursuit of those aims involved him in conflicts with nearly every other European state. Spain had fought for 80 years to preserve the Burgundian inheritance in the Low Countries. By the Peace of Westphalia (1648), the northern portion of the territory became the United Provinces, while the southern portion remained loyal to the crown and became the Spanish Netherlands. That territory provided a barrier between Holland and France that both states attempted to strengthen by establishing fortresses and bridgeheads at strategic places.

■ France Under Louis XIV. France gained vital territories in the north and east including Alsace and Lorraine, which would become a source of friction for centuries.

In the east, Louis eyed the duchies of Lorraine and Alsace and the large swath of territory farther south known as Franche-Comté. The Peace of Westphalia had granted France control of a number of imperial cities in the duchies, and Louis aimed to link them together. All the territories were ruled by Habsburgs: Alsace and Lorraine by the Austrian Holy Roman Emperor, Franche-Comté by the Spanish king.

The Balance of Power.

In the late seventeenth century, ambassadors and ministers of state began to develop the theory of a **balance of power** in Europe. It was a belief that no state or combination of states should be allowed to become so powerful that its existence threatened the peace of the others. Behind the purely political idea of the balance of power lay a theory of collective security that knit together the European state system. French expansion in either direction not only threatened the other states directly involved but also posed a threat to European security in general.

Louis showed his hand clearly enough in the Franco-Dutch war that had ended in 1679. Although he withdrew his forces from the United Provinces and evacuated most of the territories he had conquered, France absorbed Franche-Comté by the Treaty of Nijmegen, as well as portions of the Spanish Netherlands. Louis began plotting his next adventure almost as soon as the treaty was signed. During the next several years, French troops advanced steadily into Alsace, ultimately forcing the city of Strasbourg, a vital bridgehead on the Rhine, to recognize French sovereignty. Expansion into northern Italy was similarly calculated. Everywhere Louis looked, French engineers rushed to construct fortresses and magazines in preparation for another war.

War finally came in 1688 when French troops poured across the Rhine to seize Cologne. A united German Empire led by Leopold I, archduke of Austria, combined with the maritime powers of England and Holland, led by William III, to form the Grand Alliance, the first of the great balance-of-power coalitions. In fact, the two sides proved so evenly matched that the Nine Years' War (1688–1697) settled very little, but it demonstrated that a successful European coalition could be formed against France. It also signified the permanent shift in alliances that resulted from the Revolution of 1688 in England. Although the English had allied with France against the Dutch in 1672, after William became king he persuaded the English Parliament that the real enemy was France. Louis's greatest objective, to secure the borders of his state, had withstood its greatest test. He might have rested satisfied but for the vagaries of births, marriages, and deaths.

Like his father, Louis XIV had married a daughter of the king of Spain. Philip IV had married his eldest daughter to Louis XIV and a younger one to Leopold I of Austria, who subsequently became the Holy Roman Emperor (1658–1705). Before he died, Philip finally fathered a son, Charles II (1665–1700), who attained the Spanish crown at the age of four but was mentally and physically incapable of ruling his vast empire. For decades it was apparent that there would be no direct Habsburg successor to an empire that, despite its recent losses, still contained Spain, South America, the Spanish Netherlands, and most of Italy. Louis XIV and Leopold I both

■ The ratification of the Treaty of Münster (1648). Under the treaty, Spain finally recognized Dutch independence.

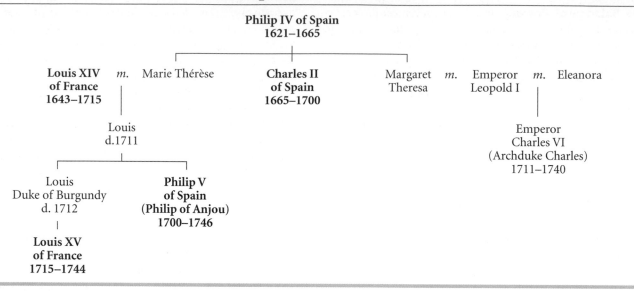

GENEALOGY

The Spanish Succession

Philip IV of Spain
1621–1665

Louis XIV *m.* Marie Thérèse   **Charles II**   Margaret *m.* Emperor *m.* Eleanora
of France   **of Spain**   Theresa   Leopold I
1643–1715   **1665–1700**

Louis   Emperor
d.1711   Charles VI
                                                           (Archduke Charles)
                                                           1711–1740

Louis   **Philip V**
Duke of Burgundy   **of Spain**
d. 1712   **(Philip of Anjou)**
                   1700–1746

Louis XV
of France
1715–1744

had legitimate claims to an inheritance that would have irreversibly tipped the European balance of power.

The War of the Spanish Succession. As Charles II grew increasingly feeble, efforts to find a suitable compromise to the problem of the Spanish succession were led by William III, who, as stadtholder of Holland, was vitally interested in the fate of the Spanish Netherlands and, as king of England, in the fate of the Spanish American colonies. In the 1690s, two treaties of partition were drawn up. The first achieved near universal agreement but was nullified by the death of the German prince who was to inherit the Spanish crown. The second, which would have given Italy to Louis's son and everything else to Leopold's son, was opposed by Leopold, who had neither naval nor commercial interests and who claimed most of the Italian territories as imperial fiefs.

All the plans had been made without consulting the Spanish. If it was the aim of the European powers to partition the Spanish Empire in order to prevent any one state from inheriting too much of it, it was the aim of the Spanish to maintain their empire intact. To this end, they devised a brilliant plan. Charles II bequeathed his entire empire to Philip of Anjou, the younger grandson of Louis XIV, with two stipulations: first, that Philip renounce his claim to the French throne; and second, that he accept the empire intact, without partition. If he—or more to the point, if his grandfather Louis XIV—did not accept the conditions, then the empire would pass to Archduke Charles, the younger son of Leopold I. Such provisions virtually ensured war between France and the empire unless compromise between the two powers could be reached. But before terms could even be suggested, Charles II died and Philip V (1700–1746) was proclaimed king of Spain and its empire.

■ War of the Spanish Succession. The great British victories in this war were in the Spanish Netherlands and the Holy Roman Empire, establishing Britain as a great power.

Thus the eighteenth century opened with the War of the Spanish Succession (1702–1714). Emperor Leopold rejected the provisions of Charles's will and sent his troops to occupy

Italy. Louis XIV confirmed the worst fears of William III when he provided his grandson with French troops to "defend" the Spanish Netherlands. William III revived the Grand Alliance and initiated a massive land war against the combined might of France and Spain. The allied objectives were twofold: to prevent the unification of the French and Spanish thrones and to partition the Spanish Empire so that both Italy and the Netherlands were ceded to Austria. The objective of Louis XIV was simply to preserve as much as possible of the Spanish inheritance for the house of Bourbon.

William III died in 1702 and was succeeded by Anne (1702–1714). John Churchill (1650–1722), duke of Marlborough and commander in chief of the army, continued William's policy. England and Holland again provided most of the finance and sea power, but, in addition, the English also provided a land army nearly 70,000 strong. Prussia joined the Grand Alliance, and disciplined Prussian troops helped offset the addition of the Spanish army to Louis's forces. In 1704, Churchill defeated French forces at Blenheim in Germany,

and in 1706 at Ramillies in the Spanish Netherlands. France's military ascendancy was over.

Between 1713 and 1714, a series of treaties at Utrecht settled the War of the Spanish Succession. Spanish possessions in Italy and the Netherlands were ceded to Austria; France abandoned all its territorial gains east of the Rhine and ceded its North American territories of Nova Scotia and Newfoundland to England. England also acquired from Spain Gibraltar, on the southern coast of Spain, and the island of Minorca in the Mediterranean. Both were strategically important to English commercial interests. English intervention in the Nine Years' War and the War of the Spanish Succession did not result in large territorial gains, but it did result in an enormous increase in English power and prestige. During the next 30 years England would assert its own imperial claims.

The Colonial Wars

The Treaty of Utrecht (1713–1714) ushered in almost a quarter century of peace in western Europe. Austrian rule in the Netherlands and Italy remained a major irritant to the Spanish, but Spain was too weak to do more than sulk and snarl. The death of Louis XIV in 1715 quelled French ambitions for a time and even led to an Anglo-French accord that guaranteed the preservation of the settlement reached at Utrecht. Peace allowed Europe to rebuild its shattered economy and resume the international trade that had been so severely disrupted during the last 40 years. The Treaty of Utrecht had resolved a number of important trading issues, all in favor of Great Britain (as England was known after its union with Scotland in 1707). In addition to receiving Gibraltar and Minorca from Spain, Britain was also granted the monopoly to provide slaves to the Spanish American colonies and the right to send one trading ship a year to them. In east and west, Britain was becoming the dominant commercial power in the world.

At least some of the reason for Britain's preeminence was the remarkable growth of the Atlantic colonies. The colonial economy was booming, and consumer goods that were in demand in London, Paris, and Amsterdam were also in demand in Boston, Philadelphia, and New York. Like every other colonial power, the British held a monopoly on their colonial trade. They were far less successful than the Spanish and French in enforcing the notion that colonies existed only for the benefit of the parent country, but the English Parliament continued to pass legislation aimed at restricting colonial trade with other nations and other nations' colonies. Like almost all other mercantile restrictions, the efforts were stronger in theory than in practice. Tariffs on imports and customs duties on British goods provided a double incentive for smuggling.

France emerged as Britain's true colonial rival. In the Caribbean, the French had the largest and most profitable of the West Indian sugar islands, Saint Domingue (modern-day Haiti). In North America, France not only held Canada but laid claim to the entire continent west of the Ohio River. The French did not so much settle their colonial territory as

MAP DISCOVERY

The Treaty of Utrecht

What critical gains did Britain make as a result of the 1714 Treaty of Utrecht? Notice the extent of Austria after the treaty. What problems was the Austrian government most likely to face? What did Savoy gain?

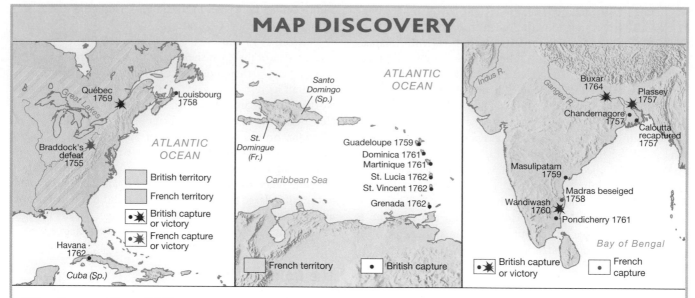

MAP DISCOVERY

The Seven Years' War

This war was fought all around the globe between Britain and France for imperial supremacy. In North America, it was called the French and Indian War. Who controlled most of North America at the beginning of the Seven Years' War? What was British strategy in the Caribbean? Who won India?

occupy it. They surveyed the land, established trading relations with the Native Americans, and built forts at strategic locations. The English, in contrast, had developed fixed communities, which grew larger and more prosperous by the decade. France determined to defend its colonies by establishing an overseas military presence. Regular French troops were shipped to Canada and installed in Louisbourg, Montreal, and Quebec. The British responded with troops of their own and sent an expeditionary force to clear the French from the Ohio River Valley. That action was the immediate cause of the Seven Years' War (1756–1763).

Although the Seven Years' War had a bitter Continental phase, it was essentially a war for empire between the English and the French. There were three main theaters: the North American mainland, the West Indian sugar plantations, and the eastern coast of India. All over the globe, the British won smashing victories. The British navy blockaded the water route to Canada, inflicting severe hardship on French settlers in Montreal and Quebec. British forces ultimately captured both towns. After some initial successes, the French were driven back west across the Mississippi River, and their line of fortresses in the Ohio Valley fell into English hands. The English also succeeded in taking all the French sugar islands except Saint Domingue. British success in India was equally complete. The French were chased from their major trading zone and English dominance was secured.

By the end of the Seven Years' War, Britain had become a global imperial power. In the Peace of Paris (1763), France ceded all of Canada in exchange for the return of its West

Indian islands. British dominion in the East Indian trade was recognized and led ultimately to British dominion of India itself. In less than a century, the ascendancy of France was broken and Europe's first modern imperial power had been created.

CONCLUSION

European commercial expansion was the first step in a long process that would ultimately transform the material life of all human beings. The quest for new commodities led to increased sophistication in transportation, marketing, and distribution—all vital developments for agricultural changes in the future. The ability to move large quantities of goods from place to place and to exchange them between different parts of the globe laid the foundation for organized manufacturing. The practical impact of scientific discovery, as yet only dimly glimpsed, would soon spur the transformation of handicrafts into industries. In the eighteenth century, the material world was still being conquered, and the most unattractive features of that conquest were all too plainly visible. Luxuries for the rich were won by the labors of the poor. The pleasures of sugar and tobacco were purchased at the price of slavery for millions of Africans. The greed of merchants and the glory of princes was an unholy alliance that resulted in warfare around the globe. But it was a shrinking globe, one whose peoples were becoming increasingly interdependent, tied together by the goods and services that they could provide to each other.

QUESTIONS FOR REVIEW

1. What was new about the methods and ideas of Copernicus, Brahe, Kepler, and Galileo, and why were they threatening to Roman Catholic doctrine?
2. In what ways did the new science build upon traditional ideas associated with alchemy, astrology, and Hermetic thinking? In what ways was it a departure?
3. What new technologies, trading practices, and financial devices assisted the expansion of long-distance trading?
4. Why were the Dutch especially well suited to participate in the worldwide expansion of European commerce?
5. How did the governments of the various European nations promote their own commercial interests?

KEY TERMS

alchemy, *p. 507*

balance of power, *p. 525*

Cartesianism, *p. 511*

entrepôt, *p. 511*

giro banking, *p. 513*

joint-stock companies, *p. 518*

materialism, *p. 502*

mercantilism, *p. 518*

monopoly, *p. 518*

Navigation Acts, *p. 519*

scientific revolution, *p. 502*

triangular trade, *p. 513*

DISCOVERING WESTERN CIVILIZATION ONLINE

You can obtain more information about science and commerce in early modern Europe at the Websites listed below. See also the Companion Website that accompanies this text, www.ablongman.com/kishlansky, which contains an online study guide and additional resources.

The New Science

Internet Modern History Sourcebook: Scientific Revolution

www.fordham.edu/halsall/mod/modsbook09.html

Links to sources and other sites dealing with the scientific revolution.

The Art of Renaissance Science

www.crs4.it/Ars/arshtml/arstoc.html

An interesting site dealing with the relations between Renaissance art and early modern science.

Sir Isaac Newton

www-gap.dcs.st-and.ac.uk/~history/Mathematicians/Newton.html

A miscellany of material on Sir Isaac Newton.

The Galileo Project

es.rice.edu/ES/humsoc/Galileo/

A site devoted to Galileo that contains pictures of his instruments and guides to his experiments.

Empires of Goods

Trade Products in Early Modern History

www.bell.lib.umn.edu/Products/Products.html

A site describing the new products introduced to Europe during the period of global expansion.

Holland Museums

www.hollandmuseums.nl/

An online gallery of Dutch art, with text available in English.

SUGGESTIONS FOR FURTHER READING

General Reading

Jeremy Black, *The Rise of the European Powers, 1679–1793* (New York: Edward Arnold, 1990). A look at diplomatic history from an English point of view.

Jan de Vries, *The European Economy in an Age of Crisis* (Cambridge: Cambridge University Press, 1976). A comprehensive study of economic development, including long-distance trade and commercial change.

K. H. D. Haley, *The Dutch in the Seventeenth Century* (London: Thames and Hudson, 1972). A well-written and well-illustrated history of the golden age of Holland.

A. Rupert Hall, *The Revolution in Science, 1500–1750* (London: Longman, 1983). The best introduction to the varieties of scientific thought in the early modern period. Detailed and complex.

Derek McKay and H. M. Scott, *The Rise of the Great Powers, 1648–1815* (London: Longman, 1983). An outstanding survey of diplomacy and warfare.

The New Science

H. F. Cohen, *The Scientific Revolution* (Chicago: University of Chicago Press, 1994). The history of the idea of the scientific revolution and of the events that comprised it.

Lorraine Daston and Katherine Park, eds., *The Cambridge History of Science, Volume 3: Early Modern Science*. (London: Cambridge University Press, 2006). A massive and detailed collaborative history of science in the early modern world.

Stillman Drake, *Galileo* (New York: Hill and Wang, 1980). A short but engaging study of the great Italian scientist.

Margaret C. Jacob, *The Cultural Meaning of the Scientific Revolution* (New York: Alfred A. Knopf, 1988). Scientific thought portrayed in its social context.

Lisa Jardine, *Ingenious Pursuits: Building the Scientific Revolution* (New York: Anchor Books, 1999). A study emphasizing the technical contexts of the scientific revolution and interactions between its major figures.

Londa Schiebinger, *The Mind Has No Sex? Women in the Origins of Modern Science* (Cambridge, MA: Harvard

University Press, 1990). The role of women in the scientific revolution.

Steven Shapin, *The Scientific Revolution* (Chicago: University of Chicago Press, 1996). An excellent brief introduction.

Richard Westfall, *The Construction of Modern Science: Mechanisms and Mechanics* (Cambridge: Cambridge University Press, 1977). A survey of scientific developments from Kepler to Newton. A good introduction to both mechanics and mathematics.

Richard Westfall, *The Life of Isaac Newton* (Cambridge: Cambridge University Press, 1993). The best short biography.

Empires of Goods

Julia Adams, *The Familial State: Ruling Families and Merchant Capitalism in Early Modern Europe.* (Ithaca, NY: Cornell University Press, 2005). An historical sociologist discusses the paternalist power structure among the Dutch trading elite.

J. N. Ball, *Merchants and Merchandise: The Expansion of Trade in Europe* (London: Croom Helm, 1977). A good overview of European overseas economies.

K. N. Chaudhuri, *The Trading World of Asia and the English East India Company* (Cambridge: Cambridge University Press, 1978). A brilliant account of the impact of the Indian trade on both Europeans and Asians.

Philip Curtin, *The Atlantic Slave Trade* (Madison: University of Wisconsin Press, 1969). A study of the importation of African slaves into the New World, with the best estimates of the numbers of slaves and their destinations.

Ralph Davis, *The Rise of the Atlantic Economies* (Ithaca, NY: Cornell University Press, 1973). A nation-by-nation survey of the colonial powers.

Jonathan Israel, *Dutch Primacy in World Trade, 1585–1740* (Oxford: Oxford University Press, 1989). The triumph of Dutch traders and techniques, written by the leading authority.

Joseph Miller, *Way of Death: Merchant Capitalism and the Angolan Slave Trade, 1730–1830* (Madison: University of Wisconsin Press, 1988). An illuminating portrait of the eighteenth-century slave trade, with an unforgettable account of the slave voyages.

Sidney Mintz, *Sweetness and Power* (New York: Viking Press, 1985). An anthropologist explores the lure of sugar and its impact on Western society.

Simon Schama, *The Embarrassment of Riches* (New York: Alfred A. Knopf, 1987). A social history of the Dutch Republic that explores the meaning of commerce in Dutch society.

The Wars of Commerce

Jeremy Black, *A System of Ambition? British Foreign Policy, 1660–1793* (London: Longman, 1991). The best survey of Britain's international relations during the long eighteenth century.

A. C. Carter, *Neutrality or Commitment: The Evolution of Dutch Foreign Policy, 1667–1795* (London: Edward Arnold, 1975). A tightly written study of the objectives and course of Dutch diplomacy.

Paul Langford, *The Eighteenth Century, 1688–1815* (New York: St. Martin's Press, 1976). A reliable guide to the growth of British power.

J. A. Lynn, *The Wars of Louis XIV, 1667–1714* (London: Longman, 1999). A comprehensive study by a leading military historian of France.

Richard Pares, *War and Trade in the West Indies, 1739–1763* (Oxford: Oxford University Press, 1936). A blow-by-blow account of the struggle for colonial supremacy in the sugar islands.

For a list of additional titles related to this chapter's topics, please see http://www.ablongman.com/kishlansky.

18 THE BALANCE OF POWER IN EIGHTEENTH-CENTURY EUROPE

A DASHING OFFICER
THE RISE OF MILITARISM

From the middle of the seventeenth century Britain was a great sea-faring power. Its navy, built up during the reign of Charles I and the rule of Oliver Cromwell, challenged the Dutch for imperial supremacy in the East and the Spanish for colonial supremacy in the West. Louis XIV actually paid the British government a subsidy to remain neutral in his commercial and territorial wars and even attempted to rent British ships on occasion. The British flag flew on seas worldwide, and it would not be long before Britannia ruled the waves. But beginning at the end of the seventeenth century Great Britain also became a feared landed military power. Under its Dutch king, William III, British armies successfully held the French at bay in the Nine Years' War and inflicted defeat upon them in the brutal War of the Spanish Succession (1702–1714). British generals, such as the Duke of Marlborough, became Europeanwide celebrities, their feats the subject of story, song, and painting.

THE VISUAL RECORD

Britain's rise to military greatness was as swift as it was unexpected, and it lasted for more than one hundred years. The titanic struggle with France dominated the lives of four successive generations and was not finally concluded until the Battle of Waterloo in 1815. Throughout the eighteenth century, the military was present in British society in a way in which it never had been before or would be again. A society that had openly condemned the concept of a standing army now gave way to one in which the presence of uniformed officers was everywhere. Where younger sons had once gone into the church, now they joined the guards. Where the impoverished and luckless had once migrated to London, now they took the King's shilling, as voluntary enlistment was called. The excess agricultural populations of Scotland and Ireland, once doomed to hunger and starvation, now became the raw materials for the greatest fighting men Europe had known.

One indication of the new prominence given soldiers was the painting of their portraits by the most talented artists of the day. This portrait of Captain Robert Orme was painted by Sir Joshua Reynolds, founder and first president of the Royal Academy and one of the greatest portrait artists of the age. Reynolds revived the long tradition of English portrait painting that had reached its height with the Fleming Van Dyck and the Dutch Kneller. But Reynolds was no foreign import. He was born and raised in Devonshire, learned his trade by painting sailors at Plymouth Docks, and even sailed on a naval expedition. Reynolds's military portraits capture that spirit of patriotism, of strength, and of courage that the British expected from their officers. Captain Orme, a member of the prestigious Coldstream Guards, is portrayed in a moment of action, his steed foaming and winded, the message that he carries admitting no delay. Slaughter rages behind him. In his haste, his hair has come undone and his extended right arm suggests that he is about to mount and gallop away. But in his pause there is a great stillness and confidence. His gaze is suffused with reassurance, the jaw solid, the eyes piercing. This is the image of flesh and blood that carried Britain to its greatness in the wars of the eighteenth century.

LOOKING AHEAD

The balance of power established by the European monarchies in the eighteenth century was achieved on the battlefield. As we shall see in this chapter, in Russia, Prussia, and Austria, noblemen flocked to military service and the military portion of national economies multiplied dramatically. In the east, its neighbors three times carved up Poland. In the west, the continuing struggle between France and Britain resulted in the destabilization of French society that prepared the way for the French Revolution. In the Atlantic, Britain casually lost its North American colonies in a war it fought half-heartedly for a prize it no longer appreciated.

■ Portrait of Captain Robert Orme (1756) by Sir Joshua Reynolds.

GEOGRAPHICAL TOUR
A Grand Tour of Europe in 1714

In the eighteenth century young noblemen from every European nation completed their education by taking a grand tour. Usually in company with a tutor, they would visit the palaces, castles, and churches of their neighboring countries, learn a little of the language, and mingle with others of their class who were engaged in a similar experience. Noblemen were prepared for the grand tour by reading history, studying antiquities—many of them would purchase ancient Roman sculptures to place in their gardens—and viewing great works of art, normally religious decorations in cathedrals and urban churches. The grand tour made them cosmopolitan or at least European. They learned French language, Italian art, German music, and British science. Some even visited more exotic locations such as Prague or Moscow where language, architec-

■ **Map A. Europe in 1714.** Europe as established by the Treaty of Utrecht.

ture, and music all had an eastern tinge. Noblemen who took the grand tour in the second decade of the century witnessed the redrawing of Europe's political map as well as a new balance of power among the European states.

Within a relatively short span of time at the beginning of the eighteenth century, two treaties brought about a considerable reorganization of the political geography of Europe. The Treaty of Utrecht (1713–1714) created a new Europe in the west. The Treaty of Nystad (1721) created a new Europe in the east. Both agreements reflected the dynamics of change that had taken place over the previous century. The rise of France on the Continent and Britain's colonial empire around the globe were facts that could no longer be ignored. The decline of Sweden and Poland and the emergence of Russia as a great power were the beginning of a long-term process that would continue to dominate European history.

All of these changes could be seen on a map of Europe in the early eighteenth century (see **Map A**). France's absorption of Alsace and encroachments into Lorraine would be bones of contention between the French and the Germans for two centuries and would ultimately contribute to the outbreak of World Wars I and II. The political footballs of the Spanish Netherlands and Spanish Italy, now temporarily Austrian, continued to be kicked about until the nationalist movements of the nineteenth century gave birth to Belgium, Luxembourg, and a united Italy. The emergence of Brandenburg-Prussia on the north German coast and the gradual decline of the Holy Roman Emperor's power were both vital to the process that created a unified Germany and a separate Austria. In the southeast, the slow but steady reconquest of the Balkans from Ottoman dominion restored the historic southern border of the Continent. The inexorable expansion of Russia was also already apparent.

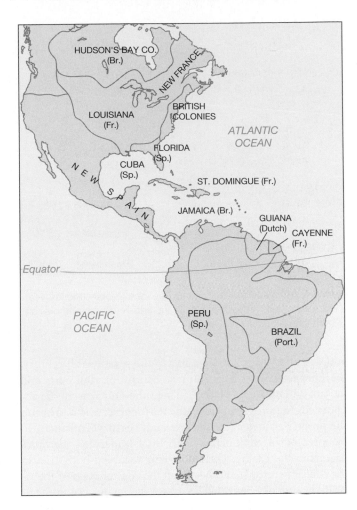

■ **Map B. The Americas.** Much of the American continents was still uncharted with most settlements in the coastal areas.

Expansion of Western Europe

Few noblemen would have traveled to the new outposts of the European empires, and only scholars, missionaries, and adventurers included the colonies among their travels. Yet perhaps the most obvious transformation in the political geography of western Europe was the expansion of European power around the globe.

Colonies in the Americas. In the Atlantic, Spain remained the largest colonial power. Through its vice-royalty system it controlled all of Mexico and Central America; the largest and most numerous of the Caribbean islands; North America from Colorado to California (as well as Florida); and most of South America (see **Map B**). The other major colonial power in the region was Portugal, which shared dominion over the South American continent. In the Portuguese colony of Brazil, production of sugar, dyestuffs, timbers, and exotic commodities amply repaid the meager investment the Portuguese had made.

In North America, the French and British shared the eastern half of the continent (see **Map B**). The French controlled

most of it. They had landed first in Canada and then slowly made their way down the Saint Lawrence River. New France, as their colonial empire was called, was a trading territory, and it expanded along the greatest of the waterways: the Great Lakes and the Ohio, Missouri, and Mississippi rivers. French settlements had sprung up as far south as the Gulf of Mexico. France also claimed the territory of Louisiana, named for Louis XIV, which stretched from New Orleans to Montana. The British settlements were all coastal, stretching from Maine to Georgia on the Atlantic seaboard. Unlike the French, the British settled their territory and were only interested in expansion when their population, which was doubling every 25 years, outgrew its resources. By the early eighteenth century, the ports of Boston, New York, Philadelphia, and Charleston were thriving commercial centers.

Colonies in the Far East. Europeans managed their eastern colonial territories differently from the way they did those in the Atlantic. Initially, the Portuguese and the Dutch had been satisfied with establishing trading factories—coastal fortresses in Africa and Asia that could be used as warehouses

■ **Map C. India and the East Indies.** The famous Spice Islands were still controlled by the Dutch while the British gained footholds on both coasts of India.

■ **Map D. Great Britain and the Low Countries.** Great Britain and the Low Countries were the two leading European commercial nations.

and defended against attack. But in the seventeenth century, the European states began to take control of vital ports and lucrative islands (see **Map C**). There the Dutch were the acknowledged leaders, replacing the Portuguese, who had begun the process at the end of the sixteenth century. Holland held by force or in conjunction with local leaders all the Spice Islands in the Pacific. The Dutch also occupied both sides of the Malay Peninsula and nearly all the coastal areas of the islands in the Java Sea. Dutch control of Ceylon was strategically important for its Indian trade. Compared to the Dutch Republic, all other European states had only a minor territorial presence in the East, with the exception of Spain, which still controlled the Philippines. The British had originally limited their eastern outposts to trading establishments, and through those they maintained a significant presence in India. During the eighteenth century, however, the British began to colonize the Indian subcontinent directly (see **Map C**).

Great Britain.

Imperial expansion was the most obvious change in the geopolitical boundaries of Europe, but it was not the only one. A brief tour of the western states after the Treaty of Utrecht reveals some others. In 1707, England and Scotland formally joined together to form Great Britain (see **Map D**). In addition to its eastern and western colonies, Britain had also gained control of Gibraltar at the foot of Spain and the island of Minorca in the Mediterranean (see **Map E**). Both territories were strategically important to British commerce. More and more, Europeans visited Britain in the eighteenth century. Though it was a site of neither great palaces nor cathedrals, London was acknowledged to be one of the greatest cities in the world.

The Low Countries.

Across the English Channel were the Low Countries, now permanently divided between the United Provinces in the north, led by Holland, and those provinces in

the south that had remained loyal to the Spanish crown in the sixteenth century (see **Map D**). By 1714 the golden age of the Dutch was over. Although the Dutch continued as a colonial and maritime power, their small numbers and meager natural resources eventually outweighed their abilities as innovators and managers. They lost their eastern empire to Britain and their predominance in European trade to France. What the Dutch gained at Utrecht was the right to maintain their forces in the towns along the border between France and the old Spanish Netherlands. The Spanish Netherlands, the original Burgundian inheritance, was now being slowly dismembered. Since the accession of Louis XIV, France had plucked small pieces from the territories that had been contested between France and Spain since the fifteenth century. Between French aggression and the Dutch occupation of such important places as Ghent and Ypres, the ability of the southern provinces to maintain a separate identity suffered a grave blow. But the blow was not as grave as that delivered at Utrecht, when sovereignty over the territory was assigned to Austria, ostensibly because the emperor was a Habsburg, but really because the balance of power in western Europe demanded it.

France.

To the south lay France, still the most powerful nation in Europe despite its losses in the War of the Spanish Succession (see **Map E**). No grand tour was complete without a sight of one of the king's great palaces, either the Louvre in Paris or monstrous Versailles, now considered one of the wonders of the world. Those with imagination could tour

■ **Map E. France and Spain.** The War of the Spanish Succession permanently separated France and Spain.

grand chateaux or visit vast cathedrals in every part of the nation. By 1714, Louis XIV had broken forever the danger of Spanish encirclement that had been the worry of every French king since Francis I in the early sixteenth century. Louis had methodically set out to occupy those territories that were strategically necessary to defend his state from invasion by the Dutch, the Spanish, the British, or the Holy Roman Emperor. In the northeast, he absorbed the Duchy of Bar. In the north, he absorbed a healthy portion of Flanders, including Dunkirk on the English Channel and the prosperous clothing town of Lille. He pushed the eastern boundary of his state to the Rhine by overrunning Alsace and parts of Lorraine (see **Map E**). Strasbourg remained French under the settlement of 1714, testimony to the fact that it was possible to hold France only at the western banks of the Rhine. Finally, farther to the south, Louis had won and held Franche-Comté, once the center of Burgundy. In 1714, France was larger, stronger, and better able to defend its borders than ever before. It was also exhausted.

Spain.   As France expanded, so Spain contracted. Less than two centuries earlier, a Spanish king had dreamed of being monarch of all of Europe. Instead, a French Bourbon sat on the great Habsburg throne and Spain was slowly being sliced to pieces. By 1714 the European territories of the Spanish empire had been reduced to Iberia itself (see **Map E**). But the loss of its European empire was to prove a blessing in disguise for

Spain, which now entered a new and unexpected phase of growth and influence. Grand tourists did not always find Spain a congenial destination; a trek across the Pyrenees and on to an arid plain was a deterrent to reaching Madrid and Toledo, but those who ventured forth were richly rewarded by the sight of great walled castles, Philip II's palace of L'Escorial, and some of the greatest cathedrals on the Continent.

The Empire.   The center of Europe remained occupied by the agglomeration of cities, bishoprics, principalities, and small states known collectively as the Holy Roman Empire, but now more accurately called the German Empire (see **Map F**). There were still more than 300 separate jurisdictions, most of them vulnerable to preying neighbors such as Louis XIV. Bavaria in the south and Saxony, Brandenburg, and Hanover in the north were among the most important of the large states, with the added twist that Hanover was now ruled by the king of Great Britain. The emperor, now officially prohibited from interference in the internal administration of the large states, was less dominant in German affairs than he had been before the Thirty Years' War. Grand tourists were welcomed into dozens of palaces occupied by the princes of the empire and while most churches were devoid of the rich decorations to be found in Catholic countries, German cities were finally recovering from the devastation of the Thirty Years' War.

Increasingly, Habsburg power centered on Austria, Bohemia, and Hungary (see **Map F**). That was especially true during the reign of Leopold I (1655–1705). Withstanding threats on all sides, Leopold was able to expand his state both to the west and to the south and to bring Austria into the ranks of the great European powers. Such an outcome could hardly have been foreseen in the middle of the seventeenth century, when the Ottomans made their last great thrust into the interior of Europe. In 1683, the Ottomans besieged Vienna itself, and only the arrival of 70,000 Polish-led troops saved it from falling. But from that time forward, Austrian forces scored stunning victories. By 1699 almost all of Hungary had been retaken by Austria; with the Treaty of Passarowitz in 1718 Austria gained the rest of Hungary and Serbia. When the Treaty of Utrecht granted Austria control of the Netherlands, Lombardy, and Naples, the Austrian Habsburgs became rulers of a European empire (see **Map F**).

Austria's Italian possessions included the vast southern territories of Naples (including Sicily after 1720) and the rich industrial area surrounding Milan in the north. Alongside the Austrian territories, a number of independent city-states continued to flourish on the Italian peninsula. Both Venice and Genoa remained prosperous and independent. The Grand Duchy of Tuscany, with its great city of Florence, and the Papal States had both expanded over the course of the seventeenth century, absorbing their smaller neighbors until both were large consolidated territories (see **Map F**). Florence was one of the traditional destinations of those on the grand tour and a place to purchase great works of art from all periods. The palaces of the Medici on both sides of the Arno River were among the most opulent to be seen and the public art of masters such as

■ **Map F. The Holy Roman Empire.** It was still a conglomeration of towns, principalities, and bishoprics, but increasingly the empire was losing political and administrative control over its lands.

Leonardo da Vinci and Michelangelo was as popular then as it is now. To the west of the Italian states was the Duchy of Savoy (see **Map F**). Savoy had pursued a flexible foreign policy, pleasing whichever of its powerful neighbors was most dangerous and accepting the patronage of whichever seemed most friendly. As a client of the Spanish, French, and Austrians, Savoy grew and prospered. After the War of the Spanish Succession, Savoy was counted among the victors, though it had fought on both sides. Duke Victor Amadeus II became a king when he received the island of Sicily, which he exchanged with Austria for Sardinia in 1720 (see **Map F**).

Thus the Treaty of Utrecht signaled a new configuration of political power. England, France, Prussia, and Austria were the ascending powers, Holland and Spain the declining ones. Italy and the southern Netherlands were the bones over which the biggest dogs fought, sometimes playfully, sometimes in deadly earnest.

Realignment in Eastern Europe

In eastern Europe, the Treaty of Nystad (1721) ended the Great Northern War (1700–1721) and fixed the political geography in the east. There the emerging powers were Russia and Prussia, while those in decline were Sweden and Poland. The critical factor in eastern European politics remained access to the sea. Outlets to the Baltic Sea in the north and the Black Sea in the south were the vital lifeline for that part of the Continent, and

control of those outlets was the central motivation for the long years of war fought among the eastern states.

Russia. The expansion of Russia is one of the central events in European history, and the early eighteenth century is its pivotal period. During the long years of social and economic recovery after the death of Ivan the Terrible in 1584, Russia had been easy prey for its powerful neighbors Sweden and Poland. Through a series of wars and political pacts, Russia had ceded most of its Baltic territories to Sweden, while it had relinquished land and population in the west to Poland. Peter the Great (1682–1725) set out to reclaim what had been lost. As a result of the Great Northern War, Russia regained the eastern Baltic coastline from the southeastern end of Finland to Riga in the west (see **Map G**). Russia now controlled all of the vital Baltic ports in the east. Peter built a new capital on the Gulf of Finland. In the new city, named Saint Petersburg, he laid the foundation for the Russian navy. Russia was still an unusual destination for traveling noblemen but there was much curiosity about the new city that Peter and his successors were building. Russian monarchs did all they could to Westernize their state, even purchasing some of the greatest works of Italian art for the new royal palace L'Hermitage.

Sweden. What Russia gained, Sweden lost (see **Map G**). At the height of its power in the middle of the seventeenth century, Sweden had dominated the Baltic. It occupied all of Finland, controlled the important eastern coast of Norway, and had gained a foothold in Germany. Most importantly, Sweden had captured the southern tip of its own peninsula from the Danes, making the mainland portion of its state whole. But Sweden's century-long rise to power was followed by a rapid period of decline. The small and relatively poor population could not long succeed in governing an empire. The Great Northern War ended whatever pretensions Sweden still had. It lost all of its German territories: those on the North Sea went to Hanover, those on the Baltic to Prussia. Livonia, Estonia, and the eastern provinces were returned to Russia, but Sweden was able to hold on to its vital gains from the Danes. Sweden had built its own window to the west at Göteborg on the North Sea, and from there it could carry on a direct trade with Britain and the Netherlands (see **Map G**).

Prussia. Since the end of the Thirty Years' War, Brandenburg-Prussia had been growing steadily. A strange configuration of a state, with its geographical heart in Brandenburg, it was one of the domains of the Holy Roman Empire (see **Map G**). From the capital at Berlin the princes of Brandenburg directed the accumulation of small neighboring German lands: Magdeburg and Halle to the southwest, a piece of Pomerania to the northeast. But while Brandenburg expanded in every direction, it could do little to join itself to the kingdom of Prussia. A huge swath of Poland, cutting between the two, stood in the way. That division of Brandenburg-Prussia was its most important geopolitical fea-

■ **Map G. Russia and Sweden.** Sweden's age of territorial expansion was over by the beginning of the eighteenth century.

ture. In the eighteenth century, the determination to join together dominated Prussian history.

Poland. That aim, of course, meant eventual conflict with Poland. Despite its political weakness, Poland was one of the largest landmasses in Europe (see **Map G**). On its southern border it held back Ottoman expansion; on its eastern border it held back the Russians. Its great port of Gdansk on the Baltic dominated the grain and timber trade with northern Europe as well as local Baltic commerce between Scandinavia and the mainland. Sweden and Russia, the eastern powers, controlled Poland politically, helping nominate its elected kings and ensuring that its decentralized form of aristocratic government kept Poland weak. Poland served as a useful counterweight in the balance of power in eastern Europe. Except for its Baltic territories, Poland was not yet seen as a great prize to be fought over. But by the beginning of the eighteenth century it was a helpless giant ready to be toppled.

Thus a potent Prussia and Russia and a prostrate Poland characterized the realignment of the eastern portion of Europe. Most importantly, the separation between east and west was narrowing. Prussia's German orientation and the Westernization of Russia led to closer ties with the west. More and more grand tourists visited the Prussian palace of Sans Souci or ventured as far east as St. Petersburg or Moscow. More and more they became part of a single European aristocratic culture.

CAPTAIN COOK ENCOUNTERS THE TAHITIANS

The English explorer Captain James Cook, trained as a map maker, was sent by the Royal Navy on an astronomical expedition to the South Pacific. While there he decided to explore islands to the east and discovered Australia and New Zealand. He was the first European to make contact with Pacific islanders, and he kept a diary of his experiences. This entry is from 14 April 1769.

Focus Questions

What is Captain Cook's attitude toward the Tahitians? How do chiefs differ from ordinary islanders? What kind of names did Cook bestow upon the Tahitian chiefs? What qualities might they have reflected?

This morning we had a great many canoes about the ship, the most of them came from the westward but brought nothing with them but a few Cocoa-nuts. Two that appeared to be chiefs we had on board together with several others for it was a hard matter to keep them out of the ship as they climb like monkeys, but it was still harder to keep them from stealing but every thing that came within their reach. In this they are prodigious expert. I made each of the two chiefs a present of a hatchet, things that they seemed mostly to value. . . .

As soon as we had partly got clear of these people, I took two boats and went to the westward. Here the natives flocked about us in great numbers and in as friendly a manner as we could wish, only that they showed a great inclination to pick our pockets. We were conducted to a chief who for distinction sake we called Hercules. After staying a short time with him and distributing a few presents about us, we proceeded further and came to a chief who I shall call Lycurgus. This man entertained us with broiled fish, breadfruit, cocoa-nuts etc. with a great hospitality, and all the time took great care to tell us to take care of our pockets, as a great number of people had crowded about us.

From *The Journals of Captain Cook* by James Cook. Edited by Philip Edwards (Penguin, 1999), pp. 39–41.

THE RISE OF RUSSIA

At the beginning of the eighteenth century, Russia was scarcely known or cared about in the rest of Europe. Peter the Great changed that. The Treaty of Nystad had confirmed the magnitude of his victory over the Swedes in the Great Northern War, both in territory and prestige. The change created consternation in the courts of Europe. Just a quarter century before, no one had cared very much what the king of Russia called himself. In fact, little was known for sure about the Russian ruler or his state. What little mercantile contact there was between Russia and the West was conducted entirely by Westerners. Foreign merchants were allowed to live in Moscow in a separate ghetto called "Germantown." Their letters were the main source of Western knowledge about the vast Muscovite empire.

Peter the Great brought Europe to Russia and Russia to Europe. Twice he visited Europe to discover the secrets of Western prosperity and might. He arranged marriages between the closest heirs to his throne, including his son Alexis, and the sons and daughters of German princes and dukes. By 1721 he had established 21 separate foreign embassies. The sons of the Russian gentry and nobility were sent west—sometimes forcibly—to further their education and to learn to adapt to Western outlooks. Peter recruited Europeans to fill the most important skilled positions in the state: foreign engineers and gunners to serve in the army; foreign architects to build the new capital at Saint Petersburg; foreign scholars to head the new state schools; foreign administrators to oversee the new departments of state. Peter borrowed freely and adapted sensibly. If necessary, he would drag his countrymen kicking and screaming into the modern world.

By 1721, Russia was recognized all over Europe as an emerging power. The military defeat of the seemingly invincible Swedes had made monarchs from Louis XIV to William III sit up and take notice. And the great Russian victory over Sweden at Poltava in 1709 was no fluke. Peter's forces followed it up with several strong campaigns, which proved that Russia could organize, equip, finance, and train an up-to-date military force. Moreover, Peter's absorption of Sweden's Baltic territories made Russia a power in the north. The Russian navy, built mostly by foreigners, was now capable of protecting Russian interests and defending important ports such as Riga and Saint Petersburg. Even the Dutch,

■ *The Apotheosis of Peter the Great* (1710). Here Peter the Great is depicted in all his glory as a lawgiver, military commander, and leader of a new Russia.

The Rise of Russia   541

who had long plotted the decline of Swedish might, became nervous. Thus it was unsettling that Peter wanted to be recognized as emperor.

The Reforms of Peter the Great

Peter the Great was not the first Russian tsar to attempt to borrow from Western developments. The process had been under way for decades. The opening of the northern port of Archangel in 1584 led to direct contact with British and Dutch traders, who brought with them new ideas and useful products. But Russia was a vast state, and Europe was only one of its neighbors. Russia's religion had come from Byzantium rather than Rome, thus giving Russian Christianity an eastern flavor. Its Asian territories mixed the influence of Mongols and Ottomans; its southern borders met Tatars and Cossacks. While most European states were racially and ethnically homogeneous, Russia was a loose confederation of diverse peoples. Yet the western states posed the greatest threat to Russia in the seventeenth century, and it was to the West that Peter, like his father before him, turned his attention.

It would be wrong to see Peter's Westernizing innovation as a systematic program. More to the point, nearly all of his reforms—economic, educational, administrative, social, military—were done to enhance military efficiency rather than civil progress. In his 30 years of active rule there was only one year—1724—during which he was not at war. Vital reforms such as the poll tax (1724), which changed the basis of taxation from the household to the individual adult male, had enormous social consequences. The new policy of taxing individuals officially erased whole social classes. A strict census taken (and retaken) to inhibit tax evasion became the basis for further governmental encroachments on the tsar's subjects. Yet the poll tax was not designed for any of those purposes. It was instituted to increase tax revenue for war. Similarly, compulsory lifetime military service required of the landowning classes (the nobility and gentry) was established to provide officers and state servants for an expanding military machine.

Although Peter's reforms were developed from little other than military necessity, they constituted a fundamental transformation in the life of all Russian people. The creation of a gigantic standing army and an entirely new navy meant conscription of the Russian peasantry on a grand scale. In a ten-year period of the Great Northern War, the army absorbed 330,000 conscripts, most of whom never returned to their homes. Military service was not confined to the peasantry. Traditionally, the rural gentry raised and equipped the local conscript forces and gave them what training they could. Most gentry lived on estates that had been granted to them, along with the resident peasants, as a reward for their military contributions. Peter the Great intensified the obligations of the gentry. Not only were they to serve the state for life, but they were to accompany their regiments to the field and lead them in battle. When too old for active military service, they were to perform administrative service in the new departments of state.

The expansion of military forces necessitated an expansion of military administration as well. Peter's first innovation was the creation of the Senate, a group of nine senior administrators who were to oversee all aspects of military and civil government. The Senate became a permanent institution of government led by an entirely new official, the Procurator-General, who presided over its sessions and could propose legislation as well as oversee administration. From the Senate emanated 500 officials known as the *fiscals*, who traveled throughout the state looking for irregularities in tax assessment and collection. They quickly developed into a hated and feared internal police force.

Peter's efforts to reorganize his government went a step further in 1722, when he issued the **Table of Ranks,** an official hierarchy of the state that established the social position or rank of individuals. It was divided into three categories: military service, civil service, and owners of landed estates. Each category contained 14 ranks, and it was decreed that every

■ St. Petersburg, the new capital city Peter the Great had built on the Gulf of Finland to facilitate contact with western and northern Europe, testified to the growing strength of Russia in the eighteenth century.

person who entered the hierarchy did so at the bottom and worked his way up. The creation of the Table of Ranks demonstrated Peter's continued commitment to merit as a criterion for advancement. This standard had been shown in the military, where officers were promoted on the basis of service and experience rather than birth or background. Equally important was Peter's decision to make the military service the highest of the three categories. This reversed the centuries-old position of the landed aristocracy and the military service class. Although the old nobility also served in the military and continued to dominate state service, the Table of Ranks opened the way for the infusion of new elements into the Russian elite.

On Corruption of Morals in Russia

Peter's reforms of government and society were matched by his efforts to energize the economy. No state in Europe had as many natural resources as did Russia, yet manufacturing barely existed there. As with everything else he did, Peter took a direct hand in establishing factories for the production of textiles, glass, leather, and, most importantly, iron and copper. The state directly owned about half of the establishments, most of them on a larger scale than any known in the West. By 1726, more than half of all Russian exports were manufactured goods and Russia had become the largest producer of iron and copper in the world.

In all those ways and more, Peter the Great transformed Russia, but the changes did not come without cost. The traditions of centuries were not easily broken. Intrigue against Peter led first to confrontation with the old military elite, and later to conflict with his only son, Alexis. It remains unclear whether the plot with which Alexis was connected actually existed or whether it was a figment of Peter's imagination, but it is abundantly clear that Alexis's death from torture plunged the state into a succession crisis in 1725. In the end, the great costs of Westernization were paid by the masses of people, who benefited little from the improvement in Russia's international standing or from the social and economic changes that affected the elites.

Panegyric to Peter the Great

Life in Rural Russia

At the beginning of the eighteenth century, nearly 97 percent of the Russian people lived on the land and practiced agriculture. Farming techniques and agrarian lifestyles had changed little for centuries. Most of the country's soil was poor. Harsh climate and low yields characterized Russian agriculture. Thirty-four of the 100 Russian harvests during the eighteenth century can be termed poor or disastrous, yet throughout the century state taxation was making larger and larger demands upon the peasantry. During Peter's reign alone, direct taxation increased by 500 percent.

The theory of the Russian state was one of service, and the role of Russian peasants was to serve their master. Beginning in the mid-seventeenth century, the peasantry had undergone a change in status. The law code of 1649 formalized a process that had been under way for more than a century whereby peasants were turned into the property of their landlords. During the next century, laws curtailed the ability of peasants to move freely from one place to another, eliminated their right to hold private property, and abolished their freedom to petition the tsar against their masters. At the same time that landlords increased their hold over peasants, the state increased its hold over landlords. They were made responsible for the payment of taxes owed by their peasants and for the military service due from them. By the middle of the eighteenth century, more than half of all peasants—6.7 million adult males by 1782—had thus become serfs, the property of their masters, without any significant rights or legal protection.

The Enlightened Empress Catherine

Of all the legacies of Peter the Great, perhaps the one of most immediate consequence was that government could go on without him. During the next 37 years, six tsars ruled Russia, "three women, a boy of twelve, an infant, and a mental weakling," as one commentator acidly observed. More to the point, each succession was contested, as there were no direct male heirs to the throne in this period. Nevertheless, despite turmoil at the top, government continued to function smoothly and Peter's territorial conquests were largely maintained. Russia also experienced a remarkable increase in numbers during this period. Between 1725 and 1762, the population increased from 13 to 19 million, a jump of nearly 50 percent in a single generation. The explosion of people dramatically increased the wealth of the landholding class, who reckoned their status by the number of serfs they owned.

The expansion of the economic resources of the nobility was matched by a rise in legal status and political power. This was the period sarcastically dubbed "the emancipation of the nobility," a phrase that captures not only the irony of the growing gap between rich and poor but also the contrast between the social structures of Russia and those of western Europe. In return for their privileges and status, Peter the Great extended the duties the landowning classes owed to the state. By granting unique rights, such as the ownership of serfs, to the descendants of the old military service class, Peter had forged a Russian nobility. Lifetime service, however, was the price of nobility.

In order to gain and hold the throne, each succeeding tsar had to make concessions to the nobility to gain their loyalty. At first it was a few simple adjustments. The sons of wealthy landowners who completed a course of education at one of the state academies were allowed to enter the Table of Ranks in the middle of the hierarchy rather than at the bottom. Then life service was commuted to a term of 25 years, still a long time in a world of short lives and sudden deaths. But the concessions were not enough.

Twenty-five years of service did not solve the problem of estate management, especially as the tasks of management grew along with the population of serfs. Thus the next capitulation was that a single son could remain on the estate and escape service altogether. The births of younger sons were concealed; owners of multiple estates claimed the exemption of one son for each. Most decisively, the talented remained at home to serve the family while the wastrels were sent to serve the state. Finally, in 1762, the obligation for state service by the nobility was abolished entirely.

Catherine's Accession.   The abolition of compulsory service was not the same as the abolition of service itself. In fact, the end of compulsory service enabled Catherine II, "the Great" (1762–1796), to enact some of the most important reforms of her reign. At first, Catherine's accession seemed nothing more than a continuation of monarchical instability—her first two acts were to have her husband, Peter III, murdered and to lower the salt tax. Each brought her a measure of security.

Catherine was a dynamic personality who alternately captivated and terrified those with whom she came into contact. Her policies were as complex as her personality, influenced on the one hand by the new French ideas of social justice and the nobility of the human race, and on the other hand by the traditional Russian ideas of absolute rule over an enserfed and subhuman population. Catherine handled the contrasting di-

■ Catherine II of Russia sought first to consolidate her power and then to use it to reform Russian government. Here she is painted with orb, crown, and scepter as symbols of her legitimacy as empress.

mensions of her rule masterfully, gaining abroad the reputation as the most enlightened of European monarchs and at home the sincere devotion of her people.

The most important event in the early years of Catherine's reign was the establishment of a legislative commission to review the laws of Russia. Catherine herself wrote the *Instruction* (1767), by which the elected commissioners were to operate. She borrowed her theory of law from the French jurist Baron de Montesquieu (1689–1755) and her theory of punishment from the Italian reformer Cesare Beccaria (1738–1794). Among other things, Catherine advocated the abolition of capital punishment, torture, serf auctions, and the breakup of serf families by sale. Few of the radical reforms were ever put into practice.

DOCUMENT

Catherine the Great's Constitution

But in 1775 Catherine did restructure local government. Russia was divided into 50 provincial districts, each with a population of between 300,000 and 400,000 inhabitants. Each district was to be governed by both a central official and elected local noblemen. The reform was modeled upon the English system of justices of the peace. Previous local reforms had failed because of the absence of a resident local nobility. The abolition of compulsory service finally made possible the establishment of local institutions. In 1785, Catherine issued the **Charter of the Nobility**, a formal statement of the rights and privileges of the noble class. The Charter incorporated all the gains the nobility had made since the death of Peter the Great, but it also instituted the requirements for local service that had been the basis of Catherine's reforms. District councils with the right to petition directly to the tsar became the centerpiece of Russian provincial government.

To train the local nobility for government service, Catherine introduced educational reforms. Peter had established military schools for the nobility and had staffed them with foreigners. The University of Moscow had been founded in 1755, and its faculty too was dominated by European emigrants. Catherine saw the need to broaden the educational system. Borrowing from the Austrian system, she established provincial elementary schools to train the sons and daughters of the local nobility. To staff the schools, Catherine created teachers' colleges so that the state would have its own educators. Although the program called for the equal education of women, except in Saint Petersburg and Moscow few females attended either elementary or high schools.

Catherine's reforms did little to enhance the lives of the vast majority of her people. She took no effective action either to end serfdom or to soften its rigors. In fact, by grants of state land Catherine gave away 800,000 state peasants, who became serfs. So, too, did millions of Poles who became her subjects after the partition of Poland in 1793 and 1795.

Pugachev's Revolt.   The most significant uprising of the century, Pugachev's revolt (1773–1775), took place during Catherine's reign. Emelyan Pugachev (1726–1775) was a Cossack from the frozen reaches of the Russian Empire who in his youth had been a military adventurer. Disappointed in his career, he made his way to the Ural Mountains, where he recruited Asian tribesmen and laborers forced to work in the mines. By promising freedom and land ownership, he drew peasants to his cause. In 1773, Pugachev declared himself to be Tsar Peter III, the murdered husband of Catherine II. He began with small raiding parties against local landlords and military outposts and soon had gained the allegiance of tens of thousands of peasants. In 1774, with an army of nearly 20,000, Pugachev took the city of Kazan and threatened to advance on Moscow. It was another year before state forces could effectively control the rebellion. Finally, Pugachev was betrayed by his own followers and sent to Moscow, where he was executed.

During the reigns of Peter and Catherine the Great, Russia was transformed into an international power. Saint Petersburg, a window to the West, was a capital worthy of a potent monarch, and during the course of the eighteenth century it attracted many of Europe's leading luminaries. At court French was spoken, the latest fashions were worn, and the newest ideas for economic and educational reform were aired. The Russian nobility mingled comfortably with its European counterparts, while the military service class developed into bureaucrats and administrators. But if life

Russia

■ Emelyan Pugachev led the largest uprising of Russian peasants in the eighteenth century, which was also one of the most significant revolts in Russian history. In this picture, he is shown in chains with inscriptions in Russian and German below the picture decrying the evils of rebellion.

glittered at court, it remained the same dull regimen in the country. Millions of peasants were owned either by the state or by private landlords, and their quality of life was no different at the end of the campaign of Westernization from what it had been at the beginning.

THE TWO GERMANIES

The Thirty Years' War, which ended in 1648, initiated a profound transformation of the Holy Roman Empire. Warfare had devastated imperial territory. It was decades before the rich imperial lands recovered, and then the political consequences of the war had taken effect. There were now two empires, a German and an Austrian, though both were ruled by the same person. In the German territories, whether Catholic or Protestant, the Holy Roman Emperor was more a constitutional monarch than the absolute ruler he was in Austria. The larger states such as Saxony, Bavaria, and Hanover made their own political alliances despite the jurisdictional control that the emperor claimed to exercise. Most decisively, so did Brandenburg-Prussia. By the beginning of the eighteenth century, the electors of Brandenburg had become the kings of Prussia, and Prussia's military power and efficient administrative structure became the envy of its German neighbors.

The Austrian Empire was composed of Austria and Bohemia, the Habsburg hereditary lands, and as much of Hungary as could be controlled. In Austria, the Habsburgs clung tightly to their power. For decades, Austria was the center of the still-flourishing Counter-Reformation, and the power and influence of the Jesuits was as strong there as it was in Spain. The War of the Spanish Succession, which gave the Habsburgs control of the southern Netherlands and parts of Italy, brought Austria an enhanced role in European affairs. Austria remained one of the great powers of Europe and the leading power in the Holy Roman Empire despite the rise of Prussia. Indeed, from the middle of the eighteenth century, the conflict between Prussia and Austria was the defining characteristic of central European politics.

The Rise of Prussia

The transformation of Brandenburg-Prussia from a petty German principality to a great European power was one of the most significant and least expected developments of the eighteenth century. Frederick William, the Great Elector (1640–1688), had begun the process of forging Brandenburg-Prussia into a power in its own right by building a large and efficient military machine. At the beginning of the eighteenth century, Prussia was on the winning side in both the War of the Spanish Succession and the Great Northern War. When the battlefield dust had settled, Prussia found itself in possession of Pomerania and the Baltic port of Stettin. It was now a recognized power in eastern Europe.

Frederick William I.   Frederick William I (1713–1740) and his son Frederick II, "the Great" (1740–1786), turned the promising beginning into an astounding success. A devout Calvinist, Frederick William I deplored waste and display as much on moral as on fiscal grounds. The reforms he initiated were intended to subordinate both aristocracy and peasantry to the needs of the state and to subordinate the needs of the state to the demands of the military.

Because of its geographical position, Prussia's major problem was to maintain an efficient and well-trained army during peacetime. Defense of its exposed territories required a constant state of military preparedness, yet the relaxation of military discipline and the desertion of troops to their homes inevitably followed the cessation of hostilities. Frederick William I solved the problem by integrating the economic and military structures of his state. First he appointed only German officers to command his troops, eliminating the mercenaries who sold their services to the highest bidders. Then he placed the noblemen at the head of locally recruited regiments. Each adult male in every district was required to register for military service in the regiment of the local landlord. The reforms dramatically increased the effectiveness of the army by shifting the burden of recruitment and training to the localities.

Yet despite all the attention that Frederick William I lavished on the military—by the end of his reign nearly 70 percent of state expenditures went to the army—his foreign policy was largely pacific. In fact, his greatest achievements were in civil affairs, reforming the bureaucracy, establishing a sound economy, and raising state revenues. Through generous settlement schemes and by welcoming Protestant and Jewish refugees, Frederick William was able to expand the economic potential of the eastern territories. Frederick William I pursued an aggressive policy of land purchase to expand the royal domain, and the addition of so many new inhabitants in Prussia further increased his wealth. While the major western European powers were discovering deficit financing and the national debt, Prussia was running a surplus.

Frederick the Great.   Financial security was vital to the success of Frederick the Great. Father and son had quarreled

MAP DISCOVERY

Brandenburg, 1440
Acquisitions to 1618
Acquisitions to 1740
Acquisitions to 1786
Holy Roman Empire

The Expansion of Prussia

Notice how Brandenburg-Prussia grew in its first phase to 1618. How did its acquisitions made between 1618 and 1740 differ from its earlier growth? Notice how the acquisition of Silesia made Prussia an inland power in control of most of the Oder River. Why was the acquisition of West Prussia strategically important?

bitterly throughout Frederick's youth—not only about music—and most observers expected that out of spite Frederick would tear down all that his father had built up. In fact, father and son were cast in the same mold, with the unexpected difference that the son was more ruthless and ambitious. With his throne, Frederick II inherited the fourth-largest army in Europe and the richest treasury. He wasted no time in putting both to use. His two objectives were to acquire the Polish corridor of West Prussia that separated his German and Prussian territories and to acquire the agriculturally and industrially rich Austrian province of Silesia to the southeast of Berlin. Just months after his coronation, Frederick conquered Silesia, increasing the size of Prussia by nearly a quarter. Within a decade, the province dominated the Prussian economy, outproducing and outconsuming all other areas of Frederick's state.

It was Frederick's military prowess that earned him the title "the Great." But that was only a part of his achievement. More than his father, Frederick II forged an alliance with the Prussian nobility, integrating them into a unified state. A tightly orga-

nized central administration, which depended upon the cooperation of the local nobility, directed both military and bureaucratic affairs. At the center, Frederick worked tirelessly to oversee his government. Where Louis XIV had proclaimed, "I am the state," Frederick the Great announced, "I am the first servant of the state." He codified the laws of Prussia, abolished torture and capital punishment, and instituted agricultural techniques imported from the states of western Europe. By the end of Frederick's reign, Prussia had become a model for bureaucratic organization, military reform, and enlightened rule.

Austria Survives

Austria was the great territorial victor in the War of the Spanish Succession, acquiring both the Netherlands and parts of Italy. Austrian forces recaptured a large part of Hungary from the Turks, thereby expanding their territory to the south and the east. As hereditary ruler of Austria and Bohemia, king of Hungary, and Holy Roman Emperor of the German na-

■ Prussian infantry officers display their uniforms in this painting from the late eighteenth century. Distinctive, colorful, and elaborate uniforms, different for each regiment, were common in European armies before the field-gray and khaki era of the twentieth century.

A KING'S-EYE VIEW

Frederick the Great wrote philosophical and military tracts as well as composing dozens of compositions for the flute. Here is his definition of the enlightened despot.

Focus Questions

What is the relation of the sovereign to the state and its people? What is enlightened about an enlightened despot?

The sovereign is attached by indissoluble ties to the body of the state; hence it follows that he, by repercussion, is sensible to all the ills which afflict his subjects; and the people, in like manner, suffer from the misfortunes which affect their sovereign. There is but one general good, which is that of the state. . . . The sovereign represents the state; he and his people form but one body, which can only be happy as far as united by concord. The prince is to the nation he governs what the head is to the man; it is his duty to see, to think,

and act for the whole community, so that he may procure it every advantage of which it is capable. . . . Such are in general the duties imposed upon a prince, from which, in order that he may never depart, he ought often to recollect that he himself is but a man, like the least of his subjects. If he be the first general, the first minister of the realm, it is not so that he should shelter in the shadow of authority, but that he should fulfill the duties of such titles. He is only the first servant of the state, who is obliged to act with probity and prudence; and to remain as totally disinterested as if he were each moment liable to render an account of his administration to his fellow citizens.

From Frederick the Great, *An Essay on Forms of Government.*

tion, Charles VI (1711–1740) was recognized as one of Europe's most potent rulers. But appearances were deceptive. The apex of Austrian power and prestige had already passed. Austria had benefited from balance-of-power politics, not so much from its own strength as from the leverage it could give to others. With the rise of Russia and Prussia, there was now more than one fulcrum to power in eastern Europe.

Decentralized Rule.

The difficulties facing Austria ran deep. The Thirty Years' War had made the emperor more an Austrian monarch than an imperial German ruler. On the Austrian hereditary estates, the Catholic Counter-Reformation continued unabated, bringing with it the benefits of Jesuit education, cultural revival, and the religious unity necessary to motivate warfare against the Ottomans. But the benefits came at a price. Perhaps as many as 200,000 Protestants fled Austria and Bohemia, taking with them their skills and capital. For centuries, the vision of empire had dominated Habsburg rule. That meant that the Austrian monarchy was a multiethnic confederation of lands loosely tied together by loyalty to a single head. The components preserved a high degree of autonomy: Hungary elected the Habsburg emperor its king in a separate ceremony. Local autonomy continually restricted the imposition of central policy, and never were the localities more autonomous than in the matter of taxation. Thus it was hard for Austria to centralize in the same way as had Prussia.

Lack of finance, human resources, and governmental control were the underlying problems of Austria, but they were not the most immediate difficulties facing Charles VI. With no sons to succeed him, Charles feared that his hereditary and elective states would go their separate ways after his death and that the great Habsburg monarchy would end. For 20 years, his abiding ambition was to gain recognition for the principle

that his empire would pass intact to his daughter, Maria Theresa. He expressed the principle in a document known as the **Pragmatic Sanction**, which stated that all Habsburg lands would pass intact to the eldest heir, male or female. Charles VI made concession after concession to gain acceptance of the Pragmatic Sanction. But the leaders of Europe licked their lips at the prospect of a dismembered Austrian Empire.

Maria Theresa.

Maria Theresa (1740–1780) inherited the imperial throne in 1740 and quickly discovered what it was like to be a woman in a man's world. In 1740, Frederick of Prussia invaded the rich Austrian province of Silesia and attracted allies for an assault upon Vienna. Faced with Bavarian, Saxon, and Prussian armies, Maria Theresa might well have lost her inheritance had she not shown her remarkable capacities so early in her reign. She appeared before the Hungarian estates, accepted their crown, and persuaded them to provide her with an army capable of halting the allied advance. Although she was unable to reconquer Silesia, Hungarian aid helped her hold the line against her enemies.

The loss of Silesia, the most prosperous part of the Austrian domains, signaled the need for fundamental reform. The new eighteenth-century idea of building a state replaced the traditional Habsburg concern with maintaining an empire. Maria Theresa and her son Joseph II (1780–1790) began the process of transformation. For Austria, state building meant first the reorganization of the military and civil bureaucracy to clear the way for fiscal reform. As in Prussia, a central directory was created to oversee the collection of taxes and the disbursement of funds. Maria Theresa personally persuaded her provincial estates both to increase taxation and to extend it to the nobles and the clergy. Although her success was limited, she finally established royal control over the raising and collection of taxes.

MILITARY DISCIPLINE

Herman Maurice de Saxe was the illegitimate son of the king of Poland. He had extensive military experience in both eastern and western Europe. He ultimately achieved the office of Marshal of France, where he was celebrated as a military reformer. He modeled many of his reforms on the Prussian army.

Focus Questions

Why would it be desirable for men in their twenties to have to perform military service? What would be the consequences of requiring men from all levels of the social hierarchy to serve in the military?

Would it not be much better to establish a law obliging men of all conditions of life to serve their king and country for the space of five years? A law, which could not reasonably be objected against, as it is both natural and just for people to be engaged in the defense of that state of which they constitute a part, and in choosing them between the years of twenty and thirty, no manner of inconvenience can possibly be the result; for those are years devoted, as it were, to libertinism; which are spent in adventures and travels, and, in general, productive of but small comfort to parents. An expedient of this kind could not come under the denomination of a public calamity, because every man,

at the expiration of his five years service, would be discharged. It would also create an inexhaustible fund of good recruits, and such as would not be subject to desertion. In course of time, everyone would regard it as an honor rather than a duty to perform his task; but to produce this effect upon a people, it is necessary that no sort of distinction should be admitted, no rank or degree whatsoever excluded, and the nobles and rich rendered, in a principal manner, subservient to it. This would effectually prevent all murmur and repining, for those who had served their time, would look upon such, as betrayed any reluctance, or dissatisfaction at it, with contempt; by which means, the grievance would vanish insensibly, and every man at length esteem it an honor to serve his term. The poor would be comforted by the example of the rich; and the rich could not with decency complain, seeing themselves on a footing with the nobles.

From Marshal de Saxe, *Memoirs on the Art of War* (1757).

The second element in Maria Theresa's reform program involved the condition of the Austrian peasantry. Maria Theresa established the doctrine that "the peasant must be able to support himself and his family and pay his taxes in time of peace and war." She limited labor service to two days per week and abolished the most burdensome feudal dues. Joseph II ended serfdom altogether. The new Austrian law codes guaranteed peasants' legal rights and established their ability to seek redress through the law. Joseph II hoped to extend reform even further. In the last years of his life, he abolished obligatory labor service and ensured that all peasants kept one-half of their income before paying local and state taxes. Such a radical reform met a storm of opposition and was ultimately abandoned at the end of the reign.

The reorganization of the bureaucracy, the increase in taxation, and the social reforms that created a more productive peasantry revitalized the Austrian state. The efforts of Maria Theresa and Joseph II to overcome provincial autonomy worked better in Austria and Bohemia than in Hungary. The Hungarians declined to contribute at all to state revenues, and Joseph II took the unusual step of refusing to be crowned king of Hungary so that he would not have to make any concessions to Hungarian autonomy. He even imposed a tariff on Hungarian goods sold in Austria. More seriously, parts of the empire already had been lost before the process of reform could begin. Prussia's seizure of Silesia was the hardest blow of all. Yet in 1740, when Frederick the Great and his allies swept

■ Maria Theresa and her family. Eleven of Maria Theresa's 16 children are posed with the empress and her husband, Francis of Lorraine. Standing next to his mother is the future emperor Joseph II.

down from the north, few would have predicted that Austria would survive.

The Politics of Power

Frederick the Great's invasion of Silesia in 1740 was callous and cynical. Since the Pragmatic Sanction bound him to recognize Maria Theresa's succession, Frederick cynically offered her a defensive alliance in return for which she would simply hand over Silesia. It was an offer she should not have refused. Although Frederick's action initiated the War of the Austrian Succession, he was not alone in his desire to shake loose parts of Austria's territory. Soon nearly the entire Continent became embroiled in the conflict.

The War of the Austrian Succession.   The War of the Austrian Succession (1740–1748) resembled a pack of wolves stalking its injured prey. It quickly became a major international conflict, involving Prussia, France, and Spain on one side and Austria, Britain, and Holland on the other. Spain joined the fighting to recover its Italian possessions, Saxony claimed Moravia, France entered Bohemia, and the Bavarians moved into Austria from the south. With France and Prussia allied, it was vital that Britain join with Austria to maintain the balance of power. Initially, the British did little more than subsidize Maria Theresa's forces, but once France renewed its efforts to conquer the Netherlands, both Britain and the Dutch Republic joined in the fray.

That the British cared little about the fate of the Habsburg Empire was clear from the terms of the treaty that they dictated at Aix-la-Chapelle (Aachen) in 1748. Austria recognized Frederick's conquest of Silesia, as well as the loss of parts of its Italian territories to Spain. France, which the British had always regarded as the real enemy, withdrew from the Netherlands in return for the restoration of a number of colonial possessions. The War of the Austrian Succession made Austria and Prussia permanent enemies and gave Maria Theresa a crash course in international diplomacy. She learned firsthand that self-interest rather than loyalty underlay power politics.

The Partitions of Poland.   Peace among the eastern European powers of Prussia and Austria did not mean that they abandoned their territorial ambitions. All over Europe, absolute rulers reformed their bureaucracies, streamlined their administrations, increased their sources of revenue, and built enormous standing armies. All over Europe, except in Poland. There the autonomous power of the nobility remained as strong as ever. No monarchical dynasty was ever established, and each elected ruler not only confirmed the privileges of the nobility but usually was forced to extend them. In the Diet, the Polish representative assembly, small special-interest groups could bring legislative business to a halt by exercising their veto power. Given the size of Poland's borders, its army was pathetically inadequate for the task it had to face. The Polish monarchy was helpless to defend its subjects from the destruction on all sides.

■ This painting by Pierre L'Enfant (1704–1787) depicts the Battle of Fontenoy (1745), an important engagement in the War of the Austrian Succession. The French won a victory over the English army that was defending Austrian territory in the Netherlands.

■ This engraving by Le Mire is called *The Cake of the Kings: First Partition of Poland, 1773.* The monarchs of Russia, Austria, and Prussia join in carving up Poland. The Polish king is clutching his tottering crown.

In 1764, Catherine the Great and Frederick the Great joined to place one of Catherine's former lovers on the Polish throne and to turn Poland into a weak dependent. Russia and Prussia had different interests in Poland's fate. For Russia, Poland represented a vast buffer state that kept the German powers at a distance from Russia's borders. It was more in Russia's interest to dominate Polish foreign policy than to conquer its territory. For Prussia, Poland looked like another helpless flower, "to be picked off leaf by leaf," as Frederick observed. Poland seemed especially appealing because Polish territory, including the Baltic port of Gdansk, separated the Prussian and Brandenburg portions of Frederick's state.

By the 1770s the idea of carving up Poland was being actively discussed in Berlin, Saint Petersburg, and Vienna. Austria, too, had an interest in a Polish partition, especially to maintain its power and status with the other two states, and perhaps to use Polish territory as a potential bargaining chip for the return of Silesia. Finally, in 1772, the three great eastern powers struck a deal. Russia would take a large swath of the grain fields of northeast Poland, which included more than one million people, while Frederick would unite his lands by seizing West Prussia. Austria gained both the largest territories, including Galicia, and the greatest number of people, nearly two million Polish subjects.

In a half century, the balance of power in central Europe had shifted decisively. Prussia's absorption of Silesia and parts of Poland made it a single geographical entity, as well as a great economic and military power. Austria, despite its lost territory, proved capable of surviving the accession of a female ruler and of fighting off an attempt to dismember its empire. Its participation in the partition of Poland strengthened its role in the politics of the eastern powers, while its alliance with France fortified its role in the west. From one empire there were now two states, and the relationship between Prussia and Austria would dominate central Europe for the next century.

THE GREATNESS OF GREAT BRITAIN

By the middle of the eighteenth century, Great Britain had become the leading power of Europe. It had won its spurs in Continental and colonial wars. Britain was unsurpassed as a naval power, able to protect its far-flung trading empire and to make a show of force in almost any part of the world. Perhaps more impressively for a nation that did not support a large standing army, British soldiers had won decisive victories in the European land wars. Until the American Revolution, Britain came up a winner in every military venture it undertook. But might was only one part of British success. Economic preeminence was every bit as important. British colonial possessions in the Atlantic and Indian Oceans poured consumer products into Britain for export to the European marketplaces. (See "The West and the Wider World: The British Raj in India," pp. 554–555.) Growth in overseas trade was matched by growth in home production. British advances in agricultural technique had transformed Britain from an importer to an exporter of grain. The manufacturing industries that other European states attempted to create with huge government subsidies flourished in Britain through private enterprise.

British military and economic power was supported by a unique system of government. In Britain, the nobility served the state through government. The British constitutional system, devised in the seventeenth century and refined in the eighteenth, shared power between the monarchy and the ruling elite through the institution of Parliament. Central government integrated monarch and ministers with chosen representatives from the localities. Such integration not only provided the Crown with the vital information necessary to formulate national policy, but it eased acceptance and enforcement of government decisions. Government was seen as

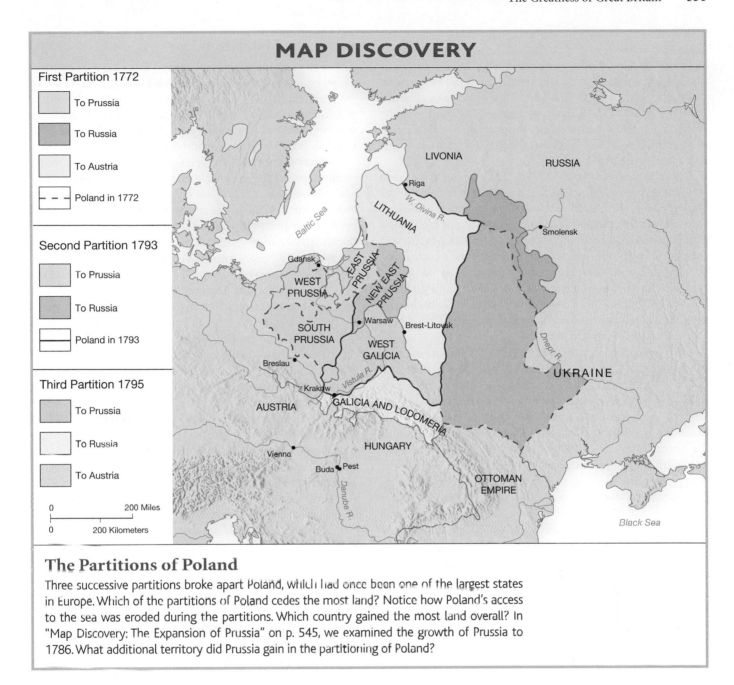

MAP DISCOVERY

First Partition 1772

- To Prussia
- To Russia
- To Austria
- - - - Poland in 1772

Second Partition 1793

- To Prussia
- To Russia
- Poland in 1793

Third Partition 1795

- To Prussia
- To Russia
- To Austria

0   200 Miles
0   200 Kilometers

The Partitions of Poland

Three successive partitions broke apart Poland, which had once been one of the largest states in Europe. Which of the partitions of Poland cedes the most land? Notice how Poland's access to the sea was eroded during the partitions. Which country gained the most land overall? In "Map Discovery: The Expansion of Prussia" on p. 545, we examined the growth of Prussia to 1786. What additional territory did Prussia gain in the partitioning of Poland?

the rule of law that, however imperfect, was believed to operate for the benefit of all.

The parliamentary system gave Britain some of its particular strengths, but they came at a cost. Politics was a national pastime rather than the business of an elite group of administrators and state servants. Decentralization of decision making led to half-measures designed to placate competing interests. Appeals to public opinion, especially by candidates for Parliament, often played upon fears and prejudices that divided rather than united the nation. Moreover, the relative openness of the British system hindered diplomatic and colonial affairs, in which secrecy and rapid changes of direction were often the monarch's most potent weapons. The weaknesses came to light most dramatically during the struggle for

independence waged by Britain's North American colonists. There the clash of principle and power was most extreme and the strengths and weaknesses of parliamentary rule were ruthlessly exposed.

The British Constitution

The British Constitution was a patchwork of laws and customs that was gradually sewn together to form a workable system of government. At the apex of the government stood the monarch, not an absolute monarch like his European counterparts, but not necessarily less powerful for having less arbitrary power. The British people revered monarchy and the monarch. The theory of mixed government depended upon the balance of interests represented by the monarchy in the Crown, the aristocracy in the House of Lords, and the people in the House of Commons. Less abstractly, the monarch was still regarded as divinely ordained and a special gift to the nation. The monarch was the actual and symbolic leader of the nation as well as the Supreme Head of the Church of England. Allegiance to the Anglican Church, whether as a political creed among the elite or as a simple matter of devotion among the populace, intensified allegiance to the Crown.

The partnership between Crown and representative body was best expressed in the idea that the British government was composed of **King-in-Parliament**. Parliament consisted of three separate organs: monarch, lords, and commons. Although each existed separately as a check upon the potential excesses of the others, it was only when the three functioned together that parliamentary government could operate. The king was charged with selecting ministers, initiating policy, and supervising administration. The two houses of Parliament were charged with raising revenue, making laws, and presenting the grievances of subjects to the Crown.

There were 558 members of the House of Commons after the union with Scotland in 1707. Most members of the lower house were nominated to their seats. The largest number of seats were located in small towns where a local oligarchy, or neighboring patron, had a customary right to make nominations that were invariably accepted by the electorate. Even in the largest cities, influential citizens made arrangements for nominating members in order to avoid the cost and confusion of an actual election. Campaigns were ruinously expensive for the candidates—an election in 1754 cost the losing candidates £40,000—and potentially dangerous to the local community, where bitter social and political divisions boiled just below the surface.

The British gentry dominated the Commons, occupying more than 80 percent of the seats in any session. Most of the members also served as unpaid local officials in the counties, as justices of the peace, captains of the local militias, or collectors of local taxes. They came to Parliament not only as representatives of the interests of their class, but as experienced local governors who understood the needs of both Crown and subject.

Nevertheless, the Crown had to develop methods to coordinate the work of the two houses of Parliament and facilitate the passage of governmental programs. The king and his ministers began to use the deep royal pockets of offices and favors to bolster their friends in Parliament. Despite its potential for abuse, it was a political process that integrated center and locality, and at first it worked rather well. Those with local standing were brought into central offices, where they could influence central policy making while protecting their local constituents. The officeholders, who came to be called *placemen,* never constituted a majority of the members of Parliament. They formed the core around which eighteenth-century governments operated, but it was a core that needed direction and cohesion. It was such leadership and organization that was the essential contribution of eighteenth-century politics to the British Constitution.

Parties and Ministers

Although parliamentary management was vital to the British Crown, it was not the Crown that developed the basic tools of management. Rather, those techniques originated within the political community itself, and their usefulness was only slowly grasped by the monarchy. The first and, in the long term, most important tool was the party system.

Political **parties** initially developed in the late seventeenth century around the issue of the Protestant succession. Those who opposed James II because he was a Catholic attempted to exclude him from inheriting the crown. They came to be called by their opponents **Whigs,** which had come to mean "horse thieves" (the term originally derived from *Wiggamore,* a name for Western Isle Scots who cried "Whig, whig!" to spur their horses on). Those who supported James's hereditary rights but who also supported the Anglican Church came to be called by their opponents **Tories,** which in Gaelic meant "cattle rustlers."

The Tories cooperated in the Revolution of 1688 that placed William and Mary on the throne because James had threatened the Anglican Church by tolerating Catholics and because Mary had a legitimate hereditary right to be queen. After the death of Queen Anne in 1714, the Tories supported the succession of James III, James II's Catholic son, who had been raised in France, rather than of George I (1714–1727), prince of Hanover and Protestant great-grandson of James I. An unsuccessful rebellion to place James III on the throne in 1715 discredited the leadership of the Tory party but did not weaken its importance in both local and parliamentary politics.

The Whigs supported the Protestant succession and a broad-based Protestantism. They attracted the allegiance of large numbers of dissenters, heirs to the Puritans of the seventeenth century who practiced forms of Protestantism different from that of the Anglican Church. The struggle between Whigs and Tories was less a struggle for power than it was for loyalty to their opposing viewpoints. As the Tories opposed the Hanoverian succession and the Whigs supported it, it was no mystery which party would find favor with George I. Moreover, as long as there was a pretender to the British throne—another rebellion took place in Scotland in 1745 led by the grandson of James II—the Tories continued to be tarred with the brush of disloyalty.

The division of political sympathies between Whigs and Tories helped create a set of groupings to which parliamentary leadership could be applied. A national rather than a local or regional outlook could be used to organize support for royal policy as long as royal policy conformed to that national outlook. The ascendancy of the Whigs enabled George I and his son George II (1727–1760) to govern effectively through Parliament, but at the price of dependence upon the Whig leaders. Although the monarch had the constitutional freedom to choose his ministers, realistically he could choose only Whigs, and practically none but the Whig leaders of the House of Commons. Happily for the first two Georges, they found Sir Robert Walpole, who was able to manage Parliament but desired only to serve the Crown.

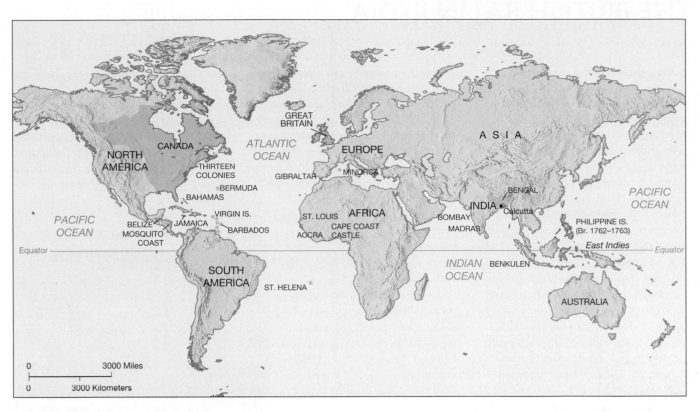

■ The First British Empire (ca. 1763). The empire was the result of commercial enterprise and Britain's military successes.

Sir Robert Walpole (1676–1745) came from a long-established gentry family in Norfolk. Walpole was an early supporter of the Hanoverian succession and an early victim of party warfare. But once George I was securely on the throne, Walpole became an indispensable leader of the House of Commons. His success rested upon his extraordinary abilities: he was an excellent public speaker, he relished long working days and the details of government, and he understood better than anyone else the intricacies of state finance. Walpole became First Lord of the Treasury, a post that he transformed into first minister of state. From his treasury post, Walpole assiduously built a Whig parliamentary party. He carefully dispensed jobs and offices, using them as bait to lure parliamentary supporters. Walpole's organization paid off both in the passage of legislation desired by the Crown and at the polls, where Whigs were returned to Parliament time and again.

From 1721 to 1742, Walpole was the most powerful man in the British government. He refused an offer of a peerage so that he could continue to lead the House of Commons. He brought a measure of fiscal responsibility to government by establishing a fund to pay off the national debt. In foreign policy he pursued peace with the same fervor with which both his predecessors and successors had pursued war. The long years of peace brought prosperity to both the landed and merchant classes, but they also brought criticism of Walpole's methods. The way in which he used government patronage to build his parliamentary party was attacked as corruption. So, too, were the ways in which the pockets of Whig officeholders were lined. During his last decade in office, Walpole struggled to survive. His attempt to extend the excise tax on colonial goods nearly led to his loss of office in 1733. His refusal to respond to the clamor for continued war with Spain in 1741 finally led to his downfall.

Walpole's 20-year rule established the pattern of parliamentary government. The Crown needed a "prime" minister who was able to steer legislation through the House of Commons. It also needed a patronage broker who could take control of the treasury and dispense its largess in return for parliamentary backing. Walpole's personality and talents had combined the two roles. Thereafter they were divided. Those who had grown up under Walpole had learned their lessons well. The Whig monopoly of power continued unchallenged for nearly another 20 years. The patronage network Walpole had created was vastly extended by his Whig successors. Even minor posts in the customs or the excise offices were now exchanged for political favor, and only those approved by the Whig leadership could claim them. The cries of corruption grew louder not only in the country houses of the long-disfranchised Tories, but in the streets of London, where a popular radicalism developed in opposition to the Whig oligarchy. They were taken up as well in the North American colonies, where two million British subjects champed at the bit of imperial rule.

America Revolts

Britain's triumph in the Seven Years' War (1756–1763) had come at great financial cost to the nation. At the beginning of

THE BRITISH RAJ IN INDIA

In the middle of the eighteenth century, the focus of the British Empire shifted from west to east. Up to that point, Britain had only been a bit player in the scramble for the spice trade and had lost the competition for nearly all of the Caribbean and South American commodities, but it had managed to claim much of the Atlantic seaboard of the inhospitable North American continent. There, English, Scots, and Irish settled colonies and built villages and towns. Thousands and then tens of thousands of Britons had made the transatlantic journey throughout the seventeenth century seeking their fortunes in the wilderness. By the middle of the eighteenth century, British North America was a flourishing society that provided a ready market for manufactured and luxury commodities. Over 25 percent of all British exports went to North America, nearly £1 million by 1740.

By contrast, English ventures in the East had resulted in only one success: the right of the East India Company to trade in India. The Mughal emperors granted this right in the early seventeenth century, as much a slight to the Portuguese as a favor to the English. Here, a classic mercantile venture was established. A few hundred Englishmen were placed in forts that contained warehouses for the accumulation of Asian goods and that kept the Westerners largely segregated from the indigenous population. English trade in India grew slowly. Each year the Company would send its fleet of ships to be laden with the merchandise that had been collected from the hinterland. Purchases were made mostly with bullion that was carried to India by the Company's expedition. Brightly colored cottons called chintzes, porcelain, woven carpets, spices, and tea were the most highly prized goods, with tea becoming the most profitable by the beginning of the eighteenth century. The English had taken up residence on the east coast of India where they established their largest base at Calcutta, and it was not long before those who stayed behind became involved in the lucrative trans-Asian trade, especially with China.

Company employees supplemented their meager wages by using their privileged position to exchange Indian goods for Chinese goods. The Indian commodity most prized in China was the drug opium because its production was illegal in China. Other Company members traded with Persia, the great Middle Eastern Empire whose contacts with India went back centuries. In this way, British products like North American tobacco made their way around the globe. Trading on their own accounts while awaiting the arrival of the Company's annual fleet, English merchants in India could make enormous fortunes. If they were lucky enough to survive the perils of Eastern climes and diseases they could return to Britain as wealthy men, "nabobs" in eighteenth-century parlance, belittled for the source of their wealth but tolerated for its quantity.

The British went to India to trade and stayed to rule. The Raj (a Hindi word for kingdom) came about accidentally and by degrees. At the beginning no one would have thought that India could have been conquered and few thought that it could be ruled. It was governed throughout the seventeenth century by the Mughals, Persians who had fled marauding Afghans and who had slowly expanded their power until they established a capital at Agra, where one of their emperors built a palace for his wife known ever after as the Taj Mahal. The Mughals created a magnificent court and were protected by an effi-

■ Oudh watercolor (1782) of British colonial administrator Warren Hastings with a servant. Hastings was the first governor-general of all India, 1773–1784.

ciently trained army. In the areas that they controlled directly they extracted a tax on land—the dirwani—from the entire peasant population. But their hold over the South Asian subcontinent was precarious and ever shifting.

Most of India was ruled by independent princes known as nawabs. They paid a cash tribute to the Mughals when they had to but otherwise fiercely guarded their independence. The East India Company was treated similarly. They had been granted trading rights in return for an annual payment, but unlike the nawabs they had no incentive to weaken Mughal power.

This arrangement worked smoothly until the 1760s. By then the India trade had become essential to the English economy and the number of Englishmen living in Company forts in Bengal had grown to number in the thousands. To protect their large investment and their teeming warehouses, the Company employed former British military officers and soldiers and equipped them with the latest armaments. Not surprisingly, Company leaders were drawn into local disputes where their power was often decisive. As Mughal influence declined, British prestige rose and inevitably a clash occurred. It began not between the British and the Indians, but between the British and the French, the other European nation with a strong presence in India. Wars in Europe that pitted Britain against France expanded to become world wars throughout their colonial empires.

In India it was the military brilliance of a young cavalry officer, Robert Clive, that eventually led to British dominance and the expulsion of the French in the 1760s. Clive was simply an employee of the East India Company and not an agent of the British government. His actions were designed to protect the Company's trading factories—the French had captured Madras in the 1740s—and defend its employees. But British successes made the Mughals wary. In 1756 Mughal forces besieged and captured Calcutta, the most important British trading settlement. The city's governor fled the town and those officials captured by the Mughals were imprisoned in the local jail known descriptively as the Black Hole. The imprisonment of Englishmen in the Black Hole of Calcutta demanded retribution, and Clive inflicted it. Not only

■ In this painting by Edward Penny (1773), Robert Clive is shown receiving a grant from a nawab of Bengal.

did his forces recapture Calcutta, but Clive also connived to oust the Mughal emperor and have him replaced by a rival willing to reconfirm all of Britain's trading rights and also to grant it political control over the province of Bengal. As if he were a local ruler, Clive was offered the dirwani—the right to collect local taxes from the entire population. It was an offer he could not refuse.

It was also the most poisoned of all chalices for the British. Quickly and inevitably the East India Company was drawn into governing Bengal and soon other provinces of India as well. The yield from the dirwani changed the balance of trade in Asia dramatically. Now it was the British who were exporting bullion and creating a drain on the local Indian economy. On the other hand, the Company needed to send thousands of administrators east to

protect their rights and to offer government to the tangle of feuding religious, ethnic, and class interests. Shares of the Company's stock declined while the cost of administering an empire rose. After the American War of Independence, it was in India that British imperial interest and efforts were focused, forging a relationship quite different from the trading partnership with which it had begun.

QUESTIONS FOR DISCUSSION

What was Britain's initial interest in India? What European nation challenged this interest? How did the British East India Company come to rule the province of Bengal and other Indian provinces? How did these developments change Britain's relationship with India?

IMAGE DISCOVERY

The BOSTONIAN'S Paying the EXCISE-MAN, or TARRING & FEATHERING
Plate I.

Bostonians Pay the Excise Man

This 1774 print illustrates Bostonians mocking the loyal British tax collector as a protest against taxed imports. They have tarred and feathered him and are pouring tea into his mouth. Tea is also in the chests that others are dumping into the harbor in the background. What do you know about the revolution in Britain's North American colonies that would explain why tea is featured here? What is the paper pasted to the tree in the background, and what does it mean? Why is there a noose hanging from the Liberty Tree? There are a number of pro-revolutionary symbols in this picture. How might revolutionaries have used this image?

want of trying. In 1763, the king and his ministers agreed that reform of colonial administration was long overdue. Such reform would have the twin benefit of shifting part of the burden of taxation from Britain to North America and of making the commercial side of colonization pay.

That was sound thinking all around, and in due course Parliament passed a series of duties on goods imported into the colonies, including glass, wine, coffee, tea, and, most notably, sugar. The so-called Sugar Act (1764) was followed by the Stamp Act (1765), a tax on printed papers such as newspapers, deeds, and court documents. Both acts imposed taxes in the colonies similar to those that already existed in Britain. Accompanying the acts were administrative orders designed to cut into the lucrative black market trade. The government instituted new rules for searching ships and transferred authority over smuggling from the local colonial courts to Britain's Admiralty courts. Although British officials could only guess at the value of the new duties imposed, it was believed that with effective enforcement £150,000 would be

CHRONOLOGY

The New European Powers

1707	England and Scotland unite to form Great Britain
1713–1714	Peace of Utrecht ends War of the Spanish Succession (1702–1714)
1714	British crown passes to House of Hanover
1721	Treaty of Nystad ends Great Northern War (1700–1721)
1721–1742	Sir Robert Walpole leads British House of Commons
1722	Peter the Great of Russia creates Table of Ranks
1740	Frederick the Great of Prussia invades Austrian province of Silesia
1748	Treaty of Aix-la-Chapelle ends War of the Austrian Succession (1740–1748)
1756–1763	Seven Years' War pits Prussia and Britain against Austria, France, and Russia
1773–1775	Pugachev's revolt in Russia
1774	Boston Tea Party
1775	American Revolution begins
1785	Catherine the Great of Russia issues Charter of the Nobility

the eighteenth century, the national debt stood at £14 million; by 1763, it had risen to £130 million, despite the fact that Walpole's government had been paying off some of it. Then, as now, the cost of world domination was staggering. George III (1760–1820) came to the throne with a taste for reform and a desire to break the Whig stranglehold on government. He was to have limited success on both counts, though not for raised. All that would go to pay the vastly greater costs of colonial administration and security.

British officials were more than perplexed when the mild measures met with a ferocious response. Assemblies of nearly every colony officially protested the Sugar Act. They sent petitions to Parliament begging for repeal and warning of dire economic and political consequences. Riots followed passage of the Stamp Act. Tax collectors were hounded out of office, their resignations precipitated by threats and acts of physical violence. In Massachusetts, mobs that included political leaders in the colony razed the homes of the collector and the lieutenant-governor. However much the colonists might have regretted the violence that was done, they believed that an essential political principle was at stake. It was a principle of the freedom of an Englishman.

At their core, the protests of the American colonists underscored the vitality of the British political system. The Americans argued that they could not be taxed without their consent and that their consent could come only through representation in Parliament. Since there were no colonists in Parliament, Parliament had no jurisdiction over the property of the colonists. Taxation without representation was tyranny. There were a number of subtleties to the argument that were quickly lost as political rhetoric and political action heated up. In the first place, the colonists did tax themselves through their own legislatures, and much of that money paid the costs of administration and defense. Second, as a number of pamphleteers pointed out, no one in the colonies had asked the British government to send regiments of the army into North America. The colonists had little reason to put their faith in British protection. Hard-fought colonial victories were tossed away at European negotiating tables, while the British policy of defending Indian

rights in the Ohio Valley ran counter to the interests of the settlers. When defense was necessary, the colonists had proved themselves both able and cooperative in providing it. A permanent tax meant a permanent army, and a standing army was as loathed in Britain as it was in the colonies.

In opposing the Stamp Act, colonists also tried to draw a distinction between internal and external taxation. They deemed regulation of overseas commerce a legitimate power of Parliament but argued that the regulation of internal exchange was not. But that distinction was lost once the issue of parliamentary representation was raised. If the colonists had not consented to British taxation, then it made no difference whether taxation was internal or external. The passion generated in the colonies was probably no greater than that generated in Britain. The British government also saw the confrontation as a matter of principle, but for Britain the principle was parliamentary sovereignty. That, above all, was the rock upon which the British Constitution had been built over the previous century. Parliament had entered into a partnership with the Crown. The Crown had surrendered—willingly or not—many of its prerogatives. In return, Parliament had bound the people to obedience. There were well-established means by which British subjects could petition Parliament for redress of grievances against the monarch, but there were no channels by which they could question the sovereignty of Parliament.

Once the terms of debate had been so defined, it was difficult for either side to find a middle ground. Parliamentary moderates managed repeal of the Stamp Act and most of the clauses of the Sugar Act, but they also joined in passing the **Declaratory Act** (1766), which stated unequivocally that Parliament held sovereign jurisdiction over the colonies "in all

UNALIENABLE RIGHTS

The Declaration of Independence, written by Thomas Jefferson (1776), succinctly summarized the principles on which the American colonists were to build a new form of democratic government.

Focus Questions

Why is it a "duty" to oppose an oppressive government? What is the purpose of government?

We hold these truths to be self-evident, that all men are created equal, that they are endowed by their Creator with certain unalienable Rights, that among these are Life, Liberty, and the pursuit of Happiness. That to secure these rights, Governments are instituted among Men, deriving their just powers from the consent of the governed. That whenever any Form of Government becomes destructive of these ends, it is the Right of the People to alter or to abolish it, and to institute new Government, laying its foundation on such princi-

ples and organizing its powers in such form, as to them shall seem most likely to effect their Saftey and Happiness. Prudence, indeed, will dictate that Governments long established should not be changed for light and transient causes; and accordingly all experience hath shown that mankind are more disposed to suffer, while evils are sufferable, that to right themselves by abolishing the forms to which they are accustomed. But when a long train of abuses and usurpations pursuing invariably the same Object evinces a design to reduce them under absolute Despotism, it is their right, it is their duty, to throw off such Government, and to provide new Guards for their future security.

From The Declaration of Independence.

cases whatsoever." That was a claim that became more and more difficult to sustain as colonial leaders began to cite the elements of resistance theory that had justified the Revolution of 1688. Then the protest had been against the tyranny of the king; the new protest was against the tyranny of Parliament. American propagandists claimed that a conspiracy existed to deprive the colonists of their property and rights and to enslave them for the benefit of special interests and corrupt politicians.

The techniques of London radicals who opposed parliamentary policy were imported into the colonies. Newspapers were used to whip up public support; boycotts brought ordinary people into the political arena; public demonstrations such as the Boston Tea Party (1774) were carefully designed to intimidate; mobs were occasionally given free rein. Although the government had faced down those tactics when they were used in London to support John Wilkes (1725–1797), an ardent critic of royal policy, it was less successful when the crisis lay an ocean away. When, in 1770, British troops fired on a Boston mob, American propagandists were provided with empirical evidence that Britain intended to enslave the colonies. Violence was met by violence, passion by passion. In 1775, full-scale fighting was under way. Eight years later, Britain withdrew from a war it could not win, and the American colonies were left to govern themselves.

CONCLUSION

By the end of the third quarter of the eighteenth century, Europe had a new political configuration. A continent once dominated by a single power—Spain in the sixteenth century and France in the seventeenth—was now dominated by a state system in which alliances among several great powers held the balance. Despite the loss of its American colonies, Great Britain had proved the most potent of the states. Its victories over the French in the Seven Years' War and over France and Prussia in the War of the Austrian Succession secured its position. But it was a position that could be maintained only through alliances with the German states, with either Prussia or Austria. The rise of Prussia provided a counterweight to French domination of the Continent. Although those two states became allies in the middle of the century, the ambitions of their rulers made them natural enemies, and it would not be long before French and Prussian armies were again pitted against each other. France, still the wealthiest and most populous of European states, had slumbered through the eighteenth-century reorganization. The legacies of Louis XIV took a long time to reach fruition. He had claimed glory for his state, giving the French people a sense of national identity and national destiny, but making them pay an enormous price in social and economic dislocation. Thus the mid-eighteenth century was to be an age of the greatest literary and philosophical achievement for France, but the late eighteenth century was to be an age of the greatest social upheaval that Europe had ever known.

QUESTIONS FOR REVIEW

1. What were the great powers of Europe in the eighteenth century, and in what ways was there a "balance of power" among them?
2. What did Peter I and Catherine II of Russia accomplish during their reigns that justifies the title "the great"?
3. How was the tiny state of Brandenburg-Prussia able to make itself into one of Europe's major powers, and what did that mean for the Austrian Empire?
4. How did Britain's theory of mixed government and its parliamentary party system assist its rise to become Europe's great imperial power?
5. How and why did the "balance of power" shift during the eighteenth century?

KEY TERMS

Charter of the Nobility, *p. 543*
Declaratory Act, *p. 557*
King-in-Parliament, *p. 552*
parties, *p. 552*
Pragmatic Sanction, *p. 547*
Table of Ranks, *p. 541*
Tories, *p. 552*
Whigs, *p. 552*

DISCOVERING WESTERN CIVILIZATION ONLINE

You can obtain more information about the balance of power in eighteenth-century Europe at the Websites listed below. See also the Companion Website that accompanies this text, www.ablongman.com/kishlansky, which contains an online study guide and additional resources.

The Rise of Russia

Russia
www.english.upenn.edu/~jlynch/FrankenDemo/Places/russia.html
A site detailing the history of Russia from the time of Peter the Great. Links to the building of St. Petersburg.

Modern History Sourcebook: Catherine the Great
www.fordham.edu/halsall/mod/18catherine.html
Sources from the reign of Catherine the Great.

The Two Germanies

Friedrich II, the Great (1712–1786)
www.hfac.uh.edu/gbrown/philosophers/leibniz/FriedrichGreat/FriedrichGreat.html
A hyper-linked biographical essay on Frederick the Great of Prussia.

The Greatness of Great Britain

The American Revolution
www.revolution.h-net.msu.edu/

A site with extensive links to all aspects of the American Revolution.

Declaring Independence: Drafting the Documents
www.loc.gov/exhibits/declara/declara1.html
An online exhibit at the Library of Congress on the drafting of the Declaration of Independence.

SUGGESTIONS FOR FURTHER READING

General Reading

M. S. Anderson, *Europe in the Eighteenth Century, 1713–1783*, 3d ed. (London: Longman, 1987). A country-by-country survey of political developments.

Jeremy Black, *Europe and the World 1650–1830* (New York: Routledge, 2002). An intelligent survey of Europe in a wider perspective.

David Kirby, *Northern Europe in the Early Modern Period* (London: Longman, 1991). Political history from a Baltic perspective, with excellent chapters on Sweden and Russia.

Nicholas Riasanovsky, *A History of Russia* (New York: Oxford University Press, 1993). The best one-volume history of Russia.

Geographical Tour: Europe in 1714

Derek McKay and H. M. Scott, *The Rise of the Great Powers* (London: Longman, 1983). An outstanding survey of diplomacy and warfare.

The Rise of Russia

John T. Alexander, *Catherine the Great: Life and Legend* (Oxford: Oxford University Press, 1989). A lively account of the public and private life of the Russian Empress.

M. S. Anderson, *Peter the Great* (London: Thames and Hudson, 1978). A well-constructed, comprehensive biography.

James Cracraft, *The Revolution of Peter the Great* (Cambridge: Harvard University Press, 2006). The latest biography of Russia's Westernizing ruler.

Paul Dukes, *The Making of Russian Absolutism, 1613–1801* (London: Longman, 1982). An extensive survey of the Russian monarchy in its greatest period.

Lindsey Hughes, *Russia in the Age of Peter the Great* (New Haven, CT: Yale University Press, 1998). A detailed, thematically organized reappraisal of Russia in the era of Peter's reign.

William B. Whisenhunt and Peter Stearns, *Catherine the Great: Enlightened Empress of Russia* (New York: Longman, 2006). The very latest biography of Russia's female "Enlightened Despot."

The Two Germanies

Reed S. Browning, *The War of the Austrian Succession* (London: Macmillan, 1995). A comprehensive history of a complicated event.

David Fraser, *Frederick the Great: King of Prussia* (New York: Allen Lane, 2001). A recent biography that is very readable.

J. Gagliardo, *Germany Under the Old Regime* (London: Longman, 1991). The best single-volume history.

H. W. Koch, *A History of Prussia* (London: Longman, 1978). A study of the factors that led to Prussian dominance of Germany.

C. A. Macartney, *Maria Theresa and the House of Austria* (Mystic, CT: Verry Inc., 1969). Still the best introductory study.

The Greatness of Great Britain

Bernard Bailyn, *The Ideological Origins of the American Revolution* (Cambridge, MA: Harvard University Press, 1967). A brilliant interpretation of the underlying causes of the break between Britain and the North American colonies.

Jeremy Black, *Britain as a Military Power* (London: UCL Press, 1999). A reliable survey of military developments in Britain.

John Brewer, *The Sinews of Power: War, Money, and the English State, 1688–1783* (Cambridge, MA: Harvard University Press, 1990). An influential and clearly written book on the fiscal and military innovations that underwrote English power in the eighteenth century.

J. C. D. Clark, *English Society, 1688–1832* (Cambridge: Cambridge University Press, 1985). A bold reinterpretation of the most important features of English society.

Linda Colley, *Britons* (New Haven, CT: Yale University Press, 1992). A lively account of how a nation was forged from Welsh, Scots, and English and how unity and diversity intermixed.

Paul Langford, *A Polite and Commercial People: England 1727–1783* (Oxford: Oxford University Press, 1989). The standard survey in the Oxford history series.

Charles Spencer, *Battle for Europe: How the Duke of Marlborough Masterminded the Defeat of the French at Blenheim* (Hoboken, NJ: Wiley, 2005). An exciting popular account of the climactic battle of Blenheim.

Gordon Wood, *The Radicalism of the American Revolution* (New York: Alfred A. Knopf, 1992). How the ideals of the American Revolution shaped an emerging nation.

For a list of additional titles related to this chapter's topics, please see http://www.ablongman.com/kishlansky.

19 CULTURE AND SOCIETY IN EIGHTEENTH-CENTURY EUROPE

HAPPY FAMILIES

AN ENLIGHTENMENT INSTITUTION

"Happy families are all alike," wrote Lev Tolstoy in the nineteenth century when the idea of a happy family was already a cliché. Such an idea would never have occurred to his eighteenth-century forebears. For them the happy family was new. Personal happiness was an invention of the Enlightenment, the result of novel attitudes about human aspirations and human capabilities. "Happiness is a new idea in Europe," wrote Louis de Saint-Just (1767–1794). It emerged in response to

THE VISUAL RECORD

the belief that what was good brought pleasure and what was evil brought pain. Happiness, both individual and collective, became the yardstick by which life was measured. That meant a reorientation in personal conduct and, most of all, a reorientation of family life. Especially for those with an economic cushion, a pleasurable family life became essential. Husbands and wives were to be companions, filled with romantic love for each other and devoted to domestic bliss. Children, the product of their affection, were to be doted on, treated not as miniature adults to be lectured and beaten, but as unfilled vessels into which was poured all that was good.

Were ever a couple more in love than the husband and wife depicted in *A Visit to the Wet Nurse* by Jean-Honoré Fragonard (1732–1806)? In the painting, the man clasps his wife's arm to his cheek, she lays her hand on his shoulder. Their sighs are almost audible! Together they admire the fruit of their love, the baby asleep in the cradle. It is hard to guess which parent dotes more, the mother with her rapturous expression or the father with his intensity as he kneels on a cushion in almost religious devotion, his hands folded as if in prayer. Who would doubt their companionship or their love for their babe? They have come together to see how the wet nurse is caring for their child.

At the beginning of the eighteenth century, the use of a wet nurse was still common among the families of the French bourgeoisie, the class to which the couple pictured belonged. As time passed, however, more and more families began to keep their children at home and more mothers began to nurse their babies themselves. In part this change was a response to the higher mortality rate among infants sent out to wet nurses. But a wet nurse who could be supervised, that is, one who lived near enough to be visited, but far enough away from the town to enjoy wholesome air, might be the best of both worlds. That is just what the couple here found, and in the picture they come, with their other child (the boy in the hat), to see their baby sleeping peacefully, the wet nurse sitting attentively at the infant's side.

But there are two families in this picture, and they are hardly alike. At first glance, the wet nurse looks like an old woman, perhaps even an aging nanny. She sits with her distaff in her hand, for the arrival of her clients has interrupted her spinning. It is shocking to realize that she cannot be much older than 30, an age beyond which wealthy families would not hire her for fear either that she would not have much milk or that it would be sour. The two younger children on the far right are undoubtedly hers, the youngest probably just weaned so that all of the milk would go to the baby. No adoring husband sits beside the wet nurse. Her husband, if he is still alive, is hard at work with no leisure time for visits to the country. Not only does the wet nurse have to sell her milk, but she also spins, to keep her family clothed and to earn a little extra to put away for hard times.

The newest fads of the age have passed her family by. While the child in the cradle will be spoiled by toys manufactured especially for children—puzzles, games, rocking horses, and balls—the children of the wet nurse must make do with household objects and their own imaginations. A ball of yarn thrown to the cat helps the elder child while away the hours.

LOOKING AHEAD

Like much else in the eighteenth century, the world of the family was divided between high and low. As we shall see in this chapter, it was changes to the middle that were most characteristic of eighteenth-century social and cultural developments. The spirit of Enlightenment was spreading from the elites throughout all social ranks, improving education, health, and social welfare. The rapid growth of the bourgeoisie, or the middle class, enhanced the quality of life for tens of thousands and transformed values in the most basic institutions of society.

■ Jean Honoré Fragonard, *A Visit to the Wet Nurse*.

EIGHTEENTH-CENTURY CULTURE

The eighteenth century spawned a rich and costly culture. Decorative architecture, especially interior design, reflected the increasing sociability of the aristocracy. Entertainment became a central part of aristocratic life, losing its previous formality. Music became a cultural passion. The string quartet made its first appearance in the eighteenth century, and chamber music enjoyed unparalleled popularity. Only the wealthiest could afford to stage private operas, the other musical passion of the age. The Esterhazys of Hungary employed 22 musicians and a conductor, who for most of the late eighteenth century was Joseph Haydn (1732–1809), the father of the modern symphony. Haydn's post was not an honorary

one. In addition to hiring and managing the orchestra, he was expected to direct two operas and two concerts a week, as well as the music for Sunday services. An aristocratic patron was essential for the aspiring composer. If he could not find one or if, like Wolfgang Amadeus Mozart (1756–1791), he could not bend his will to one, he could not flourish. While Haydn lived comfortably in a palace, Mozart, probably the greatest musical genius in Western history, lived impoverished in a garret and died at age 35 from lack of medical attention.

Musical entertainments in European country houses were matched by the literary and philosophical entertainments of the urban **salons.** Papers on scientific and literary subjects were read at gala dinner parties and discussed with great seriousness in drawing rooms. In the salons, most of which were organized by the wives and daughters of the nobility, were to be found the most influential thinkers of the day presenting the ideas of the **Enlightenment,** a new European outlook on religion, society, and politics.

The Enlightenment

The Enlightenment was less a set of ideas than it was a set of attitudes. At its core was criticism, a questioning of traditional institutions, customs, and morals. In 1762, the French philosopher Jean-Jacques Rousseau (1712–1778) published one of the most important works on social theory, *The Social Contract*, which

■ Painting of the Mozart family by Johann Nepomuk della Croce, ca. 1781. Wolfgang Amadeus Mozart plays the harpsichord, accompanied by his father Leopold and his sister Nannerl. As a boy, Mozart won great ovations on concert tours throughout Europe and persistently challenged authority.

■ During the Enlightenment, salons showcased the most influential thinkers of the day. Here, a lecture is being given at the house of Madame Geoffrin.

THE ALL-KNOWING

The Encyclopedia *was one of the great collaborative ventures of the new spirit of reason that so characterized the Enlightenment. Following is the* Encyclopedia's *entry on itself, the purpose of compiling human knowledge in book form.*

Focus Questions

What is the purpose of an encyclopedia according to Diderot? Why can an encyclopedia only be attempted in a "philosophical" age, and what kind of age is that?

Encyclopedia . . . in truth, the aim of an *encyclopedia* is to collect all the knowledge scattered over the face of the earth, to present its general outlines and structure to the men with whom we live, and to transmit this to those who will come after us, so that the work of past centuries may be useful to the following centuries, that our children, by becoming more educated, may at the same time become more virtuous and happier, and that we may not die without having deserved well of the human race. . . .

I have said that it could only belong to a philosophical age to attempt an *encyclopedia*; and I have said this because such a work constantly demands more intellectual daring than is commonly found in [less courageous periods]. All things must be examined, debated, investigated without exception and without regard for anyone's feelings. . . . We must ride roughshod over all these ancient puerilities, overturn the barriers that reason never erected, give back to the arts and sciences the liberty that is so precious to them. . . . We have for quite some time needed a reasoning age when men would no longer seek the rules in classical authors but in nature. . . .

From Denis Diderot, *Encyclopedia* (1751–1772).

opened with the gripping maxim, "Man is born free and everywhere he is in chains." But most of the great thinkers of the Enlightenment were not so much philosophers as savants, knowledgeable popularizers whose skills were in simplifying and publicizing a hodgepodge of new views.

In France, Enlightenment intellectuals were called **philosophes** and claimed all the arts and sciences as their purview. The *Encyclopedia* (35 volumes, 1751–1780), edited by Denis Diderot (1713–1784), was one of the greatest achievements of the age. Titled *Systematic Dictionary of the Sciences, Arts, and Crafts,* it attempted to summarize all acquired knowledge and to dispel all imposed superstitions. There was no better definition of a philosophe than that given them by one of their enemies: "Just what is a philosophe? A kind of monster in society who feels under no obligation towards its manners and morals, its proprieties, its politics, or its religion. One may expect anything from men of their ilk."

The influence of French counterculture on enlightened thought was great, but the Enlightenment was by no means a strictly French phenomenon. Its greatest figures included the Scottish economist Adam Smith (1723–1790), the Italian legal reformer Cesare Beccaria (1738–1794), and the German philosopher Immanuel Kant (1724–1804). In France, it began among anti-establishment critics; in Scotland and the German states, it flourished in the universities; in Prussia, Austria, and Russia, it was propagated by the monarchy. The Enlightenment began in the 1730s and was still going strong a half century later when its attitudes had been absorbed into the mainstream of European thought.

No brief summary can do justice to the diversity of enlightened thought in eighteenth-century Europe. Because it was an attitude of mind rather than a set of shared beliefs, there are many contradictory strains to follow. In his famous essay *What Is Enlightenment?* (1784), Immanuel Kant described it simply as freedom to use one's own intelligence. "I hear people clamor on all sides: Don't argue! The officer says: Don't argue, drill! The tax collector says: Don't argue, pay. The pastor says: Don't argue, believe." To all of them Kant replied: "Dare to know! Have the courage to use your own intelligence."

DOCUMENT

Kant, *What Is Enlightenment?*

The Spirit of the Enlightenment

In 1734, there appeared in France a small book titled *Philosophical Letters Concerning the English Nation.* Its author, Voltaire (1694–1778), had spent two years in Britain, and while

---

CANDIDE

Voltaire's great comic novel Candide *told the story of a too credulous boy and his too other-worldly tutor Dr. Pangloss, whose philosophy was summed up in the statement "this is the best of all possible worlds and all things turn out for the best."*

Focus Questions

Why does Pangloss remind Candide of the fate of kings? How does Cunegund reckon that everything turns out for the best? What is Voltaire's philosophy for the individual?

"Human grandeur," said Pangloss, "is very dangerous, if we believe the testimonies of almost all philosophers; for we find Eglon, King of Moab, was assassinated by Aod; Absalom was hanged by the hair of his head, and run through with three darts; King Nadab, son of Jeroboam, was slain by Baaza; King Ela by Zimri; Okosias by Jehu; Athaliah by Jehoiada; the Kings Jehooiakim, Jeconiah, and Zedekiah, were led into captivity: I need not tell you what was the fate of Croesus, Astyages, Darius, Dionysius of Syracuse, Pyrrhus, Perseus, Hannibal, Jugurtha, Ariovistus, Caesar, Pompey, Nero, Otho, Vitellius, Domitian, Richard II of England, Edward II, Henry VI, Richard III, Mary Stuart, Charles I, the three Henrys of France, and the Emperor Henry IV."

"Neither need you tell me," said Candide, "that we must take care of our garden."

"You are in the right," said Pangloss; "for when man was put into the garden of Eden, it was with an intent to dress it; and this proves that man was not born to be idle."

"Work then without disputing," said Martin; "it is the only way to render life supportable."

The little society, one and all, entered into this laudable design and set themselves to exert their different talents. The little piece of ground yielded them a plentiful crop. Cunegund indeed was very ugly, but she became an excellent hand at pastrywork: Pacquette embroidered; the old woman had the care of the linen. There was none, down to Brother Giroflee, but did some service; he was a very good carpenter, and became an honest man. Pangloss used now and then to say to Candide:

"There is a concatenation of all events in the best of possible worlds; for, in short, had you not been kicked out of a fine castle for the love of Miss Cunegund; had you not been put into the Inquisition; had you not traveled over America on foot; had you not run the Baron through the body; and had you not lost all your sheep, which you brought from the good country of El Dorado, you would not have been here to eat preserved citrons and pistachio nuts."

"Excellently observed," answered Candide; "but let us cultivate our garden."

Voltaire, *Candide* (1759).

there he had made it his business to study the differences between the peoples of the two nations. In a simple but forceful style, Voltaire demonstrated time and again the superiority of the British. They practiced religious toleration and were not held under the sway of a venal clergy. They valued people for their merits rather than their birth. Their political constitution was a marvel: "The English nation is the only one on earth that has succeeded in controlling the power of kings by resisting them." They made national heroes of their scientists, poets, and philosophers. In all of this, Voltaire contrasted British virtue with French vice. He attacked the French clergy and nobility directly, the French monarchy implicitly. Not only did he praise the genius and accomplishments of Sir Isaac Newton above those of René Descartes, but he also graphically contrasted the Catholic Church's persecution of Descartes with the British state's celebration of Newton. "England, where men think free and noble thoughts," Voltaire enthused.

Voltaire.   It is difficult to recapture the psychological impact that the *Philosophical Letters* had on the generation of educated Frenchmen who first read them. The book was officially banned and publicly burned, and a warrant was issued for Voltaire's arrest. The *Letters* dropped like a bombshell upon the moribund intellectual culture of the Church and the universities and burst open the complacent, self-satisfied Cartesian worldview. The book ignited in France a movement that would soon be found in nearly every corner of Europe.

DOCUMENT

Voltaire on Relations Between Church and State

Born in Paris in 1694 into a bourgeois family with court office, François-Marie Arouet, who later took the pen name Voltaire, was educated by the Jesuits, who encouraged his poetic talents and instilled in him an enduring love of literature. He was a difficult student, especially as he had already rejected the core of the Jesuits' religious doctrine. He was no less difficult as he grew older and began a career as a poet and playwright. It was not long before he was imprisoned in the Bastille for penning verses that maligned the honor of the regent of France. Released from prison, he insulted a nobleman, who retaliated by having his servants publicly beat Voltaire. Voltaire issued a challenge for a duel, a greater insult than the first, given his low birth. Again he was sent to the Bastille and was only released on the promise that he would leave the country immediately.

Thus Voltaire found himself in Britain, where he spent two years learning English, writing plays, and enjoying his celebrity free from the dangers that celebrity entailed in France. When he returned to Paris in 1728, it was with the intention of popularizing Britain to Frenchmen. He wrote and produced a number of plays and began writing the *Philosophical Letters,* a work that not only secured his reputation but also forced him into exile at the village of Cirey, where he moved in with the Marquise du Châtelet (1706–1749).

The Marquise du Châtelet, though only 27 at the time of her liaison with Voltaire, was one of the leading advocates of Newtonian science in France. She built a laboratory in her home and introduced Voltaire to experimental science. While she undertook the immense challenge of translating Newton into French, Voltaire worked on innumerable projects: poems, plays, philosophical and antireligious tracts (which she wisely kept him from publishing), and histories. It was one of the most productive periods of his life, and when the Marquise du Châtelet died in 1749, Voltaire was crushed.

Then older than 50, Voltaire began his travels. He was invited to Berlin by Frederick the Great, who admired him most of all the intellectuals of the age. The relationship between the two great egotists was predictably stormy and resulted in Voltaire's arrest in Frankfurt. Finally allowed to leave Prussia, Voltaire eventually settled in Geneva, where he quickly became embroiled in local politics and was none too politely asked to leave. He was tired of wandering and tired of being chased. His youthful gaiety and high spirits, which remained in Voltaire long past youth, were dealt a serious blow by the tragic earthquake in Lisbon in 1755, when thousands of people attending church services were killed.

Optimism in the face of such a senseless tragedy was no longer possible. His black mood was revealed in *Candide* (1759), which was to become his enduring legacy. *Candide* introduced the ivory-tower intellectual Dr. Pangloss, the overly optimistic Candide, and the very practical philosophy, "We must cultivate our own garden." It was Voltaire's capacity to challenge all authority that was probably his greatest contribution to Enlightenment attitudes. He held nothing sacred. He questioned

■ Portrait of Voltaire, the most famous of the *philosophes*. Voltaire sought to reinvent the universe of knowledge.

his own paternity and the morals of his mother; he lived openly with the Marquise du Châtelet and her husband; and he spoke as slightingly of kings and aristocrats as he did of his numerous critics. At the height of the French Revolution, Voltaire's body was removed from its resting place in Champagne and taken in great pomp to Paris, where it was interred in the Panthéon, where the heroes of the nation were put to rest. "Voltaire taught us to be free" was the slogan that the Parisian masses chanted during the funeral procession. It was an ending perhaps too solemn and conventional for one as irreverent as Voltaire. When the monarchy was restored after 1815, his bones were unceremoniously dumped into a lime pit.

Hume. Some enlightened thinkers based their critical outlook on **skepticism**, the belief that nothing could be known for certain. When the Scottish philosopher David Hume (1711–1776) was accused of being an atheist, he countered the charge by saying he was too skeptical to be certain that God did not exist. Hume's first major philosophical work, *A Treatise of Human Nature* (1739), made absolutely no impres-

■ Scottish philosopher David Hume argued that neither matter nor mind could be proved to exist with any certainty.

sion upon his contemporaries. For a time he took a post as a merchant's clerk, then he served as a tutor, and finally he found a position as a private secretary. During the course of his various employments he continued to write, publishing a series of essays on the subject of morality and rewriting his treatise into *An Enquiry Concerning Human Understanding* (1748), his greatest philosophical work.

Hume made two seminal contributions to Enlightenment thought. He exploded the synthesis of Descartes by arguing that neither matter nor mind could be proved to exist with any certainty. He believed that only perceptions existed, either as impressions of material objects or as ideas and if human understanding was based on sensory perception rather than on reason, then there could be no certainty in the universe. Hume's second point launched a frontal attack upon established religion: if there could be no certainty, then the revealed truths of Christian religion could have no basis. In his historical analysis of the origins of religion, Hume argued that "religion grows out of hope or fear." He attacked the core of Christian explanations based on either Providence or miracles by arguing that to anyone who understood the basis of human perception it would take a miracle to believe in miracles.

Montesquieu. In 1749, Hume received in the mail a work from an admiring Frenchman, titled *The Spirit of the Laws*. The sender was Charles-Louis de Secondat, Baron Montesquieu (1689–1755). Born in Bordeaux, he ultimately inherited both a large landed estate and the office of president of the Parlement of Bordeaux. His novel *Persian Letters* (1721) was a brilliant satire of Parisian morals, French society, and European religion all bound together by the story of a Persian despot who leaves his harem to learn about the ways of the world. The use of the Persian outsider allowed Montesquieu to comment on the absurdity of European customs in general and French practices in particular. The device of the harem allowed him to titillate his audience with exotic sexuality.

After that success, Montesquieu decided to sell his office and make the grand tour. He spent nearly two years in England, for which, like Voltaire, he came to have the greatest admiration. Back in Bordeaux, Montesquieu began to assemble his thoughts for what he believed would be a great work of political theory. The two societies that he most admired were ancient Rome and the then present-day Britain, and he studied the forms of their government and the principles that animated them. *The Spirit of the Laws* was published in 1748, and despite its gargantuan size and densely packed examples, it was immediately recognized as a masterpiece. Catherine the Great of Russia kept it at her bedside, and it was the single most influential work for the framers of the United States Constitution.

In both *Persian Letters* and *The Spirit of the Laws* Montesquieu explored how liberty could be achieved and despotism avoided. He divided all forms of government into republics, monarchies, and despotisms. Each form had its own peculiar spirit: virtue and moderation in republics, honor in monarchies, and fear in despotisms. Like each form, each spirit was prone to abuse and had to be restrained if re-

IMAGE DISCOVERY

The Spirit of the Laws

The frontispiece of Montesquieu's major work of political philosophy, *The Spirit of the Laws*, has a medallion of the author surrounded by allegorical figures of classical, often Greek, mythology. If you had lived in the eighteenth century, what would you have imagined about the author and the book from looking at this title page? The blindfolded figure is Justice, and Montesquieu argued that a people define justice and principles of good laws according to their environment. If Montesquieu thought that justice was fluid and did not exist except as defined collectively by a society, why would he have featured the personification of Justice at the beginning of his book?

strate how moderation could be maintained through rules and restraints, through the spirit of the law.

For Montesquieu, a successful government was one in which powers were separated and checks and balances existed within the institutions of the state. As befit a provincial magistrate, he insisted on the absolute separation of the judiciary from all other branches of government. The law needed to be independent and impartial, and it needed to be just. Montesquieu advocated that law codes be reformed and reduced mainly to regulate crimes against persons and property. Punishment should fit the crime but should be humane. Montesquieu was one of the first to advocate the abolition of torture. Like most Europeans of his age, he saw monarchy as the only realistic form of government, but he argued that for a monarchy to be successful, it needed a strong and independent aristocracy to restrain its tendency toward corruption and despotism. He based his arguments on what he believed was the case in Britain, which he praised as the only state in Europe in which liberty resided.

Enlightened Education and Social Reform. Enlightened thinkers attacked established institutions, above all the Church. Most were deists who believed in the existence of God on rational grounds only. Following the materialistic ideas of the new science, **deists** believed that nature conformed to its own material laws and operated without divine intervention. God, in a popular Enlightenment image, was like a clockmaker who constructed the elaborate mechanism, wound it, and gave the pendulum its first swing. After that the clock worked by itself. Deists were accused of being anti-Christian, and they certainly opposed the ritual forms of both Catholic and Protestant worship. They also opposed the role of the Church in education, for education was the key to an enlightened view of the future. That meant, above all, conflict with the Jesuits. "Let's eat a Jesuit," was Voltaire's half-facetious comment.

Jean-Jacques Rousseau attacked the educational system. His tract on education, disguised as the romantic novel *Émile* (1762), argued that children should be taught by appealing to their interests rather than with strict discipline. Education was crucial because the Enlightenment was dominated by the idea of the British philosopher John Locke (1632–1704) that the mind was blank at birth, a *tabula rasa*—"white paper void of all characters"—and that it was filled up by experience. Contrary to the arguments of Descartes, Locke wrote in *An Essay Concerning Human Understanding* (1690) that there were no innate ideas and no good or evil that was not conditioned by experience. For Locke, as for a host of thinkers after him, good and evil were defined as pleasure and pain: people did good because it was pleasurable and avoided evil because it was painful. Morality was a sense experience rather than a theological experience. It was also relative rather than absolute, an observation that derived from increased interest in non-European cultures. The *Persian Letters* of Baron Montesquieu was the most popular of a genre describing non-European societies that knew nothing of Christian morality.

publics were not to give way to vice and excess, monarchies to corruption, and despotisms to repression. Montesquieu classified regimes as either moderate or immoderate, and through the use of extensive historical examples attempted to demon-

■ Jean-Jacques Rousseau produced one of the greatest works of the Enlightenment, *The Social Contract* (1762), in which he envisioned a society capable of controlling evil. This portrait was painted by Maurice Quentin around 1740.

By the middle of the eighteenth century, the pleasure/pain principle enunciated by Locke had come to be applied to the foundations of social organization. If personal good was pleasure, then social good was happiness. The object of government, in the words of the Scottish moral philosopher Francis Hutcheson (1694–1746), was "the greatest happiness of the greatest number." The principle was at the core of *Crimes and Punishments* (1764), Cesare Beccaria's pioneering work of legal reform. Laws were instituted to promote happiness within society. They had to be formulated equitably for both criminal and victim. Punishment was to act as a deterrent to crime rather than as retribution. Therefore, Beccaria advocated the abolition of torture to gain confessions, the end of capital punishment, and the rehabilitation of criminals through the improvement of penal institutions. By 1776, happiness was established as one of the basic rights of man, enshrined in the American Declaration of Independence as "life, liberty, and the pursuit of happiness."

It was in refashioning the world through education and social reform that the Enlightenment revealed its orientation toward the future. *Optimism* was a word invented in the eighteenth century to express the feeling of liberation from the weight of centuries of traditions. "This is the best of all possible worlds and all things turn out for the best," was the satirical slogan of Voltaire's *Candide*. But if Voltaire believed that enlightened thinkers had taken optimism too far, others believed that it had to be taken further still.

Progress, an idea that not all enlightened thinkers shared, was another invention of the age. It was expressed most cogently by the French philosopher the Marquis de Condorcet (1743–1794) in *The Progress of the Human Mind* (1795), in which he developed an almost evolutionary view of human development from a savage state of nature to a future of harmony and international peace.

The Impact of the Enlightenment

As there was no single set of Enlightenment beliefs, so there was no single impact of the Enlightenment. Its general influence was felt everywhere, even seeping to the lowest strata of society. Its specific influence is harder to gauge. Paradoxically, enlightened political reform took firmer root in eastern Europe, where the ideas were imported, than in western Europe, where they originated. It was absolute rulers who were most successful in borrowing Enlightenment reforms.

It is impossible to determine what part enlightened ideas and what part practical necessities played in the eastern European reform movement that began around midcentury. In at least three areas, the coincidence between ideas and actions was especially strong: law, education, and religious toleration. Law was the basis of Enlightenment views of social interaction, and the influence of Montesquieu and Beccaria spread quickly. In Prussia and Russia, the movement to codify and simplify the legal system did not reach fruition in the eighteenth century, but in both places it was well under way. The Prussian jurist Samuel von Cocceji (1679–1755) initiated the reform of Prussian law and legal administration. Cocceji's project was to make the enforcement of law uniform throughout the realm to prevent judicial corruption and to produce a single code of Prussian law. The code, finally completed in the 1790s, reflected the principles of criminal justice articulated by Beccaria. In Russia, the Law Commission summoned by Catherine the Great in 1767 never completed its work. Nevertheless, profoundly influenced by Montesquieu, Catherine attempted to abolish torture and to introduce the Beccarian principle that the accused was innocent until proved guilty. In Austria, Joseph II presided over a wholesale reorganization of the legal system. Courts were centralized, laws codified, and torture and capital punishment abolished.

Enlightenment ideas also underlay the efforts to improve education in eastern Europe. The religious orders, especially the Jesuits, were the most influential educators of the age, and the Enlightenment attack upon them created a void that had to be filled by the state. Efforts at compulsory education were first undertaken in Russia under Peter the Great, but those were aimed at the compulsory education of the nobility. It was Catherine who extended the effort to the provinces, at-

THE GOOD OF ALL

The Social Contract (1762) was one of the greatest visionary tracts of the eighteenth century. In it Jean-Jacques Rousseau envisioned a harmonious society capable of eliminating want and controlling evil. Here he discusses his famous idea of the general will.

Focus Questions

What benefits flow from unity and simplicity? How large a "state" do you think could be effectively organized in the way Rousseau sets out here?

As long as men united together look upon themselves as a single body, they have but one will relating to the common preservation and general welfare. Then all the energies of the state are vigorous and simple: its maxims are clear and luminous; there are no mixed contradictory interests; the common prosperity shows itself everywhere, and requires only good sense to be appreciated. Peace, union, and equality are enemies of political subtleties. Upright, honest men are difficult to deceive, because of their simplicity: decoys and pretexts do not impose upon them, they are not cunning enough to be dupes. When we see among the happiest people in the world troops of peasants regulating the affairs of state under an oak, and conducting themselves wisely, can we help despising the refinements of other nations, who make themselves illustrious and miserable with so much art and mystery?

From Jean Jacques Rousseau, *The Social Contract.*

tempting to educate a generation of Russian teachers. She was especially eager that women receive primary schooling, although the prejudice against educating women was too strong to overcome. Austrian and Prussian reforms were more successful in extending the reach of primary education, even if its content remained weak.

Religious toleration was the area in which the Enlightenment had its greatest impact in Europe, though again it was in the eastern countries that it was most visible. Freedom of worship for Catholics was barely whispered about in Britain, while neither France nor Spain was moved to tolerate Protestants. Nevertheless, within those parameters there were some important changes in the religious makeup of the western European states. In Britain, Protestant dissenters were no longer persecuted for their beliefs. By the end of the eighteenth century, the number of Protestants outside the Church of England was growing; and by the early nineteenth century discrimination against Protestants was all but eliminated. In France and Spain, relations between the national church and the papacy were undergoing a reorientation. Both states were asserting more independence—both theologically and financially—from Rome. The shift was symbolized by disputes over the role of the Jesuits, who were finally expelled from France in 1764 and from Spain in 1767.

In eastern Europe, enlightened ideas about religious toleration did take effect. Catherine the Great abandoned persecution of a Russian Orthodox sect known as the Old Believers. Prussia had always tolerated various Protestant groups, and with the conquest of Silesia it acquired a large Catholic population. Catholics were guaranteed freedom of worship, and Frederick the Great even built a Catholic church in Berlin to symbolize the policy. Austria extended enlightened ideas about toleration the furthest. Maria Theresa was a devout Catholic and had actually increased religious persecution in

her realm, but Joseph II rejected his mother's dogmatic position. In 1781, he issued the **Patent of Toleration**, which granted freedom of worship to Protestants and members of the Eastern Orthodox Church. The following year he extended the toleration to Jews. Joseph's attitude toward toleration was as practical as it was enlightened. He believed that the revocation of the Edict of Nantes—which had granted limited toleration to Protestants—at the end of the seventeenth century had been an economic disaster for France, and he encouraged religious toleration as a means to economic progress.

A science of economics was first articulated during the Enlightenment. A group of French thinkers known as the **Physiocrats** subscribed to the view that land was wealth and thus argued that agricultural activity, especially improved means of farming and livestock breeding, should take first priority in state reforms. As wealth came from land, taxation should be based only on land ownership, a principle that was coming into increased prominence despite the opposition of the landowning class. Physiocratic ideas combined a belief in the sanctity of private property with the need for the state to increase agricultural output. Ultimately the Physiocrats, like the great Scottish economic theorist Adam Smith, came to believe that government should cease to interfere with private economic activity. They articulated the doctrine *Laissez faire, laissez passer*—"Let it be, let it go." The ideas of Adam Smith and the Physiocrats, particularly the **laissez-faire** doctrine, ultimately formed the basis for nineteenth-century economic reform.

If the Enlightenment did not initiate a new era, it did offer a new vision, whether in Hume's psychology, Montesquieu's political science, Rousseau's sociology, or Smith's economic theory. All of the subjects, which have such a powerful impact on contemporary life, had their modern origins in the

CHRONOLOGY

Major Works of the Enlightenment

1690	*An Essay Concerning Human Understanding* (Locke)
1721	*Persian Letters* (Baron Montesquieu)
1734	*Philosophical Letters Concerning the English Nation* (Voltaire)
1739	*A Treatise of Human Nature* (Hume)
1740	*Pamela* (Richardson)
1748	*An Enquiry Concerning Human Understanding* (Hume); *The Spirit of the Laws* (Baron Montesquieu)
1751–1780	*Encyclopedia* (Diderot)
1759	*Candide* (Voltaire)
1762	*Émile; The Social Contract* (Rousseau)
1764	*Crimes and Punishments* (Beccaria)
1784	*What Is Enlightenment?* (Kant)
1795	*The Progress of the Human Mind* (Marquis de Condorcet)
1798	*An Essay on the Principles of Population* (Malthus)

Enlightenment. As the British poet Alexander Pope (1688–1744) put it: "Know then thyself, presume not God to scan/The proper study of mankind is man." Enlightened thinkers challenged existing ideas and existing institutions. A new emphasis on self and on pleasure led to a new emphasis on happiness. All three fed into the distinctively Enlightenment idea of self-interest. Happiness and self-interest were values that would inevitably corrode the old social order, which was based upon principles of self-sacrifice and corporate identity. It was only a matter of time.

EIGHTEENTH-CENTURY SOCIETY

Eighteenth-century society was a hybrid of old and new. It remained highly stratified socially, politically, and economically. Birth and occupation determined wealth, privilege, and quality of life as much as they had in the past. But in the eighteenth century the gulf between top and bottom was being filled by a thriving middle class, a **bourgeoisie,** as they were called in France. There were now more paths toward the middle and upper classes, more wealth to be distributed among those above the level of subsistence. It was bourgeois culture and bourgeois values that were new in the eighteenth century. At the bottom of society, poverty still gripped the mass of

European people. Changes in agriculture allowed more to survive than ever before, but their survival was still perilous, dependent upon chance rather than effort.

The Nobility

Nobles were defined by their legal rights. They had the right to bear arms, the right to special judicial treatment, the right to tax exemptions. In Russia, only nobles could own serfs; in Poland, only nobles could hold government office. In France and Britain, the highest court positions were always reserved for noblemen. Nobles dominated the Prussian army. In 1786, of nearly 700 senior officers only 22 were not noblemen. The Spanish nobility claimed the right to live idly. Rich or poor, they shunned all labor as a right of their heritage. Swedish and Hungarian noblemen had their own legislative chambers, just as the British had the House of Lords. Noble privilege was as vibrant as ever.

Although all who enjoyed the special rights were noble, not all nobles were equal. In many states, the noble order was subdivided into easily identifiable groups. The Spanish grandees, the upper nobility, numbered in the thousands; the Spanish hidalgos, the lower nobility, in the hundreds of thousands. In Hungary, out of 400,000 noblemen only about 15,000 belonged to the landed nobility, who held titles and were exempt from taxes. The landed nobility were personally members of the upper chamber of the Hungarian Diet, while the lesser nobility sent representatives to the lower chamber.

The situation was similar in England, where the elite class was divided between the peerage and the gentry. The peerage held titles, were members of the House of Lords, and had a limited range of judicial and fiscal privileges. In the mid-eighteenth century, there were only 190 British peers. The gentry, which numbered more than 20,000, dominated the House of Commons and local legal offices but were not strictly members of the nobility. The French nobility was informally distinguished among the small group of peers known as the Grandes, whose ancient lineage, wealth, and power set them apart from all others; a rather larger service nobility whose privileges derived in one way or another from municipal or judicial service; and what might be called the country nobility, whose small estates and local outlook made their fiscal immunities vital to their survival.

The distinctions among the nobilities of the European states masked a more important one: wealth. As the saying went, "All who were truly noble were not wealthy, but all who were truly wealthy were noble." In the eighteenth century, despite the phenomenal increase in mercantile activity, wealth was still calculated in profits from the ownership of land, and it was the wealthy landed nobility who set the tone of elite life in Europe.

Maintaining Wealth. Eighteenth-century Europe was a society of orders gradually transforming itself into a society of classes. At the top, as vigorous as ever, was the nobility, the privileged order in every European state. In different parts of Europe the nobility used different methods to maintain their land-based wealth. In places such as Britain, Spain, Austria, and Hungary, forms of entail were the rule. In simple terms, an entail was a restriction prohibiting the breakup of a landed estate either through sale or inheritance. The owner of the estate was merely a caretaker for his heir, and while he could add land, he could not easily subtract any. Entailed estates grew larger and larger and, like magnets, attracted other entailed estates through marriage. In Britain, where primogeniture—inheritance by the eldest son—accompanied entail, 400 families owned one-quarter of the entire country. Yet the concentration of landed wealth paled into insignificance when compared to the situation in Spain, where just four families owned one-third of all the cultivable land. In the east, where land was plentiful, the Esterhazys of Hungary and the Radziwills of Poland owned millions of acres.

The second method by which the European nobility ensured that the wealthy would be noble was by absorption. There were several avenues to upward mobility, but by the eighteenth century the holding of state offices was the most common. In France, for example, a large number of offices were reserved for the nobility. Many of those were owned by their holders and passed on to their children, but occasionally an office was sold on the market and the new holder was automatically ennobled. The office of royal secretary was one of the most common routes to noble status. The number of secretaries increased from 300 to 900 during the course of the eighteenth century, yet despite the dilution the value of the offices continued to skyrocket. An office that was worth 70,000 French pounds at the beginning of the century was worth 300,000 by the 1780s. In fact, in most European societies there was more room for new nobles than there were aspiring candidates because of the costs that maintaining the new status imposed. In Britain, anyone who could live like a gentleman was accounted one. But the practice of entail made it very difficult for a newcomer to purchase the requisite amount of land. Philip V increased the number of Spanish grandees in an effort to dilute their power, yet when he placed a tax on entrance into the lower nobility, the number of hidalgos dropped precipitously.

Increased Consumption. For the wealthy, aristocracy was becoming an international status. The influence of Louis XIV and the court of Versailles lasted for more than a century and spread to town and country life. Most nobles maintained multiple residences. The new style of aristocratic entertainment required more public space on the first floor, while the increasing demand for personal and familial privacy necessitated more space in the upper stories. The result was larger and more opulent homes. There the British elite led all others. More than 150 country houses were built in the early eighteenth century alone, including Blenheim Palace, which was built for John Churchill, duke of Marlborough, at a cost of £300,000. To the expense of architecture was added the expense of decoration. New materials such as West Indian mahogany occasioned new styles, and both drove up costs. The high-quality woodwork and plastering made fashionable by the English Adam brothers was quickly imitated on the Continent. Only the Spanish nobility shunned country estates, preferring to reside permanently in towns.

The building of country houses was only one part of the conspicuous consumption of the privileged orders. Improvements in travel, both in transport and roads, permitted increased contact between members of the national elites. The stagecoach linked towns, and canals linked waterways. Both made travel quicker and more enjoyable. The grand tour of historical sites continued to be used as a substitute for formal education. Young men would pass from country house to country house buying up antiquities, paintings, and books along the way. The grand tour was a means of introducing the European aristocracies to each other, and also a means of communicating taste and fashion among them. Whether it was a Russian noble in Germany, a Swede in Italy, or a Briton in Prussia, all spoke French and shared a cultural outlook.

The Salons. Much of that outlook was cultivated in the salons, a social institution begun in the seventeenth century by French women that gradually spread throughout the Continent. In the salons, especially those in Paris, the aristocracy and bourgeoisie mingled with the leading intellectuals of the age. There wit and insight replaced polite conversation. At formal meetings, papers on scientific or philosophical topics were read and discussed. At informal gatherings, new ideas were examined and exchanged. The British ambassador to Spain was appalled to discover that men and women were still kept separate in the salons of Madrid and that there was no serious conversation during evenings out. It was in the salons that the impact of the Enlightenment was first felt.

The Bourgeoisie

Bourgeois is a French word, and it carried the same tone of derision in the eighteenth century that it does today. The bourgeois was a man on the make, scrambling after money or office or title. He was neither well-born nor well-bred, or so said the nobility. Yet the bourgeoisie served vital functions in all European societies. They dominated trade, both nationally and internationally. They made their homes in cities and did much to improve the quality of urban life. They were the civilizing influence in urban culture, for unlike the nobility, they were the city's permanent denizens. Perhaps most importantly, the bourgeoisie provided the safety valve between the nobility and those who were acquiring wealth and power but lacked the advantages of birth and position. By developing their own culture and class identity, the bourgeoisie provided successful individuals with their own sense of pride and achievement and eased the explosive buildup of social resentments.

During the eighteenth century, the bourgeoisie grew in both numbers and importance. An active commercial and urban life gave many members of the group new social and political opportunities, and many of them passed into the nobility through the purchase of land or office. But for those whose aspirations or abilities were different, the social group began to define its own values, which centered on the family and the home. A new interest in domestic affairs touched both men and women of the European bourgeoisie. Their homes became social centers for kin and neighbors, and their outlook on family life reflected new personal relationships. Marriages were made for companionship as much as for economic advantage. Romantic love between husbands and wives was newly valued. So were children, whose futures came to dominate familial concern. Childhood was recognized as a separate stage of life and the education of children as one of the most important of all parental responsibilities. The image of the affectionate father replaced that of the hard-bitten businessman; the image of the doting mother replaced that of the domestic drudge.

Urban Elites.   In the society of orders, nobility was the acid test. The world was divided into the small number of those who had it and the large number of those who did not. At the apex of the non-noble pyramid was the bourgeoisie, the elites of urban Europe whose place in the society of orders was ambiguous. *Bourgeois*, or *burgher*, simply meant "town dweller," but as a social group it had come to mean wealthy town dweller. The bourgeoisie was strongest where towns were strongest: in western rather than in eastern Europe and in northern rather than southern Europe, with the notable exception of Italy. Holland was the exemplar of a bourgeois republic. More than half of the Dutch population lived in towns, and there was no significant aristocratic class to compete for power. The Regents of Amsterdam were the equivalent of a European court nobility in wealth, power, and prestige, though not in the way in which they had accumulated their fortunes. The size of the bourgeoisie in various European states cannot be determined absolutely. At the end of the eighteenth century, the British middle classes probably constituted around 15 percent of the population, the French bourgeoisie less than 10 percent. By contrast, the Russian or Hungarian urban elites were less than 2 percent of the population in those states.

Like the nobility, the bourgeoisie constituted a diverse group. At the top were great commercial families engaged in the expanding international marketplace and reaping the profits of trade. In wealth and power they were barely distinguishable from the nobility. At the bottom were the so-called petite bourgeoisie: shopkeepers, artisans, and small manufacturers. The solid core of the bourgeoisie was employed in trade, exchange, and service. Most were engaged in local or national commerce. Trade was the lifeblood of the city, for by itself the city could neither feed nor clothe its inhabitants. Most bourgeois fortunes were first acquired in trade. Finance was the natural outgrowth of commerce, and another segment of the bourgeoisie accumulated or preserved their capital through the sophisticated financial instruments of the eighteenth century. While the very wealthy loaned directly to the central government or bought shares in overseas trading companies, most bourgeois participated in government credit markets. They purchased state bonds or lifetime annuities and lived on the interest. The costs of war flooded the urban credit markets with high-yielding and generally stable financial instruments. Finally, the bourgeoisie were members of the burgeoning professions that provided services for the rich. Medicine, law, education, and the state bureaucracy were all bourgeois professions, for the cost of acquiring the necessary skills could be borne only by those already wealthy.

During the course of the eighteenth century, the combination of occupational groups was expanding, both in numbers

■ William Hogarth was famous for his satirical series paintings. *Marriage à la Mode*, ca. 1743, depicts the complicated negotiations between a wealthy merchant and an aristocrat for a marriage between their families and shows the progress of the arranged match to its end. In this scene of domestic disarray, second in the series, the marriage quickly proves to be a disaster.

and in importance, all over Europe. So was the bourgeois habitat. The urbanization of Europe continued steadily throughout the eighteenth century. A greater percentage of the European population were living in towns, and a greater percentage were living in large towns of more than 10,000 inhabitants, which, of necessity, were developing complex socioeconomic structures. In France alone there were probably more than a hundred such towns, each requiring the services of the bourgeoisie and providing opportunities for their expansion. And the larger the metropolis, the greater the need. In 1600, only 20 European cities contained as many as 50,000 people; in 1700, that number had risen to 32, and by 1800 it reached 48. During the course of the eighteenth century, the number of cities with 75,000 inhabitants doubled. London, the largest city, had grown to 865,000, a remarkable feat considering that in 1665 more than one-quarter of the London population had died in the Great Plague. In such cities, the demand for lawyers, doctors, merchants, and shopkeepers was almost insatiable.

Besides wealth, the urban bourgeoisie shared another characteristic: mobility. The aspiration of the bourgeoisie was to become noble, either through office or by acquiring rural estates. In Britain, a gentleman was still defined by lifestyle: "All are accounted gentlemen in England who maintain themselves without manual labor." Many trading families left their wharves and countinghouses to acquire rural estates, live off rents, and practice the openhanded hospitality of gentlemen. In France and Spain, nobility could still be purchased, though the price was constantly going up. For the greater bourgeoisie, the transition was easy; for the lesser, the failure to move up was all the more frustrating for being just beyond their grasp. The bourgeoisie did not only imagine their discomfort, they were made to feel it at every turn. They were the butt of jokes, theater, and popular songs. They were the first victims in the shady financial dealings of crown and court, the first casualties in urban riots. Despised from above and envied from below, the bourgeoisie were uncomfortable with their present yet profoundly conservative about their future. The one consolation to their perpetual misery was that as a group they became richer and richer. And as a group they began to develop a distinctive culture that reflected their qualities and aspirations.

Bourgeois Values.   Many bourgeoisie viewed their condition as temporary and accepted the pejorative connotations of the word *bourgeois*. They had little desire to defend a social group out of which they fervently longed to pass. Others, whose aspirations were lower, were nevertheless uncomfortable with the status that they had already achieved. They had no ambition to wear the silks and furs reserved for the nobility or to attend the opening night at the opera decked in jewels and finery. In fact, such ostentation was alien to their existence and to the success that they had achieved. There was a real tension between the values of noble and bourgeois. The ideal noble was idle, wasteful, and ostentatious; the ideal bourgeois was industrious, frugal, and sober. Voltaire, who made his fortune as a financial speculator rather than as a man of letters, aped the lifestyle of the nobility. But he could never allow himself to be cheated by a trades-

man, a mark of his origins. When Louis XVI tried to make household economies in the wake of a financial crisis, critics said that he acted "like a bourgeois."

Even if the bourgeoisie did not constitute a class, they did share certain attitudes that constituted a culture. The wealthy among them participated in the new world of consumption, whether they did so lavishly or frugally. For those who aspired to more than their birth allowed, there was a loosening of the strict codes of dress that reserved certain fabrics, decorative materials, and styles to the nobility. Merchants and bankers could now be seen in colored suits or with piping made of cloth of gold; their wives could be seen in furs and silks. They might acquire silverware, even if they did not go so far as the nobility and have a coat of arms engraved upon it. Coaches and carriages were also becoming common among the bourgeoisie, to take them on the Sunday rides through the town gardens or to their weekend retreats in the suburbs. Parisian merchants, even master craftsmen such as clockmakers, were acquiring suburban homes, although they could not afford to retire to them for the summer months.

But more and more, the bourgeoisie was beginning to travel. In Britain, whole towns were established to cater to leisure travelers. The southwestern town of Bath, which was rebuilt in the eighteenth century, was the most popular of all European resort towns, famous since Roman times for the soothing qualities of its waters. Bath was soon a social center as notable for its marriage market as for its recreations. Brighton, a seaside resort on the south coast, quadrupled in size in the second half of the eighteenth century. Bathing—what we would call swimming—either for health or recreation, became a middle class fad, displacing traditional fear of the sea.

Leisure and Entertainment.   The leisure that wealth bestowed on the bourgeoisie, in good bourgeois fashion, quickly became commercialized. Theater and music halls for both light and serious productions proliferated. By the 1760s, an actual theater district had arisen in London and was attracting audiences of more than 20,000 a week. London was unusual, both for its size and for the number of well-to-do visitors who patronized its cultural events. The size of the London audiences enabled the German-born composer Georg Friedrich Handel (1685–1759) to earn a handsome living by performing and directing concerts. He was one of the few musicians in the eighteenth century to live without noble patronage. But it was not only in Britain that theater and music flourished. Voltaire's plays were performed before packed houses in Paris, with the author himself frequently in attendance to bask in the adulation of the largely bourgeois audiences who attended them. In Venice, it was estimated that more than 1200 operas were produced in the eighteenth century. Rome and Milan were even better known, and Naples was the center for Italian opera. Public concerts were a mark of bourgeois culture, for the court nobility was entertained at the royal palaces or great country houses. Public concerts began in Hamburg in the 1720s, and Frederick the Great helped establish the Berlin Opera House some decades later.

Theater and concert going were part of the new attitude toward socializing that was one of the greatest contributions of the Enlightenment. Enlightened thinkers spread their views in the salons, and the salons soon spawned the academies, local scientific societies that, though led and patronized by provincial nobles, included large numbers of bourgeois members. The academies sponsored essay competitions, built up libraries, and became the local centers for intellectual interchange. A less structured form of sociability took place in the coffeehouses and tearooms that came to be a feature of even small provincial towns. In the early eighteenth century, there were more than 2000 London coffee shops where men—for the coffeehouse was largely a male preserve—could talk politics, read the latest newspapers and magazines, and indulge their taste for this still-exotic beverage. More exclusive clubs were also a form of middle-class sociability, some centering on political issues, some (such as the chambers of commerce) centering on professional interests. Parisian clubs, called *sociétés,* covered a multitude of diverse interests. Literary sociétés were the most popular, maintaining their purpose by forbidding drinking, eating, and gambling on their premises.

Above all, bourgeois culture was literate culture. Wealth and leisure led to mental pursuits—if not always to intellectual ones. The proliferation of relatively cheap printed material had an enormous impact on the lives of those who were able to afford it. Holland and Britain were the most literate European societies and also, because of the absence of censorship, the centers of European printing.

It was the first great period of the newspaper and the magazine. The first daily newspaper appeared in London in 1702; 80 years later, 37 provincial towns had their own newspapers, while the London papers were read all over Britain. Then as now, the newspaper was as much a vehicle for advertisement as for news. News reports tended to be bland, avoiding controversy and concentrating on general national and international events. Advertising, on the other hand, tended to be lurid, promising cures for incurable ills and the most exquisite commodities at the most reasonable prices.

For entertainment and serious political commentary, the British reading public turned to magazines, of which there were more than 150 separate titles by the 1780s. The most famous were *The Spectator,* which ran in the early part of the century and did much to set the tone for a cultured middle-class life, and *The Gentleman's Magazine,* which ran in mid-century and was said to have had a circulation of nearly 15,000. The longest-lived of all British magazines was *The Ladies' Diary,* which continued in existence from 1704 to 1871 and doled out self-improvement, practical advice, and fictional romances in equal proportion.

The Ladies' Diary was not the only literature aimed at the growing number of leisured and lettered bourgeois women. Although enlightened thinkers could be ambivalent about the place of women in the new social order, they generally stressed the importance of female education and welcomed women's participation in intellectual pursuits. Whether it was new ideas about women or simply the fact that more women had leisure, a growing body of both domestic literature and light entertainment was available to them. The literature included a vast number of teach-yourself books aimed at instructing women how best to organize domestic life and how to navigate the perils of polite society. Moral instruction, particularly on the themes of obedience and sexual fidelity, was also popular. But the greatest output directed toward women was in the form of fanciful romances, from which a new genre emerged. The novel first appeared in its modern form in the 1740s. Samuel Richardson (1689–1761) wrote *Pamela* (1740), the story of a servant girl who successfully resisted the advances of her master until he finally married her. It was composed in long episodes, or chap-

■ This scene shows activity at a London coffeehouse. Coffeehouses became increasingly popular in European cities in the eighteenth century. As a forum for discussion and for reading newspapers, they were important sites for the dissemination of Enlightenment ideas.

ters, that developed Pamela's character and told her story at the expense of the overt moral message that was Richardson's original intention. Richardson's novels were printed in installments and helped to drive up the circulation of national magazines.

Family Life and Companionate Marriage.

Whereas the public life of the bourgeoisie can be measured in the sociability of the coffeehouse and the academy, private life must be measured in the home. There a remarkable transformation was under way, one that the bourgeoisie shared with the nobility. In the pursuit of happiness encouraged by the Enlightenment, one of the newest joys was domesticity. The image—and sometimes the reality—of the happy home, where love was the bond between husband and wife and care the bond between parents and children, came to dominate both the literary and visual arts. Only those wealthy enough to afford to dispense with women's work could partake of the new domesticity; only those touched by Enlightenment ideas could attempt to make the change. But where it occurred, the transformation in the nature of family life was one of the most profound alterations in eighteenth-century culture.

The first step toward the transformation of family relationships was in centering the conjugal family in the home. In the past, the family was a less important structure for most people than the social groups to which they belonged or the neighborhood in which they lived. Marriage was an economic partnership and a means to carry on lineage. Individual fulfillment was not an object of marriage, and that attitude could be seen among the elites in the great number of arranged marriages, the speed with which surviving spouses remarried,

and the formal and often brutal personal relationships between husbands and wives.

Patriarchy was the dominant value within the family. Husbands ruled over wives and children, making all of the crucial decisions that affected both the quality of their lives and their futures. As late as the middle of the eighteenth century, a British judge established the "rule of thumb," which asserted that a husband had a legal right to beat his wife with a stick, but the stick should be no thicker than a man's thumb. It was believed that children were stained with the sin of Adam at birth and that only the severest upbringing could clean some of it away. In nearly 200 child-rearing advice books published in England before the middle of the eighteenth century, only three did not advise the beating of children. John Wesley (1703–1791), the founder of Methodism, remembered his own mother's dictum that "children should learn to fear the rod and cry softly." Children were sent out first for wet-nursing; then at around the age of seven for boarding, either at school or in a trade; and finally into their own marriages.

There can be no doubt that the profile of family life began to change, especially in western Europe, during the second half of the eighteenth century. Although the economic elements of marriage remained strong—newspapers actually advertised the availability of partners and the dowries or annual income that they would bring to the marriage—other elements appeared. Fed by an unending stream of stories and novels and a new desire for individual happiness, romantic and sexual attraction developed into a factor in marriage. Potential marriage partners were no longer kept

■ *The Snatched Kiss*, or *The Stolen Kiss* (1750s), by Jean-Honoré Fragonard, was one of the "series paintings" popular in the late eighteenth century. A later canvas entitled *The Marriage Contract* shows the next step in the lives of the lovers.

away from each other or smothered by chaperons. The social season of polite society, in which prospective partners could dance, dine, and converse with each other to determine compatibility, gave greater latitude to courtship. Perhaps more importantly, the role of potential spouses in choosing a partner appears to have increased. That was a subtle matter, for even in earlier centuries parents did not simply assign a spouse to their children. But by the eighteenth century, adolescents themselves searched for their own marriage partners and exercised a strong negative voice in identifying unsuitable ones.

The quest for compatibility, no less than the quest for romantic love, led to a change in personal relationships between spouses. The extreme formality of the past was gradually breaking down. Husbands and wives began spending more time with each other, developing common interests and pastimes. Their personal life began to change. For the first time, houses were built to afford a couple privacy from their children, servants, and guests. Rooms were designed for specific functions and were set off by hallways. Corridors were an important innovation in creating privacy. In earlier architecture, one walked through a room to the next one behind it. In new

LOVE AND MARRIAGE

Frances Brooke (1724–1789) was one of the earliest women novelists in Britain, publishing her first novel, The History of Lady Julia Mandeville, *in 1763. Orphaned at an early age, she settled in London and earned her living as a translator, writer, and editor. Brooke also participated in the thriving magazine culture of mid-eighteenth-century London. In her essay periodical,* The Old Maid, *she addressed domestic and public issues through the voice of a fictional mouthpiece, "Mary Singleton, Spinster." In this excerpt from the first issue of the magazine, the "Old Maid" reflects on her personal history and the circumstances that led to her unmarried state.*

Focus Questions

How does the passage of time affect the Old Maid's recollections about her past? According to this selection, how do parents control the destiny of their children and heirs? What appears to be the role of love in eighteenth-century marriages?

I was born in the north of England, being the eldest daughter of an honest country justice, who having no children but me and a younger sister, proposed leaving his estate, a clear eight hundred a year, betwixt us. My sister married a neighboring gentleman, and I might perhaps have followed her example, having very good offers (upon my word it's true, I have several love letters by me, which I read once a year, on my birthday, by the help of spectacles) but unluckily, at the age of twenty three, I was addressed by a gentleman so very agreeable, and so passionately fond of me, that though he had not a shilling, I unknown to any body, partly from inclination, partly for fear the poor man should hang himself, which he often threatened, engaged myself to him. As it was impossible to get my father's consent, we agreed to wait till his death; and my lover, who was bred to no employment, went in the meantime to reside with an old relation, in a distant country, who had a good estate, and whose son had a friendship for him. After two years of expectation, during which my faithful admirer, who contrived to see me as often as the distance of the place, and his dependent situation would permit, had frequently pressed me to marry him privately, my father died. Though my concern for his death was real, love soon dried

up my tears: no one who is not as romantic as I then was can imagine the joy I felt at being able to give my lover such a proof of the disinterestedness of my passion: I sent a servant post with a letter full of fine sentimental rhapsodies which I am now convinced were very foolish, and received the following answer,

MADAM,

I am sorry for your loss: I have also been so unhappy as to lose my uncle and cousin, who both died of the smallpox within this week: the excess of my grief, and the multiplicity of business I am at present engaged in, by being left heir to my uncle's estate, render it impossible for me to wait upon you. I am much obliged to you for the expressions of regard in your's [sic], and am sorry to tell you, my uncle when dying, insisted on my promise to marry Miss Wealthy, who was intended for my cousin. The will of the dead ought to be sacred therefore it is impossible for me to fulfill the engagement into which we, perhaps imprudently, entered. I expect from your known candor that you will do me the justice to believe no motive but the gratitude and respect I own to the memory of this dear relation, to whose generosity I am so much obliged, could make me give up the hope of being yours. I doubt not your good sense and religion will enable you to bear with becoming fortitude, a shock, which I have need of all the strength of manly reason to support. I sincerely wish you every happiness, and that you may whenever you marry, meet with a man more worthy of you . . .
—J.C.

From *The Old Maid*, Number 1 (November 15, 1755).

design, rooms were separated and doors could be closed, which allowed for an intimate life that earlier generations did not find necessary and that they could not, in any case, have put into practice.

Couples had more time for each other because they were beginning to limit the size of their families. There were a number of reasons for that development, which again pertained only to the upper classes. For one thing, child mortality rates were declining among wealthy social groups. Virulent epidemic diseases such as the plague, which knew no class lines, were gradually disappearing. Moreover, though there were few medical breakthroughs in the period, sanitation was improving. Bearing fewer children had an enormous impact on the lives of women, reducing the danger of death and disablement in childbirth and giving them leisure time to pursue domestic tasks. However, that did not mean that the early part of a woman's marriage was not dominated by children; in fact, because of new attitudes toward child-rearing it may have been dominated more than ever by children. Many couples appear to have made a conscious decision to space births,

though success was limited by the fact that the most common technique of birth control was coitus interruptus, or withdrawal.

New Attitudes Toward Children. The transformation in the quality of relationships between spouses was mirrored by an even greater transformation in attitudes toward children. There were many reasons why childhood now took on a new importance. Decline in mortality rates had a profound psychological impact. Parents could feel that their emotional investment in their children had a greater chance of fulfillment. But equally important were the new ideas about education, especially Locke's belief that the child enters the world a blank slate whose personality is created through early education. That view not only placed a new responsibility on parents but also gave them the concept of childhood as a stage through which individuals passed. The idea could be seen in the commercial sphere as well as in any other. In 1700, there was not a single shop in London that sold children's toys exclusively; by the 1780s, there

■ English wax doll with silk gown, 1757. The eighteenth century saw a transformation in family life, including new attitudes toward children that created a market for new products such as books, toys, and games.

■ The eighteenth century was a transitional period in family life. The children in this picture dress like undersized adults, and the oldest girl is posed like an adult as well, but there are also toys included in the scene, which signify the emerging notion that childhood was a separate and more playful stage in a person's development.

were toy shops everywhere, three of which sold nothing but rocking horses. Children's toys abounded: soldiers and forts, dolls and dollhouses. The jigsaw puzzle was invented in the 1760s as a way to teach children geography. There were also shops that sold nothing but clothes specifically designed for children, no longer simply adult clothes in miniature.

Most important of all was the development of materials for the education of children, which took place in two stages. At first, so-called children's books were books whose purpose was to help adults teach children. Later came books directed at children themselves, with large print, entertaining illustrations, and nonsensical characters, usually animals who taught moral lessons. In Britain, the Little Pretty Pocket Book series, created by John Newbery (1713–1767), not only encompassed educational primers but also included books for the entertainment of the child. Newbery published a Mother Goose book of nursery rhymes and created the immortal character of Miss Goody Two-Shoes. Instruction and entertainment also lay behind the development of children's playing cards, in which the French specialized. Dice games, such as one in which a child made a journey across Europe, combined geographical instruction with the amusement of competition.

The commercialization of childhood was, of course, directed at adults. The new books and games that were designed to enhance a child's education not only had to be purchased by parents but had to be used by them as well. More and more mothers were devoting their time to their children. Among the upper classes, the practice of wet-nursing began to decline. Mothers wanted to nurture their infants—both literally, by breast-feeding, and figuratively, by teaching them. Children became companions to be taken on outings to the increasing number of museums or shows of curiosities, which began to discount children's tickets by the middle of the century.

The preconditions of the transformation of family life could not be shared by the population at large. Working women could afford neither the cost of instructional materials for their children nor the time to use them. Ironically, they now began using wet nurses, once the privilege of the wealthy, for increasingly a working woman's labor was the margin of survival for her family. Working women enjoyed no privacy in the hovels in which they lived, with large families in single rooms. Wives and children were still beaten by husbands and fathers and were unacquainted with enlightened ideas of the worth of the individual and the innocence of the child. By the end of the eighteenth century, two distinct family cultures coexisted in Europe: one based on companionate marriage and the affective bonds of parents and children; the other based on patriarchal dominance and the family as an economic unit.

The Masses

Although more Europeans were surviving than ever before, with more food, more housing, better sanitation, and even better charities, there was also more misery. Those who would have succumbed to disease or starvation a century before now survived from day to day, beneficiaries—or victims—of increased farm production and improved agricultural marketing. The market economy organized a more effective use of land, but it created a widespread social problem. The landless agrarian laborer of the eighteenth century was the counterpart of the sturdy sixteenth-century beggar, capable of working but incapable of finding work. In the cities, the plight of the poor was as desperate as ever. Even the most openhearted charitable institutions were unable to cope with the massive increase in the poor. Thousands of mothers abandoned their children to the foundling hospitals, hoping that they would have a better chance of survival, even though hospital death rates were nearly 80 percent.

Despite widespread poverty, many members of the lower orders were able to gain some benefit from existing conditions. The richness of popular culture, signified by a spread of literacy into the lower reaches of European society, was one indication of the change. So, too, were the reforms urged by enlightened thinkers to improve basic education and the quality of life in the cities. For the segment of the lower orders that could keep its head above water, the eighteenth century offered new opportunities and new challenges.

Breaking the Cycle. Of all the legacies of the eighteenth century, none was more fundamental than the steady increase in European population that began around 1740. It was not the first time that Europe had experienced sustained population growth, but it was the first time that such growth was not checked by a demographic crisis. Breaking the cycle of population growth and crisis was a momentous event in European history, despite the fact that it went unrecorded at the time and unappreciated for centuries after.

The figures tell one part of the story. In 1700, European population is estimated to have been 120 million. By 1800, it had grown 50 percent, to more than 180 million. And the aggregate hides significant regional variations. While populations in France, Spain, and Italy expanded between 30 and 40 percent, the population of Prussia doubled and those of Russia and Hungary may have tripled in number. Britain's population increased by 80 percent, from about 5 to 9 million, but the rate of growth was accelerating. In 1695, the English population stood at 5 million. It took 62 years to add the next million and 24 years to add the million after that. In 1781, the population was 7 million, but it took only 13 years to reach 8 million and only 10 more years to reach 9 million. Steady population growth had continued without significant checks for more than a half century.

Ironically, the traditional pattern of European population found its theorist at the very moment that it was about to disappear. In 1798, Thomas Malthus (1766–1834) published *An Essay on the Principles of Population*. Reflecting on the history of European population, Malthus observed the cyclical pattern by which growth over one or two generations was checked by a crisis that significantly reduced population. From the lower levels new growth began until it was checked and the cycle repeated itself. Because the number of people increased more quickly than did food supplies, the land could only sustain a certain level of population. When that level was near, population became prone to a demographic check.

DOCUMENT

Malthus, Laws of Population Growth

Malthus divided population checks into two categories: positive and preventive. Positive checks were famine, war, and disease, all of which Malthus believed were natural, although brutal, means of population control. Famine was the obvious result of the failure of food supplies to keep pace with demand; war was the competition for scarce resources; disease often accompanied both. It was preventive checks that most interested Malthus. Those were the means by which societies could limit their growth to avoid the devastating consequences of positive checks. Celibacy, late marriages, and sexual abstinence were among the choices that Malthus approved, although abortion, infanticide, and contraception were also commonly practiced.

Patterns of Population. In the sixteenth and seventeenth centuries, the dominant pattern of the life cycle was high infant and child mortality, late marriages, and early death. All controlled population growth. Infant and child mortality rates were staggering: only half of all those born reached the age of ten. Late marriage was the only effective form of birth control—given the strong social taboos against sexual relations outside marriage—for a late marriage reduced a woman's childbearing years. Women in western Europe generally married between the ages of 24 and 26; they normally ceased bearing children at the age of 40. But not all marriages lasted that 14- or 16-year span, as one or the other partner died. On average, the childbearing period for most women was between 10 and 12 years, long enough to endure six pregnancies, which would result in three surviving children. (See "A Closer Look: Giving Birth in the Eighteenth Century," pp. 582–583.)

Three surviving children for every two adults would, of course, have resulted in a 50 percent rise in population in every generation. Celibacy was one limiting factor; cities were another. Perhaps as much as 15 percent of the population in western Europe remained celibate, either by entering religious orders that imposed celibacy or by lacking the personal or financial attributes necessary to make a match. Religious orders that enforced celibacy were still central features of Catholic societies, and spinsters, as unmarried women were labeled, were increasing everywhere. Cities were like sticky webs, trapping the surplus rural population for the spiders of disease, famine, and exposure to devour. Throughout the early modern period, urban areas grew through migration. Settled town dwellers might have been able to sustain their own numbers despite the unsanitary conditions of cities, but it was migrants who brought about the cities' explosive growth. Rural migrants accounted for the appallingly high urban death rates. The largest European cities were continuously growing—London from 200,000 in 1600 to 675,000 in 1750; Paris from 220,000 to 576,000; Rome from 105,000 to 156,000; Madrid from 49,000 to 109,000; Vienna from 50,000 to 175,000—and many countless thousands of immigrants perished before

marriage. If urban perils were not enough, there were still the so-called positive checks. Plagues carried away hundreds of thousands, wars halved populations of places in their path, and famine overwhelmed the weak and the poor. The worst famine in European history came as late as 1697, when one-third of the population of Finland starved to death.

The late seventeenth and early eighteenth centuries were a period of population stagnation, if not actual decline. It was not until the third or fourth decade of the eighteenth century that another growth cycle began. It rapidly gained momentum throughout the Continent and showed no signs of abating after two full generations. More important, the upward cycle revealed unusual characteristics. In the first place, fertility was increasing, for several reasons. In a few areas, most notably in Britain, women were marrying younger, thereby increasing their childbearing years. That pattern was also true in eastern Europe, where women traditionally married younger. In the late eighteenth century, the average age at marriage for Hungarian women had dropped to 18.6 years. Elsewhere, most notably in France, the practice of wet-nursing was becoming more common among the masses. As working women increasingly took jobs outside the house, they were less able to nurse their own children. Finally, sexual activity outside marriage was rising. Illegitimacy rates, especially in the last decades of the century, were spurting everywhere. Over the course of the century, they rose by 60 percent in France, more than doubled in England, and nearly quadrupled in Germany. So, too, were the rates of premarital pregnancy on the rise. The number of couples rushed to the altar in 1800 was nearly double that before 1750 in most of western Europe.

But increasing fertility was only part of the picture. More significant was decreasing mortality. The positive checks of the past were no longer as potent. European warfare not only diminished in scale after the middle of the century, it changed location as well. Rivalry for colonial empires removed the theater of conflict from European communities. So did the increase in naval warfare. The damage caused by war had always been more by aftershock than by actual fighting. The destruction and pillage of crops and the wholesale slaughter of livestock created food shortages that weakened local populations for the diseases that came along with the armies. As the virulence of warfare abated, so did that of epidemic disease. The plague had all but disappeared from western Europe by the middle of the eighteenth century. The widespread practice of quarantine—especially in Hungary, which had been the crucial bridge between eastern and western epidemics—went far to eradicate the scourge of centuries.

Public health improvements also played a role in population increases. Urban sanitation, at least for permanent city dwellers, was becoming more effective. Clean water supplies, organized waste and sewage disposal, and strict quarantines were increasingly part of urban regulations. The use of doctors and trained midwives helped lower the incidence of stillbirth and decreased the number of women who died in childbirth. Almost everywhere levels of infant and child mortality were decreasing. More people were being born, more were surviving the first ten dangerous years, and thus more were marrying and reproducing. Increased fertility and decreased mortality could have only one result: renewed population growth. No wonder Malthus was worried.

Agricultural Improvements.   In the past, if warfare or epidemic diseases failed to check population growth, famine would have done the job. How the European economy conquered famine in the eighteenth century is a complicated story. There was no single breakthrough that accounts for the ability to feed the tens of millions of additional people who inhabited the Continent. Holland and Britain, at the cutting edge of agricultural improvement, employed dynamic new techniques that would ultimately provide the means to support continued growth, but most European agriculture was still mired in the time-honored practices that had endured for centuries. Thus, not everyone could be fed or fed adequately. Widespread famine might have disappeared, but slow starvation and chronic undernourishment had not. Hunger was more common at the end of the eighteenth century than at the beginning, and the nutritional content of a typical diet might have reached its lowest point in European history.

Nevertheless, the capacity to sustain rising levels of population can only be explained in terms of agricultural improvement. Quite simply, European farmers were now producing more food and marketing it better. In the most advanced societies, that was a result of conscious efforts to make agriculture more efficient. In traditional open-field agriculture, communities quickly ran up against insurmountable obstacles to growth. The three-field crop rotation system left a significant proportion of land fallow each year, while the concentration on subsistence cereal crops progressively eroded the land that was in production. Common farming was only as strong as the weakest

member of the community. There was little incentive for successful individuals to plow profits back into the land, either through the purchase of equipment or the increase of livestock. Livestock was a crucial variable in agricultural improvement. As long as there was only enough food for humans to eat, only essential livestock could be kept alive over the winter. Oxen, which were still the ordinary beasts of burden, and pigs and poultry, which required only minimal feed, were the most commonly

MAP DISCOVERY

Wheat

Oats

Rye

Winter Barley

Barley

Cereal Crops in Europe

Soil, climate, and agricultural techniques all combined to determine the diet of Europeans in different parts of the Continent. What were the predominant cereal crops in eastern Europe? Where were the heaviest concentrations of grain grown? If wheat was the most expensive cereal crop, which do you think were the richest parts of Europe?

kept livestock. But few animals meant little manure, and without manure the soil could not easily be regenerated.

It was not until the middle of the seventeenth century that solutions to those problems began to appear. The first change was consolidation of landholdings so that traditional crop rotations could be abandoned. A second innovation was the introduction of **fodder crops,** some of which—such as clover—added nutrients to the soil, while others—such as turnips—were used to feed livestock. Better grazing and better winter feed increased the size of herds, while new techniques of animal husbandry, particularly crossbreeding, produced hardier strains. It was quite clear that the key to increased production lay in better fertilization, and by the eighteenth century some European farmers had broken through the "manure barrier." Larger herds, the introduction of clover crops, the use of human waste from towns, and even the first experiments with lime as an artificial fertilizer were all part of the new agricultural methods. The impact of new farming techniques was readily apparent. In Britain and Holland, where they were used most extensively, grain yields exceeded ten kernels harvested for each one planted, while in eastern Europe, where the techniques were hardly known, yields were less than five to one.

The New Staples.   Along with the new crops that helped nourish both soil and animals came new crops that helped nourish people. Indian corn, or maize, was a staple crop for Native Americans and gradually came to be grown in most parts of western Europe. Maize not only had higher nutritional value than most other cereals, it also yielded more food per acre than traditional grains, reaching levels as high as 40 to 1. So, too, did the potato, which also entered the European diet from the New World. The potato grew in poor soil, required less labor, and yielded an abundant and nutritious harvest. It rapidly took hold in Ireland and parts of Prussia, from where it spread into eastern Europe. French and Spanish peasants reluctantly introduced it into their diet. Wherever it took root, the potato quickly established itself as survival food. It allowed families to subsist on smaller amounts of land and with less capital outlay. As a result, potato cultivation enabled people in some parts of Europe to marry younger, and thus to produce more children.

However, the new developments involved only a very narrow range of producers. The new techniques were expensive, and knowledge of the new crops spread slowly. Change had to overcome both inertia and intransigence. With more mouths to feed, profits from agriculture soared without landowners having to lift a finger. Only the most ambitious were interested in improvement. At the other end, peasant farmers were more concerned with failure than success. An experiment that did not work could devastate a community; one that did work only meant higher taxes. Thus the most important improvements in agricultural production were more traditional ones. Basically, there was an increase in the amount of land that was utilized for growing. In most of western Europe there was little room for agricultural expansion, but in the east there remained great tracts of uncultivated land. In Russia, Prussia,

and Hungary, hundreds of thousands of new acres came under the plow, although some of it simply went to replace land that had been wastefully exhausted in previous generations. In one German province, nearly 75 percent more land was in cultivation at the end of the eighteenth century than had been at the beginning. Even in the west, drainage schemes and forest clearance expanded productive capacity.

There was also an upswing in the efficiency with which agricultural products were marketed. From the seventeenth century onward, market agriculture was gradually replacing subsistence agriculture in most parts of Europe. Market agriculture had the advantage of allowing specialization on farms. Single-crop farming enabled farmers to benefit from the peculiarities of their own soil and climate. They could then exchange their surplus for the range of crops they needed to subsist. Market exchange was facilitated by improved transportation and communication, and above all by the increase in the population of towns, which provided demand. On a larger scale, market agriculture was able to respond to regional harvest failures in a way that subsistence agriculture could not. The most hated figure in the eighteenth century was the grain engrosser, a middleman who bought up local surplus and shipped it away. Engrossers were accused of driving up prices—which they did—and of creating famines—which they did not. In fact, the national and international trade in large quantities of grain evened out regional variations in harvests and went a long way toward reducing local grain shortages. The upkeep of roads, the building of canals, and the clearing of waterways created a national lifeline for the movement of grain.

Finally, the increase in agricultural productivity may have owed something to a change in climate that took place in the late eighteenth century. It is thought that the annual ring of growth inside tree trunks is an indicator of changes in climate. Hot years produce markedly different rings than cold ones; wet years are etched differently from dry ones. Examination of trees that are centuries old seems to indicate that the European climate was unusually cold and wet during the seventeenth century—some have even called it a little ice age—and that it gradually warmed during the eighteenth century. Even moderate climatic change, when combined with new techniques, new crops, expanded cultivation, and improved marketing, would go a long way toward explaining how so many more people were being fed at the end of the eighteenth century.

The Plight of the Poor.   "Of every ten men one is a beggar, five are too poor to give him alms, three more are ill at ease, embarrassed by debts and lawsuits, and the tenth does not represent a hundred thousand families." So observed an eighteenth-century Frenchman about the distribution of wealth in his country. There can be no doubt that the most serious social problem of the eighteenth century was the explosion of poor people throughout Europe. There was grim irony in the fact that advances in the production and distribution of food and the retreat of war and plague allowed more people to survive hand-to-mouth than ever before. Whereas their ancestors

GIVING BIRTH IN THE EIGHTEENTH CENTURY

"In sorrow thou shalt bring forth children." Such was Eve's punishment for eating of the forbidden tree, and that sorrow continued for numberless generations. Childbirth was painful, dangerous, and all too often deadly. Although successful childbirth needed no outside intervention, without the accumulated wisdom of the ages, babies and mothers routinely perished. The wisdom was passed from mother to daughter and finally was collected by skilled women who practiced the craft of midwifery. Every village, no matter how small, had women who were capable of assisting others in childbirth. Midwives' skills ranged widely, from the use of herbal potions and strong drink to ease the pain of labor to a rudimentary understanding of how to assist a complicated delivery when the fetus was not in the proper position.

■ Early application of forceps.

Midwives, who until the late seventeenth century were always women, were part of the support group that attended a woman during her labor. Typically, childbirth was a social occasion. Along with the midwife would be a wet nurse and female kin and neighbors, who would offer encouragement, bring refreshments, and tend to the chores that the pregnant woman would have performed herself. Without chemicals to induce contractions and without the ability to intervene in the delivery, labor was usually long. Ordinarily, it did not take place in bed, but rather in a room or a part of a room that had been set aside for the occasion. By the eighteenth century, at least in larger urban areas, poor women who had no separate space for labor could give birth in lying-in hospitals. Within the birthing room, the conclave of women was much like a social gathering. The pregnant woman was advised to adopt any position that made her feel comfortable; standing and walking were favored in the belief that the effects of gravity helped the baby move downward. The woman might sit on a neighbor's lap or on a birthing stool, a chair open at the bottom, during contractions and delivery.

Most midwives subscribed to the philosophy of letting nature take its course. Because the difficulties and length of labor differed markedly from woman to woman, the midwife's most important contribution was to offer comfort and reassurance based on her long experience. By the seventeenth century, manuals for midwives were being published, some of them written by women, but most by male doctors with surgical experience. Midwives and doctors were always at daggers drawn. Trained physicians increasingly saw childbirth as a process that could be improved by the application of new medical knowledge, but as childbirth was a female experience, midwives jealously guarded their role in it. No matter how skilled they were, they were denied access to medical training that might have enabled them to develop lucrative practices on their own. Thus they had no intention of letting male doctors into their trade. For a time, the compromise was the handbooks, which contained guides to anatomy, descriptions of the most common complications, and the direst warnings to call trained physicians when serious problems arose.

By the beginning of the eighteenth century, the "man-midwife" had made his appearance in western Europe. Medically trained and usually experienced in other forms of surgery, the emergence of the man-midwife led to a number of breakthroughs in increasing the safety of childbirth. There can be no question that more mothers and children survived as a result of the man-midwives' knowledge and skills. But at the same time, the social experience of childbirth changed dramatically. What had been a female rite of passage, experienced by and with other women, now became a private event experienced by an individual woman and her male doctor. As female midwives were still excluded from medical training and licensing, their ability to practice their trade eroded in the face of new techniques and information to which they were denied access.

Although most man-midwives trained in hospitals where the poor came to give birth, they practiced among the rich. New attitudes toward marriage and children made the pain and danger of childbirth less acceptable to husbands, who sought every remedy they could afford. British and French man-midwives made fortunes practicing their trade. Their first task was to ascertain that the fetus was in the proper position to descend. In order to do this, however, they had to make an examination that was socially objectionable. Although advanced thinkers could face their man-midwife with the attitude that shame was better than death—"I considered that through modesty I was not to give up my life," as one English noblewoman reasoned—many women and more husbands were unprepared for the actual practice of a man. Thus students were taught as much about bedside manner as about medicine. They were not to examine the patient unless there was another person present in the room, they were not to ask direct questions, and they were not to face the patient during any of their procedures. They were taught to keep a linen cloth on top of the woman's abdomen and to make the examination only by touch—incredulous students were reminded that the most famous French man-midwife was blind! If the fetus were in the correct position, nothing further would be done until the delivery itself. It was only when the fetus was in what was labeled an "unnatural" position that the skill of the physician came into play.

For the most part, a child that could not be delivered head first, face down was in serious risk of being stillborn and the mother in serious risk of dying in labor. That was the problem to which the physicians addressed themselves in the eighteenth century and for which they found remarkable solutions. Most answers came from better understanding of female anatomy and a better visualization of the way in which the fetus moved during labor. The first advance was the realization that the fetus could be turned while still in the womb. Pressure applied on the outside of the stomach, especially in early stages of labor, could help the fetus drop down correctly. A baby who emerged feet first had to be turned face down before it was pulled through the birth canal.

For babies who could not be manually manipulated, the greatest advance of the eighteenth century was the invention of the forceps, or the *tire-tête*, as the French called them. With forceps, the physician could pull the baby by force when the mother was incapable of delivery. Forceps were used mostly in breech births but were also a vital tool when the baby was too large to pass through the cervix by contraction. The forceps were invented in Britain in the middle of the seventeenth century but were kept secret for more than 50

Childbirth with assistance from a man-midwife seated in a chair.

years. During that time they were used by three generations of a single family of man-midwives. In the eighteenth century, they came into general use when the Scotsman William Smellie (1697–1765) developed a short, leather-covered instrument that enabled the physician to do as little damage as possible to either mother or child. Obstetrics now emerged as a specialized branch of medical practice. If neither the pain nor the sorrow of childbirth could be eliminated, its dangers could be lessened.

■ *The Governess*, by Jean Baptiste Simeon Chardin. Many unmarried women moved to cities and found employment as maids. If a single woman or a widow had some education, she might serve as a governess, supervising the upbringing of children in a wealthy family.

subsistence producers. Perhaps another 40 percent of the population in western Europe was described by contemporaries as those without a fixed interest: in the country, those without land; in the towns, those without steady jobs.

It was easy to see why poverty was increasing. The relentless advance of population drove up the price of food and drove down the price of wages. In the second half of the eighteenth century, the cost of living in France rose by more than 60 percent while wages rose only by 25 percent. In Spain, the cost of living increased by 100 percent while wages rose only 20 percent. Only in Britain did wages nearly keep pace with prices. Rising prices made land more valuable. At the beginning of the eighteenth century, as the first wave of population expansion hit western Europe, small holdings began to decrease in size. The custom of partible inheritance, by which each son received a share of land, shrank the average size of a peasant holding below that necessary to sustain an average-size family, much less one that was growing larger. In one part of France it was estimated that 30 acres was a survival plot of land in good times. At the end of the seventeenth century, 80 percent of the peasants there owned less than 25 acres.

As holdings contracted, the portion of the family income derived from wage labor expanded. In such circumstances, males were more valuable than females, both as farmers and laborers, and there is incontrovertible evidence that European rural communities practiced female infanticide. In the end, however, it became increasingly difficult for the peasant family to remain on the land. Mediterranean sharecroppers fell further and further into debt until they finally lost their land entirely. Small freeholders were forced to borrow against future crops until a bad harvest led to foreclosure. Many were allowed to lease back their own lands, on short terms and at high rents, but most swelled the ranks of agricultural laborers, migrating during the planting and harvest seasons and suffering cruelly during winter and summer. In Britain, the rural landless outnumbered the landed by two to one. In France, as many as 8 million peasants no longer owned their own land.

Emigration was the first logical consequence of poverty. In places where rural misery was greatest, such as Ireland, whole communities pulled up stakes and moved to America. Frederick the Great attracted hundreds of thousands of emigrants to Prussia by offering them land. But most rural migrants did not move to new rural environments. Rather, they followed the well-trodden paths to the cities. Many traditional domestic crafts were evolving into industrial activities. In the past, peasants had supplemented their family income by processing raw materials in the home. Spinning, weaving, and sewing were common cottage industries in which the workers took in the work, supplied their own equipment, and were paid by the piece. Now, especially in the cloth trades, a new form of industrial activity was being organized. Factories, usually located in towns or larger villages, assembled workers together, set them at larger and more efficient machines, and paid them for their time rather than for their output. Families

had succumbed to quick death from disease or starvation, they eked out a miserable existence of constant hunger and chronic pain, with death at the end of a seemingly endless corridor.

It is impossible to gauge the number of European poor or to separate them into categories of greater and greatest misery. The truly indigent, the starving poor, probably composed 10 to 15 percent of most societies, perhaps as many as 20 million people throughout the Continent. They were most prevalent in towns but were an increasing burden on the countryside, where they wandered in search of agricultural employment. The wandering poor had no counterpart in the east, where serfdom kept everyone tied to the land, but the hungry and unsheltered certainly did. Yet the problem of poverty was not only to be seen among the destitute. In fact, the uniqueness of the poor in the eighteenth century was that they were drawn from social groups that even in the hungry times of the early seventeenth century had been successful

Eighteenth-Century Society   585

unable to support themselves from the land had no choice but to follow the movement of jobs.

Caring for the Poor. Urban poverty seemed more extreme to observers because there were more poor to observe. They crowded into towns in search of work or charity, though they were unlikely to find much of either. Urban areas were better equipped to assist the poor than were the rural communities from which they came, but the likelihood of finding aid only attracted more and more poor, straining and finally breaking the capacities of urban institutions. The death rate of the migrants and their children was staggering. It is perhaps best typified by the dramatic increase in the numbers of abandoned babies throughout western European cities. The existence of foundling hospitals in cities meant that unwed or poor mothers could leave their children in the hope that they would receive better care than the mother herself could provide. In fact, that was rarely the case. In the largest foundling hospital in Paris, only 15 percent of the children survived their first year of "care." But that did little to deter abandonment. In 1772, more than 7500 babies were left at that charnel house, representing 40 percent of all the children born in Paris that year. The normal rates of abandonment of between 10 and 15 percent of all children born in cities as diverse as Madrid and Brussels were little better.

Neither state nor private charities could cope with the flood of poor immigrants. Although the English pundit Samuel Johnson (1709–1784) opined that "a decent provision for the poor is the true test of civilization," what he meant was provision for the deserving poor, those unfortunates who were physically or mentally unable to support themselves. The distinction between the worthy and unworthy poor was one involved with changing definitions of charity itself. In earlier times, charity was believed to benefit the soul of the giver as much as the body of the recipient. Thus the poor were socially useful, providing the rich with the opportunity to do good works. But the poor were coming to be viewed as a problem of social administration. Hospitals, workhouses, and, more ominously, prisons were established or expanded to deal with them.

Hospitals were residential asylums rather than places for health care. They took in the old, the incapacitated, and, increasingly, the orphaned young. Those in France were aptly named "Hotels of God," considering their staggering death rates. "There children dwell who know no parents' care/Parents who know no children's care dwell there," one poet lamented. Workhouses existed for those who were capable of work but incapable of finding it. They were supposed to improve the values of the idle by keeping them busy, though in most places they served only to improve the profits of the industrialists, who rented out workhouse inmates at below-market wages. Prisons grew with crime. There were spectacular increases in crimes against property in all eighteenth-century cities, and despite severe penalties that could include hanging for petty theft, more criminals were incarcerated than executed. Enlightened arguments for the reform of pris-

ons and punishment tacitly acknowledged the social basis of most crime. As always, the victims of crime were mostly drawn from the same social backgrounds as the perpetrators. Along with all of their other troubles, it was the poor who were most commonly robbed, beaten, and abused.

Popular Culture. However depressing the story of the unrelieved misery of the poor is, the masses of eighteenth-century society were not only the downtrodden victims of social and economic forces beyond their control. For the peasant farmer about to lose his land or the urban artisan without a job, security was an overwhelming concern. But while many were to endure such fates, many others lived comfortably by the standards of the age, and almost everyone believed that things were better than they had ever been before. Popular culture was a rich mixture of family and community activities that provided outlets

■ A 1781 colored mezzotint by J. R. Smith shows a lady leaving a lending library with a book.

from the pressures of work and the vagaries of fortune. It was no less sustaining to the population at large than was the purely literate culture of the elite, no less vital as a means of explanation for everyday events than the theories of the philosophers or the programs of the philosophes.

In fact, the line between elite and popular culture in the eighteenth century was a thin one. For one thing, there was still much mixing of social classes in both rural and urban environments. Occasions of display such as festivals, village fairs, and religious holidays brought entire communities together and reinforced their collective identities. Moreover, there were many shared elements between the two cultures. All over Europe, literacy was increasing, the result of primary education, of new business techniques, and of the millions of books that were available in editions tailored to even the most modest purse. Nearly half of the inhabitants of France were literate by the end of the eighteenth century, perhaps 60 percent of those in Britain. Men were more likely to have learned to read than women, and those who lived in urban areas were more likely to

■ The poverty of eighteenth-century London slums was a favorite subject of the English artist William Hogarth. *Gin Lane* depicts the London poor in alcoholic delirium, their only escape from the misery of their daily lives.

be literate than those living in the countryside. More than a quarter of French women could read, a number that had doubled over the century. As the rates of female literacy rose, so did overall rates, for women took the lead in teaching children.

Popular literacy spawned popular literature in remarkable variety. Religious works remained the most important, but they were followed by almanacs, romances, and (perhaps surprisingly) chivalric fiction. Religious tracts aimed at the populace were found throughout Europe. They contained stories of the saints in Catholic countries and of the martyrs in Protestant ones, proverbs intended to increase spirituality, and prayers to be offered for all occasions. Almanacs combined prophecies, home remedies, astrological tables, predictions about the weather, and advice on all varieties of agricultural and industrial activities. In the middle of the century, just one of the dozens of British almanacs was selling more than 80,000 copies a year. Romances were the staple of lending libraries, which were also becoming a common feature of even small towns. The books were usually published in inexpensive installments spaced according to the time working families needed to save the pennies to purchase them. Written by middle-class authors, popular romances had a strong moral streak, promoting chastity for women and sobriety for men. Yet the best-selling popular fiction, at least in western Europe, was melodramatic tales of knights and ladies from the age of chivalry. The themes had seeped into popular consciousness after having fallen out of favor among the elites. But cultural tastes did not only trickle down. The masses kept the chivalric tradition alive during the eighteenth century; it would percolate up into elite culture in the nineteenth.

Nevertheless, literate culture was not the dominant form of popular culture. Traditional social activities continued to reflect the violent and even brutal nature of day-to-day existence. Many holidays were celebrated by sporting events that pitted the inhabitants of one village against those of another. The events almost always turned into free-for-alls in which broken bones were common and deaths not unknown. In fact, the frequent breakdown of sporting activities into gang wars was the principal cause for the development of rules for soccer, as well as more esoteric games such as cricket in Britain. Well-organized matches soon became forms of popular entertainment. More than 20,000 spectators attended one eighteenth-century cricket match, and soccer and cricket soon became as popular for gambling as horse racing was among the wealthy.

Even more popular were the so-called blood sports, which continued to be the most common form of popular recreation. Those were brutal competitions in which, in one way or another, animals were maimed or slaughtered. Dogfighting and cockfighting were among those that survive today. Less attractive to the modern mind were blood sports such as bearbaiting or bull running, in which the object was the slaughter of a large beast over a prolonged period of time. Blood sports were certainly not confined to the masses—foxhunting and bullfighting were pastimes for the very rich—but they formed a significant part of local social activity.

The local tavern or alehouse also became a significant part of social activity, and in town or country was the site for local communication and recreation. There women and men gossiped and gambled to while away the hours between sundown and bedtime. Discussions and games became animated as the evening wore on, for staggering amounts of alcohol were consumed. "Drunk for a penny, dead drunk for two pennies, straw for nothing," advertised one of the thousands of British gin mills that dominated the poorer quarters of towns. The increased use of spirits—gin, brandy, rum, and vodka—changed the nature of alcohol consumption in Europe. Wine and beer had always been drunk in quantities that we would find astounding, but those beverages were also an important part of diet. The nutritional content of spirits was negligible. People drank spirits to get drunk. The British reformer Francis Place (1771–1854), who grew up in a working-class family, commented that the British masses had only two pleasures, "sex and drinking. And drunkenness is by far the most desired." The level to which it rose in the eighteenth century speaks volumes about the changes in social and economic life that the masses of European society were then experiencing.

CONCLUSION

Eighteenth-century society was a hybrid of old and new. It remained highly stratified. Birth and occupation determined wealth, privilege, and quality of life as much as they had in the past, but there were now more paths toward the middle and upper classes, more wealth to be distributed among those above the level of subsistence. Opulence and poverty increased in step as the fruits of commerce and land enriched the upper orders while rising population impoverished the lower ones. Enlightenment ideas highlighted the contradictions. The attack on traditional authority, especially the Roman Catholic Church, was an attack on a conservative, static world view. Enlightenment thinkers looked to the future, to a new world shaped by reason and knowledge, a world ruled benevolently for the benefit of all human beings. Government, society, the individual—all could be improved if only the rubble of the past was cleared away. Those thinkers could hardly imagine how potent their vision would become.

QUESTIONS FOR REVIEW

1. What were the main elements of Enlightenment thought?
2. What social, moral, and religious traditions were challenged by the ideas of thinkers such as Voltaire, Hume, Montesquieu, and Rousseau?
3. How did the European nobility maintain its social eminence in the face of a new bourgeois culture created by an expanding middle class?
4. Why did Europe's population begin to grow so dramatically in the eighteenth century, and how did society respond to the challenges that such an increase posed?

KEY TERMS

bourgeoisie, *p. 570*
deists, *p. 567*
Enlightenment, *p. 562*
fodder crops, *p. 581*
laissez-faire, p. 569
Patent of Toleration, *p. 569*
philosophes, *p. 564*
Physiocrats, *p. 569*
progress, *p. 568*
salons, *p. 562*
skepticism, *p. 566*

DISCOVERING WESTERN CIVILIZATION ONLINE

You can obtain more information about culture and society in eighteenth-century Europe at the Websites listed below. See also the Companion Website that accompanies this text, www.ablongman.com/kishlansky, which contains an online study guide and additional resources.

Eighteenth-Century Culture

NM's Creative Impulse: Enlightenment
www.history.evansville.net/enlighte.html
The best starting point for the culture and history of the age of Enlightenment.

Eighteenth-Century Resources
andromeda.rutgers.edu/~jlynch/18th/
A gateway to a wealth of sources on many different aspects of eighteenth-century culture.

Eighteenth-Century Studies
eserver.org/18th/
A list of links to a wide range of material relating to eighteenth-century literature and culture.

Internet Modern History Sourcebook: The Enlightenment
www.fordham.edu/halsall/mod/modsbook10.html
An outstanding collection of texts of Enlightenment writers.

Eighteenth-Century Society

The New Child: British Art and the Origins of Modern Childhood
www.bampfa.berkeley.edu/exhibits/newchild/
A site devoted to the nature of childhood in eighteenth-century Britain.

Voice of the Shuttle: Restoration and 18th Century
vos.ucsb.edu/browse.asp?id=2738
An inclusive page of links and resources for the study of English literature in the eighteenth century.

SUGGESTIONS FOR FURTHER READING

General Reading

T. C. W. Blanning, *The Culture of Power and the Power of Culture: Old Regime Europe 1660–1789* (New York: Oxford University Press, 2002). An outstanding example of the new cultural history.

William Doyle, *The Old European Order, 1660–1800,* 2d ed. (Oxford: Oxford University Press, 1992). An important essay on the structure of European societies and the ways in which they held together.

Henry Kamen, *Early Modern European Society* (New York: Routledge, 2000). A concise social history by a leading historian.

Eighteenth-Century Culture

A. J. Ayer, *Voltaire* (New York: Random House, 1986). A brief and vibrant study.

James Buchan, *Crowded With Genius: The Scottish Enlightenment: Edinburgh's Moment of the Mind* (New York: Harper Perennial, 2004). A history of the exciting literary, economic, and philosophical innovations of later eighteenth-century Scotland.

Robert Darnton, *The Forbidden Best-Sellers of Pre-Revolutionary France* (New York: W. W. Norton, 1995). A look at the underbelly of the Enlightenment that both provides gripping reading and makes us think about the Enlightenment in new ways.

Nicholas Dent, *Rousseau* (Routledge, 2005). The best general introduction to an exceptional eighteenth-century Frenchman's life and thought.

John G. Gagliardo, *Enlightened Despotism* (New York: Thomas Y. Crowell, 1967). A sound exploration of the impact of Enlightenment ideas on the rulers of Europe, with emphasis on the east.

Norman Hampson, *The Enlightenment* (London: Penguin Books, 1982). The best one-volume survey.

Patrick Mauries, *Cabinets of Curiosities* (London: Thames and Hudson, 2002). A fascinating account of collectors and collecting.

Dorinda Outram, *The Enlightenment* (London: Cambridge University Press, 2005). A brief thematic and global treatment of the Enlightenment in its social context.

Daniel Roche, *France in the Enlightenment* (Cambridge, MA: Harvard University Press, 1998). A wide-ranging survey of everything from politics to popular culture.

Judith Shklar, *Montesquieu* (Oxford: Oxford University Press, 1987). A concise, readable study of the man and his work.

Eighteenth-Century Society: The Nobility

Jonathan Dewald, *The European Nobility, 1400–1800* (Cambridge: Cambridge University Press, 1996). An insightful survey.

Jerzy Lukowski, *The European Nobility in the Eighteenth Century* (New York: Palgrave MacMillan, 2003). Especially valuable for its treatment of eastern Europe.

Eighteenth-Century Society: The Bourgeoisie

John Brewer, *The Pleasures of the Imagination: English Culture in the Eighteenth Century* (London: HarperCollins, 1997). A fascinating study of the making of high culture in England.

Peter Earle, *The Making of the English Middle Class* (London: Methuen, 1989). The manners, mores, and mindset of the group that would come to dominate nineteenth-century Britain.

Jean-Louis Flandrin, *Families in Former Times* (Cambridge: Cambridge University Press, 1979). Strong on family and household organization.

Olwen Hufton, *The Prospect Before Her: A History of Women in Western Europe* (New York: Alfred Knopf, 1996). A survey of women's history that is particularly strong on the eighteenth century.

Simon Shama, *The Embarrassment of Riches* (Berkeley: University of California Press, 1987). The social life of Dutch burghers, richly portrayed.

Lawrence Stone, *The Family, Sex and Marriage in England, 1500–1800* (New York: Harper & Row, 1979). A controversial but extremely important argument about the changing nature of family life.

Eighteenth-Century Society: The Masses

Peter Burke, *Popular Culture in Early Modern Europe* (New York: Harper & Row, 1978). A wide survey of practices throughout the Continent.

Olwen Hufton, *The Poor in Eighteenth-Century France* (Oxford: Oxford University Press, 1974). A compelling study of the life of the poor.

E. A. Wrigley and R. S. Schofield, *The Population History of England* (Cambridge, MA: Harvard University Press, 1981). The most important reconstruction of a national population, by a team of researchers.

For a list of additional titles related to this chapter's topics, please see http://www.ablongman.com/kishlansky.

CHAPTER

20 THE FRENCH REVOLUTION AND THE NAPOLEONIC ERA, 1789–1815

THE TENNIS COURT OATH: THE BEGINNING OF THE FRENCH REVOLUTION

Imagine the world of Jacques-Louis David (1748–1825), who was an influential painter in the royal court in France during the 1780s. A leading artist who studied in France and Italy and perfected his own neoclassical style that bestowed dignity on his historical paintings and portraits alike, he was considered a leader of his generation by the liberal and aristocratic elite of the late eighteenth century.

And then the world changed. Beginning in 1789 a decade of political transformation and turmoil, beginning with the French Revolution, swept across Europe. In June of that year King Louis XVI summoned representatives of his subjects to meet at the royal residence at Versailles to deal with the fiscal crisis facing France.

THE VISUAL RECORD

Although he was not at Versailles, David has provided us with a strong visual record and interpretation of an event of particular significance that transpired there on 20 June 1789. Look at the warm sepia tones of David's *The Tennis Court Oath*, in which he captures the spirit of an important moment in the history of democracy. This scene depicts commoners, accompanied by some clergy (the three figures forming a circle in the middle foreground), taking an oath "never to separate, and to meet whenever circumstances demand until a constitution of the kingdom is established and affirmed on solid foundations." It is a jubilant scene—one of energy and camaraderie. It is a scene of hope.

How these men came to be standing together in an indoor tennis court at Versailles, the seat of the French monarchy, is a story rooted in the travails of the French king. It is also a story rooted in the optimism of the Enlightenment. Three days earlier, on 17 June 1789, the group pictured here—577 strong—declared themselves to be deputies of the **National Assembly** (see p. 595). On 20 June, finding that they were locked out of their regular meeting room by the king's guard and outraged by this insult, they moved to a nearby indoor tennis court whose high walls and high windows add drama to this scene.

The winds of change blow in from the windows on the upper left of the painting, and the common people, including women and children, crowd the windows in witness to the scene. Standing in the middle of the tableau, but by no means dominating it, and facing the viewer with his arm upraised is the deputies' president Jean-Sylvain Bailly (1736–1793), who leads the assembled in the recitation of the "oath." Many deputies indicate their enthusiastic assent with upraised arms. Despite the sense of unity that the composition and its warm tones convey, the viewer can find many different stories captured in the moment. In the lower left, see the old man being carried in on a chair. Look for those who are carrying on their own discussions with their neighbors or are caught up in their own worlds. To the right of the speaker one person grabs his chest with emotion, while another in the lower right corner sits cross-armed, perhaps the sole deputy who did not sign the oath. As well as the promise of political progress that a constitution would bring, David shows us the seeds of political dissension and in this dramatization of an event that spelled the end of absolute monarchy and the beginning of a new concept of state power that resided in the people. The revolution had begun.

590

■ *The Tennis Court Oath* By Jacques-Louis David, 1791.

LOOKING AHEAD

The revolution that took place in France in 1789 was not the first political upheaval of that era, but it proved to be the most violent. Six years earlier the American War of Independence against Great Britain ended. Other European countries were engaged in battles for liberty. All of these revolutions shared elements in common, including an awareness of the same Enlightenment philosophers and intellectuals on both sides of the Atlantic whose works questioned existing institutions and traditions and endorsed democracy, liberty, and equality. To understand the revolution in France, one must understand the distinctive nature of French society, economy, and politics in the 50 years preceding 1789 and the crisis in the Old Regime. In their revolution, the French experimented with parliamentary government and representative and participatory democracy, all the while contending with internal violence and foreign wars. The French Revolution ended with the coming to power of Napoleon, who was both the heir of the revolution and its destroyer.

THE FRENCH REVOLUTION AND THE FALL OF THE MONARCHY

Those who lived through it were sure that there had never been a time like it before. The French Revolution, or the Great Revolution, as it was known to people alive at the time, was a period of creation and discovery. The ten years from 1789 to 1799 were punctuated by genuine euphoria and democratic transformations. But the French Revolution was also a time of violence and destruction. From the privileged elites who initiated the overthrow of the existing order to the peasants and workers, men and women, who railed against tyranny, the revolution touched every segment of society.

The revolution achieved most in the area of politics. The overthrow of absolutist monarchy brought with it new social theories, new symbols, and new behavior. The excitement of anarchy was matched by the terror of repression. In the search for a new order, competing political forms followed one after the other in rapid succession: constitutional monarchy, republic, oligarchy, and dictatorship.

At the end of the eighteenth century France was a state in trouble, but it was not alone. Revolutionary incidents flared up throughout Europe in the second half of the eighteenth century in the Netherlands, Belgium, and Ireland. Absolute authority was challenged and sometimes modified. Across the Atlantic, American colonists concerned with the principle of self-rule had thrown off the yoke of the British in the War of Independence. But none of the events, including the American Revolution, was so violent in breaking with the old order, so extensive in involving millions of men and women in political action, and so consequential for the political futures of other European states as was the French Revolution. The triumphs and contradictions of the revolutionary experiment in democracy mark the end of the old order and the beginning of modern history. Politics would never be the same again.

The Political and Fiscal Crisis of Eighteenth-Century France

The French monarchy was in a state of perpetual financial crisis across the eighteenth century. Louis XV, like his great-grandfather Louis XIV, ruled as an absolute monarch; but he lacked sufficient funds to run the state. He sought loans to meet his needs as well as to pay the interest on existing debts. Borrowing at high rates required the government to pay out huge sums in interest and service fees on the loans that were keeping it afloat. The outlays in turn piled the state's indebtedness ever higher, requiring more loans, and threatening to topple the whole financial structure of the state and the regime itself. The monarchy tried to reduce expenditures, but such attempts were limited by the necessity of maintaining an effective and costly army and navy because of wars on both the Continent and in the colonies.

The nadir of Louis XV's reign came in 1763, with the French defeat in the Seven Years' War. The defeat not only left France barren of funds, it also promoted further expenditures for strengthening the French navy against the superior British fleet. The king saw taxation as the only way out of the financial trap in which he now found himself.

But raising taxes was far from an easy undertaking, and it was one that required the support of the aristocracy. The heightened tensions between the monarch and the aristocracy found expression in various institutions, especially the parlements, which were the 13 sovereign courts in the French judicial system, with their seats in Paris and a dozen provincial centers. The magistrates of each parlement were members of the aristocracy, some of them nobles of recent origin and others of long standing, depending on the locale. Following the costly Seven Years' War, the parlements chose to exercise the power of refusal by blocking a proportional tax to be imposed on nobles and commoners alike. The magistrates resisted taxation, arguing that the king was attacking the liberty of his subjects by attempting to tax those who were exempt by virtue of their privileged status.

The parlements claimed that they represented the nation; the king said the nation was himself. The king repeatedly attempted to neutralize the power of the parlements by relying instead on his own state bureaucracy, which was too weak for the task. The king's agents in the provinces, the intendants, were accountable directly to the central government. The intendants, as the king's men, and the magistrates who presided in the parlements represented contradictory claims to power. As the king's needs increased in the second half of the eighteenth century, the situation was becoming intolerable for those exercising power and those aspiring to rule in the name and for the good of the nation. The financial crisis provided the elite of notables, made up of both aristocrats and bourgeois, with the basis for asserting their own ascendancy to political power. Louis XV, who is often remembered for his cavalier prediction, "*Après moi, la déluge*" ("After me comes the

DOCUMENT

Madame de Staël on the Ancient Regime

flood"), indeed left a debt that swamped his grandson and successor Louis XVI. This tension between a growing debt that was undermining the monarchy and the increased ascendancy of an elite of nobles and bourgeois came to characterize the **Old Regime** in France.

When Louis XVI assumed the French throne in 1774, he was only 20 years old. He inherited a monarchy in a state of perpetual financial crisis. Not only did he inherit a trouble-ridden fiscal structure, but Louis XVI also made his own contributions to it, increasing the debt greatly by his involvement in the War of American Independence (1775–1783). Following the advice of a series of ministers, Louis sought structural solutions to the debt through a reformed fiscal policy, taxation, and other new sources of revenue, but each set of reforms offended different established interests. In the end he resorted to an unusual but available step—the convening of the **Estates-General**—as a means of achieving reforms and providing financial stability for the state.

Historically, the Estates-General was the representative body of the three "estates," or social groups, of France—the clergy (the First Estate), the nobility (the Second Estate), and the commoners (the Third Estate). The **Third Estate** was composed of all those members of the realm who enjoyed no special privilege—28 million French people. The Estates-General had not been convened since 1614. Through this body and its duly chosen representatives, Louis XVI sought the consent of the nation to levy taxes. In the political organizing that took place in the winter of 1788–1789 the seeds of revolution were sown.

Convening the Estates-General

When Louis XVI announced in August 1788 that the Estates-General would meet at Versailles in May 1789, people from all walks of life hoped for some redress of their miseries. The king hoped that the clergy, nobility, and commoners would solve his fiscal problems. Every social group, from the nobles to the poorest laborers, had its own agenda and its own ideas about justice, social status, and economic well-being.

One in four nobles had moved from the bourgeoisie to the aristocratic ranks in the eighteenth century; two out of every three had been ennobled during the seventeenth or eighteenth centuries. Nobles had succeeded in expanding their economic and social power and they now sought to preserve it. Furthermore, a growing segment of the nobility, influenced by Enlightenment ideas and the example of English institutions, was intent on increasing the political dominance of the aristocracy.

Members of the Third Estate, traditionally excluded from political and social power, were presented with the opportunity of expressing their opinions on the state of government and society. As commoners in the Third Estate, the bourgeoisie embraced within it a variety of professions, from bankers and financiers to businessmen, merchants, entrepreneurs, lawyers, shopkeepers, and artisans. Those who could

■ This cartoon depicts the plight of the French peasants. An old farmer is bowed down under the weight of the privileged aristocracy and clergy while birds and rabbits, protected by unfair game laws, eat his crops.

not read stood in marketplaces and city squares or sat around evening fires and had the political literature read to them. Farmhands and urban laborers realized that they were participating in the same process as their social betters, and they believed they had a right to speak and be heard.

It was a time of great hope, especially for workers and peasants who had been buffeted by the rise in prices, decline in real wages, and the hunger that followed crop failures and poor harvests. There was new promise of a respite and a solution. Taxes could be discussed and changed, the state bureaucracy could be reformed—or better, abolished. Intellectuals discussed political alternatives in the salons of the wealthy. Nobles and bourgeois met in philosophical societies dedicated to enlightened thought. Commoners gathered in cafes to drink and debate. Although the poor often fell outside the network of communication, they were not immune to the ideas that emerged. In the end, people of all classes had opinions and were more certain than ever of their right to express their ideas. Absolutism was in trouble, though Louis XVI did not know it, as people began to forge a collectively shared idea of politics. People now had a forum—the Estates-General—and a focus—the politics of taxation.

"If Only the King Knew."   In conjunction with the political activity and in scheduled meetings, members of all three estates drew up lists of their problems. This process took place in a variety of forums, including guilds and village and town meetings. The people of France drew up grievance lists—known as *cahiers de doléances*—that were then carried to Versailles by the deputies elected to the Estates-General. The grievance lists contained the collective outpouring of problems of each estate and are important for two major reasons. First, they made clear the similarity of grievances shared throughout France. Second, they indicated the extent to which a common political culture, based on a concern with political reform, had permeated different levels of French society. Both the privileged and the nonprivileged identified a common enemy in the system of state bureaucracy to which the monarch was so strongly tied. Although the king was still addressed with respect, new concerns with liberty, equality, property, and the rule of law were voiced.

"If only the king knew!" In that phrase, French men and women had for generations expressed their belief in the inevitability of their fate and the benevolence of their king. They saw the king as a loving and wise father who would not tolerate the injustices visited on his subjects if only he knew what was really happening. In 1789, peasants and workers were questioning why their lives could not be better, but they continued to express their trust in the king. Combined with their old faith was a new hope. The peasants in the little town of Saintes recorded their newly formed expectations:

> Our king, the best of kings and father of a great and wise family, will soon know everything. All vices will be destroyed. All the great virtues of industriousness, honesty, modesty, honor, patriotism, meekness, friendliness, equality, concord, pity, and thrift will prevail and wisdom will rule supreme.

The elected deputies arrived at Versailles at the beginning of May 1789 carrying in their valises and trunks the grievances of their estates. The opening session of the Estates-General took place in a great hall especially constructed for the event. The 1248 deputies presented a grand spectacle as they filed to their assigned places to hear speeches by the king and his ministers. Contrasts among the participants were immediately apparent. Seated on a raised throne under a canopy at one end of the hall, Louis XVI was vested in full kingly regalia. On his right sat the archbishops and cardinals of the First Estate, strikingly clad in the pinks and purples of their offices. On his left were the richly and decorously attired nobility of the Second Estate. Facing the stage sat the 648 deputies of the Third Estate, dressed in plain black suits, stark against the colorful and costly costumes of the privileged. Members of the Third Estate had announced beforehand that they would not follow the ancient custom for commoners of kneeling at the king's entrance. Fired by the hope of equal treatment and an equal share of power, they had come to Versailles to make a constitution. The opening ceremony degenerated into a moment of confusion over whether members of the Third Estate should be able to wear their hats in the presence of the king. Many saw in the politics of clothing a tense beginning to their task.

The Crisis in Voting by Estate.   The tension between commoners and the privileged was aggravated by the unresolved issue of how the voting was to proceed. Traditionally, each of the three orders was equally weighted. The arrangement favored the nobility, who controlled the first two estates, since the clergy themselves were often noble.

The Third Estate was adamant in its demand for vote by head. The privileged orders were equally firm in insisting on vote by order. Paralysis set in, as days dragged into weeks and

■ "Abuses to Suppress." This cartoon depicts the Third Estate—represented here by the peasant following the carriage, the worker leading the horses, and the merchant driving—delivering a petition of "abuses" to be remedied by the National Assembly.

ABUS À SUPPRIMÉ

Présentée a l'Assemblée Nationale par les trois Ordres

"WHAT IS THE THIRD ESTATE?"

As an ambitious clergyman from Chartres, Abbé Emmanuel Joseph Sieyès was a member of the First Estate. Yet Sieyès was elected deputy to the Estates-General for the Third Estate on the basis of his attacks on aristocratic privilege. He participated in the writing and editing of the great documents of the early revolution: the Oath of the Tennis Court and the Declaration of the Rights of Man and Citizen. The pamphlet for which he is immortalized in revolutionary lore was his daring "What Is the Third Estate?" Written in January 1789, it boldly confronted the bankruptcy of the system of privilege of the Old Regime and threw down the gauntlet to those who ruled France. In this document the revolution found its rallying point.

Focus Questions

Why does Sieyès claim that nothing in the nation can "progress" without the Third Estate? When he states that "the nobility does not belong to the social organization at all," what point is he making about the social utility of privilege?

1st. What is the Third Estate? Everything.

2nd. What has it been heretofore in the political order? Nothing.

3rd. What does it demand? To become something therein. . . .

Who, then, would dare to say that the Third Estate has not within itself all that is necessary to constitute a complete nation? It is the strong and robust man whose one arm remains enchained. If the privileged order were abolished, the nation would not be something less but something more. Thus, what is the Third Estate? Everything; but an everything shackled and oppressed. What would it be without the privileged order? Everything; but an everything free and flourishing. Nothing can progress without it; everything would proceed infinitely better without the others. It is not sufficient to have demonstrated that the privileged classes, far from being useful to the nation, can only enfeeble and injure it; it is necessary, moreover, to prove that the nobility does not belong to the social organization at all; that, indeed, it may be a *burden* upon the nation, but that it would not know how to constitute a part thereof.

The Third Estate, then, comprises everything appertaining to the nation; and whatever is not the Third Estate may not be regarded as being of the nation. What is the Third Estate? Everything!

the Estates were unable to act. The body that was to save France from fiscal collapse was hopelessly deadlocked.

Abbé Emmanuel Joseph Sieyès (1748–1836), a member of the clergy, emerged as the critical leader of the Third Estate. Sieyès had already established his reputation as a firebrand reformer with his eloquent pamphlet, "What Is the Third Estate?" published in January 1789. (See the document above.) He understood that although eighteenth-century French society continued to be divided by law and custom into a pyramid of three tiers, these orders or estates were obsolete in representing social realities. The base of the pyramid was formed by the largest of the three estates, those who worked—the bourgeoisie, the peasantry, and urban and rural workers—and produced the nation's wealth. He argued that so long as the First and Second Estates did not share their privileges and rights, they were not a part of the French nation.

Under the influence of Sieyès and the reformist consensus that characterized their ranks, the delegates of the Third Estate decided to proceed with their own meetings. On 17 June 1789, joined by some sympathetic clergy, the Third Estate changed its name to the National Assembly as an assertion of its true representation of the French nation. They dedicated themselves to the primary task of writing a constitution and thereby ending absolute rule of the king. (See The Visual Record, pp. 590–591.)

The Importance of Public Opinion. The drama of Versailles, a staged play of gestures, manners, oaths, and attire, also marked the beginning of a far-reaching political revolution. Although it was a drama that took place behind closed doors, it was not one unknown to the general public. Throughout May and June 1789, Parisians trekked to Versailles to watch the deliberations and then brought the news back to the capital. Deputies wrote home to their constituents to keep them abreast of events. Newspapers that reported daily on the wranglings and pamphleteers who analyzed them spread the news throughout the nation. Information, often conflicting, stirred up anxiety; news of conflict encouraged action.

The frustration and stalemate of the Estates-General threatened to put the spark to the kindling of urban unrest. The people of Paris had suffered through a harsh winter and spring under the burdens of high prices (especially of bread), limited supplies, and relentless tax demands. The rioting of the spring had for the moment ceased as people waited for their problems to be solved by the deputies of the Estates-General. The suffering of the urban poor was not new, but their ability to connect economic hardships with the politics at Versailles and to blame the government was. As hopes began to dim with the news of political stalemate, news broke of the creation of the National Assembly. It was greeted with new anticipation.

The Outbreak of Revolutionary Action in 1789

The king, who had temporarily withdrawn from sight following the death of his son at the beginning of June, reemerged to meet with the representatives of each of the three estates and propose reforms, including a constitutional monarchy. But Louis XVI refused to accept the now popularly supported National Assembly as a legitimate body, insisting instead that he must rely on the three estates for advice. He simply did not understand that the choice was no longer his to make. He summoned troops to Versailles and began concentrating soldiers in Paris. Civilians continually clashed with members of the military, whom they jostled and jeered. The urban crowds recognized the threat of repression that the troops represented. People decided to meet force with force. To do so, they needed arms themselves—and they knew where to get them.

The Storming of the Bastille.   On 14 July 1789, the irate citizens of Paris stormed the Bastille, a royal armory that also served as a prison for a handful of debtors. The storming of the Bastille became the great symbol in the revolutionary legend of the overthrow of the tyranny and oppression of the Old Regime. But it is significant for another reason. It was an expression of the power of the people to take politics into their own hands. Parisians were following the lead of their deputies in Versailles. They had formed a citizen militia known as the National Guard, and they were prepared to defend their concept of justice and law.

The people who stormed the Bastille were not the poor, the unemployed, the criminals, or the urban rabble, as their detractors portrayed them. They were petty tradesmen, shop-keepers, and wage-earners, who considered it their right to seize arms in order to protect their interests. The Marquis de Lafayette (1757–1834), a noble beloved of the people because of his participation in the American Revolution, helped organize the National Guard. Under his direction, the militia adopted the tricolor flag as its standard. The tricolor combined the red and blue colors of the city of Paris with the white of the Bourbon royal family. It became the flag of the revolution, replacing the fleur-de-lis of the Bourbons. It is the national flag of France today.

The king could no longer dictate the terms of the constitution. By their actions, the people in arms had ratified the National Assembly. Louis XVI was forced to yield. The events in Paris set off similar uprisings in cities and towns throughout France. National guards in provincial cities modeled themselves after the Parisian militia. Government officials fled their posts and abandoned their responsibilities. Commoners stood ready to fill the power vacuum. But the revolution was not just an urban phenomenon: the peasantry had their own grievances and their own way of making a revolution.

Peasant Fear of an Aristocratic Plot.   The precariousness of rural life and the increase in population in the countryside contributed to the permanent displacement and destitution of a growing sector of rural society. Without savings and destroyed by poor harvests, impoverished rural inhabitants wandered the countryside looking for odd jobs and eventually begging to survive. All peasants endured common obligations placed on them by the crown and the privileged classes. A bewildering array of taxes afflicted peasants: they owed the tithe to the Church, land taxes to the state, and seigneurial dues and rents to the landlord. In some areas, peasants repaired roads

■ This lively amateur painting of the fall of the Bastille is by Claude Cholat, one of the attackers. Tradition has it that Cholat is manning the cannon in the background. The inscription proclaims that the painting is by one of the "conquerors of the Bastille."

MAP DISCOVERY

Boundaries, 1789

★ Revolutionary centers

Areas of the Great Fear, July – Aug. 1789

French boundaries, 1793

Counter-revolutionary activity

• Centers of counter-revolutionary activity

Areas of insurrection

0   200 Miles

0   200 Kilometers

Revolutionary France

The French Revolution was not merely a Parisian phenomenon, as this map shows. Locate the revolutionary centers on the map. What feature is common to all of these centers? How do you explain their distribution throughout France? Pockets of insurrection and counter-revolution were scattered for the most part in the southeast and west. What did they have in common? What territories did France gain between 1789 and 1793 and why did it expand?

and drew lots for military service. Dues affected almost every aspect of rural life. The labor of women was essential to the survival of the rural family. Peasant women sought employment in towns and cities as seamstresses and servants in order to send money back home to struggling relatives. Children, too, added their earnings to the family pot. In spite of various strategies for survival, the lives of more and more peasant families were disrupted by the end of the eighteenth century as they were displaced from the land.

News of the events of Versailles and then of the revolutionary action in Paris did not reassure rural inhabitants. By the end of June the hope of deliverance from crippling taxes and dues was rapidly fading. The news of the Oath of the Tennis Court and the storming of the Bastille terrified country folk, who saw the actions as evidence of an aristocratic plot that threatened sorely needed reforms. As information moved along postal routes in letters from delegates to their supporters, and as news was repeated in the Sunday market gatherings, distortions and exaggerations crept in. It seemed to rural inhabitants that their world was falling apart. Some peasants believed that Paris was in the hands of brigands and that the king and the Estates-General were victims of an aristocratic plot. Rural vision, fueled by empty stomachs, was apocalyptic.

That state of affairs was aggravated as increasing numbers of peasants were pushed off the land to seek employment as transient farm laborers, moving from one area to another with the cycles of sowing and harvesting. Throughout the 1780s, the number of peasants without land was increasing steadily.

Starving men, women, and children, filthy and poorly dressed, were frightening figures to villagers who feared that the same fate would befall them with the next bad harvest. As one landowner lamented, "We cannot lie down without fear, the nighttime paupers have tormented us greatly, to say nothing of the daytime ones, whose numbers are considerable."

Most peasants had lived in the same place for generations and knew only the confines of their own villages. They were uneasy about what existed beyond the horizon. Transients, often speaking strange dialects, disrupted and threatened the social universe of the village. In order to survive, wanderers often resorted to petty theft, stealing fruit from trees or food from unwatched hearths. Often traveling in groups, hordes of vagabonds struck fear into the hearts of farm workers, trampling crops and sleeping in open fields. Peasants were sure that the unfortunate souls were brigands paid by the local aristocracy to persecute a peasantry already stretched to the breaking point.

The Peasant Revolt. Hope gave way to fear. Beginning on 20 July 1789, peasants in different areas of France reacted collectively throughout France, spreading false rumors of a great conspiracy. Fear gripped whole villages and in some areas spawned revolt. Just as urban workers had connected their economic hardships to politics, so too did desperate peasants see their plight in political terms. Historians describe this period of collective panic as the **Great Fear**. Peasants banded together and marched to the residences of the local nobility, breaking into chateaux with a single mission in mind: to destroy all legal documents by which nobles claimed payments, dues, and services from local peasants. They drove out the lords and in some cases burned their chateaux, putting an end to the tyranny of the privileged over the countryside. The peasants had taken matters into their own hands. They intended to consign the last vestiges of aristocratic privilege to the bonfires of aristocratic documents.

The overthrow of privileges rooted in a feudal past was not so easy. Members of the National Assembly were aghast at the eruption of rural violence. They knew that to stay in power they had to maintain peace. They also knew that to be credible they had to protect property. Peasant destruction of seigneurial claims posed a real dilemma for the bourgeois deputies directing the revolution. If they gave in to peasant demands, they risked losing aristocratic support and undermining their own ability to control events. If they gave in to the aristocracy, they risked a social revolution in the countryside, which they could not police or repress. Liberal members of the aristocracy cooperated with the bourgeois leaders in finding a solution.

■ A contemporary print of the women of Paris advancing on Versailles. The determined marchers are shown waving pikes and dragging an artillery piece. The women were hailed as heroines of the revolution.

Depart des Heroines de Paris pour Versailles le 5 Octobre 1789.

In a dramatic meeting that lasted through the night of 4 August 1789, the National Assembly agreed to abolish the principle of privilege. The peasants had won—or thought they had. In the weeks and months ahead, rural people learned that they had lost their own prerogatives—the rights to common grazing and gathering—and were expected to buy their way out of their feudal services. In the meantime, parliamentary action had saved the day: the deputies stabilized the situation through legislating compromise.

Women on the March.   Women participated with men in both urban and rural revolutionary actions. Acting on their own, women were responsible for one of the most dramatic events of the early years of the revolution: in October 1789 they forced the king and the royal family to leave Versailles for Paris to deal in person with the problems of bread supply, high prices, and starvation. Women milling about in the marketplaces of Paris on the morning of 5 October were complaining bitterly about the high cost and shortages of bread. The National Assembly was in session, and the National Guards were patrolling the streets of Paris. But the trappings of political change had no impact on the brutal realities of the marketplace.

Women were in charge of buying the food for their families. Every morning they stood in lines with their neighbors reenacting the familiar ritual. Some mornings they were turned away, told by the baker or his assistants that there was no bread. On other days they did not have enough coins in their purses to buy the staple of their diet. Women responsible for managing the consumption of the household were most directly in touch with the state of provisioning the capital. When they were unable to feed their families, the situation became intolerable.

So it was, on the morning of 5 October 1789, that 6000 Parisian women marched out of the city and toward Versailles. They were taking their problem to the king with the demand that he solve it. Later in the day, Lafayette led the Parisian National Guard to Versailles to mediate events. The women were armed with pikes, the simple weapon available to the poorest defender of the revolution, and they were prepared to use them. The battle came early the next morning, when the women, now accompanied by revolutionary men, tired and cold from waiting all night at the gates of the palace, invaded the royal apartments and chased Marie Antoinette from her bedroom. Several members of the royal guards, hated by the people of Paris for alleged insults against the tricolor cockade, were killed by the angry crowd, who decapitated them and mounted their heads on pikes. A shocked Louis XVI agreed to return with the crowd to Paris. The crowd cheered Louis's decision, which briefly reestablished his personal popularity. But as monarch, he had been humiliated at the hands of women of the capital. Reduced to the roles of "the baker, the baker's wife, and the baker's son" by jeering crowds, the royal family was forced to return to Paris that very day. Louis XVI was now captive to the revolution, whose efforts to form a constitutional monarchy he purported to support.

Declaring Political Rights

"Liberty consists in the ability to do whatever does not harm another." So wrote the revolutionary deputies of 1789. Sounding a refrain similar to that of the American Declaration of Independence, the Declaration of the Rights of Man and Citizen appeared on 26 August 1789. The document amalgamated a variety of Enlightenment ideas drawn from the works of political philosophy, including those of Locke and Montesquieu. "Men are born and remain free and equal in rights. Social distinctions may be based only on common utility." Perhaps most significant of all was the attention given to property, which was declared a "sacred and inviolable," "natural," and "imprescriptible" right of man.

In the year of tranquility that followed the violent summer of 1789, the new politicians set themselves the task of creating institutions based on the principle of liberty and others embodied in the Declaration of the Rights of Man and Citizen. The result was the Constitution of 1791, a statement of faith in a progressive constitutional monarchy. A king accountable to an elected parliamentary body would lead France into a prosperous and just age. The constitution acknowledged the people's sovereignty as the source of political power. It also enshrined the principle of property by making voting rights dependent on property ownership. All men might be equal before the law, but by the Constitution of 1791 only wealthy men had the right to vote for representatives and hold office.

Civil Liberties.   All titles of nobility were abolished. In the early period of the revolution, civil liberties were extended to Protestants and Jews, who had been persecuted under the Old Regime. Previously excluded groups were granted freedom of thought, worship, and full civil liberties. More reluctantly, deputies outlawed slavery in the colonies in 1794. Slave unrest in Saint Domingue (modern-day Haiti) had coincided with the political conflicts of the revolution and exploded in rebellion in 1791, driving the revolutionaries in Paris to support black independence although it was at odds with French colonial interests. Led by Toussaint L'Ouverture (1743–1803), black rebels worked to found an independent Haitian state, which was declared in 1804. But the concept of equality with regard to race remained incompletely integrated with revolutionary principles, and slavery was reestablished in the French colonies in 1802.

Women's Rights.   Men were the subject of the newly defined rights. No references to women or their rights appear in the constitutions or the official Declarations of Rights. Women's organizations agitated for an equitable divorce law, and divorce was legalized in September 1792. Women were critical actors in the revolution from its very inception, and their presence shaped and directed the outcome of events, as the women's march to Versailles in 1789 made clear. The Marquis de Condorcet (1743–1794), elected to the Legislative Assembly in 1791, was one of the first to chastise the revolutionaries for overlooking the political rights of women who,

DECLARATION OF THE RIGHTS OF MAN AND CITIZEN

Sounding a refrain similar to that of the American Declaration of Independence (1776), the Declaration of the Rights of Man and Citizen was adopted by the French National Assembly on 26 August 1789. The document amalgamated a variety of Enlightenment ideas, including those of Locke and Montesquieu. The attention to property, which was defined as "sacred and inviolable," rivaled that given to liberty as a "natural" and "imprescriptible" right of man.

Focus Questions

How are individual rights defined in relation to the rights of "society" and the "nation"? What is the role of law in protecting rights?

1. Men are born and remain free and equal in rights. Social distinctions may be founded only upon the general good.

2. The aim of all political association is the preservation of the natural and imprescriptible rights of man. These rights are liberty, property, security, and resistance to oppression.

3. The principle of all sovereignty resides essentially in the nation. No body nor individual may exercise any authority which does not proceed directly from the nation.

4. Liberty consists in the freedom to do everything which injures no one else; hence the exercise of the natural rights of each man has no limits except those which assure to the other members of the society the enjoyment of the same rights. These limits can only be determined by law.

5. Law can only prohibit such actions as are hurtful to society. Nothing may be prevented which is not forbidden by law, and no one may be forced to do anything not provided for by law.

6. Law is the expression of the general will. Every citizen has a right to participate personally, or through his representative, in its formation. It must be the same for all, whether it protects or punishes. All citizens, being equal in the eyes of the law, are equally eligible to all dignities and to all public positions and occupations, according to their abilities, and without distinction except that of their virtues and talents.

7. No person shall be accused, arrested, or imprisoned except in the cases and according to the forms prescribed by law. Any one soliciting, transmitting, executing, or causing to be executed, any arbitrary order, shall be punished. But any citizen summoned or arrested in virtue of the law shall submit without delay, as resistance constitutes an offense.

8. The law shall provide for such punishments only as are strictly and obviously necessary. . . .

9. As all persons are held innocent until they shall have been declared guilty, if arrest shall be deemed indispensable, all harshness not essential to the securing of the prisoner's person shall be severely repressed by law.

10. No one shall be disquieted on account of his opinions, including his religious views, provided their manifestation does not disturb the public order established by law.

11. The free communication of ideas and opinions is one of the most precious of the rights of man. Every citizen may, accordingly, speak, write, and print with freedom, but shall be responsible for such abuses of this freedom as shall be defined by law.

12. The security of the rights of man and of the citizen requires public military forces. These forces are, therefore, established for the good of all and not for the personal advantage of those to whom they shall be entrusted.

13. A common contribution is essential for the maintenance of the public forces and for the cost of administration. This should be equitably distributed among all the citizens in proportion to their means.

14. All the citizens have a right to decide, either personally or by their representatives, as to the necessity of the public contribution; to grant this freely; to know to what uses it is put; and to fix the proportion, the mode of assessment and of collection and the duration of the taxes.

15. Society has the right to require of every public agent an account of his administration.

16. A society in which the observance of the law is not assured, nor the separation of powers defined, has no constitution at all.

17. Since property is an inviolable and sacred right, no one shall be deprived thereof except where public necessity, legally determined, shall clearly demand it, and then only on condition that the owner shall have been previously and equitably indemnified.

DECLARATION OF THE RIGHTS OF WOMAN AND CITIZEN

"Woman, wake up!" Thus did Olympe de Gouges (d. 1793), a self-educated playwright, address French women in 1791. Aware that women were being denied the new rights of liberty and property extended to all men by the Declaration of the Rights of Man and Citizen, Gouges composed her own Declaration of the Rights of Woman and Citizen, modeled on the 1789 document. Persecuted for her political beliefs, she foreshadowed her own demise at the hands of revolutionary justice in Article 10 of her declaration. The Declaration of the Rights of Woman and Citizen became an important document in women's demands for political rights in the nineteenth century, and Gouges herself became a feminist hero.

Focus Questions

Why was a separate declaration of rights necessary for women? How does this declaration differ from the "Declaration of the Rights of Man and Citizen"?

Article I Woman is born free and lives equal to man in her rights. Social distinctions can be based only on the common utility.

Article II The purpose of any political association is the conservation of the natural and imprescriptible rights of woman and man; these rights are liberty, property, security, and especially resistance to oppression.

Article III The principle of all sovereignty rests essentially with the nation, which is nothing but the union of woman and man; no body and no individual can exercise any authority which does not come expressly from it [the nation].

Article IV Liberty and justice consist of restoring all that belongs to others; thus, the only limits on the exercise of the natural rights of woman are perpetual male tyranny; these limits are to be reformed by the laws of nature and reason.

Article V Laws of nature and reason proscribe all acts harmful to society; everything which is not prohibited by these wise and divine laws cannot be prevented, and no one can be constrained to do what they do not command.

Article VI The law must be the expression of the general will; all female and male citizens must contribute either personally or through their representatives to its formation; it must be the same for all: male and female citizens, being equal in the eyes of the law, must be equally admitted to all honors, positions, and public employment according to their capacity and without other distinctions besides those of their virtues and talents.

Article VII No woman is an exception; she is accused, arrested, and detained in cases determined by law. Women, like men, obey this rigorous law.

Article VIII The law must establish only those penalties that are strictly and obviously necessary. . . .

Article IX Once any woman is declared guilty, complete rigor is [to be] exercised by the law.

Article X No one is to be disquieted for his very basic opinions; woman has the right to mount the scaffold; she must equally have the right to mount the rostrum, provided that her demonstrations do not disturb the legally established public order.

Article XI The free communication of thoughts and opinions is one of the most precious rights of woman, since that liberty assures the recognition of children by their fathers. Any female citizen thus may say freely, I am the mother of a child which belongs to you, without being forced by a barbarous prejudice to hide the truth; [an exception may be made] to respond to the abuse of this liberty in cases determined by the law.

Article XII The guarantee of the rights of woman and the female citizen implies a major benefit; this guarantee must be instituted for the advantage of all, and not for the particular benefit of those to whom it is entrusted.

Article XIII For the support of the public force and the expenses of administration, the contributions of woman and man are equal; she shares all the duties [*corvées*] and all the painful tasks; therefore, she must have the same share in the distribution of positions, employment, offices, honors and jobs [*industrie*].

Article XIV Female and male citizens have the right to verify, either by themselves or through their representatives, the necessity of the public contribution. This can only apply to women if they are granted an equal share, not only of wealth, but also of public administration, and in the determination of the proportion, the base, the collection, and the duration of the tax.

Article XV The collectivity of women, joined for tax purposes to the aggregate of men, has the right to demand an accounting of his administration from any public agent.

Article XVI No society has a constitution without the guarantee of rights and the separation of powers; the constitution is null if the majority of individuals comprising the nation have not cooperated in drafting it.

Article XVII Property belongs to both sexes whether united or separate; for each it is an inviolable and sacred right; no one can be deprived of it, since it is the true patrimony of nature, unless the legally determined public need obviously dictates it, and then only with a just and prior indemnity.

■ Slaves revolting against the French in Saint Domingue in 1791. Napoleon sent an army to restore colonial rule in 1799, but yellow fever decimated the French soldiers, and the rebels defeated the weakened French army in 1803.

he pointedly observed, were half of the human race. "Either no individual of the human race has genuine rights, or else all have the same; and he who votes against the right of another, whatever the religion, color, or sex of that other, has henceforth abjured his own." Condorcet argued forcefully but unsuccessfully for the right of women to be educated.

The revolutionaries had declared that liberty was a natural and inalienable right, a universal right that was extended to all with the overthrow of a despotic monarch and a privileged elite. The principle triumphed in religious toleration. Yet the revolutionary concept of liberty foundered on the divergent claims of excluded groups—workers, women, and slaves—who demanded full participation in the world of politics. In 1792, revolutionaries confronted the contradictions inherent in their political beliefs of liberty and equality that were being challenged in the midst of social upheaval and foreign war. In response, the revolution turned to more radical measures to survive.

The Trials of Constitutional Monarchy

The disciplined deliberations of committees intent on fashioning a constitutional monarchy replaced the passion and fervor of revolutionary oratory. The National, or Constituent, Assembly divided France into new administrative units—*départements*—for the purpose of establishing better control over municipal governments. Along with new administrative trappings, the government promoted its own rituals. On 14 July 1790, militias from each of the newly created 83 départements of France came together in Paris to celebrate the first

anniversary of the storming of the Bastille. A new national holiday was born and with it a sense of devotion and patriotism for the new France liberated by the revolution. In spite of the unifying elements, however, the newly achieved revolutionary consensus began to show signs of breaking down.

The Counterrevolution. In February 1790, legislation dissolved all monasteries and convents, except for those that provided aid to the poor or that served as educational institutions. As the French church was stripped of its lands, Pope Pius VI (1775–1799) denounced the principles of the revolution. In July 1790, the government approved the Civil Constitution of the Clergy: priests now became the equivalent of paid agents of the state. By requiring an oath of loyalty to the state from all practicing priests, the National Assembly created a new arena for dissent. Catholics were forced to choose to embrace or reject the revolution. Many "nonjuring" priests who refused to take the oath went into hiding. The wedge driven between the Catholic Church and revolutionary France allowed a mass-based counterrevolution to emerge. Aristocratic émigrés who had fled the country because of their opposition to the revolution were languishing for lack of a popular base. From his headquarters in Turin, the king's younger brother, the comte d'Artois, was attempting to incite a civil war in France. When the revolutionaries decided to attack the Church not just as a landed and privileged institution but also as a religious one, the counterrevolution rapidly expanded.

Late one night in June 1791, Louis XVI, Marie Antoinette, and their children disguised themselves as commoners, crept out of the royal apartments in the Tuileries Palace, and fled Paris. Louis intended to leave France to join royalist forces opposing the revolution at Metz. He got as far as Varennes, where he was captured by soldiers of the National Guard and brought back to a shocked Paris. The king had abandoned the revolution. Although he was not put to death for another year and a half, he was more than ever a prisoner of the revolution.

The Fiscal Crisis.   The defection of the king was certainly serious, but it was not the only problem facing the revolutionaries. Other problems plagued the revolutionary government, notably foreign war and the fiscal crisis, coupled with inflation. In order to establish its seriousness and legitimacy, the National Assembly had been willing in 1789 to absorb the debts of the Old Regime. The new government could not sell titles and offices, as the king had done to deal with financial problems, but it did confiscate Church property. In addition, it issued treasury bonds in the form of assignats in order to raise money. The assignats soon assumed the status of bank notes, and by the spring of 1790 they had become compulsory legal tender. Initially they were to be backed by land confiscated from the Church and sold by the state. But the need for money soon outran the value of the land available, and the government continued to print assignats according to its needs. Depreciation of French currency in international markets and inflation at home resulted. The revolutionary government found itself in a situation which in certain respects was worse than that experienced by Louis XVI before the calling of the Estates-General. Assignat-induced inflation produced a sharp decline in the fortunes of bourgeois investors living on fixed incomes. Rising prices meant increased misery for workers and peasants.

New counterrevolutionary groups were becoming frustrated with revolutionary policies. Throughout the winter and spring of 1791–1792, people rioted and demanded that prices be fixed, while the assignat dropped to less than half its face value. Peasants refused to sell crops for the worthless paper. Hoarding further drove up prices. Angry crowds turned to pillaging, rioting, and murder, which became more frequent as the value of the currency declined and prices rose.

Foreign war beginning in the fall of 1791 also challenged stability. Some moderate political leaders welcomed war as a blessing in disguise, since it could divert the attention of the masses away from problems at home and promote loyalty to the revolution. Others envisioned war as a great crusade to bring revolutionary principles to oppressed peoples throughout Europe. The king and queen, trapped by the revolution, saw war as their only hope of liberation. Louis XVI could be rightfully restored as the leader of a France defeated by the sovereigns of Europe. Some who opposed the war believed it would destabilize the revolution. France must solve its problems at home, they argued, before fighting a foreign enemy. Louis, however, encouraged those ministers and advisers eager for battle. In April 1792, France declared war against Austria.

Individuals, events, economic realities, and the nature of politics conspired against the success of the first constitutional experiment. The king's attempt to flee France in the summer of 1791 seriously wounded the attempt at compromise. Many feared that the goals of the revolution could not be preserved in a country at war and with a king of dubious loyalties.

EXPERIMENTING WITH DEMOCRACY, 1792–1799

The Revolution was a school for the French nation. A political universe populated by individual citizens replaced the eighteenth-century world of subjects loyal to their king. The new construction of politics, in which all individuals were equal, ran counter to prevailing ideas about collective identities defined in guilds and orders. People on all levels of society learned politics by doing it. In the beginning, experience helped. The elites, both noble and bourgeois, had served in government and administration. But the rules of the game under the Old Regime had been very different, with birth and wealth determining power.

After 1789, all men were declared free and equal, in opportunity if not in rights. Men of ability and talent, who had served as middlemen for the privileged elite under the Old Regime, now claimed power as their due. Many of them were lawyers, educated in the rules and regulations of the society of orders. They experienced firsthand the problems of the exercise of power in the Old Regime, and they had their own ideas about reform. But the school of the revolution did not remain the domain of a special class. Women demanded their places but continued to be excluded from the political arena, though the importance of their participation in the revolution was indisputable. Workers talked of seizing their rights, but because of the inherent contradictions of representation and participation, experimenting with democracy led to outcomes that did not look very democratic at all.

The Revolution of the People

The first stage of the French Revolution, lasting from 1789 through the beginning of 1792, was based on liberty—the liberty to compete, to own, and to succeed. The second stage of the French Revolution, which began in 1792, took equality as its rallying cry. It was the revolution of the working people of French cities. The popular movement that spearheaded political action in 1792 was committed to equality of rights in a way not characteristic of the leaders of the revolution of 1789. Urban workers were not benefiting from the revolution, but they had come to believe in their own power as political beings. Organized on the local level into sections, artisans in cities identified themselves as **sans-culottes**—literally, those trousered citizens who did not wear knee breeches (*culottes*)—to distinguish themselves from the privileged elite.

Who constituted the popular movement? The self-designated sans-culottes were the working men and women of Paris. Some were wealthier than others, some were wage earners, but all shared a common identity as consumers in the market-

THE GUILLOTINE AND REVOLUTIONARY JUSTICE

In the sultry summer days of 1792, Parisians found a new way to entertain themselves. They attended executions. French men, women, and children were long accustomed to watching criminals being tortured and put to death in public view. During the Old Regime, spectators could enjoy a variety of methods: drawing and quartering, strangling, or hanging. Decapitation, reputedly a less painful death, was a privilege reserved for nobles sentenced for capital crimes. The French Revolution extended that formerly aristocratic privilege to all criminals condemned to death. What especially attracted people to public squares in the third year of the revolution was the introduction of a novel method of decapitation. In 1792, the new instrument of death, the guillotine, became the center of the spectacle of revolutionary justice.

The guillotine promised to eliminate the suffering of its victims. Axes, swords, and sabers—the traditional tools of decapitation and dismemberment—were messy and undependable, producing slow and bloody ordeals when inept or drunken executioners missed their mark or victims flinched at the fatal moment. The design of the guillotine took all of that into account. On its easel-like wooden structure, victims, lying on their stomachs, were held in place with straps and a pillory. Heavy pulleys guaranteed that the sharp blade would fall efficiently from its great height. A basket was placed at the base of the blade to catch the severed head; another was used to slide the headless body through the base of the scaffolding for removal. In place of unintended torture and gore, the guillotine was devised as a humanitarian instrument to guarantee swift and painless death.

It should have been called the Louisette, after its inventor, Dr. Antoine Louis. In what now seems a dubious honor, the new machine was named instead after its greatest supporter, Dr. Joseph Ignace Guillotin, a delegate to the National Assembly. Both Guillotin and Louis were medical doctors, men of science influenced by Enlightenment ideas and committed to the revolution's elimination of the cruelty of older forms of punishment. In the spirit of scientific experimentation, Louis's invention was tested on sheep, cadavers, and then convicted thieves. In 1792, it was used for the first time against another class of offenders: political prisoners.

Early in the revolution, the Marquis de Condorcet, philosophe and mathematician, had opposed capital punishment with the argument that the state did not have the right to take life. Ironically, Maximilien Robespierre, future architect of the Reign of Terror, was one of the few revolutionaries who agreed with Condorcet. Those who favored justice by execution of the state's enemies prevailed. By the end of 1792, as revolution and civil war swept over France, 83 identical guillotines were constructed and installed in each of the départements of France. For the next two years, the guillotine's great blade was rhythmically raised and lowered daily in public squares all over France. In the name of the revolution, the "axe of the people" dispatched over 50,000 victims.

Although intended as a humanitarian instrument, the guillotine became the

■ Execution of Louis XVI on 21 January 1793.

symbol of all that was arbitrary and repressive about a revolution run amok. Day and night, the Revolutionary Tribunal in Paris delivered the death sentence to the "enemies of the people." Most of those executed were members of what had been the Third Estate: members of the bourgeoisie, workers, and peasants. Only 15 percent of the condemned were nobles and priests. During the Terror, the guillotine could be used to settle old scores. Sans-culottes turned in their neighbors, sometimes over long-standing grievances that owed more to spite than politics. The most fanatical revolutionaries had fantasies that guillotines were about to be erected on every street corner to dispense with hoarders and traitors. Others suggested that guillotines be made portable so that by putting justice on wheels, it could be taken directly to the people.

As usual, Paris set the style. The most famous of the guillotines stood on the Place du Carrousel, deliberately placed in front of the royal palace of the Tuileries. It was eventually moved to the larger Place de la Révolution in order to accommodate the growing numbers of spectators. Famous victims drew especially large crowds. The revolutionary drama took on the trappings of a spectacle as hawkers sold toy guillotines, miniature pikes, and liberty caps as souvenirs, along with the usual food and drink. Troops attended the events, but not to control the crowd. Members of the National Guard in formation, their backs to the people, faced the stage of the scaffold. They, like the citizenry, were there to witness the birth of a new nation and, by their presence, to give legitimacy to the event. The crowd entered into the ritual, cheering the victim's last words and demanding that the executioner hold high the severed head. In the new political culture, death was a festival.

■ This frontispiece from the anti-Robespierre work *Almanach des Prisons* illustrates the results of the Reign of Terror under Robespierre's leadership and the guillotine's blade.

For two centuries, Western societies have debated the legitimacy of the death sentence and have periodically considered the relative merits of the guillotine, the gas chamber, and the electric chair. For the French, the controversy temporarily ceased in 1794, when people were convinced that justice had gotten out of hand and that they had seen enough. The guillotine would return, but for the time being, the government put an end to capital punishment. At the height of its use, between 1792 and 1794, it had played a unique role in forging a new system of justice: the guillotine had been the great leveler. In the ideology of democracy, people were equal—in death as well as in life. The guillotine came to be popularly known as the "scythe of equality." It killed king and commoner alike.

place. They hated the privileged (*les gros*), who appeared to be profiting at the expense of the people. The sans-culottes wanted government power to be decentralized, with neighborhoods ruling themselves through sectional organizations. As the have-nots, they were increasingly intent on pulling down the haves, and they translated the sense of vengeance into a new revolutionary justice. On 10 August 1792, the people of Paris stormed the Tuileries, chanting their demands for "Equality!" and "Nation!" The people tramped across the silk sheets of the king's bed and broke his fine furniture, reveling in the private chambers of the royal family. Love and respect for the king had vanished. What the people of Paris demanded was the right to vote and participate in a popular democracy. Working people were acting independently of other factions, and the bourgeois political leadership became quickly aware of the need to scramble to maintain order. When they invaded the Tuileries Palace on the morning of 10 August, the sans-culottes did so in the name of the people. They saw themselves as patriots whose duty it was to brush the monarchy aside. The people were now a force to be reckoned with and feared.

"Terror Is the Order of the Day"

Political factions characterized revolutionary politics from the start. The terms *Left* and *Right,* which came to represent opposite ends of the political spectrum, originated in a description of where people sat in the Assembly in relation to the podium. Political designations were refined in successive parliamentary bodies. The Convention was the legislative body elected in September 1792 that succeeded the Legislative Assembly and had as its charge determining the best form of government after the collapse of the monarchy. On 21 September 1792, the monarchy was abolished in France; on the following day the Republic, France's first, came into being. Members of the Convention conducted the trial of Louis XVI for treason and pronounced his sentence: execution by the guillotine in January 1793.

The various political factions of the Convention were described in terms borrowed from geography. The Mountain, sitting on the upper benches on the left, was made up of members of the Jacobin Club (named for its meeting place in an abandoned monastery). The **Jacobins** were the most radical element in the National Convention, supporting democratic solutions and speaking in favor of the cause of people in the streets.

Jacobin Ascendancy.   Both **Girondins**, the more moderate revolutionary faction, and Jacobins were from the middle ranks of the bourgeoisie, and both groups were dedicated to the principles of the revolution. Although they controlled the ministries, the Girondins began to lose their hold on the revolution and the war. The renewed European war fragmented the democratic movement, and the Girondins, unable to control violence at home, saw political control slipping away. They became prisoners of the revolution when 80,000 armed Parisians surrounded the National Convention in June 1793.

Girondin power had been eroding in the critical months between August 1792 and June 1793. A new leader was working quietly and effectively behind the scenes to weld a partnership between the popular movement of sans-culottes and the Jacobins. He was Maximilien Robespierre (1758–1794), leader of the Mountain and the Jacobin Club. Robespierre was typical of the new breed of revolutionary politician. Only 31 years old in 1789, he wrote mediocre poems and attended the local provincial academy to discuss the new ideas when he was not practicing law in his hometown of Arras. Elected to the Estates-General, he joined the Jacobin Club and quickly rose to become its leader. He was willing to take controversial stands on issues: unlike most of his fellow members of the Mountain—including his rival, the popular orator Georges-Jacques Danton (1759–1794)—he opposed the war in 1792. Although neither an original thinker nor a compelling orator, Robespierre discovered with the revolution that he was an adroit political tactician. He gained a following and learned how to manipulate it. It was he who engineered the Jacobins' replacement of the Girondins as leaders of the government.

Robespierre and the Reign of Terror.   Robespierre's chance for real power came when he assumed leadership of the Committee of Public Safety in July 1793. Faced with the threat of internal anarchy and external war, the elected body, the National Convention, yielded political control to the 12-man Committee of Public Safety that ruled dictatorially under Robespierre's direction. The Great Committee, as it was known at the time, orchestrated the **Reign of Terror** (1793–1794), a period of systematic state repression that meted out justice in the people's name. Summary trials by specially created revolutionary tribunals were followed by the swift execution of the guilty under the blade of the guillotine.

Influenced by *The Social Contract* (1762) and other writings of Jean-Jacques Rousseau, Robespierre believed that sovereignty resided with the people. For him, individual wills and even individual rights did not matter when weighed against the will of the nation. The king was dead; the people were the new source of political power. Robespierre saw himself in the all-important role of interpreting and shaping the people's will. His own task was to guide the people "to the summit of its destinies." As he explained to his critics, "I am defending not my own cause but the public cause." As head of the Great Committee, Robespierre oversaw a revolutionary machinery dedicated to economic regulation, massive military mobilization, and a punitive system of revolutionary justice characterized by the slogan, "Terror Is the Order of the Day." Militant revolutionary committees and revolutionary tribunals were established throughout France to identify traitors and to mete out the harsh justice that struck hardest against those members of the bourgeoisie perceived as opponents of the government.

The guillotine became the symbol of revolutionary justice, but it was not the only means of execution. (See "A Closer Look: The Guillotine and Revolutionary Justice," pp. 604–605.)

DOCUMENT

Saint-Just on Democracy, Education, and Terror

IMAGE DISCOVERY

The Death of Marat, 1793,
by Jacques-Louis David

The revolutionary Jean-Paul Marat was killed in his medicinal tub (he suffered from a skin disease) by Charlotte Corday, a critic of the Radical politics and mob violence of the Revolution. Marat advocated the use of violence to ensure the success of the revolution. How does the use of lighting and drapery in this canvas convey the political leanings and attitude of the artist toward his subject? The canvas is dedicated to Marat (À Marat). What effect does the artist intend by listing his name—David— under Marat's? Note that the knife used to commit the attack is juxtaposed with the pen in Marat's hand. What is the overall effect of the tableau?

revolution chained to barges and drowned in the estuary of the Loire. The civil war, which raged most violently in the Vendée in the west of France, consisted often of primitive massacres that sent an estimated quarter of a million people to their deaths. The bureaucratized Reign of Terror was responsible for about 40,000 executions in a nine-month period, resulting in the image of the republicans as "drinkers of blood."

The Cult of the Supreme Being, a civic religion without priests or churches and influenced by Rousseau's ideas about nature, followed de-Christianization. The cathedral of Notre Dame de Paris was turned into the Temple of Reason, and the new religion established its own festivals to undermine the persistence of Catholicism. The cult was one indication of the Reign of Terror's attempt to create a new moral universe of revolutionary values.

Women Excluded.   Women remained conspicuously absent from the summit of political power. After 1793, Jacobin revolutionaries, who had been willing to empower the popular movement of workers, turned against women's participation and denounced it. Women's associations were outlawed and the Society of Revolutionary Republican Women was disbanded. Olympe de Gouges, revolutionary author of the Declaration of the Rights of Woman and Citizen (see p. 601), was guillotined. Women were declared unfit for political participation, according to the Jacobins, because of their biological functions of reproduction and child-rearing. Rousseau's ideas about family policy were probably more influential than his political doctrines. His best-selling books, *La Nouvelle Héloïse* (1761) and *Émile* (1762), which combined went into 72 editions before 1789, were moral works that transformed people's ideas about family life. Under his influence, the reading public came to value a separate and private sphere of domestic and conjugal values. Following Rousseau's lead, Robespierre and the Jacobins insisted that the role of women as mothers was incompatible with women's participation in the political realm.

The Thermidorian Reaction.   By attacking his critics on both the Left and the Right, Robespierre undermined the support he needed to stay in power. He abandoned the alliance with the popular movement that had been so important in bringing him to power. Robespierre's enemies—and he had many—were able to break the identification between political power and the will of the people that Robespierre had

In Lyon, officials of the Reign of Terror had prisoners tied to stakes in open fields and fired on with cannons. In Nantes, a Parisian administrator of the new justice had enemies of the established. As a result, he was branded a traitor by the same process that he had used against many of his own enemies. He saved France from foreign occupation and internal collapse, but he could not save democracy through terror. In the summer of 1794, Robespierre was guillotined. The Reign of Terror ceased with his death in the revolutionary month of Thermidor 1794.

The revolution did not end with the **Thermidorian Reaction,** as the fall of Robespierre came to be known, but his execution initiated a new phase. For some, democracy lost its legitimacy. The popular movement was reviled, and sans-culotte became a term of derision. Jacobins were forced underground. Price controls were abolished, resulting in extreme hardship for most urban residents. Out of desperation, in April 1795 the Jacobins and the sans-culottes renewed their alliance and united to demand "bread and the Constitution of 1793." The politics of bread had never been more accurately captured in slogan. Those who took to the streets in 1795 saw the universal manhood suffrage of the unimplemented 1793 constitution as the way to solve their economic problems. But their demands went unheeded; the popular revolution had failed.

The End of the Revolution

In the four years after Robespierre's fall, a new government by committee, called the Directory, appeared to offer mediocrity, caution, and opportunism in place of the idealism and action of the early years of the revolution. No successor to Robespierre stepped forward to command center stage. There were no heroes like Lafayette or the great Jacobin orator Georges-Jacques Danton to inspire patriotic fervor. Nor were there women like Olympe de Gouges to demand in the public arena equal rights for women. Most people, numbed after years of change, barely noticed that the revolution was over. Ordinary men in parliamentary institutions effectively did the day-to-day job of running the government. They tried to steer a middle path between royalist resurgence and popular insurrection. This nearly forgotten period in the history of the French Revolution was the fulfillment of the liberal hopes of 1789 for a stable constitutional rule.

The Directory, however, continued to be dogged by European war. A mass army of conscripts and volunteers had successfully extended France's power and frontiers. France expelled foreign invaders and annexed territories, including Belgium, while increasing its control in Holland, Switzerland, and Italy. But the expansion of revolutionary France was expensive and increasingly unpopular. Military defeats and the corruption of the Directory undermined government control. The Directory might have succeeded in the slow accretion of a parliamentary tradition, but reinstatement of **conscription** in 1798 met with widespread protest and resistance. No matter what their political leanings, people were weary. They turned to those who promised stability and peace.

In the democratic experiment at the heart of the second stage of the French Revolution, the sovereign will of the peo-

CHRONOLOGY	
The French Revolution	
August 1788	Louis XVI announces meeting of Estates-General to be held May 1789
5 May 1789	Estates-General convenes
17 June 1789	Third Estate declares itself the National Assembly
20 June 1789	Oath of the Tennis Court
14 July 1789	Storming of the Bastille
20 July 1789	Revolution of peasantry begins
26 August 1789	Declaration of the Rights of Man and Citizen
5 October 1789	Parisian women march to Versailles; force Louis XVI to return to Paris
February 1790	Monasteries, convents dissolved
July 1790	Civil Constitution of the Clergy
June 1791	Louis XVI and family attempt to flee Paris; are captured and returned
September 1791	France's first Constitution
April 1792	France declares war on Austria
10 August 1792	Storming of the Tuileries
22 September 1792	Revolutionary calendar implemented
January 1793	Louis XVI executed
July 1793	Robespierre assumes leadership of Committee of Public Safety
1793–1794	Reign of Terror
1794	Robespierre guillotined
1795	Directory rules France
1799	Napoleon overthrows the Directory and seizes power

ple permanently replaced the monarch's claim to divine right to rule. Yet with democracy came tyranny. The severe repression of the terror revealed the pressures that external war and civil unrest created for the new Republic. The Thermidorian Reaction and the elimination of Robespierre as the legitimate interpreter of the people's will ushered in a period of conciliation, opportunism, and a search for stability. Ironically, the savior that France found to answer its needs for peace and a just government was a man of war and a dictator.

THE REIGN OF NAPOLEON, 1799–1815

The great debate that rages to this day about Napoleon revolves around the question of whether he fulfilled the aims of the revolution or perverted them. In his return to a monarchical model, Napoleon resembled the enlightened despots of eighteenth-century Europe. In a modern sense, he was also a dictator, manipulating the French population through a highly centralized administrative apparatus. He locked French society into a program of military expansion that depleted its human and material resources. Yet, in spite of destruction and war, he dedicated his reign to building a French state according to the principles of the Revolution. Napoleon is one of those individuals about whom one can say that if he had not lived, history would have been different. He left his mark on an age and a continent.

Bonaparte Seizes Power

In Paris in 1795 a young, penniless, and unknown military officer moved among the wealthy and the beautiful of Parisian society and longed for fame. Already nicknamed at school "the Little Corporal" on account of his short stature, he was snubbed because of his background and ridiculed for his foreign accent. His story is typical of all stories of thwarted ambition. Yet the outcome of his story is unique: within four years, that young man would become ruler of France. The story of his ascent to power is also a story of the demise of the revolution.

Napoleon's Training and Experience.
Napoleon Bonaparte (1769–1821) was a true child of the eighteenth century. He shared the philosophes' belief in a rational and progressive world. Born in Corsica, which until a few months before his birth was part of the Republic of Genoa, he received his training in French military schools. As a youth, he was arrogant and ambitious. But he could have never aspired to a position of leadership in the army during the Old Regime because he lacked the noble birth necessary for advancement. The highest rank Napoleon could hope to achieve was that of captain or major.

DOCUMENT
The Rise of Napoleon

The revolution changed everything for him. First, it opened up careers previously restricted by birth, including those in the military, to those with talent. Second, the revolution made new posts available when aristocratic generals defected and crossed over to the enemy side, both before and after the execution of the king. Finally, the revolution created great opportunities for military men to test their mettle.

Foreign war and civil war required military leaders devoted to the revolution. Forced to flee Corsica because he had sided with the Jacobins, Napoleon and his troops were given the task of crushing Parisian protesters who rioted against the Directory in 1795. His victories in the Italian campaign in 1796–1797 launched his political career. As he extended French rule into central Italy, he became the embodiment of revolutionary values and energy.

The revolutionary wars had begun as wars to liberate humanity in the name of liberty, equality, and fraternity. Yet concerns for power, territory, and riches soon replaced earlier concerns with defense of the nation and of the revolution. The aggrandizement was nowhere more evident than in the Egyptian campaign of 1798, in which Napoleon Bonaparte headed an expedition whose goal was to enrich France by hastening the collapse of the Turkish Empire, crippling British trade routes, and handicapping Russian interests in the region. With Napoleon's highly publicized campaigns in Egypt and Syria, the war left the European theater and moved to the East, leaving behind its original revolutionary ideals. The Egyptian campaign, which was in reality a disaster, made Napoleon a hero at home.

Napoleon as First Consul.
In 1799, Napoleon Bonaparte readily joined a conspiracy that pulled down the Directory, the government he had earlier preserved, and became the First Consul of a triumvirate of consuls. Napoleon set out to secure his position of power by eliminating his enemies on the Left and weakening those on the Right. He guaranteed the security of property acquired in the revolution, a move that undercut royalists who wanted to return property to its original owners. Through policing forces and special criminal courts, law and order prevailed and civil war subsided. The First Consul promised a balanced budget and appeared to deliver it. Bonaparte spoke of healing the nation's wounds, especially those opened by de-Christianization during the revolution. Realizing the importance of religion in maintaining domestic peace, Napoleon reestablished relations with the pope in 1801 by the Concordat, which recognized Catholicism as the religion of the French and restored the Roman Catholic hierarchy.

Napoleon's popularity as First Consul flowed from his military and political successes and his religious reconciliation. He had come to power in 1799 by appealing for the support of the army. In 1802, Napoleon decided to extend his power by calling for a plebiscite in which he asked the electorate to vote him First Consul for life. Public support was overwhelming. An electoral landslide gave Napoleon greater political power than any of his Bourbon predecessors. Using revolutionary mechanisms, Napoleon laid the foundation for a new dynasty.

Napoleon at War with the European Powers

Napoleon was either at war or preparing for war during his entire reign. He certainly seemed up to the task of defeating the European powers. His military successes before 1799, real and apparent, had been crucial in his bid for political power. By 1802, he had signed favorable treaties with both Austria and Great Britain. He appeared to deliver a lasting peace and to establish France as the dominant power in Europe. But the

■ This engraving, from the series *Disasters of War* by Francisco Goya, depicts the horrors of war. The series was inspired by Napoleon's invasion and occupation of Spain from 1808 to 1814.

peace was short-lived. In 1803, France embarked on an 11-year period of continuous war. Under Napoleon's command, the French army delivered defeat after defeat to the European powers. Austria fell in 1805, Prussia in 1806, and the Russian armies of Alexander I were defeated at Friedland in 1807. In 1808, Napoleon invaded Spain to drive out British expeditionary forces intent on invading France. The great painter of the Spanish court, Francisco Goya (1746–1828), produced a series of etchings, *The Disasters of War*, that depicted the atrocities accompanying the Napoleonic invasion. Spain became a satellite kingdom of France, though the conflict continued.

Britain was the one exception to the string of Napoleonic victories. Napoleon initially considered sending a French fleet to invade the island nation. Lacking the strength necessary to achieve that, he turned to economic warfare, blockading European ports against British trade. Beginning in 1806, the **Continental System**, as the blockade was known, erected a structure of protection for French manufactures in all continental European markets. The British responded to the tariff walls and boycotts with a naval blockade that succeeded in cutting French commerce off from its Atlantic markets. The Continental System did not prove to be the decisive policy that Napoleon had planned: the British economy was not broken and the French economy did not flourish when faced with restricted resources and the persistence of a black market in smuggled goods.

Still, by 1810 the French leader was master of the Continent. French armies had extended revolutionary reforms and legal codes outside France and brought with them civil equality and religious toleration. They had also drained defeated countries of their resources and had inflicted the horrors of war with armies of occupation, forced billeting, and pillage. Napoleon's empire extended across Europe, with only a diminished Austria, Prussia, and Russia remaining independent. He placed his relatives and friends on the thrones of the new satellite kingdoms of Italy, Naples, Westphalia, Holland, and Spain. It was a fine empire, Napoleon later recalled in the loneliness of exile. Napoleon's empire did not endure, but at its acme, it seemed as though it would never fall.

The First Empire and Domestic Reforms

Napoleon measured domestic prosperity in terms of the stability of his reign. Through the 1802 plebiscite that voted him First Consul for life, he maintained the charade of constitutional rule while he ruled as virtual dictator. In 1804, he abandoned all pretense and had himself proclaimed emperor of the French. Mimicking the rituals of kingship, he staged his own coronation and that of his wife Josephine at the cathedral of Notre Dame de Paris. Breaking the tradition set by Charlemagne, Napoleon took the crown from the hands of Pope Pius VII (1800–1823) and placed it on his own head.

MAP DISCOVERY

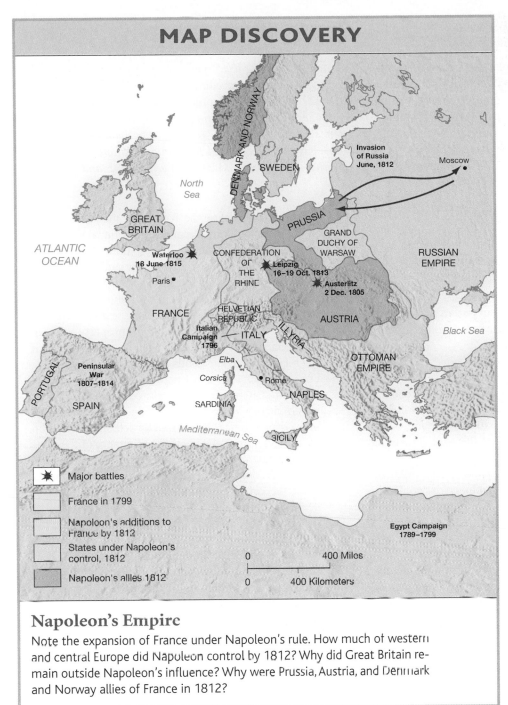

Napoleon's Empire

Note the expansion of France under Napoleon's rule. How much of western and central Europe did Napoleon control by 1812? Why did Great Britain remain outside Napoleon's influence? Why were Prussia, Austria, and Denmark and Norway allies of France in 1812?

measures. The metric system was established by 1799. But Napoleon felt the need to go further: France must be first in scientific research and application. To assure French predominance, Napoleon became a patron of science, supporting important work in the areas of physics and chemistry. Building for the future, Napoleon made science a pillar in the new structure of higher education.

The Directory had restored French prosperity through stabilization of the currency, fiscal reform, and support of industry. Napoleon's contribution to the French economy was the much needed reform of the tax system. He authorized the creation of a central banking system. French industries flourished under the protection of the state. The blockade forced the development of new domestic crops such as sugar beets and indigo, which became substitutes for colonial products. Napoleon extended the infrastructure of roads necessary for the expansion of national and European markets.

The New Legal System. Perhaps his greatest achievement was the codification of law, a task begun under the revolution. Many of the new articles of the **Napoleonic Code** were hammered out in Napoleon's presence, as he presided regularly over meetings with legal reformers. Combined with economic reforms, the Napoleonic Code facilitated trade and the development of commerce by regularizing contractual relations and protecting property rights and equality before the law.

The civil laws of the new code carved out a family policy characterized by hierarchy and subordination. Married women were neither independent nor equal to men in ownership of property, custody of children, or access to divorce. Women also lacked political rights. In the Napoleonic Code, women, like children, were subjected to paternal authority. The Napoleonic philosophy of woman's place is well captured in an anecdote told by Madame Germaine de Staël

The Importance of Science and Economic Reforms. Secure in his regime, surrounded by a new nobility that he created based on military achievement and talent and that he rewarded with honors, Napoleon set about implementing sweeping reforms in every area of government. Like many of the men of the revolutionary assemblies who had received scientific educations in their youth, he recognized the importance of science for both industry and war. The revolution had removed an impediment to the development of a national market by creating a uniform system of weights and

THE *CIVIL CODE* OF THE *CODE NAPOLÉON* (1804)

While still First Consul, Bonaparte assembled a group of the country's leading legal specialists to replace the vast agglomeration of feudal, customary, and canon laws, all with their own courts and procedures, with a unified system based on Roman law. The Civil Code, *along with the* Criminal Code, *made up the* Code Napoléon, *and consisted of 2281 articles intended to cover all aspects of civil life from birth to death, all civic aspects relating to family and property, contractual responsibilities, and civil liberties. A unified legal system became the basis for economic development and was arguably Napoleon's greatest achievement as ruler of France. The* Civil Code *replaced the Roman Catholic Church as having authority over marriage, and although divorce was permitted in the* Code, *it was outlawed in 1816 and not permitted again until 1884.*

Focus Questions

What rights do men enjoy in this passage that women do not? What are you able to conclude about the rights of married women who work?

Of the respective rights and duties of parent and children

212. Husband and wife owe each other fidelity, support, and assistance.

213. A husband owes protection to his wife; a wife owes obedience to her husband.

214. A wife is bound to live with her husband and to follow him wherever he deems proper to reside. The husband is bound to receive her, and to supply her with whatever is necessary for the wants of life, according to his means and condition.

215. A wife cannot sue in court without the consent of her husband, even if she is a public tradeswoman or if there is no community or she is separated as to property.

216. The husband's consent is not necessary when the wife is prosecuted criminally or in a police matter.

217. A wife, even when there is no community, or when she is separated as to property, cannot give, convey, mortgage, or acquire property, with or without consideration, without the husband joining in the instrument or giving his written consent.

218. If a husband refuses to allow his wife to sue in court, the Judge may grant the authorization.

219. If a husband refuses to allow his wife to execute an instrument, the wife can cause her husband to be summoned directly before the Tribunal of the First Instance of the common domicile, and such Tribunal shall grant or refuse its consent in the Judges' room after the husband has been heard or has been duly summoned.

220. A wife may, if she is a public tradeswoman, bind herself without the husband's consent with respect to what relates to her trade, and in that case she also binds her husband if there is a community of property between them. She is not considered a public tradeswoman if she merely retails the goods of her husband's business, but only when she has a separate business.

221. When a sentence has been passed upon a husband which carries with it a degrading corporal punishment, even if it has been passed by default, a wife, even of full age, cannot, during the continuance of the punishment, sue in court nor bind herself, unless she has been authorized by the Judge, who may in such cases grant the consent without the husband having been heard or summoned.

222. If a husband has been interdicted or is absent, the Judge may with proper knowledge of the case, authorize the wife to sue in court or to bind herself.

223. Any general authorization, even given by marriage contract, is only valid as to the management of the wife's property.

224. If the husband is a minor, the authorization of the Judge is necessary to the wife, either to sue in court or to bind herself.

225. A nullity based on the want of authorization can only be set up by the wife, the husband, or the heirs.

226. A wife can make a will without her husband's consent.

(1766–1817), a leading intellectual of her day. As the daughter of Jacques Necker, a Swiss financier and adviser to Louis XVI at the time of the revolution, she had been taught Enlightenment ideas from an early age. On finding herself seated next to Napoleon at a dinner party, she asked him what was very likely a self-interested question: Whom did he consider the greatest woman, alive or dead? Napoleon had no name to give her but responded, without pausing: "The one who has had the most children."

Napoleon turned his prodigious energies to every aspect of French life. He encouraged the arts while creating a police force. He had monuments built but did not forget about sewers. He organized French administrative life in a fashion that has endured. In place of the popular democratic movement, he offered his own singular authority. In place of elections, clubs, and free associations, he gave France plebiscites and army service. To be sure, Napoleon believed in constitutions, but he thought they should be "short and obscure." For Napoleon, the great problem of democracy was its unpredictability. His regime solved that problem by eliminating choices.

Decline and Fall

Militarily, Napoleon went too far. The first cracks in the French facade began to show in the Peninsular War (1808–1814) with Spain, in which Spanish guerrilla tactics proved costly for French troops. Napoleon's biggest mistake, the one that shattered the myth of his invincibility, occurred when he decided to invade Russia in June 1812.

The Invasion of Russia and the Battle of Nations.

Having decisively defeated Russian forces in 1807, Napoleon had entered into a peace treaty with Tsar Alexander I that guaranteed Russian allegiance to French policies. Alexander repudiated the Continental System in 1810 and appeared to be preparing for his own war against France. Napoleon seized the initiative, sure that he could defeat Russian forces once again. With an army of 500,000 men, Napoleon moved deep into Russia in the summer

---

CHRONOLOGY

The Reign of Napoleon

1799	Napoleon establishes consulate, becomes First Consul
1801	Napoleon reestablishes relations with pope, restores Roman Catholic hierarchy
1802	Plebiscite declares Napoleon First Consul for life
1804	Napoleon proclaims himself Emperor of the French
1806	Continental System implemented
1808–1814	France engaged in Peninsular War with Spain
June 1812	Napoleon invades Russia
September 1812	French army reaches Moscow; trapped by Russian winter
1813	Napoleon defeated at Battle of Nations at Leipzig
March 1814	Napoleon abdicates and goes into exile on island of Elba
March 1815	Napoleon escapes Elba and attempts to reclaim power
15 June 1815	Napoleon is defeated at Waterloo and exiled to island of Saint Helena

---

of 1812. The tsar's troops fell back in retreat. It was a strange war, one that pulled the French army to Moscow like a bird following bread crumbs. When Napoleon and his men entered Moscow in September, they found a city in flames. The people of Moscow had destroyed their own city to deprive the French troops of winter quarters.

Winter came early in Moscow, Napoleon's men discovered. They had left France basking in the warmth of summer and sure of certain and early victory. They then found themselves facing a severe Russian winter without overcoats, supplies, or food. Russia's strategy has become legendary. The Russians destroyed grain and shelter that might be of use to the French. Napoleon and his starving and frostbitten troops were forced into retreat. The horses of the French cavalry died because they were not properly shod for cold weather. The French army was decimated. Fewer than 100,000 men made it back to France.

Britain, unbowed by the Continental System, remained Napoleon's sworn enemy. Prussia joined Great Britain, Sweden, Russia, and Austria in opposing France anew. In the Battle of Nations at Leipzig in October 1813, France was forced to retreat. Napoleon refused a negotiated peace and fought on until the following March, when the victorious allies marched down the streets of Paris and occupied the French capital. Only then did Napoleon abdicate in favor of his young son, François, the titular king of Rome (1811–1832). Napoleon was exiled to the Mediterranean island of Elba.

The allies refused to accept the young "Napoleon II" and supported instead the Bourbon claimant to the throne, the brother of the guillotined Louis XVI. Naming himself Louis XVIII (skipping "XVII" in deference to his nephew dead at the hands of the Revolution), the new king claimed to rule over a "restored" France.

Napoleon's Final Defeat: Waterloo.

Still it was not quite the end for Napoleon. While the European heads of state sat in Vienna trying to determine the future of Europe and France's place in it, Napoleon returned from his exile on the Mediterranean island of Elba to reclaim leadership of France. On 15 June 1815, Napoleon once again, and for the final time, confronted the European powers in one of the most famous military campaigns in history. With 125,000 loyal French forces, Napoleon seemed within hours of reestablishing the French Empire in Europe.

DOCUMENT

Napoleon's Exile to St. Helena

But he had underestimated his opponents. The defeat of Napoleon's forces at Waterloo was decisive. Napoleon later explained, "Everything failed me just when everything had succeeded!" He had met his Waterloo, and with his defeat a new expression entered the language to describe devastating, permanent, irreversible downfall. Napoleon's return proved brief—it lasted only 100 days. An era had come to an end. Napoleon was exiled to the inhospitable island of Saint Helena in the South Atlantic. For the next six years, Napoleon wrote his memoirs under the watchful eyes of his British jailers. He died a painful death on 5 May 1821 from what today is believed to have been cancer.

■ "The Song of the End." Napoleon is depicted in flight with the whole world chasing him as he stumbles through a graveyard of bones and fallen symbols of power. Behind the globe is the masonic symbol of Providence, a shining eye within a triangle, a symbol also used by the American founding fathers on the Great Seal.

CONCLUSION

The period of revolution and empire from 1789 to 1815 radically changed the face of France. A new, more cohesive elite of bourgeois and nobles emerged, sharing power based on wealth and status. Ownership of land remained a defining characteristic of both old and new elites. A new state bureaucracy, built on the foundations of the old, expanded and centralized state power.

The people as sovereign now legitimated political power. Napoleon at his most imperial never doubted that he owed his existence to the people. In this sense, Napoleon was the king of the revolution—an apparently contradictory fusion of old forms and new ideology. Napoleon channeled democratic forces into enthusiasm for empire. He learned his lessons from the failure of the Bourbon monarchy and the politicians of the revolution. For 16 years, Napoleon successfully reconciled the Old Regime with the new France. Yet he could not resolve the essential problem of democracy: the relationship between the will of the people and the exercise of political power. The picture in 1815 was not dramatically different from the situation in 1789. The revolution might have been over, but changes fueled by the revolutionary tradition were just beginning. The struggle for a workable democratic government continued in France for another century and elsewhere in Europe throughout the twentieth century.

QUESTIONS FOR REVIEW

1. To what extent was the French nobility responsible for the crisis that destroyed the Old Regime?

2. How did commoners, men and women, transform a crisis of government into a revolution?
3. Why did the leaders of the Revolution resort to a "reign of terror," and what effect did that have on the Revolution?
4. What problems in France and beyond contributed to the rise of Napoleon?
5. What did Napoleon accomplish in France, and what brought about his fall?

KEY TERMS

cahiers de doléances, p. 594

conscription, *p. 608*

Continental System, *p. 610*

Estates-General, *p. 593*

Girondins, *p. 606*

Great Fear, *p. 598*

Jacobins, *p. 606*

Napoleonic Code, *p. 611*

National Assembly, *p. 590*

Old Regime, *p. 593*

Reign of Terror, *p. 606*

sans-culottes, *p. 603*

Thermidorian Reaction, *p. 608*

Third Estate, *p. 593*

DISCOVERING WESTERN CIVILIZATION ONLINE

You can obtain more information about the French Revolution and the Napoleonic Era at the Websites listed below. See also the Companion Website that accompanies this text, www.ablongman.com/kishlansky, which contains an online study guide and additional resources.

The French Revolution and the Fall of the Monarchy

Creating French Culture

www.loc.gov/exhibits/bnf/bnf0001.html

Different aspects of French culture as a form of elite power from Charlemagne to Charles de Gaulle are presented by the Library of Congress. Most of the material is from the collections of the Bibliothèque Nationale de France.

Liberty, Equality, Fraternity: Explaining the French Revolution

Chnm.gmu.edu/revolution/

This site contains an extraordinary archive of key images, maps, songs, timelines, and texts from the French Revolution. The site is authored by Professors Lynn Hunt and Jack Censer, leading scholars in the field of French revolutionary history.

Château de Versailles

www.chateauversailles.fr/en/

Devoted to the history and images of Versailles, this site provides brief essays about the people and events significant to court culture during the seventeenth and eighteenth centuries. It also explores the role of Versailles in French culture after the French Revolution.

Experimenting with Democracy, 1789–1792

St. Just

history.hanover.edu/texts/stjust.html

Texts by St. Just, a close colleague of Robespierre and a member of the Committee of Public Safety, which orchestrated the Reign of Terror.

Modern History Sourcebook: Robespierre: The Supreme Being

www.fordham.edu/halsall/mod/robespierre-supreme.html

This site contains Robespierre's words on The Cult of the Supreme Being and links to other sites.

The Reign of Napoleon, 1799–1815

Internet Modern History Sourcebook: French Revolution

www.fordham.edu/halsall/mod/modsbook13.html

This site will direct students to the Modern History Sourcebook section of documents on the French Revolution, Napoleon, and the Napoleonic Wars.

Napoleon

www.napoleon.org/en/home.asp

Sponsored by the Foundation Napoleon for "the furtherance of study and research into the civil and military achievements of the First and Second Empires," this site is aimed at a nonacademic audience providing chronologies, essays, images, videos, and links to other sites on Napoleon.

SUGGESTIONS FOR FURTHER READING

The French Revolution and the Fall of the Monarchy

Keith Michael Baker, *Inventing the French Revolution* (Cambridge: Cambridge University Press, 1992). The author views the French Revolution as a basically political event that can only be understood in the context of the changing political culture of the eighteenth century, with special attention to the use of language and the role of public opinion as a political invention.

Roger Chartier, *The Cultural Origins of the French Revolution*, tr. Lydia G. Cochrane (Durham, NC: Duke University Press, 1991). Argues for the importance of the rise of critical modes of thinking in the public sphere in the eighteenth century and of long-term de-Christianization in shaping the desire for change in French society and politics.

William Doyle, *Origins of the French Revolution* (Oxford: Oxford University Press, 1988). An excellent introduction devoted to the historiography of the Revolution since 1939, followed by an analysis of the breakdown of the Old Regime and the struggle for power.

Lynn Hunt, ed., *The French Revolution and Human Rights*: A *Brief Documentary History* (Bedford: St. Martins, 1996). This edited work contains 38 primary documents on citizenship and civil rights.

Georges Lefebvre, *The Great Fear of 1789* (New York: Pantheon Books, 1973). This classic study analyzes the rural panic that swept through parts of France in the summer of 1789 as a distinct episode in the opening months of the Revolution that had its own internal logic.

Colin Lucas, ed., *Rewriting the French Revolution* (Oxford: Clarendon Press, 1991). Eight scholars present interpretations in the areas of social development, ideas, politics, and religion.

Daniel Roche, *The People of Paris* (Berkeley: University of California Press, 1987). An essay on popular culture in the eighteenth century in which the author surveys the lives of the Parisian popular classes—servants, laborers, and artisans—and examines their housing, furnishings, dress, and leisure activities.

Timothy Tackett, *Becoming a Revolutionary: The Deputies of the French National Assembly and the Emergence of a Revolutionary Culture* (Princeton: Princeton University Press, 1996). This collective biography of the cohort of deputies to the National Assembly demonstrates that their practical experience was distinct from that of the nobility.

Michel Vovelle, *The Fall of the French Monarchy* (Cambridge: Cambridge University Press, 1984). A social history of the origins and early years of the Revolution, beginning with a brief examination of the Old Regime and paying special attention to social and economic changes initiated by the

Revolution, the role of the popular classes, and the creation of revolutionary culture.

Experimenting with Democracy, 1792–1799

Jack Censer and Lynn Hunt, *Liberty, Equality, Fraternity: Exploring the French Revolution* (University Park: Pennsylvania State University Press, 2001). This book is accompanied by a CD-ROM and provides a unique multimedia introduction to the French Revolution.

François Furet, *Interpreting the French Revolution* (Cambridge: Cambridge University Press, 1981). A series of essays challenging many of the assumptions about the causes and outcome of the Revolution and reviewing its historiography.

Dominique Godineau, *The Women of Paris and Their French Revolution* (Berkeley: University of California Press, 1998). A compelling account of the lives of women revolutionaries. Godineau presents women's protests as a mass movement within the Revolution.

Patrice Higonnet, *Goodness Beyond Virtue: Jacobins During the French Revolution* (Cambridge: Harvard University Press, 1998). The author considers the Jacobin politics as a model for modern democrats, not to be reduced to the tragedy of the Terror.

Michael L. Kennedy, *The Jacobin Clubs in the French Revolution, 1793–1795* (New York: Berghahn Books, 2000). The final volume of Kennedy's three-volume history of the Jacobin Club focusing on the period between May 1793 and August 1795.

Sara E. Melzer and Leslie Rabine, eds., *Rebel Daughters: Women and the French Revolution* (New York: Oxford University Press, 1992). Contributors from a variety of disciplines examine the importance of women in the French Revolution, with special attention to the exclusion of women from the new politics.

Albert Soboul, *The Sans-Culottes* (New York: Anchor, 1972). A study of the artisans who composed the core of popular political activism in revolutionary Paris.

The Reign of Napoleon, 1799–1815

David Patrick Geggus, *Haitian Revolutionary Studies* (Bloomington: Indiana University Press, 2002). Using archives from several countries, the author examines little-known aspects of black rebellion from French rule.

Jean Tulard, *Napoleon: The Myth of the Saviour* (London: Weidenfeld and Nicolson, 1984). In this biography of Napoleon, the Napoleonic Empire is presented as a creation of the bourgeoisie, who desired to end the Revolution and consolidate their gains and control over the lower classes.

Isser Woloch, *Napoleon and His Collaborators: The Making of a Dictatorship* (New York: Norton, 2001). Woloch explains the success of Napoleon's regime in terms of the support of his civilian collaborators.

Isser Woloch, *The New Regime: Transformations of the French Civic Order* (New York: Norton, 1994). Woloch's study emphasizes the break of the new regime from the old, placing the institutions created or revamped after 1789 in the context of a new civic order and citizenship.

For a list of additional titles related to this chapter's topics, please see http://www.ablongman.com/kishlansky.

CHAPTER 2

INDUSTRIAL EUROPE

PORTRAIT OF AN AGE
THE RAILROAD

The Normandy train has reached Paris. The coast and the capital are once again connected. Passengers in their city finery disembark and are greeted by others who have awaited their scheduled arrival. Workmen stand ready to unload freight, porters to carry luggage. Steam billows forth from the resting engine, which is the object of all human activity. The engine stares as enigmatically as any character in a Renaissance portrait. Yet the train that has arrived in *La Gare Saint-Lazare* by Claude Monet (1840–1926) is as much the central character in this portrait of the industrial age as was any individual in portraits of ages past.

THE VISUAL RECORD

The train's iron bulk dwarfs the people around it. Indeed, iron dominates; tons of it are in view. The rails, the lampposts, the massive frame of the station, no less than the train itself, are all formed from iron—pliable, durable, inexpensive iron—the miracle product of industrialization. The iron station with its glass panels became as central a feature of nineteenth-century cities as stone cathedrals were in the Middle Ages. Railway stations changed the shape of urban settings, just as railway travel changed the lives of millions of people.

There had never been anything like it before. Ancient Romans had hitched four horses to their chariots; nineteenth-century Europeans hitched four horses to their stagecoaches. The technology of overland transportation had hardly changed in 2000 years. Coach journeys were long, uncomfortable, and expensive, and they were governed by the elements and muddy, rutted roads that caused injuries to humans and horses with alarming regularity. First-class passengers rode inside, where they were jostled against one another and breathed the dust that the horses kicked up in front of them. Second-class passengers rode on top, braving the elements and risking life and limb in an accident.

Railway travel was a quantum leap forward. It was faster, cheaper, and safer. Overnight it changed conceptions of time, space, and, above all, speed. People could journey to what once were distant places in a single day. Voyages be-

came trips, and the travel holiday was born. Commerce was transformed, as was the way in which it was conducted. Large quantities of goods could be shipped quickly from place to place; orders could instantly be filled. The whole notion of locality changed, as salesmen could board a morning train for what only recently had been an unreachable market. Branch offices could be overseen by regional directors, services and products could be standardized, and the gap between great and small cities and between town and countryside could be narrowed.

Wherever they went, the railroads created links that had never been forged before. In Britain, the railroad schedule led to the creation of official time. Trains that left London were scheduled to arrive at their destinations according to London time, which was now kept at the royal observatory in Greenwich. Trains carried fresh fish inland from the coasts and fresh vegetables from rural farms to city tables. Mail moved farther and more quickly; news spread more evenly. Fashionable ideas from the capital cities of Europe circulated everywhere, as did new knowledge and discoveries. The railroads brought both diversity and uniformity.

They also brought wonderment. The engine seemed to propel itself with unimaginable power and at breathtaking speed. The English actress Fanny Kemble (1809–1893) captured the sensation memorably: "You can't imagine how strange it seemed to be journeying on thus, without any visible cause of progress other than the magical machine, with its flying white breath and rhythmical, unvarying pace. I felt no fairy tale was ever half so wonderful as what I saw." For many, the railroad symbolized the genius of the age in which they were living, an age in which invention, novelty, and progress were everywhere to be seen. It combined the great innovations of steam, coal, and iron that were transforming nearly every aspect of ordinary life. But for others, the railway was just as much a symbol of disquiet, of the passing of a way of life that was easier to understand and to control. "Seated in the old mail-coach we needed no evidence out of ourselves to indicate the velocity," wrote the English author Thomas De

■ Claude Monet, *Arrival of the Normandy Train, Gare Saint-Lazare, 1877*

Quincey (1785–1859) in his obituary for the passing of horse travel. "We heard our speed, we saw it, we felt it. This speed was not the product of blind, insensate agencies, that had no sympathy to give, but was incarnated in the fiery eyeballs of the noblest among brutes."

The fruits of the railways, like the fruits of industrialization, were not all sweet. As the nineteenth century progressed, there could be no doubt that, year by year, one way of life was being replaced by another. More and more laborers were leaving the farms for the factories; more and more products were being made by machines. Everywhere there was change, but it was not always or everywhere for the better. Millions of people poured into cities that mushroomed up without plan or intention. Population growth, factory labor, and ultimately the grinding poverty that they produced overwhelmed traditional means of social control. Families and communities split apart; the expectations of ordinary people were no longer predictable. Life was spinning out of control for individuals, groups, and even whole societies. It was an engine racing down a track that only occasionally ended as placidly as did the Normandy train at the Gare Saint-Lazare.

LOOKING AHEAD

As this chapter will discuss, industrialization began in Great Britain, spurred by its mineral wealth and entrepreneurial skill. It was the result of changes in agricultural practices that allowed for a larger population to be supported by fewer farmers. It was powered first by coal and its use in the production of iron and then by steam that allowed for powerful engines to mechanize production. The steam engines also allowed for a revolution in transportation as seen in the painting of the Gare Saint-Lazare. Industrialization transformed every aspect of the British economy and soon spread throughout Europe.

619

THE TRADITIONAL ECONOMY

The curse of Adam and Eve was that they would earn their daily bread by the sweat of their brows. For generation after generation, age after age, economic life was dominated by toil. Man, woman, and child labored to secure their supply of food against the caprice of nature. There was nothing even vaguely romantic about the backbreaking exertion needed to crack open the hard ground, plant seeds in it, and protect the crops from the ravages of insects, birds, and animals long enough to be harvested. Every activity was labor-intensive. Wood for shelter or fuel was chopped with thick, blunt axes. Water was drawn from deep wells by the long, slow turn of a crank or dragged in buckets from the nearest stream. Everything that was consumed was pulled or pushed or lifted. French women carried soil and water up steep terraces in journeys that could take as long as seven hours. "The women seemed from their persons and features to be harder worked than horses," Arthur Young (1741–1820), the English agricultural expert, observed with a combination of admiration and disgust. The capital that was invested in the traditional economy was human capital, and by the middle of the eighteenth century nearly eight out of every ten Europeans still tilled the soil, earning their bread by the sweat of their brow.

Although the traditional economy was dominated by agriculture, an increasing amount of labor was devoted to manufacture. The development of a secure and expanding overseas trade created a worldwide demand for consumer goods. In the countryside, small domestic textile industries grew up. Families would take in wool for spinning and weaving to supplement their income from agriculture. When times were good, they would expend proportionately less effort in manufacturing; when times were bad, they would expend more. Their tasks were set by an entrepreneur who provided raw materials and paid the workers by the piece. Wages paid to rural workers were lower than those paid to urban laborers because they were not subject to guild restrictions and because the wages supplemented farm income. Thus entrepreneurs could profit from lower costs, although they had to bear

the risk that the goods produced in that fashion would be of lesser quality or that markets would dry up in the interval. Although domestic industry increased the supply of manufactured commodities, it demanded even more labor from an already overworked sector of the traditional economy.

Throughout the traditional economy, the limits on progress were set by nature. Good harvests brought prosperity, bad harvests despair. Over the long run, the traditional economy ran in all-too-predictable cycles. Sadly, the adage, "Eat, drink, and be merry, for tomorrow we may die," was good advice. Prosperity was sure to bring misery in its train. The good fortune of one generation was the hard luck of the next, as more people competed for a relatively fixed quantity of food. No amount of sweat and muscle and, as yet, ingenuity could rescue the traditional economy from its pendulum swings of boom and bust.

By the eighteenth century, the process that would ultimately transform the traditional economy was already under way. It began with the **agricultural revolution**, one of the great turning points in human history. Before it occurred, the life of every community and of every citizen was always held hostage to nature. The struggle to secure an adequate food supply was the dominant fact of life to which nearly all productive labor was dedicated. After the agricultural revolution, an inadequate food supply was a political rather than an economic fact of life. Fewer and fewer farmers were required to feed more and more people. In Britain, where nearly 70 percent of the population was engaged in agriculture at the end of the seventeenth century, fewer than 2 percent today work on farms. By the middle of the nineteenth century, the most advanced economies were capable of producing vast surpluses of basic commodities. The agricultural revolution was not an event, and it did not happen suddenly. It would not deserve the label "revolution" at all were it not for its momentous consequences: Europe's escape from the shackles of the traditional economy.

Farming Families

Over most of Europe, agricultural activity in the eighteenth century followed methods of crop rotation that had been in place for more than a thousand years. Fields were divided into strips of land, and each family "owned" a certain number of strips, which they cultivated for their livelihood. Between one-half and one-third of village land lay fallow each year so that its nutrients could be restored. Open-field farming, as the system was called, was communal rather than individual. Decisions about which crops to grow in the productive fields, where animals would be pastured, or how much wood could be cut from the common wastes affected everyone. Moreover, many activities, such as plowing, gleaning, and manuring, could not conveniently observe the distinctions of ownership of separate strips. Nor, given the realities of nature, could individual families be self-sustaining without the services of a village tanner or milkmaid or hog minder drawn from the closely intertwined group of kin and neighbors that consti-

MAP DISCOVERY

Percentage increase

- Over 80
- 60 – 79
- 40 – 59
- 20 – 39
- Under 20

Population Growth in Europe, 1800–1850

Notice which parts of Europe experienced the largest growth in population in the first half of the nineteenth century. Compare the rate of population growth in Spain and Norway and Sweden. Which grew faster? In which parts of Europe did the population increase the most during this period? What impact would you expect such growth to have on the agricultural economy? On the rate of industrialization?

potatoes in the mistaken belief that they caused leprosy. Yet both potatoes and corn became peasant crops and spread rapidly throughout southern Europe, not least because as new commodities they were untaxed. Peasants bartered their surplus, hoarded their profits, and took what few advantages they could out of a system in which the deck was stacked against them.

As the European population entered a new cycle of growth in the second quarter of the eighteenth century, the traditional economy began to increase agricultural productivity in traditional ways. In the east, new lands were colonized and slowly brought under cultivation. Frederick the Great welcomed immigrants to Prussia, where land was plentiful, if not very fertile. In settled communities, less productive land, which had provided fodder for animals at the end of the seventeenth century, now had to provide food for humans. Scrubland was cleared and hillsides terraced. Dry ground was irrigated manually by women and children working in bucket brigades. As always, an increase in population initially meant an increase in productivity. For a time, more able-bodied workers produced more food. In the half century that ended in the 1770s, French peasants increased agricultural production by nearly 60 percent. The intensification of traditional methods rather than innovation accounted for the increase. The number of strips held by each family declined, but each strip was more carefully cultivated.

By the end of the eighteenth century, the European population was reaching the point at which another check on its growth might be expected. Between 1700 and 1800, total European population had increased by nearly 50 percent, and the rate of growth was continuing to accelerate. The vast expansion of rural population placed a grave strain on agricultural production. Decade by decade, more families attempted to eke out an existence from the same amount of land. The gains made by intensive cultivation were now lost to overpopulation. In areas that practiced partible inheritance, farms were subdivided into units too small to

tuted the community. Communal agriculture was effective, but it also limited the number of people that could survive on the produce from a given amount of land.

Agriculture was a profoundly conservative occupation, for the risk of experimentation was nothing less than survival. Lords and peasants both practiced defensive innovation, introducing change only after its practical benefits were easily demonstrable. For example, in the mid-seventeenth century two French provincial parlements banned the cultivation of provide subsistence. Competition for the "morsels" of land, as the French called them, was intense. Older sons bought out younger brothers; better-off families purchased whatever came on the market to prevent their children from slipping into poverty. Even in areas in which primogeniture was the rule, portions for younger sons and daughters ate into the meager inheritance of the eldest son. Over much of Europe, it was becoming increasingly difficult to live by bread alone.

Rural Manufacture

The crisis of overpopulation meant that not only were there more mouths to feed, there were more bodies to clothe. That increased the need for spun and woven cloth, and thus for spinners and weavers. Traditionally, commercial cloth production was the work of urban artisans, but the expansion of the marketplace and the introduction of new fabrics, especially cotton and silk, had eroded the monopoly of most of the clothing guilds. Merchants could sell as much finished product as they could find, and the teeming rural population provided a tempting pool of inexpensive labor for anyone willing to risk the capital to purchase raw materials. Initially, farming families took manufacturing work into their homes to supplement their income. Spinning and weaving were the

■ The European Linen Industry. By the eighteenth century, linen production was dominated by the Low Countries and the north German principalities where skilled labor could still be found for the complicated process of linen weaving.

most common occupations, and they were treated as occasional work, reserved for the slow times in the agricultural cycle. This was known as cottage industry. It was side-employment, less important and less valuable than the vital agricultural labor that all members of the family undertook.

But by the middle of the eighteenth century, cottage industry was developing in a new direction. As landholdings grew smaller, even good harvests did not promise subsistence to many families. The oversupply of labor was soon organized into the **putting-out system**, which mobilized the resources of the rural labor force for commercial production of large quantities of manufactured goods. The characteristics of the putting-out system were similar throughout Europe, whether it was undertaken by individual entrepreneurs or lords of the manor, or even sponsored by the state. The process began with the capital of the entrepreneur, which was used to purchase raw materials. The materials were "put out" to the homes of workers where the manufacture, most commonly spinning or weaving, took place. The finished goods were returned to the entrepreneur, who sold them at a profit, with which he bought raw materials to begin the process anew.

The simplicity of the putting-out system was one of its most valuable features. All of its essential elements were already present in rural communities. The small nest egg of a prosperous farmer or small trader was all the money needed to make the first purchase of raw materials. The raw materials could be put out to his kin or closest neighbors and the finished goods then delivered to market along with surplus crops. Not only could a small amount of cash begin the cycle of putting-out, but that capital continued to circulate to keep the process in motion.

The small scale of the initial enterprise can be seen in the fact that many entrepreneurs had themselves begun as workers. In Bohemia, for example, some of the largest putting-out operations were run by serfs who paid their lords fees for the right to engage in trade. At the end of the eighteenth century, there were more than one-quarter million spinners in the Bohemian linen industry alone, most of them organized into small groups around a single entrepreneur, though one monastery employed more than 650 women spinners. Putting-out also required only a low level of skill and common, inexpensive tools. Rural families did their own spinning and rural villages their own weaving. Thus, putting-out demanded little investment, either in plant, equipment, or education. Nor did it inevitably disrupt traditional gender-based tasks in the family economy. In most places spinning was women's work, weaving was done by men, and children helped at whichever task was under way. In fact, certain occupations, such as lacemaking in France, were so gender-based that men would not even act as entrepreneurs. In Austria, lacemaking was considered less honorable than other forms of clothmaking because of its association with women and household-based production. Performed at home, rural manufacture remained a traditional family-oriented occupation.

Gradually, the putting-out system came to dominate the lives of many rural families. From small networks of isolated

■ Linen production is the subject of this 1705 engraving by Franz Philipp Florin. To make linen, it was necessary to soak the stems of the flax plant to soften its tough outer fibers, which were then removed by beating. The more delicate inner fibers were spun into thread, and then were woven into linen cloth on handlooms.

villages, domestic manufacture grew to cover entire regions. Perhaps as many as one-quarter of the inhabitants of the Irish province of Ulster were engaged in manufacturing linen by the end of the eighteenth century. Spinning and weaving became full-time occupations for families that kept no more than a small garden. But without agricultural earnings, piecework rates became starvation wages, and families unable to purchase their subsistence were forced to rely upon loans from the entrepreneurs who set them at work. Long hours in dank cottages performing endlessly repetitive tasks became the lot of millions of rural inhabitants, and their numbers increased annually. While the sons of farmers waited to inherit land before they formed their families, the sons of cottage weavers needed only a loom to begin theirs. They could afford to marry younger and to have more children, for children could contribute to manufacturing from an early age.

Consequently, the expansion of the putting-out system, like the expansion of traditional agriculture, fueled the continued growth of population. Like traditional agriculture, putting-out contained a number of structural inefficiencies. Both entrepreneur and worker were potential victims of unscrupulousness. Embezzlement of raw materials was a problem for the entrepreneur, arbitrary wage cuts for the laborers. Because the tasks were performed at home, the entrepreneur could not supervise the work. Most disputes in domestic manufacturing arose over specifications of quality. Workers would not receive full pay for poorly produced goods that could not be sold for full value. Inexperienced, aged, or infirm workers could easily spoil costly raw materials. One Bohemian nobleman created village spinning rooms on his estates so that young girls could be given four weeks of train-

ing before they set up on their own. Finally, the putting-out system was labor- rather than capital-intensive. As long as there were ready hands to employ, there was little incentive to seek better methods or more efficient techniques.

The Agricultural Revolution

The continued growth of Europe's population necessitated an expansion of agricultural output. In most places that was achieved by intensifying traditional practices, bringing more land into production and more labor to work the land. But in the most advanced European economies, first in Holland and then in England, traditional agriculture underwent a long but dynamic transformation, an agricultural revolution. It was a revolution of technique rather than technology. Humans were not replaced by machines nor were new forms of energy substituted for human and animal muscle. Indeed, many of the methods that were to increase crop yields had been known for centuries and practiced during periods of population pressure. But they had never been practiced as systematically as they came to be from the seventeenth century onward, and they were never combined with a commercial attitude toward farming. It was the willingness and ability of owners to invest capital in their land that transformed subsistence farming into commercial agriculture.

Enclosures.   As long as farming was practiced in open fields, there was little incentive for individual landowners to invest in improvements to their scattered strips. Although the community as a whole could enclose a small field or plant some fodder crops for the animals, its ability to change

IMAGE DISCOVERY

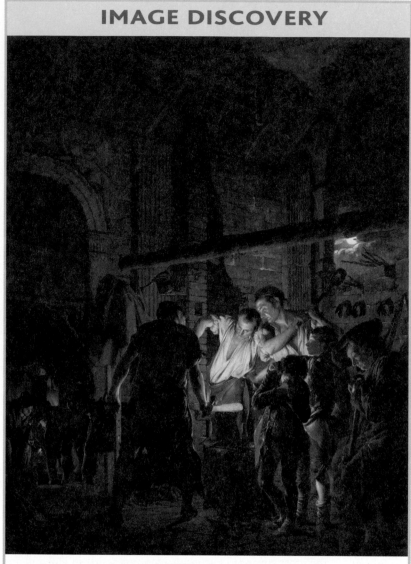

The Blacksmith's Shop

Joseph Wright of Derby depicts a blacksmith working without many of the technological advances of the eighteenth century. The smith is housed in an abandoned religious building, most likely an old church. What clues in the background would lead one to that conclusion? The image, as a whole, recalls an oft-painted scene from Christianity involving figures gathered around and bending over a source of light. Can you identify it? Why would Joseph Wright have imitated depictions of that foundational Christian event in painting a traditional English blacksmith?

The consolidation of estates along with the enclosure of fields was thus the initial step toward change. It was a long-term process that took many forms. In England, where it was to become most advanced, **enclosure** was already under way in the sixteenth century. Prosperous families had long been consolidating their strips in the open fields, and at some point the lord of the manor and the members of the community agreed to carve up the common fields and make the necessary exchanges to consolidate everyone's lands. Perhaps as much as three-quarters of the arable land in England was enclosed by agreement before 1760. Enclosure by agreement did not mean that the breakup of the open-field community was necessarily a harmonious process. Riots preceding or following agreed enclosures were not uncommon.

Paradoxically, it was the middling rather than the poorest villagers who had the most to lose. The breakup of the commons initially gave the poor more arable land from which to eke out their subsistence, and few of them could afford to sacrifice present gain for future loss. The smallholders were quickly bought out. It was the middle-size holders who were squeezed hardest. Although prosperous in communal farming, those families did not have access to the capital necessary to make agricultural improvements such as converting grass to grain land or purchasing large amounts of fertilizer. They could not compete in producing for the market, and gradually they, too, disappeared from the enclosed village. Their opposition to enclosure by agreement led, in the eighteenth century, to enclosure by act of Parliament. Parliamentary enclosure was legislated by government, a government composed for the most part of large landowners. A commission would view the community's lands and divide them, usually by a prescribed formula. Between 1760 and 1815, more than 1.5 million acres of farmland were enclosed by act of Parliament. During the late eighteenth century, the Prussian and French governments emulated the practice by ordering large tracts of land enclosed.

The enclosure of millions of acres of land was one of the largest expenses of the new commercial agriculture. Hedging or fencing off the land and plowing up the commons required extra labor beyond that necessary for basic agrarian activities. Thus many who sold the small estates that they received on the breakup of the commons remained in villages as agricultural laborers or leaseholders. But they practiced a different form of farming. More and more agricultural activity became market-oriented. Single crops were sown in large enclosed fields and ex-

traditional practice was limited. In farming villages, even the smallest landholder had rights in common lands, which were jealously guarded. Rights in commons meant a place in the community itself. Commercial agriculture was more suited to large rather than small estates and was more successful when the land could be utilized in response to market conditions rather than to the necessities of subsistence.

■ Surveyors measure a field for land enclosure. The enclosure movement eliminated large areas of what had formerly been communal land.

changed at market for the mixture of goods that previously had been grown in the village. Market production turned attention from producing a balance of commodities to increasing the yield of a single one.

Agricultural Innovations. The first innovation was the widespread cultivation of fodder crops such as clover and turnips. Crops like clover restore nutrients to the soil as they grow, shortening the period in which land has to lie fallow. Moreover, farm animals grazing on clover or feeding on turnips return more manure to the land, further increasing its productivity. Turnip cultivation had begun in Holland and was brought to England in the sixteenth century. But it was not until the late seventeenth century that Viscount Charles "Turnip" Townsend (1675–1738) made turnip cultivation popular. Townsend and other large Norfolk landowners developed a new system of planting known as the four-crop rotation, in which wheat, turnips, barley, and clover succeeded one another. The method kept the land in productive use, and both the turnip and clover crops were used to feed larger herds of animals.

The ability of farmers to increase their livestock was as important as their ability to grow more grain. Not only were horses and oxen more productive than humans—a horse could perform seven times the labor of a man while consuming only five times the food—but the animals also refertilized the land as they worked. Light fertilization of a single acre of arable land required an average of 25,000 pounds of manure. But animals competed with humans for food, especially during the winter months when little grazing was possible. To conserve grain for human consumption, lambs were led to the slaughter and the fatted calf was killed in the autumn. Thus

the development of the technique of meadow floating was a remarkable breakthrough. By flooding low-lying land near streams in the winter, English and Dutch farmers could prevent the ground from freezing during their generally mild winters. When the water was drained, the land beneath it would produce an early grass crop on which the beasts could graze. That meant that more animals could be kept alive during the winter.

The relationship between animal husbandry and grain growing became another feature of commercial agriculture. In many areas farmers could choose between growing grain and pasturing animals. When prices for wool or meat were relatively higher than those for grain, fields could be left in grass for grazing. When grain prices rose, the same fields could be plowed. Consolidated enclosed estates made convertible husbandry possible. The decision to hire field-workers or shepherds could be taken only by large agricultural employers. Whatever the relative price of grain, the open-field village continued to produce grain as its primary crop. Farmers who could convert their production in tune to the market not only could maximize their profits but also could prevent shortages of raw materials for domestic manufacturers or of foodstuffs for urban and rural workers.

Convertible husbandry was but the first step in the development of a true system of regional specialization in agriculture. Different soils and climates favored different use of the land. In southern and eastern England the soil was thin and easily depleted by grain growing. Traditionally, the light soil areas had been used almost exclusively for sheep rearing. On the other hand, the clay soils of central England, though poorly drained and hard to work, were more suited to grain growing. The new agricultural techniques reversed the

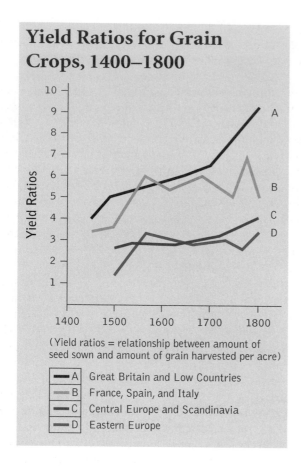

Yield Ratios for Grain Crops, 1400–1800

(Yield ratios = relationship between amount of seed sown and amount of grain harvested per acre)

——A	Great Britain and Low Countries
——B	France, Spain, and Italy
——C	Central Europe and Scandinavia
——D	Eastern Europe

pattern. The introduction of fodder crops and increased fertilization rejuvenated thin soils, and southeastern England became the nation's breadbasket. Large enclosed estates provided a surplus of grain throughout the eighteenth century. By the 1760s, England was exporting enough grain to feed more than a half million people. Similarly, the midland clays became the location of great sheep runs and cattle herds. Experiments in herd management, crossbreeding, and fattening all resulted in increased production of wool, milk, meat, leather, soap, and tallow for candles.

There can be no doubt about the benefits of the transformation of agricultural practices that began in Holland and England in the seventeenth century and spread slowly to all corners of the Continent over the next 200 years. Millions more mouths were fed at lower cost than ever before. In 1700, each person engaged in farming in England produced enough food for 1.7 people; in 1800, each produced enough for 2.5 people. Cheaper food allowed more discretionary spending, which fueled the demand for consumer goods, which in turn employed more rural manufacturers. But there also were costs. The transformation of agriculture was also a transformation in a way of life. The open-field village was a community; the enclosed estate was a business. The plight of the rural poor was tragic enough in villages of kin and neighbors, where face-to-face charity might be returned from one generation to the next. With their scrap of land and their common rights, even the poorest villagers laid claim to a place of their own. But as landless laborers, either on farms or in rural manufacturing, they could no longer make that claim and many soon became fodder for the factories, the "dark satanic mills" that came to disfigure the land once tilled in open-field villages. For the destitute, charity was now visited upon them in anonymous parish workhouses or in the good works of the comfortable middle class. In all of those ways the agricultural revolution changed the face of Europe.

THE INDUSTRIAL REVOLUTION IN BRITAIN

Like the changes in agriculture, the changes in manufacturing that began in Britain during the eighteenth century were more revolutionary in consequence than in development. But their consequences were revolutionary indeed. A work force that was predominantly agricultural in 1750 had become predominantly industrial a century later. A population that for centuries had centered on the south and east was now concentrated in the north and west. Liverpool, Manchester, Glasgow, and Birmingham mushroomed into giant cities. While the population of England grew by 100 percent between 1801 and 1851, from about 8.5 million people to more than 17 million, the populations of Liverpool and Manchester grew by more than 1000 percent.

It was the replacement of animal muscle by hydraulic and mineral energy that made the continued population growth possible. Water and coal drove machinery that dramatically increased human productivity. In 1812, one woman could spin as much thread as 200 women had in 1770. What was most revolutionary about the Industrial Revolution was the wave after wave of technological innovation, a constant tinkering and improving of the ways in which things were made, which could have the simultaneous effects of cutting costs and improving quality. It was not just the great breakthrough inventions such as the steam engine, the smelting of iron with coke, and the spinning jenny that were important, but also the hundreds of adjustments in technique that applied new ideas in one industry to another, opened bottlenecks, and solved problems. Ingenuity rather than genius was at the root of the **Industrial Revolution** in Britain.

The Industrial Revolution was a sustained period of economic growth and change brought about by the application of mineral energy and technological innovations to the process of manufacturing. It took place during the century between 1750 and 1850, though different industries moved at different paces and sustained economic growth continued in Britain until World War I. It is difficult to define the timing of the Industrial Revolution with any great precision because, unlike a political event, an economic transformation does not happen all at once. Nor are new systems and inventions ever really new. Coal miners had been using rails and wheeled carriages to move ore since the seventeenth century. In the sixteenth century, "Jack of Newbury" had housed his cloth workers in a large shed. The one was the precursor of the railroad and the other the precursor of the factory, but each preceded the Industrial Revolution by more than a century. Before 1750, innovations made their way slowly into general use, and after 1850 the pace of growth slowed appreciably. By then, Britain had a manufacturing economy: fewer than one-quarter of its labor force engaged in agriculture and nearly 60 percent were involved in industry, trade, and transport.

Britain First

The Industrial Revolution occurred first in Britain, but even in Britain **industrialization** was a regional rather than a national phenomenon. There were many areas of Britain that remained untouched by innovations in manufacturing methods and agricultural techniques, although no one remained unaffected by the prosperity that industrialization brought. That was the result of both national conditions and historical developments. When industrialization spread to the Continent, it took hold—as it had in Britain—in regions where mineral resources were abundant or where domestic manufacturing was a traditional activity. There was no single model for European industrialization, however often contemporaries looked toward Britain for the key to unlock the power of economic growth. There was as much technological innovation in France, as much capital for investment in Holland. Belgium was rich in coal, while eastern Europe enjoyed an agricultural surplus that sustained an increase in population. The finest cotton in the world was made in India; the best iron was made in Sweden. Each of those factors was in some way a precondition for industrialization, but none by itself proved sufficient. Only in Britain did those circumstances meld together.

Water and Coal. Among Britain's blessings, water was foremost. Water was its best defense, protecting the island from foreign invasion and making it unnecessary to invest in a costly standing army. Rather, Britain invested heavily in its navy to maintain its commercial preeminence around the globe. The navy protected British interests in times of war and transported British wares in times of peace. Britain's position in the Asian trade made it the leading importer of cottons, ceramics, and teas. Its colonies, especially in North America, not only provided sugar and tobacco but also formed a rich market for British manufacturing.

But the commercial advantages that water brought were not confined to oceanic trade. Britain was favored by an internal water system that tied inland communities together. In the eighteenth century, no place in Britain was more than 70 miles from the sea or more than 30 miles from a navigable river. Water transport was far cheaper than hauling goods overland; a packhorse could carry 250 pounds of goods on its back but could move 100,000 pounds by walking alongside a river and pulling a barge. Small wonder that river transport was one of the principal interests of merchants and traders. Beginning in the 1760s, private concerns began to invest in the construction of canals, first to move coal from inland locations to major arteries and then to connect the great rivers themselves. Over the next 50 years several hundred miles of canals were built by authority of Navigation Acts, which

■ Pictured here is the mouth of the underground tunnel for the Worsley-Manchester Canal, as depicted in Arthur Young's *Six Months' Tour Through the North of England* (1770). Here at Worsley the canal led to a significant coal mine, enabling increased coal production that would improve England's new industrial economy.

allowed for the sale of shares to raise capital. In 1760, the Duke of Bridgewater (1736–1803) lived up to his name by completing the first great canal. It brought coal to Manchester and ultimately to Liverpool. It cost more than £250,000 and took 14 years of labor to build, but it repaid the duke and his investors many times over by bringing an uneconomical coal field into production. Not the least of the beneficiaries were the people of Manchester, where the price of coal was halved.

Coal was the second of Britain's natural blessings on which it improved. Britain's reserves of wood were nearly depleted by the eighteenth century, especially those near centers of population. Coal had been in use as a fuel for several centuries, and the coal trade between London and the northern coal pits had been essential to the growth of the capital. Coal was abundant, much of it almost at surface level along the northeastern coast, and easily transported on water. The location of large coalfields along waterways was a vital condition of its early use. As canals and roadways improved, more inland coal was brought into production for domestic use. Yet it was in industry rather than in the home that coal was put to its greatest use. There again Britain was favored, for large seams of coal were also located near large seams of iron. At first, the coincidence was of little consequence, since iron was smelted by charcoal made from wood and iron foundries were located deep in forests. But ultimately ironmakers learned to use coal for fuel, and then the natural economies of having mineral, fuel, and transport in the same vicinity were given full play.

Economic Infrastructure.   The factors that contributed to Britain's early industrialization were not only those of natural advantage. Over the course of years, Britain had developed an infrastructure for economic advancement. The transformation of domestic handicrafts to industrial production depended as much on the abilities of merchants as on those of manufacturers. The markets for domestic manufacturing had largely been overseas, where British merchants built up relationships over generations. Export markets were vital to the success of industrialization as production grew dramatically and most ventures needed a quick turnaround of sales to reinvest the profits in continued growth. The flexibility of English trading houses would be seen in their ability to shift from reexporting Eastern and North American goods to exporting British manufactures. Equally important, increased production meant increased demand for raw materials: Swedish bar iron for casting, Egyptian and American cotton for textiles, and Oriental silk for luxuries. The expansion of shipping mirrored the expansion of the economy, tripling during the eighteenth century to more than one million tons of cargo capacity.

The expansion of shipping, agriculture, and investment in machines, plant, and raw material all required capital. Not only did capital have to exist, but it had to be made productive. Profits in agriculture, especially in the south and east, somehow had to be shifted to investment in industry in the north and west. The wealth of merchants, which flowed into London, had to be redistributed throughout the economy.

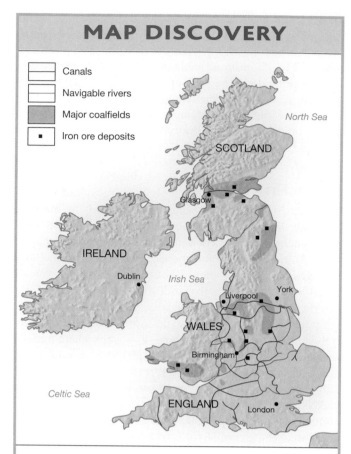

MAP DISCOVERY

Canals
Navigable rivers
Major coalfields
Iron ore deposits

Great Britain: Canals and Natural Resources
Examine the locations of canals, navigable rivers, and coal and iron ore deposits in Great Britain. Which parts of Great Britain did not develop canals? Why? Where are the canals concentrated? What is the relationship between canals and major navigable rivers? What about the relationship between the canals and the coal and iron ore deposits? Where would you expect railroads to be built?

More importantly, short-term investments had to give way to long-term financing. At the end of the seventeenth century, the creation of the Bank of England had begun the process of constructing a reliable banking system. The Bank of England dealt almost entirely with government securities, but it also served as a bill broker. It bought the debts of reputable merchants at a discount in exchange for Bank of England notes; Bank of England notes could then be exchanged between merchants, which increased the liquidity of the English economy, especially in London. It also became the model for provincial banking by the middle of the eighteenth century.

Private family banks also grew in importance in London, handling the accounts of merchants and buying shares in profitable enterprises, of which the canals were a favorite. Regional banks, smaller and less capitalized, began to use the private London banks as correspondents, that is, as extensions of their own banks in the city. That allowed local manufacturers and city merchants to do business with one another. The connections between the regional banks and London facilitated the flow of capital from one section of the nation to the other. In 1700, there were just 12 provincial banks; by 1790, there were nearly 300. Banks remained reluctant to invest for the long term, preferring to discount bills for a few months, but after they developed a relationship with a particular firm, they were usually willing to continue to roll the debt over. Although the banking system was vital to large enterprises, in fact the capital for most industry was raised locally, from kin and neighbors, and grew by plowing back profits into the business. At least at the beginning, manufacturers were willing to take risks and to work for small returns to ensure the survival and growth of their business.

Minerals and Metals

There could have been no Industrial Revolution without coal. It was the black gold of the eighteenth century, the fuel that fed the furnaces and turned the engines of industrial expansion. The coal produced by one miner generated as much energy as 20 horses. Coal was the first capital-intensive industry in Britain, already well developed by the seventeenth century. Owners paid the costs of sinking shafts, building roads, and erecting winding machines. Miners were brought to a pit and paid piecework for their labor. Only the very wealthy could afford to invest in coal mining, and it was by chance that British law vested mineral rights in owners rather than users of the land, as was the case on the Continent. That meant that the largest English coalfields were owned by landed families of means who were able to invest agricultural profits in mining. Britain's traditional elites thus played a crucial role in the industrial transformation of the agrarian economy from which their wealth and social standing had derived.

Early Coal Mining. The technical problems of coal mining grew with demand. As surface seams were exhausted it became necessary to dig deeper shafts, to lower miners farther underground, and to raise the coal greater heights to the surface. Men loosened the coal from the seam; women and children hauled it to the shaft. They also cleared the tons of debris that came loose with the coal. Underground mining was extremely dangerous. In addition to all-too-frequent cave-ins, miners struggled against inadequate ventilation and light. Better ventilation was achieved by the expensive method of sinking second and third shafts into the same seam, allowing for cross breezes. Candles and sparks created by flint wheels addressed the problem of light, though both methods suffered from the disadvantage that most pits contained combustible gases. Even after a fireman walked through the mine exploding gas with a long lighted stick, many miners preferred to work in total darkness, feeling the edges of the seam.

But by far the most difficult mining problem was water. As pits were sunk deeper they reached pools of groundwater, which enlarged as the coal was stripped away from the earth. Dripping water increased the difficulty of hewing, standing water the difficulty of hauling. The pit acted like a riverbed and filled quickly. Water drainage presented the greatest obstacle to deep-shaft mining. Women and children could carry the water out in large skin-lined baskets, which were attached to a winding wheel and pulled up by horses. Primitive pumps, also horse-powered, had been devised for the same purpose. Neither method was efficient or effective when shafts sank deeper. In 1709, Thomas Newcomen (1663–1729) introduced a steam-driven pump that enabled water to be sucked through a pipe directly from the pit bottom to the surface. Although the engine was expensive to build and needed tons of coal to create the steam, it could raise the same amount of water in a day as 2500 humans. Such economies of labor were enormous, and within 20 years of its introduction there were 78 engines draining coal and metal mines in England.

Innovations such as Newcomen's engine helped increase output of coal at just the time that it became needed as an industrial fuel. Between 1700 and 1830, coal production increased tenfold despite the fact that deeper and more difficult seams were being worked. Eventually, the largest demand for coal came from the iron industry. In 1793, just two ironworks consumed as much coal as the entire population of Edinburgh. Like mining coal, making iron was both capital- and labor-intensive, requiring expensive furnaces, water-powered bellows, and mills in which forged iron could be slit into rods or rolled into sheets. Ironmaking depended upon an abundance of wood, for it took the charcoal derived from 10 acres of trees to refine 1 ton of iron ore. After the ore was mined, it was smelted into pig iron, a low-grade, brittle metal. Pig iron was converted to higher-quality bar iron in charcoal-powered forges that burned off some of its impurities. From bar iron came the rods and sheets used in casting household items such as pots and nails or in making finer wrought iron products such as plows and armaments. Because each process in the making of iron was separate, furnaces, forges, and mills were located near their own supplies of wood. The shipping of the bulky ore, pig iron, and bar iron added substantially to its cost, and it was cheaper to import bars from Sweden than to carry them 20 miles overland.

The great innovations in the production of iron came with the development of techniques that allowed for the use of coal rather than wood charcoal in smelting and forging. As early as 1709, Abraham Darby (ca. 1678–1717), a Quaker nail maker, experimented with smelting iron ore with coke, coal from which most of the gas has been burned off. Iron coking greatly reduced the cost of fuel in the first stages of production, but because most ironworks were located in woodlands rather than near coal pits, the method was not widely adopted. Moreover, although coke made from coal was cheaper than charcoal made from wood, coke added its own impurities to the iron ore. Nor could it provide the intense heat needed for smelting without a large bellows. The cost of

Britain's ample coal deposits were one of the country's assets as it industrialized. This painting of the pithead of an eighteenth-century coal mine shows the coexistence of the new steam technology with aspects of older forms of production, such as the use of beasts of burden.

the bellows offset the savings from the coke until James Watt (1736–1819) invented a new form of steam engine in 1775.

The Steam Engine. Like most innovations of the Industrial Revolution, James Watt's steam engine was an adaptation of existing technology made possible by the sophistication of techniques in a variety of fields. Although Watt is credited with the invention of the condensing steam engine, one of the seminal creations in human history, the success of his work depended upon the achievements of numerous others. Watt's introduction to the steam engine was accidental. An instrument maker in Glasgow, he was asked to repair a model of a Newcomen engine and immediately realized that it would work more efficiently if there were a separate chamber for the condensation of the steam. Although his idea was sound, Watt spent years attempting to implement it. He was continually frustrated that poor-quality valves and cylinders never fit well enough together to prevent steam from escaping from the engine.

Watt was unable to translate his idea into a practical invention until he became partners with the Birmingham ironmaker and manufacturer Matthew Boulton (1728–1809). At Boulton's works, Watt found craftsmen who could make precision engine valves, and at the foundries of John Wilkinson (1728–1808) he found workers who could bore the cylinders of his engine to exact specifications. Watt's partnership with Boulton and Wilkinson was vital to the success of the steam engine. But Watt himself possessed the qualities necessary to ensure that his ideas were transformed into reality. He persevered through years of unsuccessful experimentation and searched out partners to provide capital and expertise. He saw beyond bare mechanics, realizing the practical utility of his invention long before it was perfected. Watt designed the mechanism to convert the traditional up-and-down motion of the pumping engine into rotary

James Watt's rotary beam steam engine. This model was built in 1788 to provide rotary power to the lapping and polishing machines at Matthew Boulton's Soho Engineering Works in Birmingham, England, where Watt and Boulton manufactured steam engines from 1775 to 1810.

motion, which could be used for machines and ultimately for locomotion.

Watt's engine received its first practical application in the iron industry. Wilkinson became one of the largest customers for steam engines, using them for pumping, moving wheels, and ultimately increasing the power of the blast of air in the forge. Increasing the heat provided by coke in the smelting and forging of iron led to the transformation of the industry. In the 1780s, Henry Cort (1740–1800), a naval contractor, experimented with a technique for using coke as fuel in removing the impurities from pig iron. The iron was melted into puddles and stirred with rods. The gaseous carbon that was brought to the surface burned off, leaving a purer and more malleable iron than even charcoal could produce. Because the iron had been purified in a molten state, Cort reasoned that it could be rolled directly into sheets rather than first made into bars. He erected a rolling mill adjacent to his forge and combined two separate processes into one.

Puddling and rolling had an immediate impact upon iron production. There was no longer any need to use charcoal in the stages of forging and rolling. From mineral to workable sheets, iron could be made entirely with coke. Ironworks moved to the coalfields, where the economies of transporting fuel and finished product were great. Moreover, the distinct stages of production were eliminated. Rather than separate smelting, forging, and finishing industries, one consolidated manufacturing process had been created. Forges, furnaces, and rolling machines were brought together and powered by steam engines. Cort's rolling technique alone increased output 15 times. By 1808, output of pig iron had grown from 68,000 to 250,000 tons and of bar iron from 32,000 to 100,000 tons.

Cotton Is King

Traditionally, British commerce had been dominated by the woolen cloth trade, in which techniques of production had not changed for hundreds of years. Running water was used for cleaning and separating fleece; crude wooden wheels spun the thread; simple handlooms wove together the long warp threads and the short weft ones. It took nearly four female spinners to provide the materials for one male weaver, the tasks having long been gender-specific. During the course of the seventeenth century, new fabrics appeared on the domestic market, particularly linen, silk, and cotton. It was cotton that captured the imagination of the eighteenth-century consumer, especially brightly colored, finely spun Indian cotton.

Domestic Industries.   Spinning and weaving were organized as domestic industries. Work was done in the home on small, inexpensive machines to supplement the income from farming. Putters-out were especially frustrated by the difficulty in obtaining yarn for weaving in the autumn, when female laborers were needed for the harvest. Even the widespread development of full-time domestic manufacturers did not satisfy the increased demand for cloth. Limited output and variable quality characterized British textile production throughout the early part of the eighteenth century. The breakthrough came with technological innovation. Beginning in the mid-eighteenth century, a series of new machines dramatically increased output and, for the first time, allowed English textiles to compete with Indian imports.

The first innovation was the flying shuttle, invented by John Kay (1704–1764) in the 1730s. A series of hammers drove the shuttle, which held the weft, through the stretched warp on the loom. The flying shuttle allowed weavers to work alone rather than in pairs, but it was adopted slowly because it increased the demand for spun thread, which was already in

■ In the eighteenth century, a number of British inventors patented new machines that transformed the British textile industry and marked the beginning of the Industrial Revolution. Among the inventions was the spinning jenny, invented by James Hargreaves in 1764, and named for his daughter. The jenny, which permitted the spinning of a number of threads at the same time, made possible the automatic production of cotton thread.

■ Great Britain: Textile Centers. Textiles had been the traditional industrial activity in Britain and almost every region of the country had organized textile production.

short supply. The spinning bottleneck was opened by James Hargreaves (d. 1778), who devised a machine known as the jenny. The jenny was a wooden frame containing a number of spindles around which thread was drawn by means of a hand-turned wheel. The first jennies allowed for the spinning of eight threads at once, and improvements brought the number to more than 100. Jennies replaced spinning wheels by the tens of thousands. The jenny was a crucial breakthrough in redressing the balance between spinning and weaving, though it did not solve all problems. Jenny-spun thread was not strong enough to be used as warp, which continued to be wheel spun. But the jenny could spin cotton in unimaginable quantities.

As is often the case with technological change, one innovation followed another. The problem set by improvements in weaving gave rise to solutions for increasing the output of spinners. The need to provide stronger warp threads posed by the introduction of the jenny was ultimately solved by the development of the water frame. It was created in 1769 by Richard Arkwright (1732–1792), whose name was also to be associated with the founding of the modern factory system. Arkwright's frame consisted of a series of water-driven rollers that stretched the cotton before spinning. The stronger fibers could be spun into threads suitable for warp, and English manufacturers could finally produce an all-cotton fabric. It was not long before another innovator realized that the water frame and the jenny could be combined into a single machine, one that would pro-

duce an even finer cotton yarn than that made in India. The **mule**, so named because it was a cross between a frame and a jenny, was invented by Samuel Crompton (1753–1827), who sold its rights for only £60. It was the decisive innovation in cotton production. By 1811, ten times as many threads were being spun on mules as on water frames and jennies combined.

The original mules were small machines that, like the jennies, could be used for domestic manufactures. But increasingly the mule followed the water frame into purposely built factories, where it became larger and more expensive. The need for large rooms to house the equipment and for a ready source of running water to power it provided an incentive for the creation of factories, but secrecy provided a greater one. The original factories were called "safe-boxes," and whether they were established for the manufacture of silk or cotton, their purpose was to protect trade secrets. Innovators took out patents to prevent their inventions from being copied and fought long lawsuits to prevent their machines from being used. Workers were sworn to secrecy about the techniques they were taught. Imitators practiced industrial espionage as sophisticated as the age would allow: enticing knowledgeable workers; employing spies; copying inventions. Although the factory was designed to protect secrets, its other benefits were quickly realized. Manufacturers could maintain control over the quality of products through strict supervision of the work force. Moreover, workers in shifts could keep the costly machines in continuous use.

Cotton Factories.   Richard Arkwright constructed the first cotton factories in Britain, all of which were designed to house water frames. The first was established in 1769 at Cromford near Nottingham, which was the center of stocking manufacture. The site was chosen for its isolation, since stockings were an article of fashion in which secrecy was most important. The Cromford mill was a four-story building that ultimately employed more than 800 workers. During the next quarter century, Arkwright built more than a dozen other mills, most in partnership with wealthy manufacturers. Arkwright's genius lay in industrial management rather than mechanical innovation. As others switched from frames to mules, Arkwright stubbornly stuck to his own invention. When steam power began to replace water, he failed to make the shift. But his methods of constructing and financing factories were undeniably successful. From a modest beginning as a traveling salesman of wigs, Sir Richard Arkwright died in possession of a fortune worth more than £500,000.

The organization of the cotton industry into factories was one of the pivotal transformations in economic life. Domestic spinning and weaving took place in agricultural villages; factory production took place in mill towns. The location of the factory determined movements of population, and from the first quarter of the eighteenth century onward a great shift toward northeast England was under way. Moreover, the character of the work itself changed. The operation of heavy machinery reversed the traditional gender-based tasks. Mule spinning became men's work, while handloom weaving was taken over by

DOCUMENT

Industrial Society and Factory Conditions

THE WEALTH OF BRITAIN

Cotton was the first of the new industries that led to British economic domination in the nineteenth century. In cotton production, new inventions such as the spinning jenny and the water frame revolutionized manufacture, and the factory system was born. Britain's domination of cotton production impressed contemporaries. In this excerpt, a contemporary tries to explain why Britain took the lead in industrialization.

Focus Questions

How important does the author think geography and natural resources have been to Britain's industrial success? What is the relation between industrialization and forms of government?

In comparing the advantages of England for manufactures with those of other countries, we can by no means overlook the excellent commercial position of the country—intermediate between the north and south of Europe; and its insular situation, which, combined with the command of the seas, secures our territory from invasion or annoyance. The German ocean, the Baltic, and the Mediterranean are the regular highways for our ships; and our western ports command an unobstructed passage to the Atlantic, and to every quarter of the world.

A temperate climate, and a hardy race of men, have also greatly contributed to promote the manufacturing industry of England.

The political and moral advantages of this country, as a seat of manufactures, are not less remarkable than its physical advantages. The arts are the daughters of peace and liberty. In no country have these blessings been enjoyed in so high a degree, or for so long a continuance, as in England. Under the reign of just laws, personal liberty and property have been secure; mercantile enterprise has been allowed to reap its reward; capital has accumulated in safety; the workman has "gone forth to his work and to his labour until the evening"; and, thus protected and favoured, the manufacturing prosperity of the country has struck its roots deep, and spread forth its branches to the ends of the earth.

England has also gained by the calamities of other countries, and the intolerance of other governments. At different periods, the Flemish and French protestants; expelled from their native lands, have taken refuge in England, and have repaid the protection given them by practising and teaching branches of industry, in which the English were then less expert than their neighbours.

From Edward Baines, *The History of the Cotton Manufacture in Great Britain* (1835).

women. The mechanization of weaving took longer than that of spinning, both because of difficulties in perfecting a power loom and because of opposition to its introduction by workers known as **Luddites**, who organized machine-breaking riots in the 1810s. The Luddites attempted to maintain the traditional organization of their industry and the independence of their labor. For a time, handloom weavers managed to survive by accepting lower and lower piece rates. But their competition was like that of a horse against an automobile. In 1820, there were more than 250,000 handloom weavers in Britain; by 1850, the number was less than 50,000. Weaving as well as spinning became factory work.

The transformation of cotton manufacture had a profound effect on the overall growth of the British economy. It increased shipping because the raw material had to be imported, first from the Mediterranean and then from America. American cotton—especially after 1794, when American inventor Eli Whitney (1765–1825) patented his cotton gin—fed a nearly insatiable demand. This appetite was met primarily because American cotton plantations used slave labor to plant and harvest their crop. In 1750, Britain imported less than 5 million pounds of raw cotton; a century later the volume had grown to 588 million pounds. And to each pound of raw cotton, British manufacturers added the value of their technology and their labor. By the mid-nineteenth century, nearly a half million people earned their living from cotton, which alone accounted for more than 40 percent of the value of all British exports. Cotton was undeniably the king of manufactured goods.

The Iron Horse

The first stage of the Industrial Revolution in Britain was driven by the production of consumer goods. Pottery, cast-iron tools, clocks, toys, and textiles, especially cottons—all were manufactured in quantities unknown in the early eighteenth century. The products fed a ravenous market at home and abroad. The greatest complaint of industrialists was that they could not get enough raw materials or fuel, nor could they ship their finished products fast enough to keep up with demand. Transportation was becoming a serious stumbling block to continued economic growth. Even with the completion of the canal network that linked the major rivers and improvement in highways and tollways, raw materials and finished goods moved slowly and uncertainly. It was said that it took as long to ship goods from

Manchester to Liverpool on the Duke of Bridgewater's canal as it did to sail from New York to Liverpool on the Atlantic Ocean. Furthermore, once the canals had a monopoly on bulk cargo, transportation costs began to rise.

It was the need to ship increasing amounts of coal to foundries and factories that provided the spur for the development of a new form of transportation. Ever since the seventeenth century, coal had been moved from the seam to the pit on rails, first constructed of wood and later of iron. Broadwheeled carts hitched to horses were as much dragged as rolled, but that still represented the most efficient form of hauling, and those railways ultimately ran from the seam to the dock. By 1800, there was perhaps as much as 300 miles of iron rail in British mines.

In the same year, Watt's patent on the steam engine expired, and inventors began to apply the engine to a variety of mechanical tasks. Richard Trevithick (1771–1833), whose father managed a tin mine in Cornwall, was the first to experiment with a steam-driven carriage. George Stephenson (1781–1848), who is generally recognized as the father of the modern railroad, made two crucial improvements. In mine railways the wheels of the cart were smooth and the rail was grooved. Stephenson reversed the construction to provide better traction and less wear. Perhaps more importantly, Stephenson made the vital improvement in engine power by increasing the steam pressure in the boiler and exhausting the smoke through a chimney. In 1829, he won a £500 prize with his engine "The

Rocket," which pulled a load three times its own weight at a speed of 30 miles per hour and could actually outrun a horse.

The First Railways. In 1830 the first modern railway, the Manchester-to-Liverpool line, was opened. Like the Duke of Bridgewater's canal, it was designed to move coal and bulk goods, but surprisingly its most important function came to be moving people. In its first year, the Manchester–Liverpool line carried more than 400,000 passengers, which generated double the revenue derived from freight. The railway was quicker, more comfortable, and ultimately cheaper than the coach. Investors in the Manchester–Liverpool line, who pocketed a comfortable 9.5 percent when government securities were paying 3.5 percent, learned quickly that links between population centers were as important as those between industrial sites. The London–Birmingham and London–Bristol lines were both designed with passenger traffic in mind.

Railway building was one of the great boom activities of British industrialization. Since it came toward the end of the mechanization of factories, investors and industrialists were psychologically prepared for the benefits of technological innovation. By 1835, Parliament had passed 54 separate acts to establish more than 750 miles of railways. Ten years later, more than 6000 miles had been sanctioned and more than 2500 miles built; by 1852, more than 7500 miles of track were in use. The railways were built on the model of the canals. Private bills passed through Parliament, which allowed a company to raise money through the sale of stock. Most railways were trunk lines, connecting one town to another or joining two longer lines together. They were run by small companies, and few ultimately proved profitable. Only because of the dominant influence of George Stephenson and his son Robert (1803–1859) was there an attempt to establish a standard gauge for tracks and engines. Britain was the only country in which the government did not take a leading role in building the railways. Hundreds of millions of pounds were raised privately, and in the end it is calculated that the railroads cost £40,000 a mile to build, more than three times the cost per mile of railroads on the Continent and in the United States.

From Goods to Passengers. Nevertheless, the investment paid huge dividends. By the 1850s, the original purpose of the railways was being realized as freight revenues finally surpassed passenger revenues. Coal was the dominant cargo shipped by rail, and the speedy, efficient service continued to drive down prices. The iron and steel industries were modernized on the back of demand for rails, engines, and cast-iron seats and fittings. In peak periods—and railway building was a boom-and-bust affair—as much as a quarter of the output of the rolling mills went into domestic railroads, and much more into Continental systems. The railways were also a massive consumer of bricks for beddings, sidings, and especially bridges, tunnels, and stations. Finally, the railways were a leading employer of labor, surpassing the textile mills in peak periods. Hundreds of thousands worked in tasks as varied as engineering and ditch digging, for even in that most ad-

■ Great Britain: Railroads (ca. 1850). All rails led to London as the major lines were built to transport passengers as well as goods.

■ Honoré Daumier (1808–1879), *The Third-Class Carriage*. Daumier captured a human condition peculiar to the modern era: "the lonely crowd."

vanced industry, sophisticated mechanized production went hand in hand with traditional drudgery. More than 60,000 workers were permanently engaged in the industry to run trains, mind stations, and repair track. Countless others were employed in manufacturing engines, carriages, boxcars, and the thousands of components that went into making them.

Most of all, the railroads changed the nature of people's lives. Whole new concepts of time, space, and speed emerged to govern daily activities. As Henry Booth, an early railroad official, observed, "Notions which we have received from our ancestors and verified by our own experience are overthrown in a day. What was slow is now quick; what was distant is now near." Coach travel had ordinarily been limited to those with means, not only because it was expensive, but also because it was time-consuming. Ordinary people could not take off the days necessary to complete relatively short round-trip journeys. When passenger rail service began, there was even a debate over whether provision should be made for third-class passengers, a class unknown on the coaches, where the only choices were riding inside for comfort or outside for savings.

Third-class passengers quickly became the staple of railroad service. The cheap excursion was born to provide short holidays or even day trips. The career of Thomas Cook (1808–1892), who became the world's first travel agent, began after he took a short excursion. More than six million people visited London by train to view the Crystal Palace exhibition in 1851, a number equivalent to one-third of the population of England and Wales. The railways did more than link places; they brought people together and helped develop a sense of national identity by speeding up all forms of communication.

Entrepreneurs and Managers

The Industrial Revolution in Britain was not simply invented. Too much credit is given to a few breakthroughs and too little to the ways in which they were improved and dispersed. The Industrial Revolution was an age of gadgets when people believed that new was better than old and that there was always room for improvement. "The age is running mad after innovation," the English moralist Dr. Johnson wrote. "All the business of the world is done in a new way; men are hanged in a new way." Societies for the advancement of knowledge sprang up all over Britain. Journals and magazines promoted new ideas and techniques. Competitions were held for the best invention of the year; prizes were awarded for agricultural achievements. Practical rather than pure science was the hallmark of industrial development.

Yet technological innovation was not the same as industrialization. A vital change in economic activity took place in the organization of industry. Putters-out with their circulating capital and hired laborers could never make the economies necessary to increase output and quality while simultaneously lowering costs. That was the achievement of industrialists, producers who owned workplace, machinery, and raw materials and invested fixed capital by plowing back their profits. Industrial enterprises came in all sizes and shapes. A cotton mill could be started with as little as £300 or as much as £10,000. As late as 1840, fewer than 10 percent of the mills employed more than 500 workers. Most were family concerns with less than 100 employees, and many of them failed. For every story with a happy ending, there was another with a sad one. When Major Edmund Cartwright (1740–1824) erected a cotton mill, he was offered a Watt steam engine built for a distiller who had gone bankrupt. He acquired his machinery at the auction of another bankrupt mill. Cartwright's mill, engine, and machinery ended on the auction block less than three years later. There were more than 30,000 bankruptcies in the eighteenth century, testimony both to the risks of business and to the willingness of entrepreneurs to take them.

To survive against the odds, successful industrialists had to be both entrepreneur and manager. As entrepreneurs, they raised capital, almost always locally from relatives, friends, or members of their church. Quakers were especially active in financing each other's enterprises. The industrial entrepreneur also had to understand the latest methods for building and powering machinery and the most up-to-date techniques for performing the work. One early manufacturer claimed "a practical knowledge of every process from the cotton-bag to the piece of cloth." Finally, entrepreneurs had to know how to market their goods. In those functions, industrial entrepreneurs developed logically from putters-out.

But industrialists also had to be managers. The most difficult task was organization of the workplace. Most gains in productivity were achieved through the specialization of function. The processes of production were divided and subdivided until workers performed a basic task over and over. The education of the work force was the industrial manager's greatest challenge. Workers had to be taught how to use and maintain their machines and disciplined to apply themselves continuously. At least at the beginning, it was difficult to staff the factories. Many employed children as young as seven from workhouses or orphanages, who, though cheap to pay, were difficult to train and discipline. It was the task of the manager to break old habits of intermittent work, indifference to quality, and petty theft of materials. Families were preferred to individuals, for then parents could instruct and supervise their children. There is no reason to believe that industrial managers were more brutal masters than farmers or that children were treated better in workhouses than in mills. Labor was a business asset, what was sometimes called "living machinery," and its control with carrots and sticks was the chief concern of the industrial manager.

Who were the industrialists who transformed the traditional economy? Because British society was relatively open, they came from every conceivable background: dukes and orphans, merchants and salesmen, inventors and improvers. Although some went from rags to riches—such as Richard Arkwright, who was the thirteenth child of a poor barber—it was extremely difficult for a laborer to acquire the capital necessary to set up a business. Wealthy landowners were prominent in capital-intensive aspects of industries—for example, owning ironworks and mines—but few established factories. Most industrialists came from the middle classes, which, while comprising one-third of the British population, provided as much as two-thirds of the first generation of industrialists. That first generation included lawyers, bankers, merchants, and those already engaged in manufacturing, as well as tradesmen, shopkeepers, and self-employed artisans. The career of every industrialist was different, as a look at two—Josiah Wedgwood and Robert Owen—will show.

Josiah Wedgwood. Josiah Wedgwood (1730–1795) was the thirteenth child of a long-established English potting family. He worked in the potteries from childhood, but a deformed leg

■   Jasperware copy of the Portland vase by Josiah Wedgwood. The Portland vase is one of the most famous ancient vases. It was found near Rome in the seventeenth century in a tomb believed to be that of Alexander Severus.

made it difficult for him to turn the wheel. Instead he studied the structure of the business. His head teemed with ideas for improving ceramic manufacturing, but it was not until he was 30 that he could set up on his own and introduce his innovations, which encompassed both technique and organization, the entrepreneurial and managerial sides of his business.

Wedgwood developed new mixtures of clays that took brilliant colors in the kiln and new glazes for both useful and ornamental ware. His technical innovations were all the more remarkable in that he had little education in mineral chemistry and made his discoveries by simple trial and error. But there was nothing of either luck or good fortune in Wedgwood's managerial innovations. He was repelled by the disorder of the traditional pottery, with its waste of materials, uneven quality, and slow output. When he began his first works, he divided the making of pottery into distinct tasks and assigned separate workers to them. One group did nothing but throw the pots on the wheel; another painted designs; a third glazed. To achieve the division of function, Wedgwood had to train his own workers almost from childhood. Traditional potters performed every task from molding to glazing and prized the fact that no two pieces were ever alike. Wedgwood wanted each piece to replicate another, and he stalked the works breaking defective wares on his wooden leg. He invested in schools to help train young artists, in canals to transport his products, and in London shops to sell them. Wedgwood was a marketing genius. He named his famed cream-colored pottery Queen's Ware and made special coffee and tea services for leading aristocratic families. He would then sell replicas by the thousands. In less than 20 years, Wedgwood pottery was prized all over Europe and Wedgwood's potting works were the standard of the industry.

Robert Owen.   Robert Owen (1771–1858) did not have a family business to develop. The son of a small tradesman, he was apprenticed to a clothier at the age of 10. As a teenager he worked as a shop assistant in Manchester, where he audaciously applied for a job as a manager of a cotton mill. At 19, he was supervising 500 workers and learning the cotton trade. Owen was immediately successful, increasing the output of his workers and introducing new materials to the mill. In 1816, he entered a partnership to purchase the New Lanark mill in Scotland. Owen found conditions in Scotland much worse than those in Manchester. More than 500 workhouse children were employed at New Lanark, where drunkenness and theft were endemic. Owen believed that to improve the quality of work one had to improve the quality of the workplace. He replaced old machinery with new, reduced working hours, and instituted a monitoring system to check theft. To enhance life outside the factory, he established a high-quality company-run store, which plowed its profits into a school for village children.

Owen was struck by the irony that in the mills, machines were better cared for than were humans. He thought that with the same attention to detail that had so improved the quality of commodities he could make even greater improvements in the

■ Great Britain: Manufacturing Centers. The growth of manufacturers in the Midlands led to a massive population shift and the development of major urban areas such as Manchester.

quality of life. He prohibited children under 10 from mill work and instituted a 10-hour day for child labor. His local school took infants from one year old, freeing women to work and ensuring each child an education. Owen instituted old-age and disability pensions, funded by mandatory contributions from workers' wages. Taverns were closed and workers were fined for drunkenness and sexual offenses. In the factory and the village, Owen established a principle of communal regulation to improve both the work and the character of his employees. New Lanark became the model of the world of the future, and each year thousands made an industrial pilgrimage to visit it.

The Wages of Progress

Robert Owen ended his life as a social reformer. His efforts to improve the lot of his workers at New Lanark led to experiments to create ideal industrial communities throughout the world. He founded cooperative societies, in which all members shared in the profits of the business, and supported trade unions in which workers could better their lives. His followers planted colonies where goods were held in common and the fruits of labor belonged to the laborers. Owen's agitation for social reform was part of a movement that produced results of lasting consequence. The **Factory Act (1833)** prohibited factory work by children under nine, provided two hours of daily education, and effectively created a 12-hour day in the mills

THE SIN OF WAGES

Robert Owen was both a successful manufacturer and a leading philanthropist. He believed that economic advance had to take place in step with the improvement of the moral and physical well-being of the workers. He organized schools, company shops, and ultimately utopian communities in an effort to improve the lives of industrial laborers. Owen was one of the first social commentators to argue that industrialism threatened the fabric of family and community life.

Focus Questions

What effect does the luxury market have on "the lower orders"? Why are commercial competition and its effects becoming more intense?

The acquisition of wealth, and the desire which it naturally creates for a continued increase, have introduced a fondness for essentially injurious luxuries among a numerous class of individuals who formerly never thought of them, and they have also generated a disposition which strongly impels its possessors to sacrifice the best feelings of human nature to this love of accumulation. To succeed in this career, the industry of the lower orders, from whose labour this wealth is now drawn, has been carried by new competitors striving against those of longer standing, to a point of real oppression, reducing them by successive changes, as the spirit of competition increased and the ease of acquiring wealth diminished, to a state more wretched than can be imagined by those who have not attentively observed the changes as they have gradually occurred. In consequence, they are at present in a situation infinitely more degraded and miserable than they were before the introduction of these manufactories, upon the success of which their bare subsistence now depends. . . .

The inhabitants of every country are trained and formed by its great leading existing circumstances, and the character of the lower orders in Britain is now formed chiefly by circumstances arising from trade, manufactures, and commerce; and the governing principle of trade, manufactures, and commerce is immediate pecuniary gain, to which on the great scale every other is made to give way. All are sedulously trained to buy cheap and to sell dear; and to succeed in this art, the parties must be taught to acquire strong powers of deception; and thus a spirit is generated through every class of traders, destructive of that open, honest sincerity, without which man cannot make others happy, nor enjoy happiness himself.

From Robert Owen, *Observations on the Effect of the Manufacturing System* (1815).

---

until the Ten Hours Act (1847). The Mines Act (1842) prohibited women and children from working underground.

Nor was Owen alone in dedicating time and money to the improvement of workers' lives. The rapid growth of unplanned cities exacerbated the plight of those too poor and overworked to help themselves. Conditions of housing and sanitation were appalling even by nineteenth-century standards. The *Report on the Sanitary Condition of the Laboring Population of Britain* (1842), written by Edwin Chadwick (1800–1890), so shocked Parliament and the nation that it helped to shift the burden of social reform to government. The Public Health Act (1848) established boards of health and the office of medical examiner, while the Vaccination Act (1853) and the Contagious Diseases Act (1864) attempted to control epidemics. (See "A Closer Look: Industry and the Environment," pp. 640–641.)

The movement for social reform began almost as soon as industrialization. The Industrial Revolution initiated profound changes in the organization of British society. Cities sprang up from grain fields almost overnight. The lure of steady work and high wages prompted an exodus from rural Britain and spurred an unremitting boom in population. In the first half of the nineteenth century, the population of

DOCUMENT

Chadwick, *The Sanitary Condition of the Laboring Population of Britain*

England doubled from 9 to 18 million, with growth most rapid in the newly urban north and west. In 1750, about 15 percent of the population lived in urban areas; by 1850, about 60 percent did. Industrial workers married younger and produced more children than their agricultural counterparts. For centuries, women had married in their middle twenties, but by 1800, age at first marriage had dropped to 23 for the female population as a whole and to nearly 20 in the industrial areas. That was in part because factory hands did not have to wait until they inherited land or money, and in part because they did not have to serve an apprenticeship. But early marriage and large families were also a bet on the future, a belief that things were better now and would be even better soon, that the new mouths would be fed and the new bodies clothed. It was an investment on the part of ordinary people similar to that made by bankers and entrepreneurs when they risked their capital in new businesses. Was it an investment that paid off?

Expansion of Wealth.   It is difficult to calculate the benefits of the Industrial Revolution or to weigh them against the costs. What is certain is that there was a vast expansion of wealth as well as a vast expansion of people to share it. Agricultural and industrial change made it possible to support comfortably a population more than three times larger than that of the seventeenth century, when it was widely believed that England had reached the limits of expansion. Despite the fact that population doubled between 1801 and 1851, per capita income rose by 75 percent. Had the population remained stable, per capita income would have increased by a staggering 350 percent. At the same time, untold millions of pounds had been sunk into canals, roads, railways, factories, mines, and mills.

But the expansion of wealth is not the same as the improvement in the quality of life, for wealth is not equally distributed. An increase in the level of wealth may mean only that the rich are getting richer more quickly than the poor are getting poorer. Similarly, economic growth over a century involved the lives of several generations, each of which experienced different standards of living. One set of parents may have sacrificed for the future of their children; another may have mortgaged it. Moreover, economic activity is cyclical. Trade depressions, such as those induced by the War of 1812 and the American Civil War, which interrupted cotton supplies, could have disastrous short-term effects. The "Great Hunger" of the 1840s was a time of agrarian crisis and industrial slump. The downturn of 1842 threw 60 percent of the factory workers in the town of Bolton out of work at a time when there was neither unemployment insurance nor a welfare system. Finally, quality of life

cannot be measured simply in economic terms. People with more money to spend may still be worse off than their ancestors, who may have preferred leisure to wealth or independence to the discipline of the clock.

Thus there are no easy answers to the quality-of-life question. In the first stages of industrialization, it seems clear that only the wealthy benefited economically, though much of their increased wealth was reinvested in expansion. Under the impact of population growth, the Napoleonic wars, and regional harvest failure, real wages seem to have fallen from the levels reached in the 1730s. Industrial workers were not substantially better off than agricultural laborers when the high cost of food and rent is considered. But beginning around 1820, there is convincing evidence that the real wages of industrial workers were rising despite the fact that more and more work was semi- and unskilled machine-minding and more of it was being done by women, who were generally paid only two-thirds the wages of men. Although the increase in real wages was still subject to trade cycles, such as the Great Hunger of the 1840s, it continued nearly unabated for the rest of the nineteenth century. Thus, in the second half of the Industrial Revolution, both employers and workers saw a bettering of their economic situation, which was one reason why

EXPLOITING THE YOUNG

The condition of child laborers was a concern of English legislators and social reformers from the beginning of industrialization. Most of the attention was given to factory workers, and most legislation attempted to regulate the age at which children could begin work, the number of hours they could be made to work, and the provision of schooling and religious education during their leisure. It was not until the early 1840s that a parliamentary commission was formed to investigate the condition of child labor in the mines. In this extract, the testimony of the child is confirmed by the observations of one of the commissioners.

Focus Questions

How does Mr. Franks's account differ from Ellison Jack's own? Why do you think Ellison offers information about her level of literacy and knowledge of the Bible?

Ellison Jack, 11-years-old girl coal-bearer at Loanhead Colliery, Scotland: I have been working below three years on my father's account; he takes me down at two in the morning, and I come up at one and two next afternoon. I go to bed at six at night to be ready for work next morning: the part of the pit I bear in the seams are much on the edge. I have to bear my burthen up four traps, or ladders, before I get to the main road which leads to the pit bottom. My task is four or five tubs; each tub holds 4G cwt. I fill five tubs in twenty journeys.

I have had the strap when I did not do my bidding. Am very glad when my task is wrought, as it sore fatigues. I can read, and was learning the writing; can do a little; not been

at school for two years; go to kirk occasionally, over to Lasswade: don't know much about the Bible, so long since read.

R. H. Franks, Esq., the sub-commissioner: A brief description of this child's place of work will illustrate her evidence. She has first to descend a nine-ladder pit to the first rest, even to which a shaft is sunk, to draw up the baskets or tubs of coals filled by the bearers; she then takes her creel (a basket formed to the back, not unlike a cockle-shell flattened towards the neck, so as to allow lumps of coal to rest on the back of the neck and shoulders), and pursues her journey to the wall-face, or as it is called here, the room of work. She then lays down her basket, into which the coal is rolled, and it is frequently more than one man can do to lift the burden on her back. The tugs or straps are placed over the forehead, and the body bent in a semicircular form, in order to stiffen the arch.

"Child Labor in the Coal Mines," Testimony to the Parliamentary Investigative Committee (1842).

INDUSTRY AND THE ENVIRONMENT

The Industrial Revolution changed the landscape of Britain. Small villages grew into vast metropolises seemingly overnight. The rates of growth were absolutely staggering: in 1801, there were 75,000 people in Manchester; by 1851, the number had more than quadrupled. The unremitting boom in population did more than strain the resources of local authorities: it broke them apart. It was not that the new industrial cities were unplanned; they were beyond the capacity of planning. Every essential requirement for human survival became scarce and expensive. Shortages of food, water, and basic accommodation were commonplace.

Shantytowns sprang up wherever space would allow, making the flimsily built habitations of construction profiteers

A CLOSER LOOK

seem like palaces. There was loud complaint about those nineteenth-century rip-off artists, but in truth the need for housing was so desperate that people willingly lived anywhere that provided shelter. Houses were built back to back and side by side, with only narrow alleyways to provide sunlight and air. In Edinburgh, one could step through the window of one house into the window of the adjoining one. Whole families occupied single rooms where members slept as others worked, in shifts. In Liverpool, more than 38,000 people were estimated to be living in cellars—windowless underground accommodations that flooded with the rains and the tides.

Most cities lacked both running water and toilet facilities. Districts were provided with either pumps or capped pipes through which private companies ran water for a few hours each day. The water was collected in buckets and brought to the home, where it would stand for the rest of the day and serve indifferently for washing, drinking, and cooking. Outhouse toilets were an extravagant luxury; in one Manchester district, 33 outhouses had to accommodate 7095 people. They were a mixed blessing even in the middle-class districts where they were more plentiful, as there was no system of drainage to flush away the waste. It simply accumulated in cesspools, which were emptied manually about every two years. The thing that most impressed visitors as they approached an industrial city was the smoke; what impressed them most when they arrived was the smell.

The quality of life experienced by most of the urban poor who lived in the squalid conditions has been recorded by a number of contemporary observers. Friedrich Engels was a German socialist who was sent to England to learn the cotton trade. He lived in Manchester for two years and spent much of his time exploring the working-class areas of the city. "In this district I found a man, apparently about sixty years old, living in a cow stable," Engels recounted from one of his walking tours in *The Condition of the Working Class in England in 1844.* "He had constructed a sort of chimney for his square pen, which had neither windows, floor, nor ceiling, had obtained a bedstead and lived there, though the rain dripped through his rotten roof. This man was too old and weak for regular work, and supported himself by removing manure with a hand-cart; the dung-heaps lay next door to his palace!" From his own observations Engels concluded that "in such dwellings only a physically degenerate race, robbed of all humanity, degraded, reduced morally and physically to bestiality, could feel comfortable and at home." And as he was quick to point out, his own observations were no different from those of parliamentary commissioners, medical officers, or civic authorities who had seen the conditions firsthand.

Among the observers, the most influential by far was Sir Edwin Chadwick, who began his government career as a commissioner for the poor law and ended it as the founder of a national system of public health. Chadwick wrote the report of a parliamentary commission, *The Sanitary Condition of the Laboring Population of Britain* (1842), which caused a sensation among the governing classes. Building on the work of physicians, overseers of the poor, and the most technical scholarship available, Chadwick not only painted the same grim picture of urban life as Engels did, he proposed a comprehensive solution to one of its greatest problems, waste management.

■ Drawings of workers constructing London's sanitation system.

Chadwick was a civil servant, and he believed that problems were solved by government based on the conclusions of experts. He had heard doctors argue their theories about the causes of disease, some believing in fluxes that resulted from combinations of foul air, water, and refuse; others believing disease was spread by the diseased, in this case Irish immigrants who settled in the poorest parts of English industrial towns. Although medical research had not yet detected the existence of germs, it was widely held that lack of ventilation, stagnant pools of water, and the accumulation of human and animal waste in proximity to people's dwellings all contributed to the increasing incidence of disease. Chadwick fixed upon the last element as crucial. Not even in middle-class districts was there any effective system for the removal of waste. Chamber pots and primitive toilets were emptied into ditches, which were used to drain rain off into local waterways. The few underground sewers that existed were square containers without outlets that were simply emptied once filled. Chadwick's vision was for a sanitation system, one that would carry waste out of the city quickly and deposit it in outlying fields where it could be used as fertilizer.

Chadwick realized that the key to disposing of waste was a constant supply of running water piped through the system. Traditionally, only heavy rainstorms cleared the waste ditches in most cities, and those were too infrequent to be effective. The river had to be the beginning of the sewerage system as well as its end. River water had to be pumped through an underground construction of sewage pits that were built to facilitate the water's flow. Civil engineers had already demonstrated that pits with rounded rather than angular edges were far more effective, and Chadwick advocated the construction of a system of oval-shaped tunnels, built on an incline beneath the city. Water pumped from one part of the river would rush through the tunnels, which would empty into pipes that would carry the waste to nearby farms.

Chadwick's vision took years to implement. He had all of the zeal of a reformer and none of the tact of a politician. He offended nearly everyone with whom he came into contact, because he believed that his program was the only workable one and because he believed that it had to be implemented whatever the price. He was uninterested in who was to pay the enormous costs of laying underground tunnels and building pumping stations and insisted only that the work begin immediately. In the end, he won his point. Sanitation systems became one of the first great public-works projects of the industrial age.

rural workers flocked to the cities and Irish peasants emigrated in the hundreds of thousands to work the lowest paid and least desirable jobs in the factories.

Social Costs.   But economic gain had social costs. The first was the decline of the family as a labor unit. In both agricultural and early industrial activity, families labored together. Workers would not move to mill towns without the guarantee of a job for all members of their families, and initially they could drive a hard bargain. The early factories preferred family labor to workhouse conscripts, and it was traditional for children to work beside their parents, cleaning, fetching, or assisting in minding the machines. Children provided an essential part of family income, and youngest children were the agency of care for infirm parents. Paradoxically, it was agitation for improvement in the conditions of child labor that spelled the end of the family work unit. At first, young children were barred from the factories and older ones allowed to work only a partial adult shift. Although reformers intended that schooling and leisure be substituted for work, the separation of children from parents in the workplace ultimately made possible the substitution of teenagers for adults, especially as machines replaced skilled human labor. The individual worker now became the unit of labor, and during economic downturns it was adult males with their higher salaries who were laid off first.

The decline of the family as a labor unit was matched by other changes in living conditions when rural dwellers migrated to cities. Many rural habits were unsuited to both factory work and urban living. The tradition of "Saint Monday," for example, was one that was deeply rooted in the pattern of agricultural life. Little effort was expended at the beginning of the work week and progressively more at the end. Sunday leisure was followed by Monday recovery, a slow start to renewed labor. The factory demanded constant application six days a week. Strict rules were enforced to keep workers at their stations and their minds on their jobs. More than efficiency was at stake. Early machines were not only crude, they were dangerous, with no safety features to cover moving parts. Maiming accidents were common in the early factories, and they were the fault of both workers and machines. Similarly, industrial workers entered a world of the cash economy. Most agricultural workers were used to being paid in kind and to barter exchange. Money was an unusual luxury that was associated with binges of food, drink, and frivolities, which made adjustment to the wage packet as difficult as adjustment to the clock. Cash had to be set aside for provisions, rent, and clothing. On the farm, the time of a bountiful harvest was the time to buy durable goods; in the factory, "harvest time" was always the same.

Such adjustments were not easy, and during the course of the nineteenth century a way of life passed forever from England. For some, its departure caused profound sorrow; for others, it was a matter of rejoicing. A vertically integrated society in which lord of the manor, village worthies, independent farmers, workers, and servants lived together interdependently was replaced by a society of segregated social classes. By the middle decades of the nineteenth century, a class of capitalists and a class of workers had begun to form and had begun to clash. The middle classes abandoned the city centers, building exclusive suburban

■ *Dudley Street, Seven Dials, London,* by Gustave Doré, depicts life in the London slums of the early nineteenth century.

communities in which to raise their children and insulate their families. Conditions in the cities deteriorated under the pressure of overcrowding, lack of sanitation, and the absence of private investment. The loss of interaction between the different segments of society had profound consequences for the struggle to improve the quality of life for everyone. Leaders of labor saw themselves fighting against profits, greed, and apathy; leaders of capital against drunkenness, sloth, and ignorance. Between the two stereotypes there was little middle ground.

THE INDUSTRIALIZATION OF THE CONTINENT

Industrialization in Europe

Although Britain took the first steps along the road to an industrial economy, it was not long before other European nations followed. There was intense interest in "the British miracle," as it was dubbed by contemporaries. European ministers, entrepreneurs, even heads of state visited British factories and mines in hope of

learning the key industrial secrets that would unlock the prosperity of a new age. The **Crystal Palace Exhibition** of manufacturing and industry held in London in 1851 was the occasion for a Continentwide celebration of the benefits of technology and a chance for ambitious Europeans to measure themselves against the mighty British. By then many European nations had begun the transformation of their own economies and had entered a period of sustained growth.

There was no single model for the industrialization of the Continental states. Contemporaries continually made comparisons with Britain, but in truth the process of British industrialization was not well suited to any but the coal-rich regions in Belgium and the Rhineland. Nevertheless, all of Europe benefited from the British experience. No one else had to invent the jenny, the mule, or the steam engine. Although the British government banned the export of technology, none of the path-breaking inventions remained a secret for long. Britain had demonstrated a way to make cheap, durable goods in factories, and every other state in Europe was able to skip the long stages of discovery and improvement. Thus, while industrialization began later on the Continent, it could progress more quickly.

MAP DISCOVERY

Industrial Revolution on the Continent

What were the least industrial parts of Europe outside of Great Britain? In what directions did the major railroads run? How did the progress of industrialization in continental Europe compare with that in Britain? What impact did industrialization have on Spain and Italy?

France and Germany were building a railroad system within years of Britain despite the fact that they had to import most of the technology, raw materials, and engineers.

Britain shaped European industrialization in another way. Its head start made it very difficult for follower nations to compete against British commodities in the world market. Thus European industrialization would be directed first and foremost to home markets, where tariffs and import quotas could protect fledgling industries. Although European states were willing to import vital British products, they placed high duties on British-made consumer goods and encouraged higher-cost domestic production. Britain's competitive advantage demanded that European governments become involved in the industrialization of their countries, financing capital-intensive industries, backing the railroads, and favoring the establishment of factories.

European industrialization was therefore not the thunderclap it was in Britain. In France, it was a slow, accretive development that took advantage of traditional skills and occupations and gradually modernized the marketplace. In Germany, industrialization had to overcome the political divisions of the empire, the economic isolation of the petty states, and the wide dispersion of vital resources. Regions rather than states industrialized in the early nineteenth century, and parts of Austria, Italy, and Spain imported machinery and techniques and modernized their traditional crafts. But most of the states and most of the eastern part of Europe remained tied to a traditional agrarian-based economy that provided neither labor for industrial production nor purchasing power for industrial goods. The areas quickly became sources for raw materials and primary products for their industrial neighbors.

France: Industrialization Without Revolution

The experience of France in the nineteenth century demonstrates that there was no single path to industrialization. Each state blended together its natural resources, historical experiences, and forms of economic organization in unique combinations. While some mixtures resulted in explosive growth, as in Britain, others made for steady development, as in France.

French industrialization was keyed to domestic rather than export markets and to the application of new technology to a vast array of traditional crafts. The French profited, as did all of the Continental states, from British inventions, but they also benefited from the distinct features of their own economy. France possessed a pool of highly skilled and highly productive labor, a manufacturing tradition oriented toward the creation of high-quality goods, and consumers who valued taste and fashion over cost and function. Thus while the British dominated the new mass market for inexpensive cottons and cast-iron goods, a market with high sales but low profit margins, the French were producing luxury items whose very scarcity kept both prices and profits high. Two decisive factors determined the nature of French industrialization: population growth and the French Revolution.

Slow Growth. From the early eighteenth to the mid-nineteenth centuries, France grew slowly. In 1700, the French population stood at just less than 20 million; in 1850, it was just less than 36 million, a growth rate of 80 percent. In contrast, Germany grew 135 percent, from 15 to 34 million, and England 300 percent, from 5 to 20 million, during the same period. Nevertheless, France remained the most populous nation in western Europe, second on the Continent only to Russia. There is no simple explanation for France's relatively sluggish population growth. The French had been hit particularly hard by subsistence crises in the seventeenth century, and there is reliable evidence that the rural population consciously attempted to limit family size by methods of birth control as well as by delaying marriages. Moreover, France urbanized slowly at a time when city dwellers were marrying younger and producing larger families. As late as the 1860s, a majority of French workers were farmers. Whatever the cause of the moderate population growth, its consequences were clear. France was not pressured by the force of numbers to abandon its traditional agricultural methods, nor did it face a shortage of traditional supplies of energy. Except during crop failures, French agriculture could produce to meet French needs, and there remained more than enough wood for domestic and industrial use.

The Impact of the French Revolution. The consequences of the French Revolution are less clear. Throughout the eighteenth century, the French economy performed at least as well as the British, and in many areas better. French overseas trade had grown spectacularly until checked by military defeat in the Seven Years' War (1756–1763). French agriculture steadily increased output, while French rural manufactures flourished. A strong guild tradition still dominated urban industries, and although it restricted competition and limited growth, it also helped maintain the standards for the production of high-quality goods that made French commodities highly prized throughout the world. The Revolution disrupted every aspect of economic life. Some of its outcomes were unforeseen and unwelcome. For example, Napoleon's Continental System, which attempted to close European markets to Britain, resulted in a shipping war, which the British won decisively and which eliminated France as a competitor for overseas trade in the mid-nineteenth century. But other outcomes were the result of direct policies, even if their impact could not have been entirely predicted. Urban guilds and corporations were abolished, opening trades to newcomers but destroying the close-knit groups that trained skilled artisans and introduced innovative products. Similarly, the breakup of both feudal and common lands to satisfy the hunger of the peasantry had the effect of maintaining a large rural population for decades.

Despite the efforts of the central government, there had been little change in the techniques used by French farmers over the course of the eighteenth century. French peasants clung tenaciously to traditional rights that gave even the smallest landholder a vital say in community agriculture.

Landlords were predominantly absentees, less interested in the organization of their estates than in the dues and taxes that could be extracted from them. Thus the policies of successive revolutionary governments strengthened the hold of small peasants on the land. With the abolition of many feudal dues and with careful family planning, smallholders could survive and pass a meager inheritance on to their children. Even prosperous farmers could not grow into the large-scale proprietors that had enclosed English fields, for little land came on the market, and many parts of France practiced partible inheritance, which, over time, tended to even out the size of holdings. French agriculture continued to be organized in its centuries-old patterns. While it was able to supply the nation's need for food, it could not release large numbers of workers for purely industrial activity.

Stages of Industrial Progress. Thus French industrial growth was constrained on the one hand by the relatively small numbers of workers who could engage in manufacturing and on the other by the fact that a large portion of the population remained subsistence producers, cash-poor, and linked only to small rural markets. Throughout the eighteenth century, the French economy continued to be regionally segregated rather than nationally integrated. The size of the state inhibited a highly organized internal trade, and there was little improvement of the infrastructure of transportation. Although some British-style canals were built, canals in Britain were built to move coal rather than staple goods, and France did not have much coal to move. Manufacturing concerns were still predominantly family businesses whose primary markets were regional rather than international. Roads that connected the short distances between producers and consumers were of greater importance to the producers than arterial routes that served the markets of others. Similarly, there was no national capital market until the mid-nineteenth century, and precious few regional ones. French producers were as thrifty and profit-oriented as any others, but they found it more difficult to raise the large amounts of capital necessary to purchase the most expensive new machinery and build the most up-to-date factories. Ironworks, coal mines, and railroads, the three capital-intensive ventures of industrialization, were financed either by government subsidy or by foreign investment.

All those factors determined the slow, steady pace of French industrialization. Recovery after 1815 came in fits and starts. British inventors, manufacturers, and entrepreneurs were enticed to France to demonstrate new machinery and industrial techniques, but in most places the real engine of growth was skilled workers' steady application of traditional methods. By 1820, only 65 French factories were powered by steam engines, and even water-powered machinery was uncommon. Industrial firms remained small and were frequently a combination of putting-out and factory production. It was not until midcentury that sustained industrial growth became evident. This was largely the result of the construction of railroads on a national plan, financed in large part by the central government. Whereas in Britain the railways took advantage of a national market, in France they created one. They also

■ Pierre Denis Martin's *Waterworks and Aqueduct at Marly* makes clear the transformation of the landscape wrought by the infrastructure of industry in eighteenth-century France.

gave the essential stimulation to the modernization of the iron industry, in which much refining was still done with charcoal rather than coke; of machine making; and of the capital markets. Imported iron and foreign investment were vital ingredients in a process that took several decades to reach fruition.

The disadvantages of being on the trailing edge of economic change were mitigated for a time by conventional practices of protectionism. Except in specialty goods, agricultural produce, and luxury products, French manufactures could not compete with either British or German commodities. Had France maintained its position as a world trader, the comparative disadvantage would have been devastating. But defeat in the wars of commerce had led to a drawing inward of French economic effort. Marseille and Bordeaux, once bustling centers of European trade, became provincial backwaters in the nineteenth century. But the internal market was still strong enough to support industrial growth, and domestic commodities could be protected by prohibitive tariffs, especially against British textiles, iron, and, ironically, coal. Despite the fact that France had to import more than 40 percent of its meager requirements of coal, it still insisted upon slapping high import duties on British supplies. That was in part to protect French mine owners, who had never integrated their operations with iron production and therefore had no interest in keeping fuel costs low. Moreover, the slow pace of French industrialization allowed for the skipping of intermediate stages of development. France had hardly entered the canal age when it began to build its railways. Ultimately, industry moved from hand power to steam power in one long step.

While France achieved industrialization without an industrial revolution, it also achieved economic growth within the context of its traditional values. Agriculture may not have modernized, but the ancient village communities escaped the devastation modernization would bring. The orderly progression of generations of farming families characterized rural France until the shattering experiences of the Franco-Prussian War (1870) and World War I (1914–1918). Nor did France experience the mushroom growth of new cities with all of their problems of poverty, squalor, and homelessness. Slow population growth ameliorated the worst of the social diseases of industrialization while traditional rural manufacturing softened the transformation of a way of life. If France did not reap the windfall profits of the Industrial Revolution, neither did it harvest the bitter crop of social, economic, and spiritual impoverishment that was pulled in its train.

Germany: Industrialization and Union

The process of industrialization in Germany was dominated by the historic divisions of the empire of the German peoples. Before 1815, there were more than 300 separate jurisdictional units within the empire, and after 1815 there were still more than 30. Those included large advanced states such as Prussia, Austria, and Saxony as well as small free cities and the personal enclaves of petty nobles who had guessed right during the Napoleonic wars. Political divisions had more than politi-

cal impact. Each state clung tenaciously to its local laws and customs, which favored its citizens over outsiders. Merchants who lived near the intersection of separate jurisdictions could find themselves liable for several sets of tolls to move their goods and several sets of customs duties for importing and exporting them. The tolls and duties would have to be paid in different currencies at different rates of exchange according to the different regulations of each state. Small wonder that German merchants exhibited an intense localism, preferring to trade with members of their own state and supporting trade barriers against others. Such obstacles had a depressing effect on the economies of all German states but pushed with greatest weight against the manufacturing regions of Saxony, Silesia, and the Rhineland.

Agriculture.   Most of imperial Germany was agricultural land suited to a diversity of uses. The mountainous regions of Bavaria and the Austrian alpine communities practiced animal husbandry; there was a grain belt in Prussia, where the soil was poor but the land plentiful, and one in central Germany in which the soil was fertile and the land densely occupied. The Rhine Valley was one of the richest in all of Europe and was the center of German wine production. The introduction of the potato was the chief innovation of the eighteenth century. While English farmers were turning farms into commercial estates, German peasants were learning how to make do with less land.

Agricultural estates were organized differently in different parts of Germany. In the east, serfdom still prevailed. Peasants were tied to the land and its lord and were responsible for labor service during much of the week. Methods of cultivation were traditional, and neither peasants nor lords had much incentive to adopt new techniques. The vast agricultural domains of the Prussian Junkers, as those landlords were called, were built on the backs of cheap serf labor, and the harvest was destined for the Baltic export trade, where world grain prices rather than local production costs would determine profits. In central Germany, the long process of commuting labor service into rents was nearly completed by the end of the eighteenth century. The peasantry was not yet free, as a series of manorial relationships still tied them to the land, but they were no longer mere serfs. Moreover, western Germany was dominated by free farmers who either owned or leased their lands and who had a purely economic relationship with their landlords. The restriction of peasant mobility in much of Germany posed difficulties for the creation of an industrial work force. As late as 1800, more than 80 percent of the German population was engaged in agriculture, a proportion that would drop slowly over the next half century.

Although Germany was well endowed with natural resources and skilled labor in a number of trades, it had not taken part in the expansion of world trade during the seventeenth century, and the once bustling Hanseatic ports had been far outdistanced by the rise of the Atlantic economies. The principal exported manufacture was linen, which was expertly spun and woven in Saxony and the Prussian province of Silesia. The linen industry was organized traditionally, with a mixture of domestic production managed on the putting-out system and some factory spinning, especially after the introduction of British mechanical innovations. But even the most advanced factories were still being powered by water, and thus they were located in mountainous regions where rapidly running streams could turn the wheels. In the 1840s there were only 22 steam-driven spinning mills in Germany, several of them established by the Prussian government, which imported British machines and technicians to run them. Neither linens nor traditional German metal crafts could compete on the international markets, but they could find a wider market within Germany if only the problems of political division could be resolved.

The Zollverein.   The problems of political division were especially acute for Prussia after the reorganization of European boundaries in 1815 (see Chapter 22). Prussian territory included the coal- and iron-rich Rhineland provinces, but a number of smaller states separated those areas from Prussia's eastern domain. Each small state exacted its own tolls and customs duties whenever Prussian merchants wanted to move goods from one part of Prussia to the other. Such movement became more common in the nineteenth century as German manufacturing began to grow in step with its rising population. Between 1815 and 1865, the population of Germany grew by 60 percent to more than 36 million people. It was an enormous internal market, nearly as large as the population of France, and the Prussians resolved to make it a unified trading zone by creating a series of alliances with smaller states known as the **Zollverein** (1834). The Zollverein was not a free-trade zone, as was the British Empire, but rather a customs union in which member states adopted the liberal Prussian customs regulations. Every state was paid an annual portion of receipts based upon its population, and every state—except Prussia—increased its revenues as a result. The crucial advantage the Prussians received was the ability to move goods and materials from east to west, but Prussia reaped political profits as well. It forced Hanover and Saxony into the Zollverein and kept its powerful rival Austria out. Prussia's economic union soon proved to be the basis for the union of the German states.

The creation of the Zollverein was vital to German industrialization. It permitted the exploitation of natural advantages, such as plentiful supplies of coal and iron, and it provided a basis for the building of railroads. Germany was a follower nation in the process of industrialization. It started late and it self-consciously modeled its success on the British experience. British equipment and engineers were brought to Germany to attempt to plant the seeds of an industrial economy. German manufacturers sent their children to England to learn the latest techniques in industrial management. Friedrich Engels (1820–1895) worked in a Manchester cotton factory, where he observed the appalling conditions of the industrial labor force and wrote *The Condition of the Working Class in England in 1844* (1845). Steam

THE SLAVERY OF LABOR

Although born in Germany, Friedrich Engels witnessed industrialization in England firsthand. His father owned a factory in Manchester of which Engels was put in charge. By day he oversaw industrial production, and by night he wandered the city streets overwhelmed by the suffering of the working classes. His analysis of industrialization developed from his own observations. He became first a socialist and then, with Karl Marx, a founder of the Communist party.

Focus Questions

Why is capital "the all-important weapon in the class war"?
Why does Engels view wage labor as a kind of slavery?

Capital is the all-important weapon in the class war. Power lies in the hands of those who own, directly or indirectly, foodstuffs and the means of production. The poor, having no capital, inevitably bear the consequences of defeat in the struggle. Nobody troubles about the poor as they struggle helplessly in the whirlpool of modern industrial life. The working man may be lucky enough to find employment, if by his labour he can enrich some member of the middle classes. But his wages are so low that they hardly keep body and soul together. If he cannot find work, he can steal, unless he is afraid of the police; or he can go hungry and then the police will see to it that he will die of hunger in such a way as not to disturb the equanimity of the middle classes. . . .

The only difference between the old-fashioned slavery and the new is that while the former was openly acknowledged the latter is disguised. The worker *appears* to be free, because he is not bought and sold outright. He is sold piece-meal by the day, the week, or the year. Moreover he is not sold by one owner to another, but he is forced to sell himself in this fashion. He is not the slave of a single individual, but of the whole capitalist class. As far as the worker is concerned, however, there can be no doubt as to his servile status. It is true that the apparent liberty which the worker enjoys does give him some *real* freedom. Even this genuine freedom has the disadvantage that no one is responsible for providing him with food and shelter. His real masters, the middle-class capitalists, can discard him at any moment and leave him to starve, if they have no further use for his services and no further interest in his survival. . . .

From Friedrich Engels, *The Condition of the Working Class in England in 1844* (1845).

engines were installed in coal mines, if not in factories, and the process of puddling revolutionized ironmaking, though most iron was still smelted with charcoal rather than coke. Although coal was plentiful in Prussia, it was found at the eastern and western extremities of Germany. Even with the lowering of tolls and duties, it was still too expensive to move over rudimentary roads and an uncompleted system of canals.

Thus the railroads were the key to tapping the industrial potential of Germany. There they were a cause rather than a result of industrialization. The agreements hammered out in the creation of the Zollverein made possible the planning necessary to build single lines across the boundaries of numerous states. Initially, German railroads were financed privately, with much foreign investment. But ultimately governments saw the practical advantages of rail transport and took an active part in both planning and financing the system. More than a quarter of the track constructed in Prussia before 1870 was owned directly by the government, and most of the rest had been indirectly financed by the government, which purchased land and guaranteed interest on stock issues.

Germany imported most of its engines directly from Britain and thus adopted standard British gauge for its system. As early as 1850 there were more than 3500 miles of rail in Germany, with important roads linking the manufacturing districts of Saxony and the coal and iron deposits of the Ruhr. Twenty years later, Germany was second only to Britain in the amount of track that had been laid and opened. By then it was no longer simply a follower. German engineers and machinists, trained in Europe's best schools of technology, were turning out engines and rolling stock second to none. And the railroads transported a host of high-quality manufactures, especially durable metal goods that came to carry the most prestigious trademark of the late nineteenth century: "Made in Germany."

The Lands That Time Forgot

Nothing better demonstrates the point that industrialization was a regional rather than a national process than a survey of those states that did not develop industrial economies by the middle of the nineteenth century. The states ranged from the Netherlands, which was still one of the richest areas in Europe, to Spain and Russia, which were the poorest. Also included were Austria-Hungary, the states of the Italian peninsula, and Poland. In all those nations there was some industrial progress. The Bohemian lands of Austria contained a highly developed spinning industry; the Spanish province of Catalonia produced more cotton than did Belgium, and the Basque region was rich in iron and coal. Northern Italy mechanized its textile production, particularly silk spinning, while in the regions around both Moscow and Saint Petersburg, factories were run on serf labor. Nevertheless, the economies of all the states remained nonindustrial and, with the exception of the Netherlands, dominated by subsistence agriculture.

There were many reasons why the states were unable to develop their industrial potential. Some, such as Naples and Poland, were simply underendowed with resources; others, such as Austria-Hungary and Spain, faced difficulties of transport and communications that could not easily be overcome. Spain's modest resources were located on its northern and eastern edges, while a vast, arid plain dominated the center. To move raw materials and finished products from one end of the country to the other was a daunting task, made more difficult by lack of waterways and the rudimentary condition of Spanish roads. Two-thirds of Austria-Hungary was either mountains or hills, a geographic feature that presented obstacles not even the railroads could easily solve. But there was far more than natural disadvantage behind the failure of those parts of Europe to move in step with the industrializing states. Their social structure, agricultural organization, and commercial policies all hindered the adoption of new methods, machines, and modes of production.

Despite the fact that industrialization created new and largely unmanageable social problems, the follower states were eager for its benefits. All imported the latest products of technology, and the ruling elites in even the most traditional economies lived a material life similar to those in the most advanced. British entrepreneurs and artisans were courted by heads of state and their ministers and were offered riches in exchange for their precious knowledge. British industrialists set up textile factories in Moscow, built spinning machines in Bohemia, and taught Spanish miners how to puddle iron. Railroad pioneer George Stephenson himself surveyed the prospect of creating a passenger rail system in Spain, though he concluded pessimistically, "I have not seen enough people of the right sort to fill a single train." In the later part of the nineteenth century, French, Belgian, and German industrialists served similar roles. There were no traditional economies by choice. Industrialization was seen as a miracle, and the latecomers worshiped avidly at its shrine.

It was work rather than faith that would produce economic salvation. The most common characteristic of the latecomers was a traditional agrarian structure that consumed the lion's share of labor and capital while producing little surplus for any but a small dominant class. In areas as dissimilar as Spain, Italy, and Russia, agriculture was organized in vast estates, which kept the mass of peasants perpetually poor. Sharecropping systems in the west and serfdom in the east differed only in formal organization. Both conditions made it impossible for peasants to accumulate the land necessary to invest in capital improvements or to send their children to towns to engage in industrial occupations. In Hungary, Poland, and Russia, it was illegal for people to change occupations, and serfs who engaged in industrial activity paid their lords for the privilege. Although a number of serfs amassed considerable fortunes in organizing domestic or factory spinning, legal constraints restricted the efforts of potential entrepreneurs.

Similarly, the leaders of traditional economies maintained tariff systems that insulated their own producers from competition. Austrian tariffs were not only artificially high, they were accompanied by import quotas to keep all but the smallest fraction of foreign products from Austrian consumers. The Spanish government prohibited the importation of grain, forcing its eastern provinces to pay huge transport costs for domestic grain despite the fact that cheaper Italian grain was readily available. Such policies sapped much needed capital from industrial investment. There were many reasons for so-called protective tariffs, and it was not only the follower states that imposed them. France and the Zollverein protected domestic industry while Britain was converted to free trade only in the 1840s. But protection was sensible only when it protected rather than isolated. Inefficiently produced goods of inferior quality were the chief results of the protectionist policies of the follower nations. Failure to adopt steam-powered machines made traditionally produced linens and silks so expensive that smuggling occurred on an international scale. Although the goods might find buyers in domestic markets, they could not compete in international trade, and one by one the industries of the follower nations atrophied. Such nations became exporters of raw materials and foodstuffs. The export of Russian linen was replaced by the export of Russian flax. Spain, once the largest exporter of woolen cloth in Europe, exported mainly wines and fruits. Those economies that remained traditionally organized came to be exploited for their resources by those that had industrialized.

The international situation was not all that different from the dual system that came into effect within the nonindustrialized states. In Austria-Hungary, for example, it was Hungary that was kept from industrializing, first by the continuation of serf-based agriculture, then by the high internal tariffs that favored Austrian over Hungarian manufactures. In Italy, the division was between north and south. In Lombardy and Tuscany, machine-based manufacturing took hold alongside mining and metallurgy; in 1860, northern Italy contained 98 percent of the railways and 87 percent of the roads that existed on the entire peninsula. In Naples and Sicily, half-starved peasants eked out a miserable existence on once-rich soil that had become depleted from overuse. It was estimated that of the 400,000 people living in Naples, more than 100,000 were destitute beggars. In Spain, Catalonia modernized while Castile stagnated. Until the loss of its Latin American empire in the first half of the nineteenth century, Spain had a ready market for Catalonian textiles and handicrafts. But since Castile remained the cultural and administrative center of the state, it did little to encourage change, and much government policy was actually counterproductive. The chief problem faced by the dual economies was that neither part could sustain the other. Traditional agriculture could not produce the necessary surplus of either labor or capital to support industry, and industry could not economize sufficiently to make manufactured goods cheap enough for a poor peasantry.

Thus the advantages of being a follower were all missed. Technology could not be borrowed or stages skipped because the ground was not prepared for widespread industrial activity to be cultivated. Even by standing still, followers fell behind. While over the course of the nineteenth century male illiteracy dropped dramatically in the industrialized states—to 30 percent in Britain and France and 10 percent in Prussia—it remained at 75 to 80 percent in Spain and Italy and more than 90 percent in Russia. There was more than irony in the fact that one of the first railroads built on the Continent was built in Austria but was built to be powered by horses rather than engines. The first railways in Italy linked royal palaces to capital cities. Those in Spain radiated from Madrid and bypassed most centers of natural resources. In those states, the railroads

■ A Russian peasant tills a field with a primitive horse-drawn wooden plow. Russian fields produced low yields, partly because of the use of such crude farming methods.

were built to move the military rather than passengers or goods. They were state-financed, occasionally state-owned, and almost always lost money. They were symbols of the industrial age, but in those states they were symbols without substance.

CONCLUSION

The industrialization of Europe in the eighteenth century was an epochal event in human history. The constraints on daily life imposed by nature were loosened for the first time. No longer did population growth in one generation mean famine in the next; no longer was it necessary for the great majority of people to toil in the fields to earn their daily bread. Manufacture replaced agriculture as humanity's primary activity, though the change was longer and slower than the burst of industrialization that took place in the first half of the nineteenth century. For the leaders, Britain especially, industrialization brought international eminence. British achievements were envied, British inventors celebrated, Britain's constitutional and social organization lauded. A comparatively small island nation had become the greatest economic power in Europe. Industrialization had profound consequences for economic life, but its effects ran deeper than that. The search for new markets would result in the conquest of continents; the power of productivity unleashed by coal and iron would result in the first great arms race. Both would reach fruition in World War I, the first industrial war. For better or worse, the industrial era that began in Britain in the middle of the eighteenth century continues today.

QUESTIONS FOR REVIEW

1. Why did early manufacturing develop in the countryside, and what effect did that have on manufacturing practices and social relations?
2. In what ways were the ideas about organization of manufacturers such as Josiah Wedgwood and Robert Owen as significant as new technology in the development of industry in Britain?
3. How did British society address some of the changes in people's lives that were brought about by industrialization?
4. How did industrialization on the Continent differ from industrialization in England?
5. Why did some nations develop little industry at all?

KEY TERMS

agricultural revolution, *p. 620*	Industrial Revolution, *p. 626*
Crystal Palace Exhibition, *p. 643*	Luddites, *p.633*
enclosure, *p. 624*	mule, *p. 632*
Factory Act (1833), *p. 637*	putting-out system, *p. 622*
industrialization, *p. 627*	Zollverein, *p. 647*

DISCOVERING WESTERN CIVILIZATION ONLINE

You can obtain more information about industrial Europe at the Websites listed below. See also the Companion Website that accompanies this text, www.ablongman.com/kishlansky, which contains an online study guide and additional resources.

The Industrial Revolution in Britain

Reminiscences of James Watt

www.history.rochester.edu/steam/hart/
A nineteenth-century account of the life of James Watt and his role as inventor of the steam engine with links to the history of the steam engine.

Women in World History Curriculum: Industrial Revolution

www.womeninworldhistory.com/lesson7.html
Sponsored by Women in World History Curriculum, this site details the plight of working women in industrial England.

Child Labour in the 19th Century

www.spartacus.schoolnet.co.uk/IRchild.main.htm
This site chronicles child labor in Britain, including life in the factory and first-hand experiences.

The Industrialization of the Continent

Modern History Sourcebook: Tables Illustrating the Spread of Industrialization

www.fordham.edu/halsall/mod/indrevtabs1.html
Charts and statistics about industrialization in Europe.

Internet Modern History Sourcebook: Industrial Revolution

www.fordham.edu/halsall/mod/modsbook14.html
An outstanding collection of documents on the Industrial Age with links.

SUGGESTIONS FOR FURTHER READING

General Reading

T. S. Ashton, *The Industrial Revolution* (Oxford: Oxford University Press, 1997). A compelling brief account of the traditional view of industrialization.

Niall Ferguson, *The Cash Nexus: Money and Power in the Modern World, 1700–2000* (New York: Basic Books, 2001). A transnational history of the role of finance in the making of the modern world.

Jordan Goodman and Katrina Honeyman, *Gainful Pursuits: The Making of Industrial Europe, 1600–1914* (London: Edward Arnold, 1988). A brief overview of the entire process of industrialization.

Pat Hudson, *The Industrial Revolution* (London: Oxford University Press, 2007). The latest account of the technological innovation that began the modern era.

The Traditional Economy

Richard Brown, *Society and Economy in Modern Britain, 1700–1850* (London: Routledge, 1991). A comprehensive survey.

J. D. Chambers and G. E. Mingay, *The Agricultural Revolution* (London: Batsford, 1966). The classic survey of the changes in British agriculture.

The Industrial Revolution in Britain

N. F. R. Crafts, *British Economic Growth During the Industrial Revolution* (Oxford: Oxford University Press, 1986). A highly quantitative study by an economic historian arguing the case that economic growth was slow in the early nineteenth century.

François Crouzet, *The First Industrialists* (Cambridge: Cambridge University Press, 1985). An analysis of the social background of the first generation of British entrepreneurs.

Martin Daunton, *Progress and Poverty: An Economic and Social History of Britain, 1700–1850* (Oxford: Oxford University Press, 1995). The best single-volume survey on the Industrial Revolution and its effects on British society.

Phyllis Deane, *The First Industrial Revolution*, 2d ed. (Cambridge: Cambridge University Press, 1979). The best introduction to the technological changes in Britain.

Judith Flanders, *Inside the Victorian Home: A Portrait of Domestic Life in Victorian England* (New York: W. W. Norton, 2005). A detailed depiction of homes and families in nineteenth-century England.

Richard Price, *British Society, 1680–1880: Dynamism, Containment, and Change* (New York: Cambridge University Press, 1999). An argument about the nature of British society in the age of the Industrial Revolution.

John Rule, *The Vital Century: England's Developing Economy, 1714–1815* (London: Longman, 1992). A comprehensive survey of the British economy.

E. P. Thompson, *The Making of the English Working Class* (New York: Random House, 1966). A brilliant and passionate study of the ways laborers responded to the changes brought about by the industrial economy.

The Industrialization of the Continent

W. O. Henderson, *The Rise of German Industrial Power* (Berkeley: University of California Press, 1975). A chronological study of German industrialization that centers on Prussia.

Tom Kemp, *Industrialization in Nineteenth-Century Europe*, 2d ed. (London: Longman, 1985). Survey of the process of industrialization in the major European states.

Sidney Pollard, *Peaceful Conquest* (Oxford: Oxford University Press, 1981). Argues the regional nature of industrialization throughout western Europe.

Roger Price, *The Economic Transformation of France* (London: Croom Helm, 1975). A study of French society before and during the process of industrialization.

Wolfgang Schivelbusch, *The Railway Journey* (Berkeley: University of California Press, 1986). A social history of the impact of railways, drawn from French and German sources.

Clive Trebilcock, *The Industrialization of the Continental Powers, 1780–1914* (London: Longman, 1981). A complex study of Germany, France, and Russia.

For a list of additional titles related to this chapter's topics, please see http://www.ablongman.com/kishlansky.

22 POLITICAL UPHEAVALS AND SOCIAL TRANSFORMATIONS, 1815–1850

POTATO POLITICS

THE PLIGHT OF THE POOR IN EUROPEAN SOCIETIES

Vegetables have histories too. But none has a more interesting history in the West than the humble potato. First introduced to northern Europe from the Andean highlands of South America at the end of the sixteenth century, it rapidly became a staple of peasant diets from Ireland to Russia. The potato's vitamins, minerals, and high carbohydrate content provided a rich source of energy to Europe's rural poor. It was simple to plant, required little or no cultivation, and did well in damp,

THE VISUAL RECORD

cool climates. Best of all, it could be grown successfully on the smallest plots of land. One acre could support a peasant family of four for a year. Potato peelings helped sustain the family cow and pig, further supplementing family income.

In *Potato Planters,* shown here, the French painter Jean-François Millet (1814–1875) provided a view of the peasant labor involved in planting potatoes. Millet, the son of a wealthy peasant family, understood well the importance of the potato crop in the peasant diet. The man and woman in the painting plant their potatoes as a reverent act, bowing as field laborers might in prayer. (Laborers actually do pray in Millet's more sentimental work *The Angelus.*) The primitive nature of the process is striking: the man uses a short hoe to scrape at what seems to be unyielding soil. The peasants seem part of the nature that surrounds them, patient as the beast that waits in the shade, bent and gnarled and lovely as the tree that arches in the background.

The fleshy root not only guaranteed health, it also affected social relations. Traditionally, peasants delayed marrying and starting families because of the unavailability of land. The potato changed that behavior. Now the potato allowed peasants with only a little land to marry and have children earlier. Millet's depiction of the man and woman working together in the field resonates with the simple fact that potato cultivation aided in the formation of the couple. Millet's couple are parents whose baby sleeps swaddled in a basket and shaded by the tree. In those peasant homes where family members did putting-out work for local entrepreneurs, potato cultivation drew little labor away from the spinning wheel and loom. It permitted prosperous farmers to devote more land to cash crops, since only a small portion of land was required to feed a family. As the sole item of diet, it provided life-sustaining nutrients and a significant amount of the protein so necessary for heavy labor. The Irish adult male ate an average of 12 to 14 pounds of potatoes a day—a figure that may seem preposterous to us today.

Proverbs warned peasants against putting all their eggs in one basket, but no folk wisdom prepared the Irish, many of whom relied on the potato as a single crop, for the potato disaster that struck them. In 1845, a fungus from America destroyed the new potato crop. Although peasants were certainly accustomed to bad harvests and crop failures, they had no precedent for the years of blight that followed. From 1846 to 1850, famine and the diseases resulting from it—scurvy, dysentery, cholera, and typhus fever—killed more than a million people in what became known as the **Great Hunger**. Another million people emigrated, many to the United States. Total dependence on the potato reaped its grim harvest, devastating all levels of Irish society. Within five years, the Irish population was reduced by almost 25 percent.

LOOKING AHEAD

The Irish potato famine has been called the "last great European natural disaster," to distinguish it from the man-made horrors of war and revolution. But it was as much a social and political disas-

■ Jean-François Millet, *Potato Planters* (ca. 1861).

ter as a natural one. As the wealth of European societies expanded in the nineteenth century, so did the number of those who lived on the edge, poised between unemployment and starvation. The Great Hunger in Ireland was the most striking example of the problem that plagued all Western societies in the first half of the nineteenth century: what to do with the poor. In this chapter, we shall see that while the boundaries of European nations were redefined in order to create stability following the Napoleonic Wars, the economic hardships of peasants and workers continued to plague and disrupt European societies internally. The new ideologies of the first half of the nineteenth century grappled with the challenge of reshaping state and society. But social inequities continued to fuel protest and revolution between 1815 and 1850 and pulled down governments across Europe.

GEOGRAPHICAL TOUR
Europe in 1815

Peasants like those depicted by Millet (in this chapter's Visual Record) seldom traveled beyond their own villages. Of course, all of that was different in Napoleon's quest for empire. Napoleon had placed large armies of peasants and workers in motion, crisscrossing the continent, and giving his own troops and Europe a geography lesson. At the heart of that lesson was the fact that no one state had been able to defeat Napoleon and his conscript armies. He had made clear the territorial and political interdependence of the European powers. The lesson was not lost on the leaders of Russia, Austria, Prussia, and France as they sat down to redraw the map of Europe in 1815.

■ **Map A. Europe, 1815.** In a series of treaties following Napoleon's defeat, the European powers re-drew the map of Europe to create the most stable territorial arrangement and ensure European security. At the center of Europe stood the German confederation, outlined here in red.

Europe's rulers shared the vision of Europe as a machine that must be kept in running order. Those victorious in defeating Napoleon's Empire looked on the whole of Europe as one entity and conceived of peace in terms of a general European security.

The primary goal of European leaders was to devise the most stable territorial arrangement possible. That goal entailed redrawing the map of Europe (see **Map A**). During the negotiations, traditional claims of the right to rule came head to head with new ideas about stabilization. The equilibrium established in 1815 made possible a century-long European peace. Conflicts erupted, to be sure, but they took on the characteristics of the new system that was constructed at Vienna in 1815.

The Congress of Vienna

In September 1814, representatives of the victorious Allies agreed to convene in the Austrian capital of Vienna for the purposes of mopping up the mess created in Europe by French rule and restoring order to European monarchies.

The central actors of the **Congress of Vienna** were Austrian minister of foreign affairs Prince Klemens von Metternich (1809–1848), British foreign secretary Viscount Castlereagh (1812–1822), French minister of foreign affairs Charles Maurice de Talleyrand (1814–1815), the Russian tsar Alexander I (1801–1825), and the Prussian king Frederick William III (1797–1840). In spite of personal eccentricities, animosities, and occasional outright hostilities among Europe's leaders, all shared a common concern with reestablishing harmony in Europe.

Settling with France. Because of the concern with establishing harmony at the time of Napoleon's defeat, the peace enforced against France was not a punitive one. After Napoleon's abdication in 1814, the victorious powers of Great Britain, Russia, Prussia, and Austria decided that leniency was the best way to support the restored Bourbon monarchy. After 1793, royalist émigrés referred to the young son of the executed Louis XVI as Louis XVII, although the child died in captivity and never reigned. In 1814, the four powers designated the elder of the two surviving brothers of Louis XVI as the appropriate candidate for the restored monarchy. Because of the circumstances of his restoration, the new king, Louis XVIII (1814–1815; 1815–1824), bore the ignominious image of returning "in the baggage car of the Allies." Every effort was made not to weigh down Louis XVIII with a harsh settlement. The First Peace of Paris, signed by the Allies with France in May 1814, had reestablished the French frontiers at the 1792 boundaries, which included Avignon, Venaissin, parts of Savoy, and German and Flemish territories—none of which had belonged to France in 1789.

Even after the hundred-day return of Napoleon, the "Usurper," the Second Peace of Paris of November 1815 declared French frontiers restricted to the boundaries of 1790 (see **Map B**) and exacted from France an indemnity of 700

■ **Map B. France, 1815.** In determining the borders of France, European heads of state were torn between the need to punish and control France and the importance of reconciliation with France for a stable Europe. The Second Peace of Paris of November 1815 permitted France to return to the borders of 1790 and to resume its role as one of the Great Powers.

million francs. An army of occupation consisting of 150,000 troops was also placed on French soil at French expense but was removed ahead of schedule in 1818. Contrary to the terms of the first treaty, the second treaty also required France to return plundered art treasures to their countries of origin.

New Territorial Arrangements. The dominant partnership of Austria and Britain at the Congress of Vienna resulted in treaty arrangements that served to restrain the ambitions of Russia and Prussia. No country was to receive territory without giving up something in return, and no one country was to receive enough territory to make it a present or future threat to the peace of Europe. To contain France, some steps taken prior to the Congress were ratified or expanded. In June 1814, the Low Countries had been set up as a unitary state to serve as a buffer against future French expansion on the Continent and a block to the revival of French sea power. The new Kingdom of the Netherlands (see **Map C**) created out of the former Dutch Republic and the Austrian Netherlands, was placed under the rule of William I (1815–1840). The Catholic southern provinces were thus uneasily reunited with the Protestant northern provinces, regions that had been separated since the Peace of Westphalia in 1648. Great Britain gave

■ **Map C. Kingdom of the Netherlands.** As a buffer on France's northernmost border, the new Kingdom of the Netherlands was a forced union of two regions with different languages and religions. The union lasted only until 1831 when the southern provinces revolted to form Belgium.

■ **Map D. Italian Peninsula, 1815.** Austria gained major territorial concessions on the Italian peninsula. The Austrian Empire now included Lombardy and Venetia. Austria was also influential throughout the peninsula in the Papal States, the three small duchies (Tuscany, Parma, Modena), and the Kingdom of the Two Sicilies.

William I of the Netherlands £2 million to fortify his frontier against France.

A reestablished monarchy that united the island kingdom of Sardinia with Piedmont and included Savoy, Nice, and part of Genoa contained France on its southeast border (see **Map D**). To the east, Prussia was given control of the left bank of the Rhine. Switzerland was reestablished as an independent confederation of cantons. Bourbon rule was restored in Spain on France's southwestern border.

Austria's power was firmly established in Italy, either through outright territorial control or influence over independent states (see **Map D**). The Papal States were returned to Pope Pius VII (1800–1823), along with territories that had been Napoleon's Cisalpine Republic and the Kingdom of Italy. Lombardy and the Illyrian provinces on the Dalmatian coast were likewise restored to Austria. The Republic of Venice and the Italian duchies of Tuscany, Parma, and Modena fell under the influence of Habsburg princes.

After the fall of Napoleon, the Allies made no attempt to restore the Holy Roman Empire. Napoleon's Confederation of the Rhine, which organized the majority of German territory under French auspices in 1806, was dissolved. In its place, the lands once divided into 300 petty states in central Europe

were reorganized into 38 states in the German Confederation (see **Map E**). The 38 states, along with Austria as the thirty-ninth, were represented in a new Federal Diet at Frankfurt, dominated by Austria. The German Confederation was intended as a bulwark against France, not to serve any nationalist or parliamentary function.

All of the changes were the result of carefully discussed but fairly uncontroversial negotiations. The question of Poland was another matter indeed. Successive partitions by Russia, Austria, and Prussia in 1772, 1793, and 1795 had completely dismembered the land that had been Poland. Napoleon had reconstituted a small portion of Poland as the Grand Duchy of Warsaw. The Congress faced the dilemma of what to do with the Napoleonic creation and with Polish territory in general. Fierce debate over Poland threatened to shatter congressional harmony (see **Map F**).

Tsar Alexander I of Russia argued for a large Poland that he intended to be fully under his influence, thus extending Russian-controlled territories to the banks of the Oder. He also envisioned extending Russian dominance farther into central and eastern Europe. He based his claim on the significant contribution the Russian army had made to Napoleon's defeat. But such thinking conflicted with the Austrian minis-

■ In this French cartoon satirizing the Congress of Vienna, left to right, Talleyrand is watching and waiting as Castlereagh balks, Metternich leads the "dancing," the king of Saxony clutches his crown in fear, and Genoa jumps up and down on the sidelines.

■ **Map E. German Confederation.** The league of German states created in 1815 replaced the Holy Roman Empire. The 39 states, of which 35 were monarchies and 4 were free cities, existed to ensure the independence of its member states and support in case of external attack. The member states of Austria and Prussia lay partially outside the Confederation.

ter Metternich's pursuit of equilibrium. Frederick William III of Prussia contended that if a large Poland were to be created, Prussia would expect compensation by absorbing Saxony (see **Map G**). Both Great Britain and France distrusted Russian and Prussian territorial aims.

In the final arrangement, Prussia retained the Polish territory of Posen and Austria kept the Polish province of Galicia (see **Map F**). Krakow, with its population of 95,000, was declared a free city. Finally, a kingdom of Poland, nominally independent but in fact under the tutelage of Russia, emerged from what remained of the Grand Duchy of Warsaw. It was a solution that benefited no one in particular and disregarded Polish wishes.

In addition to receiving Polish territories, Prussia gained two-fifths of the kingdom of Saxony (see **Map G**). Prussia also received territory on the left bank of the Rhine, the Duchy of Westphalia, and Swedish Pomerania. With the acquisitions, Prussia doubled its population to around 11 million people. The Junkers, the landed class of east Prussia, reversed many of the reforms of the Napoleonic period. The new territories that Prussia gained were rich in waterways and resources but geographically fragmented. The dispersal of holdings that was intended to contain Prussian power in central Europe spurred Prussia to find new ways of uniting its markets. In the endeavor, Prussia constituted a future threat to Austrian power over the German Confederation.

In Scandinavia, the members of the Congress acknowledged Russia's conquest of Finland, and in return Sweden acquired Norway from Denmark. Unlike Austria, Prussia, and Russia, Great Britain made no claim to territories at the Congress. Having achieved its aim of containing France, its

■ **Map F. Poland, 1815.** An independent kingdom in name only, Poland was under the influence of Russia. Prussia carved off Posen, and Austria maintained control of Galicia. Krakow was defined by treaty as an independent republic.

■ **Map G. Saxony.** In 1806, Saxony had sided with France against Prussia and remained allies with the French for the remainder of the Napoleonic Wars. With Napoleon's defeat in 1815, about 40 percent of Saxony became part of Prussia.

greatest rival for dominance on the seas, Britain returned the French colonies it had seized in war. For the time being, the redrawing of the territorial map of Europe had achieved its pragmatic aim of guaranteeing the peace. It was now left to a system of alliances to preserve that peace.

The Alliance System

Only by joining forces had the European powers been able to defeat Napoleon, and a system of alliances continued to be needed even after the battles were over. Two alliance pacts dominated the post-Napoleonic era: the renewed Quadruple Alliance and the Holy Alliance.

The **Quadruple Alliance** (see **Map H**), signed by the victorious powers of Great Britain, Austria, Russia, and Prussia in November 1815, was intended to protect Europe against future French aggression and to preserve the status quo. In 1818, France, having completed its payment of war indemnities, joined the pact, which now became the **Quintuple Alliance**. The five powers promised to meet periodically over the following 20 years to discuss common problems and to ensure the peace.

The **Holy Alliance** (see **Map H**) was the brainchild of Alexander I and was heavily influenced by his mystical and romantic view of international politics. In the pact, the mon-

archs of Prussia, Austria, and Russia agreed to renounce war and to protect the Christian religion. The Holy Alliance spoke of "the bonds of a true and indissoluble brotherhood . . . to protect religion, peace, and justice." Russia was able to give some credibility to the alliance with the sheer size of its army. Career diplomats were aware of its hollowness as a treaty arrangement, but it did indicate the willingness of Europe's three eastern autocracies to intervene in the affairs of other states.

The concept of Europe acting as a whole, through a system of periodic conferences, marked the emergence of a new diplomatic era. Conflict, however, was inherent in the tension between the commitment of parliamentary governments to open consultation and the need for secrecy in diplomacy. Dynastic regimes sought to intervene in smaller states to buoy up despots, as was the case in 1822, when European powers met to consider restoring the Bourbon monarchy in Spain. The British acted as a counterbalance to interventionist tendencies, refused to cooperate, and blocked united action by the Alliance. France took military action on its own in 1823, restored King Ferdinand VII, and abolished the Spanish constitution.

In both the Congress of Vienna and the system of alliances that succeeded it, European nations aimed to establish a balance of power that recognized legitimate rulers and preserved

Map H. Quadruple Alliance and Holy Alliance. The Quadruple Alliance grew out of the need of the Great Powers to create a stable Europe and had as its initial impulse the creation of a buffer against a future French threat. Austria, Great Britain, Prussia, and Russia entered into the agreement as the basis for defining the balance of power in Europe. In the Holy Alliance, Russia, Austria, and Prussia entered an agreement to treat each other according to the precepts of the Christian religion. As a counterweight to the Quadruple Alliance, the Holy Alliance served as a justification for repression against dissent.

CHRONOLOGY

The Alliance System

May 1814	First Peace of Paris
23 September 1814–9 June 1815	Congress of Vienna
26 September 1815	Formation of the Holy Alliance
20 November 1815	Second Peace of Paris; Formation of the Quadruple Alliance
November 1818	Quadruple Alliance expands to include France in Quintuple Alliance
1823	French restoration of Bourbon Monarchy in Spain

the peace. The upheaval of the French Revolution and the revolutionary and Napoleonic Wars had made clear the interdependence of one nation on another as a guarantee of survival. By maintaining an international equilibrium, Europe's statesmen hoped—erroneously, as it turned out—that by keeping the peace abroad, domestic peace would follow.

THE NEW IDEOLOGIES

After 1815, the world was changing in many ways. As national boundaries were being redefined, the ways in which Europeans regarded their world were also being transformed. Steam-driven mechanical power in production and transportation steadily replaced human and animal power. In deference to what it was replacing, the new mechanical force was measured in units of horsepower. The new technology combined with political changes to challenge old values; new definitions of worth emerged from the increasingly mechanized world of work. The fixed, castelike distinctions of the old aristocratic world were under attack or in disarray. Western intellectuals struggled with the changes as they sought to make sense of the way in which Europeans lived, looked at the world, and defined their place in it.

The political and economic upheavals of the first half of the nineteenth century encouraged a new breed of thinkers to search for ways to explain the transformations of the period. During that period, Europeans witnessed one of the most intellectually fertile periods in the history of the West. The search for understanding during this era gave birth to new ideologies—liberalism, nationalism, romanticism, conservatism, and socialism—that continue to shape the ideas and institutions of the present day.

The New Politics of Preserving Order

European states had been dealing with war for more than two decades. Now they faced the challenge of peace. The French Revolution and Napoleon had not only meant military engagements; they had also brought the force of revolutionary ideas to the political arena, and those ideas did not retire from the field after Waterloo. Nor did treaties restore an old order, in spite of claims to doing so. Governments throughout Europe had to find new ways to deal with the tension between state authority and individual liberty. Conservative and liberal thinkers took very different paths in the pursuit of political stability.

Conservatism. **Conservatism** represented a dynamic adaptation to a social system in transition. In place of individualism, conservatives stressed the corporate nature of European society; in place of reason and progress, conservatives saw organic growth and tradition. Liberty, argued British statesman Edmund Burke (1729–1797) in *Reflections on the Revolution in France* (1790), must emerge out of the gradual development of the old order, and not its destruction. On the Continent, conservatives Louis de Bonald (1754–1840) and Joseph de Maistre (1753–1821) defended the monarchical principle of authority against the onslaught of revolutionary events.

Conservatism took a reactionary turn in the hands of the Austrian statesman Metternich. The Carlsbad decrees of 1819 are a good example of the "Metternich system" of espionage, censorship, and repression in central Europe, which sought to eliminate any constitutional or nationalist sentiments that had arisen during the Napoleonic period. The German Confederation approved decrees against free speech and civil liberties and set up mechanisms to root out "subversive" university students. Students who had taken up arms in the Wars of Liberation (1813–1815) against France had done so in hope of instituting liberal and national reforms. Metternich's system aimed at uprooting those goals. Student fraternities were closed, and police became a regular fixture in the university. Political expression in central Europe was driven underground for at least a decade. Metternich set out to crush any form of democratic government, constitutionalism, and parliamentarianism in central Europe.

Liberalism. The term *liberal* was first used in a narrow political sense to indicate the Spanish party of reform that supported the constitution modeled on the French document of 1791. But the term assumed much broader connotations in the first half of the nineteenth century as its appeal spread among the European middle classes. The two main tenets of belief that underlay **liberalism** were the freedom of the individual and the corruptibility of authority. As a political doctrine, liberalism built on Enlightenment rationalism and embraced the right to vote, civil liberties, legal equality, constitutional government, parliamentary sovereignty, and a free-market economy. Liberals firmly believed that less government was better government and that noninterference would produce a harmonious and well-ordered world. They also believed that human beings were basically good and reasonable and needed freedom to flourish. The sole end of government should be to promote that freedom.

Liberal thinkers tried to make sense of the political conflicts of the revolutionary period and the economic disruptions brought on by industrialization. The Great Revolution at the end of the eighteenth century spawned a vast array of liberal thought in France. Republicans, Bonapartists, and constitutional monarchists cooperated as self-styled "liberals" who shared a desire to preserve the gains of the revolution while ensuring orderly rule. In 1807, British law attempted to eliminate the slave trade with very limited success. William Wilberforce led abolitionists in England who continued to agitate for a parliamentary law that would abolish the slave trade throughout the British Empire. Such a law was finally passed in 1833, and about £20 million was paid in compensation to British plantation owners in the Caribbean. Also influenced by liberal ideas were a variety of political movements in

■ This cameo, made by Josiah Wedgwood for the Society for the Abolition of Slavery, shows a chained and manacled slave and bears the inscription, "Am I Not a Man and a Brother?" Wedgwood sent a batch of the cameos to Benjamin Franklin for distribution among American abolitionists.

the United States, including those demanding the liberation of slaves and the extension of legal and political rights to women. Abolitionists justified their opposition to slavery on humanitarian Christian grounds and on the liberal principles of freedom and equality. American women who were active in antislavery societies extended their liberal crusade against oppression to their own legal and political status.

By the mid-nineteenth century, liberal thinking constituted a dominant strain in British politics. Jeremy Bentham (1748–1832), trained in British law, fashioned himself into a social philosopher. He founded **utilitarianism,** a fundamentally liberal doctrine that argued for "the greatest happiness of the greatest number" in such works as *Introduction to the Principles of Morals and Legislation.* Bentham believed that government could achieve positive ends through limited and "scientific" intervention. Only the pursuit of social harmony justified interference with individual liberty. He found the best testing grounds for his theories in prisons, among convicted criminals. By supporting the reform of penal codes and prison regulations in *Rationale of Punishments and Rewards* (1825), he hoped that rewards and punishments could be meted out to convicts in a measurable "geometry" of pain and pleasure. He was sure that behavior could be improved and that prisoners could be rehabilitated and returned as honest citizens to society. (See "A Closer Look: The Birth of the Prison," pp. 662–663.)

The Scottish philosopher, economist, and historian James Mill (1773–1836) met Jeremy Bentham in 1808 and dedicated the rest of his life to promulgating Bentham's utilitarian philosophy. James Mill's son John Stuart Mill (1806–1873) reacted to his early and intense education in Benthamite ideas by rejecting the tenets of utilitarianism. Forging his own brand of classical liberalism in his treatise *On Liberty* (1859), the younger Mill became the greatest liberal thinker of the age. John Stuart Mill criticized Bentham for ignoring human emotions and for the mass tyranny implicit in his ideas. Mill went beyond existing political analyses by applying economic doctrines to social conditions in *Principles of Political Economy* (1848). With his wife and collaborator Harriet Taylor (d. 1858), he espoused social reform for the poor and championed the equality of women and the necessity of birth control. By 1848, his writings on liberty and equality were questioning the sacredness of private property. In later life, John Stuart Mill came to believe that a more equitable distribution of wealth was both necessary and possible.

Mill on Enfranchisement of Women

David Ricardo (1772–1823) was a stockbroker prodigy who by the age of 20 had made his fortune. In *Principles of Political Economy and Taxation* (1817), Ricardo outlined his opposition to government intervention in foreign trade and elaborated his "iron law of wages," which contended that wages would stabilize at the subsistence level. Increased wages would cause the working classes to grow, and the resulting competition in the labor market would drive wages down to the level of subsistence. Other liberals, more concerned with social welfare than Ricardo, argued that state intervention was unavoidable but could be limited.

Romanticism and Change

Unlike liberalism and conservatism, which were fundamentally political ideologies, **romanticism** included a variety of literary and artistic movements throughout Europe that spanned the period from the late eighteenth century to the mid-nineteenth century. One could be a liberal and a romantic just as easily as one could be a conservative and a romantic.

The Romantic World View. Above all, and in spite of variations, romantics shared similar beliefs and a common view of the world. Among the first romantics were the English poets William Wordsworth (1770–1850) and Samuel Taylor Coleridge (1772–1834), whose collaborative *Lyrical Ballads* (1798) exemplified the iconoclastic romantic idea that poetry was the result of "the spontaneous overflow of powerful feelings" rather than a formal and highly disciplined intellectual exercise. Romantics, in general, rebelled against the confinement of classical forms and refused to accept the supremacy of reason over emotions.

The English gardens designed at the end of the eighteenth century provide one of the best visual examples of the new romanticism. The formal gardens that surrounded the castles and manor houses of Europe's wealthy elite throughout the eighteenth century relied on carefully drawn geometric patterns, minutely trimmed hedges and lawns, and symmetrically arranged flowers planted in rows by size and color to achieve the effect of total mastery of nature. The gardens at the great palace of Versailles are a good example of the formal landscaping chosen by France's kings and emulated by the wealthy everywhere in Europe. The romantic or English garden was, by contrast, a rebellious profusion of color in which the landscaper rejected the carefully drawn geometric patterns then in vogue and set out instead, deliberately and somewhat paradoxically, to imitate nature. The romantic aesthetic, whether in landscape gardening or in literature, recognized the beauty of untamed nature and the inspiration produced by the release of human emotions.

Intellectuals, Artists, and Freedom. By rooting artistic vision in spontaneity, romantics endorsed a concept of creativity based on the supremacy of human freedom. The artist was valued in a new way as a genius through whose insight and intuition great art was created. Intuition, as opposed to scientific learning, was endorsed as a valid means of knowing. Building on the work of the eighteenth-century philosopher Immanuel Kant (1724–1804), romanticism embraced subjective knowledge. Inspiration and intuition took the place of reason and science in the romantic pantheon of values.

Germaine de Staël (1766–1817), often hailed as the founder of French romanticism, was an extraordinary woman whose writings influenced French liberal political theory after 1815. Madame de Staël's mother had followed the principles of education spelled out by Jean-Jacques Rousseau in *Emile* (1762), according to which the child was allowed to follow his or her own path of intellectual development. De Staël authored histories, novels, literary criticism, and political tracts that opposed what she judged to be the tyranny of Napoleonic rule. She, like many other romantics, was greatly influenced by the writings of Rousseau, and through him she discovered that "the soul's elevation is born of self-consciousness." The recognition of the subjective meant for de Staël that women's vision was as essential as men's for the flowering of European culture.

"It is within oneself that one must look at what lies outside." Following de Staël's lead, Victor Hugo (1802–1885), one of the great French writers of the nineteenth century, identified another essential ingredient in romanticism. The turning "within oneself" so apparent in Hugo's poetry was profoundly influenced by the political events of the French Revolution and its principles of liberty and equality. His greatest novels, including *Notre-Dame de Paris* (1831) and *Les Misérables* (1862), offer bold panoramic sweeps of the social universe of Paris across the ages. Whether in words or in music or on canvas, romanticism conveyed a new way of understanding the world. The supremacy of the emotions over reason found its way into the works of the great romantic composers of the age. Liberation from the forms that dominated the classical

THE BIRTH OF THE PRISON

There was once a time when modern prisons, what we call penitentiaries, did not exist. Prisons, like modern hospitals and schools, were one of the great achievements of the age of reform in the first half of the nineteenth century. Thanks to the efforts of humanitarians and social reformers, a new rationale for punishment emerged, one claiming that modern prisons were capable of rehabilitating criminals. Reformers argued that the controlled environment of a new prison system would be able to fashion wrongdoers into upstanding citizens through moral instruction, hard work, constant surveillance, and, in some cases, isolation from human contact.

The principles of the new penal arrangement were silence and separation—total or partial, in order to rehabilitate prisoners through supervised activities, including productive work. In French penitentiaries, prisoners were given an occupation and produced goods for the prison system itself—shoes or mattresses, for example—or for sale on the open market. The belief was that through productive labor, prisoners could be taught to be good workers and good citizens. Idle hands were the devil's workshop, so no moment of the prisoner's day was unoccupied or, in theory, unsupervised.

A CLOSER LOOK

Some of the "new" prisons were built in the shells of ancient military garrisons, seminaries, convents, and retreat houses. Before the beginning of the nineteenth century, prisons existed but they served as waystations, holding areas for those who were about to face their "real" punishments, which could be death, mutilation, forced labor in prison ships, or banishment. After 1820, however, incarceration became a punishment in itself throughout western Europe, with the goal to deprive prisoners of liberty and freedom of movement.

A typical prisoner in the new penitentiaries was a man convicted of theft serving a sentence of five to seven years. He entered a prison world where every aspect of his life was prescribed and supervised. The experience of the prison was intended to transform the behavior of the prisoner. Prisoners for the first time were required to wear uniforms. In addition to the regimented routine of work, meals, and sleep, the prisoner now also received moral and religious instruction behind bars.

Although populations in the old prisons of the eighteenth century were mixed with women and men, adults and children confined in the same spaces, by contrast, in the nineteenth century convicted women and children were systematically separated from male prisoners and subject to separate rules of confinement. Religious orders and philanthropic groups supervised women and children in prisons and continued to watch them in their lives after prison. Reformers now spoke of the punishment being made to fit the criminal—not the crime.

The most controversial aspect of the new punishment was solitary confinement. Women were usually exempted from the initial isolation experiments, deemed as too "social" or too weak to support total separation. Young boys on the other hand were targeted for the special experimental punishment of solitary isolation, something French observers such as historian and political philosopher Alexis de Tocqueville greatly admired on his travels in the United States. In one particularly brutal period of experimentation, beginning in 1838 French prison officials confined boys between the ages of six and sixteen to their cells day and night where they were expected to follow a strict regime of silence, discipline, religious instruction, and constant occupation. Most of the children were court custody cases committed by their fathers because of unruly behavior. The results were dire. There was no accurate way to measure recidivism, and, worse, the children's mortality rates increased sharply. Children in solitary confinement may have been protected from the "moral depravity" of other inmates, but they became sick and died more frequently than their counterparts in free society and than other kinds of prisoners. What began as a humanitarian advance was soon denounced as a form of torture for juvenile offenders.

Why did penitentiaries come into being in the first half of the nineteenth century? The new punishment was considered attractive because, in an age confronted with industrial and political transformations and revolutionary upheavals, it seemed to be a way of controlling criminal disruptions and social unrest. The middle classes, whether in London or Paris, grew increasingly fearful about potential threats to their property and well-being. Industrial workers crowded into substandard urban housing could face long periods of unemployment, when it was feared that desperate men and women would commit crimes to feed themselves and their families. The fear of the poor as dangerous influenced many of the prison reforms of the early nineteenth century. Great Britain and France created growing bureaucracies of penal, policing, and judicial institutions to guarantee the safety of honest citizens. At the same time that new prisons opened their doors, policemen started walking their neighborhood beats in European capitals.

Almost from the beginning prisons were deemed a failure. Specialists concluded that prisons did not correct criminals but instead served as schools for crime. Statistics—a new scientific practice in itself—proved them right. Recidivism rates rose dramatically, as penal authorities devised new ways—eventually fingerprinting and photography—to follow the activities of released prisoners. It is very likely that what was increasing in this era was not criminality but the ability of the state to track it.

■ Vincent Van Gogh, *The Prison Courtyard* (1890). The painting is copied after a wood engraving by Gustave Doré representing Newgate—the Exercise Yard in *London, a Pilgrimage* (1872).

The science of the new punishment evolved directly in relation to political and social changes in the first half of the nineteenth century. The three major spurts of prison reform in France, for example, coincided with the revolutionary upheavals of 1789, 1830, and 1848. Social reformers and legislators turned to the prison system as a crucial mechanism in the regulation of civil society. The new prisons were part of the network of institutions created to maintain an orderly working class in the new democratic age.

■ *Liberty Leading the People* (1831) by Eugène Delacroix captures the spirit of the French romantics, who looked upon revolutionary action as a way to achieve union with the spirit of history.

era could be heard in the works of French composer Louis Hector Berlioz (1803–1869), who set Faust's damnation to music; Polish virtuoso Frédéric Chopin (1810–1849), who created lyric compositions for the piano; and Hungarian concert pianist Franz Liszt (1811–1886), who composed symphonic poems and Hungarian rhapsodies.

Artists as different as J. M. W. Turner (1775–1851), the English landscape painter, and Eugène Delacroix (1798–1863), the leader of the French romantic school in painting (see image above), shared a commitment to their iconoclastic art. Turner's intense and increasingly abstract vision of an often turbulent world (see page 665) and Delacroix's epic historical and political masterpieces shared a rebellious experimentation with color and a rejection of classical conventions and forms. Characteristic of a particular strain within romanticism was the political message of Delacroix's art. In the magnificent painting

Liberty Leading the People (1831), for example, Delacroix immortalized the revolutionary events that swept Paris in 1830 in his moving portrayal of valiant revolutionaries of different social classes led into battle by a female Liberty.

In the postrevolutionary years between 1815 and 1850, romanticism claimed to be no more than an aesthetic stance in art, letters, and music, a posture that had no particular political intent. Yet its validation of the individual as opposed to the caste or the estate was the most revolutionary of doctrines, just as its justification of subjective knowledge threatened to erode the authority of classical learning. Artists did not make revolutions, but they supported them. Some stood by on the sidelines; others mounted the barricades; but all romantics, no matter how political or apolitical, helped shape a new way of looking at the world and helped define a new political consciousness.

■ *Ulysses deriding Polyphemus*, as described in Homer's *Odyssey*. J. W. Turner, 1829, National Gallery.

Reshaping State and Society

As another legacy of the French Revolution, the concept of the *nation* as a source of collective identity and political allegiance became a political force after 1815. Just as nationalism put the needs of the people at the heart of its political doctrine, so did socialism focus on the needs of society and especially of the poor.

Nationalism. In its most basic sense, nationalism between 1815 and 1850 was the political doctrine that glorified the people united against the absolutism of kings and the tyranny of foreign oppressors. The success of the French Revolution and the spread of Napoleonic reforms boosted nationalist doctrines. In Germany, Johann Gottfried von Herder (1744–1803) rooted national identity in German folk culture. The *Fairy Tales* (1812–1814) of the brothers Jacob Ludwig Grimm (1785–1863) and Wilhelm Carl Grimm (1786–1859) had a similar national purpose. The brothers painstakingly captured in print the German oral tradition of peasant folklore. The philosophers Johann Fichte (1762–1814) and Georg Wilhelm Friedrich Hegel (1770–1831) emphasized the importance of the state.

Nationalism gave birth to a search for new symbols, just as the tricolor flag replaced the fleur-de-lis and the image of Marianne replaced the monarch as a result of the Great Revolution in France. There was a new concern with history as nationalists sought to revive a common cultural past.

The nationalist yearning for liberation sometimes meshed with the liberal political program of overthrowing tyrannical rule. Giuseppe Mazzini (1805–1872) represented the new breed of liberal nationalist. A less-than-liberal nationalist was political economist Georg Friedrich List (1789–1846), who formulated a statement of economic nationalism to counter the liberal doctrines of David Ricardo. Arguing that free trade worked only for the wealthy and powerful, List advocated a program of protective tariffs for developing German industries. He perceived British free trade as merely economic imperialism in disguise. List was one of the few nationalists who did not wholeheartedly embrace liberal economic doctrines. Beyond ideology and political practices, nationalism began to capture the imagination of groups who resented foreign domination. Expanding state bureaucracies did little to tame the centrifugal forces of nationalist feeling and probably exacerbated a desire for independence in eastern and central Europe, especially in the Habsburg-ruled lands.

YOUNG ITALY (1832)

Giuseppe Mazzini, an Italian patriot and revolutionary, was the principal theorist of national revolution in Europe in the first half of the nineteenth century. He claimed that his strong commitment to equality and democratic principles stemmed from his readings on the French Revolution of 1789 and his study of the Latin classics. As a young man, he resolved to dress always in black as a sign of mourning for his country, disunited and under foreign oppressors. In 1832 he founded the secret society Young Italy. The goal of the revolutionary group was the unification of Italy under a republican form of government through direct popular action.

Focus Questions

How is Mazzini's message about Italian nationalism reflective of the romantic world view? What is the significance of Mazzini's stress on the role of youth?

We have beheld Italy—Italy, the purpose, the soul, the consolation of our thoughts, the country chosen of God and oppressed by men, twice queen of the world and twice fallen through the infamy of foreigners/ and the guilt of her citizens, yet lovely still though she be dust, unmatched by any other nation whatever fortune has decreed; and Genius returns to seek in this dust the word of eternal life, and the spark that creates the future. . . .

Young Italy: but we chose this term because the one term seems to marshal before the youth of Italy the magnitude of its duties and the solemnity of the mission that circumstances have entrusted to it, so that it will be ready when the hour has struck to arise from its slumber to a new life of action and regeneration. And we chose it because we wanted to show ourselves, writing it, as what we are, to do battle with raised visors, to bear our faith before us, as the knights of medieval times bore their faith on their shields. For while we pity men who do not know the truth, we despise men who, though they know the truth, do not dare to speak it.

Nationalists valued the authenticity of the vernacular and folklore over the language and customs imposed by a foreign ruler. Herder and the brothers Grimm were German examples of the romantic appreciation of the roots of German culture. While French romantics emphasized the glories of their revolutionary heritage, German romantics stressed the importance of history as the source of one's identity. By searching for the self in a historic past, and especially in the Middle Ages, they glorified their collective cultural identity and national origins.

Socialism. Socialists rejected the world as it was. Socialism, like other ideologies of the first half of the nineteenth century, grew out of changes in the structure of daily life and the structure of power. There were as many stripes of socialists as there were liberals, nationalists, and conservatives. Socialists as a group shared a concern with "alienation," though they may not all have used the term.

Henri de Saint-Simon (1760–1825) rejected liberal individualism in favor of social organization and, for this reason, has been called the father of French socialism. To Saint-Simon, the accomplishments and potential of industrial development represented the highest stage in history. In a perfect and just society, productive work would be the basis of all prestige and power. The elite of society would be organized according to the hierarchy of its productive members, with industrial leaders at the top. Work was a social duty. The new industrial society that Saint-Simon foresaw would be both efficient and ethical, based on a religion similar to Christianity.

Like Saint-Simon, the French social theorist Pierre-Joseph Proudhon (1809–1865) recognized the social value of work. But unlike Saint-Simon, Proudhon refused to accept the dominance of industrial society. A self-educated typesetter of peasant origin, Proudhon gained national prominence with his ideas about a just society, free credit, and equitable exchange. In his famous pamphlet *What Is Property?* (1840), Proudhon answered, "Property is theft." That statement was not, however, an argument for the abolition of private ownership. Proudhon reasoned that industrialization had destroyed workers' rights, which included the right to the profits of their own labor. In attacking "property" in the form of profits amassed from the labor of others, Proudhon was arguing for a socialist concept of limited possession—people had the right to own only what they had earned from their own labor. Proudhon, who did not himself participate in political agitation, held a profoundly anarchistic view of society, hated government, and favored instead small self-ruling communities of producers. Proudhon's ideal world would be one of comfort but not great wealth.

At least one socialist believed in luxury. Charles Fourier (1772–1837), an unsuccessful traveling salesman, devoted himself to the study and improvement of society and formulated one of the most trenchant criticisms of industrial capitalism. In numerous writings between 1808 and his death, the eccentric, solitary man put forth his vision of a utopian world organized into units called phalanxes that took into account the social, sexual, and economic needs of their members. With a proper mix of duties, everyone in the phalanx would work only a few hours a day. In Fourier's scheme, work was not naturally abhorrent, but care had to be taken to match temperaments with tasks. Women and men fulfilled themselves and found pleasure and gratification through work. People would be paid according to their contributions in work, capital, and talent. In his vision of a better world, Fourier's phalanxes were always rural and were organized communally, though neither poverty nor property would be eliminated. Education would help alleviate discord, and rich and poor would learn to live together in perfect harmony.

Charles Fourier's work, along with that of Saint-Simon and Proudhon, became part of the tradition of utopian thinking that can be traced back to Thomas More in the sixteenth century. Because he believed in the ability of individuals to shape themselves and their world, Fourier intended his critique of society to be a blueprint for living. Fourier's followers set up communities in his lifetime—40 phalanxes were established in the United States alone—but because of financial problems and petty squabbling, all of them failed.

Women, who were active in demanding their own emancipation, were often joined by men who espoused utopian socialist and liberal views. The issue of increased civil liberties for women, tied as it often was to talk of freeing the slaves, was both a moral and political question for social reformers and

utopian thinkers, including Fourier, who put the issue of women's freedom at the center of their plans to redesign society. Saint-Simonians argued for woman's social elevation and searched for a female messiah. Other social reformers joined with conservative thinkers in arguing that women must be kept in their place and that their place was in the home. Proudhon, for example, saw women's only choices as working at home as housewives or working in the streets as prostitutes.

Socialists, along with other ideologues in the decades before the middle of the nineteenth century, were aware of how rapidly their world was changing. Many believed that a revolution that would eliminate poverty and the sufferings of the working class was at hand. Followers of Saint-Simon, Fourier, and Proudhon all hoped that their proposals and ideas would change the world and prevent violent upheaval. Not all social critics were so sanguine.

In January 1848, two young men, one a philosopher living in exile and the other a businessman working for his father, began a collaboration that would last a lifetime with the publication of a short tract entitled ***The Communist Manifesto.*** Karl Marx (1818–1883) and Friedrich Engels (1820–1895) described the dire situation of the European working classes throughout the 1840s. The growing poverty and alienation of the propertyless workers, the authors promised, would bring

THE COMMUNIST MANIFESTO

The Communist Manifesto *is one of the most important documents in world history. Translated into many languages in countless editions, it inspired worker organizations throughout Europe in the second half of the nineteenth century and fired the imagination of Communist leaders in Asia, Latin America, Africa, and Europe well into the twentieth century.*

The pamphlet, which consists of no more than 12,000 words, was written early in 1848 by Karl Marx, founder of modern communism, and his collaborator and friend, Friedrich Engels. Their intention was to urge exploited workers throughout Europe to prepare themselves for the coming revolution by uniting across national boundaries. The Communist Manifesto *is a concise statement of the basic tenets of Marxism. Although mistaken in most of its predictions about the future development of capitalism, it accurately distilled some of the most salient inequities of industrial economies whose remedies, Marx and Engels asserted, could only be found through the revolutionary overthrow of the capitalist system.*

Focus Questions
According to Marx and Engels, how do markets and capitalism promote class struggle? What is the basis of their opposition to private property and their justification of a Communist revolution?

*Bourgeois and Proletarians**

The history of all hitherto existing society is the history of class struggles.

Freeman and slave, patrician and plebeian, lord and serf, guild-master and journeyman, in a word, oppressor and oppressed, stood in constant opposition to one another, carried on an uninterrupted, now hidden, now open fight, a fight that each time ended, either in a revolutionary reconstitution

of society at large, or in the common ruin of the contending classes. . . .

The modern bourgeois society that has sprouted from the ruins of feudal society has not done away with class antagonisms. It has but established new classes, new conditions of oppression, new forms of struggle in place of the old ones.

Our epoch, the epoch of the bourgeoisie, possesses, however, this distinctive feature: it has simplified the class antagonisms. Society as a whole is more and more splitting up into two great hostile camps, into two great classes directly facing each other: Bourgeoisie and Proletariat. . . .

The bourgeoisie cannot exist without constantly revolutionizing the instruments of production, and thereby the

(continued)

relations of production, and with them the whole relations of society. Conservation of the old modes of production in unaltered form, was, on the contrary, the first condition of existence for all earlier industrial classes. Constant revolutionizing of production, uninterrupted disturbance of all social conditions, everlasting uncertainty and agitation distinguish the bourgeois epoch from all earlier ones. All fixed, fast-frozen relations, with their train of ancient and venerable prejudices and opinions are swept away, all new-formed ones become antiquated before they can ossify. All that is solid melts into air, all that is holy is profaned, and man is at last compelled to face with sober senses, his real conditions of life, and his relations with his kind.

The need of a constantly expanding market for its products chases the bourgeoisie over the whole surface of the globe. It must nestle everywhere, settle everywhere, establish connections everywhere. . . .

The proletariat goes through various stages of development. With its birth begins its struggle with the bourgeoisie. At first the contest is carried on by individual labourers, then by the work-people of a factory, then by the operatives of one trade, in one locality, against the individual bourgeois who directly exploits them. They direct their attacks not against the bourgeois conditions of production, but against the instruments of production themselves; they destroy imported wares that compete with their labour, they smash to pieces machinery, they set factories ablaze, they seek to restore by force the vanished status of the workman of the Middle Ages.

Proletarians and Communists

In what relation do the Communists stand to the proletarians as a whole?

The Communists do not form a separate part opposed to other working-class parties. They have no interests separate and apart from those of the proletariat as a whole. . . .

You are horrified at our [Communists'] intending to do away with private property. But in your existing society, private property is already done away with for nine-tenths of the population; its existence for the few is solely due to its non-existence in the hands of those nine-tenths. You reproach us, therefore, with intending to do away with a form of property the necessary condition for whose existence is the non-existence of any property for the immense majority of society. . . .

In short, the Communists everywhere support every revolutionary movement against the existing social and political order of things.

In all these movements they bring to the front, as the leading question in each, the property question, no matter what its degree of development at the time.

Finally, they labour everywhere for the union and agreement of the democratic parties of all countries.

The Communists disdain to conceal their views and aims. They openly declare that their ends can be attained only by the forcible overthrow of all existing social conditions. Let the ruling classes tremble at a Communistic revolution. The proletarians have nothing to lose but their chains. They have a world to win.

WORKING MEN OF ALL COUNTRIES, UNITE!

*By bourgeoisie is meant the class of modern Capitalists, owners of the means of social production and employers of wage labour. By **proletariat**, the class of modern wage-labourers who, having no means of production of their own, are reduced to selling their labour power in order to live. [*Note by Engels to the English edition of 1888.*]

to industrialized Europe a class war against the capitalists, the owners of the means of production. Exploited workers were to prepare themselves for the moment of revolution by joining with each other across national boundaries: "Workers of the world unite. You have nothing to lose but your chains." In light of subsequent events, the *Manifesto* appears to be a work of great predictive value. But neither Marx nor Engels realized that the hour of revolution was at hand.

Intellectuals and reformers hoped to reshape the world in which they lived with the force of their ideas. Yet the new ideologies were themselves the consequence of the changing role of government and the changing practices of daily life. The technology of industrial production influenced people's values and required a new way of looking at the world. Liberals, nationalists, romantics, conservatives, and socialists addressed the challenges of a changing economy in a political universe buffeted by democratic ideas. The new ideologies did not provide easy answers, but they did serve to incite their followers to take up arms in protests and revolutions throughout Europe.

PROTEST AND REVOLUTION

For European societies that had remained stable, if not stagnant, for centuries, the changes in the first half of the nineteenth century were undoubtedly startling and disruptive. New factories created the arena for exploitation and misery. More people than ever before lived in cities, and national populations faced the prospect of becoming urban. Urban congestion brought crime and disease; patterns of consumption demonstrated beyond dispute that people were not created equal. A new European society that challenged existing political ideas and demanded new political formulations was in the process of emerging.

Causes of Social Instability

The fabric of stability began unraveling throughout Europe in the 1820s. The forces of order reacted to protest with repression everywhere in Europe. Yet armed force proved inadequate to contain the demands for political participation and the increased political awareness of whole segments of the population. Workers, the middle class, and women's political organizations now demanded, through the vote, the right to govern themselves.

Urban Miseries.   In 1800, two of every 100 Europeans lived in a city. By 1850, the number of urban dwellers per hundred had jumped to five and was rising rapidly. In England, the shift was more concentrated than the general European pattern. With one of every two people living in a city, England had become an urban society by mid-century. London was the fastest-growing city in Europe, followed at some distance by Paris and Berlin. The numbers of smaller urban centers were also multiplying.

Massive internal migrations caused most urban growth. People from the same rural areas often lived together in the same urban neighborhoods, and even in the same boarding-houses. Irish emigrants crowded together in the "Little Dublin" section of London. Similarly, districts in other cities were set off by regional accents and native provincial dress. Workers from the same hometowns gravitated to their favorite cafes. The social networks helped make the transition from rural to urban life bearable for the tens of thousands of people who poured into Europe's cities in search of jobs and opportunity. Until mid-century, many migrants returned to their rural homes for the winter when work, especially in the building trades, was scarce in the city. Young migrant women who came to the city to work as servants sent money home to support rural relatives, or worked to save a nest egg—or dowry—with the plan of returning to the village permanently. Before 1850, 20 percent of the workers in London were domestics, and most of them were women.

Despite the support networks that migrants constructed for themselves, the city was not always a hospitable place. Workers were poorly paid, and women workers were more poorly paid than men. When working women were cut free of the support of home and family, uncounted numbers were forced into part-time prostitution to supplement meager incomes. It is conservatively estimated that in 1850 there were 34,000 prostitutes in Paris and 50,000 in London. The phenomenon of prostitution indicated changing mores about sexuality in the first half of the nineteenth century. The "angel" of middle-class households and the "whore" of the streets were subjects of fascination in fiction and nonfiction. Increased prostitution created a veritable epidemic of venereal diseases, especially syphilis, for which there was no known cure until the twentieth century.

Urban crime also grew astronomically, with thefts accounting for the greatest number of crimes. Social reformers identified poverty and urban crowding as causes of the increase in criminal behavior. In 1829, both Paris and London began to create modern urban police forces to deal with the challenges to law and order. Crime assumed the character of disease in the minds of middle-class reformers. Statisticians and social scientists, themselves a new urban phenomenon, produced massive theses on social hygiene, lower-class immorality, and the unworthiness of the poor. The pathology of the city was widely discussed. Always at the center of the issue was the growing problem of what to do with the poor.

The Role of the State.   State-sponsored work relief expanded after 1830 for the deserving poor: the old, the sick, and children. Able-bodied workers who were idle were regarded as undeserving and dangerous, regardless of the causes of their unemployment. Performance of work became an indicator of moral worth as urban and rural workers succumbed to downturns in the economic cycle. Those unable to work sought relief from the state as a last resort. What has been called a "revolution in government" took place in the 1830s and 1840s as legislative bodies increased regulation of everything from factories and mines to prisons and schools.

Poverty was not just an urban problem, although it was both more conspicuous and more feared in urban areas. Politicians, social reformers, religious thinkers, and revolutionaries all had different solutions that followed one of two general orientations. There were those who argued, as in the

■ The Irish potato famine, one of the worst famines in modern history, afflicted the European poor in the 1840s.

case of the Irish famine, that the government must do nothing to intervene because the problem would correct itself, as Thomas Malthus had predicted 40 years earlier. Malthus had argued that the "positive" means of famine and death would keep population from outgrowing available resources and food supplies. The Irish population, one of the poorest in Europe, had indeed doubled between 1781 and 1841, and for Malthusians the Irish famine was the fulfillment of their vision that famine was the only way to correct overpopulation. Some insisted that poverty was a social necessity; by interfering with it, governments could only make matters worse.

Others contended that poverty was society's problem, and perhaps society's creation, and not a law of nature. Thus it was the social responsibility of the state to take care of its members. The question of how to treat poverty—or the "social question" as it came to be known among contemporaries—underlay many of the protests and reforms of the two decades before 1850 and fueled the revolutionary movements of 1848. Parliamentary legislation attempted to improve the situation of the poor, especially the working class, during the 1830s and 1840s. In 1833, British reformers turned their attention to the question of child labor. Against the opposition of those who argued for a free market for labor, Parliament passed the Factory Act of 1833, which prohibited the employment of children under nine years of age and restricted the workweek of children aged nine to thirteen to 48 hours. No child in this age group could work more than nine hours a day. Teenagers between 13 and 18 years could work no more than 69 hours a week. By modern standards, the "reformed" workloads present a shocking picture of the heavy reliance on child labor. The British Parliament commissioned investigations, compiled in the "Blue Books," that reported the abusive treatment of men, women, and children in factories. Similar studies existed for French and Belgian industry.

British legislation marked an initial step in state intervention in the workplace. Additional legislation over the next three decades further restricted children's and women's labor in factories and concerned itself with improving conditions in the workplace. Fundamentally, the "social question" was the question of what the state's role and responsibility were in caring for its citizens.

The Revolutions of 1830

Few Europeans alive in 1830 remembered the age of revolution that spanned the period from 1789 to 1799. Yet the legends were kept alive from one generation to the next. Secret political organizations perpetuated Jacobin republicanism. Mutual aid societies and artisans' associations preserved the rituals of democratic culture. A new generation of radicals seemed to be budding in the student riots in Germany and in the revolutionary waves that swept across southern and central Europe in the early 1820s. In August of 1819, a crowd of 80,000 people gathered outside Manchester, England, in St. Peter's Field to hear speeches for parliamentary reform and universal male suffrage. The cavalry swept down on them in a bloody slaughter that came to be

known as the **"Peterloo" Massacre,** a bitter reference to the Waterloo victory four years before.

Poor harvests in 1829 followed by a harsh winter left people cold, hungry, and bitter. Misery fueled social protest, and political issues of participation and representation commanded new attention. The convergence of social unrest with long-standing political demands touched off apparently simultaneous revolutions all over Europe. Governmental failure to respond to local grievances sparked the revolutions of 1830. Highly diverse groups of workers, students, lawyers, professionals, and peasants rose up spontaneously to demand a voice in the affairs of government.

The French Revolution of 1830. In France, the late 1820s were a period of increasing political friction. Charles X (1824–1830), the former comte d'Artois, had never resigned himself to the constitutional monarchy accepted by his brother and predecessor, Louis XVIII. When Charles assumed the throne in 1824, he dedicated himself to a true restoration of kingship as it had existed before the Revolution. To this end, he realigned the monarchy with the Catholic Church and undertook several unpopular measures, including approval of the death penalty for those found guilty of sacrilege. The king's bourgeois critics, heavily influenced by liberal ideas about political economy and constitutional rights, sought increased political power through their activities in secret organizations and in public elections. The king responded to his critics by relying on his ultraroyalist supporters to run the government. In May 1830, the king dissolved the Chamber of Deputies and ordered new elections. The elections returned a liberal majority unfavorable to the king. Charles X retaliated with what proved to be his last political act, the Four Ordinances, in which he censored the press, changed the electoral law to favor his own candidates, dissolved the newly elected Chamber, and ordered new elections.

Opposition to Charles X might have remained at the level of political wrangling and journalistic protest, if it had not been for the problems plaguing the people of Paris. A severe winter in France had driven up food prices by 75 percent. Most urban dwellers were barely subsisting. The king had erred in hoping that France's recent conquest of Algeria in North Africa would keep the populace quiet. He underestimated the extent of hardship and the political volatility of the population. Throughout the spring of 1830, prices continued to rise and Charles continued to blunder. In a spontaneous uprising in the last days of July 1830, workers took to the streets of Paris. The revolution they initiated spread rapidly to towns and the countryside as people throughout France protested the cost of living, hoarding by grain merchants, tax collection, and wage cuts. In "three glorious days," the restored Bourbon regime was pulled down and Charles X fled to England.

The people fighting in the streets demanded a republic, but they lacked organization and political experience. Liberal bourgeois politicians quickly filled the power vacuum. They presented Charles's cousin Louis-Philippe, formerly the duc d'Orléans, as the savior of France and the new constitutional monarch. The July Monarchy, born of a revolution, put an end to the Bourbon Restoration. Louis-Philippe became "king of the French." The charter that he brought with him was, like its predecessor, based on restricted suffrage, with property ownership a requisite for voting. The voting age was lowered from 30 to 25, and the tax requirement was also lowered. The electorate nearly doubled, from 90,000 to 170,000, but nevertheless voting remained restricted to a small fraction of the population.

Unrest in Europe.   Popular disturbances did not always result in revolution. In Britain, rural and town riots erupted over grain prices and distribution, but no revolution followed. German workers broke their machines to protest low wages and loss of control of the workplace, but no prince was displaced. In Switzerland, reformers found strength in the French revolutionary example. Ten Swiss cantons granted liberal constitutions and established universal manhood suffrage, freedom of expression, and legal equality.

In southern Europe, Greece had languished as a subjugated country for centuries. Turkish overlords ruled Greece as part of the Ottoman Empire. The longing for independence smoldered in Greece throughout the 1820s as public pressure to support the Greeks mounted in Europe. Greek insurrections were answered by Turkish retaliations throughout the Ottoman Empire. In 1822, a Turkish fleet captured the island of Chios in the Aegean Sea off the west coast of Turkey and massacred or enslaved the population. The atrocities committed by the Turks against Greeks in Constantinople provoked international reaction in the form of a Philhellenic (literally, "lover of Greece") movement supported by two of Britain's great romantic poets,

Lord Byron (1788–1824) and Percy Bysshe Shelley (1792–1822). Byron sailed to the besieged Greek city of Missolonghi in 1824 to help coordinate the military effort, and there he contracted malaria and died. The sultan of Turkey had been able to call upon his vassal, the pasha of Egypt, to subdue Greece. In response, Great Britain, France, and Russia signed the Treaty of London in 1827, pledging intervention on behalf of Greece. In a joint effort, the three powers defeated the Egyptian fleet. Russia declared war on Turkey the following year, seeking territorial concessions from the Ottoman Empire. Following the Russian victory, Great Britain and France joined Russia in declaring Greek independence.

The concerted action of the three powers in favor of Greek independence was neither an endorsement of liberal ideals nor a support of Greek nationalism. The British, French, and Russians were reasserting their commitment made at the Congress of Vienna to territorial stability. Yet beneath the veneer of their commitment, the Russians intervened, hoping for territorial gains in the Ottoman Empire. The British favored Ottoman stability while distrusting Russian ambitions in the area. The Turks had been unable to maintain stability on their own. Finally, the three powers abandoned their policy of propping up the Ottoman Empire and supported instead the movement for Greek independence. But they did so on their own terms by creating a monarchy in Greece and placing a German-born prince on the new throne.

Belgian, Polish, and Italian Struggles.   The overthrow of the Bourbon monarch in France served as a model for revolution in other parts of Europe. Following the French lead, in the midst of the Greek crisis the Belgian provinces revolted against the Netherlands. The Belgians' desire for their own nation struck at the heart of the Vienna settlement. Provoked by a food crisis similar to that in France, Belgian revolutionaries took to the streets in August 1830. As a symbol of their solidarity with the successful French Revolution, they flew the tricolor in defiance of their Dutch rulers. Belgians protested the deterioration of their economic situation and made demands for their own Catholic religion, their own language, and constitutional rights. Bitter fighting on the barricades in Brussels ensued, and the movement for freedom and independence spread to the countryside.

The Great Powers disagreed on what to do. Russia, Austria, and Prussia were all eager to see the revolution crushed. France, having just established the new regime of the July Monarchy, and Great Britain, fearing the involvement of the central and eastern European powers in an area where Britain had traditionally had interests, were reluctant to intervene. A provisional government in Belgium set about the task of writing a constitution. All five great powers recognized Belgian independence, with the proviso that Belgium was to maintain the status of a neutral state.

Russia, Prussia, and Austria were convinced to accept Belgian independence because they were having their own problems in eastern and southern Europe. Revolution erupted to the east in Warsaw, Poland. Driven by a desire for national independence, Polish army cadets and university students revolted in November 1830, demanding a constitution.

DOCUMENT

The Books of the Polish Nation

Landed aristocrats and gentry helped establish a provisional government but soon split over how radical reforms should be. Polish peasants refused to support either landowning group. Within the year, Russia brought in 180,000 troops to crush the revolution and reassert its rule over Poland.

In February 1831, the Italian states of Modena and Parma rose up to throw off Austrian domination of northern Italy. The revolutionaries were ineffective against Austrian troops. Revolution in the Papal States resulted in French occupation that lasted until 1838 without serious reforms.

Nationalist and republican yearnings were driven underground, kept alive there in the Young Italy movement under the leadership of Giuseppe Mazzini.

Although the revolutions of 1830 are called "the forgotten revolutions" of the nineteenth century, they are important for several reasons. First, they made clear to European states how closely tied together were their fates. The events of 1830 were a test of the Great Powers' commitment to stability and a balance of power in Europe. True to the principles of the Vienna settlements of 1815, European leaders preserved the status quo. Revolutions in Poland and Italy were contained by Russia and Austria without interference from the other powers. Where adaptation was necessary, as in Greece and Belgium, the Great Powers were able to compromise on settlements, though the solutions ran counter to previous policies. Heads of state were willing to use the forces of repression to stamp out protest. Although each revolution followed its own pattern of development, all shared origins in domestic crises unsuccessfully addressed by those in power.

IMAGE DISCOVERY

Rue Transnonain by Honoré Daumier

Workers launched an insurrection in Paris in the spring of 1834 against the labor policies of the French government. An officer was killed by sniper fire in the rue Transnonain. Before dawn on the next day, 14 April 1834, troops entered an apartment building on that street and killed many of the occupants by either shooting or bayoneting them. How many bodies do you see in this lithograph? What message about the victims is Daumier, the artist, conveying by the bedroom location of the scene? What story do the dead bodies, including that of the baby, tell? Lithographs were printed in large numbers especially for newspapers and journals. Is this a work of art or propaganda?

The international significance of the revolutions reveals a second important aspect of the events of 1830: the vulnerability of international politics to domestic instability. No state could practice diplomacy in a vacuum. Grain prices and demands for democratic participation had direct impact on the balance of power of European states. The five Great Powers broke down into two ideological camps. On the one hand were the liberal constitutional states of Great Britain and France, on the other stood the autocratic monarchies of Russia, Austria, and Prussia. Yet ideological differences were always less important than the shared desire for internal stability as a prerequisite for international peace.

Finally, the 1830 revolutions exposed a growing awareness of politics at all levels of European society. If policies in 1830 revealed a shared consciousness of events and shared values among ruling elites, the revolutions disclosed a growing awareness among the lower classes of the importance of politics in their daily lives. The cry for "liberty, equality, and fraternity" transcended national borders and the French language. The demands for constitutions, national identity, and civic equality resounded from the Atlantic to the Urals. In a dangerous combination of circumstances, workers and the lower classes throughout Europe were politicized, yet they continued to be excluded from political power.

Reform in Great Britain

The right to vote had been an issue of contention in the revolutions of 1830 in western Europe. Only the Swiss cantons enforced the principle of "one man, one vote." The July Revolution in France had doubled the electorate, but still only a tiny minority of the population (less than 1 percent) enjoyed the vote. Universal male suffrage had been mandated in 1793 during the Great Revolution but not implemented. Those in power believed that the wealthiest property owners were best qualified to govern, in part because they had the greatest stake in politics and society. One also needed to own property to hold office. Because those who served in parliaments received no salary, only the wealthy had the resources and the leisure to represent the electorate. When confronted by his critics, François Guizot (1787–1874), French prime minister and chief spokesman for the July Monarchy, offered this glib advice to an aspiring electorate: "Get rich!"

The Rule of the Landed.   Landowners also ruled Britain. There the dominance of a wealthy elite was strengthened by the geographic redistribution of population resulting from industrialization. Migration to cities had depleted the population of rural areas. Yet the electoral system did not adjust to the changes: large towns had no parliamentary representation, while dwindling county electorates maintained their parliamentary strength. Areas that continued to enjoy representation greater than that justified by their population were dubbed "rotten" or "pocket" boroughs to indicate a corrupt and antiquated electoral system. In general, urban areas were grossly underrepresented and the wealthy few controlled county seats.

Liberal reformers attempted to rectify the electoral inequalities by reassigning parliamentary seats on the basis of density of population, but vested interests balked at attempted reforms and members of Parliament wrangled bitterly. Popular agitation by the lower classes provoked the fear of civil war, which helped break the parliamentary deadlock. The **Great Reform Bill of 1832** proposed a compromise. Although the vast majority of the population still did not have the vote, the new legislation strengthened the industrial and commercial elite in the towns, enfranchised most of the middle class, opened the way to social reforms, and encouraged the formation of political parties.

Years of bad harvests, unemployment, and depression, coupled with growing dissatisfaction with the government's

■ This English cartoon of 1832 is titled "The Clemency of the Russian Monster." It shows Nicholas I in the guise of a bear with menacing teeth and claws addressing the Poles after crushing their rebellion against Russian rule.

'Gentlemen,' says Nicholas I, the bear, to the Polish revolutionaries of 1830, 'I know that you wish to address me; but to spare you from delivering a pack of lies, I desire that you hold your tongues.' The Polish rebellion of 1830–31 was brutally suppressed by the Russians. However, this brutality reinforced Polish national sentiment (the Poles rebelled again in 1863) and engaged the sympathy of the West for the Poles—as this English cartoon shows. (2)

weak efforts to address social problems, put the spur to a new national reform movement in the 1830s. Radical reformers, disillusioned with the 1832 Reform Bill because it strengthened the power of a wealthy capitalist class, argued that democracy was the only answer to the problems plaguing British society.

The Chartist Movement. In 1838, a small group of labor leaders, including representatives of the London Working Men's Association, an organization of craft workers, drew up a document known as the People's Charter. The single most important demand of the charter was that all men must have the vote. In addition, Chartists petitioned for a secret ballot, salaries for parliamentary service, elimination of the requirement that a person must own property in order to run for office, equal electoral districts, and annual elections. The proposal favored direct democracy, guaranteed by frequent elections that would ensure maximum accountability of officials to their constituents.

Chartist appeal was greatest in periods of economic hardship. A violent mood swept through the movement in 1839. The Irish Chartist leader Feargus O'Connor (1794–1855) and the Irish journalist and orator James Bronterre O'Brien (1805–1864) urged an unskilled and poorly organized working class to

MAP DISCOVERY

Unrest of the 1820s and 1830s: Centers of Revolutionary Action

What geographic and political features were common to the centers of popular unrest and revolutionary action in the 1820s and 1830s? How did the French Revolution of 1830 serve as a model for revolutionary action in the Belgian provinces, Poland, and the northern Italian states? How did political actions in Great Britain differ from those of the Continent in this period?

protest inequities through strikes that on occasion became violent. O'Brien thrilled his working-class listeners by haranguing "the big-bellied, little-brained, numbskull aristocracy." **Chartism** blossomed as a communal phenomenon in working-class towns and appeared to involve all members of the family: "Every kitchen is now a political meeting house; the little children are members of the unions and the good mother is the political teacher," one Chartist organizer boasted. Chartist babies were christened with the names of Chartist heroes. When Mrs. King of Manchester, England, attempted to register the birth of her son, James Feargus O'Connor King, her choice of names was challenged. The registrar demanded,

"Is your husband a Chartist?" Mrs. King replied, "I don't know, but his wife is." Women organized Chartist schools and Sunday schools in radical defiance of local church organizations. Many middle-class observers were sure that the moment for class war and revolutionary upheaval had arrived. The government responded with force to the perceived threat of armed rebellion and imprisoned a number of Chartist leaders.

Throughout the 1840s, bad harvests and economic hardships continued to fan the flames of discontent. National petitions signed by millions were submitted to the House of Commons, which stubbornly resisted the idea of universal manhood suffrage. Strikes and attacks on factories spread throughout

England, Scotland, and Wales in 1842. Increased violence served to make the Parliament intransigent and caused the movement to splinter and weaken as moderates formed their own factions. The final moment for Chartism occurred in April 1848 when 25,000 Chartist workers, inspired by revolutionary events on the Continent, assembled in London to march on the House of Commons. They carried with them a newly signed petition demanding the enactment of the terms of the People's Charter. In response, the government deputized nearly 200,000 "special" constables in the streets. The deputized private citizens were London property owners and skilled workers intent on holding back a revolutionary rabble. Tired, cold, and rain-soaked, the Chartist demonstrators disbanded. No social revolution took place in Great Britain, and the dilemma of democratic representation was deferred.

Workers Unite

The word **proletariat** entered European languages before the mid-nineteenth century to describe those workers afloat in the labor pool who owned nothing, not even the tools of their labor, and who were becoming "appendages" to the new machines that dominated production. To workers, machines could mean the elimination of jobs or the de-skilling of tasks; almost always machines meant a drop in wages.

Luddism. Mechanization deprived skilled craft workers of control of the workplace. In Great Britain, France, and Germany, groups of textile workers destroyed machines in protest. Workers demanding a fair wage smashed cotton power looms, knitting machines, and wool-carding machines. Sometimes the machines were a bargaining point for workers who used violence against them as a last resort. Machine-breakers tyrannized parts of Great Britain from 1811 to 1816 in an attempt to frighten masters. The movement was known as Luddism after its mythical leader, Ned Ludd. Workers damaged and destroyed property for more control over the work process, but such destruction met with severe repression. From the 1820s to the 1850s, sporadic but intense outbursts of machine-breaking occurred in continental Europe. Suffering weavers in Silesia and Bohemia resorted to destroying their looms in 1844.

Craft production continued to deteriorate with the rise in industrial competition. Skilled workers, fearing that they would be pulled down into the new proletariat because of mechanization and the increased scale of production, began organizing in new ways after 1830 by forming associations to assert their control over the workplace and to demand a voice in politics.

In Britain, skilled craft workers built on a tradition of citizenship. They resisted the encroachments of factory production, and some channeled their political fervor into the Chartist movement. Skilled workers in France also built on a cultural heritage of shared language and values to create a consciousness of themselves as an exploited class. Uprisings and strikes in France, favoring the destruction of the monarchy and the creation of a democratic republic, increased dramatically from 1831 to 1834. Many French craft workers grew conscious of themselves as a class and embraced a socialism heavily influenced by their own traditions and contemporary socialist writings. Republican socialism spread throughout France by means of a network of traveling journeymen and tapped into growing economic hardship and political discontent with the July Monarchy. Government repression drove worker organizations underground in the late 1830s, but secret societies proliferated. Increasingly, workers saw the validity of the slogan of the silk workers of Lyon: "Live Working or Die Fighting!"

Women in the Work Force. Women were an important part of the work force in the industrializing societies. Working men were keenly aware of the competition with cheaper female labor in the factories. Women formed a salaried work force in the home, too. In order to turn out products cheaply and in large quantities, some manufacturers turned to subcontractors to perform the simpler tasks in the work process. The new middlemen contracted out work such as cutting and sewing to needy women who were often responsible for caring for family members in their homes. That kind of subcontracting, called "sweated labor" because of the exertion and long hours involved in working in one's own home, was always poorly paid.

Cheap female labor paid by the piece allowed employers to profit by keeping overhead costs low and by driving down the wages of skilled workers. Trade unions opposed women's work, both in the home and in the factories. Women's talents, union leaders explained, were more properly devoted to domestic chores. Unions argued that their members should earn a family wage "sufficient to support a wife and children." Unions consistently excluded women workers from their ranks.

French labor leader Flora Tristan, speaking not only as a worker but also as a wife and mother, had a very different answer for those who wanted to remove women from the workplace and assign them to their "proper place" in the home. She recognized that working women needed to work in order to support themselves and their families. Tristan told audiences in Europe and Latin America that the emancipation of women from their "slave status" was essential if the working class as a whole was to enjoy a better future. She deplored the economic competition between working men and women and denounced the degradation of women in both the home and the workplace. A working woman earned one-third or less of the average working man's wages, and women's working conditions were often deplorable. In the 1840s, British parliamentary commissions heard the horrifying testimony of one young London dressmaker from the country who was forced to work grueling hours—often 20 hours a day—under unhealthy working conditions that had destroyed her health. She concluded that "no men could endure the work enforced from the dressmakers."

Working women's only hope, according to Tristan, lay in education and unionization. She urged working men and

FLORA TRISTAN AND THE RIGHTS OF WORKING WOMEN

Flora Tristan (1803–1844) was a feminist and socialist who in the 1830s was actively involved in efforts to reintroduce divorce and to abolish the death penalty. She made her greatest political efforts for the creation of an international union of workers. The education of women was, Tristan asserted, essential for the success and prosperity of the working class. She toured slums in England and traveled across France on lecture tours to promote workers' unions and the education of women. The excerpt below is taken from her important book, L'Union Ouvriére, *1843. Tristan's argument for women's education is based not only on the claims of women to basic human rights, but on her assertion that educated women held the key to the betterment of families, the working class, and the whole society.*

Focus Questions

Why is education so important in Tristan's justification of women's rights? Would you describe Tristan as a reformer or a revolutionary?

. . . [I]t is imperative, in order to improve the intellectual, moral, and material condition of the working class, that women of the lower classes be given a rational and solid education, conducive to the development of their good inclinations, so that they may become skillful workers, good mothers, capable of raising and guiding their children, and of tutoring them in their school work, and so that they may act as moralizing agents in the life of the men on whom they exert an influence from the cradle to the grave.

Do you begin to understand, you, men, who cry shame before even looking into the question, why I demand rights for woman? Why I should like her to be placed on a footing of absolute equality with man in society, and that she should be so by virtue of the legal right every human being brings at birth?

I demand rights for women because I am convinced that all the misfortunes in the world result from the neglect and contempt in which woman's natural and inalienable rights have so far been held. I demand rights for woman because it is the only way she will get an education, and because the education of man in general and man of the lower classes in particular depends on the education of woman. I demand rights for woman because it is the only way to obtain her rehabilitation in the Church, the law, and society, and because this preliminary rehabilitation is necessary to achieve the rehabilitation of the workers themselves. All the woes of the working class can be summed up in these two words: poverty and ignorance, ignorance and poverty. Now, I see only one way out of this labyrinth: begin by educating women, because women have the responsibility of educating male and female children. . . .

As soon as the dangerous consequences of the development of the moral and physical faculties of women—dangerous because of women's current slave status—are no longer feared, woman can be taught with great care so as to make the best possible use of her intelligence and work. Then, you, men of the lower classes, will have as mothers skillful workers who earn a decent salary, are educated, well brought up, and quite capable of raising you, of educating you, the workers, as is proper for free men. You will have well brought up and well educated sisters, lovers, wives, friends, with whom daily contacts will be most pleasant for you. Nothing is sweeter or more agreeable to a man's heart than the sensible and gracious conversation of good and well educated women.

---

women to join together to lay claim to their natural and inalienable rights. In some cases, working women formed their own organizations, like that of the Parisian seamstresses who joined together to demand improved working conditions. On the whole, however, domestic workers in the home remained isolated from other working women, and many women in factories feared the loss of their jobs if they engaged in political activism. The wages of Europe's working women remained low, often below the level of subsistence. In the absence of a man's income, working women and their children were the poorest of the poor in European society in the middle of the nineteenth century.

For some men and women of the working class, the 1840s were a time of mounting unrest, increased organization, and growing protest. Workers used their unity in associations, unions, and mutual aid societies to press for full political participation and government action in times of economic distress.

Revolutions Across Europe, 1848–1850

Europeans had never experienced a year like 1848. Beginning soon after the ringing in of the New Year, revolutionary fervor swept through nearly every European country. By year's end, regimes had been created and destroyed. France, Italy, the German states, Austria, Hungary, and Bohemia were shaken to their foundations. Switzerland, Denmark, and Romania experienced lesser upheavals. Great Britain had survived re-

■ Meeting of Chartists on Kennington Common, 15 April 1848.

formist agitation, and famine-crippled Ireland had endured a failed insurrection. No one was sure what had happened. Each country's conflict was based on a unique mix of issues, but all were connected in their conscious emulation of a revolutionary tradition.

Hindsight reveals warning signs in the two years before the 1848 cataclysm. Beginning in 1846, a severe famine—the last serious food crisis Europe would experience—racked Europe. Lack of grain drove up prices. An increasing percentage of disposable income was spent on food for survival. Lack of spending power severely damaged markets and forced thousands of industrial workers out of their jobs. The famine hurt everyone—the poor, workers, employers, and investors—as recession paralyzed the economy.

The food crisis took place in a heavily charged political atmosphere. Throughout Europe during the 1840s, the middle and lower classes had intensified their agitation for democracy. Chartists in Great Britain argued for a wider electorate. Bourgeois reformers in France campaigned for universal manhood suffrage. Known as the "banquet" campaign because its leaders attempted to raise money by giving speeches at subscribed dinners, the movement for the vote appeared to be developing a mass following by taking its cause directly to the people. In making demands for political participation, those agitating for suffrage necessarily criticized those in

power. Freedom of speech and freedom of assembly were demanded as inalienable rights. The food crisis and political activism provided the ingredients for an incendiary situation.

In addition to a burgeoning democratic culture, growing demands for national autonomy based on linguistic and cultural claims spread through central, southern, and eastern Europe. The revolts in Poland in 1846, though failures, encouraged similar movements for national liberation among Italians and Germans. Even in the relatively homogeneous nation of France, concerns with national mission and national glory grew among the regime's critics. National unity was primarily a middle-class ideal. Liberal lawyers, teachers, and businessmen from Dublin to Budapest to Prague agitated for separation from foreign rule. Austria, with an empire formed of numerous ethnic minorities, had the most to lose. Since 1815, Metternich had been ruthless in stamping out nationalist dissent. However, by the 1840s, national claims were assuming a cultural legitimacy that was difficult to dismiss or ignore.

France Leads the Way.   The events in France in the cold February of 1848 ignited the conflagration that swept Europe. Bourgeois reformers had arranged for their largest banquet to date in support of extension of the vote, to take place in Paris on 22 February. City officials became nervous at the prospect of thousands of workers assembling for political purposes and canceled the scheduled banquet. That was the spark that touched off the powder keg. In a spontaneous uprising, Parisians demonstrated against the government's repressive measures. Skilled workers took to the streets, not only in favor of the banned banquet but also with the hope that the government would recognize the importance of labor to the social order. Shots were fired; a demonstrator was killed. The French Revolution of 1848 had begun.

Events moved quickly. The National Guard, a citizen militia of bourgeois Parisians, defected from Louis-Philippe. Many army troops garrisoned in Paris crossed the barricades to join revolutionary workers. The king attempted some reform, but it was too little and too late. Louis-Philippe fled. The Second Republic was proclaimed at the insistence of the revolutionary crowds on the barricades. The Provisional Government, led by the poet Alphonse de Lamartine (1790–1869), included members of both factions of political reformers of the July Monarchy: moderates who sought constitutional reforms and an extension of the suffrage, and radicals who favored universal manhood suffrage and social programs to deal with poverty and work. Only the threat of popular violence held together the uneasy alliance.

The people fighting in the streets had little in common with the bourgeois reformers who assumed power on 24 February. Workers made a social revolution out of a commitment to their "right to work," which would replace the right to property as the organizing principle of the new society. Only one member of the new Provisional Government was a worker, and he was included as a token symbol of the intentions of the new government. He was known as "Albert, the worker," and was not addressed by his surname, Martin. The government acknowledged the demand of the "right to work" and set up two mechanisms to guarantee workers' relief. First, a commission of workers and employers was created to act as a grievance and bargaining board and settle questions of common

concern in the workplace. Headed by the socialist Louis Blanc (1811–1882) and known as the Luxembourg Commission, the worker-employer parliament was an important innovation, but it accomplished little other than deflecting workers' attention away from the problems of the Provisional Government. The second measure was the creation of "national workshops" to deal with the problems of unemployment in Paris. Although the name was taken from Blanc's plan for worker control of production, the national workshops were no more than an inefficient charity program that paid men minimal wages. The national workshops quickly proved disastrous. Workers from all over France poured into Paris with the hope of finding jobs. However, the workshops had a residency requirement that even Parisians had difficulty meeting. As a result, unemployment skyrocketed. Furthermore, the government was going bankrupt trying to support the program. The need to raise taxes upset peasants in the provinces. National pressure mounted to repudiate the programs of the revolution.

French workers were too weak to dominate the revolution. The government dissolved the workshops and recalled General Louis Cavaignac (1802–1857) from service in Algeria to maintain order. In a wave of armed insurrection, Parisian workers rebelled in June. Using provincial troops having no identification with the urban population and employing guerrilla techniques he had mastered in Algeria, Cavaignac put down the uprising. The June fighting was the bloodiest that Paris had ever seen. The Second Republic was placed under the military dictatorship of Cavaignac until December, when presidential elections were scheduled.

Revolutions in Central and Eastern Europe.
The overthrow of the July Monarchy at the end of February set off shock waves of protest in central and eastern Europe. Long-suppressed desires for civil liberties and constitutional reforms erupted in widespread popular disturbances through-

■ Club-wielding police break up a radical demonstration in Berlin, the capital of Prussia, in 1848. In March, King Frederick William of Prussia acceded to the demands of liberal reformers. But in November, after uprisings against conservative regimes elsewhere in Europe had been put down, the monarch allowed the Prussian army to regain control of Berlin.

MAP DISCOVERY

✴ Revolutions of 1848

The Revolutions of 1848

In less than a generation, a second major wave of revolutions swept across Europe from west to east in 1848. What were the centers of revolutionary action in 1848 and what was their relationship to the seats of political power? How do you explain the timing of the eastern trajectory of successive revolutions? How did the map of Europe change as a result of these revolutions?

out Prussia and the German states. Fearing a war with France and unable to count on Austria or Russia for support, the princes who ruled Baden, Württemberg, Hesse-Darmstadt, Bavaria, Saxony, and Hanover followed the advice of moderate liberals and acceded quickly to revolutionary demands. In Prussia, Kaiser Friedrich Wilhelm IV (1840–1861) preferred to use military force to respond to popular demonstrations. Only in mid-March 1848 did the Prussian king yield to the force of the revolutionary crowds building barricades in Berlin by ordering his troops to leave the city and by promising to create a national Prussian assembly. The king was now a prisoner of the revolution.

Meanwhile, the collapse of absolute monarchy in Prussia gave further impetus to a constitutional movement among the liberal leaders of the German states. The governments of all the German states were invited to elect delegates to a national parliament in Frankfurt. The Frankfurt Assembly, which was convened in May 1848, had as its dual charge the framing of a constitution and the unification of Germany. It was composed for the most part of members of the middle class, with civil servants, lawyers, and intellectuals predominating. In spite of the principle of universal manhood suffrage, no members of the working class served among the 800 men elected. To most of the delegates, who had been trained in universities and shared a social and cultural identity, nationalism and constitutionalism were inextricably related.

As straightforward as the desire for a German nation appeared to be, it was complicated by two important facts. First, there were non-German minorities living in German states. What was to be done with the Poles, Czechs, Slovenes, Italians, and Dutch in a newly constituted and autonomous German nation? Second, there were Germans living outside the German states under Habsburg rule in Austria, in Danish Schleswig and Holstein, in Posen (Poznan), in Russian Poland, and in European Russia. How were they to be included within the linguistically and ethnically constituted German nation? No matter how small the circle was drawn, it included non-Germans; no matter how wide, it excluded Germans. After much wrangling over a "small" Germany that excluded Austrian Germans and a "large" Germany that included them, the Frankfurt Assembly opted for the small-Germany solution in March 1849. The crown of the new nation was offered to the unpredictable Friedrich Wilhelm IV of Prussia, head of the largest and most powerful of the German states. Unhappy with his capitulation to the revolutionary crowd in March 1848, the Prussian king refused to accept a "crown from the gutter." He had his own plans to rule over a middle-European bloc, but not at the behest of a liberal parliament. The attempt to create a German nation crumbled with his unwillingness to lead.

Revolution in Austrian-dominated central Europe was concentrated in three places: Vienna, where German-speaking students, workers, and middle-class liberals were agitating for constitutional reform and political participation; Budapest, where the Magyars, the dominant ethnic group in Hungary, led a movement for national autonomy; and Prague, where Czechs were attempting self-rule. By April 1848, Metternich had fallen from power and the Viennese revolutionaries had set up a constituent assembly. In Budapest, the initial steps of the patriot Lajos Kossuth (1802–1894) toward establishing a separate Hungarian state seemed equally solid as the Magyars defeated Habsburg troops. Habsburg armies were more successful in Prague, where they crushed the revolution in June 1848. In December 1848, Emperor Ferdinand I (1835–1848), whose authority had been weakened irreparably by the overthrow of Metternich, abdicated in favor of his 18-year-old nephew, Franz Josef I (1848–1916).

DOCUMENT

Metternich on Revolutions of 1848

Italian Nationalism. The Habsburg Empire was also under siege on the Italian Peninsula, where the Kingdom of the Two Sicilies, Tuscany, and Piedmont declared new constitutions in March 1848. Championed by Charles Albert of Piedmont, Venice and Lombardy rose up against Austria. Italian middle-class intellectuals and professionals championed the idea of national unification and the expulsion of the hated Austrian overlords. Nationalist sentiments had percolated underground in the Young Italy movement, founded in 1831 by Giuseppe Mazzini. A tireless and idealistic patriot,

CHRONOLOGY

Protest and Revolution

August 1819	Peterloo Massacre
1824	Charles X assumes French throne
1827	Treaty of London to support liberation of Greece
July 1830	Revolution in Paris; creation of July Monarchy under Louis-Philippe
August 1830	Revolution in Belgium
November 1830	Revolution in Poland
1831–1838	Revolutions in Italian states
1831–1834	Labor protests in France
1832	Britain's Great Reform Bill
1838	Drawing up of the first People's Charter in Britain
1846	Beginning of food crisis in Europe; revolts in Poland
1846–1848	Europewide movements for national liberation
February 1848	Revolution in France; overthrow of the July Monarchy; proclamation of the French Second Republic and creation of Provisional Government
March 1848	Uprisings in some German states; granting of a constitution in Prussia
March 1848– June 1849	Revolutions in Italy
April 1848	Revolutions in Vienna, Budapest, Prague
May 1848	Frankfurt Assembly
June 1848	Second revolution in Paris, severely repressed by army troops under General Cavaignac
December 1848	Presidential elections in France; Louis Napoleon wins

Mazzini favored a democratic revolution. In spite of his reputation as a liberal, Pope Pius IX (1846–1878) lost control of Rome and was forced to flee the city. Mazzini became head of the Republic of Rome, created in February 1849.

The French government decided to intervene to protect the pope's interests and sent in troops to defeat the republicans. One of Mazzini's disciples, Giuseppe Garibaldi (1807–1882), returned from exile in South America to undertake the defense of Rome. Garibaldi was a capable soldier who had learned the tactics of guerrilla warfare by joining independence struggles in Brazil and Argentina. Although his legion of poorly armed patriots and soldiers of fortune, known from their attire as the Red Shirts, waged a valiant effort to defend the city from April to June 1849, they were no match for the highly trained French army. French troops restored Pius IX as ruler of the Papal States.

Meanwhile, from August 1848 to the following spring, the Habsburg armies fought and finally defeated each of the revolutions. Austrian success can be explained in part because the various Italian groups of Piedmontese, Tuscans, Venetians, Romans, and Neapolitans continued to identify with their local concerns and lacked coordination and central organization. Both Mazzini and Pius IX had failed to provide the focal point of leadership necessary for a successful national movement. By the fall of 1849, Austria had solved the problems in its own capital and with Italy and Hungary by military repression.

Europe in 1850.   In 1850, Austrians threatened the Prussians with war if they did not give up their plans for a unified Germany. In November of that year, Prussian ministers signed an agreement with their Austrian counterparts in the Moravian city of Olmütz. The convention became known as "the humiliation of Olmütz" because Prussia was forced to accept Austrian dominance or go to war. In every case, military force and diplomatic measures prevailed to defeat the national and liberal movements within the German states and the Austrian Empire.

By 1850, a veneer of calm had spread over central Europe. In Prussia, the peasantry were emancipated from feudal dues, and a constitution, albeit conservative and based on a three-class system, was established. Yet beneath the surface, there was the deeper reality of Austrian decline and Prussian challenge. The great Habsburg Empire needed to call on outside help from Russia to defeat its enemies within. The imperial giant was again on its feet, but for how long? In international relations, Austria's dominance in the German Confederation had diminished, while Prussia assumed greater political and economic power.

The 1848 revolutions spelled the end to the concert of Europe as it had been defined in the peace settlement of 1815. The European powers were incapable of united action to defend established territorial interests.

The revolutions of 1848 failed in part because of the irreconcilable split between moderate liberals and radical democrats. The participation of the masses had frightened members of the middle classes, who were committed to moderate reforms that did not threaten property. In France, working-class revolutionaries had attempted to replace property with labor as the highest social value. Property triumphed. In the face of more extreme solutions, members of the middle class were willing to accept the increased authority of existing rule as a bulwark against anarchy. In December 1848, Prince Louis Napoleon, nephew of the former emperor, was elected president of the

Second Republic by a wide margin. The first truly modern French politician, Louis Napoleon managed to appeal to everyone—workers, bourgeois, royalists, and peasants—by making promises that he did not keep. Severe repression forced radical protest into hiding. The new Bonaparte bided his time, apparently as an ineffectual ruler, until the moment in 1851 when he seized absolute power.

Similar patterns emerged elsewhere in Europe. In Germany, the bourgeoisie accepted the dominance of the old feudal aristocracy as a guarantee of law and order. Repressive government, businessmen were sure, would restore a strong economy. The attempts in 1848 to create new nations based on ethnic identities were in shambles by 1850.

Nearly everywhere throughout Europe, constitutions had been systematically withdrawn with the recovery of the forces of reaction. With the French and Swiss exceptions, the bid for the extension of the franchise failed. The propertied classes remained in control of political institutions. Radicals willing to use violence to press electoral reforms were arrested, killed, or exiled. The leadership of the revolutionary movements had been decapitated, and there seemed no effective opposition to the rise and consolidation of state power. The 1848 revolutions have been called a turning point at which modern history failed to turn. Contemporaries wondered how so much action could have produced so few lasting results.

CONCLUSION

The perception that nothing had changed was wrong. The revolutions of 1848 and subsequent events galvanized whole societies to political action. Conservatives and radicals alike turned toward a new realism in politics. Everywhere governments were forced to adapt to new social realities. No longer could the state ignore economic upheavals and social dislocations if it wanted to survive. Revolutionaries also learned the lesson of repression. The state wielded powerful forces of violence against which nationalists, socialists, republicans, and liberals had all been proved helpless. Organizing, campaigning, and lobbying were newly learned political skills, as was outreach across class lines—from bourgeoisie to peasantry—around common political causes. In these ways, 1848 was a turning point in the formation of a modern political culture.

QUESTIONS FOR REVIEW

1. What problems did European peacemakers confront at the Congress of Vienna, and how did they attempt to resolve the problems?
2. How did industrialization change European families?
3. In what ways were liberalism and nationalism compatible with each other; how were they in conflict?
4. What are the connections between various ideologies—for instance, liberalism, romanticism, or socialism—and the revolutions of 1830 and 1848?

KEY TERMS

Chartism, *p. 674*

*The Communist
Manifesto, p. 667*

Congress of Vienna, *p. 655*

conservatism, *p. 659*

Great Hunger, *p. 652*

Great Reform Bill
of 1832, *p. 673*

Holy Alliance, *p. 658*

liberalism, *p. 660*

"Peterloo" Massacre, *p. 670*

proletariat, *p. 675*

Quadruple Alliance, *p. 658*

Quintuple Alliance, *p. 658*

romanticism, *p. 661*

"social question," *p. 670*

utilitarianism, *p. 660*

DISCOVERING WESTERN CIVILIZATION ONLINE

You can obtain more information about political upheavals and social transformations between 1815 and 1850 at the Websites listed below. See also the Companion Website that accompanies this text, www.ablongman.com/kishlansky, which contains an online study guide and additional resources.

Geographical Tour: Europe in 1815

Internet Modern History Sourcebook: Conservative Order
www.fordham.edu/halsall/mod/modsbook16.html
The site provides documents, discussions, and bibliographies on the Congress of Vienna and charts the development of conservative thought.

The New Ideologies

McMaster University Archive for the History of Economic Thought
socserv.mcmaster.ca/econ/ugcm/3ll3
A site for texts in modern economic theory.

Internet Modern History Sourcebook: Liberalism
www.fordham.edu/halsall/mod/modsbook18.html
A collection of links to primary documents and bibliographies on liberalism.

Internet Modern History Sourcebook: Nationalism
www.fordham.edu/halsall/mod/modsbook17.html

The Nationalism Project
www.nationalismproject.org/
These sites provide links to primary documents and bibliographies of nationalism.

Internet Modern History Sourcebook: Romanticism
www.fordham.edu/halsall/mod/modsbook15.html
This site provides links to primary texts on romantic philosophy and literature.

Voice of the Shuttle
vos.ucsb.edu/index.asp
This comprehensive database for humanities research provides links to general resources, criticism, and primary texts. Type "Romantics" into the search function for resources on romantic philosophy and literature.

Marxist Internet Archive: Marxist Writers
www.marxists.org/archive/index.htm
The site provides translated texts of Marx and Engels as well as other prominent Social Democrats and Communists.

Protest and Revolution

Child Labour in the 19th Century
www.spartacus.schoolnet.co.uk/IRchild.htm
A collection of biographies of reformers and promoters of child labor laws, electronic texts of major child labor legislation, and excerpts from primary sources concerning child labor in nineteenth-century Britain.

The Emancipation of Women: 1750–1920
www.spartacus.schoolnet.co.uk/women.htm
The site contains links to biographies of major figures, essays on the major organizations and societies, and electronic texts of the women's movement in Britain.

Internet Modern History Sourcebook: 1848
www.fordham.edu/halsall/mod/modsbook19.html
The site provides documents, discussions, bibliographies and other links on the revolutions of 1848.

SUGGESTIONS FOR FURTHER READING

Geographical Tour: Europe in 1815

Tim Chapman, *The Congress of Vienna: Origins, Processes, and Results* (New York: Routledge, 1998). A brief, comprehensive survey of how the European powers victorious against Napoleon redrew Europe's frontiers. It follows the impact of the Settlement to its demise in the twentieth century.

Robert Gildea, *Barricades and Borders, Europe 1800–1914* (Oxford: Oxford University Press, 1996). A synthetic overview of economic, demographic, political, and international trends in European society.

Robin Okey, *The Habsburg Monarchy: From Enlightenment to Eclipse* (New York: St. Martin's Press, 2001). An informative survey of Austrian rule from the mid-eighteenth century to the end of World War I, which contains an annotated bibliography and materials drawn from historiographic material in Magyar, Serbo-Croat, Czech, and other eastern European language sources.

The New Ideologies

Jonathan Beecher, *Charles Fourier: The Visionary and His World* (Berkeley: University of California Press, 1986). An intellectual biography that traces the development of Fourier's theoretical perspective and roots it firmly in the social context of nineteenth-century France.

Gareth Stedman Jones, *Languages of Class: Studies in English Working Class History, 1832–1982* (Cambridge: Cambridge University Press, 1983). A series of essays, on topics such as working-class culture and Chartism, that examine the development of class consciousness.

William H. Sewell, Jr., *Work and Revolution in France: The Language of Labor from the Old Regime to 1848* (Cambridge: Cambridge University Press, 1980). Traces nineteenth-century working-class socialism to the corporate culture of Old Regime guilds through traditional values, norms, language, and artisan organizations.

Denis Mack Smith, *Mazzini* (New Haven, CT: Yale University Press, 1994). Mazzini is presented as an important force in legitimizing Italian nationalism by associating it with republicanism and the interests of humanity.

Edward P. Thompson, *The Making of the English Working Class* (New York: Pantheon Books, 1963). A classic in social history that spans the late eighteenth to mid-nineteenth centuries in examining the social, political, and cultural contexts in which workers created their own identity and put forward their own demands.

Protest and Revolution

Maurice Agulhon, *The Republican Experiment, 1848–1852* (Cambridge: Cambridge University Press, 1983). Traces the Revolution of 1848 from its roots to its ultimate failure in 1852 through an analysis of the republican ideologies of workers, peasants, and the bourgeoisie.

Clive Church, *Europe in 1830: Revolution and Political Change* (London: Allen & Unwin, 1983). Considers the origins of the 1830 revolutions within a wider European crisis through a comparative analysis of European regions.

Dieter Dowe, H. G. Haupt, D. Langewiesche, J. Sperber, and D. Higgins, eds., *Europe in 1848: Revolution and Reform* (New York: Berghahn Books, 2001). A collection by leading nineteenth-century European historians.

R. J. W. Evans and Hartmut Pogge von Strandmann, eds., *The Revolutions in Europe, 1848–1849: From Reform to Reaction* (Oxford: Oxford University Press, 2000). A focused collection of articles on the mid-nineteenth-century collapse of authority across Europe.

Alan J. Kidd, *State, Society, and the Poor in Nineteenth-Century England* (New York: St. Martin's Press, 1999). This volume is part of the *Social History in Perspective* series; it provides an overview of poverty in industrializing England, the role of the poor laws, public welfare, and charitable organizations in the nineteenth century.

Catherine J. Kudlick, *Cholera in Post-Revolutionary Paris: A Cultural History* (Berkeley: University of California Press, 1996). Examines the cultural values of ruling elites and demonstrates the role disease played in shaping political life and class identity in nineteenth-century France.

Patricia O'Brien, *The Promise of Punishment: Prisons in Nineteenth-Century France* (Princeton: Princeton University Press, 1982). An overview of the creation of the penitentiary system in nineteenth-century France and the rise of the new science of punishment, criminology, and the eventual appearance of alternatives to the penitentiary system.

Cormac O'Grada and A. Eriksson, *Ireland's Great Famine: Interdisciplinary Essays* (Dublin: University College Dublin Press, 2006). These authors have done extensive work in the Famine Archives of Ireland.

Redcliffe N. Salaman, *The History and Social Influence of the Potato,* revised impression edited by J. G. Hawkes (Cambridge: Cambridge University Press, 1985). The classic study of the potato. A major portion of the work is devoted to the potato famine.

Jonathan Sperber, *Revolutionary Europe, 1780–1850* (New York: Longman, 2000). Considers the revolutions of 1848 within the context of economic and social changes rooted in Old Regime politics and society and from the perspective of the twenty-first century.

For a list of additional titles related to this chapter's topics, please see http://www.ablongman.com/kishlansky.

GLOSSARY

CREDITS

INDEX

GLOSSARY

absolutism   Government in which power was consolidated in the hands of a divinely ordained monarch; typified by reverence for the monarch, weakening of representative institutions, and expansion of military.

agricultural revolution   Changes in the traditional agricultural system during the eighteenth century that included enclosure, introduction of fodder crops, intensified animal husbandry, and commercial market orientation.

alchemy   Study of metals in an effort to find their essence through purification. Medieval alchemists attempted to find precious metals such as silver and gold as the essence of base metals such as lead and iron.

Allies   In World War I, the United States, Great Britain, France, and Russia—the alliance that opposed and defeated the Central Powers of Germany and Austria-Hungary and their allies.

Anabaptists   Part of the radical Reformation, Protestant groups that varied in belief but agreed on the principle of adult baptism.

anarchism   A political movement based on rejection of extant political systems; most prominent in less industrialized Western nations.

Anarcho-syndicalists   Craft workers in France combined local trade union organization with anarchist principles to oppose capitalism and maintain worker solidarity from the end of the nineteenth-century to World War I.

anti-Semitism   Hostility toward and discrimination against Jews.

appeasement   British policy of making concessions to Germany in the 1930s in order to avoid war. It allowed Hitler to militarize the Sudetenland and eventually take all of Czechoslovakia.

April Theses   Lenin's promise to the Russian people and challenge to the Provisional Government to provide peace, land, and bread. These three issues became the rallying cries for the second Russian revolution and for the withdrawal of Soviet Russia from World War I.

Arians   During the early Christological controversies, followers of the Alexandrine theologian, Arius, who believed that Jesus was not equal to God the Father.

Axis Powers   In World War II, the alliance of Germany, Italy, and later Japan.

Baby boom   The dramatic and sustained growth in the birth rate in the United States and western Europe immediately following World War II and lasting until about 1960.

Baghdad Railway   Railway Construction began at the end of the nineteenth-century to link Constantinople with Baghdad, ad was undertaken by the Ottoman abd German Empires. The railway had geopolitical goals for Germany in the Persian Gulf and the Ottoman Empire in Arabia.

balance of power   Distribution of power among nations in alliances so that any one nation is prevented from dominating the others.

Balfour Declaration   The commitment by the British government issued in 1917 to support a Jewish homeland in Palestine.

Berlin Wall   Barrier built by East Germany in 1961 to halt an exodus of skilled professionals to the West; opened in 1989 as a prelude to the reunification of East and West Germany.

Big Three   The British, Soviet, and U.S. leaders who coordinated defeat of Germany and Japan in World War II and negotiated postwar settlements. Referred to Churchill, Stalin, and Roosevelt until 1945; Attlee, Stalin, and Truman by summer 1945.

Black Death   The virulent combination of bubonic, septicemic, and pneumonic plagues that destroyed between one third and one half of the population of Europe between 1347 and 1352.

blitzkrieg   "Lightning war"; the rapid advance accompanied by armored vehicles that typified the German military during World War II.

Bolsheviks   Radical faction of Marxist Social Democrats following a political theory based on necessity of violent revolution. The Bolsheviks came to power with Lenin in November 1917.

bourgeoisie   A French term referring to the commercial classes of Europe after the seventeenth century; primarily an urban class.

Brezhnev Doctrine   Policy of Soviet leader Leonid Brezhnev that approved the use of military intervention in the internal affairs of Soviet allies to prevent counterrevolution.

broad-spectrum gathering   A technique of subsistence common in the Neolithic era that preceded permanent settlement in one place and relied on the exploitation of many seasonal sources of food over a limited area.

cahiers de doléances   Lists of grievances sent with representatives to the French Estates-General in 1789; demonstrated the existence of a widespread public political culture in France.

caliph   The successors of Muhammad who served as political and religious leaders of the Islamic world (see Umma).

capitularies   The written instructions for the implementation of royal directives at the local level produced by the clerics of the Carolingian court.

caravels   Small Portuguese ships developed in the fifteenth-century that were ideal for ocean travel.

Carnival   One of the traditional sixteenth-century festivals, the feasts and carousing of which preceded the onset of Lent.

Carolingian Renaissance   The cultural revival of classical learning sponsored by the emperor Charlemagne. New schools and the copying of manuscripts were among its important achievements.

cartels   Combinations of firms in a given industry to fix prices and establish production quotas.

Cartesianism   Philosophy of René Descartes that rested on the dual existence of mind and matter, a principle that enabled the use of skepticism to create certainty.

Central Powers   Germany and Austria-Hungary during World War I.

chartism   An English working-class reform movement that flourished in the 1830s and 1840s and that demanded universal male suffrage (right to vote), payment for parliamentary service, equal electoral districts, and secret ballots.

chivalry   The ideals of knighthood, most notably fighting, that spread from northern France across Europe in the High Middle Ages.

Christian humanism   The application of the principles of humanistic education, particularly philology, to the documents of Christianity. It resulted in a program of reform through better education.

Christological controversies   The debate about the Christian Trinity (Father, Son, and Holy Spirit) and the relationship between humanity and divinity within it. It caused great division and conflict in the Church and society from the third to the fifth centuries.

city-states   Self-governing political units centered upon an urban area. During the fifteenth and sixteenth centuries, city-states took on various forms of government, including republics such as Venice and oligarchies such as Milan.

civic humanism   The use of humanistic training and education in the service of the state. Many humanists became advisors to princes or republican governments, holding high office and helping to establish policy.

Cold War   The diplomatic and ideological confrontation between the Soviet Union and the United States that began in the aftermath of World War II, dividing the world into two armed camps.

collectivization   Soviet plan under Stalin to create large communal state farms to replace private farms owned by peasants.

coloni   Tenant farmers who worked on the estates of wealthy landowners in the Roman Empire.

colonization   Process by which colonies, or new settlements with links to a parent state, are established.

Columbian Exchange   The transfer of microbes, animals, and plants in the encounters between Europeans and Native Americans during the age of exploration.

Comecon   The Council for Mutual Economic Assistance established in 1949 with bilateral agreements between the Soviet Union and eastern European states. Comecon was Stalin's response to the U.S. Marshall Plan in western Europe, but rather than providing aid it sought to integrate and control the economies of eastern Europe for Soviet gain.

Communist Manifesto, The   A call to arms written in 1848 by Karl Marx and Frederich Engels in which they defined in general terms the class struggle in industrializing Europe.

conciliarism   The movement proposed by church lawyers in which only a general council of bishops could end the Great Schism.

condottiere   A mercenary military leader who sold his services and that of his private army to the highest bidder; used in the wars between the Italian city-states.

Congress of Vienna   A meeting of European powers after the Napoleonic wars in 1815; established a balance of power to preserve the status quo in post-revolutionary Europe.

conquistadores   "Conquerors." Spanish adventurers who led the conquests in the Americas in the sixteenth century.

conscription   Compulsory service of citizens in the army. France was the first modern state to enforce conscription. The ability to draft all able-bodied men was a key component in the Revolutionary and Napoleonic wars.

conservatism   Nineteenth-century ideology that favored tradition and stability and only gradual, or "organic," growth and change.

containment   Cold War policy of resisting the spread of Soviet communism.

Continental System   The economic boycott of England by Napoleon during the wars beginning in 1803.

Counter-Reformation   Catholic response to repel Protestantism.

Crusades   Religious wars of conquest directed against non-Christians and heretics in the eleventh through the thirteenth centuries.

Crystal Palace Exhibition   This international exhibition, held in London in 1851 in a specially built see-through exhibition hall, featured the greatest technological advances of the day and served as a spur for further industrialization.

culture   Those shared beliefs, values, customs, and practices that humans transmit from generation to generation through learning.

cuneiform   A form of writing from Mesopotamia characterized by wedge-shaped symbols pressed into wet clay tablets to record words.

Cycladic culture   The artistically and economically sophisticated culture which flourished on islands in the Aegean Sea during the early and middle Greek Bronze Age (3000–1500 bce).

Cynics   Followers of a Hellenistic Greek philosophy that rejected the world as the source of evil and unhappiness and advocated the reduction of possessions, connections, and pleasures to the absolute minimum.

Dawes Plan   The plan crafted by international financial experts in 1924 under the leadership of the American banker Charles Dawes whose aim was to end inflation and restore economic prosperity to Germany by a reform of the reparations repayment schedule.

Dayton Peace Accords   The peace agreement brokered at the end of 1995 among Bosnians, Croats and Serbs by the United States, which provided U.S. troops to support the peace. The aim was to create a unified country in Bosnia, while recognizing ethnic differences.

Declaratory Act   A statute enacted in England in 1766 that stated that Parliament held sovereign jurisdiction over the North American colonies.

decolonization   Withdrawal of Western nations from colonies in Africa and Asia after World War II.

decurions   Members of the city councils in the Roman Empire. Initially, they were the backbone of the provincial elite but by the third and fourth centuries were crippled by their personal responsibility for provincial taxes.

deists   Those who believed that God created the universe but then did not intervene in its operation.

Delian League   League of Greek cities formed to drive out the Persian invaders. Its leader, Athens, turned it into its own empire.

demesne   Land kept by a medieval lord for his direct profit and worked a specified number of days each week by his peasants.

democracy   Form of government in which the citizens choose their leaders; began in Athens, Greece, in the fifth century b.c.e.

de-Stalinization   Process initiated by Nikita Khrushchev beginning in 1956 that reversed many of Stalin's repressive policies in the Soviet Union.

détente   From the French word meaning a relaxation in tension, cooperation between the two superpowers, the Soviet Union and the United States. This policy was characterized by improved U.S.-Soviet diplomatic relationships in the 1970s to lessen the possibility of nuclear war.

dictator   In the Roman Republic, an official who was granted unlimited power to rule the state for a period up to six months in a time of emergency. Sulla and Caesar both used the dictatorship for political ends.

diplomas   The records of royal grants and decisions produced by clerics in medieval courts.

divine rights of kings   Political theory that held that the institution of monarchy had divine origin and that the monarch functioned as God's representative on earth.

doge   Chief magistrate of the Venetian Republic who served for life.

Eastern Question   The "question" posed by the Great Powers about the future of the Ottoman territories.

Edict of Nantes   The proclamation by Henry IV of France granting limited toleration to Huguenots.

ekklesia   The assembly of all free male Athenian citizens.

emirs   Local military commanders who took control of provincial administration in the Islamic world at the expense of the caliphs by the tenth century.

empiricism   The philosophy propounded by Aristotle which rejected Plato's idea of abstract Forms in favor of practical observation and explanation, building general theories from particular data.

enclosure   In the eighteenth century, the closing off of common and public land within the open field system to foster private landholding.

Enlightenment   Philosophical and intellectual movement that began in Europe during the eighteenth century. The movement was characterized by a wave of new learning, especially in the sciences and mathematics, and the application of reason to solve society's problems.

entrepôt   A place where goods were brought for storage before being exchanged; a commercial concept originated by the Dutch.

Epicureans   Those who adhered to a Hellenistic Greek philosophy that the world was a random collection of atoms (atheistic and materialistic), and that one must pursue pleasure, but only in moderation as excess causes pain.

equestrians   In the early Roman Republic, the equestrians were one of the richest classes in the Roman army, those who could afford to maintain a horse. By the late republic, their role expanded into banking and commerce.

Estates-General   An official body assembled periodically by the medieval French state, consisting of representatives from three separate groups or "estates": those who prayed (the Church), those who fought (the aristocracy), and those who worked (commoners). Long in disuse by the monarch, it was convened by Louis XVI in 1789.

ethnic cleansing   Term introduced in the Balkan war of the 1990s to describe the systematic killing and forcible removal of one ethnic group by another.

ethnos   Large rural territorial units in the Dark Age and Archaic Greece focused around a central religious sanctuary and dominated by a local oligarchy, such as in Aetolia.

Etruscans   Peoples native to Italy who influenced the formation of the Roman state.

eugenics   An ersatz scientific theory that promoted the improvement of the human race through selective breeding.

eunomia   The good order and obedience to the law which was the ideal of Sparta's militaristic society.

euro   Common currency of the European Union; accepted as common currency by all members of the European Union except the United Kingdom.

European Economic Community (EEC)   Formed in 1957 by Belgium, the Netherlands, Luxembourg, Italy, France, and West Germany to provide a single, integrated European market. Also known as the Common Market.

European Union (EU)   Formed in 1992 to succeed the European Community in terms of economic integration; members share defensive, social, and economic policies as well.

extraterritoriality   Exempted all foreigners in China from Chinese legal jurisdiction; practiced within foreign "spheres of influence" in China.

Fabians   Members of a late nineteenth-century socialist movement in Britain who advocated gradual reform rather than revolution and supported the Labour party.

Factory Act (1833)   British Parliamentary legislation that prohibited factory work by children under age nine, provided two hours of daily education for factory children, and limited labor for adults to twelve hours each day.

fascism   Rooted in mass politics of the late-nineteenth century, a totalitarian political system that glorifies the state and subordinates the individual to the state's needs. First emerging in Italy after World War I, fascism appeared in virtually all European countries, but particularly Germany.

feudalism   Anachronistic term used by early modern lawyers to describe medieval relations of vassalage.

fief   A parcel of productive land along with the serfs and privileges attached to it granted by a lord to a knightly follower (vassal) in return for loyalty and military service.

Final Solution   The term used by the Third Reich to refer to the extermination of all people deemed unfit; resulted in the execution of 11 million men, women, and children, 6 million of them Jews.

first triumvirate   Political alliance between Pompey, Crassus, and Caesar to share power in the Roman Republic.

fodder crops   Crops that were grown not for human consumption but to improve the nutrients in the soil. Some, such as turnips, were also used as animal feed.

Forms   In Plato's philosophy, the perfect ideal that underlies all worldly objects. In recollecting them from one's previous existence one communes with all that is good, true, and beautiful.

Fourteen Points   U.S. President Woodrow Wilson's idealistic set of guidelines drawn up as part of the peace process whose goal was to create a lasting peace after World War I.

French wars of religion   Violent clashes between French Catholics and Calvinists (Huguenots) from 1562–1598.

Fronde   An aristocratic revolution in France beginning in 1648 during the minority of Louis XIV, which was initiated by the tax policies of the minority government under Cardinal Mazarin.

futurists   Artists and intellectuals of the late nineteenth and early twentieth century who wished to create a new culture free from traditional Western civilization. Futurists lionized technology, the masses, violence, and upheaval.

general strike   a central concept for anarcho-syndicalism, this strike action had as a primary purpose the symbolic promotion of worker solidarity by means of a mass protest of limited duration which could mobilize workers from a variety of sectors. Unlike a strike called by a union, general strikes were of a short and defined period of time and were not aimed at improved wages or better working conditions, but were intended to signal the end of capitalism.

generation gap   The baby boom following World War II resulted in a generation that came of age in the 1960s. The gap refers to the divergence in values between a large cohort of adolescents and young adults and their parents that resulted in more liberal values and socio-cultural mores.

Geopolites   Geopolitics, or the politics of geography, is based on the recognition that certain areas of the world are valuable for political reasons—for example the Suez canal was important to Great Britain because of its economic interests in India.

Girondins   French revolutionary faction that was more moderate than the Jacobins.

glasnost   A Russian term meaning openness; one of the programs of reform initiated by Mikhail Gorbachev in the 1980s.

Glorious Revolution   Change of government in England in 1688–1689 when the Catholic monarch James II was replaced by the Dutch ruler William of Orange. Called "glorious" because it supposedly was accomplished without bloodshed.

Gnostics   An early Christian group that interpreted scripture as gnosis, or secret wisdom, and believed that Jesus had no human element. They were opposed by many bishops.

Golden Bull   The edict of emperor Charles IV in 1356 recognizing that German princes and kings were autonomous rulers.

Great Chain of Being   A hierarchic model of social organization common in the fifteenth and sixteenth centuries in which all parts of creation held a specific place in a divinely ordered universe.

Great Depression   Devastation of the global economy that began in 1929 with the U.S. stock market crash and lasted through the 1930s.

Great Fear   The term refers to that period in the summer of 1789 when French peasants, gripped by fear, revolted, attacked the chateaux of French nobility and burned documents that legally bound peasants to taxes and service.

Great Patriotic War   The term by which the Russian people referred to World War II, reflecting their sense of dedication, nationalism and sacrifice in waging the war.

Great Purge   A series of executions between 1934 and 1938 in the Soviet Union that removed all of Joseph Stalin's political enemies.

Great Reform Bill of 1832   An extension of the right to vote in England to men of the middle class that resulted in a 50 percent increase in those eligible to vote.

Great Schism   The conflict (1378–1415) between two sets of rival popes based in Rome and Avignon that divided the loyalties of states and individuals across Europe.

guilds   Professional associations of merchants or artisans that offer protection of members and regulation of a particular trade or craft.

hadith   The written form of the Sunnah, practices established by the prophet Muhammad that guide the interpretation of the Qur'an.

Hanseatic League   A commercial and political alliance of northern German towns established in the late fourteenth century to monopolize the grain and fish trade of the Baltic Sea.

Haussmannization   The radical rebuilding of the city of Paris during the Second Empire directed by the Prefect of the Seine Baron Haussmann. Wide avenues, public parks and elegant apartment buildings defined the transformation of the city of Paris from narrow medieval streets into one of the world's most beautiful cities.

Hijra   In early Islam, the journey undertaken by Muhammad from Mecca to Medina in 622 in order to govern Medina and calm its internal political dissension.

Holocaust   During World War II, mass extermination of Jews by the Nazis under Adolph Hitler.

Holy Alliance   Prussia, Austria, and Russia, under the leadership of tsar Alexander I, agreed to protect the peace and the Christian religion following the Congress of Vienna.

honestiores   The privileged classes of the later Roman Empire: senators, municipal gentry, and the military.

hoplites   In Archaic Greece, armed infantry soldiers.

Huguenots   French Calvinists led by Henry of Navarre. Huguenots were victims of the St. Bartholomew's Day Massacre, a slaughter of numerous Protestants in Paris in 1572 during the French wars of religion.

Humanists   Scholars who studied and taught the humanities, the skills of disciplines like philology—the art of language—and rhetoric—the art of expression; concentrated on ancient texts.

humiliores   The lower classes of the later Roman Empire whose status declined from the period of the Pax Romana and who suffered disproportionately from the tax increases of the period.

Hundred Years' War   A series of military engagements between England and France (1337–1452) over territorial and dynastic rivalries.

Hussites   Followers of Jan Hus who attacked the sale of indulgences and German political dominance in the kingdom of Bohemia. After his execution, they led a partially successful revolt.

iconoclasts   Breakers of icons; opponents of the mediating use of icons (religious images) in worship. Most emperors supported this faction in eighth- and early ninth-century Byzantium.

iconodules   Venerators of icons; the ecclesiastical faction that resisted the iconoclasts. Most of the people and lesser clergy were iconodules.

icons   Sacred images.

imperium   The powers conferred on magistrates by the Roman people: the supreme power to command, to execute the law, and to impose the death penalty.

indulgences   Remission of temporal punishment in Purgatory due to one's sins. Originally granted for performing pious acts, but later acquired through a grant to the church treasury. In the sixteenth century, indulgences were sold to raise money for the papacy; a critical issue in the Lutheran reform.

industrialization   Process by which production becomes mechanized.

Industrial Revolution   Sustained period of economic growth and change brought on by technological innovations in the process of manufacturing; began in Britain in the mid-eighteenth century.

intendants   Officials appointed by the central government in France to oversee the local administration of the regional aristocracy; a critical component of the centralization of the French state.

Irish Great Hunger   The famine of 1845 was caused by a potato blight that resulted in the decline by 25 percent of the Irish population within five years.

iron curtain   The term coined by former British Prime Minister Winston Churchill to describe the ideological divide between western and eastern Europe after World War II.

Jacobins   One of the political factions of the French National Convention that seized the initiative provided by the sans-culottes to take control of the radical revolution in the late eighteenth century; led by Maximilien Robespierre.

Jacquerie   The revolt of French peasants against the aristocracy and crown in 1358. It was part of the struggle for rights caused by the labor shortage after the Black Death.

jihads   Holy wars waged by Muslims against their religious enemies.

jingoism   Use of public opinion to stir support for one's own nation and hatred for another nation; used extensively by political leaders to justify imperial expansion.

joint-stock companies   Business enterprises that raise capital by selling shares to individuals who receive dividends on their investments.

Kellogg-Briand Pact   An agreement, named for the two men who devised it—the U.S. Secretary of State Frank B. Kellogg and the French Foreign Minister Aristide Briand, signed by 23 nations in 1928 whose purpose was an idealistic renunciation of war.

kouros   Nude statues of young men that were a common subject in Archaic art. The stiff posture demonstrates the influence of Egyptian sculpture.

Kristallnacht   "Crystal night" in German; refers to the night of 9 November 1938 when mobs directed by the Nazis destroyed the homes, businesses, and synagogues of German Jews.

Kulturkampf   "Struggle for civilization"; legislation of the German Empire against the Catholic Church in the 1870s.

laissez-faire   An economic theory that required government to cease interference with private economic activity; Adam Smith and the Physiocrats were its leading proponents.

latifundia   The vast rural estates of the Roman patricians which were worked by slaves or free but dependent tenant farmers.

lay investiture   The practice by which kings and emperors appointed bishops and invested them with the symbols of their office. It led to conflict between the Papacy and the emperors in the eleventh century.

League of Nations   A global, supra-national organization formed following World War I (1919) for the purpose of promoting the peaceful resolution of disputes among member nations. Even though Germany in 1926 and the Soviet Union in 1934 were permitted to join, the failure of the United States to become a member of the League undermined its effectiveness.

Lebensraum   "Living room"; one of Hitler's foreign policy objectives to extend the borders of Germany in eastern and central Europe.

lectio divina   In monastic life, the process of reading and studying the Old and New Testaments that formed an important part of each day's activities.

liberalism   A political philosophy based on freedom of the individual and the corruptibility of authority; associated with constitutional reform in the first half of the nineteenth century.

Linear B   A syllabic form of writing from the late Greek Bronze Age which preserves the earliest known form of Greek. It was used by Mycenaean elites almost entirely for record-keeping.

linear perspective   A technique developed in painting to give a flat surface the appearance of depth and dimension.

Long Parliament   An English Parliament that officially met from 1640 to 1653. It forced reforms under Charles I, defeated the royal armies during the English Civil War, and tried and executed the king.

Luddites   Workers who attacked machines in order to protest the loss of their skilled jobs.

Ludendorff Offensive   The final German offensive of World War I, named after the general who devised it, launched against the Allies on the Western Front in March 1918. The offensive ultimately failed.

maat   In Egyptian thought, the ideal state of the universe and of society which the pharaoh was supposed to uphold.

Maginot Line   A system of defensive fortifications built by France along its German border in the 1920s and 1930s.

Magna Carta   The "great charter" limiting royal power that King John was forced to sign in 1215.

manses   Farms worked by slaves, serfs, and freemen in the Middle Ages.

March on Rome   The takeover of political power in Rome by the fascists in Italy on 28 October 1922, followed by similar takeovers in Milan and Bologna.

Marchfield   The assembly of all free warriors in the early Germanic kingdoms in which the king's authority was all-powerful.

Marshall Plan   The U.S. economic aid program for European countries after World War II; intended to establish U.S. economic influence in European markets.

mercantilism   A popular state economy of the seventeenth century; involved bullionism, protective tariffs, and monopolies.

metics   The non-Athenian residents of Athens who comprised about half of the free population of the city. They were active in commerce and banking.

Minoan civilization   The culture of Crete in the Middle Bronze Age (2000–1550 b.c.e.) in which elites based at great palaces, such as Knossos, dominated the island politically, economically, and religiously.

minuscule   New style of handwriting developed in the Carolingian Renaissance to preserve texts; later adopted as standard script.

Mishnah   In Jewish law, the oral interpretation of the Torah (scripture) which was developed by the Pharisees and later developed into an extensive written body of legal interpretation.

missi dominici   Teams of counts and bishops that examined the state of each county in the Carolingian Empire on behalf of the king.

monasticism   The life of monks devoted to God, from the fourth century onwards, either as part of communal organization or in solitary life. Monasticism began in Egypt as a rejection of the worldliness of civilization.

monopoly   Exclusive control of a market or industry; a form of economic regulation in which special privileges are granted in return for financial considerations and an agreement to abide by the rules set out by the state.

Moujahedeen   An Arabic word referring to Muslim holy warriors fighting for Islam in various countries, including the Balkans and Chechnya, in the late 20th and 21st century.

Museum   The shrine to the Muses in Hellenistic Alexandria to which was added the Library containing all the great works of Greek literature and learning.

Mycenaean   Late Greek Bronze Age civilization that arose ca. 1600 b.c.e. at Mycenae and that encompassed the Greek mainland and parts of Asia Minor. Myceneans developed the Linear B script.

mystery cults   Religions that promised immediate, personal contact with a deity that would bring immortality.

Napoleonic Code   The recodification of French law carried out during Napoleon's reign.

National Assembly   That body formed on 17 June 1789 by the French Third Estate when it changed its name to the National Assembly, laying claim to being the true representatives of the French nation.

nationalities problem   The existence of numerous ethnic minorities within the borders of the Soviet Union leading to demands for self-determination and political independence.

natural selection   A theory advanced by Charles Darwin that accounted for evolution of species; a realist scientific approach.

Navigation Acts   English economic legislation providing that colonial goods could only be shipped in English ships.

Nazism   National Socialism; German variant of fascism.

Neolithic era   The New Stone Age (8000–6500 b.c.e.) in which modern man developed agriculture and the first villages.

Neoplatonism   Use of the writings of Plato to advance modern ideas about science, particularly mathematics and the health sciences.

New Economic Policy (NEP)   A state-planned economic policy in the Soviet Union between 1921 and 1928; based on agricultural productivity, it required set payments from peasants; surpluses could be sold on the free market.

new imperialism   Imperialism practiced by European countries after 1870 that was, in essence, the domination by industrial powers over the non-industrial world. Distinguished from the earlier acquisition of territory, new imperialism took a variety of forms including territorial occupations, colonization, exploitation of labor and raw materials, and development of economic spheres of influence.

New Monarchies   The more centralized European governments of western Europe created in the fifteenth and sixteenth centuries.

New Piety   An aspect of the Roman Catholic reform movement; originated among the Brethren of the Common Life with an emphasis on simplicity and more personalized religious practice.

nominalism   The doctrine of William of Ockham that argued that human reason could not aspire to certain truth.

North Atlantic Treaty Organization (NATO)   An organization founded in 1949 the members of which signed a defense pact to protect those countries bordering the North Atlantic.

nuclear club   The group of nations in possession of atomic weapons, originally consisting of the United States and the Soviet Union. By 1974, the nuclear club included Great Britain, France, the People's Republic of China, and India.

Old Regime   The old order; political and social system of France in the eighteenth century before the French Revolution.

oligarchy   Government by an elite few.

optimates   The traditionalist Roman political faction that succeeded the Gracchi and sought to preserve the senatorial oligarchy against the populares.

Orthodox Christianity   The official "right-teaching" faith of Constantinople as opposed to the heterodox peoples on the margins of the Byzantine Empire.

ostracism   A practice in Athenian democracy by which anyone deemed to threaten the constitution could, by popular vote, be exiled for ten years without the loss of property.

Pact of Steel   A military alliance formed between Hitler's Germany and Mussolini's Italy in May 1939 pledging cooperation and military and economic coordination.

Paleolithic era   The Old Stone Age (600,000–10,000 b.c.e.) in which advanced primates developed into Neanderthals and also modern man. They hunted food or collected it by gathering.

Paris Commune   Created in 1871 in the aftermath of the Franco-Prussian War; crushed by the national army after a brief struggle; symbol of revolution for radical politicians, including Marxists.

parlements   Provincial courts in France; the Parlement of Paris, the main law court of the state, was the most powerful of these.

parties   A form of political organization in which members of the British parliament divided into groups with identifiable interests. Whigs and Tories were the first political parties.

Patent of Toleration   An edict of Joseph II of Austria in 1781 that granted freedom of worship to Protestants and members of the Greek Orthodox Church, in addition to Roman Catholics.

paterfamilias   The male head of household in the Roman family. His power was absolute, including the power of life and death.

patricians   Leaders of the gentes, or clans, in early Roman society.

Pax Romana   The two centuries of peace and stability in the early Roman Empire inaugurated by the emperor Augustus.

Peace of Paris of 1856   The peace treaty that ended the Crimean War whereby Russia relinquished its claim as protector of Christians in Turkey and ceased interference in the Ottoman Empire; the British gained the neutralization of the Black Sea; Turkish control was reestablished over the mouth of the Danube; Russia gave up a portion of Bessarabia; and the Danubian Principalities were placed under guarantee of Great Britain and France.

perestroika   A Russian term meaning restructuring; part of Mikhail Gorbachev's attempts to reform the Soviet government and economy in the 1980s.

Peterloo Massacre   In August 1819, the English army troops policing a political crowd gathered near Manchester, England, lost control resulting in the deaths of 11 and the injury of hundreds of others.

phalanx   A tightly ordered and well-disciplined body of elite Greek warriors in heavy armor that attacked in close formation with long spears.

philology   The art of language; one of the most important aspects of humanist studies, based on models of ancient texts.

philosophes   A French term for the intellectuals of the eighteenth-century Enlightenment. Voltaire, Diderot, and Condorcet were leading philosophes.

phony war   The period between 3 September 1939, when Great Britain and France declared war on Germany, and the spring of 1940, when the German offensive against France commenced armed combat between France and Germany. In this strange interlude, while civilian populations waited for attack, an attitude of defeatism grew in France.

Physiocrats   A group of French thinkers who subscribed to the view that land was wealth and thus argued that improvements in agricultural activity should take first priority in state reforms.

pictograms   The earliest form of writing in Mesopotamia, ca. 3500 b.c.e., in which pictures represented particular objects, such as animals.

Pietà   A painting or sculpture of Mary mourning the dead Jesus. The most famous was carved by Michelangelo and is in St. Peter's Basilica.

plebs   Families not organized into gentes, or clans, in early Roman society. The lower classes.

pogroms   State-organized massacres of Jews.

polis   The city-state of Archaic and Classical Greece, particularly found on the shores of the Aegean. A city formed the center of government (tyranny, oligarchy, or democracy) and of religious life with temples on its citadel (Acropolis).

politiques   During the sixteenth-century French wars of religion, a group of Catholics who joined with Huguenots to demand a practical settlement of the wars.

populares   The Roman political faction that succeeded the Gracchi whose leaders appealed to the masses as a source of power.

Popular Front   Socialist governments established in both France and Spain in the 1930s; the French version failed to solve the Depression and was voted out of office; the creation of a socialist republic in Spain initiated a civil war.

Pragmatic Sanction   The document that attempted to secure the recognition of Maria Theresa as heiress to the Habsburg possessions of Charles VI

Prague Spring   Popular uprising and reform movement in 1968 Czechoslovakia, ended by Soviet invasion in August 1968.

predestination   A fundamental principle of Calvin's theology: the belief that all Christians are predestined to either heaven or hell from the act of creation.

presbyters   The priests of the early Christian tradition who were subordinated to bishops as hierarchy developed in the Church.

Price Revolution   The dramatic price inflation of the fifteenth and sixteenth centuries; caused by monetary debasement and the influx of bullion from the New World.

princeps   "First citizen"; the title assumed by the emperor Augustus to reassure public opinion by preserving the traditional constitutional forms.

Proclamation of the German Empire   The creation in 1871 of the nation-state of Germany by uniting the 38 German states into a single national entity.

proletariat The industrial working class.

pronatalism State programs implemented after the Second World War to encourage women to have larger families.

Puritans English Protestants who sought to purify the Church of England of all traces of Catholicism.

putting-out system Mobilization of the rural labor force for commercial production of large quantities of manufactured goods; raw materials put out to homes of workers where manufacture took place.

quadrivium Part of a medieval liberal arts education that included arithmetic, geometry, astronomy, and music.

Quadruple Alliance Pact signed in 1815 by the four powers who defeated Napoleon—Great Britain, Austria, Russia, and Prussia—for the purpose of protecting Europe against future French aggression.

quinine An important nineteenth-century medical advance derived from cinchona that was an effective treatment for malaria; it permitted large numbers of Europeans to travel without risking death and disease.

raison d'état Reason of state; placing the needs of the nation above the privileges of its most important groups.

realism An artistic and literary style that criticized industrialized society and rejected bourgeois concepts of morality.

Realpolitik Pragmatic political theory advanced by Otto von Bismarck; ruthless pursuit by any means, including illegal and violent ones, in the interests of the state.

reconquista The Christian reconquest of the Iberian peninsula from the Spanish Muslims or Moors; completed in 1492 under Ferdinand and Isabella.

Reformation A movement to reform and purify the Catholic Church that resulted in the creation of new religious denominations in Europe collectively known as Protestants.

Reichstag The national legislative body of the German Empire; elected by universal male suffrage.

Reign of Terror The period from 1793 to 1794 when Maximilien Robespierre assumed leadership of the Committee of Public Safety and oversaw the revolutionary tribunals that sentenced about 40,000 people to execution.

Renaissance A "rebirth" of classical learning and emphasis on humanity that characterized the period between 1350 and 1550.

revisionism A German socialist school that favored gradual reform through the parliamentary system; led by Edouard Bernstein.

rhetoric The art of expression and persuasion.

Risorgimento The nineteenth-century movement to reunite Italy.

robot Labor service that peasants owed to their lord; more typical in eastern Europe after the fifteenth century.

romanticism An artistic and literary tradition based on emotions rather than the intellect; rejection of classical traditions in favor of "nature"; often associated with nationalism.

salons Informal social gatherings during the Enlightenment, frequently organized by women, in which topics of intellectual interest were discussed.

samizdat Self-published, privately circulated manuscripts; chief vehicle for circulating information among dissidents in the Soviet Union.

sans-culottes Literally "those without knee-breeches"; working-class revolutionaries who initiated the radical stage of the French revolution in 1792.

Schlieffen Plan The strategy of the German high command at the outset of World War I, predicated on knocking France out of the war.

Scholastic method The combination of legal analysis from the new university at Bologna with Aristotelian logic; established by Peter Abelard in the twelfth century.

Schuman Plan In 1950 France and West Germany joined together to pool all their coal and steel resources. The plan is named for the French Foreign Minister Robert Schuman who was influenced by the economic vision of Jean Monney. The following year the European Coal and Steel Community, predecessor to the European Union, was formed.

scientific revolution In the sixteenth and seventeenth centuries, a period of new scientific inquiry, experimentation, and discovery that resulted in a new understanding of the universe based on mathematical principles and led to the creation of the modern sciences, particularly astronomy and physics.

scramble for Africa The colonization of Africa as part of the new imperialism. This domination of Africa by Germany, Britain, and France ended with the crisis at Fashoda.

second triumvirate Alliance of Octavian, Mark Anthony, and Lepidus following the assassination of Julius Caesar to defeat the assassins and control the Roman Empire.

seigneur Manor lord responsible for maintaining order, administering justice, and arbitrating disputes among tenants.

Semi-nomadic south A society that remains at fixed locations for extended periods but also remains migratory.

serfs Peasants of degraded status and very limited legal rights who were dependent on the lords in the High Middle Ages. They formed the great bulk of the population.

**Shi`ites** Muslims who follow the tradition that legitimate leadership of Islam can only come through the descendants of `Ali, whom they regard as the last orthodox caliph.

social Darwinists Those who applied the theory of evolutionary biology, particularly the concept of "survival of the fittest," to human society.

social question The question of how to treat poverty became a pressing issue for European societies between 1830 and 1850. The social question revolved around what the role of government and the role of private individuals should be in addressing social misery.

sola fide A fundamental principle of Luther's theology: justification of Christians by faith alone.

"Socialism in one country" The slogan employed by Joseph Stalin in the 1920s to justify his plans for rapid industrialization as a means of preserving socialism in the Soviet Union.

sola scriptura By the word alone; emphasis on scriptural authority in preference to the canons of the Church, a fundamental element of Luther's theology.

Solidarity A non-communist Polish labor organization founded by Lech Walesa in the Gdansk shipbuilding yards; legalized in 1989 as a political movement, it won a victory in the first Polish democratic elections.

Sophists Professional teachers in fifth-century Greece who traveled from city to city instructing students, for a fee, in rhetoric, the art of persuasion.

Soviets Councils of workers in Russia formed after 1905 that became one center of power after the overthrow of the tsar; source of power for Lenin and Bolsheviks.

Spanish Armada The Spanish fleet sent in 1588 to transport troops from the Low Countries for an invasion of England; defeated by the English fleets of Elizabeth I.

Spanish Inquisition An ecclesiastical tribunal utilized to combat heresy and non-Christians; used by Ferdinand and Isabella against the conversos, or converted Jews of Spain.

spheres of influence Diplomatic term used to connote territorial influence or control of weaker nations not necessarily occupied by the more powerful ones. The term was first used to explain one kind of control of western European powers in the 1800s during African imperialism, and was later used to describe European and Japanese territorial control and influence over markets in China at the end of the nineteenth century.

"Spirit of Locarno" A series of treaties, signed in Locarno, Switzerland in 1925 by Germany, France, Great Britain, Belgium and Italy, and intended to promote cooperation and respect for borders, promoted an atmosphere of good will in the international arena known as the "spirit of Locarno."

Stoics Followers of the Hellenistic Greek philosophy propounded by Zeno, which teaches that orderliness is proper to the universe and that happiness derives from embracing one's divinely ordained role and unhappiness from rejecting it.

strategoi Generals, the military commanders of themes in the Byzantine Empire. They were responsible for civil and military administration.

suffragettes Militant members of the English feminist movement led by Emmeline Pankhurst who engaged in acts of violence against private property in order to secure the vote.

sunnah In Islamic theology, the practices established by the prophet Muhammad. They were initially preserved by oral tradition.

Sunnis The majority tradition of Islam that accepts that political succession should be based on consensus, the existing political order, and a leader's merits.

synod A meeting of bishops called to debate Church policy, such as that at Whitby in 664, which established the customs of the Roman Church among Angles and Saxons.

Talmud Rabbinic discussions of the Mishna and its interpretation complied around 500 C.E.

Table of Ranks Official state hierarchy in Russia under Peter the Great that established the social position or rank of individuals according to categories of military service, civil service, and ownership of landed estates.

tetrarchy Rule by four; Diocletian's attempt to regulate the suggestion of the Roman Empire by dividing the empire into eastern and western parts, with both an augustus and a junior emperor, or caesar, ruling each part.

Taliban The fundamentalist Muslim ruling group that controlled Afghanistan for the period between 1996 to 2001, and currently waging guerilla actions against Afghanistan's democratic government. A rigid sect, the Taliban follows strict observance, denying rights to women.

Thermidorian Reaction Revolt beginning in July 1794 (the month of Thermidor) against the radicalism of the French Revolution, leading to the downfall and execution of Robespierre and the end of the Reign of Terror.

Third Estate Branch of the French Estates-General consisting of the bourgeoisie and the working classes; separated from the other estates to form the National Assembly in 1789.

Third Reich "The Third Empire"; Hitler's government, established after 1933.

third world The former colonies of European and Asian imperialism; sought to separate themselves from European economic control after independence; operated in the United Nations as a non-aligned bloc.

Thirty Years' War War lasting from 1618–1648.

three-field system An efficient agricultural system in which one-third of the land was planted in autumn with wheat or rye, one-third remained fallow, and one-third was planted in spring with a crop that added nutrients to the soil.

Time of Troubles The period of disruption within Russia following the death of Ivan the Terrible; only ended with the Polish invasion of Russia.

Torah The body of law in Hebrew scripture.

Tories Members of a political party in England that in the seventeenth century defended the principle of hereditary succession to the crown; in opposition to the Whigs. The Tories sought to preserve the traditional political structure and supported the authority of the Anglican church.

total war War that requires mobilization of the civilian population in addition to the military; typified by centralized governments with limits on economy and civil rights.

Treaty of Brest-Litovsk The Treaty between Russia and Germany signed in March 1918 whereby Soviet Russia withdrew from World War I.

Treaty of Rapallo An economic treaty signed between Weimar Germany and Soviet Russia in 1922 intended to promote economic recovery and trade.

Treaty of Tordesillas A 1494 agreement that recognized Portugal's claims to Brazil, but gave all of the remainder of the New World to Spain

Treaty of Versailles Peace settlement with Germany at the end of World War I; included the War Guilt Clause fixing blame on Germany for the war and requiring massive reparations.

triangular trade A three-way trade system during the seventeenth century involving the shipment of calicoes to Africa for slaves who were transported to the East Indies in exchange for sugar, which was shipped to Europe.

Tripartite Pact In September 1940 Japan, Germany and Italy promised mutual support against aggression and endorsed each other's expansionist aims in Europe and Asia.

Triple Alliance An alliance founded in 1882 between Germany, Austria-Hungary, and Italy at Germany's instigation for the purpose of securing mutual support on the European continent.

Triple Entente Alliance founded in 1907 between France, Britain, and Russia. With the defection of Russia from the Three Emperors' League, it hemmed in Germany on both eastern and western borders.

trivium The basic education in cathedral schools of the Middle Ages: grammar, rhetoric, and logic.

tyrants Rulers who had seized power illegally. Tyrannies replaced oligarchies in many *poleis* in Archaic Greece, such as at Corinth and Athens. The term did not have the negative connotations it does today, as many tyrants were popular leaders welcomed by their subjects.

Umma The community of all believers in the Islamic faith. Initially, it was both a political and religious supertribe of Arabs.

universitas The guilds of students that formed the first true universities from the twelfth century onwards.

utilitarianism Jeremy Bentham's philosophical plan to ensure social harmony through measurement of pleasure and pain or the greatest happiness of the greatest number; a liberal philosophy.

vassals Knights sworn to fealty or loyalty to a lord; in return the lord granted the vassal a means of support, or fief.

Velvet revolutions the term refers to the peaceful transformations from communist rule to democratic governments that occurred in 1989 in Poland, Hungary and Czechoslovakia.

Victorian Compromise The balance between freedom and protectionism achieved by liberal parliamentary reform during the reign of Queen Victoria.

Villanovans Peoples of the first Iron Age culture in Italy (1000–800 b.c.e.), which was based in the north. They made iron tools and weapons and placed the ashes of their dead in large urns.

War Guilt Clause As part of the Treaty of Versailles of 1919, the Clause assigned sole responsibility for World War I to Germany and stated that Germany must be made to pay: "Compensation will be made by Germany for all damage done to the civilian population of the Allies and their property by the aggression of Germany by land, by sea and from the air." Reparations resulted from this assignment of guilt, which the German people considered punitive.

Warsaw Pact Defensive alliance organization formed in 1955 by Albania, Bulgaria, Romania, Czechoslovakia, Hungary, Poland, East Germany, and the Soviet Union. The alliance served as a strategic buffer zone against NATO forces.

Weimar Republic German government founded at the end of the First World War; used by German general staff as scapegoat for German defeat and harsh peace terms; overthrown in 1933.

welfare state The tendency of post–World War II states to establish safety nets for citizens in areas of birth, sickness, old age, and unemployment.

wergeld In Germanic society, the payment in reparation for crimes in place of blood vengeance. Tribal leaders used it to reduce internal hostilities.

Whigs Members of a political party in England that in the seventeenth century supported the Protestant succession and a broad-based Protestantism and advocated a constitutional monarchy that limited royal power; in opposition to the Tories. The Whigs were later identified with social and parliamentary reform.

Young Plan The plan devised by the American businessman Owen Young in 1929 that replaced the Dawes Plan and transferred $100 million to Germany to assist in reparations repayments.

zemstvos Local elected assemblies in Russia during the reign of Alexander II; representatives elected by landowners, townspeople, and peasants.

ziggurat Babylonian tiered towers (or step pyramids) from ca. 2000 b.c.e. that were dedicated to gods and stood near temples. They were among the most important buildings of Babylonian cities.

Zimmermann note Arthur Zimmermann, the German foreign minister during World War I sent a telegram, or "note," in support of Mexico's territorial claims against the United States in New Mexico, Arizona and Texas in exchange for Mexico's support of Germany in the war. As a result of the interception and publication of this note, the United States declared war against Germany in April 1917.

Zionism A program initiated by Theodor Herzl to establish an independent Jewish state in Palestine.

Zollverein A unified trading zone created by Prussia in which member states adopted the liberal Prussian customs regulations; an attempt to overcome the fragmented nature of the German economy.

Zoroastrianism A monotheistic religion founded by Zoroaster in sixth-century b.c.e. Persia that emphasized the personal choice between good (light) and evil (darkness).

CREDITS

DOCUMENT CREDITS

Chapter 11
"On the Family": by Leon Battista Alberti in *The Family in Renaissance Florence* by Renee Watkins. Reprinted by permission of Renee Watkins.

Chapter 12
"The Halls of Montezuma": From Bernal Diaz Chronicles.

"The Kingdom of France": From Claude de Seyssel, *The Monarch of France* translated by J. H. Hexter and edited by Donald R. Kelley pp. 38–39, 48–54, 56–57. Copyright © 1981 by Yale University Press. All rights reserved.

Chapter 13
"A Dutch Wit": From *In Praise of Folly* by Erasmus.

Chapter 14
"Cannibals": Excerpts from Donald M. Frame, translator, *The Complete Essays of Montaigne.* Copyright © 1958 by the Board of Trustees of the Leland Stanford Junior University. All rights reserved.

"War Is Hell": Translated by A. T. S. Goodrick, from *The Adventurous Simplicissmus.*

Chapter 15
"The Peasants' Revolt": From Readings in European History.

"A Feminine Perspective": From Arcangela Tarabotti, "Innocence Undone," translated by Brendan Dooley. Reprinted by permission of Brendan Dooley.

"The Devil's Due": From "Medieval Witchcraft" in *Translations and Reprints from the Original Sources of European History*, Volume III. Reprinted by permission of The University of Pennsylvania Press.

Chapter 17
"Stargazing": From *Movement of the Earth* by Thomas S. Kuhn.

"The Telescope": From *Discoveries and Opinions of Galileo* by Galileo Galilei, translated by Stillman Drake. Copyright © 1957 by Stillman Drake. Reprinted by permission of Doubleday, a division of Random House, Inc.

"Descartes Experiments": From *Discourse on Method and Related Writings* by Rene Descartes, translated by Desmond Clarke (Penguin Classics, 1999). Copyright © 1999. Reproduced by permission of Penguin Books Ltd.

Chapter 18
"Captain Cook Encounters the Tahitians": From *The Journals of Captain Cook,* edited by Philip Edwards, pp. 39–41, Copyright © 1999. Reprinted by permission of Hakluyt Society. The Hakluyt Society was established in 1845 for the purpose of printing rare or unpublished Voyages and Travels. For further information please see their website at www.hakluyt.com.

"Military Discipline": Geoffrey Symcox, "Memoirs on the Art of War" by Marshal de saxe in *War, Diplomacy, and Imperialism, 1618–1763,* pp. 178–179. Copyright © 1974 by Geoffrey Symcox. Reprinted by permission of the author.

Chapter 20
"What Is the Third Estate?": Abbe Emmanuel Joseph Sieyes "What is the Third Estate?" in *A Documentary Survey of the French Revolution* by John Hall Stewart. Copyright © 1951. Reprinted by permission of Pearson Education, Upper Saddle River, NJ.

"The Civil Code of the Code Napoléon": "Code Napoleon, 1804" from *The French Civil Code,* trans. Henry Cachard.

Chapter 22
"Young Italy": G. Mazzine, "Young Italy" in *Metternich's Europe,* edited and translated by Mack Walker, 1968.

"Flora Tristan and the Rights of Working Women": Giselle Pincetl, "Flora Tristan" from *L'Union Ouvriere,* 3rd edition, as translated in *Harvest Quarterly,* 7 (Fall 1977). Copyright © 1977 Giselle Pincetl.

PHOTO CREDITS

Unless otherwise acknowledged, all photographs are the property of Pearson Education, Inc. Page abbreviations are as follows: (T) top, (B) bottom, (L) left, (R) right.

Chapter 11
317 Maria della Grazie, Milan, Italy/Bridgeman Art Library 320 Scala/Art Resource, NY 323 (L), (R) Galleria degli Uffizi, Florence/Dagli Orti/The Art Archive 325 Erich Lessing/Art Resource, NY 326 (L), (R), Scala/Art Resource, NY 327, 328, 329 (T), (B) Scala/Art Resource, NY 330 Scala/Art Resource, NY 333 (T) Scala/Art Resource, NY (B) Réunion des Musées Nationaux/Art Resource, NY 338, 339 Scala/Art Resource, NY 340 Erich Lessing/Art Resource, NY 343 Bibliothèque Nationale de France, Paris (MS Fr. 9087, fol. 207v)

Chapter 12
347 Walker Art Gallery, National Museums Liverpool 350 Bridgeman-Giraudon/Art Resource, NY 353 Mexicolore 354 Laurie Platt Winfrey, Inc. 356 Snark/Art Resource, NY 357 © 2006 Harvard University Peabody Museum, 2004.24.29636 358 Reproduced by courtesy of the Trustees, © The National Gallery, London (NG1287) 364 Czartoyski Collection, Krakow 365 National Portrait Gallery, London (NPG668) 366 Réunion des Musées Nationaux/Art Resource, NY 371, 372

Scala/Art Resource, NY **374** Erich Lessing/Art Resource, NY **375** Topkapi Palace Museum

Chapter 13

378, 379 Library of Congress **380** Private Collection/Bridgeman Art Library **386** Erich Lessing/Art Resource, NY **387** Kunstsammlungen der Veste Coburg, Germany **388** Rheinisches LandesMuseum, Bonn **391** Bridgeman-Giraudon/Art Resource, NY **393** University Library Geneva/Dagli Orti/The Art Archive **394** Erich Lessing/Art Resource, NY **396** National Portrait Gallery, London, UK/Bridgeman Art Library **397** University Library Geneva/Dagli Orti/The Art Archive **398** Pen drawing by Jakob Murner, 1525 © Artothek **400** Collection Rijksmuseum Amsterdam **402** Scala/Art Resource, NY **403** Erich Lessing/Art Resource, NY **404** Bridgeman-Giraudon/Art Resource, NY

Chapter 14

411 Bridgeman-Giraudon/Art Resource, NY **412** Hulton Archive/Getty Images **414** (T) Art Resource, NY (B) Musée cantonal des Beaux-Arts, Lausanne **417** National Portrait Gallery, London (NPG429) **418** Bibliothèque Nationale de France, Paris, Lauros/Giraudon/Bridgeman Art Library **420** © National Maritime Museum, London **422** Palazzo Pitti. Florence/Dagli Orti/The Art Archive **425** Collection Rijksmuseum Amsterdam **427** Erich Lessing/Art Resource, NY **432** Musées de Strasbourg **435** Kunsthistorisches Museum, Vienna (Inv.Nr.GG1071)

Chapter 15

440, 441 Roudnice Lobkowicz Collection/Bridgeman Art Library **442** © British Library Board/All Rights Reserved/Bridgeman Art Library **443** Scala/Art Resource, NY **444** Museum of Art, Tula, Russia/Bridgeman Art Library **446** Erich Lessing/Art Resource, NY **449** Bridgeman-Giraudon/Art Resource, NY **450** Private Collection, Photo © Christie's Images/Bridgeman Art Library **452** Reproduced by courtesy of the Trustees, © The National Gallery, London (NG944) **454** Erich Lessing/Art Resource, NY **455** The Granger Collection, NY **457** Collection Rijksmuseum Amsterdam **459** Victoria & Albert Museum, London/Art Resource, NY **460** Philadelphia Museum of Art: Smith, Kline and French (now SmithKline Beecham) Laboratories Collection. Photo by Lynn Rosenthal, 2000 **461** Reproduced by courtesy of the Trustees, © The National Gallery, London (NG186) **462** Erich Lessing/Art Resource, NY **466** © Mary Evans Picture Library/The Image Works

Chapter 16

471 Réunion des Musées Nationaux/Art Resource, NY **472** National Portrait Gallery, London (NPG2561) **475** (L) The National Portrait Gallery, London (NPG1449) (R) Courtesy of the Hispanic Society of America, New York **476** National Portrait Gallery, London (NPG3840) **479** The Art Archive **481** Château de Versailles, France/Bridgeman Art Library **482** Peter Willi/SuperStock, Inc. **485** By permission of the Earl of Rosebury, on loan to the Scottish National Portrait Gallery. Permission of Lord Dalmeny **486** Stock Montage, Inc. **490** © Leemage **493, 495, 496** Scala/Art Resource, NY **497** Bridgeman-Giraudon/Art Resource, NY

Chapter 17

501 Royal Cabinet of Paintings, Mauritshuis, The Hague **503** (B) © The British Library Board, All Rights Reserved, (Maps C6C3. between 22–23) **505** (L) Scala/Art Resource,NY (R) bpk/Art Resource, NY **507**

Erich Lessing/Art Resource, NY **508** National Library of Medicine **509** (T) Scala/Art Resource, NY (B) Bridgeman Art Library **511** Städelsches Kunstistitut, Frankfurt Gnamm-Arthotek **513** © V&A Images **514** Hanging (Kalamakari): Indian notable, wife and child, surrounded by household scenes, with European figures introduced. Detail #1: Bottom center, three women. Cotton, resist dyed. Whole: H. 99 1/2 in. W. 77 in. (2.53 x 1.96 m) The Metropolitan Museum of Art, Gift of Mrs. Albert Blum, 1920 (20.79) Photograph © 1980 The Metropolitan Museum of Art **515** Tate Gallery, London/Art Resource, NY **517** © David Hall/Artothek **519, 520** Collection Rijksmuseum Amsterdam **522** Peter V. Lape **523** Biblioteca Nacional, Lisbon, Portugal **524** The New York Public Library/Art Resource, NY **525** Reproduced by courtesy of the Trustees, © The National Gallery, London (NG896)

Chapter 18

533 Reproduced by courtesy of the Trustees, © The National Gallery, London (NG681) **540** Russian Historical Museum Moscow/Dagli Orti/The Art Archive **541, 543** The Granger Collection, NY **544, 546** bpk/Art Resource, NY **548** Kunsthistorisches Museum, Vienna **549** Bridgeman-Giraudon/Art Resource, NY **554** British Library/The Art Archive **555** India Office Library/The Art Archive **556** Library of Congress

Chapter 19

561 Samuel H. Kress Collection, © Board of Trustees, National Gallery of Art, Washington, D.C. (1946.7.7.[772]/PA) **562** Mozarteum Salzburg/Dagli Orti/The Art Archive **563** Erich Lessing/Art Resource, NY **565** Réunion des Musées Nationaux/Art Resource, NY **566** Scottish National Portrait Gallery (PG1057) **568** bpk/Art Resource, NY **572** Reproduced by courtesy of the Trustees, © The National Gallery, London (NG114) **574** Michael Holford Photographs **575** Scala/Art Resource, NY **577** (T) Victoria & Albert Museum, London/Art Resource, NY (B) Yale Center for British Art, Paul Mellon Collection USA/Bridgeman Art Library **584** National Gallery of Canada, Ottawa. Photo © NGC **585** © The Trustees of the British Museum

Chapter 20

591 Erich Lessing/Art Resource, NY **593** Bridgeman-Giraudon/Art Resource, NY **594** "Abus à Suprimé" ("Abuses to Suppress"), engraving by Dessal, Musée de la Révolution Française (MRF 88–133) **596** Réunion des Musées Nationaux/Art Resource, NY **598** Bridgeman-Giraudon/Art Resource, NY **602** Library of Congress **604** Bridgeman-Giraudon/Art Resource, NY **605** University of Maryland Libraries (DC 187.7 C655 [1794]) **607** Musées Royaux des Beaux-Arts de Belgique, Bruxelles **610** Goya, Francisco. Spanish, 1746-1828, *Y No Hai Remedio (And there is no remedy)*, from Los *Desastres de la Guerra*. Etching, fourth state. The Metropolitan Museum of Art, Schiff Fund, 1992 (22.60.25[15]). Photo © 2002 The Metropolitan Museum of Art **614** Olin Library, Rare Books, Cornell University (Cornell nap. 31)

Chapter 21

619 Claude Monet, French, 1840–1926, Arrival of the Normandy Train, Gare Saint-Lazare, oil on canvas, 1877, 59.6 x 80.2 cm, Mr. and Mrs. Martin A. Ryerson Collection, 1933. 1158, The Art Institute of Chicago.photography © The Art Institute of Chicago **624** Yale Center for British Art/Paul Mellon Collection USA/Bridgeman Art Library **625** Bedfordshire & Luton Archives & Records Service **627** © British Library

INDEX

A boldface entry indicates a key term and the page number where its definition can be found. Terms and definitions also appear in the Glossary on pages G-1–G-7.